Work Your Way

Around the

World

D0950968

by
Susan Griffith

Distributed in the U.S.A. by Peterson's Guides, Inc.,
202 Carnegie Center, Princeton, N.J. 08543-2123
Published by Vacation Work, 9 Park End Street, Oxford

First published 1983

Revised every other year

Seventh edition 1995
Reprinted 1996

WORK YOUR WAY AROUND THE WORLD

by Susan Griffith

ISBN 1 85458 131 7 (hardback)
ISBN 1 85458 130 9 (softback)

Cover Design and Chapter Headings by
Miller Craig & Cocking Design Partnership

Maps by William Swan

Imageset and Printed by Unwin Brothers Ltd, Old Woking, Surrey

Contents

4

Work your Way

Work Your Way in Europe

Work Your Way Worldwide

8

To our American Readers: Your fact-finding mission and job journey abroad
will differ from your British counterparts. Because the US is not a member of
the European Union (Austria, Belgium, Denmark, Finland, France, Germany,
Greece, Ireland, Italy, Luxembourg, the Netherlands, Portugal, Spain, Sweden
and the United Kingdom), there will not be the job reciprocity in these countries
or some of the special schemes which British travellers enjoy. Getting a work
permit will prove difficult for American citizens — and sometimes the best jobs
can be had without one. Remember, too, that certain British expressions may
be unfamiliar to American ears and that wages and prices are normally stated
in pounds sterling (£1=$1.55 at the time of going to press).

Preface

World developments have created both new opportunities and new problems for the working traveller. Finland, Sweden and Austria will join the European Union in January 1995 thereby opening up hitherto difficult areas to the travelling worker. The melting away of barriers in the former Soviet Union and Eastern Europe has enticed many travellers to live and work in those countries, particularly as English teachers. In the southern hemisphere, political changes in South Africa have made that country a more attractive destination for globetrotters. On the other side of the equation, the loosening of state control in Albania has resulted in a mass exodus of Albanians competing for casual work in neighbouring countries.

Since the publication of the last edition less than two years ago, readers have been writing as enthusiastically as ever. The correspondence which this book generates is one of my chief delights. Not only do I take an interest in the job opportunities which readers describe in loving detail, but I greatly enjoy the soap operatic aspect: two contributors who met in a youth hostel in Australia are now married to each other; two Americans cheerfully cut short their European working holiday when they discovered that a baby had been conceived at the organic farm in Britanny where they were working; two contributors have acquired new and exotic surnames through marrying men met abroad, a man who was considered a ne'er-do-well by his family for going off to Peru to try to teach English is now in a senior EFL post in Turkey.

There is no average profile of the working traveller. For this seventh edition of *Work Your Way Around the World* I have heard from a Northerner who gave up being a milkman to travel round the world, a Scottish lawyer who describes herself as geriatric (at age 26), a butcher, a baker (but no candlestick-maker), a Russian in Paris, a couple from the Isle of Man in Calcutta, a Pole in Luxembourg, an American in Korea and a Dane in Spain. Their common message was to urge people whatever their backgrounds to give it a go and expose themselves to the unexpected friendliness and generosity of foreign residents and fellow travellers.

Although the permanent employment situation worldwide remains difficult, travellers continue to find many temporary jobs to which they can turn their hands. Naturally, the prospect of relinquishing a regular income and tackling red tape hassles can be daunting. (I wish I had a few air miles for every time a correspondent has used the phrase catch-22 in this context.) And yet all those who have followed their inclination to take off have been unanimous in not regretting their decision to give it a whirl.

As much up-to-the-minute information as possible has been squeezed into these 512 pages. In addition to providing practical and realistic advice about where and how to get jobs abroad, this book also tries to inspire and renew optimism and spark the imagination of all potential travellers whatever their ages or backgrounds. If you are someone who feels the spirit of adventure occasionally flicker, read this book and see what you think. Many happy departures (as well as happy returns). And keep writing.

Susan Griffith
Cambridge
December, 1994

Acknowledgments

This new revised edition of *Work Your Way Around the World* would not have been possible without the help of hundreds of travellers who have generously shared their information with us. Some have been writing in to me since the early editions of this book in the mid-1980s, and their loyalty is greatly appreciated.

As well as all the people who helped with previous editions, many of whose names appear throughout these pages, we would like to thank the travellers who have made significant contributions over the past two years:

Brigitte Albrech, Brad Allemand, David Allsop, Brett Archer, Craig Ashworth, Brendan Barker, Ann Barkett, Stuart Bellworthy, Karl Beringhs, Paul Binfield, Armin Birrer, Rikke Bogensberger, Simon Bond, Jørn Borup, Laura Bowers, R Bryant, Dermot Campbell, Jan Christensen, Bruce Collier, Steven Conneely, Adam Cook, Alison Cooper, Kenneth Corcoran, Scott Corcoran, Iain Croker, Damon Das, Mark Davies, Paul Donut, Steve & Iona Dwyer, Michael Easingwood, Carolyn Edwards, Xuela Edwards, Mark Elliott, Michel Falardeau, Julie Fast, Dean Fisher, Liam Forkin, Emma Forster, Paul & Tracey Foulkes, Khristen Ghodsee, Lara Giavi, Andrew Giles, Peter Goldman, Matthew Goodman, Ian Govan, Julian Graham, Andy Green, Carl Griffith, Coral Grossman, Mary Hall, Nicola Hall, Shirine Harburn, Jason Harris, Debbie Harrison, Dustie Hickey, Jimmy Hill, Martin Hobbs, Rita Hoek, Karen Holman, Mark Horobin, David & Greeba Hughes, Mark Hurley, Michael Jordan, George Kelly, Mark Kinder, Brian Komyathy, Lita Kristensen, Bela Lal, Camilla Lambert, Bruce Lawson, Michelle Lindsay, Ian McArthur, Heather McCulloch, Jane McNally, Adda Maccich, Eric Mackness, Isak Maseide, Beth Mayer, Ian Mitselburg, Lee Morton, Ian Mudge, Vicky Nakis, Jayne Nash, Laura O'Connor, Raymond Oliver, Brenda O'Shea, Tom Parker, Joanne Patrick, PG Penn, Caroline Perry, Stephen Psallidas, Cindy Roberts, K Rounce, Nicola Sarjeant, Andrew Smith, Bethany Smith, Dawn Smith, Ken Smith, Arthur Solovev, Rhona Stannage, Julie Stanton, Hannah Start, Carina Strutt, Kristof Szymczak, Woden Teachout, Vaughan Temby, Murray Turner, Mig Urquhart, Obbe Verwer, Lindsay Watt, Jill Weseman, Safra Wightman, Matthew Williams, Paul Winter.

INTRODUCTION

The Decision to Go

For many, deciding to get up and go is the biggest stumbling-block. Often the hardest step is fixing a departure date. Once you have bought a ticket, explained to your friends and family that you are off to see the world (they will either be envious or disapproving) and packed away your possessions, the rest seems to look after itself. Inevitably first-time travellers suffer some separation anxieties and pre-departure blues as they contemplate leaving behind the comfortable routines of home. But these are usually much worse in anticipation than in retrospect. As long as you have enough motivation, together with some money and a copy of this book, you are all set to have a great time abroad.

Either you follow your first impulse and opt for an immediate change of scenery, or you plan a job and a route in advance. On the one hand people use working as a means to an end; they work in order to fund further travelling. Other people look upon a job abroad as an end in itself, a way to explore other cultures, a means of satisfying their curiosity about whether there is any truth in the clichés about other nationalities. Often it is the best way to shake off the boredom which comes with routine. Zoe Drew felt quite liberated when she decided to drop everything — her 'cushy secretarial job, Debenhams account card, stiletto heels' — and embark on a working holiday around Europe. Bruce Lawson finally kicked over the traces of the 'Office Job from Hell' and went off to Thailand to teach English.

When you are wondering whether you are the right sort to work abroad, do not imagine you are a special case. It is not only students, school-leavers and people on the dole who enjoy the chance to travel and work, but also a large number of people with a profession, craft or trade which they were happy to abandon temporarily. We have heard of a career civil servant who enjoyed washing dishes in a Munich restaurant, a physiotherapist who has packed cod in Iceland, a nurse who busked in Norway and another who has worked on a sheep station in Australia, an Australian teacher who became a nanny in Istanbul, a Scottish lawyer who worked as a chalet girl in a French ski resort, a German tourism trainee who planted trees in Canada, a chartered surveyor who took more than two years off from his job to work his way around the world and a journalist and tour operator couple who picked up casual jobs to fund their 'Stuff Mammon World Tour' and ended up living quite comfortably in Hong Kong. They were motivated not by a desire to earn money but by a craving for new and different experiences, and a conviction that not all events which make up one's life need to be career-furthering or 'success'-oriented.

PREPARATION

It is not the Mr. Micawbers of this world who succeed at getting jobs. If you sit around 'waiting for something to turn up' you will soon find yourself penniless with no prospects for replenishing your travel funds. If you wait in idleness at home or if you sit in your *pension* all day worrying about your dwindling pesetas or drachmas, hesitating and dithering because you are convinced the situation is hopeless or that you lack the necessary documents to work, you will get absolutely nowhere.

Every successful venture combines periodic flights of fancy with methodical planning. The majority of us lack the courage (or the recklessness) just to get up and go. And any homework you do ahead of time will benefit you later, if only because it will give you more confidence. But it is important to strike a good balance between slavishly following a predetermined itinerary which might deter you from grasping opportunities as they arise and setting off with no idea of what you're looking for. Many travel converts regret their initial decision to buy an air ticket with a fixed return date.

For many people, a shortage of money is the main obstacle. It is the rare individual who, like Ian McArthur, specialises in 'reckless arrivals' (Istanbul with £5, Cairo with $20 between him and a friend, New York with $1). Other people wait until they have substantial savings before they dare leave home which gives them the enviable freedom to work only when they want to. Sometimes pennilessness acts as a spur to action as it did in the case of Jason Davies. His timidity had been getting the better of him until he realised in Nice he was down to his last 100 francs, whereupon he decided to stop being so fussy about the restaurants he approached for work. The next day he found a job.

Anyone embarking on an extended trip will have to have a certain amount of capital to buy tickets, visas, insurance (see below), etc. But it is amazing how a little can go a long way if you are willing to take a wide variety of casual jobs en route and willing to weather the financial doldrums. Stephen Psallidas had £40 one December and four months later (most of which was spent working as a waiter in Paris) he had £1,600 for a planned year in Australia. An even more impressive rags to riches story came from Mark Hurley who spent his last 3,000 drachmas on the ferry from Athens to the island of Santorini, and had to borrow from some new-found travelling companions for food and accommodation:

> *The next day we all tried to find work with me trying harder than the others because I was skint and going into debt. After looking for work every possible hour of the full four days, I was just about to give it all up as a bad joke, when I pulled myself together — 200 Nos in four days doesn't do a lot for your self-esteem — and had another look in a small village called Kamari. The last hotel I came to was still under construction and said they would take me on to help the tiler which was great. I started the next day for dr5,000 a day and as much as I could eat. The job lasted five weeks, by which time I had paid back my friends. Later I got a job in a winery and settled down there. I met so many great people from all over the world, and have filled two address books. After two and a half years I had £4,500.*

Money

It is of course always a good idea to have an emergency fund in reserve if possible, or at least access to money from home should you run into difficulties (see *In Extremis*). Yet a surprising number of our correspondents have written in with the advice not to bother saving money before leaving home. Adrian McCay is just one who advocates packing your bags and going even if you have only £10 (though he later confesses that he left for Australia with £300). How much you decide to set aside before leaving will depend on whether or not you have a gambling streak. But even gamblers should take only sensible risks. If you don't have much cash, it's probably advisable to have a return ticket. For example, if you decide to crew on a yacht from the Mediterranean and don't have much money, you could buy a very cheap last minute return flight to

Rhodes or the Canaries. If you succeed and waste the return half of your charter, wonderful; if not, you will have had a few weeks in the sun — disappointing perhaps but not desperate.

Attitudes to saving vary too. A Malaysian student, T. P. Lye, thinks that there is no better feeling than planning travels while saving for them (assuming you realise your ambition). On the other hand, Ian McArthur finds saving over a long period depressing and starts to long for those pints of lager and late-night curries of which he has been deprived. But even Ian admits that 'living on the edge' is no fun when only a couple of hundreds of unattainable pounds stand between you and the air ticket you want to buy. When Xuela Edwards returned after two years of working her way around Europe, she tried to hang on to the travelling mentality which makes it much easier to save money:

> *My advice is to consider your home country in the same way as others. It makes you more resourceful. Try to avoid the car loans and high living that usually make up home life. I'm sure that the reason bulb workers in Holland for example save so much money is because they live in tents (which I admit would be tricky at home).*

Mike Tunnicliffe spent more on his world travels than he intended but didn't regret it:

> *Originally, I intended to finance my year with casual work and return to England having spent only the price of my ticket. In the end, I delved far deeper into my life's savings than I had intended to do, but I was fortunate in having savings on which to draw, and I made the conscious decision to enjoy my year while I had the chance. In other words, fun now, pay later!*

Once you are resolved to travel, set a realistic target amount to save and then go for it wholeheartedly. Estimate how long it will take you to raise the desired amount and stick to the deadline as if your home country was going to sink into the ocean the day after. Don't get just any job, get one which is either highly paid (easier said than done of course) or one which offers as much overtime as you want. Dedicated working travellers consider a 70-hour week quite tolerable (think of junior doctors) which will have the additional advantage of leaving you too tired to conduct an expensive social life. If you are already on the road and want to save, head for a place which allows this possibility, even if it won't be much fun. Adam Cook spent a miserable eight weeks picking peaches for an impossible French farmer but had saved £1,000 by the end of it. Murray Turner wrote from Hong Kong in 1994 to say that doing a night shift of labouring was killing him but that he had saved £3,000 in a few months. If you have collected some assets before setting off, you are luckier than most. Property owners can arrange for the rental money to follow them at regular intervals.

Whatever the size of your travelling fund, you should give some thought to how and in what form to carry your money. Travellers' cheques are much safer than cash, though they cost an extra 1%. The most universally recognised brands are American Express, Thomas Cook and Visa. It is advisable also to keep a small amount of cash. Sterling is fine for most countries but US dollars are preferred in much of the world such as Latin America, Eastern Europe and Israel. The easiest way to look up the exchange rate of any world currency is to look at the Monday edition of the *Financial Times*. A Currency Conversion Chart is included in the Appendices.

Credit cards are useful for many purposes, provided you will not be tempted to abuse them. Few people think of crediting their Visa, Access, etc. account before leaving and then withdraw cash on the credit card without incurring interest charges (since the money is not being borrowed). This is the most efficient and cheapest way of transferring funds abroad since you bypass bank charges for the currency exchange and for travellers' cheques. To use this method successfully, you must be able to find a bank which issues cash for credit cards and also to keep careful track of your balance to avoid paying exorbitant interest rates.

Otherwise a credit card is invaluable in an emergency and handy for showing at borders where the officials frown on penniless tourists. Several round-the-world travellers have opened a bank account in their destination country before leaving home, partly as an incentive to reach the country and also to prevent having to carry the money on their persons.

If you have been slaving over a tepid sink full of washing up every day for the last few months, it would be disappointing to have your well-gotten gains stolen. From London to La Paz there are crooks lurking, ready to pounce upon the unsuspecting traveller. Theft takes many forms, from the highly trained gangs of gipsy children who artfully pick pockets all over Europe to violent attacks on the streets of American cities. Even more depressing is the theft which takes place by other travellers in youth hostels or on beaches. Risks can be reduced by carrying your wealth in several places including a comfortable money belt worn inside your clothing, steering clear of seedy or crowded areas and moderating your intake of alcohol. If you are mugged, and have an insurance policy which covers cash, you must obtain a police report (often for a fee) to stand any chance of recouping part of your loss.

While you are busy saving money to reach your desired target, you should be thinking of other ways in which to prepare yourself, including health, what to take and which contacts and skills you might cultivate.

Baggage

While aiming to travel as lightly as possible (one pair of jeans instead of two) you should consider the advantage of taking certain extra pieces of equipment. For example many working travellers consider the extra weight of a tent and sleeping bag worthwhile in view of the independence and flexibility it gives them if they are offered work by a farmer who cannot provide accommodation. A comfortable pair of shoes is essential, since a job hunt abroad often involves a lot of pavement pounding. Stephen Hands had his shoes stolen while swimming at night and found that bleeding feet were a serious impediment to finding (never mind, doing) a job. Others pack items essential to their money-making projects such as a guitar for busking, a suit for getting work as an English teacher, a pair of fingerless gloves for cold-weather fruit-picking, and so on. Leave at home anything of value (monetary or sentimental). The general rule is stick to the bare essentials (including a Swiss army knife). One of our contributors met a woman who told him that having her rucksack stolen was the best thing that happened to her.

If you plan to work in one place for a long period of time, for instance on a kibbutz, you might allow yourself the odd (lightweight) luxury, such as a favourite tape, a short-wave radio or a jar of peanut butter. If you have prearranged a job, you can always post some belongings on ahead. You could even use poste restante for items you don't want to carry around for the first part of your trip (say hiking equipment) though you would have to have an itinerary fixed in cement for this to be an option.

Good maps and guides always enhance one's enjoyment of a trip. If you are going to be based in a major city, buy a map ahead of time. If you are in London, visit the famous map shop Edward Stanford Ltd. (12-14 Long Acre, Covent Garden, WC2E 9LP; 0171-836 1321) and Daunt Books for Travellers (83 Marylebone High Street, W1M 4DE; 0171-224 2295). The Map Shop (15 High St, Upton-on-Severn, Worcestershire WR8 0HJ; 01684 593146) does an extensive mail order business and will send you the relevant catalogue. Also write to Roger Lascelles for his catalogue of travel literature (47 York Road, Brentford, Middlesex TW8 0QP). There are dozens of travel specialists throughout North America, including the mail order company Travelers Bookstore (22 W 52nd St (Lobby), New York, NY 10019; 800-755-8728), the Complete Traveler Bookstore (199 Madison Ave, New York, NY 10016; 212-685-9007) which also issues a free mail-order catalogue and, in Canada, Wanderlust (1929 West 4th Avenue, Kitsilano, Vancouver, BC, V6J 1M7; 604-739-2182).

Health

No matter what country you are heading for, you should obtain the Department of Health leaflet T5 *Health Advice for Travellers Anywhere in the World*. This leaflet should be available from any post office or you can request a free copy on the Health Literature Line 0800 555777.

If you are a national of the European Economic Area, namely the UK, Ireland, Netherlands, Belgium, Luxembourg, Denmark, Germany, France, Italy, Spain, Portugal, Greece, Austria, Finland, Sweden, Norway and Iceland) and will be working in another EEA country, you will be covered by the European Community Social Security Regulations. Advice and the leaflet SA29 *Your Social Security Insurance, Benefits and Health Care Rights in the European Community* may be obtained free of charge from the Department of Social Security, Overseas Contributions (EC), Newcastle-upon-Tyne NE98 1YX.

The leaflet T5 contains an application form to obtain form E111 (called the 'E-one-eleven') which is a certificate of entitlement to medical treatment in the EEA. All EEA nationals going to another EEA country either on holiday or to work for a UK employer for not more than 12 months while paying UK National Insurance contributions should apply for an E111 from the post office. If you will be working for a foreign employer, you should seek advice from the DSS in Newcastle.

If you are planning to include Third World countries on your itinerary, you will want to take the necessary health precautions, though this won't be cheap unless you are able to have your injections at your local NHS surgery where most injections are free or given for a minimal charge (e.g. £13 for yellow fever). However pressure is mounting for GPs to charge the market rate which would result in travellers having to pay up to £200 for vaccines. A further problem is that GPs cannot be expected to keep abreast of all the complexities of malaria prophylaxis for different areas, etc. and many are downright ignorant.

Private specialist clinics charge both for information and for the jabs. For example the Hospital for Tropical Diseases (0171-388 8989) does not give out information over the phone but charges £15 for a consultation and approximately £8 per vaccine needed. The International Medical Centre with branches in central London (32 Weymouth St; 0171-486 3063) and Earls Court (131-135 Earls Court Road) gives minimal advice over the phone and will tell you their range of charges (from £6.50 for typhoid to £40 for the new long-lasting immunisation against hepatitis B). There are 36 British Airways Travel Clinics throughout the UK; ring the recorded message 0171-831 5333 for your nearest one. The Health Control Unit at Heathrow Airport (0181-745 7209) will give recommendations for immunisations.

Some countries have introduced HIV antibody testing for long-stay foreigners and the certificate may be required to obtain a work or residence visa. If you are going to be spending a lot of time in countries where blood screening is not reliable you should consider carrying a sterile medical kit. These are sold by MASTA (Medical Advisory Service for Travellers Abroad) at the London School of Hygiene and Tropical Medicine, keppel St, London WC1. MASTA publishes health briefs at varying prices (£10-35) depending on the depth of customised detail you require. You can ring their interactive Travellers' Health Line on 0891 224100 with your destinations and they will send you a basic health brief by return, for the price of the telephone call (about £2).

The Hospital for Tropical Diseases operates a health hotline for advice on health regulations for various destinations; ring 0839 337722 off-peak. An excellent general guide on the subject of visiting hot climates is *The Tropical Traveller* by John Hatt (Penguin, 1993). All these books emphasise the necessity of avoiding tap water and recommend ways to purify your drinking water by filtering, boiling or chemical additives. MASTA has details of a new water purifier called the 'Trekker Travel Well' for about £20. Tap water throughout Western Europe is safe to drink.

Americans seeking general travel health advice should ring the Center for Disease Control & Prevention Hotline in Atlanta on 404-332-4559. For a list of more than 100+ doctors in North America who are travel health experts, send a self-addressed envelope and and $1 in stamps to Travelers Health & Immunization Services, 148 Highland Ave, Newton, MA 02165.

Malaria is at present making a comeback in many parts of the world, due to the resistance of certain strains of mosquito to the pesticides and preventative medications which have been so extensively relied upon in the past. At the time of writing an outbreak of cerebral malaria had claimed about 250 lives in northern India. For recorded information on malaria and prophylactics, ring 0891 600350. There are two principal types of drug which can be obtained over the counter: Chloroquine-based and Proguanil (brand name Paludrine). Many areas of the world are reporting resistance to one of the drugs, so you may have to take both or a third line such as Maloprim or Mefloquine available only on prescription and with possible side effects. Unfortunately these prophylactic medications are not foolproof, and even those who have scrupulously swallowed their pills before and after their trip as well as during it have been known to contract the disease. It is therefore also wise to take mechanical precautions against mosquitoes. If possible, screen the windows and sleep under an insecti-cide-impregnated mosquito net. Marcus Scrace bought some netting intended for prams which occupied virtually no space in his luggage. If these are unavail-able, cover your limbs at nightfall with light-coloured garments, apply insect repellant with the active ingredient DEET and sleep with a fan on.

It is a good idea to join the International Association for Medical Assistance to Travellers (IAMAT) whose European headquarters are at 57 Voirets, 1212 Grand-Lancy-Geneva, Switzerland and in North America at 40 Regal Road, Guelph, Ontario, Canada N1K 1B5 (416-836-0102) with other offices in the US (417 Center St, Lewiston, NY 14092) and New Zealand (PO Box 5049, Christchurch). This organisation co-ordinates doctors and clinics around the world who maintain high medical standards at reasonable cost e.g. US$45 per consultation for IAMAT members. They will send you a directory listing IAMAT centres throughout the world as well as detailed leaflets about malaria and other tropical diseases and country-by-country climate and hygiene charts. There is no set fee for joining the association, but donations are welcome; at the very least you should cover their postage and printing costs.

Insurance

Given the limitations of state-provided reciprocal cover, you may decide to take out comprehensive private cover which will cover extras like loss of baggage and, more importantly, emergency repatriation. Every enterprise in the travel business is delighted to sell you insurance because of the commission earned. Shopping around can save you money. Ring several insurance companies with your specifications and compare prices. If you are going abroad to work, you are expected to inform your insurer ahead of time (which is often impossible). Many policies will be invalidated if you injure yourself at work, e.g. put out your back while picking plums or cut yourself in a restaurant kitchen, though it is not clear how they would know how or where the accident took place. It could be worth asking a broker to quote for a tailor-made policy.

Europ-Assistance Ltd of 252 High St, Croydon, Surrey CR0 1NF (01444 440202) specialises in travel emergency services and has a network of doctors, air ambulances, agents, vehicle rescue services etc. in 220 countries worldwide. Their Voyager Travel policy covering periods of up to 18 months is fairly comprehensive and costs £235 for 12 months in Europe and £480 worldwide. The policy is invalidated if you return home during the period insured. The American branch is Worldwide Assistance Services Inc, 1133 15th St NW, Suite 400, Washington, DC 20005-2710 (800-821-2828).

Many companies charge less, though you will have to decide whether you are satisfied with their level of cover. Most offer a standard rate which covers medical emergencies and a premium rate which covers personal baggage, cancellation, etc. Most travel policies list as one of their exclusions: 'any claims which arise while the Insured is engaged in any manual employment'. If you are not planning to visit North America, the premiums will be much less expensive. Some companies to consider are listed here with an estimate of their premiums for 12 months of worldwide cover (including the USA):

ATI Group, 37 Kings Exchange, Tileyard Road, London N7 9AH (0171-609 5000). £330.

Campus Travel Insurance, 52 Grosvenor Gardens, London SW1W 0AG (0171-730 3402) or regional branches. For people under 35 the policy costs £252 without baggage cover, £346 with.

Columbus Travel Insurance, 17 Devonshire Square, London EC2M 4SQ (0171-375 0011). Globetrotter policy (basic medical cover only) costs £180 for one year. More extensive cover is offered for £334 and £517.

Endsleigh Insurance, Endsleigh House, Cheltenham, Glos GL50 3NR. Offices in most university towns. Twelve months of cover in Europe costs from £205, worldwide £360 (£289 and £481 respectively for a higher level of cover).

Marcus Hearn & Co, 65-66 Shoreditch High St, London E1 6JL (0171-739 3444). Has a one-year package for about £100 though no trip can last longer than 120 days within the year. 12 months' continuous cover costs £270 or £305.

Travel Insurance Agency, 871 High Road, North Finchley, London N12 8QA. (0181-446 5414/5). Charges approximately £25 per month, after the first month costing £35 worldwide.

If you do have to make a claim, you may be unpleasantly surprised by the amount of the settlement eventually paid. Loss adjusters have ways of making calculations which prove that you are entitled to less than you think. For example when Caroline Langdon was mugged in Seville she suffered losses of about £100, for which her insurance company paid compensation of £22.30. The golden rule is to amass as much documentation as possible to support your application, most importantly a police report.

Americans who spend $16 on an International Student Identity Card are automatically covered by a basic accident/sickness insurance package. Contact CIEE (Council on International Educational Exchange, 205 E 42nd St, New York, NY 10017) or any US office of their affiliated travel agency Council Travel. Other recommended US insurers for extended stays abroad are International SOS Assistance Inc (1 Neshaminy Interplex, Suite 310, Trevose, PA 19053; 800-523-8930) which is used by the Peace Corps and is designed for people working in remote areas; and Hinchcliff International (11 Ascot Place, Ithaca, NY 14850). A firm which specialises in providing insurance for Americans living overseas is Wallach & Company (107 West Federal St, PO Box 480, Middleburg, VA 22117-0480; 800-237-6615).

Qualifications

These sensible precautions of purchasing maps, buying insurance, finding out about malaria, etc. are relatively straightforward and easy. Other specific ways of preparing yourself, such as studying a language, learning to sail or dive, cook, drive or type, or taking up a fitness programme, are a different kettle of fish. But the traveller who has a definite commitment may well consider embarking on a self-improvement scheme before setting off. Among the most useful qualifications you can acquire are a certificate in Teaching English as a Foreign Language (see chapter *Teaching*) and a knowledge of sailing.

The person who has a definite job skill to offer increases his or her chances of success. After working his way from Paris to Cape Town via Queensland, Stephen Psallidas concluded:

> *There are several professions which are in demand anywhere in the world, and I would say that anyone who practises them would be laughing all the way to the 747. These are: secretary, cook/chef, accountant, nurse and hairdresser.*

Nursing training is very useful and, after a year of working her way through Europe doing a variety of things, Mary Hall is glad she stuck the training since she has found that medical doors opened for her in Gibraltar, Uganda and South Africa. Childcare experience is also a highly portable skill.

It is a good idea to take documentary evidence of any qualifications you have earned. Also take along a sheaf of references, both character and work-related, if possible, all on headed notepaper. It is difficult to arrange for these to be sent once you're on the road. This was obviously a good idea in Karen Heinink's case, when she approached a coastal hotel in South Africa:

> *I showed them my CV and references which I always carry round when travelling (just in case), had a quick chat with the owners and was told I could start right away.*

Language

Having even a limited knowledge of a foreign language is especially valuable for the job-seeker. Stephen Hands thinks that this can't be overemphasised; after an unsuccessful attempt to find work in France, he returned to Britain and, even before phoning home, signed up for a language course (and received the additional perk of a student card).

Evening language classes offered by local authorities usually follow the academic year and are aimed at hobby learners. Intensive courses offered privately are much more expensive. If you are really dedicated, consider using a self-study programme with books and tapes (which start at £30), correspondence course or broadcast language course. Even if you don't make much headway with the course at home, take it with you since you will have more incentive to learn once you are immersed in a language.

There are a great many teach-yourself courses on the market from Berlitz, the BBC (Education Information 0181-746 1111), Linguaphone (0800-282417), Macmillan (01256 817245). All of them offer deluxe courses with refinements such as interactive videos and of course these cost much more (from £150). Linguaphone recommends half an hour of study a day for three months to master the basics of a language. If you are interested in an obscure language and don't know where to study it, contact the CILT Library (0171-379 5110) which has a certain amount of documentation on courses especially in London.

A more enjoyable way of learning a language (and normally a more successful one) is by speaking it with the natives. Numerous organisations offer 'in-country' language courses, though these tend to be expensive. Euroyouth (301 Westborough Road, Westcliff, Southend-on-Sea, Essex SSO 9PT; 01702 341434) tries to keep costs down on their Holiday Guest Programme by arranging language exchanges between host families (mostly in Spain, Italy and France) and billeted English-speakers. EF International Language Schools (0171-401 3660) offer the chance to study French, German, Spanish and Italian *in situ*, as does Euro-Academy, 77a George St, Croydon CR0 1LD (ask for their 'Learn the Language on Location' brochure). Americans might like to contact the National Registration Center for Study Abroad (PO Box 1393, Milwaukee, WI 53201) for a listing of language schools in 25 countries.

Another possibility is to forgo structured lessons and simply live with a family, which has the further advantage of allowing you to become known in a community which might lead to job openings later. (See *Making Contacts* below). Several agencies arrange paying guest stays which are designed for people wishing to learn or improve language skills in the context of family life. Try En Famille Agency (The Old Stables, 60b Maltravers St, Arundel, West Sussex BN18 9BG) which specialises in France. EIL or the Experiment in International Living ('Otesaga', West Malvern Road, Malvern, Worcestershire WR14 4EN) arranges home stays in over 30 countries. Administrative fees vary from £120 for a week's stay in Nepal to £350 for a week in Argentina.

Making Contacts

The importance of knowing people, not necessarily in high places but on the spot, is stressed by many of our contributors. Some people are lucky enough to have family and friends scattered around the world in positions to offer advice or even employment. Others must create their own contacts by exploiting less obvious connections. Dick Bird, who spent over a year travelling around South America, lightheartedly anticipates how this works:

> *In Bolivia we hope to start practising another survival technique known as 'having some addresses'. The procedure is quite simple. Before leaving one's country of origin, inform everyone you know from your immediate family to the most casual acquaintance, that you are about to leave for South America. With only a little cajoling they might volunteer the address of somebody they once met on the platform of Clapham Junction or some other tenuous connection who went out to South America to seek their fortunes. You then present your worthy self on the unsuspecting emigré's doorstep and announce that you have been in close and recent communication with their nearest and dearest. Although you won't necessarily be welcomed with open arms, the chances are they will be eager for your company and conversation. Furthermore these contacts are often useful for finding work: doing odd jobs, farming, tutoring people they know, etc.*

Paul Rowlatt accumulated a list of contacts all over Brazil just by being 'nosey and talkative'.

Everyone has ways of developing links with people abroad. Think of distant cousins and family friends, foreign students met in your home town, pen friends, people in the town twinned with yours, etc. Human rights groups in your home country might have links with your destination or even know about opportunities for doing voluntary work in their offices abroad. Tony Dalby of Swindon came up with an original way of forging links with Japan:

> *I wrote off to our new Honda car plant and requested some contacts in order to gain some first-hand experience of Japanese culture and language before travelling. I now have links with a Japanese family.*

School exchanges and membership in the Youth Hostels Association can also result in valuable contacts.

One way of developing contacts is to join a travel club such as the Globetrotters Club (BCM/Roving, London WC1N 3XX) for £9 a year after the joining fee of £3. The Club has no office and so correspondence addressed to the above box office address is answered by volunteers. Members receive a bi-monthly travel newsletter and a list of members in their region (Britain, Continental Europe, the Western Hemisphere and the rest). Many members are willing to extend hospitality to other globetrotters and possibly to advise them on local employment prospects. If you want a list of members outside your region send £1 for each regional list you require.

Servas International is an organisation begun by an American Quaker, which runs a worldwide programme of free hospitality exchanges for travellers, to further world peace and understanding. Normally you don't stay with one host for more than a couple of days. To become a Servas traveller or host, contact the National Secretary (Ann Greenhough, PO Box 1035, Edinburgh EH3 9JQ) who can forward your enquiry to your Area Coordinator. Before a traveller can be given a list of hosts (which are drawn up every autumn), he or she must pay a fee of £20 (£30 for couples) and be interviewed by a coordinator. Servas US is at 11 John St, Room 407, New York, NY 10038-4009 (212-267-0252). There is a joining fee of $55 and a refundable deposit of $25 for host lists in up to five countries. Janet Renard from the US stayed with 21 Servas hosts during her six months in Europe:

> We call it 'Servas Magic'. Each visit was a great experience. The houses we visited ranged from a 16th century farmhouse in Wales to a cramped apartment in Naples. While we were on an archaeological dig in France, one family hosted us for three weekends, taking us to St. Malo and even sailing in a regatta. For some hosts, we gardened, chopped wood or cooked; others insisted on waiting on us completely.

There are other hospitality clubs and exchanges worth investigating. Women Welcome Women (8a Chestnut Avenue, High Wycombe, Bucks. HP11 1DJ; tel/fax 01494 439481) enables women of different countries to visit one another. There is no set subscription cost but £20 is suggested for Western members in employment, which covers the cost of the membership list and three newsletters in which members may publish announcements.

In the US the Hospitality Exchange (1338 Foothill Drive, No. 199, Salt Lake City, Utah 84105; 1-800-580-8759) charges an annual fee of $15, whereas the Crash Network (519 Castro, No. 7, San Francisco, CA 94114) is free to join, though directories cost $5.

There are many pen friend organisations in Europe and North America which charge varying fees for matching up correspondents. After years of corresponding with a girl in a small East German town, Kathy Merz from South Carolina paid what she thought would be a brief visit and instead turned into a six month stay while she worked in the family's butcher shop. The Central Bureau for Educational Exchanges (Seymour Mews, London W1H 9PE) puts young Britons aged 12 to 20 in touch with correspondents abroad. International Pen Friends (PO 340, Dublin 12, Ireland) is a long-established club; the average charge for being sent 14 names and addresses by IPF is £8. The long-established American representative is Eileen Bouldin, PO Box 42232, Philadelphia, Pennsylvania 19101-2232, USA. A new Australian organisation Top International Mailing Connections (PO Box 590, Eltham, VIC 3095) has recently become a singles-only penfriend club; a sample of their quarterly magazine costs US$5.

Travelling Alone

Many travellers emphasise the benefits of travelling alone, such as a chance to make friends with the locals more easily. Most are surprised that loneliness is hardly an issue, since there is always congenial company to be met in travellers hostels, kibbutzim, etc. some of whom even team up with each other for short or long spells. Of course, if you are working in a remote rural area and don't speak the language fluently, you will inevitably miss having a companion and may steer away from this kind of situation if it bothers you. If you are anxious about the trials and traumas of being on your own, try a short trip and see how you like it.

Women can travel solo just as enjoyably as men, as Woden Teachout discovered:

I'm 24, female, American and like to travel alone. I have travelled with friends on occasion which is definitely more 'fun' but it lacks the perilous sense of possibility and adventure that I love most about travelling. Whatever situations you get yourself into when you are on your own, you have to get out of. I have been terribly frightened: I spent the night of my 21st birthday huddled in a cellar hole in downtown Malmo Sweden, wet and shivering, knowing that a local rapist had claimed three victims within the fortnight. But by the same token, the glorious moments, the stick-out-your-thumb-and-be-glad-for-whatever-is-going-to-happen-next moments, the feelings of triumph and absolute freedom, are uniquely yours.

Travelling Companions

You have to be fairly lucky to have a friend who is both willing and available when you are to embark on a working trip. If you don't have a suitable companion and are convinced you need one, you can publish your request in the pages of the Globetrotters Club newsletter *Globe,* the Youth Hostels Association's *Triangle* magazine, the 'Travel Link' column of *Overseas Jobs Express* (in which potential job-seekers can announce their travel plans), or the North American travellers' magazine *Great Expeditions* (PO Box 18036, Raleigh, NC 27619). A notice board which might be useful is the one in the basement of the Travellers' Bookshop in London at 25 Cecil Court.

There are also a few agencies which try to match up compatible travel companions for an annual or a one-off fee for example Odyssey International (21 Cambridge Road, Waterbeach, Cambridge CB5 9NJ; 01223 861079) whose questionnaire asks about plans vis-à-vis casual work, and whose annual fee is £25, Travelmate (52 York Place, Bournemouth, Dorset BH7 6JN; tel/fax 01202 431520) which charges a membership fee of £35. In the US, try Travel Companion Exchange, PO Box 833, Amityville, NY 11701 (516-454-0880/fax 454-01700). A sample copy of their newsletter is US$4.

Sarah Clifford describes the easiest way of all to find companions:

I think you should warn people that Work You Way Around the World is infectious. Even people who I would never have thought would want to go anywhere start flicking through the pages, then get more and more absorbed, become incredibly enthusiastic and demand to go with me on my travels!

RED TAPE

Passports and Work Visas

For travellers serious about working their way, there is no substitute for a full ten-year passport, which in Britain costs £18 for 32 pages and £27 for 48 pages, and takes up to a month to obtain from the regional passport office (longer in the lead-up to the summer holidays). Queuing in person at one of the six passport offices (in Liverpool, London, Newport, Peterborough, Glasgow and Belfast) will speed things up; addresses are listed on passport application forms (available from main post offices).

The free reciprocity of labour within the European Union means that the red tape has been simplified (though not done away with completely). See the chapter *EU Employment*. As will become clear as you read further in this book, work permits/work visas outside the EU are not readily available to ordinary mortals. In almost all cases, you must find an employer willing to apply to the immigration authorities on your behalf months in advance of the job's starting date, while you are in your home country. This is usually a next-to-impossible feat unless you are a high ranking nuclear physicist, a foreign correspondent or are participating in an organised exchange programme where the red tape is taken care of by your sponsoring organisation. Wherever possible, we have mentioned such possibilities throughout this book. The official visa information should be requested from the Embassy or Consulate; addresses in London and Washington are listed in an Appendix. For general information about visas, see *Travel*.

Student Exchange Organisations

BUNAC (16 Bowling Green Lane, London EC1R 0BD; 0171-251-3472) is a student club which helps UK students to work abroad. It has a choice of programmes in the United States, Canada, Australia and Jamaica, and in all cases assists participants to obtain the appropriate short-term working visas.

The Council on International Educational Exchange (205 East 42nd St, New York, NY 10017; 800-INTL-JOB) runs work abroad programmes for students in the following countries, for which it charges a fee of $160 and can arrange working visas: Britain, Ireland, France, Germany, Canada, New Zealand, Australia and Costa Rica. American students should contact their local Council Travel office or obtain a copy of the 'Work Abroad' booklet from CIEE.

The counterpart programmes in Canada and Australia are called SWAP (Student Work Abroad Programme). SWAP in Australia is administered by Student Services Australia in connection with STA Travel (PO Box 399, Carlton South, VIC 3053; 03-348 1777/fax 347 8070). The countries for which exchange programme work visas are available are the UK, USA, Canada, Germany and Japan. The Canadian SWAP brochure covers most of the CIEE destination countries plus Finland, USA, Japan, Australia and Eastern Europe and may be picked up at any office of Travel CUTS in Canada.

Other mainstream organisations mentioned below in *Getting a Job Before You Go* and the *Voluntary Work chapter* will also be able to help with the red tape.

Student Cards

With an International Student Identity Card (ISIC) it is often possible to obtain reduced fares on trains, planes and buses, discounted admission to museums and theatres, and other perks. To obtain a card (which is valid for 15 months from September) you will need the ISIC application form, proof of full-time student status (i.e. photocopy of an NUS card or a letter on school/college headed paper), a passport size photo and a £5 fee (£5.50 if obtained by post). Take these to a local student travel office or write to ISIC Mail Order, Bleaklow House, Howard Town Mills, Mill St, Glossop, Derbyshire SK13 8PT. With the card comes a booklet *(ISIC World Travel Handbook)* giving a country-by-country guide to the discounts available and also information about the ISIC Helpline, a special service for travelling students who need advice in an emergency. Americans can obtain an ISIC or youth identity card from CIEE for $16.

If you are not eligible, people have been known to walk into their local college, say that they are about to start a course and request a student card. There are a great many forgeries in circulation, most of which originate in Cairo or Bangkok.

Bureaucracy at Large

Having your papers in order is a recurring problem for the working traveller. Andrew Winwood thinks that this book underestimates the difficulties:

I wish that you would be honest about immigration, obtaining the proper visas, etc. But having said that, I wouldn't have had the nerve to go in the first place if I'd known how hard it would be.

It is easy to understand why every country in the world has immigration policies which are principally job protection schemes for their own nationals. Nevertheless it can be frustrating to encounter bureaucratic hassles if you merely intend to teach English for a month or so, and there is really no local candidate available with your advantages (e.g. fluency). In all the countries with which we deal, we have tried to set out as clearly as possible the official position regarding visas and work and/or residence permits for both EU and non-EU readers.

If you are cautious by nature you may be very reluctant to transgress the regulations. People in this category will feel much happier if they can arrange things through official channels, such as approved exchange organisations or agencies which arrange permits for you, or by finding an employer willing to get them a work permit, which must normally be collected outside the country of employment. Arranging things this way will require extra reserves of patience.

It seems that a great many decisions are taken at the discretion (or whim) of the individual bureaucrat. Whether or not a document is issued seems to depend more on the mood of the official than on the rulebook. Leeson Clifton from Canada followed all the rules for getting official status as a temporary employee in Norway. When she took her passport to the police for their stamp she was told it would take two weeks and she could not work in the meantime. She returned to the same office the next day and got it done on the spot. She concludes:

The left hand didn't know what the right hand was doing, but of course this is the same in any country. When dealing with government authorities always be patient and pleasant, but keep on asking for what you want and in most cases you'll get it (eventually). Losing your cool gets you nowhere; after all they have no obligations to you.

Other travellers are prepared to throw caution to the winds and echo Helen Welch's view that 'government bureaucracy is the same anywhere, i.e. notoriously slow; by the time the system discovers that you are an alien you can be long gone.' This is more serious in some countries and in certain circumstances than in others, and we have tried to give some idea in this book of the enthusiasm with which the immigration laws are enforced from country to country and the probable outcome for employer and employee if the rules are broken. The authorities will usually turn a blind eye in areas where there is a labour shortage and enforce the letter of the law when there is a glut of unemployed foreign workers. If you do land an unofficial job (helping a Greek islander build a taverna, picking kiwifruit in New Zealand, doing odd jobs at an orphanage in central Africa) try to be as discreet as possible. Noisy boasting has been the downfall of many a traveller who has attracted unwelcome attention. It is always important to be as sensitive as possible to local customs and expectations.

Julian Peachey is another veteran traveller who is suspicious of the value of using official channels:

One of my conclusions is that going through the official channels and taking advice from officialdom is often a mistake. 'Officially' (i.e. the view of the British Council in Paris) it is very hard to get teaching work, as there are so many highly qualified English people living in Paris. The French agricultural information office warns that there is very little in the way of farm work for foreigners.

And yet Julian had a variety of teaching and agricultural jobs throughout France. He claims that if he had believed all that he had been told by officialdom and had taken all the suggested precautions, he would never have been able to go in the first place.

GETTING A JOB BEFORE YOU GO

The subsequent chapters contain a great deal of advice and a number of useful addresses for people wishing to fix up a job before they leave home. If you have ever worked for a firm with branches abroad (e.g. Virgin Records, Alfred Marks, even McDonalds) it may be worth writing in advance to ask about prospects. There is a lot to recommend prior planning especially to people who have never travelled abroad and who feel some trepidation at the prospect. There are lots of 'easy' ways to break into the world of working travellers, for instance working on an American summer camp, joining a two-week voluntary workcamp on the Continent or going on a kibbutz, both of which can be fixed up at home with few problems. Inevitably these will introduce you to an international circle of travellers whose experiences will entertain, instruct and inspire the novice traveller.

Professional or skilled people have a chance of prearranging a job. For example nurses, plumbers, architects, motor mechanics, piano tuners, teachers, divers, secretaries and computer programmers can sometimes find work abroad within their profession by answering adverts in British newspapers and specialist journals, by writing direct to hospitals, schools and businesses abroad, and by registering with the appropriate professional association. For example the Royal College of Nursing (20 Cavendish Square, London W1M 0AB) has an International Officer who can offer advice to members seeking to work overseas.

But the majority of people who dream about working their way around the world do not have a professional or trade qualification. Many will be students who are on the way to becoming qualified, but are impatient to broaden their horizons before graduation. The main requirement seems to be perseverance. Dennis Bricault sent off 137 letters in order to fix up a summer job as a volunteer at an alpine youth hostel.

For many other jobs, it is not at all easy to fix something up in advance. In an ideal world, you could stop in at your local branch of an international employment agency, impress them with your talent and keenness and be assigned your choice of job whether entertainments manager on a Caribbean cruise or ski tow operator in New Zealand. But it just isn't like that and people who expect jobs abroad to be handed to them on a platter by some agency or other are naïve in the extreme. Very very few employers anywhere in the world are willing to hire someone they haven't met. Some cynics would maintain that an employer who cannot fill vacancies locally, and who hires foreign people sight unseen, must be suspect. John Linnemeier worked at a Norwegian hotel, 'for a guy who had such a terrible reputation that none of the locals would work for him'.

Stephen Hands envisions another possibility in an ideal world:

Wouldn't it be great if someone set up a scheme, whereby people could forward correspondence to an exchange of some kind, for people to swap addresses of places they've worked abroad. For example someone planning to work in Nice could write to some agency to obtain the address of another traveller who could tell him what the manager's like or if the chef is an axe-wielding homicidal maniac or that the accommodation is a hole in the bottom of the local coal mine. This would enable working travellers to avoid the rip-off places; also it might save them turning up in places where the work potential is zero.

But axe-wielding chefs get replaced and coal mines are occasionally refurbished. By its nature the kind of detailed knowledge of specific working situations can only be discovered by personal on-the-spot experience. Until such time as Stephen's miracle agency is set up, *Work Your Way Around the World* will have to suffice as the repository of working travellers' information.

Employment Agencies

Adverts which offer glamorous jobs and high wages abroad should be treated with scepticism. They are often placed by one-man companies who are in fact selling printed bumph about jobs on cruise ships, in the United States or whatever, which will not get you much closer to any dream job whatever their ads promise (e.g. 'Earn up to £400 a week in Japan' or 'Would you like to work on a luxury cruise ship?'). A not infrequent con is to charge people for regular job listings in their chosen destination, which may consist of adverts lifted from newspapers long out of date.

According to the Employment Agencies Act of 1973, UK employment agencies (with a couple of exceptions) are not permitted to charge job-seekers an upfront fee. They make their money from the company or organisation seeking staff. (The exceptions are au pair agencies and modelling or theatrical agencies.) Every so often a bogus agency will place false recruitment advertisements in the tabloid press charging a 'registration fee', say of £15 for building workers in the Middle East, and possibly an extra sum for a magazine about living and working in the Middle East. They then disappear without trace. Some operate as clubs offering members certain services such as translating and circulating CVs. Before joining any such club, try to find out what their success rate is. You could even ask to be put in touch with someone whose membership resulted in their getting a job.

There are of course reputable international recruitment agencies in Britain, the USA and elsewhere. Specialist agencies for qualified personnel can be very useful, for example the British Nursing Association (a commercial agency which can assist UK nurses to work abroad) or other agencies for accountants, tradesmen who want to work in Russia, etc. Agencies with a range of specialities from disc jockeys for international hotels to English teachers for language schools abroad are mentioned in the relevant chapters which follow.

In Britain, the Federation of Recruitment & Employment Services (FRES, 36-38 Mortimer St, London W1N 7RB) publishes lists of its members according to specialisation; send a £2 postal order and request the list of overseas placement agencies (which covers topics like catering, nanny, agriculture, petrochemical, etc.) These are almost invariably seeking highly qualified professionals, technicians and managers. A good source of addresses for such agencies is *Jobs & Careers Abroad* (Vacation-Work, £9.95) and the classified advertisements in the fortnightly newspaper *Overseas Jobs Express* (address below). The latter makes an honest attempt to vet agencies and invites any reader who is dissatisfied with the service offered by an advertiser or comes across one which attempts to charge a fee to complain.

International Exchange Organisations

BUNAC, CIEE and SWAP are mentioned in the section above on *Red Tape*, since they have the authority to help participants to obtain work visas. Other organisations (commercial and charitable) offer a package which helps young people take advantage of the work permit rules. Rita Hoek is one person who decided to participate in an organised programme, i.e. Travel Active's 'Work & Travel Australia' programme (address below):

Though I'm not suggesting these programmes are perfect for everybody's specific plans, it's been of great help to me. You join a discount-group airfare (cheaper and easier), they help with getting a visa and most programmes provide a first week of accommodation, assistance in getting a tax file number and opening a bank account, a service to forward your mail, general information about work and travelling and heaps more. If you don't want to feel completely lost at the airport while travelling for the first time (as I was), I can surely recommend it.

Other organisations fix up actual jobs for qualifying applicants. In fact many of the placements arranged through such organisations are tantamount to voluntary work since remuneration may consist in not much more than board and lodging. See the chapter *Voluntary Work* and also the country chapters for organisations which are active in specific countries. The organisations mentioned here operate in a number of countries.

The Central Bureau for Educational Visits and Exchanges (Seymour Mews House, Seymour Mews, London W1H 9PE; 0171-486 5101) is a goldmine of information about official work schemes and exchanges, many of them aimed at students. IAESTE is the acronym for the International Association for the Exchange of Students for Technical Experience. It provides international course-related vacation training for thousands of university-level students in over 60 member countries. Placements are available in engineering, science, agriculture, architecture and related fields. British undergraduates should apply directly to IAESTE UK at the Central Bureau (0171-486 5101 ext 259/60) in the autumn term for placements commencing the following summer. The US affiliate is the Association for International Practical Training (AIPT, 10400 Little Patuxent Parkway, Suite 250, Columbia, Maryland 21044-3510; 301-997-2200) which can consider applications from graduates and young professionals as well as college students.

Also for Americans, the InterExchange Program (161 6th Ave, New York, NY 10013; 212-924-0446/fax 924-0575) can provide work placements in Europe. Students can be placed in resort jobs in Germany (for which the deadline is mid-February) and both students and non-students aged 18-30 can be placed as camp counselors in France, farm workers in Scandinavia and Switzerland, interns in Finland, English teachers in Eastern Europe and au pairs in a range of countries. Placement fees range from $125 to $300.

Similarly, Worldwide Internships & Service Education was incorporated in November 1993 to arrange placements for Americans as au pairs in Europe, camp counsellors in the Netherlands, community volunteers in the UK, farm assistants in Norway and interns in Paris and London. Details are available from WISE, 303 S Craig St, Suite 202, Pittsburgh, PA 15213 (412-681-8120/fax 681-8187).

Exchange organisations in various European countries can help their nationals to work on American summer camps, become au pairs, etc. For example EXIS (see *Netherlands* chapter) publish a free Working Holiday Newsletter for young Dutch people and also arrange a few summer programmes. Travel Active Programmes (PO Box 107, 5800 AC Venray, Netherlands) arrange for 1,000 English-speaking people to work on US summer camps, 1,000 more as au pairs in many countries, and even more on a Work & Travel Australia programme.

Various work exchanges and training programmes exist within the European Union such as the ones administered by Interspeak Ltd (see page 133) and ProEuropa (see page 84).

Useful Publications

Apart from contacting specific organisations, you should consider consulting reference books on the subject and directories of jobs. Publications covering specific countries or specific kinds of work (e.g. *Teaching English Abroad* or *Kibbutz Volunteer*) are mentioned in the relevant chapters. Of general interest are:

The Directory of Summer Jobs Abroad (Vacation Work, 9 Park End Street, Oxford OX1 1HJ; £7.95 plus £1 postage). Published each November.

Working Holidays (Central Bureau for Educational Visits and Exchanges, Seymour Mews House, Seymour Mews, London W1H 9PE at £8.99). Also publish *A Year Between* for £7.99 plus £1 and other work-related titles.

A Year Off... A Year On? (Careers Research & Advisory Centre/Hobsons plc, Bateman St, Cambridge CB2 1LZ at £7.99 from the Biblios Orderline on 01403 710851).

Opportunities in the Gap Year (Independent Schools Careers Organisation, 12a-18a Princess Way, Camberley, Surrey GU15 3SP, at £3.50).

GAP Year Book (Cavendish Educational Consultants, Oddfellow Cottage, Setley, Brockenhurst, Hants, SO42 7UF; 01590 622195). Updated annually.

Central Services Unit, Graduate Careers & Appointments Services, Crawford House, Precinct Centre, Manchester M13 9EP; 0161-273 4233). Publishes a range of booklets and directories including a few about working abroad.

Work Study Travel Abroad: The Whole World Handbook (Council on International Educational Exchange, 205 East 42nd St, New York, NY 10017, USA at $13.95). Not particularly strong on work.

Directory of International Internships, Career Development & Placement Services, Michigan State University, 113 Student Services, East Lansing, Michigan 48824-1113, USA). Third edition 1994. Describes itself as a 'comprehensive guide to international internships sponsored by educational institutions, government agencies and private organisations,' mainly for American undergraduates.

Internships (Peterson's Guides, Inc. 202 Carnegie Center, Princeton, NJ 08543, USA). Although the majority of listings are for on-the-job training opportunities in the US, there is a chapter on international internships. Available from Vacation-Work at £19.95 + £2.50 postage.

Overseas Jobs Express (Premier House, Shoreham Airport, Sussex BN43 5FF; 01273 440220/fax 440229). Fortnightly newspaper for international job hunters. Subscription costs are £18 for three months, £43 for 12 months.

Transitions Abroad, (Dept. TRA, Box 3000, Denville, NJ 07834, USA). Annual subscription (six issues) costs $19.95 within the US, $26 in Canada; $38 outside North America. Valuable resource guide for Americans. The editorial address is 18 Hulst Road, PO Box 1300, Amherst, MA 01004.

Advertisements

While you are still at home you can either try to find job advertisements you might be in a position to answer or you can advertise yourself abroad (or both). Some embassies have a reading room where you can browse in that country's national newspapers (though these will be somewhat out of date). Specialist newsagents do often carry foreign papers, though in some cases bulky Saturday supplements (including classified employment ads) have been jettisoned before shipping.

Unless you have very specialised skills, it is probably not worth advertising your services and availability for work in a foreign newspaper since anyone interested in hiring you would probably want to meet you first. If you have set your sights on finding work in a specific region, it is possible to advertise in the classified sections of local journals either directly or through their UK-based representatives. Among the largest publishers' representatives is Publicitas Ltd. (517-523 Fulham Road, London SW6 1HD), which deals with a number of overseas dailies. Other agencies include Powers Overseas Ltd (Duncan House,

Dolphin Square, London SW1V 3PS) and Smyth International (234 Aylmer Parade, London N2 0PQ). Check in *Willings Press Guide* in any library for the agent which handles advertising in the paper you wish to contact. Advertising rates are high, ranging from £50-200.

Another paper which might be worth checking is *LOOT* (24 Kilburn High Road, London NW6 5UJ; 0171-328 1771) which bills itself as 'London's notice-board,' though there are regional editions in Nottingham, Derby, Leicester, Mansfield, Liverpool and Manchester. Among its many categories of classified ads (which are free to private advertisers) are 'International Jobs Offered/ Wanted' (which doesn't usually contain anything very exciting) and 'Au Pair Jobs Offered/Wanted.' The paper is published daily Monday to Friday and costs £1.10. It is just one of many free newspapers worldwide in the Free Ads Paper International Association, usually printed on coloured newsprint. It is possible to advertise free of charge in any of these papers (from San Diego to Sofia, Rio to Ravenna) which are listed in each issue of *LOOT* with instructions for placing ads.

If you use a foreign newspaper's box office service, there may be delays in receiving replies. In any case, you must allow plenty of time to receive replies and (with luck) negotiate a suitable position. If possible talk to your prospective employer on the telephone and ascertain as many details as possible, to prevent what happened to Kev Vincent:

That summer I decided to try and set up a working holiday in Hawaii for the winter. I obtained the addresses of local newspapers from the Hawaii State tourist board in London and put an advertisement in several of the daily publications on the islands. I asked for free accommodation, food and a small wage in exchange for work, preferably outside on a ranch or farm. I received very few replies (five to be exact) of which only one sounded OK.

So in November I flew to Maui where I had arranged to be picked up at the airport in Kahului. They weren't there so I phoned and after about six hours the mother came to pick me up, mentioning that the charge would be $15. On arrival I was shown to my 'room' — a small space at the rear of their garage, very dirty and ugly, for which they expected me to pay $150 a month in advance. They did not have a small farm, only a few fruit trees in the yard. It didn't take me long to realise that they were only after my money and had taken me for a ride. So I left and hitched back to the capital of Maui, and after an unsuccessful week of looking for work in Honolulu I flew home again. I know this is not the case in all pre-arranged jobs abroad, but I have heard from many travellers that often it's not quite what one thought it might be.

Another disappointed international job-seeker was Josephine Norris who had been assured over the phone that a job would be waiting for her in a bulb packing factory in the Netherlands. So she gave up her housing and unemployment benefit in Glasgow to go to Holland, only to discover that the number she had dialled did not belong to a bulb employer at all but to a Dutch citizen who was so peeved by the number of wrong numbers she had been receiving that she maliciously gave false information over the phone. The story has a happy ending though: Josephine was eventually hired by the bulb processing factory in question. Always try to obtain a written promise of work and terms of employment before making any life-changing decisions.

GETTING A JOB ON ARRIVAL

For those who leave home without something fixed up, a lot of initiative will be needed. Many travellers find it easier to locate casual work in country areas rather than cities, and outside the student holiday periods (although just before Christmas is a good time, when staff turnover is high). But it is possible in cities too, on building sites, in restaurants and in factories. If you go for the jobs which are least appealing (e.g. an orderly in a hospital for the criminally insane, a loo attendant, pylon painter, assistant in a battery chicken farm, salesman of encyclopaedia, dog meat factory worker, dog policemen (in Berlin, people are hired to follow dog-walkers) or just plain dogsbodies, the chances are you will be taken on sooner rather than later.

It always helps to have a neat appearance in order to dissociate yourself from the image of the hobo or hippy. You must show a keenness and persistence which may be out of character but are often essential. Even if a prospective employer turns you down at first, ask again since it is human nature to want to reward keenness and he or she may decide that an extra staff member could be useful after all. Polite pestering pays off. For example, if your requests for work down on the docks produce nothing one day, you must return the next day. After a week your face will be familiar and your eagerness and availability known to potential employers. If nothing seems to be materialising, volunteer to help mend nets (thereby adding a new skill to the ones you can offer) and if an opening does eventually arise, you will be the obvious choice. If you want a job teaching English in a school but there appear to be no openings, volunteer to assist with a class one day a week for no pay and if you prove yourself competent, you will have an excellent chance of filling any vacancy which does occur. So patience and persistence should become your watchwords, and before long you will belong to the fraternity of experienced, worldly-wise travellers who can maintain themselves on the road for extended periods.

Casual work by its very nature is changeable and unpredictable and can best be searched out on the spot. You may follow our advice to go to Avignon France in August, for example, to pick plums or to Magnetic Island Australia to get bar work. When you arrive you may be disappointed to learn that the harvest was unusually early or the resort has already hired enough staff. But your informant may go on to say that if you wait two weeks you can pick grapes or if you travel to the next reef island, there is a shortage of dining room staff. In other words, one thing leads to another once you are on the track.

A certain amount of bravado is a good, even a necessary, thing. If you must exaggerate the amount of experience you have had or the time you intend to stay in order to get a chance to do a job, then so be it. There is little room for shyness and self-effacement in the enterprise of working your way around the world. (On the other hand, bluffing is not recommended if it might result in danger, for example if you pretend to have more sailing experience than you really do for a transatlantic crossing.) After circumnavigating the globe and working in a number of countries David Cooksley comments:

All the information and contacts in the world are absolutely useless unless you make a personal approach to the particular situation. You must be resourceful and never retiring. If I were the manager of a large company which needed self-motivating sales people, I'd hire all the contributors to Work Your Way Around the World *since they have the ability to communicate with anyone anywhere in any language.*

Meeting People

The most worthwhile source of information is without question your fellow travellers. After you have hurled yourself into the fray you will soon become connected up with kindred spirits more experienced at the game than you, whose advice you should heed. Other travellers are surprisingly generous with their information and assistance. David Hewitt claims that this cannot be overemphasised; he and his Brazilian wife have been consistently helped by their compatriots from Berlin to Miami. A Mexican correspondent who arrived in Toronto cold sought out the Latino community and, after taking their advice, was soon comfortably housed and employed.

Hitch-hiking is a good means for getting leads on work, providing you pump the local people who give you lifts for any useful information. If you arrive in a new place without a prearranged contact, there are many ways of meeting the locals and other travellers to find out about job possibilities. Youth hostels are universally recommended, especially out of season, and many hostel wardens will be well versed in the local opportunities for casual jobs. Membership in the Youth Hostels Association costs £9 if you're over 18; you can join at any hostel or at their London office (14 Southampton St, WC2E 7HY; 0171-836 1036).

Private hostels outside the IYHF are sometimes even better sources of information on local work opportunities. Backpacker Resorts of Australia (PO Box 1000, Byron Bay, NSW 2481, Australia) are associated with over 200 other hostels in New Zealand, USA, Europe and Africa. They sell a 'VIP Kit' for $20 which includes a list of international hostel addresses and discounts at all member hostels.

Universities and polytechnics are good meeting places in term-time and also during the vacations when it is often possible to arrange cheap accommodation in student residences. Seek out the overseas student club to meet interesting people who are foreigners just like you. Investigate the student or bohemian parts of town where the itinerant community tends to congregate. Go to the pubs and cafés frequented by worldly-wise travellers (often the ones serving Guinness).

If you have a particular hobby or interest, ask if there is a local club, where you will meet like-minded people; join local ramblers, cyclists, cavers, environmental activists, train spotters, jazz buffs — the more obscure the more welcome you are likely to be. Join evening language courses, frequent the English language bookshop (which may well have a useful notice board) or visit the functions of the English language church, where you are likely to meet the expatriate community or be offered free advice by the vicar. Marta Eleniak introduced herself to the local Polish club, since she has a Polish surname and a fondness for the country, to ask if she could put up a notice asking for accommodation. The kindly soul to whom she was speaking told her not to worry about it; she'd find her something she could move into the next day. She has come to the conclusion that learning to be a 'fog-horn' is an invaluable characteristic.

Not that the people you will meet in this way will necessarily be able to give you a full-time job, but it sets the wheels in motion and before too long you will be earning your way by following their advice and leads. Provided your new friends speak the local language better than you, they can make telephone calls for you, translate newspaper advertisements, write out a message for you to show possible employers and even act as interpreters. One young Englishman was dragged along to the local radio station by his Italian hosts who persuaded the station to have him co-host an afternoon programme. The manager of another traveller's hostel in Cairo wrote out an Arabic notice for him, offering private English lessons.

If your contacts can't offer you a real job they might know of a 'pseudo job' or 'non-job' which can keep you afloat: guarding their yacht, doing odd jobs around their property, babysitting, typing, teaching the children English, or just staying for free. These neatly avoid the issue of work permits, too, since they are arranged on an entirely unofficial and personal basis. Human contacts are usually stronger than red tape.

Chance

When you first set off, the possibility of being a sheep-catcher in the Australian outback or an English tutor in Turkey may never have crossed your mind. Chance is a fine thing and is one of the traveller's greatest allies. Brigitte Albrech had saved up two years' leave from her job in the German tourist industry to go on holiday in Mexico. While there, she became friendly with some Québecois who invited her to join them as tree planters in Western Canada, and she never made it back to her job.

There will be times when you will be amazed by the lucky chain of events which led you into a certain situation. 'Being in the right place at the right time' would have made a suitable subtitle to this book, though of course there are steps you can take to put yourself in the right place, and this book tries to point out what these might be. Here are some examples of how luck, often in combination with initiative, has resulted in travellers finding paid work:

Mark Kilburn took up busking in a small Dutch town and was eventually asked to play a few nights a week in a nearby pub for a fee.

Stuart Britton was befriended by a fisherman in a dusty little town in Mexico and was soon tutoring some of the fisherman's friends and acquaintances (and living in his house).

While standing in a post office queue in the south of France, Brian Williams overheard the word *boulot* (which he knew to mean odd job) and *cerises*. He tapped the lady on the shoulder and offered his cherry picking expertise. After a protracted search for the address she had given him, he finally asked directions of someone who offered him a job in their orchard instead.

On a flight to Reykjavik, Caroline Nicholls happened to sit next to the wife of the managing director of a large fish-packing cooperative in Iceland who told her they were short of staff.

After finishing his summer stint as a camp counsellor in the US, Mark Kinder decided to try one parachute jump. He enjoyed it so much that he learned how to pack parachutes and was able to fund himself at the aerodrome for months afterwards.

While looking for work on a boat in Antibes, Tom Morton found a job as a goatherd for six weeks in the mountains near Monte Carlo.

Dominic Fitzgibbon mentioned to his landlady in Rome that he intended to leave soon for Greece since he had been unable to find a job locally in six weeks of looking. She decided he was far too nice to become a washer-up in a taverna and arranged for him to work as a hall porter at a friend's hotel.

I. A. Gowing was a little startled to wake up one evening in Frankfurt station to find a middle-aged women staring down at him. She offered him the chance of working with her travelling fun-fair.

While getting her jabs for Africa at a clinic in Gibraltar, Mary Hall (a nurse cycling across Europe) noticed a door marked 'District Nurses', barged in and the following week had moved in as a live-in private nurse for a failing old lady.

While shopping in a supermarket in Cyprus, Rhona Stannage noticed a local man with a trolley full of wine and beer, and assumed it could not be for his own consumption. She approached him, ascertained that he ran a restaurant and a day or two later was employed as a waitress.

Connie Paraskeva shared a taxi in Bangkok with an American nurse who told her about a vacancy in a refugee camp.

While sunbathing on an isolated Greek beach, Edward Peters was approached by a farmer and asked to pick his oranges.

The examples could be multiplied *ad infinitum* of how travellers, by keeping their ears open and by making their willingness to help obvious, have fallen into work. One of the keys to success is total flexibility. Within ten minutes of a chance conversation with a family sharing her breakfast table in an Amsterdam hotel, Caroline Langdon had paid her bill, packed her bags and was off to Portugal with them as their mother's help.

Of course there is always such a thing as bad luck too. You may have received all sorts of inside information about a job on a Greek island, a vineyard or in a ski resort. But if a war has decimated tourism (as the Gulf War did) or if there was a late frost which killed off the grapes or if the snowfalls have been poor, there will be far fewer jobs and your information may prove useless. Unpredictability is built into the kinds of jobs which travellers do.

Design

But you cannot rely on luck alone; you will have to create your own luck at times. You may have to apply to 20 hotels before one will accept you and you may have to inform 20 acquaintances of your general plans before one gives you the address of a useful contact. Public libraries can be helpful as proved by the traveller who found a directory of wildlife and environmental organisations in a South African library and went on to fix up a board-and-lodging job at a game reserve.

You must check notice boards and newspaper advertisements, register with agencies and most important of all use the unselective 'walk-in-and-ask' method, just like job-seekers anywhere. The most important tools for an on-the-spot job hunt are a copy of the Yellow Pages and a phone card. When Mary Hall was starting her job search in Switzerland, a friend gave her an odd piece of advice which she claims works, to smile while speaking on the phone. Some people say that all initial approaches are best made by telephone since refusals are less demoralising than in person and you need not worry about the scruffiness of your wardrobe.

One old hand Alan Corrie, describes his approach:

The town of Annecy in the French Alps looked great so I found a fairly cheap hostel and got down to getting organised. This meant I was doing the rounds of the agencies, employment office, notice boards and cafés for a few days. After a matter of minutes in a town, I begin to sprout plastic bags full of maps, plans, lists, addresses and scraps of advice from people I have met on the road.

Alan sounds unusually cheerful and optimistic about job-hunting and the result is that he worked in Europe for the better part of a decade. He concludes:

Looking for work in Annecy was an enjoyable pastime in early autumn. Making contacts and job hunting in a new place is a whole lot more fun than actually working and worrying about the bills as I've often found before.

Our working wanderers have displayed remarkable initiative and found their jobs in a great variety of ways:

Waiter in Northern Cyprus: *I arranged my job by writing direct to the restaurant after seeing a two-minute clip on a BBC travel programme. Rita wrote back and here I am.*

Farmhand on a Danish farm: *I placed an advert in* Landsbladet, *the farmers' weekly, and chose one from four replies.*

Au pair to a family in Helsinki: *I found work as a nanny in Finland simply by placing advertisement cards in a few playgroups.*

Teacher at a language school in southern Italy: *We used the Yellow Pages in a Sicilian Post Office and from our 30 speculative applications received four job offers without so much as an interview.*

Winery guide in Spain: *I composed a modest and polite letter and sent it to an address copied from one of my father's wine labels. I was astonished at their favourable reply.* Several years later the same contributor wrote to say, *I sent a*

copy of the page in your book where I am mentioned to prospective employers in Australia, and I was offered a job on a vineyard near Melbourne.
Factory assistant in Ghana: *I asked the local Amnesty International representative for any leads.*
Implicit in all these stories is that you must take positive action.

REWARDS AND RISKS

The Delights

The rewards of travelling are mostly self-evident: the interesting characters and lifestyles you are sure to meet, the wealth of anecdotes you will collect with which you can regale your grandchildren and photos with which you can bore your friends, a feeling of achievement, an increased self-reliance and maturity, a better perspective on your own country and your own habits, a good sun tan... the list could continue. Stephen Psallidas summed up his views on travelling:

Meeting people from all over the world gives you a more tolerant attitude to other nationalities, races, etc. More importantly you learn to tolerate yourself, to learn more about your strengths and weaknesses. While we're on the clichés, you definitely 'find yourself, man'.

One traveller came back from a stint of working on the Continent feeling a part of Europe rather than just an Englishman. (Perhaps some Brussels bureaucrat should be subsidising this book.) After working in Sydney with Chinese exiles who had left their country after the Tiannanmen Square massacre, Ken Smith felt that his own problems had dwindled into insignificance compared to what his workmates had suffered.

One of the best aspects of the travelling life is that you are a free and unfettered agent. Albert Schweizer might have been thinking of the working traveller instead of equatorial Africans when he wrote:

He works well under certain circumstances so long as the circumstances require it. He is not idle, but he is a free man, hence he is always a casual worker.

Jane Roberts has travelled the world and got into some very sticky situations from the Malaysian countryside to downtown Toronto, but her last letter ended with a little impromptu poem:

I can go
Wherever I like
Whenever I like
With whoever I like
I am totally free
Are you as lucky as me?

(She has since married a Croatian man she met on the road, so may have taken on some new constraints, but never mind.)

The Dangers

Of course there are dangers too as emphasised by the tragic case of the 18-year old from Lancashire who was stabbed and left for dead when she was hitch-hiking through Bordeaux to do some fruit-picking. Any women who are feeling especially anxious about the risks of travelling and working abroad might be cheered by the statistic that of all the letters addressed to the editor of this book in the last 18 months, 40% were from women, and not one hinted that she was sorry she had gone. In many ways a solo woman traveller gains extra respect from the people she meets and in many cases finds it easier to get work. A worthwhile book to browse in for advice and encouragement is *Women Travel* (Penguin, £6.95).

A much less remote possibility is that you might be robbed or lose your luggage. You may get sick or lonely or fed up. (Always arrange to receive mail from time to time via poste restante or American Express to avoid becoming completely alienated from your roots.) You might have a demoralising run of bad luck and fail to find a job, and begin to run out of money (if this is the case, consult the chapter *In Extremis*).

Many unofficial jobs carry with them an element of insecurity. You may not be protected by employment legislation and may not be in a position to negotiate with the boss. Often the work may be available to travellers like you because the conditions are unacceptable to a stable local population (or because the place is too remote to have a local population). Phil New is probably right when he says that the travellers who worry that they won't get paid or won't get hired are the very ones who do encounter problems. If you have cultivated the right attitude, you will not hesitate to drift on to a new situation if the old one should become undesirable for any reason.

Exploitative working conditions will show you how much you are prepared to tolerate. Paul Bridgland was not sorry to have worked for a tyrannical and abusive boss in Crete, since he now thinks he has developed such a thick skin that no future employer could penetrate it.

Much is now said about 'socially responsible tourism' and perhaps working travellers who put up with dreadful employers are doing both their host community and other travellers a disservice. Stephen Psallidas's advice (based on his own experience of exploitative Greek bosses) is not to put up with it:

> *My advice when you are mistreated or your employer acts unprofessionally is to shout back when they shout at you. If things don't improve threaten to walk out and then do so. You will be doing a favour to future working travellers, and you will almost ceratinly be able to find something else if you try hard enough.*

Charlotte Jakobson's worst employer was a hotelier in the middle of nowhere in Norway. When she discovered how underpaid she was she contacted a union official who was shocked and wanted to take action. Today she regrets that she was so keen to get away that she didn't stay to present the case and thinks of other girls who were probably subjected to the same bad experiences as a result.

Travellers have a responsibility towards future travellers in other respects. Robert Mallakee felt that he should work especially hard for a Cypriot farmer who had lent his previous English helper £200 just before the fellow absconded. The respect and sensitivity you should show to other cultures is even more important in a working context.

Some people set off with false expectations about the life of the working traveller. Armin Birrer (who has travelled long enough to have earned his right to make such pronouncements) says that some of the enthusiasm with which travel writers tend to glorify travel should be moderated a little. The travelling life is full of uncertainty and hardship. To quote the inveterate working traveller Stephen Psallidas once more, 'I would say that the bad times even outnumber the good times, but the good times are *great* and the bad times are good for you in the end.'

Even when a planned working holiday does not work out successfully, the experience will be far more memorable than just staying at home. This view is held by Stephen Hands who didn't regret his decision to go abroad to look for work (although it didn't work out) but he did regret boasting to all his friends that he was off for an indefinite period to see the world. After writing pages about her dodgy and difficult jobs in Australia, Emma Dunnage concluded with a typical paradox: 'But we did have the best time of our lives'.

Though travelling itself is never dull, a job which you find to help out your finances along the way may well be. True 'working holidays' are rare: one example is to exchange your labour for a free trip with an outback Australian camping tour operator (see *Australia* chapter) or for a cruise to the midnight sun (see *Scandinavia*). But in many cases, the expression 'working holiday' is an oxymoron (like 'cruel kindness' or 'caring Tory'). Jobs are jobs wherever you do them. David Anderson, who found himself working on an isolated Danish farm where he didn't feel at home in any way, recommends taking (a) your time to decide to accept a job, (b) a copy of *War and Peace* and (c) enough money to facilitate leaving if necessary. The best policy is to leave home only after you have the reserves to be able to work when you want to.

Coming Home

Kristin Moen thinks that there should be a big warning at the beginning of *Work Your Way Around the World:* WHEN YOU FIRST START TO TRAVEL THERE IS NO WAY YOU CAN STOP! Correspondents have variously called travel an illness and an addiction. Once you set off you will probably come across a few restless souls for whom the idea of settling down is anathema and for whom the word 'vagabondage' was invented. Undoubtedly some use it as a form of escapism, believing it to be a panacea for all their problems. But these are the exceptions.

In the majority of cases, homesickness eventually sets in, and the longing for a pint of bitter, a bacon sandwich, a baseball game, Radio 4's 'Today' programme, green fields, Marks & Spencer or Mum's home cooking will get the better of you. Or perhaps duty intervenes as in the case of Michael Tunison:

I had planned to go on to South America this summer, but I had to return home under emergency circumstances. Not one, but two of my best friends were getting married. What is a poor globetrotter to do with people rather inconsiderately going on with their lives when he isn't even there? But after a year it was actually quite nice to have a chance to organise my things and repack for further adventures.

At some point your instinct will tell you that the time has come to hang up your rucksack (assuming you haven't sold it).

Settling back will be difficult especially if you have not been able to set aside some money for 'The Return'. It can be a wretched feeling after some glorious adventures to find yourself with nothing to start over on. Life at home may seem a little dull and routine at first, while the outlook of your friends and family can strike you as narrow and limited. If you have been round the world between school and further study, you may find it difficult to bridge the gulf between you and your stay-at-home peers who may feel a little threatened or belittled by your experiences. After travelling the length of Latin America (including some off-the-beaten-track teaching in Mexico), David Brown from Tayside volunteered to contribute articles on 'how not to lose the rag while queuing for sandwiches in Boots' and 'the psychosomatic reaction to wearing a collar and tie again' for any future book with the working title 'Life after Travel: How to Cope.' But the reverse culture shock normally wears off soon enough and you will begin to feel reintegrated in your course or job. In some cases the changes which travel have brought about may be more than just psychological; for example David Hewitt set off on his travels a bachelor, married a fellow volunteer from Brazil met on his kibbutz and then had a child whom they were trying to make into a working traveller before she reached her first birthday by putting her forward for promotions in the US.

People often wonder whether a long spell of travelling will damage their future job prospects. According to numerous surveys on graduate employment, most employers are sympathetic to people who defer entry to the labour market. In the majority of cases, travel seems to be considered an advantage, something that makes you stand out from the crowd. Marcus Scrace found that even in his profession of chartered surveying, employers looked favourably on someone who had had the get-up-and-go to work his way around the world. Jeremy Pack chose to join the computing industry upon his return and claimed that he did not meet one negative reaction to his two years off. Naturally it helps if you can present your experiences positively, if only to prevent the potential employer from imagining you out of your skull on a beach in Goa for 12 months. Your travels must be presented constructively and not as an extended doss. Stephen Psallidas, who recently returned to a more settled existence after three years on the road, is convinced that he would never have got a good job (as Projects Manager in Computer Education) before he left. Not that he gained any relevant experience on his travels but he had learned how to be persistent and pester employers for an interview.

Some hostility is probably inevitable especially when the job market is shrinking making employers more conservative. Jane Thomas knew that it would be tough finding a job when she got back to England, but she didn't know how tough. Some interviewers did express their concern and suspicion that she would want to take off again (which at that time was exactly what she did want to do). But she also found that she could adapt the short-term jobs she had done in the US and Australia to fit whatever job she was trying to get. And after a certain period of time has elapsed, your absence from the conventional working world ceases to be an issue. At last report Jane had a job making videos with the possibility of some work with the BBC.

In some cases the jobs you have found abroad are a positive boost to your 'real life' prospects, as in the case of Michael Tunison from Michigan:

> *Newspaper work was exactly what I thought I was leaving behind by globetrotting. I'd temporarily sacrificed (I believed) my career as a journalist. The last place I thought I'd be working was at a daily in Mexico. But things never work out as planned and before I knew it I was the managing editor's assistant and a month or so later the managing editor of the paper's weekend editions. How ironic. By taking a step my newspaper friends believed to be an irresponsible career move, I was soon years ahead of where I'd have been following the old safe route back home.*

Conclusion

While some identify the initial decision to go abroad as the hardest part, others find the inevitable troughs (such as finding yourself alone in a sleazy hotel room on your birthday, running out of money with no immediate prospect of work, etc.) more difficult to cope with. But if travelling requires a much greater investment of energy than staying at home, it will reward the effort many times over.

A host of travellers have mentioned how much they value their collection of memories. Since we have been guided by the experiences of ordinary travellers throughout the writing of this book, let one of their number, Steve Hendry, end the *Introduction*:

> *I left home with about £100 and no return ticket. I spent two years in Israel, three years in Thailand, one year in Japan. I have lived in the sun for years, with Arabs on the seashore and with wealthy Japanese. If I can do it, you can too. I've learned so very much. Travelling is 100% fun and educational. What are you waiting for?*

WORKING
A PASSAGE

Many people setting out on their world travels assume, not unreasonably, that a large chunk of their savings must inevitably be swallowed up by airlines, railways and shipping companies. This need not be so. With a little advance planning, a fair amount of bravado and a dose of good fortune you can follow the example of thousands of travellers who have successfully voyaged around the globe for next to nothing.

Hitch-hiking is an excellent way to cross several continents (see *Travel*), but usually fails to solve the problem of sea crossings. Since it is a relatively slow means of travel, it also eats into your funds since you need to sustain yourself en route. Stowing away on an ocean-going freighter is not what it was, or at least what it was reputed to be. The harsh reality of modern shipping means that stowaways are certainly not tolerated as romantic rogues. Recent stories told in maritime circles include cases of stowaways being tossed into shark-infested waters or burned alive.

Fortunately, if you are serious about travelling free or cheaply in ways other than hitch-hiking, there are several methods of working a passage by land, sea or air.

SEA

Commercial Shipping

Sadly, the days have long since gone when you might have gone to the docks at Southampton or Tilbury, New York or San Francisco, expecting to be given a job on the first steam packet to the Orient. Only registered seafarers are allowed to work on British-registered ships. The only realistic hope for casual employment and attendant transport lies with the more far-flung lines of Scandinavia and the Far East, or with the numerous ships sailing under flags of convenience e.g. Panama, Liberia and the great maritime nation of Liechtenstein. More and more UK ships are being flagged out (i.e. registered abroad) to avoid the high cost of unionised British labour. Very occasionally a medium-sized cargo ship takes on an individual who has petitioned the captain for work, though in the vast majority of cases, merchant ships are fully staffed with low paid, non-unionised workers, many of whom are recruited from Third World countries.

If you are asking captains for work, you will stand a better chance of impressing him (almost never her) if you can offer reliable references and some needed skill such as catering or carpentry, any necessary visas, a certificate of good health and comprehensive insurance. If you do join a ship's crew you will probably be the general dogsbody, and be given the jobs nobody else wants to do. Shifts are normally 12 hours, or you may be working a double shift, six hours on and six hours off.

We have heard of very few intrepid travellers who have succeeded with this method. After spending six months in India one such traveller, who chooses to call himself Steve Smith, went down to the enormous bustling harbour of Bombay and asked the captain of a cargo boat from Ghana to take him on as an assistant; within an hour of asking he had set sail for Egypt. His duties were simply to run messages, keep watch and share the cooking duties. Later during his travels around Africa, Steve tried the same technique, this time in Conakry the capital of Guinea on the coast of West Africa. He started at one end of the commercial harbour and the fifth boat agreed to take him to Casablanca (a nine-day trip) in exchange for his labour and about £20 towards expenses. This was not nearly as enjoyable a voyage as the one across the Arabian Sea since he was given the most unpleasant jobs like cleaning the cargo hold and pumping out the bilge, plus he wasn't given a proper berth.

According to Steve, the harbour authorities can be very helpful, especially in countries off the beaten track. (Be careful not to confuse them with customs officers.) They will sometimes show you a list of all the ships arriving and departing, since commercial shipping is almost as carefully regulated as air traffic. Sometimes you will have to ask their permission to go on to the docks, for example in Port Sudan you need to get a permit from the wharf police before you can ask captains for a lift to Mombasa or India. It is worth getting on the right side of the harbour-master since captains may tell him about their need of extra crew. At least, they can advise you about the tides. When it is coming up to high tide (spring tide) boats leave, and so this is a good time to ask around. Steve disagrees with the theory that habourside bars are a good place to introduce yourself to captains. In his experience captains are there to escape the responsibilities of the ship, and are much more likely to consider your offer seriously when they are aboard their vessel. It is a good idea, however to chat up the barman in the local harbour bar, buy him a drink and ask him to keep his ears open.

Cruise Liners

The luxury cruise liner business has (surprisingly) not been affected by the recession and over a thousand liners sail the world's oceans at present. Each ship requires a full range of staff, just as a fancy hotel does. Most recruitment takes place through agencies or 'concessionaires', all of whom say that they are looking only for qualified and experienced staff. But in many cases it is sufficient to be over 21 and have an extrovert personality and plenty of stamina for the very long hours of work on board.

According to Jane Roberts, who crossed the Atlantic from Venezuela to Estonia as a cruise liner croupier, not all employees are experienced professionals:

I worked in the casino department of four different cruise ships and met many people doing jobs as waiters, bar tenders, stewards and stewardesses. These jobs are very easy to come by. In fact 80% of all crew members are people who have never done that particular job in their lives. The turn-over of staff is high, even when people sign year-long contracts, since few people complete them. It is difficult to live and work with the same people 24 hours a day. Crew don't get days off, perhaps just the odd breakfast or lunch off once a month. Patience levels have to be extremely high, since people who take holidays on cruise ships seem to think that they own the damn ship. Having to be sickeningly nice can take its toll very quickly.

Contract lengths (some as short as four months) and conditions vary from ship to ship. The smaller, classier ships are your best bet. On larger ships you may have four to a cabin and communal, smelly showers/toilets. Wages are usually US$300-400 a month but can be increased with tips.

In most cases it is essential to be hired through an agency. When Stephen Cleary was in Acapulco he decided he wanted to work on a ship. When he asked a ship owned by the British company Princess Cruises he was told that he would have to go to Los Angeles because they could not sort out the paperwork and when he enquired in LA he was told he had to apply in Southampton. On the other hand some local cruise ships may hire people on-the-spot. When Stephen Psallidas was working on the Greek island of Mykonos, he noticed that several Aegean cruise ships were looking for staff.

Some UK agencies which recruit for the most prestigious liners (like Logbridge in Southampton which has the concession for the QE2 among others) do recruit only professional hotel and catering staff through advertisements in the specialist press like *The Caterer* and *Hotel Keeper*. In the UK, the following companies recruit cruise ship personnel:

Alison MacLeod Associates, Navigator House, 60 High St, Hampton Wick, Surrey KT1 4DB (0181-943 9994). Recruits personnel for over 75 cruise liners and ferry companies worldwide.

Carnival Cruise Lines, Walter House, 418-422 Stand, London WC2R 0PT. Service trainees with bar or restaurant experience, cooks with City & Guilds qualifications and junior pursers with hotel management qualification.

Crews International, Dormer House, 45 The Village, Berryharbor, North Devon EX34 9SE. Waiters and assitant waiters with at least two years experience.

Lawson Marine Services Ltd., Royale House, 2 Palmyra Place, Newport, Gwent NP9 4EJ (01633 257558). Experienced management personnel only for hotels, bars and as pursers on worldwide cruises. College graduates with no practical work experience cannot be considered.

Quest Appointments (Eastleigh) Ltd., Binning House, 4-6 High St, Eastleigh. Hants. SO5 5LA (01703 618825). Mainly catering staff.

Supersearch International Ltd, Suite 8, 1 Pink Lane, Newcastle upon Tyne NE1 5DW (0191-233 0404). All categories of hotel staff.

VIP International, 17 Charing Cross Road, London WC2H 0EP (0171-930 0541). Silver service waiters, chefs, hotel managers, bartenders, bar waiters (male and female), and bar managers placed.

Berkeley Bureau, 11 Cranmer Road, Hampton Hill, Middlesex TW12 1DW (0181-941 7110). Casino staff with at least one year's experience on land.

Steiner, 57-65 The Broadway, Stanmore, Middlesex HA7 4DU. Beauty therapists, hairdressers, massage therapists, etc. for 52 ships.

In the US, Blue Seas International Cruise Services Inc (530 East 84th St, Suite 5R, New York, NY 10028-7355; 212-734-6749) screens, interviews and recruits candidates for shipboard cruise staff positions worldwide on 58 cruise lines. They charge a consultation fee of $40 for half an hour, and then 15% of your gross wage if hired. Ship Services International Inc (370 West Camino Gardens Boulevard, Third Floor, Boca Raton, Florida 33432; 407-391-5500) is a concessionaire to the cruise industry specialising in entertainment. There is a $25 fee for reviewing the resumés of any aspiring singers, DJs, magicians, etc.

The Norwegian Seabourn Cruise Line (PO Box 275, Lysaker, Norway) employs international crew members who have a professional catering background.

Do not be misled by advertisements which read 'Cruise Ships are Hiring Now.' These are almost always placed by someone trying to sell a book about employment on cruise ships, and these are of varying quality. If you have £14.95 to spend on a specialist book, then the book from Innovative Cruise Services (36 Midlothian Drive, Waverley Park, Glasgow G41 3QU; 0141-649 8644) is worth considering because they receive monthly updates from an agent in Florida and will send these to purchasers of their book free of charge on request. Another possibility is *Crews for Cruise* from Harp Publications Ltd (Thames House, Swan St, Old Isleworth, Middlesex TW7 6RG) which costs £14.95. The best one in the US is *How to Get a Job with a Cruise Line* (third edition 1994) by Mary Fallon Miller (Ticket to Adventure Inc, PO Box 41005, St Petersburg, FL 33743-1005) which costs $14.95 plus $3 US postage/$6 overseas. It contains a directory of cruise line headquarters and employment agencies, most of which are in Florida.

Private Yachts

People who sail the seas for pleasure are not subject to the same restrictions as merchant or cruise ship owners. They may hire and fire a crew member whenever they like, and work permits are not a problem. If you display a reasonable level of common sense, vigour and amiability, and take the trouble to observe yachting etiquette, you should find it possible to persuade a yachtsman that you will be an asset to his crew. It should be stressed that inexperienced crew are almost never paid; in fact most skippers expect some contribution towards expenses, up to £20 a day for food, drink, fuel, harbour fees, etc. though US$20 is more usual.

Obviously, it is much easier to become a crew member if you have some experience. Once you have worked on one yacht it will be much easier to get on the next one. The yachting world is a small one. The more experience you have, the more favourable arrangements you will be able to negotiate. If you are embarking on a serious round-the-world-on-a-shoestring venture, it might be worth doing a short sailing course (and take your certificate with you). The first level, Competent Crew, can be reached in about a week at any Royal Yachting Association recognised centre for from £200; details from the RYA, Romsey Road, Eastleigh, Hants. SO5 4YA, who can also send you a leaflet 'Careers in Sailing' and a list of crew registers in Britain. A similar course offered by the ASA in the US costs about $350. Anyone who is a confident cook, carpenter or sewing machine operator (for sail-mending) may be able to market those skills too.

One experienced sailing traveller recommends preparing yourself for working on ships before you set off:

It is a good idea, before leaving home, to read a couple of informative yachting books which contain invaluable information on technical sea terms, and the very basics of navigation. Any information you have or claim to have can often be put to the test for real, and I would strongly advise would-be seafarers to look into the fundamentals of sea travel. Her Majesty's Stationery Office (HMSO) publish The Seaway Code *which is the equivalent of* The Highway Code *and contains much information on ships, priority traffic and navigation lights at night, etc. Whilst it is unlikely that you will be left alone on the bridge, you may be (as I was) required to keep second watch, which is a sort of back-up watch when it is quiet.*

As one skipper comments, 'A beginner ceases to be a passenger if he or she can tie half a dozen knots and hitches, know how to read the lights of various kinds of ships and boats at night, and isn't permanently seasick.' Sometimes the arrangement is halfway between working and hitching a lift. There may not be much actual work to do but you could make cups of coffee, sand deck chairs or play Scrabble with the captain's wife. Women must take care in defining their role on board before they set sail, and should make sure they are not going to be exploited in any way. Adverts which read something like, 'Mature male 40 years of age looking for attractive young lady to help on board with cooking and entertaining on cruise to Med' should probably be treated with some suspicion.

Some solo women sailors concentrate on job-hunting on cruisers sailed by retired couples partly for this reason and also because they are often the ones looking for a young deck hand.

A good way of getting started is to base yourself in a marina or boatyard and undertake hard and tedious maintenance work, sanding, painting, varnishing or scraping barnacles from the hull. If you are completely unfamiliar with the techniques, offer to work for free in exchange for instruction. Later you can aim for an easier life looking after a boat for an absent skipper by living onboard and checking anchors and bilges.

Nearer destinations should be easier to reach than distant and exotic ones, both because of the larger numbers of yachts sailing short distances, and their greater willingness to take a chance on you. If you merely want to get from Tangiers to Gibraltar, from the Bahamas to the United States, from one Pacific Island to another or from Rhodes to Turkey, any small yacht harbour might provide the appropriate lift. On the other hand skippers are more likely to want extra crew on long journeys on the open seas (sometimes just to satisfy insurance requirements) rather than on the more enjoyable and leisurely coastal cruising.

If you are planning your trip a long way in advance, scour the classified columns of *Yachting Monthly, Yachting World* or *Practical Boat Owner*, though advertisers are likely to require a substantial payment or contribution towards expenses on your part. Camilla Lambert was attracted by an advert in *The Times* which read 'young people in search of adventure needed to help sail a tall ship back from the Caribbean'. When she made enquiries she was disgusted to learn that they were looking for people willing to pay £3,000 for three weeks and felt that they should have been more honest in their advert.

Crewing agencies exist in Britain, France, America and elsewhere to match yacht captains and crew. These are mostly of use to professional experienced sailors, though occasionally an entry such as the following will be included:

> *39' teak sloop moored Ipswich heading for Adriatic Ionian Greek waters for 1994 summer season. Amateurs aged 25-35 needed with some offshore experience. Must be prepared to help clean/cook. Food and drink provided, no expenses required.*

The Cruising Association (CA House, 1 Northey St, Limehouse Basin, London E14 8BT; 0171-537 2828) runs a crewing service to put skippers in touch with unpaid crew. Monthly meetings are held between February and July for this purpose. They claim to offer a variety of sailing (including two or three week cruises to the Mediterranean and transatlantic passages) to suit virtually every level of experience. The fee for this service is £18.

Other crewing registers for professional yachtsmen and women to try are:

Crewseekers Crew Introduction Agency, Hawthorn House, Hawthorn Lane, Saris-bury Green, Southampton, Hants. SO3 6BD (tel/fax 01489 578319). £30 for six months, £35 for a year. Claim to be the largest crewing agency in Europe.

Crew Search International, 17 Gillingham St, London SW1 (01582 477906).

Travelmate, 52 York Place, Bournemouth BH7 6JN (01202 431520). A travel companion agency which has a special Crewfinder section for boat owners and potential crew. £25 per year. Reciprocal arrangement with Caribbean Crews of Florida which will put forward details of Travelmate clients when appropriate.

Once you're abroad, you'll have to track down your own sailing adventures. Frank Schiller split expenses with the New Zealand couple who took him (a complete sailing novice) aboard their yacht bound for Tonga and he ended up spending NZ$400 for four months of cruising. Always be sure to discuss the details of payment before setting sail. Many captains will ask you to pay a bond (say $500) for a long journey.

Whenever you end up finding a yacht to crew on, you may be letting yourself in for discomfort and danger, not to mention boredom, especially if you find yourself painting the boat in dock for the umpteenth time. Yachts require a surprising amount of maintenance. Offshore sailing is a risky business and you should be sure that the skipper to whom you have entrusted your life is a veteran sailor. A well-used but well-kept boat is a good sign. Don't be afraid to ask about safety procedures; this will also make you look like a sober and responsible kind of person.

Make sure before you leave the safety of dry land that your personality and politics do not clash with that of the Captain. Quickly tiring of Gibraltar, Nicola Sarjeant and her Dutch boyfriend decided to join the hordes of people looking for a working passage on a yacht:

We asked around from boat to boat but most people weren't interested or wanted experienced people. We also put up a note in a shop in the harbour. This was answered by an Englishman who wanted a couple to help him crew to the Canaries and on to the West Indies. We had to contribute to food and expenses as well as do two four-hour watches per day. We also scrubbed and painted the bottom of the yacht. Because we were inexperienced we weren't paid which at the time seemed the best deal going in Gibraltar as there were many experienced people looking for crewing positions.

I must caution anybody considering this kind of thing to think seriously about whether they can get along with the other people on the boat for a period of several weeks without throwing someone overboard. It turned out the captain had wanted a couple because he assumed a woman would cook dinner, wash dishes, etc. By the time we reached Gran Canaria (after three weeks because we made so many stops) the four of us were at each others' throats. My boyfriend and I hopped off (penniless). The trip had turned out to be quite expensive, though we saw islands I wouldn't otherwise have seen (Madeira in particular) and we got to learn a little about sailing. However the sailing is mostly quite boring (a yacht is very slow moving) and when you don't like the people, a lot of the fun goes out of the trip.

Also try to ascertain in advance whether you will be subjected to any unfair pressures or unexpected fees. While travelling in Fiji, Melanie Grey met a man who had had a disastrous time crewing from Cairns:

After having paid in full for the entire sail from Cairns to New Zealand, Derek was forced to leave the vessel in Vanuatu along with several other crew members. This was due to the Hitler-style regime of the Belgian skipper and his girlfriend. After parting with large amounts of money (A$25 a day), the crew were treated like slaves, every morsel of food consumed was closely monitored, and the female members of the crew were often reduced to tears. The skipper obviously took on crew purely for the financial gain and not for the company or the pleasure of sailing. The crew members who left the trip prematurely were not reimbursed.

It is also not unknown for crew to be thrown off a boat, perhaps on a remote island, if there is a personality clash. Never underestimate the stress of life afloat. Always make sure that you sign a contract entitling you to some compensation if you do not complete all the legs of the journey. And don't do anything which could get the Captain into trouble. (Carrying drugs is the most extreme example; a boat that is found to be carrying drugs will be confiscated.)

The chartering business is booming in holiday resorts and many are owned by companies rather than individuals, which means that you will have to submit a formal application. If looking for work on a charter yacht, Paula Hurwitz suggests compiling a list of yacht brokers by impersonating a high-spending tourist and asking for brochures. This will give you a useful starting place for selling your services to charter companies. Pauline Power, an experienced sailor from Ireland, noticed a beautiful 4-masted tall ship called *Sea Cloud* while she was crewing in the Canaries. When she later applied for work to the Hamburg-registered charter ship (040-369 0272), she was given one of the 80 contracts available to experienced sailors and cabin and restaurant staff.

Charming the Captain

In every marina and harbour there are people planning and preparing for long trips. There may be requests for crew posted on harbour notice boards, in yacht clubs or chandlery shops from Marina Bay in Gibraltar to Rushcutter's Bay in Sydney. Or you may have to approach skippers on spec. The most straightforward (and usually the most successful) method is to head for the nearest yacht marina and ask captains directly. To locate the yacht basin in an unfamiliar town, simply ask at your hotel or the tourist office. The harbour water supply or dinghy dock is usually a good place to meet yachties. One sailor looking for a berth in Thailand found that he had to swim out to the anchored yachts to knock on their hulls, which culminated in a free ride to Malaysia.

Since many of the yachts moored are used for local pleasure sailing only, concentrate on the yachts with foreign flags. Some travellers contend that boat-owners appreciate a straightforward approach: 'Good morning. I'd like to work for you.' Others think that this might catch captains off guard, and that it is better to approach the question in a more roundabout fashion. Many British, North American and Australian travellers are working their way around by cleaning boats and then participating as crew members as a means of alleviating travel expenses to their next destination. If you are not afraid to ask, your options can be greatly increased. Nothing can be lost by asking and much may be gained.

A yacht is a home, so an unwelcome intrusion on board is as bad as entering a house uninvited. The accepted phrase is 'permission to board?'. Once on board, behave as politely and as deferentially as you would in any stranger's home. Once you get to know both the boat and its owner, you can find ways to make yourself useful, whether washing up or scraping barnacles from the hull. You are then more likely to be offered a berth when the yacht finally sails.

Unless you are exceptionally lucky, you must expect to face a lot of competition for crewing positions and be prepared for repeated rejections and humiliations. Posting a notice on a marina notice board is usually not enough: you must visit the docks and sell yourself. This is one time when it is *not* a good idea to exaggerate your qualifications, since skippers who find out that they have been misled will be justifiably furious and, at worst, it could be life-endangering. Britons will probably do better with yachts sailing the British flag, and women often have an edge if only because of their relative novelty in a world dominated by men.

Women sailors encounter special problems and in fact are usually trying *not* to charm the captain to excess. Mirjam Koppelaars, who responded to a notice posted by a yachtsman in Gibraltar, spells out the problems:

> *I must put some words of warning, especially for the female sailors. Most captains who are actively looking for crew are not really interested in finding competent crew, but in finding female company for day — and nighttime. Be aware of this and think it over before boarding a boat. Elise from Norway and I sailed with this extremely peculiar captain and a third crew member (Simon from England) over to the Canary Islands. I shouldn't complain too much about it, since we were one of the only boats which actually made this trip without any damage that year, but anyway, we were all three very glad that we could jump over to another boat in Las Palmas.*

Crewing From Britain

There are many yacht basins along the south coast of Britain, from Burnham-on-Crouch in Essex to Falmouth, Cornwall, with Brighton, Chichester Harbour, Lymington, Hamble and other marinas in between. Cruising yachtsmen set sail from all these marinas to various destinations across the Channel or across the Atlantic. After finding out which bars the yachting fraternity frequents, you should make your face and your requirements known (assuming you do not use a crewing agency).

Boat owners who leave in the spring are probably planning to cruise around the Mediterranean for the summer; those leaving in late October/early November may well be going to spend the winter in the Caribbean. Some are also heading to Scandinavia as Adam Cook reports:

After a heart-stopping 11 days to windward from Gibraltar to Lymington, I stayed on as crew for the trip to Norway. Wow, the North Sea, it really is yellow sou'wester country out there. The sea is full of oil rigs, Danish fishing boats and the infamous 'stealth' tanker, the kind that only turns on its running lights when you're right up its blunt end.

Crewing in the Mediterranean

The standard pattern is for a traveller to get a job on a yacht for the summer charter season on the Mediterranean and then sail with the same yacht or power boat (the latter are generally more boring) to the Americas or (occasionally) South Africa. Hundreds of boats descend on Gibraltar in the spring, many of which will be ready for a crew change. Hundreds more leave each autumn from the French Riviera, the Costa del Sol, the Canary Islands, etc.

But there are still plenty of captains with vacancies in the autumn and asking from boat to boat is the only way of discovering one of these. Committed travellers often take a cheap charter flight to a likely Mediterranean resort to look for crewing work. If they fail, the consolation prize of a couple of weeks in the sun isn't so bad. One of the favoured routes for yachts travelling from the eastern Mediterranean towards the Atlantic includes Rhodes, Malta, Palma (Majorca), Alicante, Gibraltar, Las Palmas in the Canaries and the Azores before going on to the Caribbean, the Eastern Seaboard of the US or Brazil.

The month-long Atlantic crossing is usually begun in October/November in order to reach the West Indies by Christmas. Gran Canaria is the last traditional victualling stop for about 400 yachts before the Atlantic crossing; the contemplation of thousands of miles of Atlantic Ocean often encourages owners and skippers to take on extra crew.

On the other hand they may have decided that a crew member they picked up on the Riviera or Gibraltar is never going to get his or her sea legs and they may be seeking replacements. If the competition in Las Palmas is too discouraging, take a bus to some of the smaller marinas on the island such as Puerto de Mogan. Many skippers of course do not wait until the last minute to find crew, and Gibraltar is recommended for finding a yacht (despite the two unsuccessful accounts quoted above). Check the notice boards at Marina Bay and Sheppards Marina (see Gibraltar chapter). The main crewing agencies in Antibes are housed in the same building, viz. La Galerie du Port, 8 boulevard d'Aguillon, 06600 Antibes. Try contacting the Blue Water Yacht Crew Agency (93-34 34 13) or Peter Insull's Yacht Crew Agency (93-34 64 64).

Tom Morton included a transatlantic sailing trip in his year between school and university:

Anyone wishing to cross the Atlantic should seriously consider investigating the annual Atlantic Rally for Cruisers (ARC) which leaves from Las Palmas in Gran Canaria on the last Sunday of November. It's good to get down there at least two weeks before the start and get to know the people and boats. The atmosphere is extremely friendly and most hopefuls find a passage, even if it is only two days before departure. It must be borne in mind that nearly all the boats are run by families who will want a contribution towards food.

Crewing from the Americas and the Caribbean

Yachts leaving the American east coast to cross the Atlantic tend to jump off from their home ports in the early autumn or spring according to the weather. Your best bet is to look in Miami or Fort Lauderdale (Florida), Newport (Rhode Island), Bridgeport (Connecticut) or Annapolis (Maryland). Again you might want to check or place adverts in the relevant journals such as the glossy *Cruising World* (Box 3400, Newport, Rhode Island 02840-0992). There are a number of crewing agencies in the US normally charging a modest fee of $20-$75, though experienced crew often find that asking captains directly is more efficient and produces more results. Chefs/cooks are especially in demand. If interested in registering with an agency, try Hassel Free Inc Crew Services (1550 SE 17th St, Suite 5, Fort Lauderdale, FL 33316; 305-763-1841). Fort Lauderdale is reputed to be a hard place in which to find work.

Yachts sail from the west coast of North America to Hawaii, Tahiti and beyond in April/May or September/October. In October there are several organised gatherings of 'yachties' in California which provide an excellent chance to fix up a crewing position. As well as running relevant classified adverts, the monthly yachting magazine *Latitude 38* (PO Box 1678, Sausalito, CA 94966; 415-383-8200) compiles a Mexico Only Crew List in October which costs just $5 for inclusion — the deadline is September 15th — and also hosts a 'Crew List Party'. Try also the Pacific Marine Supply store in San Diego (2804 Cannon St) for crewing information.

Elsewhere in California try the San Francisco Yacht Club, Santa Barbara and Marina del Rey in Los Angeles. Ports along Baja California (the long Mexican peninsula) are surprisingly popular because skippers want to avoid the high mooring fees of California just to the north. It has been estimated that there are as many as 400 foreign yachts moored in La Paz at any one time, a Baja town 22 hours by bus from Tijuana.

Further south, Panama is a good place to find a westward passage in January and February. Helping yachts to negotiate the locks of the Panama Canal as a 'linehandler' enables you to make the acquaintance of prospective skippers. Try also the Eden Yacht Club or the Balboa Yacht Clubs in Panama City. Near the Balboa Club is a small white booth where you can find out which boats are departing the next day. A motor boat shuffles out to yachts from which you can make your requirements known to captains. The vast continent of South America may afford possibilities. For example notices placed by yacht owners seeking crew for trips to the Caribbean or the US have been observed in the tourist office in Salvador, Brazil.

Yachts arrive in the Caribbean in September/October at the end of the hurricane season and leave again in April. A multitude of yachts gathers at the biggest end-of-season event, Antigua Race Week (end of April/beginning of May), which affords excellent opportunities to arrange a berth to Venezuela, Europe or the South Pacific. If you have accumulated experience during the season you should have little difficulty in finding a passage back to the Mediterranean or the UK.

The most active yachting centres in the West Indies, where you have the best chance of seeing a notice on a marina notice board or meeting a short-handed skipper in a yachties' bar are St. Thomas (try the Yacht Haven Marina), St. Maarten (Philipsburg), Antigua (especially English Harbour), St. Vincent, Tortola (Road Town), Martinique (Fort de France) and St. Lucia (Vigie Cove and Castries). The Virgin Islands (both British and American) are the main centres for chartering in the Caribbean.

Between May and August, hundreds of yachts congregate in Puerto la Cruz and Cumaná in Venezuela to avoid the hurricanes in the Caribbean. Elsewhere in South America try the yacht clubs in Buenos Aires and Rio.

After crewing in the Caribbean for a year, Marcus Edwards-Jones summarised the experience: 'If you are keen on sun, sea and sand and do not have much money, crewing on yachts is a fantastic way of seeing the world, getting brown and enjoying yourself while being paid to do so.' See the chapter on the *Caribbean* for more information on crewing.

Crewing in the South Pacific

After several exhausting but lucrative months of fruit-picking in Australia and New Zealand, Frank Schiller from Germany was all set to fulfil one of his dreams:

I was hellbent on scoring a ride on an ocean-going yacht for any Pacific destination — after all I'd read alluring stories of Joseph Conrad and Jack London. In June I stood in front of a 4-Square shop window in Russell in New Zealand's Bay of Islands when by pure chance a notice was put up by the shop keeper: 'Crew wanted for Tonga.' Less than an hour later I found myself sailing across the bay back to Opua. After a week of doing odd jobs on the boat I was en route to Nukualofa. Pure magic. All this despite never having set foot on a yacht before, once more stressing the theme of your book that nothing's impossible!

Since the New Zealand owners had two kids, they needed someone to give them a hand. In no time I was doing night watches, taking sights with the sextant (the skipper taught me a few lessons on navigation which I was very keen on), cooking and washing up and most important of all — I became 'Uncle Frankie' to the kids. If you get along well with everyone on board, there are no worries going sailing in a matchbox. (But if there are hassles — no escape, even on a 100 footer.) Yachting, in fact, can be a very rewarding and adventurous thing to embark on.

In New Zealand the best place by far to find crewing jobs is the Westhaven Marina in Auckland Harbour, which is one of the biggest in the southern hemisphere. Marcus Scrace saw many ads for crew (mostly on a share-expenses basis) bound for Australia, Tonga, Fiji, and the USA. As for the timing, April to mid-June are the months to pick up a boat leaving Westhaven or the Bay of Islands. The early departures are usually heading further east (i.e. to Tahiti) while the later ones are likely to be destined for the Tonga/Samoa/Fiji triangle. Many end up in Australia at the end of the season, i.e. late October when all South Pacific sailors head for shelter from cyclones.

To leave eastern Australia, head for Airlie Beach and the Whitsunday Islands in Queensland (especially during the Fun Race held in September), Cairns or Townsville; check adverts in the *Cairns Post* most of which specify a payment of $15-30 a day. Marcus Scrace, who was teaching at the Pacific Sailing School in Rushcutters Bay, Sydney, noticed an advert for crew on the notice board and was soon on his way to New Zealand. From Darwin boats leave for Indonesia from May; the Darwin-Ambon race between Australia and Indonesia in July is especially promising.

Suva, the capital of Fiji, and Papeete in Tahiti are hubs of much yachting activity in the South Pacific, especially between July and September when boats head off to Hawaii or New Zealand. Try the Royal Suva Yacht Club or

Tradewinds Marina (Suva). Frank Schiller provides more detailed advice on crewing between South Pacific Islands:

> *As good as Neiafu harbour in Tonga is in July, Malolo-Lailai has got to be the best in September when the annual yacht race to Port Vilal/Vanuatu starts. There were quite a few 'crew wanted' signs in evidence, since everyone's getting the hell out of the Pacific at that time.*

Other stops in the Pacific include Mauna Kea and Ala Wai (Hawaii) and Majuro in the Marshall Islands.

Crewing from Other Countries

Many yachts travelling around Africa lose their crew in Cape Town and need new crew for the onward journey. January is not a good time to look however judging from the number of notices from people looking for crewing positions which Stephen Psallidas noticed in the Cape Town Yacht Club. Yachts leave the East African coast for the Seychelles in January or February and for Madagascar and South Africa in August/September. Visit the yacht clubs in Dar es Salaam and Mombasa. Similarly private yachts heading east or west from the Indian subcontinent which stop at tropical Sri Lanka are often short of hands. Ask around the visitors' yacht basins in Colombo or Galle. Both ports are part of the popular South-East Asia yachting circuit which also takes in Bali (Port Benoa), Singapore (try the Changi Sailing Club or Sembawang Yacht Club), Penang and Phuket. Dustie Hickey noticed quite a few notices stuck to palm trees on the less-touristy islands of southern Thailand, i.e. the ones without roads, looking for crew to sail to Australia and elsewhere. The best time to try in South-East Asia is September/October. West of Sri Lanka there are crewing opportunities each spring to the Red Sea, Mauritius, the Seychelles and East Africa.

In fact the possibilities are infinite for people without a fixed timetable. For example the author of this book met by chance a charming sailor in a post office in Cochin, South India and could have crewed across the Indian Ocean to Dar es Salaam had it not been for the tyranny of publisher's deadlines (alas).

Yacht Delivery

Once you have some basic crewing experience you might go upmarket and try to get a job delivering yachts. Britain is still a major distributor and exporter of yachts and the easiest way to export a yacht is to sail it. This necessitates a crew, ideally one which considers the journey itself sufficient payment for the work, though licensed skippers often earn $1 a mile and the crew 50 cents. It is normally the purchaser's responsibility to arrange delivery and so he will want to get in touch with willing volunteers. Hence the yachting magazines carry adverts requesting crew for such journeys; again *Yachting Monthly* offers the most scope and carries a number of advertisements for delivery agencies in Britain. A typical advert might read: 'Sailing Crew required for yacht deliveries to Tahiti departing October/November. All onboard expenses paid but not airfares. Crew must be experienced.'

You can also contact British charter companies on the slight chance that they may know of yachts to be delivered. Lists are obtainable from the Yacht Charter Association (c/o D. R. Howard, 60 Silverdale, New Milton, Hants. BH25 7DE; 01425 619004).

LAND

If you possess a heavy goods vehicle (HGV) or passenger carrying vehicle (PCV) licence, then you will have a distinct advantage wherever you go. These are costly in money and time to acquire, but open opportunities throughout the world. People with enough mechanical knowledge to make running repairs to their vehicle are especially in demand.

You might still be able to work for a trucking company even if you do not have any driving qualifications, by being taken on as day labour to help load and unload international lorries. It may be worth ringing around nearby haulage companies (addresses in the *Yellow Pages* under 'Road Haulage' or 'Freight Forwarding and Warehousing'). Julian Peachey found that a local firm in Oxford merely satisfied themselves that he looked respectable before fixing him up with a ride to Italy. Like Julian, you might have to accept the first lift on an unpaid basis. But once you have established yourself as a reliable worker, you might be asked to accompany the driver to his European destination in order to help unload at the other end. Make sure that the arrangement is flexible enough to allow you to stay abroad after fulfilling your duties.

When the time comes for you to return to Britain you ring your transport company and ask if they intend to send any lorries requiring an assistant in your direction in the near (or distant) future. After James Spach became friendly with the dispatcher in one firm, he found it easy to arrange one way trips to and from Europe provided his dates were flexible enough. Or seek out the large international truck depots throughout Europe such as the one which Julian Altshul came across just south of Barcelona (at Vilanova y la Geltru).

Overland Tours

If you do have one of the specialist licences and some knowledge of mechanics, you may be eligible to work as an expedition driver. Competent expedition staff (including cooks) are greatly in demand by the many overland companies and youth travel specialists which advertise in magazines such as *TNT* and *Overseas Jobs Express*. Leaders have to contend with vehicle breakdowns, border crossings, black market money exchanges and the trip whinger (who, according to Brett Archer who spent eight months in Africa as an expedition leader, is always the female half of a couple from New Zealand carrying a calculator).

Here is a list of overland operators:

Encounter Overland, Wren Park, Shefford, Beds. SG17 5JD (01462 811470). Full-time expedition leader/drivers in Africa, Asia and South America are expected to work for at least three years. Applicants must have or be prepared to obtain a PCV licence. Training lasts ten months including time in their workshops, learning to repair the modified Bedford trucks they use.

Guerba Expeditions, 101 Eden Vale Road, Westbury, Wilts. BA13 3QX). Africa specialist.

Dragoman Overland Expeditions, Camp Green, Kenton Road, Debenham, Suffolk IP14 6LA (01728 861133). Have a good reputation and look for leader drivers with a PCV licence and a minimum commitment of two years for expeditions to Africa, Asia, South and Central America.

Explore Worldwide Ltd, 1 Frederick St, Aldershot, Hants. GU11 1LQ (01252 333031). Tour leaders for Europe, Africa, Asia and the Americas. Must have first aid certificate and preferably a second language. Training given.

Journey Latin America, 16 Devonshire Road, London W4 2HD. Applicants should be familiar with Latin America and fluent in Spanish or Portuguese.

Tracks, The Flots, Brookland, Romney Marsh, Kent TN29 9TG (01797 344343).

Top Deck, 131-135 Earls Court Road, London SW5 9RH (0171-244 8641). Will help promising candidates to get their coach licence. Trips across Europe and to Kathmandu.

After getting past the interview stage as an adventure tour leader, you may be invited to go on a training trip of at least six weeks at your expense — at least several hundred pounds. This money is generally returned to you after you have been accepted and completed an agreed term of work. Procedures vary for choosing and training couriers. One old hand, writing in the *Traveller* magazine, claims that to be a good tour leader you have to be 'a cross between a Butlins redcoat and Scott of the Antarctic'.

The pay on your training trip will be low, as Guerba admits in its standard reply to applicants:

The pay for this arduous job is a miserable £35 per week. However, being accepted for this position does give you the opportunity to see Africa. All incidental expenses such as visas, passports, air tickets, etc. are paid for. Guerba will also pay your kitty contributions and will cover any compulsory money changes that may exist en route. Although it is hard work being a trainee tour leader on one of our trips, I can only say that it is hard to imagine a more interesting or exciting job.

Once you are a full expedition leader, you will be paid at least £60 and possibly over £150 per week in addition to expenses. If you do land an overland job, you may find yourself driving a converted Bedford or Mercedes truck across the Sahara.

Brett Archer from New Zealand enjoyed his stint of working for an African overland company though found it a little daunting to have 18 people dependent on him in such circumstances. After eight months, his contract was not renewed because of a drop in bookings.

Expeditions

One romantic idea for working your way around the world is to become part of an expedition venturing into the more remote and unspoiled parts of the world from Tierra del Fuego to Irian Jaya. It would be nice if you could be invited to join a party of latter-day explorers in exchange for some menial duty such as portering or cooking. However expedition organisers and leaders nowadays demand that participants have some special skills or expertise to contribute beyond mere eagerness. No one will accept you for the ride. For example an advert for people needed on an Arctic expedition included among its volunteer requirements a post-doctoral archaeologist, an electronics officer for proton magneto-meter maintenance and an antenna theorist. One suspects that they weren't inundated with applications.

The Royal Geographical Society (1 Kensington Gore, London SW7 2AR) encourages and assists as many British expeditions as it can. Occasionally there are requests from expedition leaders for specialists with either scientific or medical skills, preferably with past expedition experience, and for this a register of personnel is maintained. Those who have a particular skill to offer and wish to be included on the register should send an s.a.e. to the Expedition Advisory Centre at the RGS for the appropriate form and a copy of their booklet *Joining an Expedition* (£5). If you would like advice on how to mount an expedition, consult their *Expedition Planner's Handbook* or attend their annual seminar in November on Planning a Small Expedition. If you want personal advice ring 0171-581 2057 with your questions, or make an appointment to visit. (The Centre deals with 10,000 enquiries a year.)

Another organisation worth contacting is the World Expeditionary Association or WEXAS (45 Brompton Road, London SW3 1DE) who not only make awards to worthwhile expeditions but, more to the point, carry advertisements and announcements in their quarterly publication *Traveller* where you can advertise your skills (free to members) and hope that a potential expedition leader sees it.

Raleigh International (formerly Operation Raleigh) is a UK-based charity which aims to develop young people aged 17-25 by offering them the chance to undertake demanding environmental and community projects on expeditions overseas. Applicants attend an assessment weekend and if successful are asked to raise funds (several thousand pounds) to help towards costs. Recent destinations included Chile, Zimbabwe, Guyana and Malaysia. For further information contact Raleigh House, 27 Parsons Green Lane, London SW6 4HZ (0171-371 8585).

World Challenge Expeditions (Soane House, 305-315 Latimer Road, London W10 6RA; 0181-964 1331) takes on about 40 expedition leaders to supervise school expeditions to developing countries. Applicants must be experienced hill-walkers and first aiders, and have some experience of travelling in the Third World. No wage is paid but expenses are covered.

When joining any expedition you are unlikely to escape a financial liability, for most expeditions levy a fee from each participant. Sponsorship, and the amount of it, from companies, trusts and other sources will depend upon the aims of the expedition and the benefits to the donor. And once the money and equipment are forthcoming the expedition then has obligations to its sponsors and forfeits much of its freedom. Raising sponsorship, a job with which all expedition members should help, is probably the biggest headache of all and involves endless letter-writing and the visiting, cap in hand, of dozens of commercial establishments and other possible sources of income.

AIR COURIERS

Every day international courier companies undertake to move tons of 'time sensitive documents' between countries and continents. Because of airline restrictions, these packages cannot travel as passenger baggage unless they are indeed accompanied by a passenger who will clear them through customs as 'excess passenger baggage'. At one time casual couriers could travel free but in recent years the prices of pre-booked courier flights have been rising so that there is no longer much advantage in it. Furthermore virtually all courier flights are return flights, with a maximum stay of four weeks and often less, so they are of little interest to the job-seeker. Changes in customs rules and improved technology mean that the demand for casual couriers is likely to diminish in coming years, and some predict extinction within the next four years. Still, it is worth describing the system.

The industry is taking advantage of the huge supply of hopeful couriers by charging them a hefty proportion of the fare which they call an 'administration fee.' In many cases this is nearly as much as an ordinary cheap flight. The only hope of a real bargain is if you are lucky and are free to travel at a moment's notice. Most courier flights are now sold through 'on-board courier broker' firms which supply couriers to a specific company or airline/s. Prices vary according to the time of year, just like other air tickets: November and February are the cheapest times while Christmas and summer are most expensive. It is worth noting that once you have been a successful courier you will find it easier to arrange another flight. One traveller had a marvellous fortnight's holiday in Brazil (having taken advantage of a £300 courier return from London) and several weeks later was rung up by the courier company asking her if she would like to go again, this time for £200.

Here are the companies which will send a list of their destinations in return for a self-addressed envelope. Some will be booked up months in advance. This information changes constantly.

CTS (Courier Travel Services Ltd.), 346 Fulham Road, London SW10 9UH (071-351 0300). Broker for British Airways. Wide range of destinations. Recent return fares include £150-200 to New York, £270 to Nairobi, and £400 to Rio de Janeiro. Unusually, they have been selling one-way tickets to Tokyo starting at £225. Telephone numbers abroad are Hong Kong: 852-305 1413; Sydney: 02-698 3753.

Polo Express 45 Church Street, Weybridge, Surrey KT13 8D6 (01932 820960). Destinations with return fares include New York and Boston (from £159 in November), Hong Kong (£450) and Lisbon (£65). Personal baggage allowance of 23kg. All flights are on British Airways. Large volume means that there are last-minute bargains (called 'late list flights').

Jupiter Air, Horton Road, Colnbrook, Slough SL3 0BB (01753 689989). Sydney (£450-650). In 1994 they won a big contract away from Polo Express for United Airlines so now fly to the US: New York (£270 in high summer) and San Francisco (£350).

Bridges Worldwide, Unit 61G, Building 521, Heathrow Airport, Hounslow, Middlesex TW3 3UK (0181-759 5040). Virgin Atlantic, China Airlines, Singapore Airlines and Swiss Air. Returns to Bangkok from £220, Miami for £250, etc. One-way flights are available and cost about 60% of return fare.

Linehaul Express, Building 200, Section D, Enfield Road, Heathrow, Hounslow, Middlesex TW6 2PR (0181-759 5969). Hong Kong and Sydney from £450.

Once you have booked a courier flight the procedure is as follows: you turn up in plenty of time wearing smart clothes at the company's office or the relevant airport with your passport, visa (if necessary), insurance and luggage (most companies nowadays allow their couriers the full 23kg allowance). There you will be met by the company's agent who is frequently very late, thereby causing severe anxiety to the hopeful courier. He goes through the paperwork with you, checks in up to a score of mail bags and sees you through customs. At the other end, another agent greets you (at least in theory), escorts you through customs and disappears with the packages, while you congratulate yourself on your good fortune.

If you're already abroad it is also worth trying for reduced flights as Marcus Scrace reports:

> *During my trip around the world I saw many ads for air couriers. The way to get a job as a courier is to look up in the* Yellow Pages *under 'International Couriers' and ring or visit in person the companies which are usually based very close to the airport. For instance there are about 20 companies in Mascot, Sydney. (I used Airpack Couriers for a return trip to New Zealand at a cost of $200 which is about half price). This company also had flights to the States, Singapore and Hong Kong. In Auckland all the courier offices are situated in the airport suburb of Mangere.*

That fare has not changed in the past couple of years; try Polo Express in Sydney (02-319 6011).

In the Far East, the *South China Morning Post* of Hong Kong often carries adverts for couriers. Most quoted fares are for return trips only (e.g. Bangkok for HK$800, New York for HK$4,500 and London for HK$5,500). In Hong Kong ring Jupiter (735 1946/7) which was charging HK$1,800 return to Tokyo and HK$3,800 to Los Angeles. The cheapest way to leave Taiwan is also as a 'freight forwarding courier'.

JFK Airport in New York (like Heathrow) is buzzing with air courier activity. It is harder to get a domestic courier flight within the US than an international one but both are possible. The biggest courier broker in the US is Now Voyager Freelance Couriers (74 Varrick St, Suite 307, New York, NY 10013; 212-431-1616) which charges $50 annually and a refundable deposit of $100. Recently they have been offering returns to Caracas for $220 and to Copenhagen for $400 in high summer. One of the best courier deals available at the time of writing was a return fare of $300 to Milan available from World Courier (718-978-9408); couriers are allowed to carry on hand luggage only.

If in New York, try the following, which may have flights to London or other international destinations like Frankfurt, Brussels and Amsterdam for from $200 one way, $400 return: Discount Travel International (212-362-3636) and Halbart Express (718-656-5000). For flights from the West Coast, try International Bonded Couriers (310-607-0125) and Way to Go (213-466-1126) both in Los Angeles.

If you are interested in researching this subject thoroughly, a company called Travel Unlimited (PO Box 1058, Allston, MA 02134) publishes an excellent monthly update of domestic and worldwide courier services plus general low-budget travel info which costs $35 per year in the US and $40 overseas or $5 for a single issue.

The International Association of Air Travel Couriers (PO Box 1349, Lake Worth, Florida 33460; 407-582-8320) publishes a bi-monthly bulletin which is very clearly laid out and up-to-date. IAATC also publishes the *Shoestring Traveler* newsletter for freelance couriers. Annual membership costs $35 in the US, $45/£30 in the UK.

Obviously this is a burgeoning field since several British and American companies are selling directories of air courier deals which are unlikely to prove as useful or as good value as frequently updated bulletins but may provide a useful starting point. One of the best is the *Insider's Guide to Air Courier Bargains* which the author Kelly Monaghan updates every 12-15 months. It is published in the US by The Intrepid Traveler, Box 438L, New York, NY 10034 ($14.95) and available in the UK from ASAP Publications, Prospect House, Downley Common, High Wycombe, Bucks. HP13 5XG (£10.95 plus £1 postage). Two others are *The Air Courier's Handbook,* by Jennifer Basye from Big City Books, 7047 Hidden Lane, Loomis, CA 95650 ($12) and *The Air Courier's Guide Book* by Roger Wilson from Owen Publications, Box 32172, Charleton, SC 29417 ($10.95). The Air Courier Association (191 University Boulevard, Suite 300T, Denver, CO 80206) invites people to ring 303-278-8810 for a free information and enrolment kit.

Of course there are outfits not listed in the *Yellow Pages* which employ couriers to transport more exotic substances. Unless you want an extended holiday in one of H.M. prisons or a long vacation making licence plates in San Quentin, you should steer clear of this sort of operation.

TRAVEL

Not everyone has the time nor the stamina to work a passage. There follow some general guidelines for finding bargains in train, coach, ship and air travel. Greater detail is available in books such as the *Rough Guide to Student Travel*. But first the greatest bargain of all: hitch-hiking.

Hitch-hiking

In the experience of many travellers, hitching is cheap, safe and fascinating (and what else could anyone ask for?) The uncertainty of the destination is one of its great attractions to the footloose traveller. While hitching from France to Germany in pursuit of work, Kevin Boyd got a lift with a Russian truck bound for Leningrad. He was tempted to stay for the whole trip but, as the lorry averaged 35km an hour on the autoroute, he decided to stick with his original idea. Hitch-hiking has one positive virtue for job seekers: you can sound out the driver for advice on local job opportunities. Friendly drivers often go miles out of their way and may even ask in villages about work possibilities on your behalf, as happened to Andrew Winwood in Switzerland during the *vendange*. Lorry drivers often know of temporary jobs you could do.

Some readers have expressed disapproval that we recommend hitch-hiking as a good way of getting around. Hitch-hiking, like any form of transport, has its dangers, but by following a few rules these can be minimised. Never accept a lift from a driver who seems drunk, drowsy or suspicious. Women should try not to hitch alone. A small dose of paranoia is not a bad thing, whether at midnight in Manchester or midday in Manila, especially in view of the murders of several hitch-hiking travellers in Australia and stories like the following from a reader of this book:

> After my friend had decided to go back to Thailand and (by mistake) took most of my money, I continued on alone. I was offered a ride to Kuala Lumpur by what seemed like a very pleasant Malaysian guy. After about an hour he pulled over to the side of the road. I thought he was stopping to get a drink and something to eat. Before I knew it, he'd central-locked the doors (this truck was like Fort Knox) and pulled the curtains round, turned off the lights and undressed. For the next two hours he proceeded to tell me in graphic details how he was going to rape me and throw my dead body from the truck. Panic set in quickly, but I managed not to show it too much. I told the guy that he was frightening me and that I had people waiting for me in Singapore, and if I wasn't back by a certain time, they would not hesitate to call the police. I also started to tell him all about myself and my family. This makes the person see you as a human being and not just a lump of meat. Eventually he let me go.

Try to put the risks into perspective. It is worth mentioning that the author of *Hitch-hikers Manual: Britain* and *Europe: a Manual for Hitch-hikers* has found cycling in London a far more dangerous and damaging pursuit than thumbing lifts (and has lived to become the Travel Editor of the *Independent* newspaper).

Usually the worst danger is of boredom and discouragement when you have a long wait. A few readers have written to say that they cannot understand how people manage to enjoy hitching especially across Europe. It is of course a game of patience. Eventually you will get a lift, but whether you have the stamina to wait for it is another matter.

But many hitchers have been amazed at their good fortune. Isak Maseide met nothing but nice people on the 3,200km between Oban in Scotland and Copenhagen via the Bavarian Alps. He was worried just once when he noticed a shoulder hoster on a driver who had stopped for him; this man turned out to be an undercover policeman on his way home. On F. Dixon from Nottingham's first trip abroad, he hitched, and was pleasantly surprised by the ease with which great distances could be covered:

I thought the odds were against me from the start. I am 6'6 tall, black and 18 stone. Who the hell is going to pick me up? Once in Denmark we got good lifts. One nice couple put me up at their home for the night and phoned her father who picked me up and took me to where I was going. I am now making my way to France getting good lifts. Can you tell other black people not to be afraid to travel?

The word hitch-hiking is of American derivation and the concept is primarily Western. In North America, Europe and Australia, a person standing by the side of the road with an outstretched thumb can expect (eventually) to be offered a free lift. It is essential to look neat and enthusiastic, and try to make eye contact with drivers. Hi-tech hitchers often use aids such as destination signs, flags (which indicate you are a genuine visitor from afar) and attention-attracting costumes such as a boiler suit or kilt. Ben Nakoneczny took up juggling by the side of the road and, if his 2,190km lift from Thessaloniki to Cologne is anything to go by, this attracts the right sort of attention. Eye-catching signs are especially recommended such as the one used by Malcolm Green in his quest for a grape-picking job in Australia; LONDON TO MILDURA PLEASE. R. J. Hill used a sign 'Moon'; eventually a vicar stopped, presumably because he had some inside information. Try to look respectable without looking too prosperous.

Elsewhere, there may be no tradition of giving free lifts and if you are picked up, a small payment will be expected. Since the local people often get lifts with private vehicles and pay for them, there is no reason why you should be driven free of charge. In some Western countries this technique has been formalised by organisations which fix drivers up with cost-sharing passengers upon payment of a small fee (see the section on Europe below).

An interesting variation is to prearrange a ride by talking to lorry drivers at local depots, lorry parks, truckers' cafés, pubs or wherever you see them. Antony Hunt describes his success in the northern suburbs of London:

The first time I tried hitching, I got a lift from the Scratchwood Services in a German lorry heading for Heidelberg. I got a free ferry crossing, a free cabin and a dinner ticket. The driver gave me his phone number and promised me a lift home when I wanted it since he did a weekly trip to Manchester.

If possible find out in which pubs lorry drivers tend to drink. For example Andrew Giles found that Rodolfo's Bar and the Pig and Whistle in Gibraltar were good places to get to know drivers. Drivers are increasingly wary of offering lifts to complete strangers, since there are several drivers in foreign prisons for having done just that.

Driving

In some countries you might decide to buy a cheap car and hope that it lasts long enough for you to see the country. This worked well for Frank Schiller, a German traveller in Australia:

How about becoming a car owner yourself if you just wanna roll along for a while? After two successful months of hitching in Tasmania (including a combined Landrover and yacht lift to Maria Island), the three of us decided to change our means of transport. We bought a Holden off a Canadian guy for $500 which included insurance, a few spare parts, a tool kit and some snorkelling equipment. (I'd suggest buying a standard model rather than an E-type Jaguar for ease of finding spares.) After ten weeks and 10,000 kilometres, we sold it to a wrecker in Alice Springs for $250. So each of us had paid $80 for the car plus about $120 for petrol — all in all a much better bargain than a bus pass.

A camper van is also an appealing idea, especially if you are interested in chasing fruit harvests around. It is possible to pick up a reliable vehicle for less than £1,000 in the UK if you're lucky. Australians like Ben Hockley are devoted van users:

My girlfriend and I were spending a lot of money looking for work in Spain so we decided we needed a campervan to help cut the accommodation costs. Vans are not very cheap in Spain and the casual relaxed attitude of the locals makes car hunting a nightmare. So we hopped a train to Amsterdam where I had learnt that vehicles were 40% cheaper. It was true and after three weeks we had an old Bedford camper for about £1,000. Life in the van was great, we could just park on any street and we had a home for the night.

The main van market in London takes place daily on York Way at Market Road near the Caledonian Road tube station.

Those who own their own vehicle might consider taking it with them. Certainly a car or motorcycle on the Continent will make life easier when it comes to visiting potential employers, especially in the countryside. On the negative side, it will be an expensive luxury (petrol often costs even more in most European countries than in Britain) and a serious encumbrance if you decide to travel outside continental Europe. If you are considering taking your car, contact your local AA or RAC office for information about International Driving Permits, motor insurance, green cards, etc.

Train

The conventional wisdom is that trains are preferable to buses because they allow you to walk around or lie down on long journeys. Anyone who has experienced travelling unreserved on Indian trains or on long distance Italian trains in high summer (where theft is rife) will be aware of the limitations of this generalisation. Besides which, the traveller working his or her way around the world is more interested in financial considerations than in ones of comfort. So you will probably choose a slow, cheap bus in preference to a luxurious high-speed train. But in areas which have a dreadfully creaky and overcrowded rail service (running to a calendar rather than a timetable), it may well be the cheapest way of getting around. Even in developed nations, you may find rail fares rivalling coach ones especially if you are eligible for discounts. Rail passes are generally not much use to job-seeking travellers since they benefit people who want to do a great deal of travelling. However other youth and student discounts can be very useful; for example the Carissmo pass in France which can be bought by people up to the age of 26 for less than £25 gives up to half-price off off-peak rail journeys for up to a year.

The Thomas Cook *Overseas Timetable* is the bible for overland travellers outside Europe; within Europe, consult the *Continental Timetable*.

Coach

Coach travel has never enjoyed a favourable press. After buying a cheap coach ticket from London to Athens, Mark Hurley's conclusion was 'never again': even after the on-board loo packed up, there were only two rest stops every 24 hours. The last leg of the journey through Greece was done on another coach which was already full when Mark's lot turned up. On the other hand, coaches have some confirmed fans who positively relish long-distance journeys when life is reduced to its constituent pleasures of sleeping, eating, reading and socialising. The great advantage of course is the low cost.

In many areas of the world such as Afghanistan, Nepal and Papua New Guinea, public road transport is the only way to get around the country short of flying. Fortunately this monopoly of the travel market is not generally reflected in high fares, usually because of competing companies. Such free enterprise is wonderfully apparent at the Topkapi Gate Bus Station in Istanbul where salesmen for a host of competing companies call out their destinations and prices. Bus prices are below a penny per mile in much of the Third World (possibly to compensate for the purgatory of non-stop Kung Fu videos in some parts of the world) and increase rapidly to nearly a pound for a half mile in Central London. Except where smooth air-conditioned buses provide an alternative to sub-third class rail travel, coaches are generally less expensive than trains. The Thomas Cook *Overseas Timetable* is valuable for coach as well as train travellers.

Another informative reference book for those who anticipate crossing international waters is the quarterly *ABC Cruise & Ferry Guide* which lists both domestic and international shipping companies, their routes and timings but scant information on prices. Ask for it in your library.

Air

Scheduled air fares as laid down by IATA, the airlines' cartel, are best avoided. They are primarily designed for airline accountants and businessmen on expense accounts. You should be looking at standby flights, cheap charters and discounted tickets. Air travel within individual countries and continents is not always subject to this choice, though some special deals are available.

For longhaul flights, especially to Asia, Australasia and most recently Latin America, discounted tickets are available in plenty and there should never be any need to pay the official full fare. Previously the sale of these tickets was restricted to the original 'bucket shops', often seedy discount agencies. Now high street travel agents such as Thomas Cook, Hogg Robinson and Pickfords are openly selling discounted tickets and because of their enormous turnover and sophisticated computer systems can often offer the best deals. Some reckon that the bucket shop is on the brink of extinction.

But the very lowest fares are still found by doing some careful shopping around. Bucket shops advertise in London weeklies like *TNT* and *Time Out*, and also the London *Evening Standard*. Phone a few outfits and pick the best price. The cheapest flights are available from airlines like Aeroflot or Evia (a Taiwanese airline) which are considered dubious by cautious and conservative types. East European and Asian carriers like Bangladesh Biman, Gulf Air and Garuda are often worth investigating. Try to overcome your reluctance, since flying with them is guaranteed to be more interesting than flying on KLM, Air Canada or British Airways. You may find that your flight leaves at 7am on a Sunday morning with a 12-hour stopover in Dhaka, but these inconveniences are a small price to pay for savings of a hundred pounds or more.

Once you accept a price, check that the fare will not be increased between paying the deposit (typically £50) and handing over the balance in exchange for the ticket; if the agency is unable to make such a guarantee, ask for a written promise that you can reclaim the deposit in the event of a fare increase. Similarly, if the agency claims that your ticket is refundable if unused, request a letter confirming this: any legitimate agency should be happy to comply. Buying dodgy tickets is always worrying since it is impossible to grasp all the complexities of international air travel. Hand over the balance only when you are satisfied that the dates and times agree with what you anticipated. But don't expect the fare shown on the ticket to bear any relation to the price you actually paid.

If your travelling time is limited, there are many worse possibilities than a yearly validity round-the-world (RTW) air ticket. The cheapest start at around £800. For about £900 you can get a RTW ticket combining the services of Thai International and Continental which permits stopovers in any or all of the following: Delhi, Bangkok, Sydney, Auckland, Honolulu, Los Angeles and New York. By paying more, you have a greater choice of routes and stopovers. The principal agencies specialising in longhaul travel for student and budget travellers are:

Campus Travel, 52 Grosvenor Gardens, London SW1W 0AG (0171-730 3402; or 0161-273 1721 in Manchester, 0131-668 3303 in Edinburgh). Britain's largest student and youth travel specialist with 36 branches in high streets, at universities and in YHA shops. They sell discounted rail and coach tickets for Europe as well as air fares.

STA Travel, Priory House, 6 Wrights Lane, London W8 6TA (0171-937 9962 longhaul; 0171-9921 Europe). The other main chain of youth and student travel offices with 20 offices around the UK. Main London branches at 86 Old Brompton Road SW7 and 117 Euston Road NW1.

Trailfinders Ltd, 42-50 Earls Court Road, London W8 6EJ (0171-938 3366 longhaul; 0171-937 5400 Europe and transatlantic). Also 194 Kensington High St, London W8 7RG (071-938 3939), plus offices in Manchester, Bristol and Glasgow.

Travel Cuts, 295a Regent St, London W1 7YA (0171-255 2082 longhaul; 0171-637 3161 North America).

Flight Dealders, 15 Gillingham Row, Victoria, SW1V 1HR (0171-630 9494). Advertise remarkably cheap fares.

All of these offer a wide choice of fares including RTW. Telephone bookings are possible, though these agencies are often so busy that it can be difficult to get through. In the north try the Travel Bug in Manchester (0161-721 4000) or London (0171-835 2000).

In the US, contact any of Council Travel's 42 offices throughout the US, a subsidiary of the Council on International Educational Exchange) or STA (1-800-925-4777) for cheap flights, including round-the-world fares. Some examples of student fares are: New York-London $418 (between April and June) and Los Angeles-Paris $549. Worldtek Travel (800-247-0846) offers competitive fares and donates some of its profits to developing countries. Air Brokers International in San Francisco (800-883-3273) specialise in RTW fares.

But by far the cheapest air fares from the US are available to people who are flexible about departure dates and destinations. Airhitch (2472 Broadway, Suite 200, New York, NY 10025; 1-800-326 2000/212-864-2000) has been repeatedly recommended as offering the best fares to Europe. The passenger chooses a block of possible dates (usually a five-day 'window') and a preferred destination. The company then tries to match these requirements with empty airline seats being released at knock-down prices. Mig Urquhart was happy to take potluck and ended up in Dublin:

Airhitch gets you from the States to Europe; you just don't know where or when. I put down Paris, Amsterdam or Athens on the registration form and got offered Zurich or Dublin. In 30 seconds I had to decide that Switzerland was too expensive and I had never been to Ireland. I'm very happy with the decision and with life in Donnybrook.

Airhitch can also get you from Europe to America. They have representatives in Europe, including France (1-46 86 47 73), Bonn (0228-47 65 14), Amsterdam (020-62 59 082) and Prague (02-730 603).

Recently a similar company has been set up called Air-Tech (584 Broadway, Suite 1007, New York, NY 10012; 212-219-7000) which advertises its fares by saying 'if you can beat these prices, start your own damn airline'. The transatlantic fares being advertised at the time of writing were $169 one way from/to the east coast, $269 from/to the west coast and $229 from/to the Midwest. Discounted fares of $139 return between the US and Mexico and $189 to the Caribbean are also available.

While Britain, Benelux, Switzerland, the States, Australia and other bastions of the free world have highly developed discount ticket markets, most countries do not. While hundreds of agents in Britain will sell you a cheap flight to Rio, no Brazilian is able to reciprocate. So beware of being stranded if you fly out to an exotic destination on a one-way ticket. You can get a friend in London to send you a discounted ticket for your homeward journey, but this is a tricky, risky and time-consuming business. On the other hand it is probably cheaper in the end and more flexible to piece together your own longhaul itinerary by buying cheap tickets en route, provided you have plenty of time wait around for the best deals.

The best cities abroad for buying cheap longhaul flights are Athens (try Consolas Travel at 100 Eolou St, USIT Student Travel or any of the discount agents competing in the streets south-west of Syntagma Square), Colombo (e.g. George Travel, 29 Bristol St; 422345), Hong Kong (Hong Kong Student Travel, Room 1021, Star House, Tsimshatsui, Kowloon; 7303269) and Bangkok (any along Khao San Road, Banglamphu such as Olavi Tours). Most of these agencies quote prices in US dollars; for example in the summer of 1994 George Travel was offering Colombo-Bangkok or Singapore to Europe on a one-year open ticket for just over $600 and Colombo-Sofia-New York for $675.

If someone tries to sell you the unwanted half of their ticket, be warned that airline tickets are not transferable and with increased airline security, check-in staff will almost certainly compare the name on the passport and the boarding pass to the name on the ticket.

Even for those with a thoroughly legitimate ticket, there are still a few pitfalls to avoid. Reconfirm your booking with the airline at least 72 hours before each flight and arrive at the airport by the latest time shown for check-in. Otherwise, you forfeit your rights to compensation if the flight happens to be overbooked. Also, find out whether airport tax is included in the fare or has to be paid upon departure. The UK Government imposed an air passenger duty in November 1994: travellers to Europe are charged £5 and to the rest of the world £10.

Bicycle

Cycling is not only healthy and free, it can simplify the business of finding work, as Adam Cook discovered in France:

Looking for work by bicycle is one of the very best methods as it allows you free unlimited travel far from the big towns and the competition. You can so easily visit the small villages and farms, some of which are off the beaten track.

In addition, employers may realise that people who have been cycling for a while are at least moderately fit and may choose them for the job, ahead of the flabbier vehicle-bound competition. In many parts of the world you will also

become an object of fascination, which can only aid your job-finding chances.
If you do decide to travel extensively by bicycle, you might consider joining the
Cyclists' Touring Club (69 Meadrow, Godalming, Surrey GU7 3HS) which
provides free technical, legal and touring information to members; membership
costs £25.

EUROPE

The European land mass is one of the most expensive areas of the world to
traverse. Fortunately, hitch-hiking is at its easiest, cheapest and safest in Europe.
Of course not all European countries are equally hitchable: Greece and Italy are
fine — if you're blonde and female; Portugal is good, Germany is far easier than
France, while Ireland, Denmark and Switzerland are excellent, and so on.
Readers of this book have turned in some impressive times: Jason Davies
hitched from Barcelona to Frederikshavn in $3\frac{1}{2}$ days, while in the opposite
direction Tony Davies-Patrick got from Denmark to Avignon in a day. Meanwhile Kevin Vincent wonders if he might hold a world record: it took him nine
days to hitch from Cadiz to Barcelona, a distance of less than 800 miles. The
toll booths on French and Italian motorways are heartily recommended by
seasoned hitchers as the best place to stand.

An underrated alternative is to use a lift-sharing agency of which there are
dozens of outlets across Europe, especially in Germany, where there are Citynetz
offices in Berlin, Bonn, Bremen, Dusseldorf, Munich, etc. For a varying fee
(typically £10 plus a share of the petrol) they will arrange a lift to your chosen
destination. The national car-sharing organisation in the UK is not yet well
known but is a valuable source of information for Europe as well as Britain.
Freewheelers 25 Low Friar St, Newcastle-upon-Tyne NE1 5UE; 0191-222 0090/
fax 261 5746) attempts to match drivers with fee-paying passengers; membership
costs £5 per year and the intercity passenger pays 3.5 pence per mile.

Here are some phone numbers abroad provided by Freewheelers: Allostop
Provoya Paris 1-42 46 00 66/1-47 70 02 01; Citynetz Brussels 02-512 1015;
Eurostop Amsterdam 020-22 43 42; Eurolift Portugal 01-888 5002; Citynetz
Spain Granada 058-29 29 20; Eurostop Budapest 01-13 77 124 and Eurostop
Prague 02-20 43 83. Lift-sharing agency numbers are often posted on youth
hostel notice boards. Nicola Hall made good use of this service when she wanted
to leave Germany:

There is a liftsharing place in Munich next to the main station behind one
of the main hotels which is very cheap. They charge a fee and the rest
depends on how many people will be in the car to share the cost of petrol. I
paid DM70 for a ride to Amsterdam.

Matches can seldom be made straightaway, so this system is of interest to those
travelling at a leisurely pace.

If you're starting from Britain, you have a problem. Despite the much
publicised increase in competition since the opening of the Channel Tunnel
among companies eager to transfer passengers from Britain to the Continent,
the English Channel is still a very costly stretch of water to cross. At one time
it was not too difficult to hitch free of charge with a lorry, but increased security
on the English side means that this is now much harder, though still possible as
Ian Govan from Glasgow reports:

It is still possible to hitch a lift with a trucker across the Channel. A good
place is the services on the Dover road just after the Dartford Tunnel. Ask
a trucker and if he's not interested ask him to get on the CB. Try to avoid
the truck parks next to the ports, as the drivers there are either booked on
or are in a hurry to do so. I waited nine hours in Calais once. The main

fear of the truckers is that you are carrying dope, so try to avoid the 'hippy look'. The driver can often fix you up with an onward lift via the trusty CB.

The cheapest ferry deal is an out-of-season day return from Ramsgate, Dover or Folkestone to a French or Belgian channel port for £5-10 (as opposed to the standard one-way fare of over £20). Andy Green recommends joining the Travel Market Ltd (Channel View Road, Dover, Kent CT17 9TP) for £6 which gives members access to cheap day-returns of £1 to £5. If you want to buy a day return, it is important to avoid showing up with a large rucksack or they won't believe you're coming back the same day. Stephen Hands, who was refused a day-trip ticket, suggests transferring your belongings into plastic bags. Philip O'Hara was approached by a German girl at the Dover ferry terminal offering to sell him the unused portion of her return ferry ticket for £7. Alternatively you can try to sell the unused part of your own day return at the other side. If you are leaving Britain by ferry to Scandinavia, there are substantial student discounts available. If you want to cross cheaply from France, Andy Green says try to buy a cheap day-return (from F50) from a travel agent in advance rather than waiting till you get to the ferry port.

Alternatively, buy a through ticket by bus or train which includes a much-reduced element of the ferry fare. On the whole the railways of Europe are expensive and in many cases it is cheaper to fly over a long distance. However there are worthwhile discounts to be found, especially for those under 26 through schemes such as Eurotrain (0171-730 3402) which has connections with Campus Travel, Euro-Youth (0171-834 2345), which is linked with British Rail International, and Route 26 from Wasteels Travel (0171-834 7066).

The most comprehensive network of coach services in Europe is operated by Eurolines, a consortium of some of the largest coach operators in Europe including National Express in Britain. Their services cover more than 270 destinations throughout Europe. The UK head office of Eurolines is 23 Crawley Road, Luton, Beds LU1 1HX (01582 404511). Ring this number to request their very useful brochure which is available annually from late April. In London personal callers can book tickets at 52 Grosvenor Gardens, Victoria, London SW1 (0171-730 0202); to make credit card bookings call 0171-730 8235. Passengers under the age of 26 are eligible for modest discounts of about 10%.

For smaller independent coach operators, check advertisements in London magazines like *TNT*. For example Olympic Bus Ltd (0171-837 9141) was offering one-way fares to Greece of £50 and to Italy £40 (winter 1994/5), departing London every Friday at 6.30pm and arriving three days later (give or take 12 hours). Kingscourt Express (0181-673 7500) specialises in Prague and charge £47 single, £85 return.

Air travel to the Continent from Britain can be absurdly expensive or cheaper than going by land, depending on which ticket you buy. Tickets on schedules carriers are routinely discounted and are available from all travel agencies. Next come the scheduled 'charters': regular, unrestricted flights run by agencies hiring entire planes and flying at half IATA fares. Germany and Switzerland are favourite destinations, reflecting the use that business people make of them. Thirdly, the holiday charter market: seats are available on flights to resorts (mostly May to October) including a nominal accommodation package.

For cheap flights to Europe try Globepost in London (0171-587 0303). The agency Eastways (6 Brick Lane, London E1 6RF: 0171-247 3823) has the franchise for discounting tickets throughout the CIS. For the cheapest flights of all, you need to be prepared to leave at a day or two's notice. Holiday companies out of peak season try to fill up seats on charter flights, usually by advertising in the London *Evening Standard:* such as 'Tenerife £59, leaving tomorrow' was just one of the thousands noticed recently.

If you are on the southern edge of Europe and heading east, consider taking the weekly boat from Greece to Israel. Poseidon Lines take 2½-3 days and charge from dr15,000 for the journey between Piraeus and Haifa.

NORTH AMERICA

Transatlantic fares continue to be very competitive especially in the low season (January to March). One-way tickets to the east coast start at not much more than £100 and returns from £200 plus arrival and departure taxes of £12-14 each (which represent a considerable proportion of the total price). Outside summer and the Christmas period you should have no problems getting a seat; at peak times, a reliable alternative is to buy a discounted ticket on one of the less fashionable carriers which fly to New York, such as Air India or El Al. A one-year return London-New York on Kuwait Air in 1994 started at £195 plus taxes. Recommended specialist agencies in the UK are Unijet in Haywards Heath (01444 458531) and Major Travel in London (0171-485 7017) for the US and Globespan at Gatwick Airport (01293 595910) and Unijet for Canada.

The USA and Canada share the longest common frontier in the world, which gives some idea of the potential problems and expense of getting around. You will want to consider Driveaway (see *United States* chapter) and also bus and air travel which are both cheaper than in Europe. If you intend to travel widely in the States check out air passes. One working holidaymaker timed long journeys to coincide with night flights to save on accommodation and food. Hitch-hiking in the USA is often unnerving and sometimes fraught with danger, danger not only from crazy drivers but also from the law, especially in the north where 'No Hitch-hiking' signs abound. It is a more reasonable proposition in Canada.

South of the Canadian border, bus passes are a travel bargain for people who want to cover a lot of ground. Phone Greyhound (01342 317317) for details. In 1994/5, Greyhound are offering 4, 7, 15 and 30 day passes for £50, £90, £135 and £180; these must be purchased outside the US. Once you are in the US timetable and fare information is available 24 hours a day on the toll-free number 1-800-231-2222. Discounts are normally available to anyone who purchases a ticket three weeks in advance. After taking advantage of this discount and paying $68 for the trip El Paso-New York (normal price $200), Colin Rothwell was amazed to discover that Greyhound let him change the date. Greyhound also offer a Canada Pass (valid west of Montreal) which costs £92 for 7 days, £120 for 15 days and £165 for 30 days.

Other forms of transport in the USA are probably more expensive but may have their own attractions, such as the trips run by Green Tortoise (Box 24459, San Francisco, California 94124) which use vehicles converted to sleep about 35 people and which make interesting detours and stopovers. There may even be an option to swap your labour for a free ride.

The deregulation of US domestic airlines which happened in 1979 has led to lunatic discounting ever since. Air fare restructuring in the early 1990s squeezed the market bringing bankruptcy to several domestic airlines thereby reducing competition. South-West Airlines based in Dallas is one of the survivors and it is to be hoped will set a precedent with their cheap fares and no-frills service. A new discount domestic airline Leisure Air (800-538-7688) joined the fray mid-1994 and offered special summer one-way deals of $99 Boston-Los Angelse and $79 Boston-Orlando. Normally the cheapest advance purchase coast-to-coast fares are about $200 ($129 with Air-Tech mentioned above). The best advice within the USA is to study local newspapers, as fare wars are usually fought using full page advertisements. Also contact STA or Council Travel.

Attempts to revive long-distance train travel in the US have had some beneficial effects resulting in some good value rail passes, though trains are still largely the domain of tourists. The basic four-day rail journey from Toronto to Vancouver costs C$375 off-season. This is more than the cheapest flight and coach fares between these cities. Phone Leisure Rail (01733-335599) for current prices and bookings. Amtrak's toll-free number in the US is 1-800-USA-RAIL.

In both Canada and the USA there is an alternative way to ride the rails, as Marcel Staats found:

> *An absolutely great way to see North America is by train. However , if you don't have that much money on you, do it the illegal way and 'hobo'. I left most of my luggage in a cloakroom and hoboed my way across the States. To hobo' (also known as freight-hopping — Ed) means that you jump on goods trains (called freight trains) and stay there as long as possible. Hoboing is not what it was in the 40s and 50s. There's much tighter security, including frequent checks and padlocked doors. However there are possibilities.*

The *Freighthoppers' Manual for North America* is in its third edition and is available from the author Daniel Leen at Box 191, Seattle, WA 98111 for $8.95. According to the author, freight trains are still carrying 'hobos'; however security measures and tolerance of freight-hopping vary from place to place and are always changing.

For further information on cutting travel costs in North America, consult the *Travellers Survival Kit: USA & Canada* (Vacation-Work, £9.95).

LATIN AMERICA

In some seasons you can get to South America for under £200 one way; buying onward or return travel out there will cost vastly more, so buy these in advance if possible. Open-dated returns are available as are open jaw tickets (where you fly into one point and back from another). Having a return ticket makes it much easier to cross borders.

A fully-bonded agency which specialises in travel to and around this area of the world is Journey Latin America (14-16 Devonshire Road, London W4 2HD; 0181-747 3108) who consistently offer the lowest fares. Another advantage is that they deal exclusively with Latin America and hence are the best source of up-to-date travel information. Two other specialist agencies to try are H&H Herran (0171-437 3664) and Dellstar (0181-868 2968). Possible routings include travelling to Lima via Caracas, Santiago via Bogota and Central America via Houston. An open return to Latin America costs in the region of £550. The Venezuelan airline Viasa were offering good fares to Caracas, Quito and San José at the time of writing; ring Iberia Group Reservations on 0171-830 0011 for details. It is possible to connect onwards to Australia and Asia though this is expensive.

Heavy taxes are levied on international flights within South America: the cheapest way to fly from one capital to another (assuming you have plenty of time) is to take a domestic flight (within, say, Brazil), cross the border by land and then buy another domestic ticket (within, say, Peru). The alternatives include the remnants of a British-built railway system and the ubiquitous bus, both of which are extremely cheap and interesting. A rough estimate of the price of bus travel in South America is US$1.50 for every hour of travel. Hitch-hiking is highly unpredictable, and usually the cost depends upon your bargaining ability. The degree of safety depends upon sheer good fortune. Not that taking public transport guarantees a safe journey. Dick Bird describes the bus system of Rio de Janeiro:

> *Bus drivers are paid on a piece rate basis, so understandably they drive like speed-crazed lunatics. The first problem is to flag down one of these monsters*

as it hurtles along six inches from the kerb sucking old ladies, debris and small dogs into its slipstream. Just as you are meekly offering your cruzeiros to the conductor at the rear of the bus, you are suddenly slammed back against the emergency exit as the bus takes off in a flurry of G-forces worthy of a medium-sized moon rocket. On your second attempt to pay, you find yourself jack-knifed and doubled up over the turnstile. At last you manage to flop into the upholstery like a landed fish and find yourself in a position of uncomfortable intimacy with the inevitable fat lady in the window seat. You sit quivering, vowing to go by DC-10 next time.

Rio newspapers regularly lead with headlines like *Onibus no Canal* (bus in the canal) or *Onibus Mergulho da Ponte — 50 Mortos* (bus dives off bridge killing 50).

For information on travel in Latin America contact the South America Explorers' Club (Av. Portugal 146, Brena, Postal Casilla 3714, Lima 100, Peru; 31 44 80, or Toledo 1254 y Cordero, Postal Apartado 21-431, Quito, Ecuador; 566 076. US office: 126 Indian Creek Rd, Ithaca, NY 14850. UK agent: Bradt Publications, 41 Nortoft Road, Chalfont St Peter, Bucks SL9 0LA). In addition to travel information they also keep some info on job opportunities in peru and Ecuador in the relevant clubhouses. Their magazine has a classified section which could be useful.

AFRICA

Flights to Cairo are advertised from £130 single, £190 return, while the special offers to Nairobi start as low as £169 single, £300 return. A specialist agency for South Africa is Melhart Travel in East London (0171-739 1636). Johannesburg on Olympic via Athens was available recently for £435 plus taxes (including £16 Greek departure tax with a Greek stopover); unusually for Africa this ticket was valid for a year. Another agency to try is the Africa Travel Shop (4 Medway Court, Leigh St, London WC1; 0171-387 1211). Note that there is no regular ferry service between Greece and Alexandria, Egypt.

The overland routes are fraught with difficulties, and careful research must be done before setting off via the Sahara (the route through the Sudan is virtually impossible at present). Jennifer McKibben, who spent some time in East Africa, recommends trying to negotiate a cheap seat in one of the overland expedition vehicles which are so much in evidence in that part of the world, assuming 'half their number have stormed off the bus or truck, unable to bear each other any longer'.

ASIA

The famous hippy overland route to Nepal has been problematical for many years though not impossible. Although Afghanistan is still off-limits, it is possible to cross Iran into Pakistan (a very rigorous but very cheap trip, assuming you can get a transit visa for Iran). Once you're in Pakistan, you might assume that the freedom of the sub-continent was before you, but due to the problems in the Punjab, the Indo-Pakistan border cannot be relied upon to be open. An alternative is to make the journey with an established overland company which charge between £100 and £150 a week not including the food kitty. Most travellers simply take advantage of the competitive discount flight market from London to Asian destinations. For example the cheapest quoted return price London to Delhi is £300. The cheapest carrier to Bangkok is Tarom the Romanian airline which has a one-year return for £330 with a stopover in Bucharest. A specialist consolidator for India is Greaves Travel in Manchester (0161-487 5687). Flights to Japan have dropped significantly in the past few years. An off-season winter one-way fare with Aeroflot was priced at just £250 in 1994/5 and an open return was £565.

Once you're installed in Asia, travel is highly affordable. The railways of the Indian sub-continent are a fascinating social phenomenon and also dirt cheap. Throughout Asia, air fares are not expensive, particularly around the discount triangle of Bangkok, Hong Kong and Singapore. Lifts with trucks or private vehicles are likely to cost a nominal sum, so usually it's preferable to rely on public transport. The notable exception to the generalisation about cheap public transport in Asia is Japan, where the possibility of hitching marginally compensates for the high cost of living and travelling.

Travel within the People's Republic of China can initially be exasperating as you struggle with the inscrutable bureaucracy and the utterly incomprehensible nature of stations and airports (where no allowance is made for those who do not understand Chinese characters). But like most things in the East, once you come to terms with the people and their way of life, travelling once more becomes a pleasurable experience. With upheavals in Russia, the Trans-Siberian rail journey is not as cheap as it used to be. One Europe Travel (0181-566 9424) sell tickets London-Beijing for £475. Tickets bought in Hong Kong for the trip in the opposite direction are cheaper.

AUSTRALASIA

The Australian Tourist Commission's *Traveller's Guide* contains a lot of hard information and useful telephone numbers; you can request a free copy by ringing 0181-780 1424. An excellent free guide for backpackers is the booklet *Budget Travel Australia* published three times a year and available from Red Sky Distribution, 70 Brunswick St, Stockton-on-Tees, Cleveland TS18 1DW (send £1 for postage). Once you arrive in Australia, look out for the very useful free booklets *For Backpackers by Backpackers* for most of the states; they all contain a section on working.

Per mile, the flight to the Antipodes is cheaper than most. The Indonesian carrier Garuda has traditionally been the cheapest; for example a 12-month return on Garuda might be £685 compared to £875 on the next cheapest Cathay Pacific. The cheapest advertised fares are on charter flights (from £399 return with Austravel 0171-734 7755) but for these you must return within eight weeks. One-way fares to Sydney with Britannia start at £300, and one-way to Auckland starts at about £375, £675 return in low season. A specialist agency to try is Airline Network on 0800 727747.

Your transport problems are by no means over when you land in Perth or Sydney. The distances in Australia may be much greater than you are accustomed to and so you will have to give some thought to how you intend to get around. Even with increased airline comptetition, flying is costly, though you should look into the 55% discounts offered by the major domestic airlines (Ansett and Australian) to overseas visitors who buy a certain number of domestic flights. There are also other discounts for booking at the last minute, and for travelling at unsocial hours or standby.

If you plan a major tour of the country you might consider purchasing a Greyhound, Pioneer or Bus Australia coach pass valid for between seven and 120 days, which can be bought after arrival. If you just want to get from one coast to another as quickly as possible and qualify for the very cheapest deals, you will pay around A$275 one way on the coach or train (excluding berth and meals).

Having your own transport is a great advantage when job-hunting in Australia. Places like Mach I Autos in Sydney and Deals on Wheels in Perth often have second-hand camper vans for sale which they will buy back at the end of your stay. Also in Sydney check the car market in Kings Cross (corner of Ward Avenue and Elizabeth Bay Road). A reliable vehicle would cost $2.500 or more.

If you can't afford the luxury of organised transport or buying your own vehicle, you might be drawn to the idea of hitch-hiking. A coast to coast journey won't take you much less than a week, so it's a major undertaking. Be careful about being dropped on isolated stretches of the road across the Nullarbor Plain where, without water, you might just expire before the next vehicle comes along. On the other hand, you might be lucky and get one of those not uncommon lifts which covers 3200km in 96 hours.

Many women travellers have expressed their reluctance to travel alone with a long-distance lorry driver in remote areas, especially after the well-publicised backpacker murders a couple of years ago. According to a policeman Lucy Slater spoke to, drivers are less inclined to pick up hitchers in view of the trouble. (Nevertheless, Lucy and her boyfriend hitched from Perth to Kalgoorlie and found that the people who gave them lifts were mines of information about job possibilities.) The Queensland coastal road is notoriously dangerous. Violence is rare, but if you are unlucky you might be evicted from the truck unless you comply with the driver's wishes. All backpackers' hostels are a good bet for finding drivers going your way, provided you are able to wait for a suitable ride.

You need not confine yourself to cars and lorries for hitching. Adrian McCay hitched a lift on a private plane from remote Kununurra to Mildura. While working at a remote property in Western Australia, David Irvine hitched a couple of lifts with the flying doctor service. Earlier in his travels he got stranded in Norseman after a truck ride across the Nullarbor. Here he met an aboriginal swagman who advised him to hop a freight which he did, which turned out to be a coal train. Suddenly there was a very rare rainstorm which turned the coal dust on which he was sitting in his open hopper to disgusting sludge.

Unfortunately the flight from Australia to New Zealand is not particularly cheap (about A$380 one way) although if bought in conjunction with a longhaul flight it is much less. But once in New Zealand it is difficult to imagine a country more favourable to hitch-hikers. Travellers regularly cover the whole country, using youth hostels and hitching, and spend about £200 a month.

A day return on the ferry between North and South Island costs the same as the single, so it is worth trying to sell the return half when you reach the other side. It also provides a good opportunity for finding drivers heading in your direction.

FORMALITIES AT BORDERS

Whichever mode of transport you choose, there are a number of formalities, which must be tackled before you set off, to ensure that your journey is not fraught with an unexpected range of disasters. It is always preferable to have a full passport rather than a one-year Visitor's passport. On a coach journey from London to Athens, Mark Hurley was the only passenger not to have a full passport; at the Hungarian border they made him buy a visitor's visa for £24 (which represented a fifth of his worldly wealth).

Visas

With over 150 nations crammed onto this minor planet, you can't continue in one direction for very long before you are impeded by border guards demanding to see your papers. EU nationals who confine their travels to Europe have little to worry about. Everyone else should do their homework. Always check with the Consulate or (second best) a travel agent who will have a copy of the monthly *Travel Information Manual (TIM)* which contains all visa, customs and other information. Alternatively consult Thomas Cook's timetables or the quarterly *Guide to International Travel* in local libraries. You will then be in a position to bore your friends and fellow travellers with your knowledge of the documentation required by North Korean visitors to the United Arab Emirates. Getting visas is a headache anywhere, but is usually easier in your home country. Fees are rising. For example, from October 1994, the US Embassy is charging a flat processing fee of £13 (which will not be returned if your visa application is unsuccessful for any reason).

If you are short of time or live a long way from the Embassies in London, there are private visa agencies such as Worldwide Visas (9 Adelaide St, Charing Cross, London WC2 4HZ: 0171-379 0419) and the Visa Service, 2 Northdown St, London N1 9BG; 0171-833 2709) which will obtain the relevant visa for fees from £12 per visa. Details of work permit regulations and so on can be found in the country chapters in this book. See also the introductory section *Red Tape*.

The two pariah nations of the world, Israel and South Africa, have gone some way to diminishing their international isolation and stamps in your passport from those countries may no longer guarantee problems at 'enemy borders'. The Foreign and Commonwealth Office are in the process of reviewing their list of incompatible countries and it may be that the United Kingdom Passport Agency (Clive House, 70-78 Petty France, London SW1H 9HD) will no longer be willing to issue a second passport to people who intend to travel both to Israel and hostile Arab countries (unless you can prove you need it for business). For up-to-date information on this subject, ask the Passport Office's Policy Section (0171-271 8632).

The Foreign Office has a Travel Advice Unit which can be contacted on 0171-270 4129. North Americans who are planning to visit a war zone or other potentially dangerous region might like to contact the US State Department's Hotline on 202-647-5225 (fax 202-647-3000) in case a relevant 'travel advisory' concerning epidemics, civil wars or unrest has been issued (which often errs on the side of caution).

If you intend to cross a great many borders, especially on an overland trip through Africa, ensure that you have all the relevant documentation and that your passport contains as many blank pages as frontiers which you intend to cross. Travellers have been turned back purely because the border guard refused to use a page with another stamp on it.

Money

Money can be a problem at borders: on the one hand having too little to support yourself, or on the other, carrying a non-transferable currency. You may need to prove that a) you have enough to support yourself for the duration of your proposed stay, and b) that you have the means to leave the country without undermining the economy by engaging in unauthorised activities (e.g. working, changing money on the black market, smuggling, etc.). The authorities are more likely to take an interest in a scruffy impecunious looking backpacker. Sometimes border personnel wish to see proof of absurdly large sums such as $500 before you can board the boat between Greece and Israel or $1,000 for each month of your proposed stay in New Zealand. Remember that well-dressed travellers who carry suitcases rather than rucksacks will be challenged less often. Because Michel Falardeau was travelling on one-way tickets without all that much money, he wore a business suit whenever he was due to meet an immigration official, and this worked for him on his round-the-world trip. You can get away with having less money if you have an onward ticket, and the names and addresses of residents whom you intend to visit.

There are several ways round the problem. Some travellers have gone so far as to declare the loss of their travellers cheques, in order to use the duplicate set as 'flash money'. As soon as the duplicates have done their duty at the border, the supposedly lost originals can then be burned. A less dramatic technique is to show off your range of credit cards. Or take a IATA miscellaneous charges order. This is effectively a voucher for a specified amount (say £100) worth of air travel. It may be bought from any IATA airline, and has several advantages: it is usually accepted as proof of your intention to leave the country in lieu of a straight airline ticket and may be used as such across virtually any border, plus it adds an extra £100 to your worth, i.e. the money you're supposed to be injecting into the country's flagging economy. When you get home you may cash it in at face value. The only difficulty is that officials in the off-the-beaten track countries may not recognise the document.

After reconfirming your booking with your airline 72 hours before a flight, find out whether there is a departure tax. For example to fly out of Lebanon you must pay £20, Bangkok 200 baht, etc. This can be an unexpected nuisance or a total disaster. Information about transferring emergency funds from home is given in *In Extremis* at the end of this book.

ENTERPRISE

You don't have to spend eight hours a day washing dishes in order to earn money abroad. Many travellers have found or made opportunities to go into business for themselves, exchanging steady wage packets for less predictable sources of income. The people who have succeeded in this type of work tend to have a large degree of initiative, determination and often creativity; they have identified some local need and exploited it.

Often they find themselves on the borderline of the law. If you paint the sun setting over a harbour you are an artist; sell the painting to someone who stops to admire it and you may, in law, become a street trader requiring a permit. Normally no one will object to this type of misdemeanour, and at worst you should find yourself being moved along by the police. Exceptions are noted in the country chapters.

The chapter will first deal with importing and exporting: the ways in which you can make money by buying cheaply in one country and selling in another. The second part of the chapter will deal with the kinds of marketing opportunities which you should watch out for within the country you're visiting, many of which involve pandering to the desires of homesick tourists. The final two sections deal with odd-jobbing and gambling.

IMPORT/EXPORT

The experienced traveller soon discovers what items can be bought cheaply in one country and profitably sold in another. On his trip out to a far-flung corner of the world he will stock up on the kinds of duty-free goods or other items he knows are in demand. (Johnny Walker Red Label seems to be a universally prized brand of whisky.) Wherever something is exorbitantly priced, it is possible to sell informally to local people or fellow tourits at a profit. One of the most portable and profitable items to carry around is cigarette papers which are fiendishly expensive in Scandinavia for example, and unobtainable in Greece, Brazil, etc. Ian McArthur planned to take about 500 packets to Goa where he'd heard that the selling price was five times higher than in Britain.

Some travellers think it's worthwhile to load up on bronze trinkets, alpaca sweaters, jade jewellery, rosewood boxes, Tibetan woollens, Turkish carpets or anything else which they know are more expensive or unobtainable elsewhere. Before engaging in this sort of activity you'll have to master the art of haggling, which involves patience and good humour. Also, you should be thoroughly acquainted with customs regulations. Usually it is difficult to make much of a profit on one-off trips abroad.

Do not believe every foreign trader who promises you vast profits in your home country, for example selling Tahitian pearls or Sri Lankan gems, or who assures you that you will have no difficulty at customs. In fact do not believe any of them. Almost invariably they are inventing a story in order to make a bulk sale. No consumer protection is available to their gulls. Bangkok seems to be the capital of smooth-talking swindlers. A warning notice in a Bangkok hostel, which reads 'These people are vicious and evil and all they say is lies' was written by a German who parted with US$1,100 for '$3,000 plus' of sapphires, only to be told by his 'guaranteed buyer' (an unwitting jeweller in Sydney) that their true value was $250.

Yet there is a host of travellers successfuly selling exotica as Kristen Moen reports:.

I was in Corfu selling jewellery I had bought in India, Nepal, Thailand and China. Quite a lot of my friends do similar things. When they come home from Asia and South America they sell jewellery and other things and they make almost enough money to finance their trip. Of course you have to be careful when you buy so you don't get cheated but you learn along the way.

You don't have to wait until you get home to sell. Many travellers successfully sell jewellery and knicknacks from Thailand and India in Taiwan and Hong Kong. Westerners can be seen selling leather goods and other items brought from India in European markets.

Duty-Free

Selling your duty-free tobacco, alcohol and consumer durables is probably the most obvious and simple way of earning money. In some Asian countries, Scotch whisky and European cigarettes are so widely coveted that you will be approached on the streets. In other countries, these products are available in the shops but for a colossal price. You can make as much as four times your outlay, for example, if you manage to sell a box of high quality cigars brought from Cuba to Europe. Be very cautious about taking alcohol into strict Islamic countries where it is forbidden. There is a good market in 'softer' Islamic countries too; for example touts and guides in Tangiers are willing buyers. Beware of highly organised local competition, for example along international trading routes where drivers and overland couriers will know all the tricks. Exploiting price differentials across international borders can be lucrative if you are well situated. For example people who live in Spain and work in Gibraltar can make a sizeable profit on cartons of Winston cigarettes bought in Gibraltar and sold in bars in La Linea. (Officially you are entitled to carry one carton a month across the border.)

Some travellers are content with modest profits and confine themselves to trading within their duty free allowance (normally one bottle of spirits and 200 cigarettes, except of course within the European Union). Others are after bigger gains and exceed their allowance tenfold, thereby risking heavy customs duties or having the goods confiscated at entry, with the possibility of a fine. Of course a reasonable quantity of personal effects may be imported e.g. one camera with five rolls of film, one record player, one hair dryer 'for the use of lady tourist only' (in the case of Bangladesh), and so on, in addition to personal clothing, jewellery and 'medals bestowed by foreign countries'. Few officials will accept that you really need to bring back nine stereo cassette players for your own use from your holiday in Hong Kong, though people leaving Australia can plausibly have a number of opals for 'gifts'. Many countries where illegal trading is a common practice stipulate that property of high value (e.g. camera, video recorder) must be entered on your passport or on a tourist baggage re-export form on which you undertake to re-export the named articles. If something you wish to sell is marked on your passport upon entry, you must report it stolen and obtain an official police statement to this effect to avoid undue problems when you try to leave.

Currency Exchange

In countries where there is a soft currency, i.e. one which cannot officially be used to buy dollars or sterling, or where the government attaches an unjustifiably high value to its currency, a black market often develops, as in Malawi and Ethiopia. Hong Kong dollars have been fetching twice the bank rate from street dealers in currency in Chinese cities.

Tempting as the rewards might be, you should be aware of the pitfalls (apart from the arguable unethicality of depriving banks of hard currency which helps poor economies to keep ticking over). The black market attracts all sorts of shady characters who very regularly cheat even the canniest travellers, making them regret their greed. Favourite ploys include handing the tourist an envelope full of shredded newspaper or one large denomination bill wrapped cleverly around a wad of lower bills, or pretending to spot a policeman and then vanishing after taking your dollars but before giving you your pesos, rupees, shillings, etc. Even more worrying situations can arise if you realise that the black marketeer is an *agent provocateur* who is in cahoots with the police. The law will appear instantly either to arrest you (unlikely) or to demand some baksheesh. To guard against such an outcome, always avoid trading on the street. By asking around at budget hotels, you'll soon learn where to find legitimate traders, often in shops or travel agencies. Familiarise yourself with the appearance of all denominations of currency and take along a friend to assist you.

Second-hand Gear

Outside the consumer societies of the West, there is a fluctuating demand for gadgets and gewgaws, and various items we take for granted can be sold or traded. T-shirts with Western slogans are universally popular. Even if you don't get cash, you might trade for goods and services or an interesting souvenir.

If you are a frequent visitor to a country, you might try to learn what kinds of used items are in demand at markets. Foreigners in Britain could reserve a table at a car boot sale (for about £5-10) to try to sell any items of interest from their country. Elfed Guyatt from Wales thinks that Sweden is a particularly promising destination for any would-be entrepreneurs:

In the weekend market stalls people just set up their own table and sell off all sorts of odds and ends. The prices are incredibly high compared to Britain for certain things. You should make 500% profit on selling things like medals, caps, British and American books in subjects that interest the Swedes, in fact anything that looks different and not easily available in their country. They do like showing off possessions here. Souvenirs of London or Shakespeare go well. I saw a very cheap, small brass Big Ben table bell sell for £12.50 and an old battered cricket bat went for £25.

The switch to free market economies throughout the old eastern Bloc has wiped out the old black market in designer clothes, pop music, books, cosmetics, chewing gum, etc.

Trading in Cars

Pricing policies within the single European market have reduced the price differentials on cars bought in different countries, so it is no longer worth considering this trade. (The Consumers' Association has ceased publishing its booklet *Importing a Car Action Pack*.)

Car buffs who know the market well still might profit on specialist vehicles, though this level of investment is advisable only if you have a buyer fixed up in advance. Furthermore customs regulations make this very difficult without having well-informed contacts in your selling country, as Elfed Guyatt had in Sweden a few years ago:

One of my Swedish friends asked me to buy him an old car for about £2,000. We drove this 1969 MGb through Europe and into Sweden. I said it was mine and drove straight through customs. The car here is worth £5,000. It is common for Swedes to drive their boring Saabs and Volvos in the winter and have a snazzier car for the summer. Swedish kroner go a long way in England and even the not-so-well-off are on the lookout for a 'summer car'.

During Frank Schiller's year in Egypt he couldn't help admiring the classic motorbikes being ridden around, and it dawned on him that he could make a handsome profit exporting these to his native Germany:

It all began on a hot Cairene day in a dusty street in Mohandessin when this guy rolled up riding a classic early sixties British-made BSA, and I was intrigued. Immediately I had ideas of myself riding around the Pyramids on a classic. A little later I was. I bought a 1949 single cylinder 500cc BSA. In Germany and presumably England it is inconceivable to just pick up a bike like that and go. It usually involves lots of work, mechanical skills and a very nicely stacked wallet. Yet Egyptians would frequently laugh at me and my antiquated machine and shout 'milkseller' (because milk vendors use these bikes for hauling milkcans around Cairo's back streets).

When a couple of friends and I decided to try to export four or five of these, galactical problems were in store for us, especially the notorious Epyptian bureaucracy. Knowing Arabic was utterly necessary. But we persevered with the form filling and hassles, shipped them out from Alexandria and picked them up in Hamburg a month later. Well, people in Germany were interested, including one of Germany's best known cartoonists who bought them all. We hadn't exactly made a killing but the margin was big enough for us not to be disappointed.

SPOTTING LOCAL OPPORTUNITIES

The opportunities for finding eager customers on whatever doorstep you find yourself are endless and we can only give some idea of the remarkable range of ways to earn money by using your initiative and your imagination. If you see a gap in the market, try to fill it. For example Stephen Psallidas toyed seriously with the idea of buying a bicycle in the tomato-growing capital of Queensland in order to hire it out to job-seeking tomato pickers since at the time Bowen was, if not a one-horse town, a one-bicycle town. After getting to know the Greek island of Levkas fairly well, Camilla Lambert hired a jeep at weekends for £35 a day and took three paying passengers out for a day's excursion. One Englishmen acquired a chain saw in Spain and made a killing by hiring himself out to farmers to prune their olive trees. A Canadian who was having trouble being hired by a language school in a provincial city in Taiwan set up his own English immersion social club which easily covered his costs in the two months he ran it. You just need to exploit any manual or artistic or public relations skill you already have or which you have cultivated for the purpose.

Homemade Handicrafts

A number of people have successfully supported themselves abroad by selling home-made jewellery on the street. Careful preparations can pay dividends; for example Jennifer Tong picked up shells from a beach near Eilat and invested £5 in a pair of pliers and some wire, clips and beads when she was in Israel. With these materials she made simple earrings which were bought for £2 a pair on the Greek Islands. Steve Pringle sold earrings in Madrid which he had made from a stock of cheap imitation diamonds he had brought over from London. Braided or knotted friendship bracelets are popular in travellers' resorts and can usually be sold for £2-3 and take 15 minutes to make. It is worth looking out for cheap and unusual raw materials such as coral from South America, beads from Morocco, shells from Papua New Guinea or bamboo from Crete. Grimly Corridor taught himself how to make pan pipes from the local bamboo and sold them for about £5 (which included a recitation of the Pan legend which American tourists found difficult to resist).

If you can draw, knit, sew, sculpt or work with wood or leather then you may be able to produce something that people want to buy in holiday resorts. The skill of braiding hair with beads or 'hair wraps' can make a lot of money. All you need is the expertise, some cheap multi-coloured beads and thread with which to tie off the ends. One contributor met a girl making the equivalent of £35 a day in a Cape Town market doing this. While on holiday on the island of Formentera off the coast of Spain, Georgina Bayliss-Duffield found that braiding people's hair was a lucrative pastime, especially with a companion on whom to demonstrate. Eventually she was able to complete a head whether male or female in about 20 minutes (depending on the hair) for which she charged the equivalent of £8.

Beaches and Mobs

You should learn to look on any crowd of people as a potential market for what you have to sell. People emerging from a disco are often grateful for a sandwich or skiers queuing for a lift might appreciate some chocolate. If you loiter in a place where people regularly emerge from a remote place, as at the end of treks in Nepal or New Zealand, you could probably sell some interesting food and drink of which they have been deprived. Stephen Psallidas decided to become a portable off-licence with a view to selling wine to the devotees who flock to see Jim Morrison's grave in Paris. Unfortunately this was not a popular idea with the local cannabis sellers and he ended up drinking the wine himself.

Sunbathers on a wide unspoilt beach may be longing for a cold bottle of beer, sun tan lotion, a donut, or a few pre-stamped postcards and a ballpoint pen, and won't mind paying over the odds for them (especially if you have printed up your own postcards from your travel photos). Choose your beach carefully: if a beach is already swarming with cold drinks salesmen (as is the case along much of the French and Spanish Mediterranean), you're unlikely to be welcomed by potential customers. If a beach has none, selling may well be forbidden, as one reader discovered at Sydney's Bondi Beach, when the beach inspector chased them off after a few minutes.

If a crowd is scheduled to gather for a special occasion, think of the things they will want to buy. For example you could buy a few dozen roses in Niagara Falls, 'honeymoon capital of the world', and sell them individually to the happy couples at a high mark-up. The award for the most original salesman should go to the person who spotted an unruly crowd waiting for the arrival of the then Canadian Prime Minister in Sudbury, Ontario. He got hold of some eggs and sold them for use as missiles. Another situation which could be exploited is the refusal to allow scantily clad tourists into some European churches: renting out a pair of trousers would be a valuable service.

If you have the right product, you can sell to a wider market. One traveller earned his way in South America by selling peanut butter he'd made himself from local peanuts to American tourists outside the archaeological sites of Colombia. Ski bums regularly make pocket-money by delivering croissants from the local bakery to self-catering holiday-makers. Meanwhile another traveller sold popcorn to fishermen in Crete. If you are a fisherman yourself, you can try to sell your catch door to door in residential areas. Tessa Shaw picked snails at night by the River Ardèche in southern France and then set up a stall in the market at Carpentras. She found that Fridays were particularly profitable, since restaurateurs and shopkeepers drove down from Paris to buy stock for the weekend.

Anyone who owns and can use a pack of Tarot cards can sell his or her expertise. Leda Meredith had noticed people doing this in Florence and Avignon (where the going rate for a reading was F30) and set herself up on the Greece-Italy ferry with a table, two chairs and a sign in English.

Selling tickets to popular sporting or entertainment events is probably best left to locals in the know like Floyd Creamer Jr. from Wisconsin. He made $867 by spending less than two hours before seven college football and hockey games buying unwanted tickets for a pittance and selling them at (or almost at) face value, even for games which were not sold out. He found that it was even possible to buy a single day vendor's permit for $10 which made his activities all perfectly legal.

Julian Peachey landed a job as warden in a youth hostel in Marseille, and soon began supplementing his income by selling wine at the hostel. The local supermarket delivered supplies at 40p per bottle, which he sold to the hostellers for 80p. Even though they realised he was selling at a substantial profit, the hostellers were happy to patronise his store when their own supplies had run out late at night. People staying in hostels often leave behind belongings (intentionally or otherwise) which could perhaps be sold, as Dustie Hickey did at an Avignon flea market earning herself £30 in an hour. Meanwhile Brett Archer was working as an assistant warden at the youth hostel in Bruges (Belgium) and began hiring out abandoned bicycles on a daily basis.

Writing and the Media

A few lucky people manage to subsidise their journeys abroad by selling articles or photographs based on their travels. There are two main markets for your creative work: local English language publications abroad, and newspapers and magazines in your home country. A trip to Northern Queensland might not seem newsworthy to you when you're there, but Frank Schiller sold an account of his trip to a German magazine for several hundred dollars. You can best find out about local publications by studying news-stands when you are abroad. For contacts in Britain, consult *The Writers' and Artists' Yearbook* (published by A&C Black, 35 Bedford Row, London WC1R 4JH) and in the US *The Guide to Travel Writing & Photography* or *Photographer's Market* both published by Writer's Digest Books (1507 Dana Ave., Cincinnati, Ohio 45207) for $22.95. You can also try the in-flight magazines of foreign airlines.

If you have already published take along a cutting book. Before you go abroad, it is a good idea to study the market, to get an idea of what editors are looking for. Many magazines issue editorial guidelines. One such is *Lookout* published in Malaga which describes the kind of travel article which it (like many others) is looking for:

> *We try to achieve a fresh view, a new angle, on travel destinations. Feel free to use the first person singular in a travel article. Describe those interesting or curious little incidents which, while not being of earth-shaking significance, help to brighten up the story. Quote the people you met on the trip: the innkeeper, the museum guard... Of course, you must also give practical information on how to get there, what to see, where to stay and where to eat, but this information should be delivered in a light, readable manner.*

Illustrated travel articles are best of all. Black and white prints are best for this purpose, or colour transparencies. Remember that editors are less interested in arty effects than in photos which tell a story.

English language newspapers around the world are a real source of potential casual work from South America to Eastern Europe, Mexico to Turkey. There is an entire sub-culture of bright young travellers working their way around these papers. Some are using it as a short-cut in a journalism career; others are merely adventurers. Many of the people working on these papers had never been inside a newsroom before. Anyone who can read the language should be able to find a job at least as a proofreader, and anyone who shows any competence at this level will quickly advance to copy-editor or even reporter. Editors may not want to hire globetrotters, but staff turnover is often so high that they don't have any choice.

International firms with branches abroad are less glamorous employers of writing skills, but they may need someone to edit their newsletter or brochures. If you notice a badly written company report or piece of publicity it might be worth introducing yourself (especially in Japan), though make your point as tactfully as possible. Even such a long-established English language publication as the *Athens News* was so full of mistakes that a traveller from Los Angeles was taken on as a proofreader after circling and correcting all the errors in a randomly chosen issue and presenting it to the editor. You can always offer to correct the English of museum labels, menus or travel brochures. You might get a free meal in exchange for your grammatical expertise, though you may unwittingly be depriving future travellers of a source of amusement. If you have a knack for penning catchy phrases, you might get hired as Helen Welch did by a Taiwanese businessman, to invent slogans for badges.

You do not necessarily have to be sensational; the local paper in Windsor, Ontario may like to print the opinions of a visitor from Windsor, Berkshire about its fair city. Research can pay off. For example, Tony Davies-Patrick established from local libraries and bookshops that there was a shortage of material on the subject of freshwater angling abroad. So he spent a year travelling around Europe and the Middle East taking photographs and assembling information to sell to freshwater angling magazines. Andrew Vincent intended to concentrate on radio journalism in which he had some local experience. At last report he had been promised £20 a week by his local BBC station to send weekly telephone pieces from North America.

All you readers who imagine that the ideal job would be to write a travel guide should pay attention to the following description by Woden Teachout who spent one summer researching Ireland for the well-known *Let's Go* series:

I got lucky and was hired by Harvard Student Agency (which hires only students) to update their chapter on Ireland. They gave me $600 for air travel and $40 a day for expenses and profit. It was a mixed blessing. I spent most of each day visiting local historical societies and talking to all the Mrs. O'Learys who run B&Bs, checking their bathrooms for cleanliness and trying to figure out how to vary descriptions of fluffy white bedrooms. At night I would run around to three or four pubs, trying to encapsulate each atmosphere in a good one-liner and then back to the hostel to write up the day's work. When you're writing a guidebook you can never quite relax, since you are always evaluating in your head. And since you have a fixed itinerary, you are not as free to follow the whims of chance and circumstance. It was definitely nice to get paid to travel, and go to places I otherwise would have missed, but on the whole it felt like indentured servitude.

Photography

There are several photo libraries in the UK which accept high quality travel photographs. The photos are lent or leased to the agencies who in turn rent them to clients such as publishers and advertising agencies. Most photo libraries offer a 50-50 split of the earnings from the photographs. They also usually demand a minimum initial submission of at least 50 photos, a minimum period of time for keeping your photos with the agency and at least a year's notice of withdrawal. They also prefer a contributor to send photos regularly.

Even if you have no particular skill with a camera or pen you may be able to profit from being in the right place at the right time. Earl Young has strong opinions on the subject:

Anyone who fails to carry a camera in foreign countries is a fool. What if an international incident happens to take place in the street in front of you one day and you don't happen to be carrying your camera?

If you do get a photo of an assassination attempt or any newsworthy event, don't waste a second contacting the news wire services; Reuters, Agence France Presse and Associated Press have offices or representatives in most capital cities. If your photograph is the one which is syndicated in newspapers world-wide, you need not work your way any further.

An easier way of setting yourself up as a photographer would be to take portraits with a Polaroid instant camera in cafés, on beaches near monuments, etc. Nudist beaches are reported to provide willing customers for these but check with your subjects before you snap them or they may snap back. Michael Jenkins had the bright idea of taking photos of tourists on their first parascending ride in Corfu. Most who expressed mild interest beforehand were so pleased with the photos (which Michael had developed in town) that they were delighted to spend 1200 drachmas for three.

Busking

If you can play an instrument, sing, tap dance, juggle, conjure, draw cartoons or act, you may be able to earn money on the streets. Most successful buskers say that musical talent is less important than the spot you choose and the way you collect. Two Americans busking in Morocco dediced that the local man they employed to collect money for them was more entertaining than they were so gave him the money.

To busk, you need the tools of your trade, perhaps an accomplice to collect money and an audience. A favourable climate helps, though some of the most successful buskers we have heard from have played in Northern Europe in mid-winter. One of the keys to success (in addition to talent) is originality. We have had reports from opposite ends of the world (Sweden and Northern Queensland) that kilted bagpipe-playing buskers are always a hit. (We're assuming that it wasn't the same busking Scot.) Mary Hall is one busker who is convinced that talent is not essential, as she discovered in Bergen, Norway:

I finally plucked up the courage to do a bit of busking on my pennywhistle. I'd only just bought it so was only able to play two songs 'Amazing Grace' and 'The Sounds of Silence'. Still I made £15 in 15 minutes. With a couple of extra songs I could well be on the way to my first million. It helped that my audience were pretty drunk.

Most international buskers say that people abroad (especially Scandinavia, Germany and Switzerland) are more generous than in Britain, that there is less trouble with being moved on and it is not too difficult to keep yourself by busking around the cafés of Europe. Helen Chenery was very sorry that she had not taken her accordian with her to Greece, since she soon saw that she could have elevated her diet of bread and jam if she'd had her instrument with her. Some advise that if you have to choose between carting around an instrument or your luggage, leave your luggage at home. You need a great deal of confidence in your abilities, to go abroad specifically to busk; it may be better to regard performing as a possible way of subsidising a holiday.

Festivals and other large gatherings of merry-makers are potentially lucrative; bear in mind that the more potential a position has, the greater the competition is liable to be for it. Armin Birrer made his living by busking around Norway, Wales, Ireland and New Zealand (including a 15-hour stint in an Invercargill hair salon); in fact he even saved enough in Europe for his air fare to New Zealand. (One assumes he has more musical talent than most.) He generally found busking best in small towns where buskers were seldom seen. Your main enemies are the weather and the police. David Hughes who busked with a borrowed guitar in Taipei encountered a more mysterious obstacle in the form of red graffiti appearing near his spot in the subway and veiled threats from people he could only guess were local gangsters or traders. He didn't hang around to find out.

Regulations about street performing vary from country to country, but in general you will be tolerated if you are causing no obstruction or other harm. There are a few places where it is positively encouraged if you meet a high enough standard: buskers in the Covent Garden precinct in London and the Centre Georges Pompidou in Paris have to be judged worthy before they can perform. In contrast, you may be prosecuted if you perform in the London Underground (but are more likely to be moved on). You may even find that busking leads to better things: Mark Kilburn was offered a job playing guitar in a night club in Holland on the basis of his street performances, Armin Birrer was encouraged by a film writer who heard him to try for a job as a film extra in Melbourne (see below), and Kev Vincent was invited to leave the streets of San Tropez behind to entertain on a millionaire's gin palace. If you can perform, there is no harm in offering your talents, particularly to pubs in Ireland and bars and cafés in Turkish resorts frequented by what Ian McArthur calls the 'Marlboro, Levis and Coca Cola generation'.

Artists

An artist who paints local scenes or copies local post cards can do well in holiday resorts. If you can draw a reasonable likeness you could set yourself up as a street portraitist. Two friends Belinda and Pandora found it fairly easy to make money both in Britain and the Continent especially among holiday-makers. Belinda used unlined brown paper bought in an industrial roll and oil pastels or children's crayons. You can also use driftwood or smooth pebbles. It is awkward to carry around two chairs with you so she relied on borrowing them from an adjacent café or church hall. Artistically you shouldn't be overscrupulous; when a disappointed subject asked 'Do I really look that old?' Belinda didn't hesitate to erase a few wrinkles. Once you become known, you may get more lucrative portrait commissions in people's houses. Serious artists may wish to look at a book *Across Europe: The Artist's Personal Guide to Travel and Work* published by AN Publications, PO Box 23, Sunderland SR4 6DG at £9.95 plus £1 postage.

Apparently boat owners are a particularly vain bunch and will often jump at the chance to have their vessel immortalised on canvas, so loiter around yacht marinas with your sketchbook. Wealthy home owners might also be interested in commissioning a sketch of their homes and a professionally produced leaflet might unearth some customers. Stephen Psallidas noticed a trend in Mykonos for tavernas, banks and other public buildings to display paintings of themselves. John Kilmartin's decorations of buildings on his kibbutz were so highly valued they were praised in an Israeli newspaper which prompted people to pay him to draw their portraits.

Even if you can't make any money from your artistic endeavours, you may bring pleasure to the locals. While in Ching Kong in northern Thailand, Dustie Hickey sat outside a hut painting Winnie the Pooh and blowing up balloons for the children. When the local English teacher noticed how spellbound the children were, she asked Dustie if she would like to teach at the school on a voluntary basis. She did the same at a children's hospital in Calcutta which so impressed both the children and nuns that she was invited back as a longer term volunteer.

Film Extras

If you like the idea of mingling with the stars in Hollywood for a few days and being well paid for it — forget it. In most international film studios even extras belong to trade unions which exclude outsiders. When a film is being shot on location you may have the opportunity of helping to fill out a crowd scene — in fact the accepted term is 'crowd artist' — but it is a matter of luck coming across these, though your chances are better in some places than others. The picturesque streets of old Budapest together with the relatively lower shooting costs make it a favourite location (in fact the author spotted Ben Kingsley in a restaurant in Pest). Acapulco and Tel Aviv are other favourite destinations for movie-makers.

In the massive Asian film industry, film-makers actively seek out Caucasian faces, especially to be villains, dupes or dissolutes. Agents for film companies usually look for their supernumerary staff among the budget hotels of Bombay, Hong Kong, Cairo, etc. knowing that they will find plenty of travellers only too willing to spend one or two days hanging around a film set in exchange for a few rupees or dollars. In fact by local standards the wage is generous. (See the chapter on *Asia* for further details.)

Armin Birrer followed up the tip to visit film studios in Melbourne and was paid $80 after tax for a day's work, which mostly consisted of hanging around:

In Melbourne there are always films and movies being made. If you are interested you should make the rounds of the studios. They take a photo of you and put you in their file, which usually means wait. But you might be the character they've been looking for and get work straight away.

Another traveller phoned up several Melbourne advertising agencies and was told that they did need some extras on location in the Northern Territory. Although jobs are normally found by word of mouth there are agencies in some places which will register you as potential extras. Apparently there are at least three agencies in Bangkok, one of which was successfully used by Vaughan Temby. Be wary of an agency which charges a fee. David Hughes found one in Vancouver which charged $50 and 'guaranteed' work. It turned out that if you didn't get hired by a film company, you didn't get a refund, your period of registration was simply extended.

Whether you work as an extra in the East or West you are unlikely to be given a part that will stretch your acting talents. But the work can still be demanding: hours can be erratic (for example in Hong Kong filming normally begins at midnight), and you may have to undergo a lengthy session in the make-up and costume departments. Make sure you take along a good book to fill in the idle hours.

If you hear rumours of a film being shot, try to find the crew and ask who you should see about work. Dave Bamford asked at the police station in Geneva but their directions came to nothing. By chance the next day he found the film vans, talked to someone in charge and was paid £40 to appear in the background of *The Unbearable Lightness of Being*. He was also invited to a hotel meal where he made lots of contacts for future work.

ODD JOBS

If you can't or don't want to get a steady job you could consider offering your services as an odd job person. By all accounts there is a world shortage of emergency plumbers, car and bike mechanics and piano tuners, so someone with these special skills who puts up notices locally should have no trouble finding paying customers. However there are plenty of jobs for the unskilled too: you don't have to study art to paint a garden fence. You may not earn a lot, but you should at least be promptly paid in cash, with no questions asked. There should be no problems about work permits unless you knock on the door of an immigration officer. Another odd job craze which started in New York is to offer to wash windscreens while motorists sit at red lights. A prize venue in South London has been known to earn some lucky windscreen operatives £70 a day.

It is a good policy to suggest a specific job when you are on the doorstep, rather than just to ask vaguely if there is anything to be done. Householders are more likely to respond favourably if you tactfully suggest that their garden is not devoid of weeds, or that the hinges on the gate could be brought into the twentieth century. You should never underestimate the laziness of other people: in summer lawns need mowing, garages need cleaning, cars need washing, and in winter snow needs clearing. If you propose to specialise in something like window cleaning you should invest in some basic equipment: people prefer to hire a window cleaner who has his own bucket, shammy and ladder. Some people have adopted a gimmick to attract custom, for example they offer their window-washing services while wearing roller skates. Dean Fisher had none of these when he had a brainwave in the south of France:

I was running out of money in Aix in Provence and got talking to an English guy who was working as a petrol attendant. I started washing windscreens for the people coming into the garage and ended up earning more money in tips than the petrol attendants' wages. Once a guy in a jeep gave me a 100 france tip which was amazing. I was my own boss (and didn't tell the guys how much I was getting).

The best areas to look for odd jobs and household maintenance jobs are middle class residential suburbs. The smaller the house the less potential there will be for odd jobs (and money). On the other hand, if you tour round country estates you will find it a long walk between rejections. Richard Adams did best in the semi-rural areas of Germany, where he found the population were less hasty to turn you away than fast-living city dwellers. You should consider your appearance carefully. An old age pensioner in Munich may not trust someone who looks as if has arrived on foot from Morocco. On the other hand, a housewife in Los Angeles has every right to be suspicious of someone wearing a three-piece suit who offers to clean her swimming pool.

Susan and Eric Beney took a break from travelling with their daughters overland to Australia to spend a while on the small Greek island of Halki. They arrived in April, before the tourist rush, and there was no evidence of any work around. But they successfully created a job from scratch:

The beach was a terrible mess with rubbish washed up in the winter storms, so we set ourselves the task of cleaning it up and asked the Mayor for rubbish bags. After we had been here for five weeks and our funds were sadly depleted, Eric was asked if he would like the job of 'port cleaner'. This job entailed sweeping the harbour and cleaning the streets three days a week and cleaning the loos daily. The job hadn't been done for a month so was quite a task in the beginning but I helped Eric get the loos to a reasonable standard and after that the job was quite a nice little number with plenty of time off. The pay was more than £100 a month and of course it has endeared Eric to the locals, none of whom would do such a job. Apparently a council allowance is made for this job so it could be worthwhile searching out the local Mayor and offering your services. Even the police are happy about it or turn a blind eye. Because we have now been here a while Eric has also done lots of other odd jobs for people as there is very little spare labour on the Island (or the locals are too lazy!)

Apparently Halki's beaches are in good shape these days but, according to Tom Hawthorne, Gibraltar would benefit if some future traveller could talk the council into funding a clean-up operation.

Collecting bottles and cans for their deposits is mentioned in the chapter *In Extremis* but in some countries it is lucrative enough to count as an odd job (and with a world trend towards recycling this can only increase). Tommy Karske reckons that it is possible to make a living by picking up aluminium cans in Australia which earn you $1 a kilo, while Elfed Guyatt observed that you could make £150 in three days of collecting bottles and cans during a Swedish carnival.

GAMBLING

Many countries run state lotteries but the chance of winning a prize are mostly too remote for this to be a useful way of supplementing diminished funds. Casinos and gambling on horse racing may be slightly better bets but again the percentages are always against the punter.

If you must play roulette, bet with the wheel and never against it; it is always possible that there is a slight mechanical fault which favours certain players or numbers. If there are some really big players at the table, bet last and bet against them. Crooked wheels are not unknown and if the casino plans to wipe out the high rollers you stand to profit if you keep your chips well clear of theirs.

Well used by a practised operator, a pack of cards, a backgammon board or set of poker dice are a much more promising source of extra income. Poker, bridge and backgammon, but particularly poker, are widely played for money throughout the world; if you become proficient there is every reason to use your skills for profit. The great thing about poker and backgammon is that they are comparatively simple games in which at every stage there is a mathematically correct play. The vast majority of players in amateur schools never take the trouble to learn the percentages. If you do, and so long as you keep out of the professional games, you will win. If interested, get a copy of *The Education of a Poker Player* by Herbert O. Yardley, published by Sphere Books in paperback. Clearly if you learn to deal 'seconds' or off the bottom of the pack, you will increase your chance of winning though you may well diminish your prospects of longevity.

Another gambit is to become adept at less well known games that pack neatly into your luggage like cribbage, bezique or shut-the-box and then entice your unsuspecting pals to play with you. Lose the board when they look like catching up on your expertise.

The 'Three Card Trick' or 'Spot the Lady' requires a definite element of dexterity but with regular practice you will become competent in a few weeks and can confidently invite customers to place their money on the Lady which hopefully is never the card they choose. As if you were cutting the pack, you hold one card face down lengthwise between thumb and middle finger of the left hand and two cards in a similar manner with your right hand. When releasing the cards from the right hand the top card (i.e. nearer the palm) is released first thus reversing the apparent positions of the two right hand cards when placed on the table. Keep your elbows up and let your wrist hang loose. After a while your audience will start to get wise to the game which is the time to make your apologies and leave. If you are playing with only one person, give them the three cards and you double your previous winnings as they attempt what you have been practising for weeks.

Rolling two dice for someone and getting them to bet on what number will come up is also a possible ruse. The possible numbers are 2 to 12 so the odds about any one number appear to be 10/1. In fact they range from 35/1 for a 2 or 12 to 5/1 for a 7. Actually it is better to get the pigeon to roll the dice and let you bet on 6's 7's and 8's (6/1, 5/1, 6/1) and keep him paying out at 10/1 until he can stand it no longer.

Another ploy which can be used to advantage is to fleece a con-man. It never fails but has its dangerous side and it works like this. All over the world you will find pool halls, pubs or arcades where sharks try to induce mugs to play pool, darts or some other game for money. You put on your best clothes and go into one of these alone and quietly play by yourself — obviously you are not very good and the con-artist soon spots you as a possible touch.' He invites you to play. But con-men, like the rest of us, are greedy; they don't want just to take $1 off you; they want the lot and they aim to do this by letting you think you are a match for them and even raise your hopes that you may win some money. To do this they will always lose the first and probably the second game. You take the money and leave — and make sure you know where the exit is.

Amazingly the big operators in Las Vegas and Atlantic City in the US and the Gold Coast in Australia can also be taken for a few dollars on the same principle. Always looking to get new punters into their gaming palaces they subsidise day tours or return trips to their gleaming portals in the desert or by the sea. The fare (subsidised) may be $5 and when you get there they give you free food and possibly even some chips, say $20 worth, to play the tables or the machines. Cash these in and you are a day older with all expenses paid.

EU EMPLOYMENT AND TAX

Legislation has existed for some years guaranteeing the rights of all nationals of the European Union (called the European Community until January 1994) to compete for jobs in any member country. According to Article 8a of the Maastricht Treaty, every citizen of the European Union has the right to travel, reside and work in any member state. The only reason for refusing entry is on grounds of public security and public health. But this does not mean that all the red tape and attendant hassles have been done away with. Talk of the Single Europe should not lull Euro-jobseekers into thinking that they need not worry about the formalities. EU rulings notwithstanding, barriers to the free movement of labour do remain which, it is to be hoped, the coming decade will remove.

As of autumn 1994 the EU consists of 12 member states: Belgium, Denmark, France, Germany, Greece, Ireland, Italy, Luxembourg, the Netherlands, Spain, Portugal and the United Kingdom. The European Economic Area (EEA) is a grouping of countries formed in 1994 as the result of an agreement between EU countries and five other western European countries, Austria, Finland, Norway, Sweden and Iceland. Its primary purpose is to remove trade restrictions but it has also involved the removal of the need for work permits for nationals of any one EEA member country who want to work in another member country.

Of the five, all but Iceland and Norway have ratified entry into the EU for January 1995 by referenda. Otherwise, the only Western European nation likely to remain outside the EU is Switzerland. (Liechtenstein is due to join in 1998.) For this reason the description EU is used throughout this chapter and throughout this book though technically the term EEA would be more precise (at least at the time of writing).

The standard situation among all EU countries is that nationals of any EU state have the right to look for work for up to three months. At the end of that period they should apply to the police or the local authority for a residence permit, showing their passport and job contract. The residence permit will be valid for five years if the job is permanent or for the duration of the job if it is for less than one year.

But there is no guarantee that this will be easy. Bureaucracies sometimes get in the way of progressive legislation. Many readers have written to say that it has taken, say, eight months for their *carte de séjour* in France to come through or that their Greek residence permit arrived on the last day of a nine-month contract. On his year out from university, Matt from Manchester worked in both France and Germany. In theory he should have had no problem regularising his status. In practice, he encountered many difficulties. The social security number for which he applied in France took 12 months to come through. In Germany he fared even worse, trapped in a vicious circle of 'no job — no papers — no accommodation'. Without papers he was turned away by the federal employment service, which all EU nationals are entitled to use. But resistance was useless.

Similar problems have been encountered by travellers attempting to claim unemployment benefit abroad, again in Germany. I. A. Gowing attempted to claim unemployment benefit at the *arbeitsamt* in Frankfurt, having followed the correct procedure and armed himself with his form E303 (details below). He was told that this was not possible unless he could produce a residence permit, and to get this permit he would need letters proving that he had accommodation there — and a job, which resulted in a classic Catch-22 situation; he was not allowed to collect unemployment benefit (to which he was entitled) because he was unemployed. David Ramsdale compared his attempts to get benefit from the Danish *Komune* (municipality) to trying to get blood out of a stone. Unfortunately, it requires time and energy to appeal against such decisions, which may simply be the result of bureaucratic prejudice. The DSS (now grandly called the Benefits Agency) in Britain has no control over its counterparts abroad when such problems arise and can only put forward a claimant's side of the argument, with no guarantee of success. But in light of the success of a few, it is certainly worth a try.

Another Catch-22 affects self-employed workers, particularly self-employed building workers. Although there is a demand for bricklayers, plasterers, plumbers, etc. especially in Germany, the Netherlands and Belgium, employers are reluctant to hire anyone who does not have form E101 from the relevant office of the Benefits Agency (address below) which proves that you are paying self-employed contributions in the UK and are therefore exempt from local tax and social security contributions for up to 24 months. However the Benefits Agency will issue an E101 only on the basis of a job offer with a named employer, so speculative job searches are difficult. A further problem is that some unscrupulous employers make sizeable deductions even though an E101 should mean that the worker is exempt.

This chapter is aimed exclusively at nationals of European Union member states. (Schemes and exchanges relevant to other nationalities are mentioned throughout the rest of the book.) Nancy Mitford made the U and non-U distinction famous (upper class and not upper class) but for the purposes of this book EU and non-EU has replaced it as an individual's defining characteristic. Some Americans may have access to the EU if they are fortunate enough to be of Irish or Italian descent and can prove that they have a grandparent of either nationality, in which case they can obtain an Irish or Italian passport. An increasing number of Americans are taking up this option for employment reasons and have been dubbed 'paper Europeans'. Americans of Greek extraction may be eligible for EU nationality, however they should first find out whether this will carry with it an obligation to do national service. (The United States allows its citizens to hold more than one passport, but does not recognise dual citizenship.)

NATIONAL EMPLOYMENT SERVICES IN THE EU

Every EU country possesses a network of employment offices similar to British Jobcentres, details of which are given in the individual country chapters. Although EU legislation requires national employment services to treat applicants from other member states in exactly the same way as their own citizens, it is impossible to prevent a certain amount of bias from entering the system. An employer is allowed to turn down an applicant who does not speak enough of the language to perform his job adequately for obvious reasons.

Average unemployment across Europe is predicted to rise to 11.5% in 1995 according to the OECD. No amount of positive legislation will change the attitude of the official of the Amsterdam employment office who said 'How can we help the English to find work? We do not have enough jobs for our own people' or of the French ANPE (Jobcentre) employee who told Noel Kirkpatrick that he would prefer to give a job to any Moroccan or Algerian before someone from Britain. If there are two equally qualified job applicants of different nationalities, most employers will choose their fellow countryman/woman. In the words of experienced Euroworker Paul Winter:

Please make it clear to your readers that all this talk of one Europe and a Europe without borders doesn't mean that jobs are easy and simple to get abroad. It's not easy. Plan ahead, try to learn a language and take as much money as you can. That being said, the chances of working around Europe are still there to be enjoyed, just use a little common sense.

In times of high employment some countries welcomed migrant workers because they were prepared to take jobs that no local would consider. For example the bulb-packing factories of Holland and hotel kitchens in Germany have traditionally taken on large numbers of British and Irish workers during their busiest times of year. But throughout Europe there has been a noticeable increase in the number of nationals (especially students) willing to take such jobs. And when they are not, East European migrant workers certainly are.

The UK Employment Service has a specialist office giving advice and guidance to jobseekers looking for work abroad. The Overseas Placing Unit (c/o Rockingham House, 123 West St, Sheffield S1 4ER; 0114-259 6051/2) coordinates all dealings with overseas/EU vacancies. These vacancies, distributed to Jobcentres via a computerised system called NATVACS, are usually for six months or longer, and for skilled, semi-skilled and (increasingly) managerial jobs. A random sample of job vacancies might include flying instructors for the UAE, welders and chefs for Germany, a loom turner for Ireland and (surprisingly) bar staff for Sicily.

All employment services in EU countries now have Euroadvisers, and it is worth addressing your employment queries abroad to them. The public employment services of EU countries cooperate with each other in the exchange of vacancies, usually for hard-to-fill posts or posts for which a knowledge of other EU languages is required. This computerised system is known as EURES (European Employment Services) which in Britain is located at the Overseas Placing Unit. Under the EURES scheme, well-qualified multilingual applicants can complete an application form (ES13) in the appropriate language, to be sent to the relevant EU employment service for linking with suitable posts. These speculative applications are kept on file for six months. Anyone who wants to know whether his or her qualification is acceptable in other EU countries should contact the Comparability Coordinator at the Employment Department (QS1, Room E454, Moorfoot, Sheffield S1 4PQ; 0114-259 4144).

The OPU also publishes a series of country-by-country factsheets called 'Working in...' which are free from Jobcentres or from the OPU. Although they do not contain much job-finding information which is not included in this book, they do provide some useful background information on taxation, health benefits, etc. for the job-seeker and are worth obtaining.

Information Centres for European Careers are being set up in all EU member states. The UK office Careers Europe (Ground Floor, Equity Chambers, 40 Piccadilly, Bradford BD1 3NN) produces information on training, education and employment in Europe, mostly to help careers services and their clients. This information is available in Careers Libraries on database and also in leaflet form. (These Eurofact sheets are not distributed individually but only by subscription.)

Regional offshoots of EURES exist in some cases. For example EURES Crossborder Kent (Shorncliffe Road, Folkestone, Kent CT20 2NA; 01303 220580/fax 220476) assists people looking for jobs in Belgium and Northern France.

Jobs with EU Organisations

For a list of EU-sponsored vocational and training programmes, ask the Central Bureau (Seymour Mews, London W1H 9PE) for Info Sheet 20 'Europe 1993'. These programmes have a built-in obsolescence (normally three years), but are worth investigating because most of the funding comes from the EU. The EU Action Programme known as PETRA has the main aim of providing vocational training lasting three weeks to one year to people aged 16-27 who have completed their schooling but are not university graduates. It was due to wind up in 1994 but looks set to continue, if possibly under a different name. In the summer of 1994 a new programme for vocational training was announced, to be called the Leonardo Da Vinci Programme.

Suitable applicants may participate in EU-funded packages offered by ProEuropa, Europa House, Sharpham Drive, Totnes, Devon TQ9 5HE (01803 864526). The fee of £100 includes one month's language tuition, return travel (from Totnes to the European destination), two months' work experience in your field of experience and half-board accommodation throughout. People aged 18-27 with a background in information technology are eligible for placements in France, Spain or Germany; students of marketing can choose from France, Spain or Portugal and people hoping to make a career in tourism may go to Spain, Portugal or Italy. There is also an engineering option in Germany. Participants must have some relevant vocational training or experience and a GCSE in the language. Because of their reliance on EU funding, programmes change from year to year; details are available each March.

The office of the European Commission in London (Jean Monnet House, 8 Storey's Gate, London SW1P 3AT; 0171-973 1992) issues several free Fact Sheets of interest including No. 3 'Working in the European Union' and No. 4 'Social Security in the European Union'. The European Commission has offices in Cardiff, Edinburgh and Belfast as well. All enquiries of a legal nature are dealt with by an organisation called AIRE (Advice on Individuals' Rights in Europe, 74 Eurolink Business Centre, 39 Effra Road, London SW2 1BZ: 0171-924 0927).

High flyers who would like to work for the Commission of the European Communities as administrators, translators, secretaries, etc. must compete in open competitions held at regular intervals; the London office above can advise on forthcoming dates and send application forms. The Commission runs a five-month *stagiaire* programme whereby graduates from member countries take up short-term training positions mostly in Brussels; the deadline for applications to be in to the Bureau des Stages, Commission of the European Communities, 200 rue de la Loi, 1049 Brussels, Belgium) is 30th September for positions starting in March and 31st March for *stages* beginning in October.

Short-term white-collar contracts may be available on the spot for people who are bilingual and/or have secretarial skills. Michael Jordan, an American who spent a few months in Strasbourg, met a number of people (including Americans) who were employed by the Council of Europe on temporary contracts continuously renewed. Special rules govern the red tape of employees of international organisations.

CLAIMING BENEFIT IN THE EU

It may come as a pleasant surprise to discover that it is possible to claim unemployment benefit in other EU countries. The two ways in which this can be done are covered in detail below: to understand them it is necessary to understand the principle behind unemployment benefit.

Unemployment benefit is not paid automatically to people who are out of work. It is an entitlement that has to be 'bought' by paying a certain number of contributions into a country's unemployment insurance organisation. In Britain these contributions are represented by Class 1 National Insurance contributions. Class 1 contributions are paid only by people who are employees earning at least £57 per week. Other groups of people may pay either Class 2 and 4 contributions (for the self-employed) or Class 3 contributions (a voluntary payment for those who would otherwise not be covered by National Insurance) which entitle them to some social security benefits, but not unemployment benefit.

Other EU countries have similar systems, and contributions paid in one country can be taken into account when building up an entitlement to unemployment benefit in another. Whichever of the two means of claiming unemployment benefit is relevant to you depends on where you last paid contributions, as you will be covered under that country's unemployment insurance scheme.

In Britain people who are not eligible to claim unemployment benefit may claim income support if they have no other means of support. The amount paid depends on the needs of the applicant — whether there are any relatives to support, how much is needed to pay for rent, etc. — and it is intended to cover only the essentials of life. All EU countries except Greece and Portugal have equivalents, but the right to claim these is not transferable between countries in the same way as unemployment benefit. Normally it is handled by municipal authorities who stipulate that eligibility depends on a claimant having been resident in the district for several years. Applications for income support abroad are very unlikely to succeed. Deportation is a more likely outcome.

For a general guide to unemployment benefit, get leaflet NI.12 (updated February 1994) from your local Benefits Agency, though this does not deal with the situation of working or claiming abroad. Much more detailed information is available in pink Factsheet No. 1 from the Benefits Agency office in Newcastle which specialises in claiming abroad (address below).

Claiming UK Benefit in Europe

Any EU national who has been registered unemployed for at least four weeks in the UK and is entitled to receive UK benefit can arrange to receive this benefit, paid at the UK rate, for up to three months while looking for work elsewhere in the EU. The applicant should inform his local Unemployment Benefit Office or Employment Service Jobcentre in Britain of his intention to look for work elsewhere well before departure. Note that if you go abroad on holiday and decide to stay on to work, the benefit cannot be transferred. Your local UB office or Jobcentre should have a copy of Leaflet UBL22 *Unemployment Benefit for people going abroad or coming from abroad* plus an application form for transferring benefit.

Your local UB office or Jobcentre will inform the Overseas Benefits Directorate of the Department of Social Security who will supply the applicant with a form (E303) which is the EU-wide form authorising another state to pay your benefit.

The Overseas Benefits Directorate (Room A0513, Newcastle upon Tyne, NE98 1YX; 0191-225 5251/225 5298) also gives advice on where to register when abroad. They will want to know in which EU country work is to be sought, since in some cases they send this form direct to the central liaison office of the unemployment benefit organisation abroad, viz. in the case of Belgium, Denmark, Ireland, Luxembourg, Gibraltar and the Netherlands. If the destination is France, Germany, Greece, Spain, Italy, Portugal, Austria, Finland, Iceland, Norway or Sweden, the claimant will be given the E303 to take to the authorities.

If someone tries to claim unemployment benefit abroad without making these preparations there may be delays of several months while correspondence goes between the relevant countries before the application is cleared. Be warned that even if the correct procedure is followed there may still be delays because of the time necessary to forward and translate correspondence. You should request a copy of leaflet SA29 *Your Social Security, Insurance, Benefits and Health Care Rights in the European Community* from your local DSS or from the Overseas Contributions (EU) department of the Contributions Agency in Newcastle. The Overseas Benefits Directorate also has a series of booklets published in Brussels called *Social Security for Migrant Workers.*

In theory, people looking for work in more than one EU country can continue to receive unemployment benefit under this system in each country visited, as long as they register for work in each new country promptly on arrival and have given adequate notice to the UB Office in the country from which they wish the benefit to be transferred. Overall however payment of unemployment benefit will not exceed the three month maximum. In fact complications and delays are bound to ensue if you country-hop.

Inside the United Kingdom employed persons who have paid the appropriate UK contributions can normally receive unemployment benefit for a maximum of 312 working days, i.e. one year. It is important to note that this maximum can be affected by the length of time you claim unemployment benefit abroad; if you claim benefit abroad for the maximum period of three months and then remain abroad for a further period of time, your right to claim unemployment benefit on your return to Britain lapses, according to EU regulations. But the Benefits Agency has discretion to allow those who would still be allowed to claim if they had not left the country to do so on their return.

These arrangements are standard within the EU: thus, a German wishing to look for work in Britain must obtain form E303 from his local social security services, and so on. The EU principle of equality of treatment means that an EU citizen claiming unemployment benefit under a foreign social security scheme, can arrange to collect unemployment benefit at the rate set by the foreign unemployment insurance fund for up to three months on his return home. In the case of Britons who have worked abroad, the foreign rate might be higher or lower than the standard United Kingdom rate of benefit. If after three months the applicant has still not found employment, he is no longer eligible for foreign unemployment benefit but may then apply for income support.

Despite the attraction of claiming your UK benefit abroad rather than at home, not many people take advantage of the regulation. Tony Davies-Patrick claimed in Italy:

> *I decided to claim in Italy because I had claimed for over one month when I returned to England over Christmas. It seems I was the first person in my town who had claimed for benefit abroad, so there is definitely a lack of applicants! Italy has slightly different rules from Britain. When you have had your papers signed, you have to wait six weeks before payment. Payment for the three-month period is split into only two lump sums. This has allowed me to travel for over one month, pick up my first lump sum, travel for a further month and then pick up my second lump sum!*

Tony was particularly lucky since many people have since reported great difficult and long delays in trying to comply with Italian 'control procedures'. The UK is famously unsuspicious of EU national claiming benefit, and Greece and Belgium are reputed to be relatively easy countries in which to claim. Rob Jefferson had no trouble in the Netherlands and wrote to tell us that he received his UK benefit with no problem because he had arranged everything in England, just as *Work Your Way Around the World* advised.

Anyone who is planning to quit work (to travel), go on the dole for the requisite four weeks and then head off to Europe to collect their benefit will be disappointed. Anyone who quits work voluntarily in the UK must wait 26 weeks before they are eligible to claim unemployment benefit.

Claiming Unemployment Benefit from Another EU Country

In order to claim unemployment benefit from another EU country you must have worked there and paid contributions into its unemployment insurance fund. The length of time for which you must have worked varies from country to country: the details are listed below. It cannot be emphasised too much that contributions paid in one country can be taken into account in another, and so for some people a very short period of work abroad may be sufficient to allow them to claim unemployment benefit there. For the purposes of clarity the chart omits some of the complications, and mentions only the unemployment benefit that is normally paid to people who have just lost their jobs.

How Much?

Great Britain and Ireland differ from other EU countries in paying a flat rate of unemployment benefit (£45.45 per week for a single person in the UK at the time of going to press). Other member countries base their rates of unemployment benefit on a percentage of the wage most recently earned by the applicant, varying from 30.3% (plus a small daily allowance) in France to 90% in Denmark. There are, of course, upper and lower limits on the amount paid to make sure that low earners do not suffer and the highly paid do not benefit excessively.

This means that there is an indirect link between the cost of living and unemployment benefit on the Continent. It is fair to say that average wages increase the further north you go in Europe: at the top of the league is Denmark, with an average gross weekly wage of well over £200 while Greece is at the other extreme around £80. This does not mean that you will automatically be better off in northern Europe, as the amount of benefit you receive will depend on the size of the last wage you earned.

How to Claim Unemployment Benefit

The same principles apply when claiming unemployment benefit in all member states of the EU, although the procedures may vary from one country to another. In order to claim you must:
— have become unemployed in that country through no fault of your own
— be both fit and available to work
— possess documentary proof of your last job and (normally) a residence permit
— be registered as unemployed with the employment office
— be aged under 65
— have paid sufficient contributions into unemployment insurance organisations in the EU

Unemployment insurance funds are not always administered by a country's national employment service. A country by country guide is listed below:

Eligibility Requirements for Unemployment Benefit in EU Countries

Country	Name of unemployment benefit	Qualifying Conditions
Belgium	*Allocations de chômage*	Between 75 days employment in last 10 months and 600 days employment in last 36 months, depending on age
Denmark	*Dagpenge*	Membership of an unemployment fund during the last 12 months and in employment for at least 6 of those months
France	*Allocation d'assurance chômage* (also known as ASSEDIC)	Must be out of work or legitimately dismissed; must be capable of work and less than 60 years old, plus must have paid 3 months UB insurance in the last 12 months
Germany	*Arbeitslosengeld*	At least 480 days of insurable employment during the last 3 years
Gibraltar	Unemployment benefit	At least 30 paid contributions in the last 52 weeks
Greece	*Epidoma anergias*	At least 125 days of work during the 14 months preceding job loss
Ireland	Unemployment benefit	39 weeks paid insurance plus 48 contributions paid/credited in the year preceding the benefit year
Italy	*Indennita ordinaria*	One year during the previous 2 years: must also have been registered for at least 2 years with an unemployment insurance scheme
Luxembourg	*Allocations de chômage*	At least 26 weeks in the previous 12 months
Netherlands	*Werkloosheidswet* (also known as WW)	26 weeks in the previous 12 months
Portugal	*Subsidio de Desemprego*	
Spain	*Prestación por Desempleo*	At least 12 months employment within previous 6 years
United Kingdom	*Unemployment benefit (flat-rate)*	Contributions must have been paid in one of the 2 tax years on which the claim is based amounting to at least 25 times the minimum contribution (i.e. 25 X £54)

N.B. The information for Austria, Finland and Sweden was unobtainable at press time.

Belgium: Trade union members claim from the union's unemployment insurance-division. Non-union members should go to CAPAC (the *Caisse auxiliaire de paiement des allocations de chômage*).

Denmark: Unemployment insurance is distributed by trade unions though non-union members may join an unemployment fund *(arbedjsløshedskammer)*.

France: Local office of the national employment service *(Agence Nationale pour l'Emploi)* or the local town hall if there is no *agence* nearby.

Germany: Local office of the national employment service *(arbeitsamt)*.

Greece: OAED (Labour Office).

Ireland: Local employment exchange or employment office.

Italy: Local employment office or the local office of the *Istituto della previdenza sociale* (national social welfare institution).

Luxembourg: National labour office *(Office National du Travail)* or the secretariat of the commune where you are living.

Netherlands: Previous employer's professional or trade association.

Norway: Local employment office *(Arbeidformidling)*

Portugal: Local office of the national employment service *(Centro de Emprego) and Centro Regional de Segurança* (CRSS).

Spain: Local office of the national employment service *(Oficina de Empleo)* or *Instituto Nacional de Seguridad Social* (INSS).

United Kingdom: Local Unemployment Benefit Office/Employment Service Jobcentre.

In all countries it is essential to register as unemployed with the national employment service before claiming from the unemployment insurance fund. Unemployment benefit is only paid from three days after the date when you first register as unemployed, so it is important to register as soon as you lose your job. You will also be required to continue to register as unemployed with the insurance fund at regular (normally weekly) intervals.

If you need to have a period of work in another EU country taken into account to make you eligible for unemployment benefit you will need to provide proof of the contributions you paid there on form E301 which you should obtain from the unemployment insurance organisation of the country where you paid the contributions. If you do not have this form to hand when you apply for unemployment benefit the office at which you are claiming can obtain it for you, but this may lead to a delay in processing your application.

TAX

There really isn't any such thing as a tax-free whatever an agency or employer promises. The only people who are not liable to pay any tax are those who earn less than the personal allowance (whatever that may be). However there are ways to minimise tax. Although the details of income tax systems vary from country to country, there are some common characteristics. The traveller who works for less than the full tax year will generally find himself paying too much in tax: this section outlines the circumstances when it may be possible to reclaim some of it. Individual cases should be discussed with your local tax inspector. (The Inland Revenue's EU Unit in Somerset House deals with European leislation and is not for general advice.)

If you are working on a longer term basis abroad, your UK tax liability depends on several factors, the principal one being whether you are classed as resident in the UK for that tax year. In the simplest case, a UK citizen who works abroad full-time for an entire tax year (6 April to 5 April) is not liable for UK tax. If they work abroad for at least 365 days of which no more than 62 days are spent in the UK (i.e. one-sixth of the year), they may also be exempt.

For general information consult Inland Revenue's leaflet IR20 *Residents' and Non-Residents' Tax Liability,* and IR58 'Going to Work Abroad'.

Why you can Reclaim Tax

Countries do not charge income tax on a person's income up to a certain figure, which is known as a personal allowance or a basic deduction. The exact size of this figure varies from country to country, but it is generally at least 20% of the national average wage. For example in Germany anyone who earns less than DM530 per month (DM390 in the former East Germany) should not have to pay income tax. In theory, you won't have to pay any tax if your total earnings are below this figure.

In practice, however, most countries deduct tax under a withholding system or 'pay as you earn', which assumes that your weekly wage is typical of your annual earnings. Thus, if you work in Britain for two weeks for a weekly wage of £100, you will be taxed as if you were earning £5,200 a year. Sometimes you have the right to reclaim any tax you have paid on income up to the value of your personal allowance when you have finished work and are about to leave the country or at the end of that country's tax year. Unfortunately there are residential and other requirements in some countries which make this impossible.

This may seem to imply that you could escape from tax altogether by getting a series of short term jobs around the world and never exceeding your personal allowance in any one country. Unfortunately, there are a number of 'double taxation' agreements between most western countries which prevent this. Among other things, they ensure that the taxman can ultimately track you down in your 'country of permanent residence', where you will be liable to pay tax on all your earnings abroad at the local rate. Hence the popularity among tax exiles of countries with very low rates of tax.

How to Minimise Tax

It may be worth finding out which countries have an agreement with your country (see the IR6 leaflet 'Double Taxation Relief'); for example Sweden does not have an agreement with the UK and it is not inconceivable that you could be taxed twice on the same earnings. Keep all receipts and financial documents in case you need to plead your case at a later date.

If your tax status abroad is not completely legitimate, you will be taxed in the UK as Jamie Masters found to his cost after nine months of English teaching in Crete:

> I didn't know that if you are working abroad for less than a year, you are liable to be taxed in Britain, and had cheerfully let the tax people know that I was working in Greece. The rules state that the tax you pay in Greece can be transferred to England to offset the tax you owe at home. But I didn't pay any tax in Greece (just bribes). Stupid, stupid. I should have just told the IR that I was travelling. Rule number one: if you're working illegally, deny everything.

In many countries where you can work legitimately (e.g. EU countries) your employer will expect you to clarify your tax position with the local tax office at the beginning of your work period. This can be to your advantage, for example in Denmark where, unless you obtain a tax card *(skattekort),* you will be put on the Danish equivalent of an emergency code and 60% of your earnings will be automatically deducted at source. Glyn Evans who picked apples in Denmark returned several times to the local Radhus to complain about the excessive tax, and finally obtained a *skattekort* entitling him to a taxation rate of 31%. Germany is another country where it is customary for foreign workers to register at the tax office *(Finanzamt)*. No one is eligible for a tax rebate in the Netherlands until they have been resident for one year. Be sure to get a tax code in Gibraltar since this, together with a tax return filled in before departure, will allow you to reclaim income tax once you're back in Britain.

France has an unusual tax system, and the general advice given in this section does not apply there. Instead of deducting tax on the 'pay as you earn' system, the French authorities charge tax retrospectively: in other words, with every pay packet French workers are paying off in instalments their tax bill from the previous year. So the working traveller in France will escape any deductions for tax unless he or she is unlucky enough to be working over the end of the tax year, which is from January 1st to December 31st. However he or she will have to pay social security contributions which usually amount to about 15%.

Students should always show their employers documents proving their student status since this may exempt them from paying income tax and/or social security. For example in Germany foreign students who work for less than 183 days should be exempt from German income tax.

How to Reclaim Tax

When you have finished a job your employer should give you a form which will state the amount of tax he has taken from your wages. If he can't do this for any reason you should collect your pay slips. Even a scruffy piece of paper may be sufficient proof of your having paid tax if it states the dates you worked and the amount of tax deducted, and is signed by your employer. If your employer won't give you any written proof at all, the odds are that he has been pocketing the money he has deducted, in which case there is no point in trying to reclaim it!

You then take this evidence to the local tax office and fill in a tax rebate form. On this form you will have to state that you will not be working in that country again during the tax year, and give the date of your departure. You may be asked to surrender your residence and/or work permit to prevent you from simply moving to another town and getting a new job or you may have to show your return ticket to prove that you are leaving. Bureaucratic delays often mean that your refund will have to be posted to you abroad. It can take weeks, and frequently months, for your claim to be processed. You therefore need to be sure that you will be at the address you give them for some length of time; if you are not sure of your future movements, give the address of a relative or friend.

Some countries, e.g. Germany, Denmark and the US, stipulate that you are not allowed to reclaim any tax until the end of the tax year. The rule in Germany as in Britain is that you must have resided in Germany for at least six months of the tax year in order to qualify for a rebate. In Denmark tax refunds can be issued only six months after the year in which the tax was paid.

It is not essential that you reclaim tax directly from the authorities of the country where you have been working, since double taxation agreements state that any tax you have paid on earnings abroad can be credited as if it had been paid in your own country. So, in principle, if you have paid too much tax you can reclaim it from your own national tax authority. In practice, however, this can turn into a long drawn out process as the bureaucracies of two countries attempt to communicate with each other: it took Tessa Shaw two years to obtain a refund of tax she had overpaid in Denmark through the British Inland Revenue. You are therefore strongly advised to deal directly with the tax offices of the countries in which you have worked whenever possible.

Work Your Way

TOURISM

The long-term prospects for the tourist industry are rosy. It has been estimated that travel and tourism now employ one in every 15 workers worldwide. The tourist industry, like agriculture, is a mainstay of the traveller-cum-worker. The seasonal nature of hotel and restaurant work discourages a stable working population, and so hotel proprietors often rely on foreign labour during the busy season. Also, many tourist destinations are in remote places where there is no local pool of labour. Travellers have ended up working in hotels in some of the most beautiful corners of the world from the South Island of New Zealand to Lapland.

HOTELS AND RESTAURANTS

If you secure a hotel job without speaking the language of the country and lacking relevant experience, you will probably be placed at the bottom of the pecking order, e.g. in the laundry or washing dishes. Some hotels might confuse you by using fancy terms for menial jobs, for example 'valet runner' for collector-of-dirty-laundry or 'kitchen porter' for pot-washer. Reception and bar jobs are usually the most sought after and highly paid. However the lowly jobs have their saving graces. The usual hours of chamber staff (7am-2pm) allow plenty of free time. Some people prefer not to deal with guests (particularly if they are shaky in the language) and are happy to get on at their own speed with the job of room cleaning or laundering or vegetable chopping. The job of night porter can be excellently suited to an avid reader since there is often very little to do except let in the occasional late arrival.

Even the job of dish-washer, stereotyped as the most lowly of all jobs with visions of the down and out George Orwell as a *plongeur* washing dishes in a Paris café, should not be dismissed too easily. Nick Langley enjoyed life far more as a dish-washer in Munich than as a civil servant in Britain. Simon Canning saved enough money in five months of working as a dish-washer in an Amsterdam office block to fund a trip across Asia. Benjamin Fry spent a highly enjoyable two weeks washing dishes at the Land's End Hotel in Alaska and earned more per hour than he ever had in Britain. And Sean Macnamara was delighted with his job as dish-washer in a French hotel near Chamonix:

> *After a brief interview I was given the job of dish-washer. The conditions were excellent: F3,000 per month (£300) plus private accommodation and first class meals, including as much wine as I could drink. I earned my keep, though, working six days a week from 8am to 10pm with three hours off each afternoon. I was the only foreigner and was treated kindly by everyone. Indeed I can honestly say I enjoyed myself, but then I was permanently high on the thought of all that money.*

If your only experience of hotels is as a guest, you may be in for a surprise when you go backstage. Even the most luxurious hotels have been known to have dirty, disorganised kitchens, inadequate laundering facilities and lousy (literally) staff quarters. It is quite possible that the waitress who smilingly emerges from the kitchen bearing your food has just been threatened and abused by the chef for not working quickly enough. It may have something to do with the heat generated by the ovens in large kitchens, the pride they take in their creations, or the pressures under which they work, but chefs have a terrible reputation for having fiery tempers. S. C. Firn describes the working atmosphere in a 'rather classy restaurant and bar' in Oberstdorf in Southern Germany near the Austrian border:

> *I had to peel vegetables, wash dishes, prepare food, clean the kitchen and sometimes serve food. Everything was done at a very fast pace, and was expected to be very professional. One German cook, aged 16, who didn't come up to standard, was punched in the face three times by the owner. On another occasion the assistant chef had a container of hot carrots tipped over his head for having food sent back. During my three months there, all the other British workers left, apart from the chef, but were always replaced by more.*

So if you consider yourself to be the sensitive fragile type, perhaps you should avoid hotel kitchens altogether.

On the other hand many people thrive on the animated atmosphere and on kitchen conviviality. Nick Langley, who also worked in a German kitchen loved the atmosphere. He maintains that once you're established you'll gain more respect by shouting back if unreasonable demands are made, but adds the proviso, 'but not at the powerful head cook, please!'. Heated tempers usually cool down after a couple of beers at the end of a shift.

Applications

The earlier you decide to apply for seasonal hotel work the better are your chances. Hotels in a country such as Switzerland recruit months before the summer season, and it is advisable to write to as many hotel addresses as possible by March, preferably in their own language. A knowledge of more than one language is an immense asset for work in Europe. If you have an interest in working in a particular country, get a list of hotels from their tourist office in London and write to the largest ones (e.g. the ones with over 100 rooms). If you know someone going to your chosen country, ask them to bring back local newspapers and check adverts. Enclose international reply coupons and try to write in the language of the country. Amanda Smallwood wrote to 20 hotels in a German resort and received seven job offers out of 15 replies.

On the other hand you might not be able to plan so far ahead, or you may have no luck with written applications, so it will be necessary to look for hotel work once you've arrived in a foreign country. All but the most desperate hoteliers are far more willing to consider a candidate who is standing there in the flesh than one who writes a letter out of the blue. One job-seeker recommends showing up bright and early (about 8am) to impress prospective employers. Perseverence is necessary when you're asking door to door at hotels. One of our contributors was repeatedly rejected by hotels in Amsterdam on the grounds that she was too late in the summer (i.e. August). Her last hope was the Hilton Hotel and she thought she might as well give it a try since it might be her only chance to see the inside of a Hilton. She was amazed when she was hired instantly as a chambermaid. It also might be necessary to return to the same hotel several times if you think there's a glimmer of hope. Kathryn Halliwell described her job hunt in Les Gets in the Haute Savoie of France:

> *I had to ask from hotel to hotel for three days before finding the job, and experienced what I have come to know through experience and others' reports is the normal way to hire a casual worker. The boss told me blankly*

that he had no work. As I was leaving he said, what sort of work? I told him anything. He said I could come back the next day in case something came up. I did and was told he was out, come again tomorrow. I eventually did get the job and realised he had just been testing my attitude as he had every other employee when they first applied.

When going door to door, you should start with the biggest hotels. Try to get past the receptionist to ask the manager personally. If you are offered a position (either in person or in writing) try to get a signed contract setting out clearly the hours, salary and conditions of work. If this is not possible, you should at least discuss these issues with the boss.

Another way to get a foothold in a resort is to cultivate the acquaintance of the reps from the big travel firms. Not only will they know of immediate openings, but they can establish your position with local hoteliers who normally know and respect the reps. This is a job-finding ploy which has to be used with care since reps are constantly being asked for favours. You might volunteer to help them, meeting a group or standing in for someone who is ill. Lisa Brophy met a local tour representative in an Austrian ski resort and was soon introduced to a restaurant manager with a staff vacancy.

People with a background in hotels and catering may be able to fix up overseas contracts while still in the UK. The Overseas Placing Unit of the Employment Service registers quite a few foreign vacancies in the tourist industry (particularly in Germany and Italy) with Jobcentres. Specialist agencies will be of interest to qualified hotel staff, such as Towngate Personnel, 65 Seamoor Road, Westbourne, Bournemouth BN4 9AE (01202 752955). The FRES (see page 25) lists other specialist agencies. In a very few cases agencies and leisure groups can place people without any expertise in foreign hotels; however wages in these cases are normally negligible. For example Eurotoques, the *Communauté Européenne des Cuisiniers,* places kitchen and waiting assistants in hotels throughout Germany; staff earn no wage but are given free board and lodging (see German chapter). Travelbound (Olivier House, 18 Marine Parade, Brighton, East Sussex BN2 1TL) send 150 staff to hotels in Austria and France.

Mark Warner Ltd (George House, First Floor, 61/65 Kensington Church St, London W8 4BA; 0171-393 3178) owns beachclub hotels in Corsica, Italy, Sardinia, Greece and Turkey for which it hires club managers, receptionists, chefs, bar and waiting staff, watersports and tennis instructors, pool attendants, laundry staff, handymen, drivers, gardeners, night watchmen and nannies (but not couriers or resort representatives). All staff must be over 19 and available from mid-April to mid-October, though there is a continuous need for replacements throughout the season. The wages run from £35-150 per week; benefits include use of watersports facilities, travel, medical insurance and the potential for winter work in the Alps.

The Human Resources Department of Hilton International (01923 231333) will send enquirers an application form and will then try to match a qualified applicant with a suitable vacancy in the worldwide chain.

Advantages and Disadvantages

The same complaints crop up again and again among people who have worked in hotels: long and unsociable hours (often 8am-10pm with a few hours off in the afternoon plus lots of weekend work), exploitative wages, inadequate accommodation and food, and unbearably hot working conditions exacerbated by having to wear a nylon uniform. A great deal depends on whether or not you are the type to rough it. The working atmosphere can vary a lot from hotel to hotel. If you are lucky enough to get a job in a small friendly family hotel, you will probably enjoy the work more than if you are just one in a large anonymous group of workers in a sterile and impersonal institution where you have no job security.

It can be very aggravating to be asked to do extra duties beyond the ones specified in your contract. It seems to be a common occurrence, especially in French and German hotels, that the proprietor takes for granted that you will do unpaid overtime, without time off in lieu at a later date. If a contract is being breached in this way, you should try your best to sort it out with the employer. If this fails don't hesitate to go to the appropriate employment authorities to lodge an official complaint. This has far more chance of success if you have a written contract to show the authorities.

Not all hotels are like this and many people emphasise the benefits which they have found in the experience of working in a hotel: excellent camaraderie and team spirit, the opportunity to learn a foreign language, and the ease with which wages can be saved, including the possibility of an end-of-season bonus. Although Kathryn Halliwell was forced to share a windowless room which had an intermittently working light and water streaming down the roof beams into constantly overflowing buckets, she still enjoyed her time working at a hotel in Corsica, simply because of the conviviality of her 'fellow sufferers'.

Other Catering

Hotels represent just one aspect of the tourist trade, and there are many more interesting venues for cooking and serving, including luxury yachts, prawn trawlers, holiday ranches, safari camps and ski chalets. People with some training in catering will find it much easier to work their way around the world than others who have none. The serious traveller might even consider enrolling in a cookery course before embarking on his or her journey. With experience you could try for a job on a cruise liner (see *Working a Passage*).

Of course, there are opportunities for the unskilled. You might find a job cooking hamburgers in a chain such as McDonalds or Burger King, which can be found from Tel Aviv to Toronto. Anyone who is not confident communicating in the language of the country can still hope for employment in a fast food kitchen. Pay is low, hours unreliable or inconvenient and the attitude to discipline more worthy of school children, however it is a good way of earning while you familiarise yourself with a new place. When you are applying for jobs like this, which are not seasonal, you should stress that you intend to work for an indefinite period, make a career of fast food catering, etc. In fact staff turnover is usually very high. This will also aid your case when you are obliged to badger them to give you extra hours.

A good way of gaining initial experience is to get a kitchen job with a large organisation in Britain such as Butlins Holiday Worlds (Bognor Regis, W. Sussex) which offer a variety of jobs, including kitchen, restaurant, administration, bar and shop work, or PGL Adventure (Alton Court, Penyard Lane (874), Ross-on-Wye, Herefordshire HR9 5NR). Since they have so many vacancies (most of which pay only pocket money), the chances of being hired for a first season are reasonably good. PGL also have holiday centres abroad (mostly in France) which are staffed on the same principle.

You may also find catering jobs which have nothing to do with tourism, for example in canteens, on industrial sites, mining camps or army bases. These settings are not among the most congenial in the world, so there is often a high turnover of service staff. Railway stations and airports often have catering divisions which employ casual staff. Schiphol airport in Amsterdam is especially well known for hiring foreign young people.

OTHER OPPORTUNITIES WITHIN TOURISM

Your average big-spending pampered tourist, so often ridiculed by budget travellers, indirectly provides a great number of employment opportunities. He wants to eat ice cream on the beach or croissants in his ski chalet, so you might be the one there to sell it to him. He would be most distressed if he got dripped on in his hotel bed, so you may get hired to tar the roof before the season begins. He doesn't want to be pestered by his children, so you spend the day teaching them how to swim or draw at a holiday camp. He is not happy unless he goes home with a genuine sachet of Ardeche lavender or a Texan 10-gallon hat sold to him by a charming souvenir shop assistant, who will be you. He needs to be entertained so you get a job in an amusement arcade, the local disco or windsurfing school. His wife wants to keep up appearances so a freelance hairdresser's services are very welcome. And so it could continue. The point is that casual jobs proliferate in tourist centres.

Of course there are also many opportunities at the budget end of tourism, in travellers' hostels and so on. Dustie Hickey describes the way she went about getting a job in the Avignon Youth Hostel:

I checked out all the hostels in Avignon through the Minitel system. I had help to write a letter in French. Then I telephoned because I did not get a reply. The hostel could not promise me any work till they met me. Before I left the farm in Brittany where I was working, I telephoned again to remind them I was on my way. When I arrived the hostel was very busy. For free B & B, I just had to keep the dormitory clean, but I pitched in and helped with cleaning, laundry, breakfast, etc. The manager was pleased and gave me a little money. At the end of July the paid assistant left so I was given her job, and eventually I had a room to myself.

Many private travellers' hostels worldwide employ long-stay residents to act as PR reps at railway and bus stations, trying to persuade new arrivals to patronise their hostel. A free bed is always given and usually a small fee per successful 'convert'.

Pubs and Clubs

Bars and night clubs should not be omitted from your list of likely employers. Some backpackers even carry a set of 'black and whites' (black trousers/skirt and white shirt) in case they pick up a job as a bartender or waiter. If you have no experience, it can be worthwhile volunteering to work at your local pub before you leave home for a week and then ask for a reference. Once you are abroad, ask at English style pubs which are found from the Costa del Sol to the Zamalek district of Cairo, from Santa Monica California to Austrian ski resorts and try to exploit the British connection. Irish people are at an even greater advantage since there are Guinness pubs around the world. In ordinary bars on the Continent you may be expected to be proficient in the prevailing language, although exceptions are made, particularly in the case of glamorous-looking applicants. Girls can find jobs from Amsterdam to Hong Kong, but should be sure that they can distinguish between bars and brothels.

Places like the Canaries, Ibiza, Corfu and the Caribbean islands are bursting at the seams with 'nite spots' of one kind or another. Not only is there a high turn-over of staff but there is a rapid turn-over of clubs too, and you may not have much job security. As long as you investigate the establishments in the place you want to work before accepting a job, you should not encounter too many unpleasant surprises. Handing out promotional leaflets for bars and discos is a job which travellers frequently do, especially in Spain.

The idea that Britons know their way round the music scene better than other nationalities is fairly widespread, and anyone who knows how to use a turntable might get occasional work, not only in the obvious resorts but in farflung places like Bangkok (as Laurence Koe did). Experienced DJs who want to work abroad should request details from a specialist agency like Juliana's Leisure Group (Suite 2A, Long Island House, 1/4 Warple Way, London W3 0RQ) which also has an office in Singapore or SuperVision International Discotheque Services, Hillier House, 509 Upper Richmond Road West, London SW14 7EE). These companies supply entertainment packages to 5-star hotels and other clients. Juliana's DJ/Music Coordinator, Duncan West, distributes notes on how to become an international DJ. Premier Dance Productions (26 Chace Road, Wellingborough, Northants. NN8 1NR) hold regular auditions for dancers and other entertainers who want to work at luxury hotels and nightclubs abroad.

Special Events

Great bursts of tourist activity take place around annual festivals, major sporting events like the Adelaide Grand Prix, trade fairs and World Fairs. For example, the Oktoberfest in Munich takes place each year during the last two weeks of September and you should be able to get a few days or weeks of work either helping to set up the facilities or to dismantle them. It is not possible for an event to host over 6 million visitors without a great deal of extra labour being enlisted to prepare the 560,000 barbecued chickens, 346,000 pairs of sausages and to dispense the 1,000,000 gallons of beer consumed. One enterprising mechanic we heard of took a large number of tools and spare parts with him to Munich and set himself up in the car park to fix and adjust the thousands of travel-weary vans and cars which had assembled there, and did a roaring trade. The main problem with this sort of work is that affordable accommodation will be very difficult to find.

COURIERS & REPS

Acting as a tour guide, rep or courier is one way of combining work with travel. Two-month jobs are rare in this field since in most cases employers want staff who will stay at least for the whole summer season April to October inclusive. The peak recruitment time is the preceding September, though strong candidates can be interviewed as late as February. Knowledge of a European language is always requested, though it is unusual for reps in Greece or Portugal to speak those languages. Otherwise, personality and maturity are what count most. By all accounts interviews can be fairly gruelling as they try to weed out the candidates who will crack under the pressure of holidaymakers' complaints and problems. It is estimated that only one in forty applicant gets a job.

One way of preparing is to take a repping course, for example the one-day training sessions offered by Holiday Solutions (500 Great West Road, Hounslow, Middlesex TW5 0TE; 0181-477 1606) for £50. The company's director describes the advantage of doing their course:

> *The main objectives are to give an insight into what being a holiday rep actually involves and to give advice to candidates on how to go about applying for a job. We can help candidates with their applications. We have a strong working relationship with all major holiday companies and can often bypass the preliminary interview process.*

In the first instance, send an s.a.e. to tour operators, requesting their recruitment procedures. Large tour operators like Thomson Tour Operations (Greater London House, Hampstead Road, London NW1 7SD; 0171-387 9321) employ so many people to service their estimated three million customers that they publish a large-format brochure about their recruitment requirements, which can be requested from the Overseas Personnel office. As is the case with most of the major companies, Thomson employ reps, children's reps, entertainers and ski resort staff (mentioned later in this chapter). Their reps must have all the usual qualities (flexibility, diplomacy, etc.) and knowledge of French, Spanish, Italian, Greek, Portuguese or German (in order of numbers needed).

Two other giant tour operators are First Choice Holidays (Groundstar House, London Road, Crawley, Surrey RH10 2TB; 01293 588281) and Airtours plc (Wavell House, Holcombe Road, Helmshore, Rossendale, Lancs. BB4 4NB). First Choice (formerly Owners Abroad) is the parent company of Enterprise, Sunmed and five other companies; write to the Overseas Personnel Officer to request their leaflet about employment opportunities. There may be an assumption that you have a commitment to make tourism a career, though this is not essential.

Considering the rigours and pressures of the job of package tour company representative, wages are low, though of course accommodation is provided. Often wages (from £50 a week) are paid into a bank account at home. Meagre wages can usually be supplemented with commissions from restaurant, shops and car hire.

A number of travellers who have done some casual hotel work abroad go on to take up jobs as reps with British tour companies. On her return from her extensive travels and numerous casual jobs en route, Xuela Edwards applied for various rep jobs in February 1994:

> They all told me that September is the best time to apply. But I managed to get a few interviews on the strength of my work abroad and ended up being sent to the Greek island of Paxos. I loved Paxos but I found I was too restless and used to independent travel to settle for seven months.

There are several kinds of holiday company looking for different kinds of courier and rep. Couriers are needed to escort groups on tours within Europe by companies like Top Deck Travel, 131-135 Earls Court Road, London SW5 9RH (0171-244 8641). Jayne Nash described her season with Top Deck as 'an amazing if exhausting experience':

> It enabled me to visit nearly every part of Europe, get involved in some really exciting events and meet some wonderful people, namely the South Africans (non-whites I might add) whom I later went to visit.

Often these companies charge a training bond of £200-400 which may be non-refundable if you are considered unsuitable. Drivers need to have a Passenger Carrying Vehicle licence — the PCV has replaced the old PSV — which costs several hundred pounds to obtain. Working in Africa, Asia and Latin America as an adventure tour leader is discussed in the chapter *Working a Passage: Overland Tours*.

EF Educational Tours (118 Cromwell Road, London SW7 4ET; 0171-244 6900) specialise in tours for school children and employ 200 tour leaders over the age of 23 to accompany groups of American and Canadian students touring Eastern and Western Europe. Applications are accepted only between 1st October and 31st January. Casterbridge Tours (Bowden Road, Templecombe, Somerset BA8 0LB) run training courses for tour guides as well as employ about a dozen guides to escort groups in Britain and Europe. Travelsphere Ltd (Compass House, Rockingham Road, Market Harborough, Leicestershire LE16 7QD) employ couriers over the age of 20 to escort adult and elderly groups on coaching holidays throughout Europe.

Camping tour operators employ thousands of site representatives (see section below). Many specialist tour companies employ leaders and reps to run their programmes of hiking (e.g. Ramblers' Holidays, PO Box 43, Welwyn Garden City, Herts. AL8 6PQ; 01707 331133), sailing holidays (try Sunsail International,

The Port House, Port Solent, Portsmouth, Hants. PO6 4TH; 01705 219847/ 214330) or cycling holidays (see chapters on France and Germany for specialist tour companies). Sunsail employs over 300 staff for their flotilla and bareboat sailing holidays and watersports hotels in Greece, Turkey, Corsica and Sardinia. From March to October, positions are available as flotilla skippers, hostesses, engineers, qualified dinghy instructors, receptionists, chefs, bar staff and qualified nannies. Wages vary from £220 to £400 a month plus return flights.

Contiki (Wells House, 15 Elmfield Road, Bromley, Kent BR1 1LS; 0181-290 6777) is an Australian company (also catering for a younger clientele) which hires only EU nationals aged 22/23-30 as site representatives, tour manager/ guides and coach drivers. No prior experience is needed since full training is given.

You need not confine your aspirations to Europe. Several of our contributors who have travelled extensively in South-East Asia have been invited to shepherd tourists around the island resorts of Thailand by a tour agency. You would have to be on hand to find out about this sort of opportunity. You can even set yourself up in business as a guide or courier, as Jennifer McKibben noticed long-stay travellers doing in East Africa.

Campsite Couriers

A different kind of courier is needed by the large camping holiday operators. British camping holiday firms (addresses below) hire large numbers of people to remain on one campsite on the Continent for several months. The Eurocamp Group alone recruits more than 1,000 campsite couriers and children's couriers. The courier's job is to clean the tents and caravans between visitors, greet clients and deal with difficulties (particularly illness or car breakdowns) and introduce clients to the attractions of the area or even arrange and host social functions and amuse the children. All of this will be rewarded with on average £90-100 a week in addition to free tent accommodation. Many companies offer half-season contracts April to mid-July and mid-July to the end of September. Setting up and dismantling the campsites in March/April and September (sometimes called *montage* and *démontage*) is often done by a separate team (sometimes called 'squaddies'. The work is hard but the language requirements are nil.

Some camping holiday and tour operators based in Britain are as follows (with the European countries in which they are active):

Canvas Holidays, 12 Abbey Park Place, Dunfermline, Fife KY12 7PD (01383 644007). France, Germany, Italy.

Club Cantabrica Holidays Ltd, 146/148 London Road, St. Albans, Herts. AL1 1PQ. France, Italy, Spain and Corfu.

Eurocamp, Summer Jobs (Ref WW), PO Box 170, Liverpool L70 1ES (01685 625522). Austria, Belgium, France, Germany, Italy, Netherlands, Scandinavia, Spain, Switzerland. Telephone applications are preferred, from October.

Eurosites Recruitment/Airtours plc, Wavell House, Holcombe Road, Helmshore, Lancs. BB4 4NB. France, Spain, Italy, Austria and Germany.

Haven Europe, Northney Marina, Northney Road, Hayling Island, Hants. PO11 0NH (01705 468522). Courier and children's courier staff for France, Spain and Italy.

Keycamp Holidays, Courier Recruitment Department, 92-96 Lind Road, Sutton, Surrey SM1 4PL (0181-395 8170). France, Italy, Spain, Germany.

Successful couriers make the job look easy, but it does demand a lot of hard work and patience. Occasionally it is very hard to keep up the happy, smiling, never-ruffled courier look, but most seem to end up enjoying the job. Alison Cooper described her job with Eurocamp on a site in Corsica as immensely enjoyable, though it was not as easy as the clients thought:

Living on a campsite in high season had one or two drawbacks: the toilets and showers were dirty, with constant queues, the water was freezing cold, the campsite was very very noisy and if you're unfortunate enough to have your tent in sunlight, it turns into a tropical greenhouse. Of course we did get difficult customers who complained for a variety of reasons: they wanted to be nearer to the beach, off the main road, in a cooler tent with more grass around it, etc. etc. But mostly our customers were friendly and we soon discovered that the friendlier we were to them, the cleaner they left their tents.

I found it difficult at first to get used to living, eating, working and socialising with the other two couriers 24 hours a day. But we all got on quite well and had a good time, unlike at a neighbouring campsite where the couriers hated each other. Our campsite had a swimming pool and direct beach access, though nightlife was limited. The one disco did get very repetitive.

Despite all this, she sums up by highly recommending that others who have never travelled or worked abroad work for a company like Eurocamp which provides accommodation, a guaranteed weekly wage and the chance to work with like-minded people.

Caroline Nicholls' problems at a campsite in Brittany included frequent power failures, blocked loos and leaking tents:

Every time there was a steady downpour, one of the tents developed an indoor lake, due to the unfortunate angle at which we had pitched it. I would appear, mop in hand, with cries of 'I don't understand. This has never happened before.' Working as a courier would be a good grounding for an acting career.

She goes on to say that despite enjoying the company of the client families, she was glad to have the use of a company bicycle to escape the insular life on the campsite every so often. Some companies guarantee one day off-site which is considered essential for maintaining sanity. The companies do vary in the conditions of work and some offer much better support than others. For example a company for which Hannah Start worked ignored her pleas for advice and assistance when one of her clients had appendicitis.

The big companies advertise in the *Sunday Times,* etc. and many are listed in the *Directory of Summer Jobs Abroad.* They interview hundreds of candidates and have filled most posts by the end of January. But there is a very high dropout rate (over 50%) and vacancies are filled from a reserve list, so it is worth ringing around the companies as late as April for cancellations. Despite keen competition, anyone who has studied a European language and has an outgoing personality stands a good chance if he or she applies early and widely enough. According to Carla Mitchell, not having too posh an accent helps when applying to companies based in the North; with her Surrey accent, she was given a job without too much 'client profile'.

Children's Camps and Sports Instructors

PGL Young Adventure (Alton Court, Penyard Lane (874), Ross-on-Wye, Herefordshire HR9 5NR; 01989 767833) recruit for about 3,000 seasonal vacancies at their holiday centres mainly in Britain and France. They publish a detailed brochure of their requirements called 'Work with Children in the Outdoors' which covers vacancies for activity intructors, group leaders and support staff. The norm seems to be to pay low wages but to allow lots of free time and access to all the holiday facilities. The basic weekly rate of pay of £30 rises to £36 after six weeks, with a bonus being paid to those who can start before 24th June.

Another company worth investigating for this kind of work is Village Camps, 1854 Leysin, Switzerland (025-342338). They hire counsellors, instructors, TEFL and kitchen staff for their camps in Switzerland, Austria, France, Netherlands and Belgium.

The practice of sending children to summer camps used to be uniquely North American. However, the idea is catching on in Europe and large numbers of young people are needed to work on these camps. Anyone who has a connection with the YMCA-YWCA should enquire about international summer camp possibilities. Hostelling International — American Youth Hostels (733 15th St NW, Suite 840, Washington, DC 20005) offers a one-week leadership training course (at a cost of $350) which would stand you in good stead in the job hunt and which has a good chance of leading to a job in the AYH's North American hiking and cycling programme. For information about becoming a counsellor at an American summer camp, see the chapter on the USA.

Any competent sailor, canoeist, diver, climber, rider, etc. should have no difficulty marketing their skills abroad. A comprehensive list of adventure centres in Britain and abroad, giving details of the sports and activities offered at each, can be found in the annual *Adventure Holidays* (published by Vacation-Work at £5.95). Personality and character matter more than sporting skills and qualifications for many of the jobs.

After suffering badly from the recession at the beginning of the 1990s, Club Med (106-110 Brompton Road, London SW3 1JJ) is now back to hiring hundreds of French-speaking people to work in their holiday villages in Europe and North Africa, as sports instructors as well as hostesses, kitchen and office assistants.

WINTER RESORTS

Ski resort work is by no means confined to the Alps. There are skiing centres from Geilo in Central Norway to Mount Hermon in Israel, from the Cairngorms of Scotland to dormant volcanoes of New Zealand. If you are such an avid skier that it always depresses you to see the winter snows melt from the European Alps in April, you should consider going to seek work in the Australian and New Zealand Alps or even the Chilean Andes, where the ski season lasts from late June until early October. And there are many ski resorts in North America, in addition to the most famous ones such as Banff in the Canadian Rockies, or Aspen in Colorado.

Winter tourism offers some variations on the usual theme of hotels and catering. Staff are needed to operate the ski tows and lifts, to be in charge of chalets, to patrol the slopes, to file, wax and mend hired skis, to groom and shovel snow, and of course to instruct would-be skiers. The season in the European Alps lasts from about Christmas until late April/early May. Between Christmas and the New Year is a terrifically busy time as is the middle two weeks of February during half-term. If you are lucky you might get a kitchen or dining room job in an establishment which does not serve lunch (since all the guests are out on the slopes). This means that you might have up to six hours free in the middle of the day for skiing, though three to four hours is more usual. However the hours in some large ski resort hotels are the same as in any hotel, i.e. eight to ten hours split up inconveniently throughout the day, and you should be prepared to have only one day off per week for skiing. Because jobs in ski resorts are so popular among the travelling community, wages can be low, though you should get the statutory minimum in Switzerland. Many employees are (or become) avid skiers and in their view it is recompense enough to have easy access to the slopes during their time off.

Either you can try to fix up a job with a British-based ski tour company before you leave (which has more security but lower wages and tends to isolate you in an English-speaking ghetto), or you can look for work on the spot.

Ski Holiday Companies

In the spring preceding the winter season in which you want to work, ask the ski tour companies listed below for an application form. Their literature will describe the range of positions they wish to fill. These may vary slightly from company to company but will probably include resort representatives (who must be bilingual), chalet girls (described below), cleaners, qualified cooks, odd jobbers and ski guides/instructors. An increasing number of companies are offering nanny and creche facilities, so this is a further possibility for women with a childcare background. Most staff have been hired by mid-June, though there are always a few last minute cancellations.

Here are some of the major UK companies. Some have a limited number of vacancies which they can fill from a list of people who have worked for them during the summer season or have been personally recommended by former employees. So you should not be too disappointed if you are initially unsuccessful.

Bladon Lines Travel Ltd, 56-58 Putney High St, London SW15 1SF (0181-785 2200). Hire reps, ski guides, chalet staff, nannies, hostess/cleaners, *plongeurs* and maintenance staff for resorts in France, Italy, Austria and Switzerland. Perks include free ski pass, ski and boot hire, insurance and return travel from London.

Crystal Holidays, Crystal House, The Courtyard, Arlington Road, Surbiton, Surrey (0181-241-5111). Austria, France, Italy, Switzerland.

PGL Ski Europe, Alton Court, Penyard Lane, Ross-on-Wye, Herefordshire HR9 5NR (01989 764211). Specialise in ski courses for schools in school holidays.

Powder Byrne, 50 Lombard Road, London SW11 3SU (0171-223 0601). Switzerland, France, Italy.

Simply Ski, Chiswick Gate, 598-608 Chiswick High Road, London W4 5RT (0181-742 2541).

Skibound Ltd, Olivier House, 18 Marine Parade, Brighton, East Sussex BN2 1TL (01273 677777/647230 for information line).

Ski Esprit, Oaklands, Reading Road North, Fleet, Hants. GU13 8AA (01252 625177). France, Switzerland.

Ski Scott Dunn, Fovant Mews, 12 Noyna Road, London SW17 7PH (0181-767 0202). France, Switzerland.

Ski Thomson, Greater London House, Hampstead Road, London NW1 7SD (0171-387 9321). Applications from chalet reps and ski rangers should be sent in June.

Ski Total, 10 Hill St, Richmond, Surrey TW9 1TN (0181-948 3535). France, Austria, Switzerland.

Ski West, Eternit House, Felsham Road, London SW15 1SF (0181-789 1122). Sister company of Bladon Lines.

Skiworld/Ski Val, 41 North End Road, London W14 8SZ (0171-602 4826). Mostly in France, also Switzerland and Austria.

Snowtime, 96 Belsize Lane, London NW3 5BE (0171-433 3336).

The book *Working in Ski Resorts* (Vacation Work £8.95) contains many other addresses of ski companies and details of the job hunt in individual European and North American resorts. In response to the thousands of enquiries about alpine jobs which the Ski Club of Great Britain receives, it now distributes an information sheet; send £2 to the SCGB, 118 Eaton Square, London SW1W 9AF. You can find other ski company addresses by consulting ski guide books, magazines and travel agents. Another good idea is to attend the *Daily Mail* Ski

Show held each November at Earl's Court in London where some ski companies actually hand out job descriptions and applications.

Rhona Stannage, a Scottish solicitor, and her husband Stuart applied to all the companies they could find addresses for:

> *Only one company (Skibound) gave us an interview. No one else would touch us because we were too old (i.e. 28), married and had no experience in the catering trade. Skibound gave us both jobs as chalet girls (yes, Stuart signed a 'chalet girl' contract) working in a four-person chalet with a manageress and a qualified chef. The wages were as expected — dire (£48 a week) but we got free ski passes, accommodation in our own apartment and food. Stuart was a bit worried about the uniform but it was only a purple T-shirt.*

Another way of fixing up a job in advance is to go through the London-based agency Jobs in the Alps (PO Box 388, London SW1X 8LX). They recruit a variety of staff for Swiss ski resorts, for which good German or French is usually required. You must arrange to be interviewed by the end of September and be prepared to sign a contract for the whole season, four months in the winter December-April. (They also place young Britons for a minimum of three months during the summer season for which the interview deadline is the end of April.) As of 1994, they are no longer willing to interview male school leavers unless they have had a full-time job for at least two months or are willing to do 'hard-slog backroom jobs' for up to six months. Wages are £550 a month net for a five-day week. Under the name Alpotels, the agency carries out aptitude tests on behalf of German and French hotels for the winter season. There is an agency fee of £30 plus £15 per month of the contract up to a maximum of £100.

Applying on the Spot

The best time to look is at the end of the preceding winter season though this has the disadvantage of committing you a long way in advance. The next best time is the first fortnight in September when the summer season is finishing and there are still plenty of foreign workers around who will have helpful advice. The final possibility is to turn up in the month before the season begins when you will be faced with many refusals. In November you will be told you're too early because everything's closed, in December you're too late because all the jobs are spoken for. Some disappointed job-seekers reckon there must be a 24-hour window between these two, and if you miss it, you're out of luck.

Assuming you can afford to finance yourself for several weeks, arrive as early as you can (say early November) so that you can get to know people and let them get to know your face. Weekends are better than weekdays since more shops and other tourist establishments will be open. Apply directly to hotels, equipment rental agencies, tourist offices, etc. It is also an idea to travel to the ski resorts out of season to look for work repairing or redecorating ski chalets, for instance, and then move on to a ski tow or bar job once the season begins. If you miss out on landing a job before the season, it could be worth trying again in early January, since workers tend to disappear after the holidays.

The people who do succeed on the spot claim that it is easy and the people who fail claim that it is an impossibility. The negative version, which is put forward by Rob Jefferson on page 314, is counter-balanced by Mary Jelliffe's account of opportunities in the French resort of Méribel:

> *At the beginning of the season there were many 'ski bums' looking for work in Méribel. Many found something. People earned money by clearing snow, cleaning, babysitting, etc. for which they were paid about F30 an hour. You do need some money to support yourself while looking for work but if you are determined enough, I'm sure you'll get something eventually. One group*

of ski bums organised a weekly slalom race from which they were able to make a living. Another set up a video service; another made and sold boxer shorts for F100 a pair.

Andy Winwood asked in over 200 places in Crans Montana, Verbier and Haute-Nendaz and came up with 10 or 12 possibilities. When he finally heard the magic words, 'You can start on December 15th', he rushed outside, let out a whoop of delight and headed for the nearest bar.

Chalet Staff

Many of the ski tour operators active in France and Switzerland accommodate their clients in chalets which are looked after by a chalet girl or boy (but usually the former). The chalet maid does everything (sometimes with an assistant) from cooking first-class meals for the ten or so guests, to clearing the snow from the footpath (or delegating that job). She is responsible for keeping the chalet clean, preparing breakfast, packed lunches, tea and dinner, providing ice and advice, and generally keeping everybody happy. Fifteen-hour days are standard.

Although this sounds an impossible regimen, many chalet girls manage to fit in several hours of skiing in the middle of each day. The standards of cookery skills required vary from company to company depending on the degree of luxury (i.e. the price) of the holidays. Whereas some advertise good homecooking, others offer cordon bleu cookery every night of the week (except the one night which the chalet girl has off). In most cases, you will have to cook a trial meal for the tour company before being accepted for the job.

Pandora Balchin, who got a job as a chalet maid on the strength of her catering degree, described her job this way:

It was a fantastic experience though it was very hard work. Although I had never skied before I went to Méribel, I have to admit that I am now completely hooked, as are all the others who worked there. The spirit of comradeship in the resort was amazing, and also typical of other resorts I'm told.

The pay will be £40-60 per week, with lots of perks. Obviously your accommodation and food are free. Also you should get a season's ticket to the slopes and lifts (called an *abonnement* and worth several hundred pounds) and free ski hire. Recruitment of the 1,000+ chalet girls needed in Europe gets underway in May so early application is essential.

Ski Instructors

To become a fully-fledged ski instructor, qualified to work in foreign ski schools, costs a great deal of money (some estimate £2,000) and then competition is extremely stiff for jobs in recognised alpine ski schools. Especially in France there is a great deal of resistance to foreign instructors. Freelance or 'black' instructors — those who tout in bars offering a few hours of instruction in return for pocket money — are persecuted by the authorities in most alpine resorts. The main legitimate opportunities for British skiers without paper qualifications are as instructors for school parties or as ski guides/ski rangers.

David Robinson got an instructor's job over Easter with a company which sends 4,000 school children to Swiss and Italian resorts each winter. He found the responsibility rather nerve-racking at first since, on his first run, a beginner broke his leg and had to be rescued by helicopter. Soon after that he led a group of intermediate skiers down a hill he hadn't had a chance to explore himself and it was considerably harder than the standard they had achieved; but as it happened there was no mishap and they all found it very exhilarating. Being a ski instructor is not all swooping down slopes past pretty girls and eager students.

Groups of children can be tiresome to instruct, emergencies can arise and the job can be exhausting. But it still remains one of the most enjoyable and rewarding seasonal jobs you can hope to get abroad.

If you are interested in qualifying as an instructor, contact the British Association of Ski Instructors or BASI (Grampian Road, Aviemore, Inverness-shire PH22 1RL; 01479 810407). BASI runs training and grading courses throughout the year and also publishes a Newsletter in which job adverts appear. The most junior instructor's qualification is a Grade III which is awarded by BASI after a five-day assessment following a two-week training course on the Continent in the early winter or in Aviemore throughout the season and after logging 60 hours of teaching. After attending the course, it is sometimes difficult to be accepted at a resort in order to clock up the requisite number of hours of instruction. BASI also run Nordic ski instructor courses as well as the alpine ones. Most instructors teach from two to six hours a day depending on demand. Pay can vary from as little as £150 a week, but this often inlcudes asccommodation. Some participation in the evening entertainments is expected. It is of course much easier for Ski Teachers (Grade II) and National Ski Teachers (Grade I) to find lucrative work in Europe or beyond.

Ski Resorts Worldwide

In conclusion, there are plenty of jobs in ski resorts au pairing, cooking, guiding, selling, cleaning and so on. If you do end up in a resort looking for a job, try the ski equipment hire shops which may offer you very short term work on change-over days when lots of skis need prompt attention, or the ski-lift offices preferably in the autumn. You might even find that the tourist office in the big resorts like Zermatt and Val d'Isère may be able to help. Outside the EU you will encounter work permit difficulties (details in individual country chapters), though when there is a labour shortage, there is usually a way round the difficulties. Unfortunately labour shortages these days are becoming rarer and the drifting population looking for jobs in ski resorts can be much greater in one area than the number of jobs available. You should therefore try as hard as you can to sign a contract ahead of time, or failing this, be prepared to move around to less popular areas to find work.

For a thorough list of ski resorts in Europe, consult the *Good Skiing Guide* in a bookshop. Some major ski resorts are listed below:

France	*Switzerland*	*Austria*	*Italy*
Chamonix	Davos	Kitzbühel	Cortina d'Ampezzo
Les Contamines	St. Moritz	Söll	Courmayeur
Val d'Isère	Zermatt	Lech	Sestriere
Courchevel	Gstaad	Badgastein	Bormio
Méribel	Champery	St. Anton	Campitello
St. Christoph	Saas Grund	Mayrhofen	Canazei
Flaine	Wengen & Mürren	Lermoos	Livigno
Avoriaz	Crans-Montana	Alpbach	Abetone
Les Arcs	Kandersteg	Brand	Folgarida
La Plagne	Adelboden	Kirchberg	Forni di Sopra
Tignes	Verbier	St. Johann	Sauze d'Oulx
Montgenèvre	Grindelwald	Solden	Asiago
	Arosa	Obergurgl	S. Stefano di Cadore
	Saas Fee	Zell am See	Alleghi

Spain	*Germany*	*Norway*	*Scotland*
Sol y Nieve	Garmisch-	Voss	Aviemore
Formigal	Partenkirchen	Geilo	Glenshee (Glenisla)
Cerler		Telemark	Carrbridge
		Lillehammer	Glencoe
Andorra		Gausdal	
Arinsal		Synnfjell	
Soldeu			

New Zealand	*Australia*	*Canada*	*USA*
Queenstown	Falls Creek (VIC)	Banff	Aspen, Colorado
Coronet Peak	Mount Hotham	Lake Louise	Copper Mountain
Mount Hutt	Mount Buffalo	Waterton	Steamboat Springs
Mount Ruapehu	Baw Baw	Ottawa	Vail
	Mount Buller	Huntsville	Winter Park
	Thredbo (NSW)	Collingwood	Alpine Meadows, Calif.
	Perisher	Barrie	Lake Tahoe
	Mount Field (Tas)		Mount Batchelor,
	Ben Lomond		Oregon
			Mount Hood
			Timberline
			Park City, Utah
			Sun Valley, Idaho
			Jackson Hole, Wyoming
			Sugar Mt. Resort, NC
			Waterville Valley, NH
			Stowe, Vermont
			Sugarbush Valley
			Dore Mountain, NY

AGRICULTURE

HARVESTING

Historically, agricultural harvests have employed the greatest number of casual workers. Itinerant workers have traditionally travelled hundreds of miles to gather in the fruits of the land, from the tiny blueberry to the mighty watermelon. It might even be possible to pick your way around the world, by following the seasons and the ripening crops. The old-style gypsies, who roamed over Europe picking fruit as they went, have been joined both by nomadic young people and large numbers of East Europeans looking to earn western wages.

The well organised picker in Europe might find himself starting the year in Britain, picking mundane vegetables like cabbages and potatoes. He then moves on to strawberries and gooseberries in June, cherries, currants and raspberries in July, apples and plums in August and then on to choosing between the Kentish hop harvest in September or grape-picking in France. He could follow the *vendange* (grape harvest) north and then into Germany where grapes are picked into November, back to France for the chestnut harvest in late November and December. Tiring at last of the cold northern climate, our itinerant picker could flee south to pick oranges on the Greek Peloponnese.

Furthermore, living and working in rural areas is a more authentic way of experiencing an alien culture compared to working in tourism. It is easy to see why farms, vineyards and orchards play such a large part in the chapters which follow, since harvests provide so much scope for people working their way around the world. No serious self-funding traveller can afford to ignore the employment opportunities available at harvest time.

Although the problem of work permits does dog the footsteps of fruit pickers abroad, there is always a good chance that the urgency of the farmers' needs will overrule the impulse to follow the regulations. But if you do end up picking fruit without a permit, it is best to keep a low profile in the village pub. Even locals who would not consider doing this kind of work might feel jealous of the imagined fortune you're earning while they are unemployed.

The availability of harvesting work in Europe has been greatly reduced by the large numbers of Slovaks, Poles, Albanians, etc. now roaming every corner of Europe trying to earn the money their own struggling economies cannot provide. Often a certain amount of hostility exists between these economic migrants and working travellers, primarily because farmers have been dropping wages as a result of the new competition for jobs, and because impoverished Easterners will accept below-par wages.

Where to look for work

Once you have arrived in the right area at the right time of year, the next step is to find out which farmers are short of help. Asking in the youth hostel or campsite and in the local pub or general store is often successful; the great advantage of job-hunting in rural areas rather then in cities is that people are more likely to know their neighbours' labour requirements and often are more sympathetic and helpful in their attitudes. Adam Cook interrupted a cycling tour of the South of France to look for fruit-picking work:

Faced with the decision of hurrying north to catch up with the cherries or going south to meet the first peaches, I decided to go south. It took ten good days of asking everywhere, cafés, bars, post offices, grocery shops — one of the best places I found to look as the owners very often know who is picking what and where.

If the word of mouth technique does not work at first, you will have to visit farmers personally. Since they will be generally working out of doors it is not difficult to approach them. Farm hands and people already picking in the fields will be able to offer advice as well. If farms are widely scattered, you may have to consider hiring or borrowing a bicycle, moped or car for a day of concentrated job-hunting.

Alternatively you might be able to get a list of farms and ring around. Farm cooperatives can be useful sources of this kind of information. Local newspapers may carry advertisements for pick-your-own farms or roadside fruit stands which may provide a job or at least a lead. If there is a weekly market or cooperative at which local farmers sell their produce, this is an ideal venue for job-hunting. Even if you don't find a farmer looking for pickers, they may need people to unload the lorries or man the market stall. They may also hold an auction and it may be possible to broadcast your request for work over the public address system, auctioning yourself off to the highest bidder as it were. If you are with several friends, you may find that it is difficult to find a farmer willing to offer work to all of you. You may then be able to work out a job-sharing arrangement, although this is more likely to be acceptable to the farmer if accommodation is not his responsibility.

It may not be necessary to approach farmers directly if you can fix up a harvesting job through the district employment office. In some countries, there is a special branch of the national employment service which deals exclusively with agricultural vacancies, such as the Agricultural Employment Services of Canada and the cantonal offices of Landdienst (agricultural service) in Switzerland.

One of the job-seeker's best allies is a very detailed map. Helpful locals can then point out their suggestions on a map rather than give verbal instructions (possibly in a language you barely know). An excellent reference book for prospective grape-pickers is Hugh Johnson's *World Atlas of Wine* (published by Mitchell Beazley) which includes splendidly detailed maps of wine-producing regions from Corsica to California. It is of course much too heavy and expensive (£30) to carry around, though you could perhaps take a few good photocopies of the regions you plan to try. Alternatively, get a list of vineyards from the regional tourist offices and write to (or visit) the proprietors, asking for work.

Mechanisation

Although harvesting techniques have become increasingly mechanised, human toil continues to play a large part. The recent mechanisation of the hop harvest for example has made a dramatic difference and yet a large number of helpers are still needed for various ancillary jobs. Although more and more vineyards are employing mechanical harvesters, often the rows of vines are too close together or on too steep a gradient for the machines to be of use. There are cherry-picking machines which work by shaking the fruit off the trees; these not only leave the fruit damaged but also loosen the roots and in the long run destroy the trees. Despite advances in agricultural technology, there is no immediate danger of humans being replaced altogether. That being said, it certainly can't hurt to go abroad with some tractor-driving experience.

One job which can't be done by machinery is selective picking. There are not many fruits and vegetables which ripen all at once. Pickers soon develop the ability to spot the lettuces, cauliflowers or strawberries which are ready and leave the rest for a later onslaught. Sometimes the process of selection becomes quite complicated if you are expected to sort the size and quality of the produce as you proceed; for example pickers must sometimes drop apples through a wire loop to determine the size.

Technique

Picking fruit may not be as easy as it sounds. For many people, their only experience of fruit picking may have been on family outings to an orchard where most of the time was spent in tree-climbing or sibling-bombardment exploits. Picking fruit for your living will not be so idyllic. If you are part of a large team you may be expected to work at the same speed as the most experienced picker, which can be both exhausting and discouraging.

Having a little experience can make the whole business more enjoyable, not to mention more financially worthwhile if you are being paid piece work rates. The vast majority of picking jobs are paid piece work (with the notable exception of grape harvests in Europe), though a minimum level of productivity will be expected, particularly if you are being given room and board.

Try not to feel too discouraged at the end of the first day or even the first week of working in an orchard when you see that some old hands have picked three times as much as you. When Andrew Walford was tempted to feel envious of the people who could fill seven or eight bins of apples a day in Shepparton Australia, he consoled himself that, even if his record was only five, at least he wasn't as eccentric as they were. Rather than succumb to feelings of inferiority, watch their technique closely. Ask their advice about where to place the ladder, since moving a ladder can be time-consuming. (Note that this is not a job for anyone who suffers from vertigo.) After a week or two your confidence and your earnings will certainly have increased. Once you learn how to snap strawberries off with a quick twist of the wrist (leaving the floret intact) you will be surprised at how your speed improves. In the case of other fruits, shaking trees to dislodge fruit is almost always frowned upon by employers, though this does not prevent some pickers from resorting to it. There may even be scouts in large orchards patrolling in order to prevent this practice.

It is not merely technique which separates the professionals from the amateurs, but fitness as well. Richard Walford interrupted a cycling trip along the Rhine to pick grapes for a few weeks, and assumed that all his cycling would have prepared him for the work. He soon learned however that grape-picking uses different muscles entirely and he found the first few days gruelling. It would be taking things too far to recommend back-strengthening exercises before setting off on your world travels, but at least you should be warned that the first few days of picking can be an unwelcome reminder of your physical limitations.

There are often external limitations to the amount you can earn. Sometimes picking is called off in bad weather. Sometimes you are forced to take some days off while the next crop ripens fully or because the price on the market has dropped. Be prepared to amuse (and finance) yourself on idle days.

Some farmers prefer to hire men if the work is particularly taxing or if a lot of lifting is involved. But there are few actual picking jobs which women can't do equally well. Agility is often more important than strength and for some soft fruits, female pickers are preferred because they are assumed to have a gentler touch. If the fruit is very delicate, beginners are sometimes paid an hourly rate to discourage careless and damaging picking.

Informal competitions can enliven the tedium. Alan Corrie describes his fellow tomato-picker on a farm near Auch in the Gascony region of southern France, with undisguised admiration:

> *In August I was taken on by a farmer to join his contracted Moroccan worker picking tomatoes. This is paid by the crate, and iron discipline and single-minded determination are needed to breach the fifty crates barrier per ten-hour day, and get in amongst the good earnings. When my first half century had been verified, I was punching the air in triumphant salute. The next day, toying with extremis, fifty-three was achieved, and I had the distinct feeling while unloading at the depot that the workers there nudging one another and confiding 'c'est lui, mon dieu, comme une tempête dans les tomates!'*
>
> *Ahmed, meanwhile, was touching seventy crates a day. Any day now, I reasoned, we'd be on a par, sending the boss off to buy a calculator and to order extra crates. This was not to be however. I had peaked. Desperation set in; the crates were becoming bigger, tomatoes always lying awkwardly, the heat blistering; I began to flounder, drained and dejected in the low forties. My colleague when I last asked him was turning in a cool eighty a day, which if you knew anything about tomato picking I would not ask you to believe. You would have to see it for yourself. I'm thinking of giving guided tours of the scene of his campaign for knowing seasonal workers and afficionados: 'Yup,' I'll nod my head — greyhaired as it now is after the experience — in the direction of a little altar-like structure, 'I was there, seen it wi' m'own eyes. I swear it, them little rascals wuz up'n jumpin' in that thaar bucket of his.' Anyway, good luck to him. It was with some relief that I was transferred to the shady plum groves across the road.*

Equipment

During August in the South of France the only equipment you'll need is a sun hat. But if you are planning to apples in British Columbia or olives in the Greek winter, you will need warm clothing, waterproofs and possibly also rubber boots for muddy fields. When packing for your intercontinental fruit picking holiday, it might be an idea to pack a sturdy pair of gardening gloves for frosty mornings. Gloves can also be useful if you are picking fruit which has been sprayed with an insecticide that irritates cuts or stains your hands an unsightly colour. If it is too awkward to pick wearing gloves, you can tape up your hands with surgical tape to prevent blistering.

In each country chapter, we have dealt with the possibilities for willing and well-prepared pickers. Wherever possible we have included tables of crop locations and harvesting dates, so that you will know which specific areas to head for. This information can be more easily assimilated by examining the symbols on the sktech maps which should be used in conjunction with detailed country and regional maps.

FARMING

Not all casual work in rural areas revolves around fruit and vegetable harvests. There are a lot of miscellaneous seasonal jobs created by the agricultural industry, from castrating maize to crutching sheep, from scaring birds away from cherry orchards to herding goats (something which seems to reduce most novices to tears), from weeding olive groves to spraying banana plantations. There is always the chance of work if you knock on farmers' doors. Every working traveller ought to be able to turn his hand to the basic tasks of pruning, planting and harvesting.

Many farms, especially in Europe, are relatively small family-run businesses, and the farmer may not need to look any further than his own family for labour. But often farmers are looking for one able-bodied assistant over the summer months, and if you are fortunate to be that one, you will probably be treated as a member of the family, sharing their meals and their outings. It is more important to be able to communicate with the farmer than if you are hired as a fruit picker, since the instructions given to farm hands are more complicated. It also helps to have some tractor-driving or other farm experience or at least an aptitude for machinery.

Whereas picking a given crop can quickly become tedious, working as a general assistant provides much more variety as Ed Peters describes, based on his experience of working in mainland Greece:

The work ranged from langorous to arduous — scattering chemical fertiliser, picking up wood, digging shallow ditches for water pipes, supervising irrigation (a sinecure if ever there was one) and spraying weedkiller from ten litre containers on your back (murderous!).

Advertising

Placing an advert in the national farmers' journal is especially worthwhile for people who have had some relevant experience. Gary Tennant placed the following advert in the Danish farmers' weekly *Landsbladet*:

23 year old Englishman now in Denmark would like farm work. Have been working on a kibbutz (4 months) in the fields and tractor work. Just finished gardening work in England and want to try different farming. Telephone 06191679, ask for Gary.

Although he started his job hunt in the autumn (the worst time of year), he received four offers. An Englishwoman he met who had experience of dairy farming received 11 offers from such an advert.

Range of Opportunities

Many long term itinerant workers meet up with people who are interested in alternative lifestyles which may include organic farming or goat cheese production as a way of earning a living. In rural areas, a polite request for room and board in exchange for half a day's work often succeeds. The 'small is beautiful' philosophy may mean that smallholders will not be able to pay wages, but this can be a congenial way to pass some time, as Ken Smith from New Zealand discovered in Northern Ireland:

Through various sets of coincidences I have built up several contacts here in County Tyrone and have worked as a farmhand for about two months on several occasions. For me it has proved invaluable as a way to plan my next move while in a family environment. I enjoy the work which involves cleaning out the cattle houses, cutting silage, fencing and a thousand and one other odd jobs which need doing on a farm. The work is for board and lodging only and I'm very happy with the arrangement. It's great to be outside in the fresh air and at the ground level of Irish rural life. I am now a familiar face in the local community. When the work's done the Irish like to enjoy themselves, and the atmosphere in country pubs is great, with storytelling and music.

Although shearing itself is a skilled job, there are lots of other associated jobs, from skirting the fleece to baling the wool to cooking for the extra hands. Commercial flower production often provides opportunities in the greenhouses, transplanting, picking and packing. For the seasonal worker, the most famous is the bulb and flower industry of Holland. But we have heard of jobs in flower nurseries in Helsinki, Israel, Crete and Vancouver Island as well.

Working with flowers all day sounds a lot more acceptable than working with onions. Paul Chisnall accepted a factory job in southern Holland and was dismayed to discover upon his arrival that the job involved picking, peeling and pickling thousands of wretched onions. Conditions were so smelly and gruesome that Paul didn't last twenty-four hours. We are told that gherkin factories are not much more bearable. In fact food processing can be exhausting and unpleasant but tends to be well paid. Because of its seasonal urgency, your chances of getting casual work are better than in other kinds of factory.

Occasionally the magazine *Farmers Weekly* (published Fridays) contains advertisements for jobs abroad. A few specialist agencies exist. If you do find a job through an agency do not rely exclusively on the agency's information. It is better to talk to your future employer direct to avoid the fate which befell Lee Morton when he was placed as a trainee groom in California: the employer was so demanding that he left the day after he arrived. Experienced grooms, riding instructors and stable staff may consider registering with A World of Experience Equestrian Agency (52 Kingston Deverill, Warminster, Wilts. BA12 7HF; tel/fax 01985 844102). For people with relevant full-time experience, they have vacancies in 20 countries in Europe and worldwide which pay between £50 and £150 a week plus free accommodation. Other agencies advertise in the specialist press, for example *Horse & Hound*. Stable staff and lightweight riders are needed for work on studs and in racing establishments around the world. Check the situations vacant columns in *The Sporting Life* and *Racing Post*.

Gaining Experience

Without any formal training in agriculture, it is possible to get some preliminary experience. Many European countries have programmes whereby young people spend a month or two assisting on a farm, e.g. Norway and Switzerland. A farming background is not necessary for participating in these schemes, though of course it always helps. Israeli kibbutzim often give their volunteers exposure to a range of farming jobs. You might like to get an initial taste of farm life by having a 'farm holiday'. Rural tourism is gaining popularity and the tourist organisations of countries like Italy and New Zealand) encourage tourists to take a holiday on a working farm and participate in the daily round of activities to whatever extent they like. You then have the chance not only of having a relatively inexpensive and interesting holiday, but also of learning a little about hay-baling, cheese-making and so on.

It is not impossible to find work on farms and ranches which have diversified to accept paying visitors. This has been particularly popular in the United States (where guest ranches are called 'dude ranches') and Australia. These establishments need both domestic and outdoor assistants to lead guests on trail rides, show them places or events of local interest, etc. Tourist organisations can provide lists of guest ranches.

Organic Farms

In the wake of the Rio Summit and a growing awareness of environmental concerns, the round-the-world working traveller might be attracted to the flourishing organic farming movement. Organic farms around the world take on volunteers to help them minimise or abolish the use of chemicals and heavy machinery. There are various coordinating bodies, many of which go under the name of WWOOF which orginally meant Working Weekends on Organic Farms but now usually stands for Willing Workers on Organic Farms. National coordinators compile a list of their member farmers willing to provide free room and board to volunteers who help out and who are genuinely interested in furthering the aims of the organic movement. (If the topic arises at immigration, try to avoid the word 'working'; it is preferable to present yourself as a student of organic farming or someone looking for a cultural exchange.)

Mike Tunnicliffe joined WWOOF in New Zealand to avoid work permit hassles and his experience is typical of WWOOFers' in other countries:

My second choice of farm was a marvellous experience. For 15 days I earned no money but neither did I spend any, and I enjoyed life on the farm as part of the family. There is a wide variety of WWOOF farms and I thoroughly recommend the scheme to anyone who isn't desperate to earn money.

If you are starting in Britain, send an s.a.e. to the UK branch of WWOOF (19 Bradford Road, Lewes, Sussex BN7 1RB) who will send you a membership application form. Membership costs £8 per year and includes a subscription to their bi-monthly newsletter which contains small adverts for opportunities both in Britain and abroad. After you have proved your suitability by volunteering your labour for two weekends in Britain, you are entitled to request the WWOOF Fix-it-Yourself list which includes addresses of WWOOF headquarters around the world.

The active Australian branch of WWOOF publishes its own *Worldwide List* of farms and volunteer work opportunities in those countries with no national WWOOF group. The booklet may be obtained by sending A$15/£8/US$15 to WWOOF, Mt Murrindal Cooperative, Buchan, Vic 3885, Australia. Organic farm organisations are mentioned in the following chapters of this book: UK, Ireland, Denmark, Germany, Spain, Switzerland, Hungary, Australia, New Zealand, USA, Canada and Ghana.

Many communities (what used to be called communes) welcome foreign visitors and willingly exchange hospitality for work. Although not all the work is agricultural, much of it is. The details and possible fees must be established on a case-by-case basis. The last two listings below are relevant:

TERN (Travellers Earth Repair Network), PO Box 1064, Tonasket, WA 98855. Issue an international list of about 150 hosts and other contacts which at last report cost US$50 ($35 to students).

Diggers and Dreamers, Redfield Community, Winslow, Buckinghamshire MK18 3LZ (01296 712161). Publish a directory *Diggers and Dreamers: The Guide to Communal Living* which contains brief details of 400 contacts abroad. The 1994/5 edition costs £10 (£11 overseas) and the 1996/7 edition is due for publication in autumn 1995.

Communities, Rt 4, Box 169-W, Louisa, VA 23093, USA. Publish *Communities Directory: A Guide to Cooperative Living* (late 1994) for US$19 ($21 overseas). It lists more than 500 communities worldwide, focusing mainly on North America.

Before arranging a longish stay on an organic farm, consider whether or not you will find such an environment congenial. Many organic farmers are non-smoking vegetarians and living conditions may be primitive by some people's standards. Although positive experiences are typical, Craig Ashworth expressed reservations about WWOOF, based on his experiences in New Zealand, and claims that a proportion of WWOOF hosts are 'quite wacky'. (See page 281 for a first-hand account of total incompatibility in this context.) Bear in mind that the work you are given to do may not always be very salubrious: for example Armin Birrer, who has spent time on organic farms in many countries, claims that the weirdest job he ever did was to spend a day in New Zealand picking worms out of a pile of rabbit dung to be used to soften the soil around some melon plants.

Agricultural Exchanges

There are opportunities worldwide for students of agriculture or young people between 18 and 30 who have good practical farming experience. The International Agricultural Exchange Association (IAEA) arranges placements for European participants who have had at least a season's experience in Canada, the USA, Australia, New Zealand and Japan. Placements in Canada which are in British Columbia, Ontario and the Prairies, begin in February or April and last nine or seven months respectively. Placements in the States begin in March/April for seven months. Placements in Australia begin in April, August or September while those in New Zealand begin only in August/September and last six to nine months. Placements in Japan begin in April and last four to twelve months. There are also several round-the-world itineraries which depart in the autumn to the southern hemisphere for six to seven months followed by another six to seven months in the northern hemisphere.

These programmes cost participants between £1,500 and £3,700 but trainees are then paid a realistic wage. Categories encompass straightforward agriculture (livestock and crops), horticulture (fruit, flowers, etc.), home management and a mixture of agriculture and household management. Contact IAEA, (Young Farmers' Club Centre, National Agricultural Centre, Stoneleigh Park, Kenilworth, Warwickshire CV8 2LG; 01203 696578) for complete information about the requirements, choices of programmes, costs, etc.

North American agriculturalists are also eligible for the programmes in Europe, Japan and New Zealand or Australia. They have a similar choice of category and the address of the American office of IAEA is 1000 1st Avenue South, Great Falls, Montana 59401; and in Canada, 206, 1501-17th Avenue SW, Calgary, Alberta T2T 0E2.

The International Farm Experience Programme (YFC Centre, Stoneleigh Park, Kenilworth, Warwickshire CV8 2LG; 01203 696584)is part of the National Federation of Young Farmers' Clubs. Their programme offers a wide range of placements in agriculture and horticulture in Eastern and Western Europe, the USA and China, Australia, New Zealand and Canada. Applicants must be between 18 and 28 and have at least two years' experience, one of which may be at college. Placements last between three and 12 months starting at any time of the year and wages are paid at the local rate. Opportunities to study the language are available in Germany and France. IFEP has a good relationship with its counterparts in Ohio and Minnesota, where students can spend part of their time studying at a university in addition to gaining practical work experience. IFEP is also able to arrange visas for young agriculturists who may have found their own jobs on farms in the USA.

The counterpart organisation in the US is the National FFA Organization, PO Box 15160, Alexandria, Virginia 22309, which arranges for students with a background in agriculture from 35 countries to work and train in the US and for Americans to work on farms abroad.

TEACHING ENGLISH

This chapter used to begin with a quotation from a traveller-turned-professional-EFL-teacher, Dick Bird:

> *It is extremely difficult for anyone whose mother tongue is English to starve in an inhabited place, since there are always people who will pay good money to watch you display a talent as basic as talking. Throughout the world, native speakers of English are at a premium.*

But this rosy view of the traveller's prospects must now be moderated somewhat. Although the English language is still the language which literally millions of people around the world want to learn, finding work as an English teacher is not as easy as many people assume. Furthermore there is a worrying trend even for people with a qualification to have difficulty. The number of both public and private institutes turning out certified TEFL teachers has greatly increased in the past three years, creating a glut of teachers all chasing the same jobs, especially in recession-hit Europe.

Having sounded that warning note, it must be said that there are still areas of the world where the boom in English language learning seems to know no bounds, such as Russia and most of the old Eastern Bloc, Korea, Thailand and Turkey. In cowboy schools and back-street agencies, being a native speaker and dressing neatly are sometimes sufficient qualifications to get a job. But for more stable teaching jobs in recognised language schools, you will have to sign a contract (usually nine months) and have some kind of qualification which ranges from a simple BA to a certificate in education with a specialisation in Teaching English as a Foreign Language (known as TEFL, pronounced 'teffle'). This chapter covers both possibilities.

One of the best sources of information about the whole topic of English teaching (if I may be permitted to say so) is *Teaching English Abroad* by Susan Griffith (Vacation-Work, £9.95). This chapter can only provide the most general introduction to such topics as TEFL training and commercial recruitment agencies; for specific information about individual countries, see the country chapters.

TEFL Training

The only way to outrival the competition and make the job-hunt (not to mention the job itself) easier is to do a TEFL course. If interested, write to the English Language Information Service of the British Council (Medlock St, Manchester M15 4PR) for an information sheet 'How to Become a Teacher of EFL' and a list of approved Certificate centres.

There are two standard recognised qualifications which will improve your range of job options by an order of magnitude. The best known is the Certificate in TEFLA (Teaching English as a Foreign Language to Adults) awarded by RSA/UCLES (the University of Cambridge Local Examinations Syndicate). The other is the Certificate in TESOL (Teaching English to Speakers of Other Languages) offered by Trinity College in London (16 Park Crescent, London W1N 4AP). Both are very intensive and very expensive, averaging £700-850. These courses involve at least 100 hours of rigorous training with a practical emphasis (full-time for four weeks or part-time over several months). Although there are no fixed pre-requisites apart from a suitable level of language awareness, not everyone who applies is accepted.

A list of the more than 100 centres both in the UK and abroad offering the RSA/Cambridge Certificate course in Britain and abroad is available from UCLES (1 Hills Road, Cambridge CB1 2EU) in exchange for a large s.a.e. Here is a small selection:

Basil Paterson College School of English, Dugdale-McAdam House, 22/23 Abercromby Place, Edinburgh EH3 6QE (0131-556 7696).

International House, 106 Piccadilly, London W1V 9FL (0171-491 2598). Has several sister centres including ILC, White Rock, Hastings, East Sussex TN34 1JY. Certificate course run monthly.

EF International Langauge Schools, EF House, 1 Farman St, Hove, Sussex BN3 1AL (01273 723651). Courses held in Hastings.

Stanton Teacher Training, Stanton House, 167 Queensway, London W2 4SB (0171-221 7259). Lower fees than most.

Trinity centres to try include:

Coventry TESOL Centre, Coventry Technical College, Butts, Coventry CV1 3GD (01203 256793).

Grove House Language Centre, 9 Carlton Avenue, Horns Cross, Nr Dartford, Kent DA9 9DR (01322 386826). Also offers one-week courses for about £200 and intensive weekend/home study courses for £170.

Oxford House College, 3 Oxford St, London W1R 1RF (0171-436 4214).

Regency School of English, Royal Crescent, Ramsgate, Kent CT11 9PE (01843 591212).

A number of Certificate centres and other commercial centres offer short introductory courses in TEFL, which vary enormously in quality and price. Although they are mainly intended to act as preparatory programmes for more serious courses, many people who hold just a short certificate go on to teach. Among the best known are:

Inlingua Method Courses, Rodney Lodge, Rodney Road, Cheltenham, Glos. GL50 1YX (01242 253171). Range of courses including Trinity Certificate and two-week introductory course; the latter costs £285.

Linguarama, New Oxford House, 16 Waterloo St, Birmingham B2 5UG (0121-632 5925). 5½ day courses held in Birmingham, Manchester and Canterbury. The non-residential fee is £205 and accommodation with local families can be arranged.

Pilgrims Language Courses, 8 Vernon Place, Canterbury, Kent CT1 3HG (01227 762111). One-week courses for about £185. Also offer RSA/Cambridge Certificate course.

Primary House, 300 Gloucester Road, Bristol BS7 8PD (tel/fax 01272 429142). Weekend introductory courses in locations throughout the UK at a cost of £160. Distance learning courses also available.

RSA/Cambridge courses are offered at 50 overseas centres from Majorca to Queensland, including several in the US:

English International, 655 Sutter St (Suite 500), San Francisco, CA 94102.

St. Giles Language Teaching Center, 1 Hallidie Plaza (Suite 350), San Francisco, CA 94102.

Coast Language Academy, 20720 Ventura Blvd (Suite 300), Woodland Hills, CA 91364.

Another centre for American readers to consider is Transworld Teachers Training Center, 683 Sutter St, San Francisco, CA 94102 (1-800-241-8071/415-776-8071).

What English Teaching Involves

It is difficult to generalise about what work you will actually be required to do. At one extreme you have David Cooksley whose job it was to listen to Korean businessmen reading English novels aloud for him to correct their pronunciation. At the other extreme Gillian Forsyth, who taught for a private language school in the industrial north of Germany, had a gruelling schedule of 30 hours of teaching including evening classes, translation work and extensive preparation. Whatever the teaching you find, things probably won't go as smoothly as you would wish. After a year of teaching English in Italy, Andrew Spence had this sensible advice:

> *Teaching is perhaps the best way there is of experiencing another country but you must be prepared for periods when not all is as it should be. The work is sometimes arduous and frustrating, or it can be very exhilarating. Be prepared to take the very rough with the fairly smooth.*

Native speaker teachers are nearly always employed to stimulate conversation rather than to teach grammar. Yet a basic knowledge of English grammar is a great asset when pupils come to ask awkward questions. The book *English Grammar in Use* by Raymond Murphy has been highly recommended for its clear explanations and accompanying student exercises.

Each level and age group brings its own rewards and difficulties. Beginners of all ages usually delight in their progress which will be much more rapid than it is later on. Not everyone, however, enjoys teaching young children (a booming area of TEFL from Portugal to Japan) which usually involves sing-songs, puzzles and games. Intermediate learners (especially if they are adolescents) can be difficult, since they will have reached a plateau and may be discouraged. Adults are usually well-motivated though may be inhibited about speaking. Teaching professionals and business people is almost always well paid. Discipline is seldom a problem at least outside Western Europe. In fact you may find your pupils disconcertingly docile and possibly also overly exam-oriented.

Most schools practise the direct method (total immersion in English) so not knowing the language shouldn't prevent you from getting a job. Some employers may provide nothing more than a scratched blackboard and will expect you to dive in using the 'chalk and talk' method. If you are very alarmed at this prospect you could ask a sympathetic colleague if you could sit in on a few classes to give you some ideas. Brochures picked up from tourist offices or airlines can be a useful peg on which to hang a lesson. If you're stranded without any ideas, write the lyrics of a pop song on the board and discuss; favourites include 'Here Comes the Sun' and 'When I'm 64'.

The wages paid to English teachers are usually reasonable, and in developing countries are quite often well in excess of the average local wage. In return you will be asked to teach some fairly unsociable hours since most private English classes take place after working hours, and so schedules split between early morning and evening are not at all uncommon. There may also be extracurricular duties and you should be prepared to do anything from making sausage rolls for an international food day to revising course materials. Even without these, hours will be very long, when you take into account class preparation time. Teaching of any kind is a demanding job and those who are doing it merely as a means of supporting their travelling habit may find it a disillusioning experience.

FINDING A JOB

Teaching jobs are either fixed up from home or sought out on location. Obviously it is less nerve-racking to have everything sorted out before you leave home, but this option is available only to the qualified. It also has the disadvantage that you don't know what you're letting yourself in for.

In Advance

Check the adverts in the Education section of the *Guardian* every Tuesday and in the weekly *Times Educational Supplement (TES)* published on Fridays. The best time of year is between Easter and July. In some cases, a carefully crafted CV and enthusiastic personality are as important as EFL training and experience.

Well qualified EFL teachers will already be aware of possibilities at the prestigious end of the market, for example with the British Council and International House. other recruitment agencies create a database of teachers' CVs which they then try to match with suitable vacancies in their client schools. In order to be registered with such an agency it is normally essential to have at least the Certificate and usually some experience. One exception is the organisation Teaching Abroad (46 Beech View, Angmering, Sussex BN16 4DE) which sends volunteer teachers with no particular qualifications to Spain, Ukraine, Moldavia, Poland, Russia and India for a fee ranging from £500 to £1,250.

Recruitment agencies to try are:

ELT Banbury, 49 Oxford Road, Banbury, Oxon. OX16 9AH (01295 263480).

ILC Recruitment, White Rock, Hastings, East Sussex TN34 1JY (01424 720109).

Language Exchange, Carbeth House, Blanefield, Glasgow G63 9AS (tel/fax 01360 770847).

Nord Anglia International Overseas recruitment, 10 Eden Place, Cheadle, Cheshire SK8 1AT (0161-491 4191).

The major language school chains hire substantial numbers of teachers, many of whom will have graduated from in-house training courses:

International House, Teacher Selection Department, 106 Piccadilly, Londo W1 9FL (0171-491 2598).

inlingua Recruitment, Rodney Lodge, Rodney Road, Cheltenham, Glos. GL50 1XY (01242 253171). Has 250 schools worldwide. Most vacancies are in Germany, Spain, Italy, Thailand and Singapore.

Linguarama, Oceanic House, 89 High St, Alton, Hants. GU34 1LG (01420 80899). Mostly specialise in business English.

Berlitz, 9-13 Grosvenor St, London W1A 3BZ (0171-915 0909). US Headquarters: Research Park, 239 Wall St, Princeton, NJ 08540. Normally Berlitz schools abroad hire independently and offer their own training.

The important organisations in the US are:

TESOL Inc, 1600 Cameron St, Suite 300, Alexandria, Virginia 22314. Basic membership costs $40. For an extra $20 in North America and $30 overseas, members can subscribe to the bi-monthly *Placement Bulletin* which lists job vacancies worldwide.

ELS International Inc., 5761 Buckingham Parkway, Culver City, California 90230 (310-642-0982). International chain of language schools. US office carries out recruitment for some schools and will provide addresses for other locations.

WorldTeach, Harvard Institute for International Development, 1 Eliot St, Cambridge, Massachusetts 02138 (617-495-5527). Private non-profit organisation which recruits volunteers with university degrees to teach English for one year in Costa Rica, Ecuador, Namibia, South Africa, Russia, Poland and Thailand. WorldTeach also has a summer programme in Shanghai open to undergraduates. Volunteers pay about $3,500 for airfare, training, health insurance, orientation and field support. Housing and a small stipend are provided.

On the Spot

Jobs in any field are difficult to get without an interview and English teaching is no different. In almost all cases it is more effective to go to your preferred destination, CV in hand, and call on language schools and companies. The Mainz branch of the major Euro-Schulen-Organisation is just one language school which wants to emphasise the importance of applying locally:

Schools like ours cannot under normal operating circumstances hire someone unseen merely on the basis of his/her resumé and photo. Moreover, when the need for a teacher arises, usually that vacancy must be filled within a matter of days which, for people applying from abroad, is a physical impossibility. I would suggest that an applicant should arrange for a face-to-face interview and make him/herself available at a moment's notice. Of course, I do appreciate the compromising situation to which anyone in need of employment would thus be exposed. Regrettably, I know of no other method.

When looking for work at private language schools, it is helpful if you can claim some qualifications, though you will seldom be asked to provide proof of same (though if you happen to have a BA, take along the certificate). Steven Hendry, who taught English in Japan with no qualifications, stresses the importance of dressing smartly, having a respectable briefcase and a typed CV which exaggerates (if necessary) your experience. However these days it is rare for that to be enough.

There are many means by which you might fix up the odd spot of teaching during your travels. Russia, Thailand, Korea, Hong Kong and to a lesser extent Poland, Slovakia, Greece, Spain and Turkey are probably the best destinations for aspiring teacher-travellers. The names of specific language schools and methods of securing a job are mentioned in the various country chapters.

Accents can be important, especially in Latin America and the Far East where American English is favoured. But many foreign language speakers cannot distinguish, and Geordies and Australians are as welcome as people who speak with a BBC accent. The important factor is whether or not you speak slowly and clearly. In a few cases, Americans may have an advantage, since some groups (e.g. Japanese and Middle Eastern businessmen) who hope to do business in the US, prefer to learn the language from an American speaker. In other countries (like Spain and Italy) an English accent is preferred.

If you are job-hunting in a capital city, your first stop could be the British Council (or the USIS English Center for Americans) which may be able to provide a list of language schools or advise (informally) on the availability of teaching jobs: much depends on the good will of the staff. Some Council offices and also consulates display advertisements for private tutors on their notice boards.

Consult the *Yellow Pages* in order to gather together a list of addresses where you can ask for work. Business schools often need teachers of commercial English. Read the adverts in the English language papers. Visit centres where foreigners study the local language and check the notice board or befriend the secretary.

Several factors will affect the length of time it will take before you find something: for example at what point of the term you begin your search (e.g. late August/September is usually best followed by Christmas-time; summers are usually hopeless), whether you know the vernacular language (especially an advantage in Spanish-speaking countries) and how convincing you look carrying a briefcase. If you have no luck in the major cities, consider trying resorts popular with English speaking tourists. Here you will find plenty of locals very eager to learn enough English to secure them a job in the local tourist industry.

An alternative to working for a language school is to set yourself up as a freelance private tutor. While undercutting the fees charged by the big schools, you can still earn more than as a contract teacher. Normally you will have to be fairly well established in a place before you can attempt to support yourself by private teaching, preferably with some decent premises in which to give lessons (either private or group) and with a telephone. Laurence Koe gave after-hours conversation classes in northern Italy and charged each child 50 pence. Michel Falardeau opened his own English immersion social club in Taiwan. You should bear in mind the disadvantages of working for yourself, viz. frequent last-minute cancellations by clients, unpaid travelling time (if you teach in clients' homes or offices), no social security and an absence of professional support and teaching materials.

If you do decide to try this, you will have to promote yourself unashamedly. Try posting eye-catching bilingual notices all around town (especially the prosperous areas) or even leafletting door to door. You can be more selective, and concentrate on relevant notice boards. To find school-age pupils you could visit ordinary state schools, introduce yourself to the head teacher and ask him/her to announce your willingness to offer extra English tuition. If you are less interested in making money than integrating with a culture, exchanging conversation for board and lodging may be an appealing possibility, which usually relies on having a network of contacts. But not always. According to our contributors, invitations to participate in such an arrangement have come while chatting to a Parisian businesswoman, lying on a Turkish beach or sitting by the side of a road in Thailand.

Qualified Teachers (of any subject)

Major recruitment organisations such as the British Council (CMDT Recruitment, 10 Spring Gardens, London SW1A 2BN), the ODA (Overseas Development Administration, Abercrombie House, Eaglesham Road, East Kilbride, Glasgow G75 8EA), the Central Bureau for Educational Visits and Exchanges (Seymour Mews House, Seymour Mews, London W1H 9PE), Christians Abroad (1 Stockwell Green, London SW9 9HP) and Voluntary Service Overseas (317 Putney Bridge Road, London SW15 2PN) normally welcome applications only from trained and experienced teachers. Similarly, CfBT Education Services (Quality House, Gyosei Campus, London Road, Reading RG1 5AQ) recruit teachers on behalf of foreign Ministries of Education, mainly for Brunei, Malaysia, Oman and Turkey. Although the latter at one time specialised in EFL placements, they now maintain a recruitment database of job-seeking teachers in all subjects. Qualified American teachers seeking appointments abroad in international schools may contact International Schools Services (PO Box 5910, Princeton, NJ 08543) which offers a recruitment/placement service year round and sponsors two large international recruitment centres in the US and one overseas each year. A $600 fee is charged for each successful placement.

Qualified teachers can become an exchange teacher through the League for the Exchange of Commonwealth Teachers (Commonwealth House, 7 Lion Yard, Tremadoc Road, Clapham, London SW4 7NQ) which places British teachers with at least five years experience in Australia, Barbados, Canada, India, Jamaica, Kenya, New Zealand, and other Commonwealth countries as posts arise. The Central Bureau also organises post-to-post teacher exchanges with the United States and Europe, as well as placing university students and teachers as language assistants in schools and language institutes in Europe, North Africa and Latin America for an academic year.

If you are a qualified teacher and think you might want to teach in an English-speaking country, you should take along your diploma and any letters of reference you have. It is a good idea to correspond ahead of time with the education authority in the district which interests you, to find out what their policy is on hiring teachers with foreign qualifications.

CHILDCARE

The terms au pair, mother's help and nanny are often applied rather loosely, since all are primarily live-in jobs concerned with looking after children. Nannies may have some formal training and take full charge of the children. Mother's helps work full-time and undertake general housework and/or cooking as well as childcare. Au pairs are supposed to work for no more than 30 hours a week and are expected to learn a foreign language while living with a family.

One of the great advantages of these live-in positions generally is that they are easy to get, provided you are female. After proving to an agency or a family that you are reasonably sensible, you will in the majority of cases be able to find a placement, though it is much easier and quicker in some countries than others, e.g. easy in France, Austria, and Italy, but more difficult in Scandinavia and Portugal. Furthermore au pairs can benefit from legislation in countries which exempts them from work permit requirements.

Usually the reasons for wanting to be an au pair are that you want to improve your knowledge of the country's language and culture, that you want to take a break from the routine of studies, work or unemployment, or that you wish to get some experience of catering and children before pursuing a career along those lines. Occasionally, young men can find live-in jobs, and slowly the number of families and therefore agencies willing to entertain the possibility of having a male au pair is increasing.

Anyone interested in finding out about all aspects of this kind of work should consult *The Au Pair & Nanny's Guide to Working Abroad* (Vacation-Work, £8.95).

PROS AND CONS

The relationship of au pair to family is not like the usual employer/employee relationship; in fact the term au pair means 'on equal terms'. The Home Office leaflet on au pairs in Britain uses the terminology 'hostess' and 'hospitality'. Therefore the success of the arrangement depends more than usual on whether individuals hit it off, so there is always an element of risk when living in a family of strangers. The Council of Europe guidelines stipulate that au pairs should be aged 18-27 (though these limits are flexible), should be expected to work about five hours a day, six days per week plus a couple of evenings of babysitting, must be given a private room and full board, health insurance, opportunities to learn the language and pocket money.

Once you have arrived in the family, it is important to clarify immediately what your hours and duties will be, which day you will be paid, whether you can expect a rise and how much notice either party must give if they wish to terminate the arrangement. This gets everyone off to a business-like start. But no matter how well-defined your duties are, there are bound to be occasions when your extra services will be taken for granted. It may seem that your time is not your own. Kathryn Halliwell worked for a family in Vancouver, Canada for a year and describes this problem:

A live-in job is a very committed one. It is extremely difficult to say no when the employers ring at 6pm to say they can't be home for another two hours. Children don't consider a nanny as an employee and tension develops if a child can't understand why you won't take him swimming on your day off.

So the official five and a half days per week plus two evenings of babysitting can soon turn into an unofficial string of 14 hour days. Whether you can tolerate this depends entirely on your disposition and on the compensating benefits of the job, e.g. free use of car and telephone, nice kids, good food, lots of sunshine, etc.

No matter how carefully you try to determine your duties and privileges, there is still plenty of scope for different interpretations of how the arrangement should work. At one extreme you have the family (with one well-behaved child) who invites you along on skiing trips with them and asks you to do a mere 24 hours of child-minding and light housework a week. On the other hand you might be treated like a kitchen skivvy by the mother, and like a concubine by the father, while at the same time trying to look after their four spoiled brats. So it is advisable to find out as much as possible about the family before accepting the job. If you do not like the sound of the family at the beginning you should insist that the agency offer any available alternatives.

Even though an au pair does have her own room, there may be a definite lack of privacy. This can be the logical extension of being treated like a member of the family. For example Claire Robson, who spent a summer working as an au pair in Greece, described how the mother accused her of being unsociable because she wouldn't come and watch television (all in Greek!) when invited. Such unreasonable expectations are often the result of different national temperaments as well as simple personality clashes. In conservative countries (e.g. Turkey, southern Italy), it is unacceptable for young women to go out alone at night, so your social life may be very restricted.

On the other hand, Gillian Forsyth's experience when she au paired in Bavaria was a great success:

I had no official day off or free time but was treated as a member of the family. Wherever they went I went too. I found this much more interesting than being treated as an employee as I really got to know the country and the people. In the evenings I did not have to sit in my room, but chatted with the family. Three years later we still keep in close contact and I have been skiing with them twice since, on an au pair/friend basis.

If you do not have such a friendly arrangement with your family, you may feel lonely and cut off in a foreign country. Many au pairs make friends at their language classes. Some agencies issue lists of other au pairs in the vicinity. For those wanting to meet other au pairs in a similar situation, Leeson Clifton, who came from Canada to be a mother's help in Britain, recommends placing an advertisement in the local paper for an au pair get-together. Despite all the possible problems, au pairing does provide an easy and often enjoyable introduction to living and travelling abroad. A family placement is a safe and stable environment for young, underconfident and impecunious people who want to work abroad.

Pay

You may enjoy being an au pair but you are unlikely to get rich quick. Mind you, things have improved since pre-war days when, according to one of our older contributors, you were liable not to be paid a penny until you had completed your six-month contract, and even then it would barely cover your train fare home from Switzerland. The standard pocket money paid to au pairs in Britain nowadays is £30-35 per week and untrained mother's helps £50 plus per week.

The amount of pocket money paid abroad differs considerably with Portugal at the bottom of the league table (averaging less than £20 a week), the USA in the middle with $100 (£65) a week and Switzerland at the top (with a weekly wage of up to £80).

One reason that au pairing is exempt from the usual governmental restrictions requiring work permits (with exceptions such as Switzerland, Canada and the USA) is because it is not a salaried job and normally not subject to taxation.

Of course there are more lucrative opportunities for people with some childcare or catering experience. For example a nanny will be paid from £100 per week in the Home Counties and over C$1,000 (before deductions) per month in Canada. Having some nursery training or childcare experience can open other doors. Most large tour and campsite holiday operators (addresses in *Tourism* chapter) employ nannies to look after the children of holidaymakers. This can be an excellent passport to spending a season in a summer or winter resort (see *Tourism: Winter Resorts* for more information on holiday nannying).

Duties

Before accepting a position which involves cooking you should establish what standard your employer has in mind. Unless you do this you may end up like Sally Collins, who wrote about her experiences in the *New Zealand News*:

> *I soon began to understand that simple cooking — which I had rashly said I could do, imagining boiled eggs and toast — in fact involved a certain amount of cordon bleu knowledge. I had no idea what to do with the pheasant which was presented to me.*

Perhaps it would be a good idea to ask for a *Delia Smith's Complete Cookery Course* for your birthday.

Most au pairs' duties revolve around the children. For some, taking sole responsibility for a child can be even more alarming than cooking pheasant for the first time. You should be prepared to handle a few emergencies (for example sick or lost children) as well as the usual excursions to the park or collecting them from school. The agency questionnaire will ask you in detail what experience you have had with children and whether you are willing to look after newborn infants, etc., so your preferences should be made known early. You must also be prepared to hurt the children's feelings when you leave. Nicky Parker left a family in Majorca after just nine weeks and reported, 'I could only feel guilty and sad at the distress caused to the children by yet another in a long line of people whom they had learned to love, leaving them forever.'

APPLYING

It simplifies matters to use the services of an au pair or domestic agency. The most established agencies in the UK belong to the Federation of Recruitment and Employment Services (FRES, 36-38 Mortimer St, London W1N 7RB) who will send you a list of their member agencies in the field of childcare placement. If you are interested in a short placement (summer only) you should make your enquiries as early as possible, since there is a shortage of such positions.

In the first instance send an s.a.e. to several agencies to compare terms and conditions. If your requirements are very specific as regards location or family circumstances, ring around some agencies and ask them to be blunt about their chances of being able to fix you up with what you want. Some provide a follow-up and travel service as well as placement. In the UK agencies are permitted to charge a fee of up to £40 plus VAT only after a placement has been verified. Unfortunately this means that many prospective au pairs register with a number of agencies and simply choose the best sounding job. This high level of backing out means that UK agencies do not take the trouble over individual applications which their European counterparts do who are allowed to charge substantial registration fees.

Some people have complained that if you go through an agency, you are taking potluck, though this can be minimised by making an effort to communicate with the family by phone or letter before the job begins. Nevertheless you may prefer to arrange something on your own. The best way of doing this is to answer or place advertisements in *The Lady* (39/40 Bedford St, London WC2). Advertisements usually evoke responses from all over the world, since this magazine has a virtual monopoly in this field. For example, Julie Richards, who had had no luck with the agencies because of her lack of childcare experience, placed an advert in *The Lady* and received 30 job offers. There is a special classification of au pair jobs in the fortnightly newspaper *Overseas Jobs Express* and in the free ads paper *LOOT* and au pair jobs on farms are occasionally advertised in the *Horse & Hound* magazine.

Unfortunately it is more difficult for North Americans to arrange au pair placements in Europe. The following agencies may be able to help:

AuPair Homestay USA & Abroad, World Learning Inc, 1015 15th St NW, Suite 750, Washington, DC 20005 (301-431-1613). Sends au pairs of both sexes to Britain, France, Germany, Iceland, Netherlands, Norway, Spain and Switzerland for 3-12 months. Programme fee is $775 which includes programme support throughout. Inquiries to the Administrator, Imelda Farrell.

WISE (Worldwide Internships & Service Education, 303 South Craig St, Suite 202, Pittsburgh, PA 15213 (412-681-8120). Au pairs placed in Finland, France, Netherlands, Switzerland and Germany. Fee is $600. Enquiries to the Administrator, Linda Greenberg.

Au Pair in Europe, PO Box 68056 Blakely Postal Outlet, Hamilton, Ontario, Canada L8M 3M7 (1-800-665-6305; 905-545-6305). Also PO Box 2647, Niagara Falls, NY 14302-2647. Au pairs placed in 18 countries including most western European countries plus Israel, Australia, South Africa and Bermuda. Fee is C$300. Enquiries to the Directors, Corinne and John Prince.

Alliances Abroad, 2525 Arapahoe Ave, Suite E4-288, Boulder, Colorado 80302 (303-494-4164). Au pairs placed in France, Spain, Germany, Finland, Italy, Netherlands, Switzerland, Ireland, England and Canada. Fee is $575.

On the Spot

If you are already abroad, check in the local English language newspaper such as the *Athens News* or the *Anglo Portuguese News* in Lisbon, or visit an au pair agency office in the country where you are (addresses provided in country chapters). Other ways of hearing about openings are to check the notice boards at the local English-speaking churches, ask the headmistress of a junior school if she knows of any families wanting an au pair or visit a school at the end of the school day and chat with the mothers and au pairs who are there to collect their charges. One tip for finding babysitting jobs in resorts is to introduce yourself to the *portière* or receptionist on the desk of good hotels and ask them to refer guests looking for a babysitter to you, possibly offering 10-15% commission.

Agencies

UK agencies should be licensed by the Department of Employment (the registration number will appear on their headed paper). Agencies which specialise in one country are mentioned in the country chapters. The following au pair and/or nanny agencies all deal with a number of European countries:

Aaron Employment Agency, Suite C, The Courtyard, Stanley Road, Tunbridge Wells, Kent TN1 2RJ (01892 546601).

Academy Au Pair & Nanny Agency, 42 Cedarhurst Drive, Eltham, London SE9 5LP (0181-294 1191).

All Aboard, PO Box 12188, Benoryn 1502, South Africa (011-425-3312). Sends South African au pairs to Belgium, Netherlands, France and Germany and on student visas to Italy and Spain. R180 registration fee and R400 placement fee.

Anglo Continental Au Pair Placement Agency, 21 Middleton Ave, Hove, E. Sussex BN3 4PH (01273 705959).

Anglo Nannies, Beverley Avenue, London SW20 0RL (0181-944 6677). Specialise in Turkey but also strong on USA, Italy and Geneva area.

Anglo Pair Agency, 40 Wavertree Road, Streatham Hill, London SW2 3SP (0181-674 3605).

The Au Pair Agency, 231 Hale Lane, Edgware, Middlesex HA8 9QF (0181-958 1750).

Au Pair Connections, 20 Greenways, Stoneham Lane, Southampton SO2 2NY (tel/fax 01703 585995).

Au Pair European, 11 The Green, Rowlands Castle, Hants. PO9 6BW (01705 413071). Belgium, Germany and Greece.

Au Pair International, 23 Cowdell St, Warrington, Cheshire WA2 7PP (01925 232622).

Au Pair International, 115 High St, Uckfield, E. Sussex TN22 1RN (01825 761420).

Avalon Agency (incorporating Scattergood's Agency), Thursley House, 53 Station Road, Shalford, Guildford, Surrey GU4 8HA (01483 63640).

Childcare Europe/Childcare America, Trafalgar House, Grenville Place, London NW7 3SA (0181-959 3611/906 3116).

Daylies Agency, 7 Richmond Road, St. Annes, Lancashire FY8 1PE (01253 729762).

Euro-Pair Agency, 28 Derwent Avenue, Pinner, Middlesex HA5 4QJ (0181-421 2100).

European Connections, 164 Park Close, Ashley Park, Walton-on-Thames, Surrey KT12 1EW (tel/fax 01923 220873).

Family Match Recruitment, 7 Quarry Road, Winchester, Hants. SO23 8JF (01962 855799).

Galentina's European Childcare Consultancy, PO Box 51181, Kifissia, 14510 Athens, Greece (tel/fax 1-808 1005).

Girls About Town, 15 Maxim Road, Grange Park, London N21 1EY (0181-364 0034).

Home from Home, Walnut Orchard, Chearsley, Aylesbury, Bucks. HP18 0DA (01844 208561).

Janet White Agency, 67 Jackson Avenue, Leeds LS8 1NS (0113-266 6507).

Jolaine Agency, 18 Escot Way, Barnet, Herts. EN5 3AN (tel/fax 0181-449 1334).

Just the Job, 32 Dovedale Road, West Bridgford, Nottingham NG2 6JA (0115-945 2482).

Langtrain International, Torquay Road, Foxrock, Dublin 18, Eire (01-289 3876).

Mondial Agency, 32 Links Road, West Wickham, Kent BR4 0QW (0181-777 0510).

Quick Help Agency, 307A Finchley Road, London NW3 6EH (0171-794 8666).

Pre-Select Nanny Agency, 924 Stratford Road, Birmingham B11 4BT (0121-702 2100).

Richmond & Twickenham Au Pairs and Nannies, The Old Coach House, Kineton Road, Southam, Leamington Spa, Warks. CV33 0DH (01926 812877). France, Spain, Denmark.

Solihull Agency, 1565 Stratford Road, Hall Green, Birmingham, W. Midlands B28 9JA (0121-733 6444).

South Eastern Au Pair Bureau, 39 Rutland Avenue, Thorpe Bay, Essex SS1 2XJ (01702 601911).

Students Abroad: Whitehorse Chambers, 36 Whitehorse St, Baldock, Herts. SG7 6QQ (01462 490939).

Universal Care, Chester House, 9 Windsor End, Beaconsfield, Bucks. HP9 2JJ (01494 678811).

BUSINESS & INDUSTRY

Although work in offices, mines, shops and factories is not seasonal in the way that work in orchards and hotels is, there are plenty of casual opportunities. You might be needed in a shop during the pre-Christmas rush, or in a swimming pool firm before the summer, or on an Easter-egg production line in February/March. You may be needed to do general labouring while a new motorway is being built or to type reports after an annual conference. Temporary openings are often created during the summer months when regular staff are away on holiday, especially in large department stores and supermarkets.

In fact during a recession, the demand for temporary staff actually increases. Firms which once would not have hesitated to take on extra permanent members of staff become more cautious and prefer to hire people on a short-term basis for peak periods. In some countries the law encourages this practice; for example in Belgium employers are legally required to provide a whole range of benefits after an employee has worked for a certain length of time; to avoid this, they tend to hire people for short periods often through temporary employment agencies.

Shops

It is not only during the Christmas rush that temporary sales staff are recruited, but also for the stock-clearing sales of January and July. Many large shops take an inventory once or twice a year and you can get two days of work counting sheet music or items of women's lingerie. Large stores often advertise in local papers for extra help, whereas smaller shops are more likely to carry a card in their window. It is worth registering with the personnel departments of large stores even before they advertise. The most important qualification for shop work is a presentable appearance. Not having an extensive wardrobe can be a hindrance in some shops; for example if you have been living out of your rucksack for a while, you are unlikely to make the right sort of impression at Saks of Fifth Avenue. Since people who serve in shops have a high public profile, you will normally be expected to have your papers in order. Marcel Staats from the Netherlands has worked in shops around the world from a corner store in Manhattan to Woolworths in Sydney. According to Marcel, references are very important in the retail business. So always ask for one, no matter how short a time you have been employed.

Even monolingual people may find shop work outside the English-speaking world by approaching shopkeepers who sell primarily to tourists. You could present yourself to a carpet merchant in a coastal Turkish town or to an electronics shop in a Japanese shopping precinct favoured by American tourists and offer to sell (initially) on commission. Not only will your fluency in English be an asset but your enthusiasm about the product for sale may inspire confidence in your compatriots. Make sure the percentage you are given is worthwhile; the range will be 2%-20% depending on the value of the goods (lower for video recorders and higher for cheap souvenirs). If you have a working knowledge of the language of the country, you might try to get work in the English language bookstore in a foreign city.

Selling

Readers with well developed business instincts should read the chapter on *Enterprise* which suggests many ways to market a product independently. But if you can't make earrings or find snails to peddle, you might consider becoming a salesperson for a company. Although technically you would be working for an employer, in practice it can be close to self-employment, since the income you earn will be geared to your own efforts.

If you examine the small ads of any newspaper in the world, you'll find offers of untold riches for little effort. Often they will employ euphemisms such as 'manager's assistant' for salesperson. Employers will rarely be troubled by your lack of a work permit; as long as you sell their product, many are quite happy to pay your commission in cash with no questions asked. Even in times of high local unemployment, there is usually scope for foreign sales staff; this may be either because their accent and nationality match up with the product (e.g. selling English language courses in Italy) or, more generally, because there is a lot of inbuilt resistance to selling on commission, especially on account of the insecurity involved.

Commissioned selling usually takes place door to door. Whether it is encyclopaedia or frozen steaks which you are flogging, you will be given some training which normally includes a set spiel to learn by heart. Even sceptics have been surprised by the effectiveness of this method, and after the spiel works for you once, you can repeat it with more feeling the next time.

The two qualifications you must have to be a successful salesperson are an outgoing, confident personality and a lack of squeamishness about twisting the truth. Many products sold door to door are of dubious value, for example travellers have written from Ireland to South Africa about their employment as salesmen of 'genuine original paintings' which they soon discover are actually made in Taiwanese factories. Depending on your scruples, you might want to conduct your own little investigation into both the quality of the product and the business practices of the company before committing yourself. At least find out how long they have been in business and try to dig up a bank reference if possible, especially if they are trying to recruit from abroad.

Although there may be nothing dubious about the quality of the encyclopaedia being sold, some of the sales tactics may make you feel uncomfortable, such as accusing parents from lower income brackets that they will be harming their children's future if they don't sign on the dotted line.

Selling every day objects like brushes or fire extinguishers is less lucrative but your success rate may be higher than if you're selling something as expensive as encyclopaedia or property. Make sure you are not expected to buy the goods first, even on an alleged sale or return basis. Lodge a deposit with your wholesalers if necessary, but make clear that this is a precaution against your potential dishonesty rather than against your possible failure as a salesman.

Although some salesmen must depend solely on commission, others are paid a minimal salary before commission. Others are given quite generous perks, such as a vehicle and hotel vouchers. Working holidaymakers in Australia are regularly hired to sell pens on behalf of a Sydney charity and may even be given a caravan in which to travel and live. When people detect that you are not a career salesman but somebody funding a holiday in their country they may show hospitality (without any intention of buying your product) which will compensate for the hostility you encounter elsewhere.

Not all commissioned selling takes place door to door, and you may feel happier if you don't run the risk of being mistaken for a Mormon or a Jehovah's Witness and having doors slammed in your face. For example 'telesales' are gaining in popularity in Europe after being commonplace in North America for some time. Chris Daniels found an evening job in Minneapolis trying to persuade past members of a dinner club to rejoin:

> *There were lots of advertisements for people to sell door to door or by phone, and these firms seemed keen to hire people with an English accent. First it was necessary to learn a sales pitch which would be repeated continuously for four hours each evening to a surprisingly tolerant if somewhat uninterested audience. We were paid a fairly low wage (which suited me better than commission) and there was a very high turnover of employees. I recommend that people look into this kind of work which will provide a modest income while looking for something better. You never know, perhaps you'll discover that with the help of your foreign charm, you are a born salesman.*

Ben Nakoneczny did this job for a London newspaper but gave up after a couple of weeks when he noticed that 'the most successful salespeople were the most obnoxious and least genuine.'

There are other ways of avoiding the possibility of slammed doors. For example you might get a job selling ice cream by driving a van around suburban Detroit or by roaming the beaches of the Côte d'Azur. You might be hired as a demonstrator in a department store whose main task is merely to give away as many samples of shampoo or cheese as possible. You might get a job (though these are usually badly paid) distributing advertising leaflets around a neighbourhood, which means you don't have to confront your 'victims'. Sometimes companies hire people to 'warm up' potential customers so that the hard saleman can take over. This may consist of door to door visits or of accosting people in the street to collect their names and telephone numbers in order that others may phone them up later to sell, say, life insurance; payment is for each genuine name and number. You can always explain this system to sympathetic passers-by who may be persuaded to disclose their particulars just so you can collect your 50p.

Market Research

Many people who would baulk at approaching strangers in order to sell them something are much more willing to collect information from strangers. Surprisingly, fluency in the language of the country is not always a prerequisite since there are firms in major European cities which operate on a pan-European scale and hire English-speakers to telephone from a list of English-speakers and so on. Of course your chances of being hired are better if you are bilingual. This is a requirement of CLC Language Services (73 New Bond St, London W1Y 9DD) an important agency in the field of international market research and marketing.

Like selling, market research can be done door to door, on the street or by telephone and the latter medium can be especially pleasant. Mike Tunnicliffe scoured the local *Yellow Pages* while he was in New Zealand and secured a market research job:

> *The work proved interesting, doing door to door interviews, but there really wasn't sufficient work to sustain one. It would have been useful as a second job.*

Another variation especially in the US involves canvassing for a charity such as Greenpeace.

Commerce

Students and recent graduates in business, commerce or economics may wish to investigate career-related placements in over 75 countries with AIESEC — a French acronym for International Association for Students of Economics and Management, — whose UK headquarters are at 29-31 Cowper St, 2nd Floor, London EC2A 4AP (0171-336 7939). Participants must be active members of their campus AIESEC committee and submit their applications to their local university branch. Placements last 2-18 months; applications for summer positions must be submitted by the end of November. The US headquarters is at 135 West 50th St, 20th Floor, New York, NY 10020 (212-757-3774). An alternative for American university students is the International Student Exchange Program (University Hall Room 2214, 604 Morgan, University of Illinois, Chicago, IL 60607) which allows a limited number of accounting, marking/finance and engineering majors to work for a year in a range of countries from Holland to Hong Kong.

Interspeak Ltd (The Coach House, Blackwood Estate, Blackwood, Lanarkshire ML11 0JG; 01555 894219) may be able to arrange two to six month traineeships *(stages)* in France, Spain, Italy and Germany in the fields of marketing, international trade, computing or tourism. Successful candidates live with host families. They also arrange jobs for Europeans in the UK. Their booking fee is £250 for British students.

English is the commercial language of the world, so English speaking people with office skills and a knowledge of the country's language are often in demand. Trained secretaries who are fluent in a European language should be able to arrange work within the EU (see chapter on EU Employment for information about the recruitment procedures of the Commission of the European Communities). At one time suitable candidates could fix up work through a UK agency such as the long-established International Secretaries; however with the single market individuals are better placed going to interim agencies in their destination countries. Agencies such as Merrow Employment Agency Ltd (73 New Bond St, London W1Y 9DD) and Sheila Burgess International (4 Cromwell Place, London SW7 2JE, and 62 rue St Lazare, Paris) deal with senior bilingual and multilingual secretarial positions in Europe. Agency posts tend to be long term, and for highly experienced secretaries. If you pore over the classified ads in English language dailies abroad, you may eventually secure a job for which fluent English is needed, for example to write explanations of delays in shipment or in payment to British agents.

Secretarial and employment agencies from Brussels to Brisbane can be especially useful to travellers who are qualified to work as office temps. You will have to sit for a typing test and in some cases a spelling test. Be warned that temp agencies abroad (Australia in particular) often administer these tests more rigorously than they do in Britain. You should register with more than one agency. If you work for such an agency before travelling abroad, ask if they have any overseas branches. Multinationals such as Manpower (whose UK administration is at 66 Chilten St, London W1M 1PR), Drake and Western Staff Services can provide a list of offices and, if you have not disgraced yourself, a letter of introduction. Drake Office Overload goes further and promises anyone who works successfully for them for at least three months a Career Passport which will be recognised by their agencies worldwide. No matter how briefly you have worked for an agency, request a letter of reference. If you want to work for the same agency in another country, you can bypass the typing and other tests.

Other Opportunities in Business

One interesting area of commerce is information technology, computing and word-processing. People who have programmed or operated computers can profitably take their knowledge abroad. Accountancy skills are similarly in demand in many countries.

Another kind of job which requires an advanced skill is that of translator. If you are literate in two languages, you should register with translation agencies which can be found in most big cities abroad. You can also enquire at universities where there is a fluctuating demand for people able to translate technical and academic papers (rather than racy novels). After a year of living in Germany, James Spach had achieved the required proficiency in German and could earn about DM300 in a weekend translating a paper.

Finding a job as a delivery person is usually quite easy. Contact take-out pizza or Chinese restaurants in North America, mail order houses, stationers, Interflora, etc. If you are settled in one place and are an early riser, you can usually find a job as a newspaper boy/girl or (in countries where milk is still delivered to the doorstep) a milkman. If you run out of money on a Thursday or Friday, presenting yourself at the offices of the local newspaper as a delivery person might see you through the weekend. People are also needed by the telephone company to deliver new directories once every year or two. If you have a vehicle, even if just a bicycle, contact a courier firm or set yourself up as a messenger in the financial centre of a big city.

One enterprising business idea is to become a taxi driver. You can approach the largest taxi companies and ask if they recruit trainees. This is something you have to stick at to make a worthwhile income, since your technique will improve substantially with practice. If you already have a portable skill such as experience as a mechanic, you'll probably have no trouble finding casual opportunities wherever you go.

Labouring

Labouring jobs have traditionally been a source of instant money for men. The ease with which you can find manual industrial work depends on the local labour supply and these days a shortage is a rare thing. Anyone with some building experience and a set of tools stands a good chance of finding work abroad. *Overseas Jobs Express* carries adverts for building contractors, especially for work in Germany, which plumbers, carpenters, etc. may want to follow up. Within the EU it is also a great advantage to have an E101, documentary proof that you are self-employed (see chapter on *EU Employment*).

The best idea is to concentrate on areas of sudden expansion, such as Eurodisney in the 1980s, world exhibitions or major sporting events like the Winter Olympics, but preferably in remote or otherwise undesirable places, for example land bases for oil and gas exploration, new mining developments, motorway construction, etc. Another possibility is to offer your services in a ski resort out of season when chalets and hotels are being remodelled and expanded. Something which has worked in the past couple of years in the US is to show up after major disasters like the hurricane which flattened some Florida communities and the Los Angeles earthquake. In times of crisis the authorities might not be too bothered about working visas. Check the *Yellow Pages* for furniture removal firms. Wherever you are and especially in areas where holiday homes are being built or renovated, it is worth keeping your eyes open for buildings under construction and making enquiries.

If you are making local enquiries, make contact with the British labourers already employed by frequenting the same pubs that they do (where much of the hiring takes place). Without an industrial skill you're more likely to get taken on by cowboy firms which tend to pay higher wages to foreign workers than to locals but provide no job protection or welfare benefits. Horror stories persist of unpaid or radically reduced wages and disappearing agents.

Sometimes there is an early morning meeting place for hopeful labour, perhaps outside the casual employment office in big cities or in the town square of smaller communities. As a working holiday maker you may be rather conspicuous among the desperados, winos, and illegal immigrants waiting to be picked up by an employer. Or pay an early morning call on likely businesses such as haulage contractors. This system is of course highly erratic, and it might be less depressing to advertise yourself locally as 'Instant Labour' which could lead to something more stable.

There are lots of industrial activities apart from construction which require labourers. In large ports like Rotterdam, Hamburg, Goteborg or Seattle there is work to be had cleaning out tankers or doing general wharf work; freelance stevedores are in an ideal position to earn good money in short bursts. Unfortunately dockers in most countries belong to powerful and exclusive unions. If possible get to know a union member and ask them to contact you whenever there is a need for extra casuals.

Unskilled labourers are often needed by landscape contractors and related businesses. Writing from Florida, Floyd Creamer has a suggestion for enterprising individuals:

In any city there are tree trimming companies which will take you on temporarily if you bring customers with you. That is, if you tell a company that you know several people who want tree service, they will hire you as 'ground crew', even women and undocumented aliens. Go to a flea market or similar place with lots of pedestrians and talk to as many people as possible. Offer tree trimming/pruning, tree removal, stump grinding, hedge trimming and brush hauling. Offer a free estimate and get their name, address and phone number. After you get some leads (I got 20 in one morning at a busy Fort Lauderdale flea market), call some tree services and explain the situation. There is lots of money in trees, enough for me to start my own company.

Factory Work

Production lines impose a terrible tyranny: if you fall behind packing those Mars bars or calibrating those petrol pumps, you will cause chaos, just as falling off a ski tow causes everything to grind to a halt. But if you are willing to tackle this sort of work (and it is possible to do anything for a short period) you can save a handy sum. Factories in which the pressures are less, where your bunglings are tolerated and you are permitted to switch jobs, tend to pay lower wages but are more fun. In a factory where high standards are set you will have to expect a certain amount of abuse (usually good-natured) on account of your being a 'sloppy British workman only interested in tea and striking' or a 'naïve and dreamy student'.

Some of our contributors have thoroughly enjoyed the work they have done in factories abroad: Richard Adams who worked for a shock absorber factory in the industrial Ruhr Valley of Germany was delighted to participate in the racing department and to attend weekend rallies since these were both exciting and very well paid; Chris Daniels found interesting and rewarding work in a Minnesota factory which provided employment for handicapped people; Steve Smith, who worked in a crate-making factory in Ghana, enjoyed the challenge of seeing everything run smoothly. Another possible perk is that you may be entitled to take home free samples of whatever the factory produces, so try to get a job with Carlsberg in Copenhagen or Rowntrees in York rather than Fisons or Dulux. Even those travellers who have found little job satisfaction in their factory jobs have been pleased with the pay packets.

Canning and food processing factories are a good bet because of their highly seasonal nature. Check the brand names on tinned or frozen foods (e.g. Lock-woods, Smedleys, Bird's Eye, Green Giant) and contact them for casual work. Advertising promises such as 'Only two hours from the field to the freezer' indicate the urgency of the labour requirements in this industry.

The Manpower Agency can be a worthwhile source of employment wherever you are, since it operates in over 30 countries. In addition to factory work, it is also strong on temporary warehouse packing and clerical jobs. You can locate Manpower in the telephone directories of many big cities.

VOLUNTARY WORK

Voluntary work can provide a unique stepping stone to further adventures abroad and is often an adventure in itself. Many schemes are open to all nationalities and avoid work permit hassles. By participating in a project such as digging wells in a Turkish village, looking after orphaned Eskimo children or just helping out at a youth hostel, you have the unique opportunity to live and work in a remote community, and the chance to meet up with young people from many countries who can point you towards new job prospects. You may be able to improve or acquire a language skill and to learn something of the customs of the society in which you are volunteering. You will also gain practical experience, for instance in the fields of construction, archaeology, or social welfare which will stand you in good stead when applying for paid jobs elsewhere.

It should be pointed out that the majority of voluntary jobs undertaken abroad leave the volunteer out-of-pocket. Many organisations, especially in the US, charge volunteers large sums to cover the cost of recruiting, screening, interviewing, pre-departure orientation, insurance, etc. on top of travel, food and lodging, which can be disillusioning for anyone who thinks that a desire to help the world is enough. After participating in several prearranged voluntary projects in the United States, Catherine Brewin did not resent the fee she had paid to Involvement Volunteers (whose activities are described below):

The whole business of paying to do voluntary work is a bit hard to swallow. But having looked into the matter quite a bit, it does seem to be the norm. While it may be a bit unfair (who knows how much profit or loss these voluntary organisations make or how worthy their projects?), most people I've met did seem to feel good about the experience. The group I was with did raise the odd comment about it all, but did not seem unduly concerned. However I should mention that most were around 18 years old and their parents were paying some if not all the costs.

If you are interested in short or long term voluntary projects you might like to consult one of the following books:

The International Directory of Voluntary Work (Vacation-Work, 1993) £8.95.
Volunteer Work (Central Bureau) £8.99.
Volunteer! — The Comprehensive Guide to Voluntary Service in the US and Abroad (CIEE, 205 East 42nd St, New York, NY 10017, USA) 1992 edition, $8.95 plus postage.
Volunteer Vacations (Chicago Review Press/Independent Publishers Group, 814 N Franklin St, Chicago, IL 60610; 800-888-4741) 1993 edition, $11.95. 240 organisations listed.
Invest Yourself (Commission on Voluntary Service and Action, c/o Susan Angus, PO Box 117, New York, NY 10009). $8 including US postage.

The last three would be of special interest to Americans and to others wishing to work in the US.

An interesting possibility for working your way as a volunteer is to offer to assist people with special needs to take 'independent' holidays. The charities

Project Phoenix Trust (31a St Vincents Road, Westcliff on Sea, Essex SS0 7PP; 01702 349968) and the Disaway Trust (2 Charles Road, Merton Park, London SW19 3BD; 0181-543 3431) arrange for able-bodied volunteers to accompany disabled holidaymakers abroad for 10-14 days. The former charges volunteers a quarter of their costs, whereas the latter charges a half.

Bear in mind that voluntary work, especially in the developing world, can be not only tough and character-building but also disillusioning (see Mary Hall's description of her year at a Uganda clinic on page 450). And just as the working traveller must be alert to exploitation in paid jobs, so he or she should be careful in voluntary situations as well. Misunderstandings can arise, and promises can be broken just as easily in the context of unpaid work. Occasionally eager young volunteers are forced to conclude that the people in charge of the organisation charge volunteers well in excess of essential running costs. Fortunately the experiences of one volunteer in Afria are rare: he claims to have discovered that the community development projects described in the literature from an organisation in Sierra Leone did not exist and furthermore the director had previously jumped bail from Freetown CID.

Carina Strutt's experiences in Central America are also uncommon, but worth bearing in mind when considering joining a privately-run project sight unseen. In good faith she went to work for an environmental project and spent most of her time there painting T-shirts for the owners who wanted it in time for their holiday in Australia. Worse, they had scant regard for the local people and treated the local people with scant respect. (Needless to say, neither project is included in this book.)

Workcamps

Voluntary work in developed countries often takes the form of workcamps which accept unskilled short-term labour. As part of an established international network of voluntary organisations they are not subject to the irregularities of some privately run projects. As well as providing volunteers with the means to live cheaply for two to four weeks in a foreign country, workcamps enable volunteers to become involved in what is usually useful work for the community, to meet people from many different backgrounds and to 'increase their awareness of other lifestyles, social problems and their responsibility to society' as one volunteer has described it. According to one of the leading organisers, workcamps are a 70-year-old programme of conflict resolution and community development and an inexpensive and personal way to travel, live and work in an international setting.

Andrew Boyle, who has done a variety of jobs abroad subsequently, got off to an excellent start by joining several European workcamps:

*I participated in three voluntary workcamps: two in West Germany and one in the French Alps. The former, particularly, were excellent value, both in the nature of the work (*Umweltschutz *or environmental protection) and in that the group of about 20 became part of the local community — meeting the locals in the* kneipen *or socialising with the 'Ziwis' (conscientious objectors doing community service instead of military service). These camps are an excellent introduction to travelling for 16 to 20 year olds, say, sixth formers who have never been away from a family type social structure. I suspect that their value would be more limited to an experienced traveller.*

Within Europe, and to a lesser extent further afield, there is a massive effort to co-ordinate workcamp programmes. This normally means that the prospective volunteer should apply in the first instance to the appropriate organisation in his own country, or to a centralised international headquarters. The vast majority of camps take place in the summer months, and camp details are normally published in March/April. Understandably, these organisations charge £4-6 for a copy of their international programmes. It is necessary to pay a registration fee (usually about £50-80) to join a workcamp, which includes board and lodging (but not of course travel). In developing countries, there may be an extra charge to help finance future projects. The vast majority of placements are made between mid-April and mid-May.

The largest workcamp organisation is Service Civil International with branches in 27 countries. The UK branch is International Voluntary Service (IVS) (addresses below). Another major organisation is the Christian Movement for Peace which has its International Secretariat in Brussels with national offices in the UK, France, Italy, Germany, Netherlands, Belgium, Portugal, Switzerland, Hungary, Romania and Latvia. Occasionally in the pages of this book, we have included foreign addresses of workcamp organisations for the benefit of long-term travellers who are already in the country in which they want to join a workcamp.

Other workcamp organisations are listed below. When requesting information always send a stamped self-addressed envelope or international reply coupon, since these organisations are charities which need to keep costs to a minimum and in most cases cannot reply to letters without a stamp. (In late 1994 the long-established Quaker International Social Projects had to suspend opertions due to lack of finance.)

International Voluntary Service (IVS), Old Hall, East Bergholt, Colchester, Essex CO7 6TQ (01206 298215/fax 299043). IVS North: Castlehill House, 21 Otley Road, Headingley, Leeds LS6 3AA (0113-220 4600) and IVS Scotland (7 Upper Bow, Edinburgh EH1 2JN).

Christian Movement for Peace (CMP), 186 St. Paul's Road, Balsall Heath, Birmingham B12 8LZ (0121-446 5704/fax 446 4060). Standard participation fee is £42 plus membership of £12 (£6 unwaged). Additional national addresses are available from the CMP European Secretariat, 3 Avenue du Parc Royal, 1020 Brussels, Belgium.

Concordia, 8 Brunswick Place, Hove, Sussex BN3 1ET (01273 772086).

United Nations Association (UNA Wales) International Youth Service, Welsh Centre for International Affairs, Temple of Peace, Cathays Park, Cardiff CF1 3AP (01222 223088/fax 665557). Majority of camps cost £70 to join. Run a separate North/South Exchange Programme for selected volunteers to work in sub-Saharan Africa and Southern Asia.

Ecumenical Youth Council in Europe (EYCE), PO Box 185, 00161 Helsinki, Finland (0-180 2449). Organises work/study camps in Europe for Christians.

Internationale Bouworde/International Building Companions, rue des Carmes 24, 6900 Marche-en-Famenne, Belgium. Projects to build on behalf of disadvantaged people in Austria, Belgium, France, Germany, Italy, Netherlands, etc.

ATD Fourth World, 48 Addington Square, London SE5 7LB (0171-703 3231). Workcamps (mostly manual) and street workshops concerned with fighting poverty and social deprivation. Fee for two-week projects is F450. International headquarters: ATD Quart Monde, 107 avenue du Général Leclerc, 95480 Pierrelaye, France.

Many of these recruitment organisations are heavily over-subscribed and competition to join the camps is keen. You are not normally expected to have workcamp experience in your home country before being placed abroad, though this is not a fixed rule. However Third World camps rarely take inexperienced volunteers. It should be noted that for workcamps in Eastern Europe and developing nations, you will more than likely have to be interviewed in Britain before you can be placed, or attend orientation meetings. European organisations have traditionally accepted volunteers of all nationalities; however it has become more difficult for nationals outside the European Union to be accepted. This is due to the fact that some people have been abusing the system by applying for a workcamp, using the letter of invitation at immigration control and then not showing up.

American young people should apply to one of the major workcamp organisations in the US:

Council on International Educational Exchange (CIEE), 205 E. 42nd St, New York, NY 10017 (212-661-1414 ext 1141). Their directory of opportunities is available from April and costs $12. Placement fee is $165 for overseas workcamps.

SCI-USA (Service Civil International), c/o Innisfree Village, Route 2, Box 506, Crozet, Virginia 22932 (804-823-1826). Workcamp list and application forms costs $2. Application fee $80-100 ($200 for CIS, Mongolia and Romania).

Volunteers for Peace, 43 Tiffany Road, Belmont, Vermont 05730 (802-259-2759/fax 259-2922). Annual membership $10. VFP publish an up-to-date *International Workcamp Directory* with over 800 listings in 50 countries, available from mid-April. Camp registration normally $150.

Quaker Information Center, 1501 Cherry St, Philadelphia, PA 19102 (215-241-7024). Send minimum of $3 for details of 'Friendly Camps' in the US and workcamps around the world.

The majority of projects are environmental and involve the conversion/reconstruction of historic buildings and building community facilities. Some of the more interesting projects in 1994 included building adventure playgrounds for children, renovating an open-air museum in Latvia, organising youth concerts in Armenia, constructing boats for sea-cleaning in Japan, looking after a farm-school in Slovakia during the holidays, helping peasant farmers in central France to stay on their land, excavating a Roman villa in Germany, forest fire spotting in Italy, plus a whole range of schemes with the disabled and elderly, conservation work and the study of social and political issues. It is sometimes possible to move from project to project throughout the summer, particularly in countries such as France or Morocco where the workcamp movement is highly developed.

Living conditions (and the quality of food in particular) vary greatly. The working week is 30 hours though it can stretch to a maximum of 40 hours, spread over five or six days. On the whole, camps are under the direction of one or two leaders but participants often help in the decision making. Social events and excursions are invariably included in the programme and some organisations arrange study sessions. Although English is the language of many international camps, some of them do require knowledge of a foreign language.

Archaeology

Taking part in archaeological excavations is another popular form of voluntary work, but volunteers are usually expected to make a contribution towards their board and lodging. Also, you may be asked to bring your own trowel, work clothes, tent, etc. Archaeology Abroad (31-34 Gordon Square, London WC1H 0PY) is an excellent source of information, as they publish bulletins in March, May and October with details of excavations needing volunteers; in 1994 between 700 and 1,500 definite places on sites were offered to subscribers. They do stress however that they prefer applications from people with a definite interest in the subject. An annual subscription costs £6 ($20/£8 overseas).

Another valuable list of over 200 digs worldwide needing volunteers is the *Archaeological Fieldwork Opportunities Bulletin* published by the Archaeological Institute of America in Boston (fax 617-353-6550) and available from Kendall/

Hunt Publishing, 4050 Westmark Drive, PO Box 1840, Dubuque, Iowa 52004-1840. It is published every January and costs $12.50 (US postage included; add $4.50 for foreign air mail). It includes details of digs from Kentucky to Sri Lanka.

For those who are not students of archaeology, the chances of finding a place on an overseas dig will be greatly enhanced by having some digging experience nearer to home. Details of British excavations looking for volunteers are published in *British Archaeological News,* available for £18 (£10 for students) from the Council for British Archaeology, Bowes Morrell House, 111 Walmgate, York YO1 2UA (01904 671417). Sometimes archaeologists advertise for volunteers, mainly in the *Guardian, Independent* and *Scotsman.*

Anthony Blake joined a dig sponsored by the University of Reims and warns that 'archaeology is hard work, and applicants must be aware of what working for eight hours in the baking heat means!' Nevertheless Anthony found the company excellent and the opportunity to improve his French welcome.

Israel is a country particularly rich in archaeological opportunities, many of them organised through the universities. Digs provide an excellent means of seeing remote parts of the country much more cheaply than could otherwise be accomplished. Conditions vary, but are generally primitive. Jennifer McKibben found 'washing (apart from hands and face) was allowed only one day in four, when one enjoyed the luxury of a communal hose-pipe shower to remove all of the sand and grime that easily accumulates after four days of digging in the desert.' Archaeological digs are discussed in the chapter on Israel.

Conservation

People interested in protecting the environment can often slot into conservation organisations abroad. One enterprising traveller in South Africa looked up the 'green directory' in a local library, contacted a few of the projects listed which interested him and was invited to work at a cheetah reserve near Johannesburg in exchange for accommodation and food.

To fix up a short-term project ahead of time, contact the British Trust for Conservation Volunteers (BTCV) which runs a programme of international projects in Iceland, France, Portugal, Italy, Greece, Hungary and most other European countries, as well as North America, Brazil and Japan; further details are available from the International Development Unit, BTCV, 36 St. Mary's St, Wallingford, Oxfordshire OX10 0EU (01491 839766/fax 839646). Costs vary from £60 to £200 excluding travel from the UK.

American readers should contact Conservation International, 1015 18th St NW, Suite 1000, Washington, DC 20036; 202-429-5660) which recruits volunteers to work for between one and eight weeks to preserve rainforests and their ecosystems in Botswana, Brazil, Costa Rica and many other countries.

The international system of working-for-keep on organic farms is another good way of visiting unexplored corners of the world cheaply. A description of the organisation WWOOF (Willing Workers on Organic Farms) may be found in the *Agriculture* chapter. Also, staying on communes, peace centres and the like may be of interest, as discussed in the same chapter.

The Traveler's Earth Repair Network or TERN (c/o Michael Pilarski, PO Box 1064, Tonasket, WA 98855, USA; tel/fax 509-485-2705) invites anyone planning a journey anywhere in the world to contact them for a list of potential hosts involved in projects such as tree-planting, organic gardening, etc. Prospective travellers fill out a TERN application form for a fee of US$50 ($35 students) in return for a computer list of about 150 appropriate hosts and organisations which may be looking for volunteers or apprentices.

Involvement Volunteers Association Inc (PO Box 218, Port Melbourne, Victoria 3207, Australia; tel/fax 03-646 5504) arranges short-term individual, group and team voluntary placements in Australia, New Zealand, California, Hawaii, Fiji, Papua New Guinea, Thailand, India, Germany, Finland, Italy and Latvia. Most projects are concerned with conservation such as assisting landholders with revegetation, researchers with biology and zoology, and National Parks authorities with development. Other projects are with community-based social service organisations assisting disadvantaged people as teachers, specialists or general helpers. The programme fee is A$400 covering any number of placements (which last 2-12 weeks). North American applications should be sent to Involvement Corps Inc, 15515 Sunset Blvd. Suite 108, Pacific Palisades, CA 90272 (tel/fax 310-459 1022); while the address for placements in Europe is Postfach 110224, 3400 Göttingen, Germany.

Catherine Brewin from St. Albans joined two IV projects in the US. Her reaction is typical of many people who undertake voluntary work of any kind in exotic locations:

After a fortnight of doing general maintenance at a Conference Centre in southern California, I flew to Hawaii to work at a centre for mentally handicapped people. This was a considerably more restrictive environment than LA and involved us living with the handicapped residents ('clients') in a fenced off complex some distance from the nearest town. Again we did some physical work such as tree planting and weeding, and also took the clients on day trips and organised a disco. It was not an easy place to be and could hardly have been more of an antithesis to what the mind conjures up when you think of Hawaii, but it's amazing how your sense of humour and the people around you can pull you through, and I think we all learned from the experience.

Both the projects demanded quite a bit of flexibility. Things were seldom apparent or well organised, and there were times when we were unsure as to what we were supposed to do, or felt that we were expected to work on tasks totally outside our brief. I think anyone considering joining a voluntary work project should be aware that this may be the case. I must admit that for me, two fortnight-long projects was enough and I was happy to move on, leave a group situation and start travelling and doing what I wanted to do.

There are several organisations whose function it is to help and staff scientific expeditions, for example Earthwatch (680 Mt. Auburn Street, PO Box 403, Watertown, Massachusetts 02272-9924; or in Europe, Belsyre Court, 57 Woodstock Road, Oxford OX2 6HU), an international non-profit organisation which recruits over 4,000 volunteers a year to assist professional, scientific field research expeditions around the world. The catch is that you have to pay to participate in these fortnight-long scientific projects, anything from $500/£340 to study beavers in Minnesota National Park to $2,600/£1,765 to research dolphin intelligence in Hawaii. Prices do not include travel.

Two similar scientific expedition organisations both based in California which use paying volunteers are the Foundation for Field Research (PO Box 910078, San Diego, CA 92191-0078; 619-687-3584) and the University of California Research Expeditions Program (UREP, University of California, Berkeley CA 94720; 510-642-6586). Send $5 worth of postal coupons for details of their projects worldwide. The costs for a UREP project range from $1,000 to $2,000. A new organisation Europe Conservation Italy (Via Giusti 5, 20154 Milan, Italy; 02-33 10 33 44) sends paying volunteers to various projects including a gibbon centre in Thailand and dolphin research in Croatia.

Various organisations scattered throughout the pages of the country chapters run conservation or scientific projects. Most of these require their volunteers to be completely self-financing.

Developing Countries

Commitment, no matter how fervent, is not enough to work in an aid project in the developing world. You must be able to offer some kind of useful training or skill. In Britain, the government's aid organisation is the Overseas Development Administration (Abercrombie House, Eaglesham Road, East Kilbride, Glasgow G75 8EA), which can send a general brochure 'The ODA Guide to Working Overseas for the AID Programme'. Like other major aid organisations, the ODA requires a commitment of at least two years in addition to specialist skills.

The three main organisations in the field are:

VSO (Voluntary Service Overseas), Enquiries Unit, 317 Putney Bridge Rd, London SW15 2PN (0181-780 2266 or 0181-780 1331 24-hour answerphone). Recruits volunteers in the fields of education, health, natural resources, technical trades and engineering, business and social work. VSO pays a modest local wage, various grants, national insurance, provides accommodation, health insurance and return flights. Volunteers need to be aged 20-70, qualified and experienced, without dependent children. Also have a pilot training programme for students in higher education on shorter-term projects; details from Overseas Training Programme, 17 Lincoln St, Brighton, Sussex BN2 2UG (01273 621446).

International Cooperation for Development, Unit 3, Canonbury Yard, 190a New North Rd, Islington, London N1 7BJ (0171-354 0883).

United Nations Association International Service, (UNAIS, Suite 3a, Hunter House, 57 Goodramgate, York YO1 2LS (01904 647799). Relevant qualifications, working experience and skills are essential. Third World community work experience an advantage.

Several organisations attempt to make it possible for school-leavers (normally in their gap year) to undertake useful voluntary work for six to ten months. GAP Activity Projects Ltd. (44 Queen's Road, Reading, Berks. RG1 4BB; 01734 594914) organises voluntary work placements in 33 countries around the world for young people aged 18 or 19 in their gap year between school and further education. Volunteers undertake social work, conservation work, act as teaching assistants in schools and, increasingly, teach English as a foreign language. Among the most interesting of the mostly six month placements is an attachment to a theatre in Namibia and farm work in the Falkland Islands. Applicants pay a fee (£250-395), their own airfares and medical costs, and receive free accommodation and food. Those interested should apply in the September of their last year at school. GAP is an exchange organisation in that it brings young people from overseas to the UK to undertake social work or act as teaching assistants.

A similar range of voluntary opportunities for about 200 school leavers aged 17-19 is available through the Project Trust (Hebridean Centre, Ballyhough, Isle of Coll, Argyll PA78 6TE; 0187 93444), an educational trust which places volunteers overseas each year in posts where they have the opportunity to do useful work for a year between school and higher education. The current programme includes projects in Africa, South & Central America, Asia and the Middle East. Most of the work offered falls into the categories of English language/conversation assistants and social service. Participants must raise a proportion of the cost of the placement: £2,750 in 1994/5. The Schools Partnership Worldwide (Westminster School, 17 Dean's Yard, London SW1P 3PB) is an educational charity which places school-leavers in schools in Nepal, India, Tanzania, Zimbabwe and Namibia. Participants must raise £600. The chapter *Teaching English* mentions some other voluntary opportunities in the educational field.

Christians Abroad (1 Stockwell Green, London SW9 9HP; 0171-737 7811/ 737 3237) publishes lists of volunteer vacancies open to 'people of any faith or none' in *Opportunities Abroad*. Again, the vast majority of posts are available to people who have a skill that is not available locally. Bumper editions are published in May and October and shorter updates are issued in most other months; an annual subscription costs £5 which includes free entry on a Register of people looking for work abroad. From this you may learn that the International Intern Programme (0171-584 9696) needs volunteers to work in a mountain village in Tenerife at a cost of £30 a week or that Action Health needs a midwife in Madagascar. Their newly set up World Service Enquiry department publishes a free annual directory of voluntary organisatioons active in the Third World, and offers specialised and individual advice on a sliding scale of charges.

The Christian Service Centre (CSC, Unit 3, Holloway St W, Lower Gornal, Dudley, West Midlands DY3 2DZ; 01902 882836) publishes a booklet *Short-Term Service Directory* listing vacancies 'of interest to Christians' with an emphasis on evangelical Christianity (£2.15 including postage). They also publish *Jobs Abroad* in March and September of each year with longer term vacancies, together with the agency or missionary society which is recruiting for the post. One year's subscription costs £3.30 (including postage).

Ecumenical Youth Action is part of the youth wing of the World Council of Churches (150 route de Ferney, PO Box 2100, 1211 Geneva 2, Switzerland; 022-791 6212) and can send details of a small selection of interesting-sounding two to three week workcamps to which interested volunteers apply direct. Countries listed in the 1994 brochure were: Ghana, Togo, India, Indonesia, Myanmar, Pakistan, Philippines, Antigua, Egypt, Lebanon, Syria and Cyprus.

The International Christian Youth Exchange (International Office, Georgen-kirchstr. 70, 10249 Berlin, Germany) runs an exchange programme for people aged 18-25 in nearly 30 countries, about half of which are developing countries. Exchanges normally last one year though there are some six-month placements. In 1994, a UK committee of ICYE was formed: details of the exchange pro-gramme are available from ICYE UK, The Rectory, Princess Margaret Road, East Tilbury, Essex RM18 8PD. The costs of spending a year in the Third World are about £3,000 (and somewhat less in Europe).

The Italian-based charity Centro Studi Terzo Mondo (Via G B Morgagni 39, 20129 Milan) sends volunteers with no particular qualifications to work in a variety of projects in schools, orphanages, etc. in Africa, Asia and Latin America. Canadian Crossroads International (31 Madison Avenue, Toronto, Ont M5R 2S2) sends 200 Canadians to Third World countries to work for four months in community development, health care, agriculture or education.

Many American organisations are active in the developing world. The Partner-ship for Service Learning, 815 Second Avenue, Suite 315, New York, NY 10017 (212-986-0989) offers students and recent graduates a chance to teach or care for disadvantaged people in Jamaica, Liberia, Philippines, Mexico, India and Ecuador. The Institute for International Cooperation and Development (PO Box 103, Williamstown, MA 01267) has projects lasting 6-12 months in Angola, Mozambique, Brazil and Nicaragua which cost $4,300.

The International Rescue Committee (386 Park Avenue South, New York, NY 10016, USA) is a private voluntary agency providing assistance to refugees in Thailand, Cambodia, Georgia, the former Yugoslavia and a number of African countries. They typically hire nurses, physicians, nutritionists, engineers, educators, etc. for a minimum of six months.

Global Volunteers is a non-profit voluntary organisation which sends over 500 paying volunteers a year to various projects lasting from one to three weeks in Africa, Asia, the Caribbean, Central America and Europe (especially the emerging democracies). Trips cost between $300 (for projects in the US) and $2,200, excluding air fares. Details are available from Global Volunteers, 375 E Little Canada Road, Little Canada, Minnesota 55117, USA (toll-free 1-800-487-1074). Similarly Global Service Corps (1472 Filbert St, No. 405, San Francisco, CA 94109) cooperates with grass-roots organisations in Kenya, Thailand and Costa Rica and sends volunteers for two or three weeks (fee $1,500-1,700). World Horizons International (PO Box 662, Bethlehem, CT 06751) sends North American students — including high school pupils — on four to six week summer programmes to a number of Caribbean islands, Costa Rica, Belize, Samoa, etc.

In the course of your travels, you may come across wildlife projects, children's homes, special schools, etc. in which it will be possible to work voluntarily for a short or longer time. You may simply want to join your new Tongan, Bangladeshi or Guatemalan friends in the fields or wherever they are working. You may get the chance to trade your assistance for a straw mat and simple meals but more likely the only rewards will be the experience and the camaraderie.

Some travellers who find themselves in the vicinity of a major disaster think that their assistance will be welcomed. But with no practical skills, they often become a nuisance and a burden to professional aid workers.

People who work in the Third World often experience just as much culture shock on their return home as they did when they first had to adapt to difficult conditions abroad. For a graphic and amusing description of this process see *The Innocent Anthropologist* by Nigel Barley (Penguin).

Work Your Way
in Europe

United Kingdom

Many readers of this book will begin to plan their world travels in Britain, and it is in Britain that they will want to save up an initial travelling fund. The amount of savings will vary from a few pounds to more than a thousand, depending on the ambitiousness of the travel plans and on the individual's willingness to live rough and take risks once he or she sets out. Some people are lucky enough to have a reasonably well paid and stable job as a nurse, postman or computer programmer before they set out on their adventures and will be in a good position to save. Others will have to gather together as many funds as possible from doing casual work at home before pursuing the same activities abroad. Readers in other countries will also be interested in the information contained in this chapter if they are planning a working holiday in Britain.

RED TAPE

Nationals of the European Union (which includes Austria, Sweden, Norway, Finland and Iceland) are not subject to immigration control and are therefore entitled to enter Britain to look for work. For non-EU citizens, most of whom enter on six-month tourist visas (which can normally be renewed on reentering the country after an absence), it is difficult to find legal work. In general the Department of Employment does not issue work permits to unskilled and semi-skilled workers (though unofficial catering work is still abundantly available). Employers will probably ask for your National Insurance Number but will seldom ask to see the actual card, so it is usually sufficient to say that it has been applied for. Some temporary employment agencies are also satisfied by verbal assurances.

There are some special schemes described in this chapter for young people from the United States, Canada, Australia, New Zealand, Eastern Europe, etc. which allow them to work legally in Britain, for example the Seasonal Agricultural Workers Scheme described in the section on harvests below. Another possibility for non-EU citizens is the Training & Work Experience Scheme (TWES) which allows foreign university graduates to work in their field for up to a year. Further details are available from the Overseas Labour Service of the Employment Department (W5, Moorfoot, Sheffield S1 4PQ) whose East European Unit particularly encourages trainees from Central and Eastern Europe. The Overseas Labour Service advice line can be dialled on 0114-259 4074.

Nationals from outside the European Union who are registered as students in the UK are allowed to work up to 20 hours a week. Such students wishing to take a part-time or vacational job while studying in Britain will need to visit their local Jobcentre for a form OSS1. This is an application for an overseas student work permit and contains sections to be completed by the student's educational establishment and potential employer. The Jobcentre decides whether or not to issue a permit depending on local labour market conditions. Accusations are sometimes levelled that some dubious language schools which charge unrealistically low fees for the requisite 15 hours a week of study (as little as £500 for a year) are primarily visa factories, kept in business by the fact that enrolled students may obtain student status from the Home Office. The Home Office is increasingly aware of this dodge and may check that language students are attending classes rather than in employment.

The problem of work permits does not normally arise in the case of voluntary work, though participants will have to have a valid visa to be in Britain (where applicable). Conservation camps and other voluntary projects generally offer an enthusiastic welcome to foreign participants (see section on voluntary work at the end of this chapter). For example Community Service Volunteers (237 Pentonville Road, London N1 9NJ; 0171-278 6601) run an overseas programme in which people of all nationalities aged 18-35 are placed alongside British volunteers in projects with people who need extra help with daily living. During the projects which last from between four and 12 months, food, accommodation, pocket money and travel expenses from the point of entry are paid. The placement fee for those applying from outside Britain is £477.

Non-EU nationals who want to extend their visas or have queries about work permits and other immigration matters should contact the Immigration and Nationality Department of the Home Office at Lunar House, Wellesley Road, Croydon, Surrey CR9 2BY (0181-686 0688); be prepared to wait in a queue both on the telephone and in person. In the past year or two there has been a marked increase in the number of deportations of foreign nationals who have overstayed or are in breach of the terms of their visas. For example there were reports in 1993 and 1994 of large fruit farms being raided by police and dozens of illegal immigrants being detained. Some have suggested that since the introduction of the Single Market, many immigration officials have been under-employed and so spend their days in other pursuits.

Anyone entering the country as a visitor who intends to stay longer than a few weeks should have a water-tight story, something Woden Teachout from Vermont had not prepared:

Coming into the UK I had a horribly distressing immigration experience. On the advice of my travel agent, I had bought a six-month return ticket rather than an open return and expected no problems. Everything went awry. I think it was when I wavered over how long I meant to be in the

*country that the immigration official became suspicious. The lady-turned-
ogre forced me to produce my passport, ticket, money, address book and
wrote down my entire life's history in cramped cursive on the back of my
entrance card. I portrayed myself as a spoilt and privileged child, funded by
Mummy and Daddy in her aimless intercontinental wanderings. When she
at last grudgingly stamped me into the country, she called after me in a
voice thick with derision, 'Do you think you'll ever work for a living?'*
A few weeks later Woden had five different jobs.

Reclaiming Tax

One clear advantage of obtaining legal working holiday status is that you are
entitled to apply for a National Insurance number which you should promptly
do, from the local Department of Social Security (DSS) Benefits Agency office.
Most new employees are put onto the emergency tax code (denoted by 'X' at
the end of your tax code) and immediately begin to forfeit a quarter of their
wages. Since single people are entitled to a personal allowance of £3,445 per
year (1994/95), it is likely that the maximum tax deducted under the PAYE
system (Pay As You Earn) will be in excess of what you owe, assuming you work
for less than 12 months and that you are entitled to claim the allowance.

Both UK residents and Commonwealth nationals can claim personal allowances. Foreign nationals can claim personal allowances if they have been in the
UK for at least 183 days in any tax year. If the total is less than 183 days, they
may be able to claim as a foreign ntional and/or resident of a country with
which the UK has a double taxation agreement. Inland Revenue operates a
telephone information service for the public on 0171-588 4226. But in the world
of taxation, rules are subject to discretionary interpretation, so even if you don't
think you're eligible, it does no harm to put in a claim. When you finish work,
send both parts of the P45 which your employer will give you to your employer's
tax office. When you are ready to leave Britain, complete and submit form P85,
a leaving certificate which asks your intentions with respect to returning to the
UK to work.

Always take the precaution of making photocopies of any forms you send to
Inland Revenue for the purposes of chasing later, and be prepared to wait at
least six weeks. If you leave Britain before the refund is processed, it may be
better to nominate someone locally to forward the money to you. If you have
worked briefly, then travelled for a while and started work again, your next
employer may be able to arrange a tax rebate for you provided you can hand
over the P45 from your previous job.

You can make things easier for yourself by using an accountancy firm which
specialises in tax rebates. They normally keep a percentage (about 15%) of
whatever they get back for you. Try for example one of the following London
firms: Taxback (167 Earls Court Road, London SW5 9RF; 0171-244 6666),
Taxreturn (213 Piccadilly, London W1V 9LD; 0171-437 9182) and Appleton
Taxation Services (186 Hammersmith Road, London W6; 0181-741 1224).

Foreign students are treated the same as UK students and can be exempted
from tax. They should ask their employer for a P38(S) form which exempts
students from paying tax on vacation earnings.

In addition to income tax, you must also pay National Insurance Contributions.
People earning less than £57 per week and foreign students of English or
agriculture (who can present a certificate in English from their institution proving
that they are studying these subjects) can claim exemption. If you earn over £57
you must pay 2% on the first £57 and 9% on earnings above this. The circumstances in which contributions can be reclaimed are exceedingly rare, so companies which advertise their ability to help on this one should be treated with
some suspicion.

UNITED KINGDOM

Thurso

Ullapool

Inverness

Aviemore • Aberdeen

SCOTLAND

Ben Nevis Pitlochry Forfar
Blairgowrie
Firth of Tay

North Sea

GLASGOW EDINBURGH

Belfast

LAKE DISTRICT

Isle of Man

DUBLIN
Leixlip

IRELAND

Llandudno

Cheshire

THE FENS

BIRMINGHAM

Stourport
Worcester

Wisbech King's Lynn

WALES

Pershore
Evesham

Cambridge Lowestoft

Hereford

Saxmundham
Tiptree

Pembroke

Cardiff

BRISTOL Oxford
Abingdon

Chelmsford

River

Bridgwater

Henley LONDON

Westward Ho!

Guildford

Ramsgate

WEST COUNTRY

Southampton

Tonbridge Maidstone Sandwich

Sidmouth

Bournemouth

Kent

Cornwall

Torquay
Plymouth

Brighton

Bognor

Isle of Wight

English Channel

WILLIAM SWAN

Claimants

It is estimated that about a third of the 2.9 million unemployed in Britain are under 26. If you are claiming benefit and then find a temporary job, you will have to sign off, your rent-allowance will be stopped and your file closed. If you know in advance where your employment is going to be, you should ask for form A7 from your local benefit office which allows you to claim rent, etc. at your job destination. You may even be entitled to travel expenses to your new job (e.g. a Welsh hotel or fenland farm). Enquire at your local Jobcentre.

Voluntary or part-time work may affect certain benefits. Further information on this subject is contained in leaflet FB26 *Voluntary and Part-time Workers,* but in general you are allowed to earn no more than £2 a day in addition to out-of-pocket expenses and you cannot be away from home doing voluntary work for more than a fortnight a year. If you are doing voluntary work but are available for work at short notice, you may need to fill in form UB672V.

The rules state that visitors from EU countries qualify for income support and housing benefit if they are looking for work. Despite government attempts to crack down on so-called 'benefits tourists', it remains straightforward to claim from the DSS.

SPECIAL SCHEMES & EXCHANGE ORGANISATIONS

Students and others from EU and non-EU countries may be able to participate in work exchange programmes, many of which charge a substantial placement fee. Careers advisers in universities and colleges should be the best source of information. To take a few specific examples, the organisation BIGA in Switzerland (Sektion Auswanderung und Stagiaires, Monbijoustrasse 43, 3003 Bern; 31-322 29 03) administers a trainee exchange with Britain whereby Swiss graduates can work for up to 18 months in their field. The Spanish agency GIC (Avda. Barón de Cárcer 48, 7p, Valencia 46001) organises working holidays in the London area for Spanish people aged 18-25 for a minimum of two months; the registration fee totals 60,000 pesetas. Similarly the Scandinavian au pair agency EXIS in Denmark (see Scandinavia chapter) aranges seasonal work in England.

A company based in Scotland called Interspeak Ltd. undertakes to find traineeships *(stages)* in the UK for European students mainly in the fields of commerce, marketing, engineering, hotel work and computers. A fee of £220 is payable for placements which last from two to six months. Accommodation is arranged with host families (for about £90 a week) which helps participants to improve their English, though a good standard of English is necessary before acceptance. Details are available from the Coach House, Blackwood Estate, Blackwood, Lanarkshire ML11 0JG.

Youth and student exchange organisations in European capitals should be able to advise on au pair and voluntary work in the United Kingdom. In some cases, they may even organise their own working holidays.

Working Holidays for Americans

The programme for American students wishing to work in Britain is called the Work in Britain Program, which allows about 3,500 full-time college students over the age of 18 to look for work after arriving in Britain or pre-arranged. They must obtain a blue card for a fee of $160, which is recognised by the British Home Office as a valid substitute for a work permit. They may arrive at any time of the year and work for up to six months. Candidates must be US citizens residing in the USA and studying at a US institution at the time of application and able to prove that they have at least $600. For further information contact the Council on International Educational Exchange, 205 E 42nd St, New York, NY 10017 (212-661-1414 ext 1130). The Work in Britain programme is the counterpart of BUNAC's Work America Programme for British students (see chapter *United States*). New immigration rules mean that it is possible for participants to apply for a one-year extension provided they have a definite job offer and they return to the US for three months to apply for a new work permit through the Association for International Practical Training (Career Development Exchanges, 10 Corporate Centre, Suite 250, 10400 Patuxent Pkwy, Columbia, MD 21044-3510)

According to statistics compiled on the Work in Britain programme, about a fifth of participants arrange their jobs before leaving the States, and almost all of these are in career-related jobs, often fixed up through campus contacts. The remaining students (who numbered 2,835 in 1994) wait until they arrive, and spend an average of 4-5 days job-hunting before finding work. The majority work in offices, hotels, restaurants, pubs and shops. It is not only American style establishments which hire them, but also bastions of English tradition like Burberrys, Jaeger and Harrods. The average wage for participants is about £180 per week, though secretarial jobs pay up to £240. In 1994 single rooms in London averaged £55 and shared rooms £40 per week which compares favourably with New York. There is a special tax provision for Work in Britain students who earn less than the personal allowance and who are returning to full-time education in the US; they can claim the same student exemption as British students (see section on Tax above) and are therefore tax exempt.

The *Work in Britain Participants' Handbook* contains the addresses of scores of potential employers. The BUNAC office in London (16 Bowling Green Lane, EC1R 0BD) has files of possible employers (both in London and around the UK) as well as current vacancy lists of cheap London accommodation and job offers.

US citizens who wish to spend between six and ten weeks of the summer volunteering their time to work in youth clubs, with the homeless, HIV/AIDS sufferers and in psychiatric rehabilitation should contact the Winant & Clayton Volunteers (109 E 50th St, New York, NY 10022) before the end of January.

Working Holidays for Canadians, Australians and New Zealanders

'Working holiday-maker' status may be obtained by members of Commonwealth countries between the ages of 17 and 27 inclusive with no dependants over the age of five. It is estimated that about 25,000 do so each year. The permit entitles the holder to work in Britain with the primary intention of funding a holiday, for up to two years. It is now essential to apply in the country of origin rather than at the point of entry. Immigration officials will want to be reassured that the employment you will be seeking is incidental to your travels and that it is your firm intention to leave the UK after no more than a total of two years which, as of 1994, must be continuous from the date of entry to Britain. You may also be asked to prove that you have enough money to support yourself and fund a return airfare; for example the sum specified by some official sources is £2,000. (Australians might take note that all this would be likely to change if the Australian Republican Movement achieves its aim of making Australia a republic by the year 2000.)

Teresa Berg from rural British Columbia found the procedure remarkably straightforward: 'I contacted the British Consulate in Edmonton; and one form, two passport pictures, thirty dollars and four days later, I had the visa stamped in my passport'. Canadian students who want the security of a package arrangement may participate in the Student Work Abroad Programme (SWAP) which is comparable to the Work in Britain programme. It is administered by the Canadian Universities Travel Service (Travel CUTS) which has 30 offices across Canada. After paying the registration fee and showing that they have support funds, eligible students aged 18-27 are entitled to work in Britain for up to six months at any time of the year. As on the American Work in Britain programme, the facilities of BUNAC in London are available to SWAPPERs. The equivalent for Australians is the SWAP scheme administered by STA Travel (PO Box 399, Carlton South, VIC 3053) which is open to Australians aged 17-27 for up to two years.

EMPLOYMENT PROSPECTS

Although recovery from the recession of the early 90s is still fragile, the signs are promising. But even in the depths of the recession, seasonal and temporary work opportunities could still be found and there are always various ways of tracking work down. There are, for example, a multitude of harvests from the apples of Somerset to the soft fruit of Inverness-shire for which the local work force is not sufficient. The tourist industry provides many opportunities for bar, catering and hotel staff in London, coastal resorts, the Lake District, Scotland and Wales. The increasing demand for childcare frequently outstrips the availability of willing candidates. In the South lots of office jobs can be seen advertised in the windows of employment agencies specialising in temporary work or in the 'Sits Vac' pages of local newspapers. The main problem is the lowness of the wages compared to the cost of living, particularly in the London area. Unless you are very lucky in finding cheap accommodation, it is very difficult to save any money on an hourly wage of £3.

Agencies

Temporary job agencies continue to thrive in a recession, when employers are reluctant to hire permanent staff but have frequent temporary vacancies. There are thousands of private employment offices in Britain's main cities, several hundred of which are located along London's Oxford Street. You should not be content to register with just one, since the degree of enthusiasm with which these numerous agencies try to find suitable work for their temps varies enormously. Manpower and Alfred Marks are among the biggest general agencies; the latter has over 50 branches in London alone and many more nationwide. Colin Rothwell from South Africa found industrial agency work a very satisfactory way to save for his future travels, though he couldn't stomach all his assignments:

In England I found the easiest way to find work was through temping agencies. However, it was also the most inconvenient way as they liked you to have an address and a phone number. They were also the biggest sharks around and you got paid half the going wage as they took a very healthy cut from your hard-earned blood, sweat and tears. It did have its advantages though; you worked when and where it suited you, and some agencies sent you all over the place to do all kinds of weird jobs. For example, the worst job I did on my whole trip was at a dog meat factory. You arrived at the crack of dawn and were sent into a massive fridge where you were met with tons of semi-defrosting offal, with blood everywhere, and a stench like you wouldn't believe. So, as desperate for money as I was, I only lasted two days.

If you are a trained nurse, nanny, accountant, financial analyst, teacher, etc. there are many specialist agencies eager to sign you up. Many advertise in the papers mentioned below. Temping allows a great deal of flexibility, though most agencies you approach want to be reassured that you are not about to flit off somewhere. Most, but not all, will want to see evidence that foreign temps have working papers. Working for an agency can also be a good way to meet fellow travellers, since lots of people signed up with agencies are there to save money for an upcoming trip.

Despite the agency fees, wages are still healthy enough, e.g. £3.50 an hour for labouring and warehouse jobs, and up to £5 on a night shift. When you get a temp job through an agency, the agency generally becomes your employer and pays your wages. People who perform well on typing or shorthand tests will find that they are placed more promptly than those who lack any office skills and will be paid accordingly. For example Manpower in London (0171-834 7661) were recently offering immediate work to word processor secretaries with a typing speed of 60 words per minute. Skilled secretarial wages start at about £7 an hour, while unskilled clerical work pays approximately £4-4.50 an hour. Another recommended agency is the Australian-linked temp agency Bligh (131-135 Earls Court Road, London SW5; 0171-244 7277) which has an agricultural section to place people on farms throughout Britain, as well as vacancies for nannies, secretaries, etc.

Temping at any kind of job is a good way of exposing your skills to potential employers. It is a good idea to ask for an application form at those workplaces to which you are temporarily assigned which you enjoy, assuming you are looking for longer term work. The principal disadvantage of temping is the uncertainty of hours.

Ian Mitselburg from Sydney got so tired of the London scene that he repaired to Edinburgh where he found it was even easier to find work and that the lower wages were counterbalanced by the lower cost of living:

I put my name down at almost every agency that would take it and had all sorts of temporary jobs including washing dishes, stuffing envelopes, transferring stocks and shares, labouring and unpacking delivery bags of foreign currency.

Another foreign visitor to Scotland, Cindy Roberts, was pleased that the agency she approached did not ask to see a work permit, nor did the dowager duchess for whom she worked on the west coast of Scotland, cooking, light housekeeping and errand-running.

Newspapers and Books

In addition to private agencies, you should make use of newspapers, where up to half of all job vacancies are advertised. There are several free weekly newspapers and magazines in London for the Australian and New Zealand itinerant community which can prove to be excellent sources of casual jobs for anyone. You will find distribution boxes for *TNT* (14-15 Child's Place, Earls Court, SW5 9RX; 0171-373 3377) and *New Zealand News UK* (25 Royal Opera Arcade; 0171-930 6451) in selected locations throughout London, e.g. outside travel agencies, tube stations, favoured pubs, etc. *TNT* is published every Monday. The majority of unskilled jobs advertised are for mother's helps, salesmen, in pubs or restaurants and on farms, but occasionally there are jobs in shops, offices, sports clubs, hospitals and on building sites. Agencies also advertise in these forums. In March and September of each year *New Zealand News* publishes a supplement *Overseas*, with articles and adverts relevant to foreign job-seekers in Britain. The newspaper's office in New Zealand distributes the supplement (AMG Building, 43 High St, Auckland). Jobseekers in London can visit the *New Zealand News* London office just behind New Zealand House on Haymarket, where there is a notice board with accommodation and travel advice as well as job advertisements, which are posted before they appear in print. Newsagents' windows often carry advertisements, especially for part-time help.

If you are looking for a summer job anywhere in Britain you should have a look at two annual publications which give many addresses to which you can apply: *The Directory of Summer Jobs in Britain* (Vacation-Work at £7.95), and *Working Holidays* (published by the Central Bureau for Educational Visits and Exchanges at £8.99). The latter deals with holiday jobs around the world and includes a chapter on Britain. The majority of jobs listed in *Summer Jobs in Britain* are in hotels or holiday camps, with a further emphasis on seasonal farm work. However there are also lots of unusual and interesting jobs like market researchers, travel reservation clerks, swimming pool life guards, English teachers and monitors, marquee erectors, conservation wardens and information officers for company libraries.

When answering adverts by phone, make sure you have a phone card, since otherwise you'll constantly be worrying about running out of change.

Jobcentres

Finally, in your job search, you should not omit the obvious step of visiting your local Jobcentre. Jobcentres are notified of an estimated one-third of the job vacancies in Britain. Details of available jobs are posted on display boards so centres are primarily self-service. If things look grim one week, they might improve the next, especially in areas where there is a concentration of seasonal farm work. For example Kentish job-seekers might find a depressing scarcity of job notices in July but a great many more in August when the local hop growers are anxious to recruit extra workers for the September harvest.

HARVESTS

The principal fruit growing areas of Britain are: the Vale of Evesham over to the Wye and Usk Valleys; most of Kent; Lincolnshire and East Anglia, especially the Fens around Wisbech; and north of the Tay Estuary (Blairgowrie, Forfar). But there is intensive agricultural activity in most parts of Britain so always check with the Jobcentre or Farmers' Union in the area(s) where you are interested in finding farm work. Again *The Directory of Summer Jobs in Britain* lists many fruitgrowers, some of whom need over 100 pickers. Harvest dates are not standard throughout the country, since the raspberries of Inverness-shire ripen at least two or three weeks later than the raspberries on the Isle of Wight; nor are the starting dates the same from one year to the next.

Seasonal Agricultural Workers Scheme

The Immigration & Nationality Department (Lunar House, 40 Wellesley Road, Croydon CR9 2BY) allows several large farm camps and two agents to employ non-EU students aged 18-25 for an initial three months (renewable for a further three months up until the end of November). Successful applicants receive a workcard before entering the UK, which can be used only for working on the issuing farm camp. The two agents are Concordia and HOPS described below and the four farm camps are:

Friday Bridge International Farm Camp, March Road, Friday Bridge, Wisbech, Cambridgeshire PE14 0LR (01945 860255).

International Farm Camp, Hall Road, Tiptree, Colchester, Essex CO5 0QS (01621 815496).

Leroch Farm, Alyth, Blairgowrie, Perthshire, Scotland PH11 8NZ (018284 280).

R. & J.M. Place, International Farm Camp, Church Farm, Tunstead, Norwich, Norfolk NR12 8RQ (01692 536225).

Since the political upheaval in Eastern Europe, many young people from the emerging democracies have wanted to work in Britain. A great many fruit growers are turning to the seemingly endless supply of hard-working young people from Eastern Europe to supply their harvesting requirements. Readers in Central and Eastern Europe and other non-EU countries should be aware that the scheme is massively oversubscribed and acceptance requires early application and correct documentation. The Home Office quotas are not only much lower than the number of eager applicants, they are also significantly less than the number of workers requested by farmers. That means that many large fruit farms welcome applications from EU and UK nationals.

The Harvesting Opportunity Permit Scheme (HOPS) allows a limited number of Central and East European university students aged 20 to 25 to pick fruit, vegetables or hops on HOPS (GB) registered farms for 7-13 weeks between May and November. Applicants must have been born in the years 1970-1974 (for 1995) and be full-time university students (but not finalists). Official application forms must be obtained between August and November from the YFC Centre, National Agricultural Centre, Kenilworth, Warwickshire CV8 2LG (01203 696559) and submitted with a fee (£40 at present) before January 31st.

A longer established scheme is operated by Concordia (Youth Service Volunteers), 8 Brunswick Place, Hove, Sussex BN3 1ET (01273 772086). This organisation recruits only foreign students aged 19-25 to work on about 160 international farm camps throughout England and Scotland between May and October. Like HOPS, this scheme enables young people from outside the European Union to work legally in the UK. Instead of having to obtain fully-fledged work permits, foreign 'volunteers' (as they are inaccurately called) pay a £50 registration fee.

Fruit Farms

Although the work is hard at the beginning (and also unreliable in bad weather), the international atmosphere can be enjoyable. Some farmers even organise a social and sporting programme. You are likely to meet some veteran travellers who can offer useful advice about job-hunting in their countries or whose names you can add to your address book.

Here are a few farm camps in addition to the ones listed above which hire at least 50 fruit pickers during the season, so it may be worthwhile for British and EU people to approach them directly:

F.A.B., Spring Farm, Spring Lane, Hempnall, Norwich, Norfolk NR15 2NY 01508 499016). Strawberry planters and pickers for work in glasshouses.

Williamson (Fruit Farms) Ltd., Park Lane Farm, Park Lane, Langham, Colchester, Essex CO4 5NL (01206 230233). 50 pickers.

Hilltop Fruit Farm, Ledbury, Herefordshire HR8 1LN (01531 632830). Employs about 70 pickers for strawberry and cherry, apple and pear harvests; send an s.a.e. for details.

H. B. Lowe, Barons Place, Mereworth, Maidstone, Kent ME18 5NF (01622 812229).

A. R. Neaves & Sons, Little Sharsted Farm, Doddington, Near Sittingbourne, Kent ME9 0JT (01795 886263).

Edward Vinson, Ratling Court Farm, Aylesham, Near Canterbury, Kent CT3 3HN (01304) 840427.

W. Brice & Son Ltd., Mockbeggar Farm, Higham, Rochester, Kent ME3 8EU (01634 717425). Up to 600 fruit pickers and 40 packers.

A.P. & S.M. Parris, Cutliffe Farm, Sherford, Taunton, Somerset TA1 3RQ (01823 253808). 30+ pickers.

J. F. P. Douglas, Avon Valley Farm, Bath Road, Keynsham, Bristol BS18 1TS (0117 986 0681).

Haygrove Fruit, Redbank Farm, Ledbury, Herefordshire HR8 2JL (01531 633659). 100+ strawberry pickers and packers.

Lubstree Park Farm, The Humbers, Donnington, Telford, Shropshire TF2 8LW (01952 604320).

Brocksbushes Fruit Farm, Corbridge, Northumberland (01434 633100). 150 berry pickers.

D. & B. Grant, The Steading, Wester Essendy, Blairgowrie, Perthshire PH10 6RA (01250 884389).

The raspberry harvest in Scotland usually begins in July, but can vary by as much as three weeks. Peter Thomson's farm near Blairgowrie employs 1,000 pickers when the fruit is most plentiful and about 3,000 pickers are at work throughout Perthshire and Angus. On an exceptionally good day a picker might gather more than 150lb of fruit and earn £25. Lentran is another Scottish raspberry farm which hires many seasonal pickers and functions as an international farm camp (address above). Strawberry picking in Scotland is also abundant in July/August; try contacting Bill Henderson at Seggat, Auchterless, Turiff (01888 4223).

Even in the furthest corners of Scotland, there may be opportunities on farms. Heather McCulloch from Australia asked the owners of the hostel where she was staying on the Orkney island of South Ronaldsay if they had any work on their farm and, although she confessed to having no farm experience, was hired to join other travellers for various jobs including 'the sometimes farcical task of rounding up cattle and sheep' and cooking ('opening tins of beans and rice pudding'). For this she was paid a fair wage with food and accommodation thrown in.

One of the latest harvests is of apples which should be more lucrative than many others since the weather can be cold and wet between mid-September and mid-October. Unfortunately this is not what Paul and Tracey Foulkes from New Zealand found at an apple farm in Hampshire:

> We worked for £2.76 per hour with no overtime rate which made it hard to believe that £150 was the average weekly net wage as promised by the management before we arrived. The campsite resembled an overgrown backyard surrounded by stinging nettles. The cooking area consisted of three small sinks, two of which were blocked and no plugs. Rats as big as cats were in and out all the time. After travelling round the world and visiting nearly 20 countries, there were the most unhygienic conditions we have come across. After enduring eight days work we left, and intend to call the health department.

Related employment is available in canning and food processing plants which go into high gear in fruit growing regions during the harvests. Lucrative overtime is often available. Among the largest in the country is Salvesen Food Services with freezing works in several Lincolnshire towns (Bourne, Easton and Spalding), plus Lowestoft, Peterborough, Grimsby, Hull, Edinburgh, Dundee and Inverness.

Pay and Conditions

The two methods of payment used by farmers are according to the quantity picked, known as piece work rates, or an hourly wage. In some cases farmers operate a combination of these two methods, paying an hourly rate plus a bonus for each bin of top quality fruit (which the supermarkets demand). Most farmers abide by the minimum hourly wages as stipulated by the Agricultural Wages Board (the only Wages Board to have survived government policies). The minimum rate for casual workers over 20 is £2.76 (£4.13 overtime). For those 17 years old the basic wage is £1.78 an hour. Further details are available from the AWB, Nobel House, 17 Smith Square, London SW1P 3JR.

Pickers being paid piece work sometimes overestimate their likely earnings. Novices invariably find the first few days discouraging. Also bear in mind that picking will be curtailed by rainy weather (unless you happen to be harvesting courgettes which are unaffected by rain) and on either side of the peak harvest time. Piecework rates may not be standard in one fruit-picking area so it can be worth doing some comparison shopping before promising a farmer that you will work for him, preferably a month or so before the harvest is due to begin. Some crops pay more than others, usually because they're more difficult or painful to pick. Blackcurrants grow low on the ground and require hours of stooping at an uncomfortable height. Gooseberries share this characteristic and in addition must be picked individually from among vicious thorns. Inexperienced pickers often leave after their first long gruelling day when they find they have not even earned enough to cover living expenses.

You cannot count on accommodation being provided on fruit farms. Even fruit growers who take on large numbers of pickers may provide nothing more than a field, which may or may not be properly levelled, well-drained or cleared of nettles. Sometimes you need to work a minimum number of hours per week, e.g. 15, to be allowed to use the campsite. Others provide completely equipped caravans or bunkhouses, but may make a deduction from your wages for this luxury. If full board is also provided, the Agricultural Wages Board stipulates a maximum weekly deduction of £54.41 (£43.86 for a 17 year old).

If you do not independently enjoy camping, you are not likely to enjoy life on a Farm Camp. Mark Stephenson grew very fond of the 'wet sloping field' where he was directed to pitch his tent at a farm camp in Perthshire:

After surveying the field which was to be my home for the next few weeks, I turned and noticed the terrific view; the sky may have been all grey clouds but this didn't diminish the magnificence. Social life thrived in and around this temporary community on the Scottish hillsides. Visits to the pub were usually musical events since traditional folk music was frequently played and often we visitors were invited to contribute a southern favourite like 'Maybe it's because I'm a Londoner.' Fruit-picking in Scotland may not leave you much richer in pocket but it gives you several weeks of camping surrounded by open fields and sky, combined with the chance to meet young people not only from Scotland but from all over the world.

Agricultural Agencies

Farm staff agencies like Fletcher Relief Services in Aylesbury (01296 655777) are normally interested only in qualified agriculturalists, milkers and tractor drivers. However some agencies do occasionally deal with emergency vacancies for unskilled pickers, and two which have been advertising recently are the P.A.W. Group in Bognor Regis (01243 841674) and Staffing Solutions/English Language Solutions (Pentney House, Narborough Road, Pentney, Kings Lynn, Norfolk PE32 1JD; 01760 337771/fax 337061).

Caution is always required when accepting a picking job since conditions are notoriously rough and earnings can be disappointing, as Michael Blue reported in *TNT* magazine:

I and many others have just been conned by a very dubious employment agency. Despite promises of good wages and excellent hotel accommodation, we found starvation wages and inadequate housing, as well as other surprises, such as £45 rent in advance for sharing a small room with ten others. We didn't encounter anyone who had not ended up out of pocket after the unpleasant experience.

Although not an agency, the organisation WWOOF (Working for Organic Growers) can put members in touch with organic farmers throughout the UK who offer free room and board in exchange for help. Membership costs £8; details from Bradford Road, Lewes, Sussex BN7 1RB.

HOP-PICKING

Between 1860 and 1960, hop-picking in Kent was a social institution. Traditionally, large numbers of families from the East End of London were transported by special trains to the extensive hop gardens around Maidstone and Tonbridge. But as hop-picking machines gradually took over, the number of pickers has steadily declined. The Whitbread Brewery's hop gardens at Beltring near Tonbridge were the last bastion of hand-picking and finally went mechanical in 1969.

At present the hop market is so depressed because of an inability to compete with cheap Belgian and Dutch hops that quite a few farmers have switched to other crops, especially in Kent. Yet enough hop-growers are optimistic that the demand will revive that there are still jobs left for pickers in the hop industry. If you are free during the month of September and are willing to work hard, you might consider trying to fix up a place on a hop farm well in advance as Tom Morton did:

I wrote to hop farms in April and fixed up a job at Spelmonden Estate. Work started at 7am and finished at 6pm. Accommodation (£8 per week) was in 'portakabins' with a large common room and kitchen for about 15 people. Take leather gloves and bandages for your wrists or they will be lacerated by the hops in no time. Although the work was hard there was a great atmosphere.

The easiest job to do is to drive the tractor between the rows of hops. Other jobs include going ahead of the tractor to hack the top plants at their bases, standing on the trailer to feed the severed plants into the back, walking behind to collect the missed vines or, finally, the risky job of perching in the crow's nest attached to the tractor to cut the plants at the top. Women normally work in the machine house where the hop flowers are stripped from the vines and bagged. There is usually some pre-harvest work stringing up the vines to be cut.

Jobcentres are sometimes notified of openings. Outside Kent, hops are grown mainly in Hereford & Worcester. Hop growers normally begin their recruitment process in April or May. Both the Harvesting Opportunities Permit Scheme (with an appropriate acronym) and Concordia Youth Service Volunteers mentioned above recruit foreign students to work on hop farms. At many farms, a tent is an essential item, along with sleeping bag and cooking equipment. Just as conditions vary among vineyard proprietors in France, so some hop farms are far more congenial than others. Whereas conditions are fairly primitive at some, others offer free cottages, vegetables, logs, etc. in addition to a wage of more than £150 take home a week.

Here are some addresses of large hop producers:

Adrian Scripps Ltd., Moat Farm, Five Oak Green, Paddock Green, Tonbridge, Kent TN12 6RR (01892 832406).

S.C. and J.H. Berry Ltd., Gushmere Court Farm, Selling, Faversham, Kent (01227 752205).

Elphicks Farm, Hunton, Maidstone, Kent (01622 820758).

Poldhurst & China Farms, Upper Harbledown, Canterbury, Kent CT2 9AR (01227 464911).

Reed Court Farms, Hurst Barn, Marden, Tonbridge, Kent (01622 820232).

Spelmonden Estate, Spelmonden Farm, Goudhurst, Kent TN17 1HE.

Wakeley Brothers Ltd., Otterham Buildings, Rainham, Gillingham, Kent ME8 7XB (01634 232121).

Stocks Farm, Suckley, Worcestershire WR6 5EH (01886 884202).

TOURISM & CATERING

Despite its infamous weather and cuisine, Britain attracts millions of tourists from abroad. And during the recession, an increasing number of Britons took their holidays at home rather than abroad which gave a welcome boost to struggling resort hotels, tour companies and related businesses. It has been estimated that one in ten of the employed labour force of Britain is involved in the tourist industry and that by the turn of the century the industry will be the biggest employer in the country. (But be warned that the recession was not yet over at the time of writing in 1994, when a report appeared in a national newspaper that 1,500 people queued for 80 job vacancies in a new hotel near Derby.)

Still, somebody has to look after the needs of all those pleasure-seekers, whether selling rock candy or playing the guitar to provide entertainment. (Many buskers have found holiday resorts during the season to be far more profitable than large urban areas.) Seaside hotels normally provide staff accommodation and food, though the standard will be considerably lower than that enjoyed by the paying guests at the hotel. There is also plenty of hotel work in London from the international hotels on Park Lane to the budget hotels of Earls Court, though it is the norm in London for the staff to live out.

Wages in the hotel trade are notoriously low, and exploitation is common, especially now that the government has abolished the relevant Wages Councils which used to stipulate minimum hourly rates of pay. There are widespread reports of hotels failing to offer even the 1993 minimum (i.e. £2.92 to anyone over 21). A case was recently brought to the attention of the Low Pay Unit of a job advertised in a Kent Jobcentre for a trainee chef; the pay offered was £35 for a 39-hour week split shifts. Similarly there are no longer official guidelines on what can be deducted for accommodation (the maximum used to be £2.73 a day). Hotel staff with silver service or other specialist experience can expect to earn more than the minimum in a three or four star hotel as can restaurant staff in London who should earn approximately £4 an hour plus free food. Waiting staff can supplement their wages with tips, however chamber and bar staff will generally have to be content with their hourly wage.

People who are available for the whole season, say April to October will find it much easier to land a job than those available only for the peak months of July and August. Most hotels prefer to receive a formal written application in the early part of the year, complete with photos and references; however it can never hurt to telephone (especially later in the spring) to find out what the situation is. You may work from the selective list of hotels in the *Directory of Summer Jobs in Britain* mentioned above or work systematically through a hotel guide such as those published by the Automobile Association, the Royal Automobile Club or the English Tourist Board. The more bedrooms listed in the hotel's entry, the better the chances of a vacancy. For a list of the 200 hotels on Guernsey, write to the States Tourist Office, White Rock, St. Peter Port, Guernsey. In general, the Channel Islands are a favourite destination for seasonal workers. Towngate Personnel (65 Seamoor Road, Westbourne, Bournemouth BH4 9AE; 01202 752955) specialise in filling permanent live-in vacancies in the tourist industry of the Channel Islands.

It is worth contacting large hotel chains for up-to-date vacancy information only if you are going for senior positions like chef or manager. For example Hilton UK (01923 246464) can give advice on which of their hotels have current vacancies, although these should be applied to individually for employment.

Similarly Friendly Hotels plc (10 Greycoat Place, London SW1P 1SB; 0171-222 8866) hire between 100 and 200 room attendants, waiters, bar staff, porters, etc. for their hotels and function rooms around the country. The Sheraton Hotel chain is often looking for staff as well. Smaller chains might be worth trying too like Hatton Hotels Group Services Ltd. (Hatton Court, Upton Hill, Upton St. Leonards, Gloucester GL4 8DE) which hire staff for hotels in the Cotswolds.

Fast food restaurants around the world have many vacancies. If you are prepared to work overtime, you should be able to earn a living from McDonalds, Pizza Hut, etc. working as a 'crew member', though usually you have to be content with part-time work (at about £2.75 an hour) until you prove yourself reliable. Full-time wages are normally about £3 or slightly more. A large percentage of workers is foreign, not all of whom have National Insurance numbers. Having a reference from one of these chains can be useful if you want to move to another branch.

Many London employment agencies specialise in catering work and once you are on their books, you can earn reasonably good money. An employment agency which deals with hotels throughout Britain is Montpelier Employment, 34 Montpelier Road, Brighton, Sussex BN1 2LQ. Anyone who can acquaint themselves with EU hygiene regulations before any interview would have the edge. Those with a knowledge of French might try to contact Cross Channel Catering which were trying to recruit 900 staff for the Eurostar tunnel train in 1994.

Pubs

Live-in pub work is not hard to come by. You usually have to work throughout pub opening hours six days a week, but you should be rewarded with approximately £115-150 a week cash-in-hand in London, about £20 less elsewhere. A part-time barmaid or barman makes between £12 and £15 for an evening session 6-11pm, and many people do this in addition to a day job to boost their finances. This is one job in which there is a good demand for working couples. Women with bar experience normally find it easier to find a job than barmen, and can often negotiate a better package.

Waiting for an ad to appear is usually less productive than going pub to pub. An American traveller found himself nearly penniless in the popular tourist town of Pitlochry in Perthshire and made the rounds of the pubs asking for work. In each case the management were either fully staffed or were too concerned about his lack of a work permit. He claims that in the 34th and final pub, they asked him if he were free to start work that minute, and he gleefully stepped behind the bar and began work, without knowing shandy from Guinness. Americans may need to be reminded that you do not get tips in a British pub though you may be bought a drink now and then. Americans often have trouble with the different accents they will encounter as Woden Teachout found:

I had a hard time deciphering the orders over the music; 'Bakes' does not sound remotely like 'Becks' to the American ear.

Pub jobs vary a great deal and it is better if you can find one which you find compatible. Ken Smith from New Zealand has extensive experience:

I worked in four pubs while in England, three of which were really good. I was regularly invited into the customers' homes for meals or tea and in one pub there was a retired gentleman who would drive me around historic country pubs. The six months I spent working in a pub near Russell Square were absolutely fantastic; the money was great (£130 a week cash-in-hand of which I could comfortably save £100), excellent food, great boss and brilliant customers. On the other hand I spent two months in a Surrey pub which was terrible in every conceivablw way, but I was short on money and jobs were scarce. The final straw was when they started working on the roof in November and the freezing cold wind blew right into my bedroom. The job was only ever a roof over our heads and they even took that away.

Scotland

Although unemployment is high in Scotland (and Wales as well), there are still plenty of tourist-related jobs available. Charlotte Jakobsen from Denmark (who 'fell in love with this country, its people and lifestyle' on arrival) travelled to Edinburgh for interviews with the Hilton and Sheraton Hotels, among others, and was soon working evenings in a hotel bar. Her employer did not provide accommodation but she was able to stay longterm at the Frances Kinnaird Christian Hostel for women (14 Coates Crescent) for less than £50 a week, and concluded that although it is next to impossible to find a bar or hotel job with a decent wage, it is a very enjoyable way to pass a few months.

Many foreign job-seekers in Britain tire of the London scene or are attracted to the peace and quiet of Scotland as Isak Maseide from Norway was:

We were originally going to Edinburgh to work at the Festival, but after Athens we preferred somewhere quieter, so went to the resort of Oban on the west coast of Scotland. Even though we arrived in the middle of the season (which lasts from mid-May to the end of September) we soon found work. Apparently McTavish's Kitchens in George Street is the place to go first since it is the biggest employer and has live-in facilities, pays well and employs quite a number of young people. My New Zealand girlfriend and I preferred to have a wee feeling of freedom so we rented a bedsit for £65 a week.

Paul Binfield from Kent travelled further north in Scotland and was rewarded with a healthy choice of casual work in the Orkney Islands:

Unemployment here is about 5% and from March to September there is an absolute abundance of summer jobs. We worked in one of the several youth hostels on the islands, have done voluntary work for the Orkney Seal Rescue and I am currently earning a very nice wage working at the historical site Skara Brae on a three-month contract. There is loads of seasonal work available in hotels and bars, cutting grass for the Council and other garden contracts, etc.

Holiday Camps and Activity Centres

Anyone with a qualification in canoeing, yachting, climbing, etc. should be able to find summer work as an instructor. Since the canoeing tragedy of 1993 in which several young people were drowned at an activity centre on the south coast, directors have been looking for higher standards of training and experience. Foreign equivalents of the British Canoe Union, Royal Yachting Association, etc. should suffice. There are also plenty of jobs as general assistants for sports-minded young people, especially at children's multi activity centres. Suzanne Phillips, who worked at an adventure centre in North Devon, claims that 'a person's character and personality are far more important than their qualifications.' The trouble is that the pay is not usually very much for this kind of work, perhaps about £40-45 per week in addition to all food and accommodation costs, though this will be supplemented by an end-of-season bonus at some centres. Quite often foreign applicants will be asked to provide police clearance forms for any job working with children.

One of the largest employers is PGL Adventure, Alton Court, Penyard Lane (874), Ross-on-Wye, Herefordshire HR9 5NR (01989 764211) with a staggering 3,000 vacancies during the season which extends from March to October. The Youth Hostels Association Adventure Holidays programme (Trevelyan House,

8 St. Stephen's Hill, St. Albans, Herts.; 01727 840211), which employs a large number of sports leaders, offers only free board and lodging, rail fares and sometimes pocket money.

A comprehensive list of activity centres for children, young people and adults may be found in the annually revised book *Adventure Holidays* (Vacation-Work at £5.95). Here are some of the most important ones which may require domestic as well as leadership staff:

Action Holidays, Windrush, Bexton Lane, Knutsford, Cheshire WA16 9BP. Tel: (01565) 654775. 200 staff for Greater London, Staffordshire and Cheshire.

Ardmore Adventures, 11-15 High St, Marlow, Bucks. SL7 1AU. Tel: (01628) 890060. Multi activity and English language camps mainly in London and region.

Barracuda Summer Activity Camps, 7a High St, Huntingdon, Cambs. PE18 6TE. Tel: (01480) 435090. Various residential and day camps in southern England.

Camp Beaumont, Bridge House, Orchard Lane, Huntingdon, Cambs. PE18 6QT. 4 residential centres in Britain, plus one each in Spain and France.

Devon & Dorset Adventure Holidays Ltd., c/o London Office, 6 Kew Green, Richmond, Surrey TW9 3BH. Tel: 0181-940 7782. Holiday centre near Wareham, Dorset.

EF Language Travel, EF House 1-3 Farman St, Hove, Sussex BN3 1AL. Residential courses for European students throughout Britain.

Freetime Leisure, Park House, Moor Lane, Woking, Surrey GU21 1LS. Tel: (01483) 740242. Multi-activity and sports coaching camps for children in Hampshire and Surrey.

ISCA Children's Holidays, Bonnaford, Brentor, Tavistock, Devon PL 19 0LX. Camps in Oxfordshire.

Prime Leisure, Manor Farm House, Dunstan Road, Old Headington, Oxford OX3 9BY. Tel: (01865) 750775. 10 centres in Oxfordshire, Hampshire, Berkshire and Surrey.

Summer Sports Experience, 86 Dorset Road, Merton Park, Wimbledon SW19 3HD. Tel: 0181-715 5434. Children's activity centres in London and Southeast London.

Superchoice Adventure Ltd., 191a Freshfield Road, Brighton, East Sussex BN2 2YE. Tel: (01273) 676467.

For catering, domestic and other work at family holiday centres contact the following:

Butlins Holiday Worlds Ltd., Bognor Regis, Sussex PO21 1JJ. Tel: (01243) 842073. Their five centres are Somerwest World (Minehead, Somerset TA24 5SH), Southcoast World (Bognor Regis, Sussex P021 1JJ), Starcoast World (Pwllheli, Gwynedd LL53 6HX), Funcoast World (Skegness, Lincolnshire PE25 1NJ) and Wonderwest World (Heads of Ayr, Scotland KA7 4LB). Applications should be sent to the preferred centre.

HF Holidays, Recruitment & Training Department, Redhills, Penrith, Cumbria CA11 0DT. Tel: (01768) 899988. Operate 18 country guest houses throughout the UK for people on walking and special interest holidays.

Holiday Club Pontin's, PO Box 100, Chorley, Lancashire PR7 5QQ. Hiring takes place at eight individual centres. Among the most sought-after job is that of 'Blue Coat' or entertainer-cum-host. They are paid £90 for a 90-hour week, yet in 1994 there were 2,500 applicants for 120 vacancies.

Seasonal winter work (Christmas week apart) is not common in Britain, with one important exception. Aviemore Mountain Resort Ltd. (Aviemore, Inverness-shire PH22 1PF) in the Cairngorms of Scotland absorbs a large number of itinerants, although they prefer to hire permanent staff. Fourteen-day work packages are arranged for the Christmas/New Year period which combine festivities with work. Some jobs are registered with the Inverness Jobcentre though it is probably more efficient to apply to the Personnel Office at the Centre (01479 810624). The Centre provides staff accommodation.

American-style amusement parks, which are fast gaining popularity in Britain, have large seasonal staff requirements. As well as the usual scivvying jobs, they may also require entertainers for both children and adults, lifeguards, DJs, shop assistants, etc. The main disadvantage is that accommodation is generally unavailable. Among the largest are:

Alton Towers, Alton, North Staffordshire ST10 4DB. Tel: (01538) 703344. Approximately 1,000 vacancies between March and November.

Bourne Leisure Group, Normandy Court, 1 Wolsey Road, Hemel Hempstead, Herts. HP2 4TU. Tel: (01442) 244006. 500 staff needed at 20 holiday parks throughout Britain.

Chessington World of Adventures, Leatherhead Road, Chessington, Surrey KT9 2NE. Tel: (01372) 729560. Employs between 500 and 1,000 people each year.

Frontierland Western Theme Park, The Promenade, Morecambe, Lancs. LA4 4DG. Tel: (01524) 410024. 100+ ride operators and other assistants who are paid £2.50 per hour. Accommodation available for £25 per week.

Smarts Amusement Park Ltd., Seafront, Littlehampton, West Sussex BN17 5LL Tel: (01930) 721200.

Pleasurewood Hills Theme Park, Corton, Lowestoft, Suffolk NR32 5DZ. Tel: (01520) 508200.

Thorpe Park, Staines Road, Chertsey, Surrey KT16 8PN. Tel: (01932) 569393. No accommodation provided for the 400+ ancillary staff.

Youth Hostels

Assistant wardens are needed at many youth hostels during the busy season from Easter to October. Duties include general domestic work, cooking, manning the hostel shop and the reception desk. Pay is approximately £70 for a five-day week plus room and board. In the first instance applications should be sent (preferably in the winter) to the National Office in St. Albans (address above) who may refer it to the appropriate regional headquarters (in Matlock, Cardiff and Salisbury). It may also be worth approaching the regional offices individually: Central on 01629 825850, Wales 01222 396766 and South 01722 337515. The YHA magazine *Triangle* occasionally publishes 'Situations Vacant'.

Special Events

Events such as the Henley Regatta in June, Test Matches at Headingley in Leeds, the Edinburgh Festival in August/September and a host of golf tournaments and county shows need temporary staff to work as car park attendants, ticket sellers and in catering. Ask the local tourist office for a list of upcoming events and contact the organisers. Colin Rothwell from South Africa spent a few months in Nottingham trying to scrape together enough money to move on and recommends looking for work at fairs, horse races and rock concerts.

It's long hard work but the pay is usually not bad and there are sometimes good perks that go along with the job. I worked at a chicken and chips stand in Newcastle while Joe Cocker, Status Quo and Rod Stewart played away. During my short breaks I was allowed in to enjoy the concert. When it was all finished, there was a lot of roast chicken to take home (or sell). Then it was back to Nottingham in the early hours of the next morning with £40 in my back pocket.

CHILDCARE & DOMESTIC

One of the easiest ways for European citizens between the ages of 17 and 27 to arrange to work in the United Kingdom is to become au pairs. The list of permitted nationalities includes all European Economic Area countries plus Switzerland, Cyprus, Malta, Turkey, Hungary, Czech Republic, Slovakia and the former Yugoslavia (but not Poland or any Russian Federation states). As of February 1993, males are allowed to become au pairs in Britain. Anyone seeking entry as an au pair has to show documents at entry proving that an arrangement has been made; changing status after entry as a visitor is not permitted. The maximum stay is two years, though it is possible to change families in this time.

In October 1994 the Home Office issued new guidelines reducing the number of working days from six to five and the weekly number of hours from 30 to 25, not counting some evening babysitting. The pocket money for au pairs is currently £30-35 a week. The work should consist of childcare and light housework duties. These guidelines cannot be enforced and many families ignore them, in which case the au pair should bring the Home Office directives to the attention of the host family.

In some areas it is easy to find live-in positions after arrival, but not in all areas, where there are far more notices posted by foreign au pairs looking for jobs than families looking for au pairs.

Young women (and very occasionally men) wishing to become mother's helps have a good chance of succeeding since the market in this field is booming, especially in the Home Counties. An untrained, unqualified young woman can expect to be paid between £40 and £70 a week in addition to room and board. Mothers' helps with some experience often earn twice this amount and nannies even more.

Many au pair, nanny and mother's help agencies advertise in the weekly *Lady* magazine as well as in the free papers like *TNT* and *New Zealand News UK*. Details about working in Britain as an au pair are given in the 1993 *Au Pair & Nanny's Guide to Working Abroad* published by Vacation Work at £8.95. See the list in the introductory chapter *Childcare* for addresses to contact, though normally foreign young people contact an agency in their own country in the first instance.

A less binding variation is to babysit, for which you should receive a standard hourly rate of at least £2.50 an hour. Check notice boards, student broadsheets, etc. for such opportunities. A Malaysian student in London followed up a notice she spotted on the board next to Earls Court tube station and arranged free room and board in exchange for taking a child to and from school.

If you want a live-in position but not looking after children, there are agencies which specialise in providing carers for the elderly and disabled, for example Cura Domi-Care at Home (54 Chertsey St, Guildford, Surrey GU1 4HD). Also look for opportunities to house-sit. Obviously London is the best place for such an activity, though other provincial agencies offer this service; try Home & Pet Care Ltd. (PO Box 19, Penrith, Cumbria CA11 7AA; 016974 78515). Such agencies are normally looking for mature people with a fixed address and impeccable references.

TEACHING

Although there is a veritable epidemic of English language schools along the south coast and in places like Oxford and Cambridge, you may find it more difficult to get a job as a language tutor in Torquay than in Taipei, harder in Ramsgate than in Rio. It takes more than a tidy appearance to get one of the well-paid summer jobs in a British language school. And the situation has not been improved with the Europe-wide recession which has seen a falling off of numbers at many language schools. It is not uncommon for summer staff to be offered jobs which are contingent on student numbers, which makes it difficult to plan anything with certainty.

The majority of language schools in Britain insist on seeing a formal qualification in TEFL (Teaching English as a Foreign Language) or at the very least a university degree, teacher's certificate or fluency in a foreign language. If you satisfy any or all of these requirements you should apply to a number of language schools several months prior to the summer holiday period. Your skills and experience will be rewarded with £140-150 per week with accommodation, £175 without, making it one of the most highly paid summer jobs around. If you lack these qualifications, you might still consider blitzing the language schools, since many of them also run a programme of outings and entertainments for their foreign students and they may need non-teaching supervisors and sports instructors. Working at one of these language summer schools is an excellent way of making contact with Italian, French and Spanish young people who might offer advice or even hospitality once you set off on your travels.

A list of some 200 English language schools and colleges recognised by the British Council, may be obtained from the Association of Recognised English Language Services (ARELS) at 2 Pontypool Place, Valentine Place, London SE1 8QF. These schools tend to employ only qualified or experienced teaching staff. Also check the Tuesday *Guardian* throughout the spring. Schools are located throughout the UK, but are concentrated in the South-East, London, Oxford and Cambridge. For further addresses, check in the following *Yellow Pages* under 'Language Schools' or 'Schools — Language': Bournemouth, Brighton, Cambridge, Canterbury, Exeter, Oxford and Tunbridge Wells.

Here is a selection:

Anglo-European Study Tours, 8 Celbridge Mews, London W2 6EU 0171-229 4435.

Cicero Language International, 42 Upper Grosvenor Road, Tunbridge Wells, Kent TN1 2ET (01892 547077).

Concorde International, Arnett House, Hawks Lane, Canterbury CT1 2NU (01227 451035).

EF Language Travel, 1-3 Farman St, Hove, Sussex BN3 1AL.

Embassy Study Tours, 44 Cromwell Road, Hove, East Sussex BN3 3ER (01273 707481).

Euro-Academy, 77A George Street, Croydon, Surrey CR0 1LD 0181-681 2905.

GEOS English Academy, 55-61 Portland Road, Hove, Sussex BN3 5DQ (01723 735975).

International Language Centres, International House, Palace Court, White Rock, Hastings TN32 1JY (01424 720100). 60+ sports and activity leaders as well as 200+ EFL teachers.

King's College, 31 Poole Road, Bournemouth, Dorset BH4 9DL (01202 763615).

Living Language Centre, Highcliffe House, Clifton Gardens, Folkestone, Kent CT20 2EF (01303 58536). 50 teachers needed for centres in Kent and Oxford.

Nord-Anglia, 10 Eden Place, Cheadle, Stockport, Cheshire SK8 1AT (0161-491 4191).

OISE, OISE House, Binsey Lane, Oxford OX2 0EY (01865 792799).

Passport Language Schools, 37 Park Road, Bromley, Kent BR1 3HJ (0181-466 5925).

SUL Holidays Ltd., Beech Holm, 7 Woodland Avenue, Tywardreath, Cornwall PL4 2PL (01726 814227).

TASIS England American School, Coldharbour Lane, Thorpe, Surrey TW20 8TE. Counsellors as well as teaching aides needed.

YES Educational Centres/International Study Tours, 12 Eversfield Road, Eastbourne, East Sussex B21 2AS (01323 644830). Teachers for German and other groups in southern England.

The teacher shortage in Britain is still acute in some places though it has improved somewhat. Many local Education Authorities mainly in inner and outer London are constantly in need of supply or temporary short-term teachers who are paid a daily rate ranging from about £70 to £110. For example inner city deprived areas like Tower Hamlets depend very largely on Antipodean teachers who currently account for about half the supply teachers working in that borough. Further details are available from the Tower Hamlets Supply Agency, 3rd Floor, Mulberry Place, 5 Clove Crescent, London E14 2BG (0171-512 4381); applications are especially welcome from teachers trained to teach the early years. The Wandsworth Education Department (0181-871 7977) is another borough which advertises for teachers.

The alternative to applying direct to the relevant local boroughs is signing on with a specialist agency, to which most boroughs now turn for their supply staff. Agencies such as the Timeplan Education Group (0181-343 4488) and QED Educational Consultants (2 High St, Chesham, Bucks. HP5 1EP; 01494 773393) place thousands of teachers in state schools. Beware of disreputable agencies (one of which is rumoured to be working out of a chip shop) which do not check references or police records and are prepared to provide strike-breaking teachers. The average daily rate for an agency teacher is £75.

In order to obtain 'Qualified Teacher Status' (QTS), trained teachers from outside the EU must complete a period (typically one term) as either a licensed or an authorised teacher. These must be applied for by a local education authority or the board of governors of a self-governing school. Leaflets explaining who is eligible are available from the Department for Education, Mowden Hall, Staindrop Rd, Darlington, Co. Durham DL3 9BG.

APPLYING LOCALLY

British readers may decide that it is easiest to save money by working close to home. If you have had no luck through the Jobcentre, by answering newspaper adverts or by registering with private employment agencies such as Alfred Marks or Manpower, you may want to spread your net even wider. The *Yellow Pages* are an invaluable source of potential employers in anything from market gardening to market research. Personal visits are also a good idea, for example to the Personnel Managers of large department stores, supermarkets, the Body Shop, fast food restaurants or canneries in your area, especially as summer approaches. Marks & Spencer offer better wages than most, e.g. over £3 an hour even for 16 year olds. Staff turnover is high at DIY chain stores (where people over 18 are paid from £3.25 an hour). Or you could approach the local council, most of which hire temporary staff during the summer or at Christmas. Look for small notices advertising for house cleaners.

Market research agencies often require interviewers, though jobs in this industry are tighter than they were at the beginning of the decade. Since a few days of training are normally given, you should be available to work for at least three months, though the work is almost invariably part-time. A telephone is normally essential, a car useful. Telephone interviewers are paid from £3.50 an hour, personal interviewers from about £4 an hour. An Australian Ian Mitselburg got work in Edinburgh with a town planning consultancy (Halcrow, Fox & Associates, 4 Chester Road) interviewing people in Linlithgow on why, when and how they used their cars.

This was done in the evening and I have never been sooo cold in my life.

Knocking on doors seemed to crack my frozen fingers but the Oz accent helped a lot as it seemed to arouse curiosity and thus got me invited inside where it was warm. The same firm sent me to Oban to interview ferry passengers. Apart from the initial bout of sea-sickness, this was an excellent job as I got to see the outer Hebrides for free.

Investigate every avenue for boosting your travel fund. Brendan Barker says the oddest odd job he had in England was in police identity parades. He got £3 for 15 minutes 'work' while Thames Valley Police pay £10 per appearance. You have more chance of being called back if you are male and look fairly scruffy, though the Cambridge Constabulary have been known to flag down dons cycling to the library to fill a last-minute vacancy in a parade. Ian Mitselburg several times replied to the police request received at his Edinburgh hostel but thought that the system was unfair to the suspect since the Australasians, North Americans and Germans invariably had a healthier appearance than the Scots.

After job-seekers from abroad have been based in one place for a time, they can normally find some work. Although Woden Teachout, a young travelling American woman, did not have the benefit of a work permit, she pieced together several jobs in Cambridge within a couple of weeks:

In my terror at my shrinking funds, I accumulated five jobs: two cleaning, one nannying, one behind the bar at a red plush Turkish nightclub and one (which has stood me well) as a personal assistant to a professor.

The latter job, which was advertised on a notice board at the Graduate Student Centre, was by far the most interesting and also lucrative at £4 an hour. Similar notices for research assistants are posted in universities around the world, mostly in department offices and teaching buildings rather than in student unions.

Job Creation

If you can't find anyone to hire you, you can set yourself up in a small odd-jobbing business. Karen Weaving and Chris Blakeley, who claim to have no particular skills, set themselves up in Basingstoke as 'Spare Hands — Household & Domestic Services' and managed to save £4,000 in seven months, enough to fund a round-the-world trip. Within two months they were both working over 80 hours a week and earning an average of £2.50 an hour having found that gardening, decorating and catering were the most lucrative areas. After delivering and posting some publicity leaflets, they got a few customers, and word spread quickly that they were reliable and cheap. According to Karen and Chris, the question is not 'can I make a sandwich?' but 'can I sell a sandwich?'. Notice boards in newsagents' windows, colleges and unions sometimes give leads to potential dog-walkers, flat-cleaners, shirt-ironers, etc.

Anyone thinking of starting a new business should approach his or her local Training & Enterprise Council (TEC) which can offer advice and in some cases financial support. If your business plan is accepted and you have been unemployed for at least six weeks, you could be eligible for an Enterprise Grant which totals £1,260 over 36 weeks.

Building and Other Seasonal Work

Even the hard-hit building trade seems to be emerging from recession at the time of writing. At new building sites, ask to speak to the foreman (or gaffer) who may have powers of hiring or will at least be able to advise you on possibilities. There is more work for unskilled labourers as the foundations are being laid, though you might get hired at a later stage as a hodman carting the bricks and mortar up a ladder to the mason or bricklayer. Iain Kemble has financed several trips abroad after a spell as a self-employed hod carrier. Wages, even for the unskilled, are above average. When you are asking for work, don't admit either to being a student or having no experience.

You may prefer to build temporary rather than permanent structures. The work of erecting marquees pays fairly well, especially since time spent travelling to the destination is also paid, and there is usually some overtime. Two firms to try are Barker & Sons Ltd. (47 Osborne Road, Thornton Heath, Surrey CR7 8PD; 0181-653 1988) and M & B Marquees (Premier House, Tennyson Drive, Pitsea, Basildon, Essex SS13 3BT; 01268 558002). Check the local *Yellow Pages* for firms to contact. Keith Larner recommends a variation on this:

> *Now I can tell you about another good avenue for casual work. I've just completed a job erecting temporary grandstands for sporting events such as golf, racing and tennis. It is very physical work, extremely heavy-going, but financially rewarding: £30-40 per day, 7 days per week but only between April and October.*

Another well-paid though not necessarily desirable job is painting electricity pylons for which Mark Wilson was paid £200 a week. He can't recommend this to anyone who can't handle heights, but he certainly preferred it to chicken-catching.

> *I've done unpleasant jobs before (including four years down a coal mine) but this job really was the pits. You are expected to catch six chickens in each hand at a rate of 600 an hour. You then carry them outside (the only time the chickens ever see daylight) and load them onto lorries. While they are pecking and clawing your arms, you can often feel their legs breaking. This together with the screams and cries of the chickens and the stench in the sheds meant that I didn't keep this job up very long and have since given up eating factory-farmed products.*

Finally, don't overlook the obvious. The Post Office employs 100,000 temporary workers around Christmas. The pay is approximately £175 (gross) a week.

LONDON

Most new arrivals in the capital report that there is no shortage of work, even in a recession. The problem is finding affordable accommodation which allows you to save from what is seldom a startlingly good wage. Ian Mitselburg from Sydney went through the usual processes:

> *The first job I got was through a hostel notice board: labouring for a shifty hotel owner, who was restoring his hotel in the Paddington/Bayswater area (where else?) for a few weeks, paid cash-in-hand. After that I worked through the Everyman Agency in Earls Court which is run by a couple of Kiwis who clearly favoured Australasians.*

With over 2,000 employment agencies, London is the best place to look for temporary work. It is normally pointless to write to agencies before arrival in the capital, especially foreign applicants who have no chance of obtaining a work permit and who do not speak fluent English.

Wages start at about £3.30 per hour, but people with office skills willing to work seven days a week can take home more than £250 a week. Some like Share Staff Recruitment (0181-998 9910) specialise in placing out-of-town people in jobs as loaders and packers or silver service waiting staff and can advise on accommodation starting at £50 a week.

A number of agencies specialise in catering work, with whom you can expect to earn about £3 an hour as a kitchen porter, £3.20-3.50 as a catering assistant and £4 as an assistant cook. The Alfred Marks Agency has a branch devoted entirely to catering vacancies at 170 Fleet St, EC4A 2EA (0171-248 4281). For other agency addresses, look in the travel weeklies mentioned above, or try

Abacus Recruitment, 15 Cambridge Court, 210 Shepherds Bush Road, W6 (0171-602 9090), Coyne Agency, 60-66 Wardour St, W1 (0171-439 3851/437 3230), Reed Catering, 4 Ealing Road, Wembley (0181-903 5322), Mayday Catering Staff, 2 Shoreditch High St, E1 6PG (0171-377 1352) or Angel Recruitment, 50 Fleet St, EC4 (0171-583 1555). Also check out cleaning agencies, since there is an insatiable demand for house cleaners in the affluent suburbs of London.

Anyone who can speak a foreign language has an excellent chance of finding work at a tourist attraction. Young Europeans based in London should give this a go as Brigitte Albrech did:

With basic English and a lot of courage, I applied for a job at Madame Tussauds Museum and was surprised they accepted me without a lot of questions. They are always in need of people speaking a foreign language to work as guides and are looking for people who appear clean and patient. There is an opportunity of being trained as a cashier or planetarium operator, which would mean more money. It can be hard work but getting a work reference from Madame Tussauds is not bad at all.

There is a very high turn-over of staff at pubs (see section on pub work above), shops, wine bars, station buffets, etc. Check the classified adverts in the *London Evening Standard* (which comes out at about 11am), the free weekly *TNT* and the Employment Service's 'Call London Jobline' section in *LOOT*. As mentioned earlier in this chapter, the office of *New Zealand News* in the Haymarket has a useful notice board for job-seekers where job notices are posted as soon as they are received, often before they appear in the paper.

Modelling is a traditional way of earning cash; try the Chelsea School of Art, the St Martin's School of Art or the London College of Printing for nude or clothed jobs (£3-4 per hour).

Pubs

Anyone who has been on a pub crawl in London will know that a huge percentage of the people working behind the bar are Australian. For pub vacancies in London consult TNT and New Zealand News mentioned previously. Although there are employment agencies specialising in bar work, they aren't usually very helpful to people looking for casual bar work.

Kristen Moen from Norway describes her job in a London pub:

I loved it: the atmosphere was great, I had so much fun and met so much nice people at work. The only thing I can complain about is that the money is not very good — or maybe the rents for flats in London are too high. If I had had a work permit, I would have gotten a job immediately, but it took me two weeks. First I went around asking in pubs and restaurants. Everybody was really helpful. They would always suggest another place I could go to or tell me to come back in a few weeks. At the same time I was also reading the job ads in the Evening Standard. *70% turned me down because of my missing work permit, but finally I got something and worked happily there for four months.*

Now that EU citizens are allowed to work in Britain, Kristen's job hunt would be much easier.

Medical Experiments

There are some more unusual ways of keeping the cost of living in London down, for example making yourself the subject of medical experiments. The financial rewards can be reasonably good, e.g. £50-100 per day. Most volunteer subjects must now produce a medical certificate from their own doctor attesting to their good health, and in most cases foreign volunteers must prove that they are in the country legally. If you are not thoroughly screened, it may be that the research company does not comply with the rigorous standards set out by the Association of Independent Clinical Research Contractors and should be avoided.

One of the well-regulated clinics which carries out tests on paid volunteers is the Charterhouse Clinical Research Unit (The Royal Masonic Hospital, Ravenscourt Park, W6 0TN; 0181-741 7170); if you qualify and they have places available on any experiment you will be asked to attend for screening. The Volunteer Recruitment Officer is willing to fax anywhere in the world for the required medical history. After passing the screening you must undertake to abstain faithfully from eating or drinking anything in the 12 hours preceding the experiment. Between swallowing the experimental medications and having tests (e.g. blood tests, blood pressure, etc.), you will be given lunch and entertained with videos (e.g. *Zombie Flesheater, Coma* and *Love at First Bite*).

Guys Hospital also has a Drug Research Unit which is always looking for healthy volunteers and which, according to Michael Easingwood, pays £80-120 a day.

If the thought of subjecting your body to unknown drugs upsets you, then psychological experiments provide an easier (if less lucrative) alternative. Psychology researchers constantly need large numbers of volunteers and often receive grants specifically to pay subjects. It is worth enquiring at any university's psychology department about this opportunity. Unfortunately new regulations governing sperm donation mean that it is almost impossible for men to make an easy £10.

Couriers

Driving is a standard stop-gap job, for example of vans and mini-cabs or as a courier. Motorcycle owners might be tempted by the money which can be earned by despatch riders. For those who don't own their own bikes, they can be leased from the firm for about £60 a week. According to Ben Nakoneczny, despatch riders can earn between £200 and £500 a week:

> *Earnings are commission-only; they increase dramatically according to number of hours worked, knowledge of London streets and relationship with your controller. There is also a very high risk of serious injury, hence insurance premiums will be very high if you choose to declare your occupation for insurance and tax purposes, which many don't.*

The north London firm Moves (131 Salusbury Road, NW6; 0171-625 8565) is always looking for drivers, couriers and porters, and seems sympathetic to the erratic habits of people working for relatively short periods to fund their travels.

Although cycle couriers don't earn as much as despatch riders, it appeals to some brave souls like T. P. Lye from Malaysia who claimed that you do it for love not money:

> *After the first few weeks of courier cycling (which is the best job I've ever had) it should be possible to earn £80-150 per week. Anyone who is reasonably fit, can endure from 20 to 30 miles of cycling in a day, knows London pretty well, can read a map and loves the thrill of dodging in and out of the London traffic should try it. It can be quite scary cycling in the rain when your brakes don't work and you have to cope with cretinous pedestrians who can't see beyond their brollies, but after a while that sort of experience is part of the whole fun of courier cycling.*
>
> *The company I worked for was Arrow Express. They were always looking for new people since there is a high turnover especially during the winter months. The pay is always cash in hand and by the week. In my experience*

*the most boring days have been fine, sunny ones when everyone wants to
work and there aren't enough jobs to go round. One of the worst problems
is punctured tyres.*

Firms which advertise regularly are worth trying, e.g. D.I.D (0171-739 2722)
and Southbank Couriers (0171-729 5555).

Sales

People working in shops are often paid a commission in addition to the
average weekly wage of £150-200. Jobs in 'telesales' are also plentiful in London.
Telesales involve telephoning complete strangers and persuading them to buy a
product. Advertisements for this type of work frequently appear in the free local
newspapers in the London area, although they may not always mention the
nature of the job in the advert. The ones to look out for say things like: 'Do you
want to earn up to £X/week in your spare time?'.

Accommodation in London

If you are worried that you won't be able to afford to stay in London (short
of sleeping in Victoria Station), you might choose to stay at Tent City where the
overnight charge is £5. This hostel-under-canvas operates from early June to
late September. Their staff is made up of monthly volunteers between late May
and mid-September. They receive £30 a week pocket money plus bed and food.
Contact the administrator Maxine Lambert at Tent City (Old Oak Common
Lane, East Acton, W3; 0171-415 7143). A similar system operates at the Hackney
Camping Site (Millfields Road, E5) which also charges £4 a night to those who
have their own tent.

Squatting is still a possibility in London even though the government is trying
to rush through legislation which would allow squatters to be evicted after 24
hours notice with a possible penalty of a jail sentence or large fine if they refuse.
Ben Hockley from Australia describes his arrangement:

*After frequenting a few pubs around Kennington and talking to the locals,
a friend and I decided to get ourselves a squat. We were offered a few keys
to squats in the area for about £50, but eventually we just bought a room
from a couple of Spanish guys who were going home. The squat turned out
to be a godsend. The building we were in was full of squatters and there
was a real community atmosphere with people from all over the world
having a wonderful free London experience. Two years later I heard that
there were no problems from the police or the council.*

It might be worth bearing in mind that London's casinos serve free food to
members; membership is free but must take place 48 hours before turning up.

Free food and accommodation in exchange for some duties is a great bonus
in London. For example the charity SHAD recruits full-time volunteers to assist
people with severe physical disabilities to live independently in the community.
Volunteers are required to stay for a minimum of three or four months, and
receive a place to live and an allowance of £51 a week. A shift system is worked
by volunteers allowing plenty of free time to explore London. There are several
borough offices in London including SHAD Haringey, Winkfield Resource
Centre, 33 Winkfield Road, Haringey N22 5RP (0181-365 8528) and SHAD
Wandsworth, c/o The Nightingale Centre, 8 Balham Hill, Wandsworth SW12
9EA (0181-675 6095). Similarly Independent Living Alternatives (Fulton House,
Fulton Road, Empire Way, Wembley, Middlesex HA9 0TF) pays its full-time
volunteers £56 a week in addition to free accommodation.

VOLUNTARY WORK

Community Service Volunteers mentioned at the beginning of this chapter guarantee a voluntary placement to anyone aged 16-34 who commits him/herself to work in hostels or day centres for at least four months. Volunteers receive £22 a week in addition to accommodation and meals. Other organisations which provide board, lodging and pocket money to inexperienced volunteers willing to work at centres for the homeless are the Simon Community (PO Box 1187, London NW5 4HW; 0171-485 6639) and Homes for Homeless People (90-92 Bromham Road, Bedford, MK40 2QH; 01234 350853) whose minimum stays are three and six months respectively.

There are many shorter term opportunities for volunteers, especially during the summer months when organisations such as the Winged Fellowship Trust (Angel House, 20-32 Pentonville Road, London N1 9XD) and Mencap's Holiday Service (119 Drake St, Rochdale, Lancs. OL16 1PZ) recruit volunteers to help at their holiday centres for people with disabilities. Winged Fellowship, with centres in Southampton, Southport, Redhill, Nottingham and Chigwell, needs volunteers (British or otherwise) from February to November and pays all board, lodging and travel to the centres from within the UK. If interested in this kind of work, send 65p to the Royal Association for Disability and Rehabilitation (12 City Forum, 250 City Road, London EC1V 8AF) for Factsheet 13 'Opportunities for Volunteers on Holiday Projects'.

If you are more interested in conservation work, there are several national bodies which arrange one to three week work camps where volunteers repair dry stone walls, clear overgrown ponds, undertake botanical surveys, archaeological digs or maintain traditional woodland. You will be housed, usually in volunteer basecamps where conditions may be primitive, and you must contribute towards food. Contact the National Trust's Volunteer Unit (PO Box 538, Melksham, Wilts. SN12 8SU; 01225 790290) for a free brochure about their week-long projects which run year-round and cost £37, or the British Trust for Conservation Volunteers (36 St. Mary's St, Wallingford, Oxfordshire OX10 0EU) for a calendar of their projects. BTCV organise 600 working holidays from the Anglesey coast to the Pennines. The Scottish counterpart is the Scottish Conservation Projects Trust (Balallan House, 24 Allan Park, Stirling FK8 2QG) which organises around 80 residential Action Breaks throughout Scotland between March and November. For volunteers interested in the routine maintenance and conservation of old buildings, contact Cathedral Camps at 16 Glebe Avenue, Flitwick, Beds. MK45 1HS. These organisations charge a modest fee to cover expenses, e.g. £30-40 per week.

The need for medical volunteers is not confined to London. There are an estimated 55 clinical research units according to the Association of Independent Clinical Research Contractors. It is worth making enquiries at any teaching hospital or asking any medical student you happen to meet.

A number of organisations in Britain which require volunteers for limited periods are listed in the *International Directory of Voluntary Work* (published by Vacation Work at £8.95) and in *Volunteer Work* (from the Central Bureau at £8.99). Anyone who wants to participate on an archaeological dig should subscribe to *British Archaeological News* for £18, available from the Council for British Archaeology, Bowes Morrell House, 111 Walmgate, York YO1 2UA.

Volunteering is an excellent solution for anyone who has work permit problems. Americans, and indeed anyone, can fix up voluntary jobs independently as well as through the programmes mentioned at the beginning of this chapter. Janet Renard and Luke Olivieri are two particularly enterprising American travellers who arranged several voluntary positions before they left home.

One of the most unusual was working for the Festiniog Railway Company (Porthmadog, Gwynedd LL49 9NF) which operates a famous narrow gauge railway:

> *Many of the volunteers are railroad/steam engine fanatics, but accepted us even though we didn't know the first thing about it. We elected to work in the Parks & Gardens section and spent a week weeding, planting, clearing, etc. The work was hard and the hostel not so comfortable but everything else made the volunteer experience more than worth it. The evenings were busy — we were taken to a pub one night, asked to dinner another, visited a Welsh male voice choir and went climbing in the area. Festiniog Railway depends completely on volunteers who come from all over, all ages, all professions. But they can always use more help, so we may just go back.*

Other historic railways looking for volunteers, both in beautiful parts of the country, are the Rutland Railway Museum, Ashwell Road, Cottesmore, Oakham, Leicestershire LE15 7BX and the Swanage Railway Project, Station House, Swanage, Dorset BH19 1HB.

Communes (which are now properly called communities) may provide a good opportunity for people sympathetic to a back-to-basics lifestyle. The Centre for Alternative Technology in Wales (Machynlleth, Powys SY20 9AZ; 01654 702400) takes on volunteers between March and September, many on a short-term basis, paying £5.50 a day for food. Advance booking is essential. A directory called *Diggers & Dreamers* listing more than 80 communities in Britain and 400 contacts abroad is available for £10 (£11 overseas) from Diggers & Dreamers, Redfield Community, Winslow, Bucks. MK18 3LZ.

Laura Hitchcock from New York state managed to fix up two three-month positions in the field of her career interest by agreeing to pay her own expenses if they would take her on and help her find accommodation in local homes. Her jobs were in the publicity departments of the Ironbridge Gorge Museum (Ironbridge, Telford, Shropshire TF8 7AW) and then in a theatre-arts centre in East Anglia (The Quay at Sudbury, Quay Lane, Sudbury, Suffolk CO10 6AN):

> *I learned when writing not to ask for 'internships' but rather for 'unpaid work experience'; otherwise the British will ask you what hospital you are with! The particularly good feature of my jobs was that the people were so friendly. If you were willing to help yourself they'd do all they could for you.*

If you intend to become involved in the workcamps or organic farm movements abroad, it is advisable to get local experience first (see *Voluntary* chapter for addresses of internationally-active organisations and *Agriculture* for a description of the activities of WWOOF.

Ireland

You won't get rich in Ireland, but the warmth, friendliness and the great time you'll have will make any visit worthwhile. Although Irish people will probably express amazement that you are looking for work in their country (since so many of them flee from their galling unemployment rate of 16.9% to England and beyond), people do manage to find work. The Australian world traveller Heather McCulloch defends Ireland as a good destination:

> *Despite the high unemployment, low wages and heavy taxes, I lived and worked in Ireland for six months. The people and 'good crack' more than made up for not saving as much as I could have elsewhere. I had a wonderful time and wouldn't exchange the fun I had and the things I learned for anything.*

The Republic of Ireland is a member of the EU and so no work permit is needed by EU nationals. British citizens do not even require a passport.

North American Applicants

Foreign nationals who can prove Irish ancestry may be eligible for unrestricted entry to Ireland and even Irish nationality (which would confer all EU rights). Enquiries should be directed to the relevant Irish Embassy.

Both American and Canadian students are eligible to apply for an 'Exchange Visitor Program Work Permit' valid for up to four months at any time of the year. They must be students between the ages of 18 and 30 and have US$600/C$1,000 available to fund themselves while looking for work. Once in Ireland, the Union of Students in Ireland Travel Service (USIT) will advise on job opportunities (19 Aston Quay, Dublin 2; 1-677 8117). The work is tax-free. The Work in Ireland programme is administered by CIEE in the US (205 E 42nd St, New York, NY 10017) and the Canadian Universities Travel Service Ltd. (Travel CUTS) in Canada. The US fee is US$160.

A private organisation Dublin Internships (8 Orlagh Lawn, Scholarstown Road, Dublin 16) undertakes to find four-month internships in the student applicant's field of interest with Dublin companies and government bodies. A placement fee of $1,150 is charged.

Tourism

The tourist industry is the main source of seasonal work in Ireland. Outside Dublin, the largest demand is in the south western counties of Cork and Kerry, especially the towns of Killarney (with 107 pubs) and Tralee. Write to the addresses in any guide to hotels in Ireland. One hotel chain which hires chefs, porters and waiting/bar staff for the summer season is Sinnott Hotels, Furbo, Co. Galway (091-92108). When applying, you should mention any musical talent you have, since pubs and hotels may be glad to have a barman who can occasionally entertain at the piano. Directly approaching cafés, campsites, amusement arcades and travelling circuses is usually more effective than writing.

In Dublin, try the trendy spots in Templebar in the city centre, such as the Elephant & Castle, an eating spot which hires mostly foreign workers. The going rate for general runners and waiters/waitresses starts at just £2 but tips can be good. Also try the Tex/Mex restaurant in Nassau Street called Judge Roy Beans, downstairs from the nightclub Lillie's Bordello (where workers can earn excellent tips). The owner is said to be well informed about other Dublin restaurants and clubs so a visit to JRB can be worthwhile.

Monitors and instructors are needed for children's activity centres such as Errislannan Manor Connemara Pony Stud (Clifden, Co. Galway) where pony trek leaders are needed for three months in the summer. West of Ireland Activity Centre, a Christian outdoor adventure centre, hires qualified activity instructors for variable periods from May to September and also accepts volunteers for domestic and manual work; applications to Loughanelteen, Sligo; tel/fax 071-43528. Catering staff must have EU-recognised food hygiene certificate. Experienced assistants and instructors may be needed by riding stables and watersports centres throughout Ireland.

There are innumerable festivals throughout Ireland, mostly during the summer. Big-name bands often perform at concerts near Dublin. A small fortune can be made by amateur entrepreneurs (with or without a permit) who find a niche in the market. Heather McCulloch had two friends who sold filled rolls and sandwiches at a major concert and made a clear profit of over £1,000 in just a few hours.

'The Rose of Tralee', a large regional festival held in Tralee, Co. Kerry in the first week of September, provides various kinds of employment for enterprising workers, as Tracie Sheehan reports:

> As 50,000 people attend this festival each year, guest houses, hotels, restaurants and cafès all take on extra staff. Buskers make great money, as do mime artists, jugglers and artists. Pubs do a roaring business, so singing or performing in a pub can be very profitable.

Grafton Street in Dublin is *the* place for buskers and street traders. The Irish are a generous nation and appreciate muscial talent.

Other Possibilities

The employment service of Ireland is FAS (Foras Aiscanna Saothair) with about 70 offices throughout the country which EU nationals may consult. There are a number of private employment agencies listed in the 'Irish Golden Pages' with whom you may register. The Irish Department of Enterprise & Employment (Davitt House, Adelaide Road, Dublin 2) can send a list of all licensed employment agencies. Heather McCulloch had great success with agency work:

> It took two weeks of enlisting with every agency I could find in Dublin before one called with work in their offices. My hourly rate was £4 with plenty of overtime (though tax and PRSI are extortionate).

Heather also did a stint of door to door selling and reports that the Irish are more welcoming than most nations especially to someone with a foreign accent. Although she was enjoying this job, she soon quit, not only because it was on a commission-only basis but because she felt uncomfortable passing off mass-produced Taiwanese pictures as 'original oil paintings'.

Foreign women may wish to consider au pairing in Ireland via one of the several agencies which combine an au pair placement service with language instruction. For details contact Langtrain International (Torquay Rd, Foxrock, Dublin 18) or the Language Centre of Ireland (45 Kildare St, Dublin 2). Another agency to try in Ireland's second city is Job Options Bureau, Tourist House, 40-41 Grand Parade, Cork. The pocket money for au pairs is on a par with that in Britain, starting at IR£30 a week. One important difference between Irish and English agencies is that the ones in Dublin charge a placement fee, normally IR£40. Ireland is a popular destination for students of English from the Continent, so anyone with a background in TEFL might apply to the above addresses for a summer job as an English teacher or monitor.

There is little chance of finding paid work on farms because of high rural unemployment. Even if the occasional vacancy does arise, the farms are small, widely dispersed and have no coordinating body to facilitate recruitment. However there is a good network of farms and smallholdings which allow people to work in exchange for keep. One source of farms where you can stay for a weekend, week, month or longer is Irish WWOOF (c/o Annie Sampson, Tulla Post Office, Tulla, Co. Clare). For a membership fee of IR£5 she will send the current listing of farm members.

Some rural addresses in Ireland can be hard to track down as Armin Birrer once discovered:

> Once in Ireland I spent two days looking for an organic farm I had the address of. When I finally got there, I found out they were looking for a person to start up an organic farm and thought that I would be the man. I told them I wouldn't be that good at it, got a couple of days work in their stables and gardens for food and free camping, and then moved on.

On a more hopeful note, the American David Stamboulis writing in the magazine *Transitions Abroad* found the opportunities in rural Ireland to offer plenty of non-financial rewards:

I discovered farmers, three nursery owners and small communities with plenty of work to be done. Just politely asking was usually all it took to get four hours of work per day in exchange for room and board. Always, the work was fun, challenging and unpressured, because I was not doing it for money. The food was usually self-produced and self-prepared; and the accommodations were always interesting, ranging from small crofts to large farms.

Voluntary Opportunities

A wide range of two or three week workcamps are held all over Ireland from June to October. Recent projects include converting an old prison into a community centre, inner city playschemes and environmental work. Recruitment in Britain is done by IVS in Colchester, Leeds or Edinburgh; the camps in Ireland are organised by Voluntary Service International (30 Mountjoy Square, Dublin 1). With most workcamps, there is a registration and insurance fee of between £20 and £30 per week which covers full board.

The Roman Catholic voluntary organisation Pax Christi (9 Henry Road, London N4 2LH; 0181-800 4612) needs volunteers to staff playschemes in Northern Ireland for three to five weeks each summer. Food, accommodation and insurance are provided. The Simon Community of Ireland (PO Box 1022, Dublin 1) takes on committed volunteers for a minimum of three months to work with long-term homeless people at their shelters and residential houses in four Irish cities. Volunteers work on-site for three days and then get two days off where they stay in a separate flat. The remuneration is IR£34 per week.

With renewed hopes of peace in Northern Ireland, volunteers are especially needed by a Christian organisation which is working for reconciliation in Ireland; contact the Corrymeela Community (5 Drumaroan Road, Ballycastle, Co. Antrim BT54 6QU) which works with children and families at the Corrymeela Centre on the north-east coast of the country. Volunteers can stay from one to three weeks in July and August and receive free board and lodgings. Long-term volunteers must apply by February to work for a year starting in September or by November to work for six months staring in March. Volunteers receive £20 per week pocket money.

An Oige, the Irish Youth Hostels Association (61 Mountjoy St, Dublin 1; 830 4555) has 43 hostels throughout the country and relies to a large extent on voluntary help. Many assistant wardens are needed June to September and general assistants to help with maintenance, office work, conservation, etc. year round. As throughout the world, you can always approach busy hostels to see if they need an assistant. The hostel just outside Killarney often employs foreign travellers.

Conservation Volunteers Ireland (PO Box 3836, Ballsbridge, Dublin 4; 01-668 1844) coordinates and promotes unpaid environmental working holidays on behalf of 17 affiliated conservation organisations. A £10 annual membership fee will get you details of weekend and longer projects. The average cost for a weekend is £15. Among these are the Irish Georgian Society (74 Merrion Sqare, Dublin 2) which needs people to renovate 18th centuery properties and Groundwork Conservation Centre (132a East Wall Road, Dublin 3) which runs summer workcamps to preserve wildlife habitats.

Up to 25 volunteers with a scientific background are needed to carry out research into various aspects of the marine environment at a marine station in Ireland between April and October. Volunteers must be graduates with a relevant degree and stay between three and nine months; further details from the Sherkin Island Marine Station, Sherkin Island, Co. Cork (028 20187).

Netherlands

During the recession of the early 1990s, Holland became an even more popular destination for job-seeking Britons than ever. They poured off the ferries, checked into hostels and began looking for the highly paid jobs and liberal attitudes (e.g. to drugs and prostitution) they'd heard about. Some drew benefit while they looked and in many cases Dutch tolerance was tested. The market for unskilled non-Dutch-speaking workers was not quite saturated but it left a lot less room for manoeuvre than previously.

Yet the country still absorbs large numbers of itinerant European workers. The job search should not be confined to Amsterdam, since there are temporary employment agencies aplenty and many opportunities in Rotterdam, The Hague, Haarlem, Leiden and Utrecht; the rural east and north of the country should be avoided since unemployment there is much higher.

The state-subsidised organisation for international youth activities is Exis, Prof. Tulpstraat 2, 1018 HA Amsterdam; 020-626 2664; the postal address is Postbus 15344, 1001 MH Amsterdam. They publish a free one-page information sheet in English called *Key to the Netherlands* which gives a general outline of exchange possibilities. The only activity for foreign young people which Exis actually arranges is au pairing (described later in the chapter).

The Regulations

All job-seeking EU nationals must follow the bureaucratic procedures which are strictly followed by agencies and employers in all but a handful of cases.

Contrary to what one might have expected in the new harmonised Europe, the Dutch have been tightening up the regulations in an attempt to clamp down on squatters, drug abusers and other undesirables.

The first step is to acquire a stamp in your passport which grants permission to work for up to three months. This can be obtained from the local aliens police (*Vreemdelingenpolitie*) or Town Hall, normally over-the-counter. They will expect you to provide a local address — hostel addresses will normally suffice — and it is best to use this same address throughout your stay. The stamped passport should then be taken to the local tax office to apply for a *sofinummer* or '*sofi*' (social/fiscal number). It is also possible to apply for a *sofi* from outside the Netherlands, though this will take at least six weeks; send a copy of your passport details to Belastingdienst Particulieren/Onderneminenbuitenland, Postbus 2865, 6401 DJ Heerlen.

Only after these steps have been taken is it possible to register with employment bureaux or take up a job. To turn the initial stamp into a residence permit *(Verblijfsvergunning)* after three months, you will have to show a genuine work contract or letter of employment from an employer (not an agency) and pay a fee of 50 guilders. The contract will have to show that the legal minimum wage and holiday pay are being paid and the proper tax and deductions are being made. The registration office for foreigners in Amsterdam *(Bevolkingsregister)* is at Herengracht 531-537, 1017 BV Amsterdam, while the tax office *(Belastingdienst)* is at Kingsfordweg 1, 1043 GN Amsterdam. In rural parts of Holland, satisfying the bureaucrats may take several days and use up lots of petrol.

A further complicating factor is that job agencies may not be willing to sign you up unless you have a bank account and banks in areas frequented by short-stay workers have become reluctant to open accounts. In some cases a returnable deposit of 100 guilders has been charged. Look for the V.S.B. Bank which has been recommended.

The situation for non-EU nationals is predictably more difficult and also somewhat confusing. Whereas the official literature states categorically that non-EU visitors who enter the country as tourists are not allowed to seek or accept employment, other documents state that both you and your employer can apply for an employment permit (*tewerkstellingsvergunning*) from inside the Netherlands. In practice of course the *tewerkstellingsvergunning* is unlikely to be issued for any casual work. Jill Weseman, an America who worked as an au pair in Groningen, regretted her decision to follow the letter of the law:

> *The amount of paperwork I was required to present to the police was ridiculous. It took six visits plus several phone calls before I was 'official', at which point my passport was filled with meaningless but huge stamps.*

The Dutch have some of the most progressive laws in the world to minimise exploitation of workers. The minimum wages are very good for those over 23 but are much less for younger workers. The minimum net hourly wage is around 8 guilders. (Inevitably this prompts some employers to hire younger people whenever possible, often Dutch school children.) Compulsory holiday pay of 13% of your gross salary should also be paid on all but the most temporary casual jobs. Do not count on receiving the holiday pay immediately after finishing a job. Although one of Ian Govan's friends received his holiday pay two weeks after the vegetable harvest in Westland, Ian and another friend were told that it would be sent to their UK bank account several months later. Sure enough £250 arrived in time for Christmas.

Several travellers have recommended the *Arbeidsbureau* (Dutch equivalent of a Jobcentre) as a useful source of work. For example the one in Leiden treated Xuela Edwards and her travelling companion Nicky Brown better than any English Jobcentre they had ever been in. The helpful staff checked their computer, fixed up an interview and Xuela started work the following day. To find the local address, look up *Gewestelijk Arbeids Bureau* in the local telephone directory.

If you feel that you are not being treated fairly by an employer, you can get free legal advice from any branch of YIPS (Youth Information Points) or you can make enquiries at any Arbeidsbureau.

Private Employment Agencies

The majority of employers turn to private employment agencies (*uitzendbureaux* — pronounced 'outzend') for temporary workers, partly to avoid the complicated paperwork of hiring a foreigner directly. Therefore they can be a very useful source of temporary work in Holland. They proliferate in large towns, for example there are over 125 in Amsterdam alone.

Look up *Uitzendbureau* in the telephone directory or the *Gouden Gids* (Yellow Pages) and register with as many as you can in your area. Not all will accept non-Dutch-speaking applicants. Unless you have a telephone you must visit the office daily at opening time and perhaps twice a day since often the allocation of jobs is not systematic and once the phone is put down the agency forgets about you. Do not expect to be offered a job instantly, for the competition is stiff, especially in Amsterdam and especially during school holidays in August. Many agencies are downright discouraging, as Belinda Brzeski discovered:

The first chance we got we went round the agencies, setting off at 9am and finished exhausted at 5pm. None of them encouraged us and most said 'No chance, I'm afraid. I'm sorry but you don't speak Dutch'.

But no two travellers have the same experience. Martyn Rutter reported:

It's still quite easy to find work with the agencies. It took me two days of trying at the Manpower agency before they gave me a job in a warehouse. Most people get a job within three or four days. In fact I must have met 25 English and Irish people in the two months I was in Amsterdam, all of whom had found work through agencies. The only must is to be clean and tidy when applying.

While looking for dock work north of Haarlem, Murray Turner concluded that the *uitzendbureaux* were in the habit of promising more than they could deliver. He had just five days of work out of three weeks, and those were found by asking around at the docks, while the agencies produced nothing.

Uitzendbureaux deal only with jobs lasting less than six months. Most of the work on their books will be unskilled work such as stocking warehouse shelves, production line work in factories, washing dishes in canteens, cleaning, hotel work or fixing roofs in the snow. Most agencies are accustomed to foreign job-seekers and even in the so-called 'boondocks' will have an English-speaking member of staff.

These agencies gain their income by charging the employer a percentage of your wage, so employers are inclined to drop the wage to the worker. For example Iona Dwyer, who returned to the bulb harvest in 1994 and fixed up a job through an agency (details below), was paid 10% less than if she had been hired direct.

Among the largest *uitzendbureaux* are Randstad (with about 300 branches), Unique, Manpower, BBB and ASB. For example ASB have over 70 branches throughout the country with a main office in Amsterdam (020-664 4441), and they encourage enquiries from English speakers. The agency ASA (Algemene Studenten Arbeidsverlening) specialises in finding jobs for students. The Amsterdam branch receives many enquiries from English-speaking job-seekers and can place only a handful. You might have better luck at some of the many other branches for example the one in Leiden at Breestraat 171.

BENELUX

North Sea

Friesland

Groningen

De Koog

Emmeloord

Andijk
Alkmaar

Zwolle

Haarlem
Heemstede
Hillegom
Sassenheim
Katuijk a/Zee
Naaldwijk
Hook of Holland

AMSTERDAM
Hoofd d'orp
Lisse
Nieuwveen
Ter Aar
Leiden
The Hague
Delft
Rotterdam

NETHERLANDS

Enschede

Apeldoorn

Arnhem
Wageningen
Nijmegen

Utrecht

Gorinchem
Tiel

Breda

Vlissingen
Knokke-Heist
Bruges
Ostend

Baarland

Antwerp

GERMANY

Hasselt

Ghent

Vilvoorde
BRUSSELS
Rixensart

Liege

BELGIUM

Namur
Charleroi

FRANCE

Wiltz
Diekirch

LUXEMBOURG

Bouillon

LUXEMBOURG

Esch
Remich

The symbol for flowers
refers to packing and processing bulbs
as well as picking flowers.

WILLIAM SWAN

THE BULB INDUSTRY

Traditionally, the horticultural sector has had difficulty in finding enough seasonal labour for the processing of flower bulbs for export and related activities. Hordes of young travellers descend on the area between Leiden and Haarlem in the summer and there aren't enough jobs to go around. Still, large numbers of unskilled workers are employed in fields and factories to dig, peel, sort, count and pack bulbs.

Finding the Work

The first urgent need for casual workers takes place in mid to late June when the farmers take on people, typically for just 12 days, to peel bulbs in readiness for export. Ask at the local *Arbeidsbureau* or look for signs *(Bollenpellers Gerveggd)* in Hillegom, Lisse, Noordwijk, etc. This work is paid piece work, between 3.5 and 5.5 guilders per crate and it takes most people well over an hour to fill one. Because you are paid only according to how much you do, many workers take time off to visit the bulb factories in the neighbourhood to put their names on various waiting lists, in an attempt to secure a much more lucrative job as a bulb packer. This doesn't start until the end of July or even early August and lasts to October, when all the factories and associated campsites close down.

Anyone who shows up in July will probably find that the full-time jobs have already been allocated to the people who have been around for the peeling. The only possibility is to follow Xuela Edwards' advice which is to 'be prepared to knock on doors every day, not to be put off by the No Work signs and keep going back to factories and agencies'. At least you may find a few days work. For example Nicola Sarjeant went to the Werknet Uitzendbureau in Hillegom and got three 10-hour days of work filling and stacking boxes of bulbs, which paid a satisfying 500 guilders net, including overtime and holiday pay.

The best towns to head for are Hillegom, Lisse, Sassenheim and Bennebroek. It is becoming more difficult to be employed directly by bulb factories who prefer to use agencies such as the one Iona Taylor recommends: Tempo Team Uitzendbureau, Meerstraat 12a, 2181 BR Hillegom. They found her and many others work with J. Onderwater & Co. Export B.V., Heereweg 352, 2161 CC Lisse. They also handle vacancies at M. Van Waveren (POB 10, 2180 AA Hillegom) and various others in the area.

New arrivals will have no trouble locating the properties once they arrive. In Hillegom head for Pastoorslaan or Leidsestraat where many of the factories are concentrated and in Lisse, look along Heereweg. Previous editions have listed about 15 bulb firms, but these have not been included this year since it could not be confirmed that they reply to enquirers. The only one which did wish its vacancies to be publicised was Peter Keur BV (Noorder Leidsevaart 26, 2182 NB Hillegom; 02520-16608). It might also be worth trying the famous bulb exporter P. Bakker B.V., Postbus 601, 2180 AP Hillegom, or M.G.M. van Haaster, Lissedk 490a, 2165 AH Lissebroek. The long established firm Frylink & Zonen B.V. in Noordwijkerhout asked not to be included because they receive plenty of applications via word of mouth. They did offer Josephine Norris work in 1994, starting a month after her arrival but, as happens to many others, she could not afford to stay around.

You will be in a stronger position if you arrive with a tent. Traditionally seasonal workers congregate on big campsites, and will normally be willing to advise newcomers. A couple of years ago, campsites in the area banned bulb workers after the latter staged an 'uprising', but the situation seems to have improved somewhat. The need for workers is so urgent that employers have to find some way round the problem of accommodation. Martin and Shirine from Crawley worked for a farmer who risked trouble from the police by letting them camp in a disued field. Renting a flat is even more problematical since foreign workers have such a bad reputation for rowdiness and irresponsibility that few landlords will risk it. In the words of regular bulb worker Steve Dwyer:

> *A lot of undesirable modern hippies are going over to Holland just it seems to party, and this is bad news for the 'real travellers' like myself.*

Competition may be less acute at the more far-flung factories. Mark Wilson recommends having some transport:

> *Along with a tent, a necessity when looking for bulb work is a bicycle. While out exploring on my bike I came across an area full of factories just outside Noordwijkerhout, a village west of Lisse.*

Second-hand bicycles can be picked up for between 50 and 100 guilders.

Pay and Conditions

The bulb industry is better regulated than it once was which means that there is much less black work around. The hiring of non-EU nationals has virtually ceased and exploitation is less common. Excellent earnings are possible: Iona and Steve Dwyer return every year because in their opinion they can earn twice or three times more than they could in an equivalent time anywhere else. Overtime paid at a premium rate is what makes the big savings possible. Like most agricultural work, earnings fluctuate according to the weather; on a rainy day when the flowers don't open people are lucky to get four hours work.

Bulb-peeling is not a pleasant job as Martin and Shirine recall:

> *The work was hard on our hands and we soon resorted to wearing rubber gloves or plasters. The hours of work were 8am-5pm with an hour's lunch break and the choice to work until 10pm. That was a long time to spend crouched over a table, sitting on an old wobbly stool that was the wrong height for you.*

Mark Wilson had an even more miserable experience as a bulb peeler:

> *The first job I had was peeling the skin off the bulbs which was the most mind-numbingly boring job I have ever done. Later I was condemned to two weeks in the hyacinth shed which is kept away from the main factory. While working on a sorting machine in a loose T-shirt I found to my horror and my Dutch workmates' amusement that bulb dust is a very powerful irritant, so after a couple of hours of itching like a madman, I resigned on the spot, ran back to the campsite and dived into the shower to relieve my tormented skin.*

AGRICULTURE

Limburg

The 'deep south' of Holland is known among working travellers as more than the place where the Maastricht Treaty was signed. The area around Roermond (about 50km southeast of Eindhoven and north of Maastrict in the province of Limburg) is populated by asparagus growers and other farmers who need people to harvest their crops of strawberries, potatoes and other vegetables, especially in the spring. You can travel south from Roermond (on the N271) to villages such as Linne, St. Odilienberg, Montfort, Posterholt and as far as Susteren to find work. Going north, head for Venlo, Helden and nearby Panningen. If possible find someone to translate ads in the local paper the *De Limburger*. The agencies around here are less accustomed to dealing with non-Dutch applicants but can be all the more helpful for that. Joanne Patrick and Steve Conneely recommend an agency which deals exclusively with agricultural work: Limburgse Land-en Tuinbouwbond (LLTB), Wilhelminasingel 25, Postbus 960, 6040 AZ Roermond (04750-33243). Independently they found work picking potatoes and earned 1,600 guilders between them in two weeks in late February and early March. They were so taken aback to earn so much money that they spent it all on good times across the German border.

Asparagus picking starts just after the middle of April and lasts through to mid-June. Expect to start on the minimum of 8 or 9 guilders an hour but wages of more than double that are possible. A tent is a great advantage here. Murray Turner paid 7.5 guilders a night at a family-run campsite in Helden north of Roermond. The *uitzendbureau* he recommends is Adia Keser in the same town. According to Murray one of the biggest asparagus farms around Venlo is Teeuvan (04760-71444). Despite initial hopes that earnings would be high in the peak season, he ended up earning the standard 9 guilders an hour (or 1.20 guilders per kilo). He moved on to the strawberry harvest where earnings from piece work (2 guilders per 3-4kg crate) were very unreliable because of the weather. The asparagus harvest is similarly affected by weather; if it's hot you can work as long as you are able.

Westland

The area between Rotterdam, the Hook of Holland and Den Haag is known as the Westland. K. ('Moondog') McCausland recommends tomato picking here as another good alternative to bulb packing. The principal villages in the area are Naaldwijk, Westerlee, De Lier and Maasdijk, but the whole region is a honeycomb of greenhouses.

The tomato harvest begins in early to mid-April and this is the best time to arrive, although work is generally available all year round if you are prepared to work for at least one month. Although the work was boring and dirty with long hours — it was normal to start work at 5am and finish at 7pm or 8pm — conditions were usually good and accommodation was provided in a barn.

Once again a lot of the work in the area is registered with *uitzendbureaux*. Ian Govan recommends trying the ones in Naaldwijk, 's-Gravenzande and Poeldijk for work picking cucumbers, peppers, flowers, etc. Also try the flower and vegetable auctions *(bloemenveiling/groenteveiling)* in Westerlee/de Lier and Honselersdijk which need people to load the stock for auction buyers, etc. Ian Govan's overtime pay of up to 200 guilders was paid in cash on top of the 300-350 guilders he netted for a 38-hour week.

Work in tree and other nurseries abounds in and around Boskoop, 11km from Gouda south of Amsterdam. Anyone with any relevant experience should aim to arrive in the area between February and April. Nurseries are concentrated along Reijerskoop and Laag Boskoop. Job agencies will help; Dermot Campbell recommends the Optima Uitzendbureau on Bootstraat in Boskoop. It could also be worth advertising in the free local paper, *Gouwe Kourier*.

Hard fruits like apples and pears are picked later in the season. Try the area south of Utrecht called Betuwe (which means 'Good Land') around the towns of Culemborg and Buren.

Food Processing

Onion pickling in Baarland, near Vlissingen in Southern Holland, sounds fairly grim, so you might follow James Pollock's advice and work in apple, cherry and green bean factories instead:

There were many advantages. We did not reek of onions; we were paid fairly and directly by the factory owners rather than being ripped off by an agency; plus there were perks like the 'dead animal reward', a sum of £5 for any animal (from slugs to rabbits) found dead or alive amongst the green beans. As you can imagine many of the unfortunate creatures (often picked off roads on the way to work) completed many rounds on the conveyor belt. Some of us managed to double our wages so it was no mean perk.

There are several food canning factories in Zuid Holland (between Amsterdam and Rotterdam); make enquiries in Nieuwveen, Ter Aar and Roelofarendsveen. In the latter town try the Koelans pickle factory on De Lasso.

TOURISM

Dutch hotels and other tourist establishments employ a large number of foreign workers both full time and temporarily during the tourist season. Most are from southern Europe, but a certain number are from Britain and Ireland. According to Simon Whitehead, foreigners are the last to be hired and the first to be fired, so do not expect job security in a hotel job. Although you may be lucky enough to obtain a hotel job through an *uitzendbureau,* your chances will normally be better if you visit hotels and ask if any work is available, or keep your ears open in pubs frequented by working travellers.

While visiting a friend in the seaside resort of Zaandvoort south of Haarlem, Martin and Shirine tried to find work washing dishes for one of the many bars which line the beach. They knew that without speaking Dutch this was the only job they could reasonably expect to get. Unfortunately the poor weather that June meant that business was bad and the bars were not willing to take on extra staff. (As an aside, tradesmen looking for work should ask around at the Shamrock Bar in Zandvoort.)

OTHER WORK

Labouring work may be available in some of the massive docks of Rotterdam and Ijmuiden north of Haarlem. Murray Turner spent several weeks roaming the Ijmuiden docks and managed to get a few odd days of highly paid work. The work was too unreliable to result in impressive earnings.

Domestic cleaning is a more promising area of work. Although the job hunt in Leiden took Paul Bridgland four weeks, he finally found cleaning work (no thanks to any *uitzendbureaux*) which gave him 50 hours of not particularly strenuous work a week at 10 guilders an hour after tax. Nicola Sarjeant had a shorter wait before the Effect 2000 Uitzendbureau in Haarlem found her work cleaning banks for the same wage.

Opportunities in Amsterdam

As in Athens some Amsterdam hotels and hostelries hire 'runners' to meet the morning and afternoon international trains to persuade travellers to patronise the hostel. Enquire at budget hotels and hostels near the station. There are a number of Christian hostels in Amsterdam which allow residents who do some cleaning to stay free. Ian Mitselburg from Australia did this until he 'got sick of the niceness of the rest of the staff, especially the "whitebreds" from Ohio and Idaho.'

Advertising on notice boards is a popular way to draw attention to the service you can offer such as teaching English, typing, house cleaning, window washing and babysitting. Two of the best notice boards are at the Public Library (Prinsengracht 587, just north of Leidsegracht) and the University (the library is near the flower market at Singel 425 and the Literature Faculty is at 183 Singel behind the post office). It is worth taking some trouble over the presentation of your advert, and if you are wanting to teach English, type manuscripts, etc. it might even be worth getting a notice printed (which is quite cheap). Most people employ the technique of tear-off strips to save potential clients the trouble of copying down their name and particulars. Apparently people who can teach Spanish or creative dance are in great demand, whereas English tutors are ten a penny.

You might want to contact office cleaning services directly (see 'Schoonmaakbedrijf' in the *Gouden Gids* which are kept in public libraries but not in phone boxes), or ask cafés, of which there is no shortage in Amsterdam, if they would like you to clean their windows on a weekly or regular basis. (The Dutch are very particular about the cleanliness of their windows.)

There is an international market research agency which occasionally advertises for temporary English-speaking staff for special contracts. Contact Interview Marktonderzoekbureau, Overtoom 519/521 (020-6070707) to enquire about possibilities. Apparently there is a high turn-over of staff since persuading people to do lengthy surveys over the phone is not easy.

Busking is an ever-popular way to earn some money and the tolerance for which the Dutch are famous extends to street entertainers. The best venues are in the Vondelpark (where many Amsterdammers stroll on a Sunday) and in the city squares like Stadsplein and Leidseplein. Some pitches (like the one outside the 'smoking' coffee shop the Bulldog) are in such demand that you may have to wait your turn.

Au Pairs

Since Dutch is not a language which attracts a large number of students, au pairing in the Netherlands is not well known; however there is an established programme for those interested. The youth agency Exis mentioned above has a special unit called Exis-Klix which organises au pair placements for foreign men and women aged 18 to 30. Such placements will follow (to the letter) the agreement of the Council of Europe (see *Childcare* chapter) which means that working conditions are favourable (e.g. pocket money of 500 guilders per month and insurance costs met by host family) but you must stay at least six months with the family. Application must be made through Exis's partner agencies; the list from the above address includes about ten in the UK (e.g Childcare Europe, Quick Help and Avalon (see page 128), one in the US (Interexchange, 161 Sixth Avenue 902, New York, NY 10013) and others in Eastern and Western Europe.

There are other private agencies outside Amsterdam such as Au Pair & Activity International, Steentilstraat 25, 8711 GK Groningen (or PO Box 7097, 9701 JB Groningen); 050-130666/fax 131633, which places up to 150 au pairs a year. It organises meetings and trips for all its au pairs. Jill Weseman from the States was very pleased with the service Au Pair International provided and also with her experiences as an au pair in a village of just 500 people 30km from Groningen:

After graduation I accepted an au pairing position in Holland, mainly because there is no prior language requirement here. I really lucked out and ended up with a family who has been great to me. Though the situation sounds difficult at best — four children aged 1½, 3, 5 and 7, one day off a week and a rather remote location in the very north of Holland — I have benefitted a great deal. The social life is surprisingly good for such a rural area.

Jill's job was set up by World Learning Inc. in Washington (see page 127).

Voluntary Work

Although the Netherlands is in so many ways a progressive country, there are still undeveloped corners as Joan Regan found when she joined a farm-based project not far from Rotterdam which was affiliated to IVS. In fact all the major workcamp organisations arrange camps in Holland over the summer. Two of the main ones, ICVD and Vrijwillige Internationale Aktie, are at the same address Marius van Bouwdifj Bastiaanse straat 56, 1054 SP Amsterdam. Applications to participate in ICVD projects may be sent direct, whereas VIA is part of Service Civil International and applications should be made through IVS. If you are in the Netherlands you might also make enquiries of SIW Internationale Vrijwilligersprojekten (Willemstraat 7, 3511 RJ Utrecht; 030-317721); otherwise apply through affiliated workcamp organisations at home, e.g. Concordia, IVS and QISP in England. The registration fee for most Dutch workcamps is about 100 guilders. Archaeological and building restoration camps are arranged by NJBG (Prins Willem Alexanderhof 5, 2595 BE Den Haag; fax 070-335 2536) who are hoping to publish their brochure in English at some point.

Belgium

Belgium is a country which is often ignored. Sandwiched between France and the Netherlands, its population can be broadly divided between the French-speaking people of Wallonia in the south and those who speak Flemish (which is almost identical to Dutch) in the north. The wages in Belgium fall somewhere between the high wages of Holland and those of France.

Belgium has no large agricultural industry comparable to those of its neighbours: it needs neither the extra fruit pickers that France does, nor the unskilled processors of Dutch bulbs. Furthermore Belgium has about the same rate of unemployment as the UK, i.e. 9.7%.

As in neighbouring Holland, employment legislation is strictly enforced in Belgium with favourable minimum wages, compulsory bonuses, sickness and holiday pay for all legal workers. The demand for temporary workers is especially strong in Belgium because of the generous redundancy regulations which discourage employers from hiring permanent staff. Of course the large number of multinational companies, attracted by the headquarters of the European Union in Brussels, have a constant and fluctuating demand for bilingual office workers.

The usual rules apply to EU nationals coming to work or live in Belgium: EU nationals arriving in Belgium to look for work and who intend to stay for a period of three months or more should, as in Holland, register within eight days at the local Town Hall where the *administration communale* will issue either a temporary *certificat d'immatriculation* valid for three months or the one year certificate of registration (*certificat d'inscription au registre des étrangers* — CIRE).

Non-EU citizens will have to find an employer willing to apply for a work permit on their behalf from the Office National de l'Emploi. They must be in possession of this permit before arrival, when they can then apply for an authorisation of provisional sojourn. Brett Archer from New Zealand reports that a rising number of labour checks designed mainly to catch Belgian nationals working black have made employers much more reluctant to hire people from outside the EU. Brett was caught but was lucky enough not to be penalised.

Au pairs from outside the EU must apply to the Ministère de l'Emploi et du Travail, rue Belliard 51-53, 1040 Brussels (02-233 41 11) for a one year 'B' permit. Further details on this subject are available from the Visa Department of the Belgian Embassy (103 Eaton Square, London SW1W 9AB).

Seasonal Work

Although Belgium's seaside resorts like Knokke-Heist, Blankenberge and De Panne, and other holidays centres like Bouillon in the Ardennes are hardly household names, there is a sizeable tourist industry in Belgium where seasonal work is available. The more mainstream tourist centre of Bruges is very busy in the summer. Travellers are often given free accommodation in exchange for some duties at one of the city's four or five unofficial hostels. According to Brett Archer, who worked several seasons at the Bauhaus International Youth Hostel at Langestraat 35, there are never enough people around to work in restaurants and bars during the summer. Expect to earn at least BF200 an hour. Look also for opportunities as a seasonal guide with one of the coach tour companies which run tours of scenic and historic Belgium.

The best way of finding short term work, apart from contacting possible employers directly, is to visit a branch of the Belgian employment service in any town. A special division called 'T-Service' in French-speaking areas and T-Interim in Dutch-speaking areas specialises in placing people in temporary jobs. Most jobs obtained through the T-Service will be unskilled manual ones such as stocking supermarket shelves. They may also be able to help skilled secretaries who can function in French to find temporary office positions.

The employment services in Belgium are divided into three regional branches: Greater Brussels (ORBEM), French-speaking Belgium (FOREM) and Flemish-speaking Belgium (VDAB), with addresses as follows:

ORBEM (Office National Bruxellois de l'Emploi), Boulevard Anspach 65, 1000 Brussels (02-505 14 11). The T-Service (Service Intérim de l'ORBEM) is next door at number 69 (02-511 23 85).

FOREM due to move to Charleroi; address not known at time of writing. If writing in advance, address your enquiry to the International Relations section at rue des Poissonniers 13, 1000 Brussels (02-502 44 59/fax 513 41 70).

VDAB, Keizerslaan 11, 1000 Brussels.

Other T-Interim/T-Service branches include:

Lemonnierlaan 129-131, 1000 Brussels (02-514 5700).
Avenue des Arts 46, 1040 Brussels (02-513 7739).
Rue Général Molitor 24, 6700 Arlon (063-22 66 45).
Rue Montignies 36B, 6000 Charleroi (071-31 74 45).
Rue de la Province 22, 4020 Liege (041-41 03 10).
Jezusstraat 5-7, 2000 Antwerp (03-232 9860).
Spanjaardstraat 17, 8000 Bruges (050-440470).
Pensmarkt 2, 9000 Ghent (091-240920).
Thonissenlaan 47, 3500 Hasselt (011-221177).
Beheerstraat 68, 8500 Kortrijk (056-203079).
De Merodelei 86, 2300 Turnhout (014-422731).
21 Witherenstraat, 1800 Vilvoorde (02-252 2025).

Other T-Service offices in French-speaking Belgium can be found in Huy, La Louviere, Mons, Mouscron, Namur, Tournai, Verviers and Wavre.

People who live in the south-east of England should make use of EURES Crossborder Kent (Shorncliffe Road, Folkestone, Kent CT20 2NA; 01303 220580/fax 220476) which assists people looking for jobs in Belgium.

Agencies

Private employment agencies in Belgium are licensed either to make temporary or permanent placements but not both. Contracts through temp agencies (of which there are nearly 100 altogether in Belgium) are normally for a maximum of six months. They are required to become the employer and to provide the same benefits to temps as those to which full-time employees are entitled. Unlike Dutch *uitzendbureaux*, they are normally interested only in finding jobs for qualified and experienced workers. For example the agency Select Interim (Avenue de la Joyeuse Entrée 1-5, bte. 14, 1040 Brussels; 02-231 03 33) places secretaries and personal assistants in positions lasting at least three months. About half of these temporary assignments turn into permanent ones. Other agencies with offices throughout Belgium include GREGG Interim and Randstad Interim; the latter has 22 branches and operates an English-speaking personnel department at its office in central Brussels (Hoofdkantoor, Muntplein, Prinsen-straat 8-10; 02-209 12 11). Randstadt is particularly strong on catering personnel.

Anyone who wishes to be an au pair in Belgium has a very good chance of success since the demand far exceeds the supply and is increasing all the time. Belgian agencies which can help find au pair families are Windrose (Av. Paul Déjaer 21A, 1060 Brussels; 02-534 71 91) which charges an administrative fee of BF1,000, Stufam (Vierwindenlaan 7, 1810 Wemmel (02-460 33 95) and the Catholic organisation Services de la Jeunesse Feminine (29 rue Faider, 1050 Brussels (02-539 35 14). The current monthly pocket money for au pairs is BF10,000-14,000 whereas mother's helps should receive up to BF18,000.

Berlitz have several schools in Belgium which employ native English speakers with a university background or equivalent to teach English. A three-week training course in the Berlitz Method is compulsory. Full-time teachers earn about Br80,000 per month. Details from Berlitz, Rue St.-Michel 28, 1000 Brussels (02-219 02 74). The organisation Séjours de Vacances WIAMS (rue François Bossaertsstraat 14, 1030 Brussels; 02-735 58 83) hires English teachers to teach young Belgians during the Easter and summer holidays at a holiday centre in Turnhout not far from the Dutch border.

Another company which runs summer language courses for teenagers is Prolinguis (Institut de Langues, Place de l'Eglise, Thiaumont 6717; 63-22 04 62) for whom Philip Dray, an EFL teacher from Ireland, worked during the summer of 1994:

> *I am employed in a freelance capacity to work 90 days between April 5th and September 15th. The salary is the equivalent of £60 a day and I have a sort of hotel room in a building that houses the students' dorms. For my keep I have to check the dorms twice a week, which is not too bad since most of the kids have been cooperative. The work is grammar-based but with some emphasis on games and role play.*
>
> *At best, the food is like hospital food; at worst it is indescribable. There was a story going around that one of the students once went ape after three weeks of the food in the 'restaurant' and, when he complained, the chef came out and laid into him. The police were called but nothing was done except that the teacher who phoned the police was sacked.*

Contacts

The National Youth Information Centre (CNIJ) is a non-profit making organisation which coordinates ten youth information offices in French-speaking Belgium. These can give advice on work as well as leisure, youth rights, accommodation, etc. A leaflet listing the addresses is available from the CNIJ at Impasse des Capucins 2 bte. 8, 5000 Namur (081-22 08 72). In 1993 they published the *Guide for Young Visitors in Belgium* (with a section on employment) which is available in English for BF120 (plus BF40 for postage). In Brussels Infor-Jeunes can be found at 27 rue Marché-aux-Herbes.

Belgium's English language weekly publication *The Bulletin* occasionally carries job adverts such as live-in positions and language tuition. Its address is 329 avenue Molière, 1060 Brussels; the magazine is published on Thursays and can be bought from newsstands for BF80. *Newcomer* is a free bi-annual publication (available from the above address) which is aimed at new arrivals in Belgium. The free weekly newspaper *Vlan* is an effective advertising medium for prospective au pairs under the heading *Gens de Maison*. The daily *Le Soir* is also worth consulting for employment and au pair jobs.

Asking around for construction work, especially in Antwerp, may pay off. Wages are reported to be high, which normally means jobs will be scarce for new arrivals.

Voluntary Work

The Flemish association of young environmentalists called Natuur 2000 (Bervoetstraat 33, 2000 Antwerp; 03-231 26 04) organises summer conservation workcamps open to all nationalities. The registration fee of BF1,000 covers accommodation, food, insurance and local transport. Those interested in participating in residential archaeological digs for three weeks in July should contact Archeolo-j (Avenue Paul Terlinden 23, 1330 Rixensart; 02-653 8268/ fax 02-654 19 17). There is a charge for membership in the Society and for camp expenses. Alternatively, you can join a dig at a mediaeval castle in Flanders through Jeugd en Kultureel Erfgoed (Heidestraat 118, 3590 Diepenbeek) where two-week camps cost up to BF1,000. An excavation of an 11th century church in eastern Belgium also takes on volunteers who pay by the week; contact the Centre Stavelotain d'Archéologies, Abbaye de Stavelot, 4970 Stavelot.

WEEBIO, the Belgian equivalent of WWOOF, is now defunct.

Luxembourg

If Belgium is sometimes neglected, Luxembourg is completely by-passed. Yet it is an independent country with an unemployment rate of less than 2%, and a number of useful facilities for foreigners. The national employment service *(Administration de l'Emploi)* at 38a rue Philippe II, 3rd Floor, L-2340 Luxembourg (478 53 00) operate a *Service Vacances* for students looking for summer jobs in warehouses, restaurants, etc. To find out about possibilities, you must visit this office in person, although EU nationals looking for long-term jobs may receive some assistance by post. Other branches of the employment service are located in Esch-Alzette, Diekirch and Wiltz, but the headquarters is the only one to have a *Service Vacances* section. Paul Newcombe found the service very helpful and was delighted to be given details of a job vacancy at an American bar in the capital. While cycling through the country, Mary Hall was struck by the number of travellers working on campsites and in restaurants in Luxembourg City.

Formalities for EU nationals are minimal, though anyone who wishes to reside in the country must take a battery of documents to the *Police des Etrangers* (Ministère de la Justice, 16 boulevard Royal, Luxembourg; 479 44 50) and obtain a five-year residence permit from the Bureau des Etrangers (9 rue Chimay, L-1333 Luxembourg; 479 62 52). Non-EU nationals must obtain a work permit *(Déclaration Patronale)* from an employer (which has been approved by the Administration de l'Emploi) and submit this to the Luxembourg Embassy in his or her home country before departure (which is nearly impossible at present).

The Range of Jobs

With a population of just 395,200, job opportunities are understandably limited, but they do exist especially in the tourist industry. Even the Embassy in London at 27 Wilton Crescent, London SW1X 8SD (0171-235 6961) maintains that 'seasonal jobs are often to be found in the hotels of the Grand Duchy of Luxembourg' and will send a list of the 250+ hotels in exchange for an A4 envelope with a 50p stamp. Wages are fairly good in this sector, often about £500 per month after room and board. (The franc is identical to the Belgian franc.)

The main language is Luxembourgish (variously called Luxembourgeois and Letzeburgesch) but both German and French are spoken and understood by virtually everyone. Casual workers will normally need a reasonable knowledge of at least one of these. Temporary office work abounds since many multinational companies are based in Luxembourg, some of whom may regard a knowledge of fluent English in addition to a local language as an advantage. Addresses of potential employers can be obtained from the Luxembourg Embassy who on receipt of an s.a.e. will send lists of British and American firms, as well as of the largest local companies.

Several agencies specialise in temporary work. Manpower-Aide Temporaire, 19 rue Glesener, L-1631 Luxembourg (48 23 23) handles all types of work and Adia Travail Temporaire, Grand rue 70, L-1660 Luxembourg (46 08 68) deals mainly with office work. Officenter, 25 boulevard Royal, L-2449 Luxembourg (47 25 62) also arranges temporary office jobs, and is willing to sign up students.

Other Helpful Organisations

The youth and student office CIJ (Centre Information Jeunes, 76 Boulevard de la Pétrusse, L-2320 Luxembourg; 40 55 50) runs a holiday job service between May and August for students from the EU. They can also inform you what the national minimum wage is for someone of your age and background.

Luxembourg Accueil Information (10 Bisserwee, L-1238 Luxembourg-Grund; 4 17 17) is a centre for new arrivals and residents. Amongst other services, it provides a contact point for families looking for au pairs and for young European women looking for au pair placements. Legislation requires au pairs to submit an 'Accord Placement Au Pair' to the *Administration de l'Emploi* setting out the conditions of work signed by both the employer and the au pair.

The ecological organisation Projektzentrum Gruberierg are building a park in Pétange in southern Luxembourg and have asked the British Trust for Conservation Volunteers to help recruit paying volunteers. The cost for a ten-day workcamp in November is £120.

If you want to check newspaper adverts, buy the *Luxemburger Wort* (especially on Saturdays), *Tageblatt* or the English language *Luxembourg News* (31 allée Scheffer, L-2520 Luxembourg; 47 00 52).

Grape-Picking

Luxembourgeois wine producers need help in the vineyards along the Moselle in the southeast of the country around the town of Remich. The harvest normally begins around the middle of September and continues for four or five weeks. The only way of finding out about harvest jobs, as Ian Black discovered, is to go straight to the region and ask the farmers directly. The Institut Viti-Vinicole, Boite Postale 50, 5501 Remich (6 91 22/6 91 60) does not arrange jobs, though it may be able to estimate the starting date of the harvest and give more precise dates closer to the time. To show how the starting dates fluctuate, the past five September starting dates have been the 13th, 17th, 25th, 18th and 14th. In 1994 the harvest lasted from 17th September to 2nd October.

Kristof Szymczak has picked grapes in Luxembourg for the past four seasons: *It was very easy to find work just walking along the Moselle valley from the villages of Schengen and Wasserbillig . People are really wonderful. I always received board, lodging and about £25 per day.*

France

Although you may occasionally encounter the legendary hostility of the French towards the English, more often you will be treated with warmth and helpfulness especially in the countryside. There are so many English-speaking people resident in France that expatriate grapevines are an invaluable source of job information. There is also an unemployment rate of 12.7%, with a rate twice as high among the young, so do not expect to walk into a job just because you have a GCSE in French and enjoy eating *pains au chocolat*.

Although the French tourist industry offers many seasonal jobs, there are even more in agriculture: approximately 100,000 foreign workers are employed on the grape harvest alone. Most of these foreign workers are from Eastern Europe, North Africa, Spain and Portugal, but plenty of other nationalities can be found picking fruit too. You may find yourself working in the fields next to an office worker from Basingstoke and a student from Harvard or a young Dane or Scot who is spending a couple of years touring Europe as a nomadic worker. It is possible to support yourself throughout the year in France by combining work in the various fruit harvests with either conventional jobs such as tutoring in English, or more unusual occupations from busking to gathering snails.

One important feature of working in France is that you should be paid at least the *SMIC (salaire minimum interprofessionel de croissance)* or national minimum rate. There are slightly different rates for seasonal agricultural work and full-time employees, but at present the rates are F34 or F4,737 per month which are adjusted annually to take account of inflation. In 1994 conservatives in the French government tried to lower the SMIC by one-fifth for non-graduates under the age of 26 (in an attempt to bring down the rate of youth unemployment). But the French are so proud of their SMIC that the proposal was fiercely contested on the grounds that it would turn young people into cheap labour, and the government was forced to water it down.

THE REGULATIONS

To combat rising unemployment, a powerful political lobby wants to clamp down on black work, and the authorities have become even more committed to enforcing employment legislation. Tax inspectors and immigration officers have been doing spot checks in tourist resorts, and employers in even the most out-of-the-way places have refused to hire anyone who lacks the right documents, whether or not they are EU nationals. However, according to one source (uncorroborated by the French Embassy), anyone can work for up to seven days without a permit.

British tour operators have been exempted, at least unofficially, from many French regulations, e.g their seasonal workers are not paid the SMIC nor are they likely to be making social security payments in France. The government wants to change all that, especially in areas where Britons are seen to be taking jobs away from locals (as in the case of ski chalets).

For European Union Nationals

As in all other member states, EU nationals are permitted to stay in France for up to three months without obtaining a residence permit *(carte de séjour)*. Once you have a job and know you are going to stay longer than three months, you should apply for a *carte de séjour* at the local police station *(préfecture)* or town hall *(mairie)*. Take your passport, four photos, some proof of your local address (e.g. rental contract, receipt for rent) and a job contract or, failing that, proof of funds (F1,000 should be enough) and credit cards (with recent receipts to prove their validity). The list of requested documents differs from place to place and in some cases you will be asked to show an officially translated and authenticated copy of your birth certificate, which must show your parents' names. Geoff Halstead followed the instructions given by the French Consulate in London and ended up spending more than £25 turning his birth certificate into an acceptably 'legalised' document. If in France, ask at any of the six British Consulates. The *carte de séjour* itself is free, and should be granted automatically once you have the right documents. This can take some time to come through — eight months to be precise in Stephen Psallidas's case — but in the meantime a *récépissé* for a *carte de séjour* should satisfy most employers. If you are planning to stay in France for no more than three months, you shouldn't have to bother with any of this, though employers are often unaware of the regulations, in which case you should suggest that they contact the *préfecture* to confirm it. But having a residence permit improves your chances of being hired; for example Vicky Nakis is fairly sure that she missed out on a short-term cleaning job at Eurodisney the first time round because she lacked one.

Confusingly, some employers and job centres have insisted that prospective employees obtain a *fiche d'état civil* from the *mairie* (town hall). For this you will need the same documents as for the *carte de séjour* apart from the job contract. Brendan Barker describes his struggle to obtain one in Bordeaux:

> *We met the patron who was looking for plum pickers, but he said we needed a* fiche d'état. *So we went to the* mairie *to get one. We were asked if we had our birth certificates and we said no (my girlfriend's was lost and mine was locked up in storage in England). We were told 'no birth certificate, no* fiche d'état'. *Back to the* patron *who said 'no* fiche d'état, *no work.' We*

went back to the guest house depressed. That evening I read Work Your Way Around the World *and was sparked by some of your contributors' determination in trying again. So the next day we marched down to the* mairie *and this time we explained our situation to the mayor. As she was looking us up and down, we both gave desperate smiles and the mayor said it was OK for us to be given the FDC. We breathed a great sigh of relief and got the work picking plums.*

When you start work, your employer should apply for a social security number (usually referred to as a *sécu*). The lack of one may harm your job-finding chances and in fact most private employment agencies are not willing to register you without one. Several travellers have suggested inventing one according to the following formula: 1 for men, 2 for women, followed by your year of birth, followed by your month of birth, followed by 99 if you're not French, followed by any three digits, so for example the number for a female foreigner born in May 68 could be 2-68-05-99-222.

Legal employers will deduct approximately 18% for social security payments, even before you have a number. These can be counted towards National Insurance in Britain, if you subsequently need to claim benefit. You may also lose a further 5% in tax. A further difficulty for legal workers is the difficulty in cashing pay cheques. Stephen Psallidas reports that it is so difficult for foreigners to open a bank account, that you'll have to eat your pay cheques before you can cash them. His solution was to open an account at the Post Office which seemed much easier. After the plum harvest finished, Brendan Barker was told that he would have to wait eight days to be paid and that the cheque could be cashed only at the local village Credit Agricole.

Any EU national aged 18-27 with a vocational qualification but not a university degree should investigate the EU-funded Petra schemes. In 1994 they were offering one month's language tuition in Devon followed by three months' work experience in France for a mere £100. Details are available from ProEuropa (Europa House, Sharpham Drive, Totnes, Devon TQ9 5HE; 0803 864526). This compares favourably with the work experience scheme in which Andy Green participated for two months in Limoges through Interspeak (see page 133). Since his role was mainly to observe rather than to work, he was unpaid by the firm to which he was attached, and by the time he had paid the agency fee and for food and accommodation, he was £1,000 out-of-pocket, yet still considered it all worthwhile for the experience. The European Employment Service has a regional branch in south-eastern England (EURES Crossborder Kent, Shorncliffe Road, Folkestone, Kent CT20 2NA; 01303 220580/fax 220476) which assists people looking for jobs in Northern France.

Non-EU Formalities

Non-EU nationals must obtain work documents before they leave their home country in order to work legally. These must be applied for by the employer through the Office des Migrations Internationales (44 rue Bargue, 75732 Paris). Special exemptions exist for certain categories such as au pairs and students. For example, non-EU nationals who have been studying in France for one year can apply for a holiday work permit if they can prove that they are full-time students and have an employer willing to hire them (for a maximum of three months). Other non-EU nationals with an international student card and a definite job offer may also be eligible for a temporary work permit. For further details request the leaflet *Séjour et emploi des étudiants étrangers* (No. 5.573) from the CIDJ (address and description below).

It is impossible to generalise about whether French employers are willing to hire people off-the-books, though it is possible to find laid-back employers from

The symbol for flowers refers to the castration of maize flowers

WILLIAM SWAN

the restaurants of Nice to the mushroom farms of the Loire Valley. Michael Jordan from the United States was told by grape growers in Alsace that his nationality would present no problems, whereas Brad Allemand from Australia was told by the farmers he approached in Ste Cecile des Vignes near Orange that they were frightened of the spot-checks by the immigration authorities and so couldn't risk hiring him.

Special Schemes for Americans

There is a special scheme by which American students with a working knowledge of French (normally a minimum of two years' study at university) are allowed to look for a job in France at any time of the year and work for up to three months with an *authorisation provisoire de travail.* This scheme is organised by CIEE, at 205 East 42nd St, New York, NY10017 (212-661-1414 ext 1130). Eligible Americans already in France may apply to the CIEE office in Paris (1 Place de l'Odéon, Paris 75006; 1-44 41 74 74). There is also a possibility of extending the permit in France.

Interexchange (161 6th Avenue, New York, NY 10013; 212-924 04660) can place American people as camp counsellors and au pairs in France. Worldwide Internships & Service Education (WISE, 303 S Craig St, Pittsburgh, PA 15213) sends au pairs from the US to France and also arranges internships in Paris.

THE JOB HUNT

Anyone with access to a private telephone should be aware of the widely used French Telecom subscriber service *Minitel* similar to Ceefax. With it, ordinary people can access a variety of databases including one for job vacancies or even to advertise their own availability for work. The general Minitel number for *Offres d'Emploi* is 3615 CIJPA. There are also a few specialist numbers such as 3614 Alpes for vacancies in winter resorts.

Not all hitch-hikers rank France very highly but once you get into the countryside, the French can be remarkably generous not only in offering lifts but in helping their passengers to find work. As usual the *Pages Jaunes* (Yellow Pages) can be a great help when drawing up a list of relevant places to ask for work. If you are offered seasonal work ahead of the job starting date and plan to leave the area in the meantime, stay in constant touch with the employer; not only can starting dates vary but farmers and hotel managers don't always keep their promises.

There are various organisations and agencies described below which can help both students and others to find work.

ANPE

The *Agence National pour l'Emploi* or ANPE is the national employment service of France, with dozens of offices in Paris and hundreds throughout the country. The headquarters are at 4 rue Galilée, 93198 Noisy-le-Grand (1-49 31 74 00). Although EU nationals are supposed to have equal access to the employment facilities in other member states, this seldom seems to be the case in France and is never the case unless the job-seeker speaks flawless French. Sometimes they refuse to help you unless you have a stable local address. Furthermore ANPEs are often criticised for giving out inaccurate information, especially concerning the grape harvest (see below).

But for all the ANPEs which are unsympathetic, there are exceptions. Phil New was lucky enough to find an ANPE employee in Lyon who claimed to like the English and who gave him the address of a farmer near Belleville with an opening, and Vicky Nakis heard about a promising-sounding housekeeping job through a Paris ANPE. So if you speak French you should visit the ANPE, while being prepared for a disappointing reception. Most ANPEs display cards with potential employers to whom you can apply directly.

Seasonal offices are set up in key regions to deal with seasonal demands like the *Service Vendanges* for the grape harvest and the *Antennes Saisonnieres* set up in ski resorts. These may be more likely to assist working travellers than the permanent offices which deal primarily in full-time jobs for French citizens. The addresses of ANPE offices recommended as offering seasonal work are listed in the relevant sections later in this chapter.

CIJ

There are 32 *Centres d'Information Jeunesse* or CIJ in France which may be of use to the working traveller. Helping people to find jobs is only one of their activities: they can also advise on cheap accommodation, the legal rights of temporary workers, etc. The main Paris branch is CIDJ *(Centre d'Information et de Documentation Jeunesse)* whose foyer notice board is a useful starting place for the job-seeker in Paris. It can also provide leaflets on such subjects as seasonal agricultural work, possibilities for work in the summer or winter, and the regulations that affect foreign students in France. To obtain these by post send four international reply coupons to CIDJ at 101 Quai Branly, 75740 Paris Cedex 15 (1-44 49 12 00).

In order to find out about actual vacancies you must visit the offices in person, preferably first thing in the morning. Employers notify centres of their temporary vacancies; some offices just display the details on notice boards, while others operate a more formal system in co-operation with the local ANPE. You will find *Centres d'Information Jeunesse* in the following towns: Amiens, Angers, Bastia (Corsica), Besancon, Bordeaux, Caen, Cergy Pontoise, Claremont-Ferrand, Dijon, Evry, Grenoble, Lille, Limoges, Lyon, Marseille, Melun, Montpellier, Nancy, Nantes, Nice, Orleans, Poitiers, Reims, Rennes, Rouen, Strasbourg, Toulouse and Versailles.

Julian Peachey found the Marseille CIJ at 4 rue de la Visitation (91 49 91 55) helpful for agricultural jobs (including on the *vendange*), though they mainly hold details of jobs at holiday centres, especially as *animateurs*. Needless to say it is necessary to visit the Centre in order to find out about these.

Some CIJs publish free lists of potential employers. For example Stuart Bellworthy made good use of a list given out by the CIJ in Angers which gave all the *producteurs* in the area with estimated harvest dates. About a third of the vacancies with which the CIJs deal are for mothers' helps, for which good French is not a prerequisite.

A similar range of jobs is notified to the Centres Régional des Oeuvres Universitaires et Scolaires in all university towns. Although they primarily assist registered students to find part-time and holiday jobs, they have been known to help foreign travellers who approach them in the right way.

Private Employment Agencies

Private employment agencies in France are prohibited from dealing with permanant jobs and so all are *agences de travail temporaire* (temporary work bureaux) or *agences intérimaire*. Among the largest are Manpower, Bis and Select France. Many specialise in a field such as industrial, medical or office work, and vacancies for unskilled jobs are few and far between. To find a job through an agency you first need to register, which is not as easy as it sounds. The law requires that you have a French social security number to give them, which you will only have if you have already had a legal job in France — another of those classic working travellers' catch-22s: you can't get work in France unless you've worked in France.

Yet some travellers have made good use of them. On his year abroad during his degree course, Matthew Binns went to a job agency in Paris called Stylma on the off-chance:

I foolishly said I was prepared to do anything. The bloke in the agency looked astonished and gave me, I think, the most unpopular job on his books — plongeur *in a factory canteen in the suburbs. George Orwell's account in* Down and Out in Paris and London *about his time as a* plongeur *should be required reading for all would-be dishwashers in Paris. I did three weeks in this job until the regular* plongeur *came back, poor sod. The worst bit is arriving at work with a hangover and putting on yesterday's wet clothes. But the pay was excellent (F49 an hour).*

TOURISM

The best areas to look for work in the tourist industry of France are the Alps for the winter season, December-April, and the Côte d'Azur for the summer season, June-September, though jobs exist throughout the country. The least stressful course is to fix up work ahead of time with a UK campsite or barge holiday company in summer or ski company in winter. Horizon HPL (South Bank House, Black Prince Road, London SE1 7SJ; 0171-735 8171, and 17 rue Pache, 75011 Paris; 1-40 24 09 31) is a French-British training organisation which offers a package combining language tuition and a live-in hotel job in Paris or beyond. The wages are on a trainee scale of £40 per week though accommodation is provided. Horizon charges a fee of £240. Another possibility is Travelbound (Olivier House, 18 Marine Parade, Brighton, East Sussex BN2 1TL), which hires people, who need not have qualifications, to work in hotels in France.

If you set off without anything prearranged, one of the easiest places to find work is at fast food establishments; Americana is very trendy in France at present and English-speaking staff fit well with the image. The hardest place to find work, except at the lowest level (e.g. dishwasher) is with reputable French-owned hotels and restaurants, where high standards are maintained. Your best chances will be in small family-run hotels where the hours and conditions vary according to the temperament of the *patron*.

Hotel and Restaurant Work

People with enough time to make long term plans can write directly to the hotels in the region which interests them, listed in any tourist hotel guide. Remember that the vast majority of restaurants are staffed by waiters rather than waitresses. Newspapers in holiday towns may carry adverts, e.g. *Nice Matin*.

But most people succeed by turning up at a resort and asking door to door, and in the opinion of veteran British traveller Jason Davies, 'door-to-door' should be just that:

Before I was down to my last F100 I had been choosy about which establishments to ask at. 'That doesn't look very nice' or 'that's too posh' or 'that's probably closed' were all thoughts which ensured that I walked past at least three in five. But in Nice I discovered that the only way to do it is to pick a main street (like the pedestrianised area in Nice with its high density of restaurants) and ask at EVERY SINGLE place. I visited 30-40 one morning and I would say that at least 20 of those needed more employees. *But only one was satisfied with my standard of French, and I got the job of commis waiter.*

Speaking French to a reasonable standard greatly improves chances of finding a job, though fluency is by no means a requirement. Kimberly Ladone from the American east coast spent a summer working as a receptionist/chambermaid, also in Nice, though her job hunt did not require the same dogged determination as Jason Davies did:

I found the job in April, at the first hotel I approached, and promised to return at the start of the season in June. While there, I met many English-speaking working travellers employed in various hotels. No one seemed bothered by work permit regulations as most jobs paid cash in hand. (A friend who had a work permit from CIEE spent weeks looking for a job and once he found one, his boss paid him under the table anyway.) My advice to anyone seeking a job on the French Riviera would be to go as early in the season as possible and ask at hotels featured in English guidebooks such as Let's Go: France, *since these tend to need English-speaking staff. My boss hired me primarily because I could handle the summer influx of clueless tourists who need help with everything from making a phone call to reading a train schedule.*

If in Avignon, the Koala Bar (run by Australians, naturally) has been recommended for having a notice board useful to job-seekers.

Beach restaurants are another hopeful possibility. Julian Peachey put on his one white shirt and pair of smart trousers and began visiting the restaurants along the beach by Avenue Montredon in the eastern part of Marseille. After the third request for work he was handed a tea towel, and proceeded to work 14-16 hours a day, seven days a week. Only the thought of the money kept him sane. The wage was severely cut on days when it rained or the mistral blew and no one came to the beach.

It must be said that not everyone finds work so easily as Alison Cooper found:

Last summer I tried to find work along the French Riviera, but was unsuccessful. I met many people at campsites who were in the same position as myself. From my experience most employers wanted people who could speak fluent French, and German as well. Otherwise you have to be very very lucky.

In the opinion of Andrew Giles the best time to look for work on the Côte d'Azur is the end of February when campsites well known to working travellers, such as Prairies de la Mer and La Plage at Port Grimaud near St Tropez host representatives from camping holiday companies trying to get organised in time for Easter. If you are on the spot you can often wangle free accommodation in exchange for three or four hours of work a day. If you can't be there then, try the middle of May at the beginning of the peak season. Bars recommended by Andrew where you can meet local workers and residents include Marilyns (Prairies de la Mer), Mulligans (Holiday Marina), Finnigans (Port Grimaud) and L'Utopée (Marines Cogolin). Also, try to listen to the English station Radio Riviera based in Nice which at 9.30am and 4.30pm broadcasts job vacancies along the coast and will also announce your request for a job free of charge. When Peter Goldman couldn't find work on boats as he had hoped (because of rainy September weather) he tuned in to Radio Riviera and got a job stripping wallpaper from luxury apartments in Monte Carlo for F400 a day.

Campsites and Holiday Centres

There are 7,000 campsites in France, some of them small family-run operations which need one or two assistants, others on an industrial scale. You can write directly to the individual campsite addresses listed in any guide to French campsites (e.g. the Michelin *Camping and Caravanning Guide*), or you can simply show up. Robert Mallakee and a friend easily found campsite jobs as they hitched along the Mediterranean coast in August which is the month when almost everyone in France takes their annual holiday. There is a point in the summer at which workers who have been there since the beginning of the season are getting bored and restless, which creates a demand for emergency substitution to cover the last two months of the season. Jobs included cleaning the loos, manning the bar or snack bar, doing some maintenance, etc. Some will be especially interested in people with musical ability. Even if there are no actual jobs, you may be given the use of a tent in exchange for minimal duties.

A number of British-based travel companies offer holidaymakers a complete package providing pre-assembled tents and a campsite courier to look after any problems which arise. Since this kind of holiday appeals to families, people who can organise children's activities are especially in demand. In addition to the Europe-wide companies like Eurocamp (addresses on page 101), the following all take on couriers and other seasonal staff:

Canvas Holidays Ltd, 12 Abbey Park Place, Dunfermline, Fife KY12 7PD (01383 644007).

Carisma Holidays, Bethel House, Heronsgate, Chorleywood, Herts. WD3 5BB (01923 284235).

French Country Camping, 126 Hempstead Road, Kings Langley, Herts. WD4 8AL (01923 261316).

French Life Holidays, 26 Church Road, Horsforth, Leeds LS18 5LG (0113 258 4518).

Ian Mearns Holidays, Tannery Yard, Witney St, Burford, Oxon. OX18 4DP (01993 822655).

Keycamp Holidays, 92-96 Lind Road, Sutton, Surrey SM1 4PL (0181-395 8170). One of the biggest, with requirements for approximately 350 couriers.

Sandpiper Camping Holidays Ltd, 19 Fairmile Avenue, Cobham, Surrey KT11 2JA (01932 868658).

Select France, Fiveacres, Murcott, Oxford OX5 2RE (01865 331350).

The best time to start looking for summer season jobs in England is between November and February. In most cases candidates are expected to have at least 'A' level standard French, though some companies claim that a knowledge of French is merely 'preferred'. It is amazing how far a good dictionary and a knack for making polite noises in French can get you.

Outdoor activity centres are another major employer of summer staff, both general domestic staff and sports instructors. Try the companies mentioned in the chapter *Tourism* as well as Acorn Ventures (137 Worcester Road, Hagley, Stourbridge DY9 0NW). You might also be able to find work with a French firm like one of the numerous canoe hire centres in the Ardèche. A law was passed in 1994 (aimed primarily at unregistered ski instructors) prohibiting the teaching or supervision 'in any sport, whether as a principal, secondary, seasonal or occasional occupation' without a recognised diploma. If this were to be enforced, it would have a devastating effect on British-run holiday centres.

Keen cyclists could try to get a job with a cycling holiday company active in France such as Belle France (Bayham Abbey, Lamberhurst, Kent TN3 8BG) and Susi Madron's Cycling for Softies (2-4 Birch Polygon, Rusholme, Manchester M14 5HX).

A new company has just been launched provisionally called Active Pursuits which will run campsite and activity holidays for adults in France. The director, Jim Gibbons, is looking to hire a range of catering staff and instructors in water sports, cycling and hiking, and offers an assessment and training scheme to inexperienced applicants. Details are available from Active Pursuits, 56A London Road, Dover, Kent CT17 0SP; 01304 210130.

Ski Resorts

For several reasons France ought to be the best of all countries in Europe for British and Irish people to find jobs in ski resorts. France is the number one country for British skiers with 200,000 British skiers going there annually, and most of the resorts are high, with snow conditions reliable throughout the season. The main problem is the shortage of worker accommodation; unless you find a live-in job you will have to pay nearly holiday prices. Since many top French resorts are purpose-built, a high proportion of the holiday accommodation is in self-catering flats or designed for chalet parties. This means that not only is there a shortage of rental accommodation, but there are fewer jobs as waiters, bar and chamber staff for those who arrive in the resorts to look for work. There is an increasing number of English and Irish style pubs which are good places to find out about work.

Between 20 and 30 British tour companies are present in Méribel alone, so this is one of the best resorts in which to conduct a job hunt. It may even be worth calling into the tourist office to ask about seasonal employment at a local hotel. Resorts like this are flooded with British workers and British guests, many of them school groups. Thus, only English is spoken for most of the time and there is little chance of meeting French people. Usually, you would be given time to ski every afternoon but would be paid comparatively low wages and given only one day off a week. One of the many UK operators which recruits staff is Ski Scott Dunn (Fovant Mews, 12 Noyna Road, London SW17 7PH).

Another promising resort is Chamonix, where Sean Macnamara obtained a series of manual jobs as a dishwasher and handyman through the local ANPE office. In fact the ANPE mount a concerted campaign every winter called A£ (ANPE Alpes Action) to attract qualified resort staff. Temporary job centres are set up in most resorts and are coordinated by the permanent ANPE offices. For example the ANPE in Albertville (12 rue Claude-Genoux, BP 133, 73208 Albertville Cedex; 79 37 87 80) has a centralised placement service for vacancies in a wide range of resorts including Chamonix, Megève, Les Arcs, Tignes, Val d'Isère and Méribel. Some other relevant offices open year-round include:

Aix-les-Bains ANPE, 12 rue Isaline (79 88 48 49).

Annecy ANPE, 1 Av de Genève (50 27 99 82).

Cluses & Flaine ANPE, 10 rue Charles Poncet (50 98 92 88).

St Jean-d-Maurienne ANPE, 7 rue de l'Orme (79 64 17 88).

Sallaches ANPE, 704 Av de St Martin (50 58 37 12).

Thonon ANPE, 6 Av St Francois de Sales (50 71 31 73).

Success is far from guaranteed in any ski resort job hunt and competition is increasing for the jobs available. Val d'Isère attracts as many as 500 ski bums every November/December, many of whom hang around Dick's Bar or the ANPE for days in the vain hope that work will come their way. With such an inexhaustible supply of ski bums, some employers are ready to hire people for Christmas, work them non-stop over the high season, pay them far less than the *SMIC* and fire them if they complain. If hotels and catering jobs are in short supply, au pairing is worth considering. The agency Mary Poppins (6 rue du Camping, 73200 Albertville; 79 37 85 49) has many au pair and au pair plus positions in the main ski resorts with French families (e.g. hotel owners, shopkeepers, ski instructors). A ski-pass is usually part of the deal.

There are one or two agencies which arrange for young people to work in ski resorts. Jobs in the Alps (PO Box 388, London SW1X 8LX) carry out aptitude tests on behalf of Nouvelles Frontières and other hotels to recruit workers for various French resorts. The net salary in 1994/5 is £570.

Another agency is UK Overseas Handling (UKOH, Le Plein Soleil, 73550 Méribel-Mottaret; 79 00 42 91) which recruits for large and small self-drive

British ski companies operating in the Trois Vallées, Tignes/Val d'Isère, La Plagne and Les Arcs, as well as for a French company called Eurogroup which owns and operates hotels, restaurants and nightclubs in Méribel and Courchevel. Both agencies are looking for people with excellent French, though in the latter case fluent French is not a requirement for skilled chalet girls/boys. Lotus Supertravel (Hobbs Court, Jacob St, London SE1 2BT; 0171-962 9933) takes on winter staff for France, primarily reps, odd-jobbers, ski guides, cooks and chalet girls. All applicants must have EU passports, be over 21 and have cooking/skiing qualifications.

According to K. McCausland, four-wheel drive exhibitions like the major one held each August in Val d'Isère are increasingly popular in the French Alps. They generate plenty of casual work, so ask the tourist office for dates and venues. They also afford a good chance to talk to ski season bosses and fix something up well ahead of time. (The vast majority of ski jobs are sorted out by the end of November.) Looking for work out-of-season in October and November has the added advantage that well-placed hostels (like the one in Séez where Matthew Binns stayed) are empty and relatively cheap. Matthew also recommends a free Red Cross hostel in Bourg-St Maurice.

Selling to Tourists

One of the most well known summer jobs in the south of France consists of selling refreshments on beaches. You can find foreigners doing this on beaches in and around Port Grimaud, San Tropez, Fréjus, Pampelonne and indeed all along the Mediterranean coast. Buy one of them a drink and he or she will direct you to their boss. Many bosses allow sellers to camp on their land. Sellers are paid on commission and earnings differ enormously. Nigel Baker who worked on the beaches along the Côte d'Azur for three seasons found that, for him, the positive aspects of the job outweighed the negative ones and wrote about his experiences in *TNT* magazine:

Beach selling is not for wimps. It is hard work, competitive and sometimes risky. However, if you find a good beach (the good ones change from year to year) you can spend a great couple of months living in a beautiful place... it's a great way to make a living!

Two of the firms whose names crop up are Daniel Auclair's Ice Cream in Cogolin and Sodifa which operates between Le Lavandou and Cannes. As in many jobs, the first day or two is by far the worst. If you stay long enough to get a few regular customers and if you're selling a product which isn't too repulsive (e.g. doughnuts, ice cream) you should be able to make between £15 and £25 by working a couple of hours in the morning and again in the afternoon. It seems that you have to be a raging extrovert to do well, with the gift of the gab.

The alternative to working for a boss is to go into business for yourself, by stocking up on fizzy drinks and beer from the local hypermarket, buying blocks of ice and heading for a beach crowded with thirsty holiday-makers. To do this legally you should have a licence (which costs thousands of francs). Otherwise you must be constantly vigilant and impersonate a tourist if you see the police coming. If caught, you will lose your stock at best and be arrested and fined at worst. The advantage is that you get to keep all the profits: sellers with experience and stamina can make up to £50 a day.

Stephen Hands travelled to Marseillan Plage near Montpellier. He thought he had prepared himself well with a cool bag, but discovered that a cool box was what was required since no one would believe the drinks in his bag were cool. He sold three cans in one hour before giving up while his friend managed eight cans in five hours.

Such entrepreneurial activities often meet with opposition from those who have already staked a claim, as Stephen Psallidas found in Père Lachaise cemetery in Paris:

I really was penniless so I thought up a scheme to make (I thought) vast profits. I would sell wine to all the hippies and camera-wielding tourists around Jim Morrison's grave. Macabre huh? So I bought a few bottles of el cheapo vin rouge and set up shop, complete with a sign in six languages. Unfortunately I was very quickly moved on by the established operators, who were mostly selling more exotic substances. So I drank the wine myself and had a very jolly time for the rest of the day.

Selling treats to tourists in ski resorts has also proved a lucrative sideline for some travellers-cum-ski bums. Simon Isdell-Carpenter started in Courchevel selling chocolates to the ski queues. Other entrepreneurs have made money by delivering croissants to chalets and inns either as an independent business or as an employee of the local bakery.

As usual you might be able to sell your talent to tourists as a busker. Leda Meredith made about F300 an hour as a dancer/mime in Avignon before and during the festival in August. Dustie Hickey also found work during the festival doing promotions (i.e. selling tickets and T-shirts) for an American theatre group. After the festival is over, however, street performers need a permit, and will be moved on by the police otherwise.

Yachts

Bill Garfield headed for the south of France with the intention of finding work on a private yacht. He went round the yacht harbour at Antibes asking anybody who seemed to be in a position of authority on a boat if they had any work. After a week of failure, Bill began asking at every single boat including the ones which were already swarming with workers and also all the boats big and small in the 'graveyard' (refitting area). Two weeks after leaving Solihull this tactic paid off and he was hired for a nine-week period to help refit a yacht in preparation for the summer charter season.

Antibes is one of the best destinations, especially since there are several crewing agencies based in La Galerie du Port on boulevard d'Aguillon. Also frequent the yachties' bars. You might also pick up some job tips by listening to Radio Riviera mentioned above. Smaller places like St Tropez, according to Bill, are not nearly as good, though other people have recommended Beaulieu-sur-Mer, Villeneuve-Loubet-Plage and Cros-de-Cagnes. It is essential to start early, preferably the beginning of March, since by late April most of the jobs have been filled. Bill Garfield describes the process in Antibes:

Boats frequently take on people as day workers first and then employ them as crew for the charter season if they like them. I had no previous experience of this work, which turned out to be to my advantage because the captain wished the work to be done his way. I started on £10 a day which went up to £12 after three weeks and lived on board with plenty of food provided. This pay was quite good, though some boats were paying much more.

Look tidy and neat, be polite and when you get a job work hard. The first job is the hardest to get, but once you get in with this integrated community, captains will help you find other jobs after the refitting is finished. Of course many continue through the summer as deckhands on charter yachts and are paid £100 a week plus tips (which sometimes match the wage). The charter season ends in late September when many yachts begin organising their crew for the trip to the West Indies.

Barges

Holiday barges which ply the rivers and canals of France hire cooks, hostesses, deckhands and captains. The only place where all the barges congregate is

Amsterdam, though asking for work barge-to-barge is unlikely to be very successful. It is better to apply to the companies in the new year; addresses may be found in the travel advertisement sections of English Sunday papers.

One employer is Stella Maris Cruises with whom Pauline Power got a seasonal job in 1992. After being hired over the phone, she was flown to Amsterdam and spent April to October as a deckhand (which is unusual for women who tend to be pigeonholed as hostesses) earning £100-120 a week plus tips of up to a further £100 a week. The UK address is European Waterways Ltd, 22 Kingswood Creek, Wraysbury, Staines, Middlesex TW9 5EN; 0178 448 2439), while the French address is 1 rue de la Corderie, BP 151, 34302 Agde Cedex (67 94 94 20). In addition to crew for the hotel barges, boatyard assistants are needed at their bases in Burgundy and the south of France. Applicants for all these jobs must be at least 25 and possess a current driving licence; a knowledge of French is useful. Another company to try is Charterbarge Sarl, 'Les Langrons,' 21140 Villars et Villenotte (fax 80 97 32 28) with a UK office at Milton Mill, West Milton, Bridport, Dorset DT6 3SN.

GRAPE-PICKING

Every year the lure of the *vendange* seems to be irresistible. Past participants agree about the negative aspects of the job: the eight or nine hours a day of back-breaking work, often for seven days a week, and the weather, which is too cold and damp in the early autumn mornings and too hot at mid-day. Waterproofs are essential because you will be expected to continue picking in the pouring rain. The accommodation may consist of a space in a barn for a sleeping bag, and the sanitation arrangements of a cold water tap. But despite all this, every year the grape-growing regions of France are flooded with hopeful *vendangeurs*, some of them drawn by a romantic notion which usually evaporates by the end of the first day, though not always, as Peggy Carter from Pennsylvania describes:

We asked some people we met at a bar in Nantes (Brittany) how feasible it was for Americans to find work picking grapes. They asked if we had any connections which we did not and they said it would be very hard. Well, it was our luck that one of them was from a family who owned vineyards in the area and we ended up in a field in St Fiacre at 8am the following Monday. The first four days were backbreaking, and also a little awkward since no one spoke English and no one made an effort to find out how much we understood. But eventually we became the centre of talk and everyone tried to make us feel comfortable. It was an unparalleled view into French small town culture, plus we received an insider's view of winemaking, we were able to practise our French and we overall just had a wonderful time. They've given us an open invitiation to return for pleasure or for work.

Part of the attraction is the wage. Although it is not usually much higher than *le SMIC* of F34 (porters sometimes earn more especially when the vineyards are located on steep hills), there is little opportunity to spend your earnings on an isolated farm and most people save several hundred pounds during a typical fortnight-long harvest. Recently Martin and Shirine from Crawley earned £1,550 between them during the ten-day harvest of white grapes followed a week later by the red harvest in the first half of October. If you work for the same *patron* for seven consecutive days, you should be paid an overtime rate. Remember that at least 15% will be deducted for French social security. Jason Davies sums up his experience of the *vendange* as 'that most crippling, back-breaking, demoralising of jobs which is still well worth doing for the money and the fun.'

The major threat to jobs at present comes from mechanisation. It seems that the farmers who are not investing in the machinery are either too poor or eccentric Luddites. For example the Cognac region is now heavily mechanised. Some have suggested that it won't be long before hand-picking disappears completely, except in a few prestige areas like Champagne or on very steep slopes where machinery cannot be used.

Work and Conditions

The working and living conditions can vary greatly from farm to farm. Often the size of the farm has a bearing on this: obviously it is easier for the owner of a small vineyard with a handful of workers to provide decent accommodation than for the owner of a chateau who may have over a 100 workers to consider. Farmers almost always provide some sort of accommodation, but this can vary from a rough and ready dormitory to a comfortable room in his own house. Food is normally provided, but again this can vary from the barely adequate to the sublime: one picker can write that 'the food was better than that in a 5-star hotel, so we bought flowers for the cook at the end of the harvest', while another may complain of instant mashed potatoes or of having to depend on whatever he can buy and prepare for himself. When both food and accommodation are provided there is normally a deduction of one or two hours' pay from each day's wage.

Free wine is a frequent feature of the job, though Martin and Shirine looked in vain for it at their chateau for the pickers' rations. In addition to her wage of F220 per day, Dustie Hickey was allowed a seemingly endless supply of wine which 'lifted up the workers' spirits but often left me falling into the bushes.' (When she was offered the same perk during the olive harvest later in the autumn, she wisely sold her daily two litres of wine.)

Hours also vary. Whereas one traveller (who chooses to call himself Rizla Plus) found the structuring of the working day ridiculous, with a 1½ hour lunch break and no other breaks between 7.45am and 6pm, others have found themselves finishing the day's picking at lunchtime, especially in the far south near the Spanish border, where the sun is unbearably hot in the afternoon.

The work itself will consist either of picking or portering. Picking involves bending to get the grapes from a vine that may be only three and a half feet tall, and filling a pannier which you drag along behind you. One of the incidental perils is the inevitable cuts which you will inflict on yourself with the *vendangettes* or secateurs (and don't expect any sympathy from the locals). Plastic gloves can be useful. The panniers full of grapes are emptied into an *hotte* a large basket weighing up to 100lb which the porters carry to a trailer.

The first few days as a *cueilleur/cueilleuse* or *coupeur* (picker) are the worst, as you adjust to the stooping posture and begin to use muscles you never knew you had. The job of porter is sought after, since it does not require the constant bending and is less boring because you move around the vineyard.

Whereas Julian Peachey worked in St. Cannat (not far from Aix-en-Provence) for a *patron* whose 'attitude seemed to be to have as much entertainment as possible whilst producing enough grapes to make it viable,' Rizla Plus had a boss who spent the long day shouting 'Allez! Vite!' Although he claimed not to know English, he had mastered the phrase, 'Ze 'arvest is no 'oliday.'

The further south you go the more likely you are to find yourself competing with migrant workers from Spain, Portugal, Morocco and Algeria, though East Europeans have also found their way to most grape-growing corners of France. Large and famous chateaux (like Lafite) often use a contracted team of pickers who return every season. These immigrant workers tend to return to the same large vineyards year after year, where they work in highly efficient teams. Dave Bamford describes what he encountered in Beaujolais:

We arrived at the railway station in Villefranche to the welcome of about

*70 rather desperate looking North Africans and Spaniards, some of whom
had already been waiting for a week. The atmosphere was very tense. A van
full of English people declared war on the Arabs the night we arrived (typical)
and much violence ensued. The farmers used to drive down to the station
to choose workers. You have to get in quick since the Moroccans immediately
jump into the vans, insisting on their superiority as workers. The farmers
favour English people (especially if they speak French) and girls are guaranteed work.*

Xuela Edwards noticed many Eastern Bloc nationals being picked up by farmers
at railway stations in the south of France and suspected that they were paid
considerably less than the SMIC.

Another source of competition comes from gypsies who organise crews.
When Phil New was traipsing between unhelpful ANPEs in Champagne he was
approached by several gypsy crew leaders. He decided to ignore the warnings
he'd heard and joined a crew. He can't understand what the fuss is about: he
reckons that he earned only slightly less than if he'd worked for the farmer
directly and, contrary to what he'd been told, he was paid promptly and fairly
at the end of the fortnight's harvest. Simon Whitehead's experience was not
so happy:

*Having reached Bordeaux with £3 between us, a friend and I were told that
we ought to try Libourne for work. Although the agencies could not find us
anything we were approached by two men who shouted in a broad French
patois which was difficult to understand 'vendange' at us. Being skint we
accepted the offer of eight days work. However the next day we were told
we were no longer and meanwhile my friend had had his camera ripped off.*

How to Find Work

As mentioned near the beginning of this chapter, the ANPEs do not seem to
be the best informed source of temporary job information. Jason Davies describes
his experiences with them:

*At the end of August I phoned the ANPE at Bordeaux and was informed
that the vendange was going to start early, about September 4th or 5th. So
I worked a week's notice at my restaurant in Nice and set off for Bordeaux.
When I arrived I went to the ANPE for addresses to contact. 'Oh no, not
yet,' said the pretty girl behind the desk (whom I would have liked to put
through the window). 'The vendange won't be starting until the 25th at the
earliest. It's a bit late this year,' she added. In Avignon the ANPE was just
as unhelpful. 'We are no longer concerned with the vendange here'. Altogether
I was amazed at the incompetence and uselessness of the ANPEs. If I ever
use them again, I will be very cautious with the advice they offer.*

Provided you are prepared to disregard their negative advice, there is no harm
in visiting the local ANPE in a wine-growing region on the offchance that they
will be able (and willing) to tell you which farmers need workers. Rizla Plus was
told by the ANPE in Saumur, as well as the tourist office, a *maison de vin* and
a private employment agency 'C'est complet.' Undaunted he headed east along
the Loire and, after a ten-mile walk though the vineyards, found a job. When
Michael Jordan was looking for grape-picking work in Alsace, he noticed that
every *mairie* had a poster up advising job-seekers to present themselves to the
ANPE in Colmar. That office sets up a special *Service Vendanges* in a courtyard
where addresses are given out at the discretion of ANPE staff. They wouldn't
give Michael any addresses, not because he is American but because he confessed
that he didn't have a car and there were no more vacancies which could provide
accommodation. David Loveless was told by the ANPE in Sélestat also in the
Alsace region that 50 people searching for *vendange* jobs were being turned away

daily. David happened to meet some travellers in Riquewihr (near the main Alsatian town of Colmar) who advised him to try the local wine-grower. He was promptly hired for three weeks and was even offered F200 to come back the next season.

Below are listed the addresses of major ANPEs in the wine-producing regions, with rough guidelines as to the starting dates of the harvest. It should be stressed that these dates can vary by days or even weeks from year to year.

Alsace — October 15th
ANPE, 18 rue Auguste-Larney, 67005 Strasbourg (88 75 04 50).
ANPE, 8 rue de l'Auge, 68021 Colmar Cedex (89 23 53 23).

Beaujolais — September 10th
ANPE, 169 rue Paul Bert, 69665 Villefranche-sur-Saone Cedex (74 60 30 03).

Bordeaux — September 25th
ANPE, 1 Terrasse du Front du Médoc, 33076 Bordeaux (56 00 18 00).

Burgundy — October 6th
ANPE, 6 rue Claude Debussy, 71000 Macon.
ANPE, 7 rue des Corroyeurs, BP 1504, 21033 Dijon (80 43 17 67).

Champagne — October 1st
ANPE, 40 rue de Talleyrand, 51057 Reims Cedex (26 88 47 21).

Languedoc-Roussillon — September 15th
ANPE, 10 rue Léon Paul Fargue, BP 4055, 66042 Perpignan Cedex (68 38 47 00).
ANPE, 76 Allée d'Iéna, BP 586, 11009 Carcassonne Cedex.
ANPE, 60 rue Siegfried, Nimes Est 2, BP 3054, 30002 Nimes Cedex.
ANPE, 29 av Léon Blum, BP 65, 30205 Bagnols sur Cèze.
ANPE, 13 av Alphonse Mas, BP 4236, 34544 Beziers Cedex.

Loire — October 6th
ANPE, Champ Girault, 9 rue du Docteur Herpin, BP 2510, 37025 Tours (47-66 81 26).
ANPE, Square Lafayette, 49000 Angers (41 88 56 25).

These are the most famous wine-making regions but there are many others. K. McCausland recommends the Savoie as being off the beaten track of job-seekers. The villages of Apremont, Montmélian and Les Marches near Chambery are recommended. Furthermore he was paid a healthy F40 an hour. The harvest here begins approximately October 1st. He also recommends trying to get a job picking table grapes in the département of Lot. It is harder work (because you have to be careful not to damage the fruit) but the wages are higher and the work lasts longer than for the *vendange.*

The demand for pickers in all regions is highly unpredictable. Whereas there is usually a glut of pickers looking for work at the beginning of the harvest (early to mid-September), there is sometimes a shortage later on in the month. Harvests differ dramatically from year to year; a late spring frost can wreak havoc. The element of uncertainty makes it very difficult for individuals (let alone agents) to arrange jobs for people who are not on the spot.

Experienced grape-pickers recommend visiting or phoning farms well before the harvest starts and asking the farmer to keep a job open. Phone at agreed intervals to pin down the starting date and to remind the farmer that you are serious about coming. It is generally advisable to visit farmers in small villages far from the big towns where there is a superfluity of job seekers once the harvest starts. Also check the CIJ and university notice boards, for example the one in the cafeteria at the University of Dijon.

Written applications are probably not worthwhile though some of our contributors have succeeded this way. Brian Williams obtained the addresses of ten large vineyards from a travel article in the *Sunday Times:* he wrote to them early in the year, and received five job offers in a week. Equally useful addresses can be found either in Hugh Johnson's *World Atlas of Wine* (which costs £30 but can be found in some libraries) or simply by copying addresses from the labels on wine bottles. *The Traveller's Guide to the Wine Regions of France* bu Hubrecht Duijker at £5.95 can be useful both in the planning stages and once you are searching for work.

Sésame is the acronym for *Service des Echanges et des Stages Agricoles dans le Monde* (formerly the Centre de Documentation et d'Information Rurale) at 9 square Gabriel Fauré, 75017 Paris (1-40 54 07 08). It claims that it has stopped advising and placing people looking for seasonal agricultural work. The organisation Jeunesse et Réconstruction at 10 rue de Trévise, 75009 Paris (1-47 70 15 88) is primarily a voluntary workcamp organiser but it handles several hundred *vendange* vacancies. They charge a fee of F280, but in the first instance send two IRCs for information.

While some do succeed by trudging from vineyard to vineyard on foot to ask for work, there are alternatives. After badly blistering his feet on the country roads near Montpellier, Stephen Hands recommends borrowing or hiring a bicycle. Phoning is a more leisurely option though it can be discouraging, as one working traveller found:

> *I had nothing fixed up in advance and the ANPE in Bordeaux was no help. So I got a Yellow Pages from the main post office, picked the famous appellation controlèe of Margaux and started phoning. I got about 25 chateaux down the list, which was pretty disheartening, when Chateau Prieure-Lachine told me I could start on Monday.*

Look up *viticulteurs* or *producteurs nègociants.*

Tony Davies-Patrick obtained a list of the addresses and phone numbers of the major vineyards from the Orange tourist office *(Syndicat d'initiative)* and had the good fortune to be hired by the first one he contacted. Always enquire at the *départementale* office rather than the city one; Michael Jordan was shocked at how little the Strasbourg city tourist office near the Cathedral knew or cared about the Alsatian harvest, whereas he suspects that the regional office in the rue du Dôme would have been better informed. Many rural towns have a *chambre d'agriculture, maison d'agriculture,* a *syndicat gènèral des vignerons* or a *conseil inter-professionel du vin,* all of which may have leads.

You should also look out for the offices of wine producers' cooperatives, whose staff are often friendly and helpful to prospective pickers. Cooperatives are generally called *S.I.C.A.* followed by the name of the town, and are signposted in the street with the italic typeface also used to indicate French railway stations. Stephen Hands parked himself outside the cooperative in the village of Marseillan in Languedoc-Roussillon where a steady stream of tractors loaded high with grapes came and went. Unfortunately he was too late in the harvest to get a job. Alison Cooper was similarly disappointed with her dogged attempts to find a job through the Co-op in Limoux (between Perpignan and Toulouse). Success came in the end not through the Co-op but by a stroke of good fortune:

> *Fate intervened when a Portuguese and a Frenchman turned up at the Co-op in a car, with an address of a vineyard which might need five workers. I got into that car immediately with two Spaniards and we all ended up with jobs. First class French cuisine and a bed were provided (for a deduction of £10 a day) and I earned £250 tax free in ten days.*

As well as enquiring at youth hostels and campsites, Adam Cook recommends asking at local greengrocers for information on the *vendange,* as the shop owners very often know which of their suppliers is picking what and where.

OTHER HARVESTS

Although the *vendange* may produce the highest concentration of seasonal work, there are tremendous opportunities for participating in other harvests and with far less competition for the available work. While increasing mechanisation threatens the future of grape-picking by hand, there are not yet any machines which can cope with plums, peaches and olives.

France is an overwhelmingly rural country. The *départements* of Hérault, Drôme and Gers are among the most prolific fruit and vegetable producers, especially of plums, cherries, strawberries and apples. Crops ripen first in the south of the country, and first at lower altitudes, so it is difficult to generalise about starting dates. For example the strawberry harvest on the coastal plain around Beziers normally takes place between mid-May and late June, whereas 60km inland in the Haut Languedoc near Sauclieres, it starts in mid-July. Cherries and strawberries are the first harvests, normally taking place between May and July. Peaches are picked from June after the trees have been pruned, while pears are picked throughout the summer but especially (like apples) from mid-September to mid-October.

As well as the usual places to ask about harvesting work referred to on earlier pages, try the large fruit cooperatives and *ventrês directes* stalls on main roads including the *Route Nationale*. One additional way of finding work is to ask at the fruit and vegetable markets where farmers gather daily to watch their farming cooperative sell their produce at the height of the season. Look for the person operating the weighbridge. If there is a public address system, you may even be allowed to put out an announcement asking for immediate work. If your French is shaky you have to be especially lucky, as the Dutch traveller Mirjam Koppelaars was. After finding it difficult to communicate with farmers at a large commercial fruit market in Chanas (where farmers sell their fruit to jam factories and wholesalers), she and her Norwegian friend were on the point of giving up. A farmer who had noticed them sitting dejectedly on a stone wall turned his van around and offered them both jobs picking cherries.

Sarit Moas from Israel found it very worthwhile asking a fruit weigher at one of the open markets in Paris about harvesting work:

The owner of the market stand answered, 'Why do you want to do tedious backbreaking picking?' In the end he offered me a job working with him selling from 6am to 2pm. I'd assemble the fruit stands with him five days a week and receive F250 daily.

For working travellers who can cope with French currency and language this would be an ideal experience to improve language skills in an interesting social context. It is also possible to work unloading the trucks in the morning and cleaning up at closing time.

Harvest work is paid either hourly (normally the SMIC) or by piece rates. If you are floundering with piece work, you may be transferred to a different job where you can earn an hourly wage as happened to Brendan Barker when he was picking plums in the Bordeaux area:

For the first two days we were on picking duty as part of a team, though we were marked down individually for each crate we filled. The rate was F10 a crate and some of the people were doing 30-35 even 40 crates a day. My girlfriend and I were hitting a measly 15 crates — inexperienced and unfit. So on the third day we were put on the factory line where the incoming wounded plums were sorted out and put onto wooden trays for the three giant furnaces that would shrivel them into prunes. For this work we were put on the SMIC which was better for us financially though we had the patron *(an ex-military man) barking down our necks 'Allez vite, quick, rapido' for the benefit of the French, the Portuguese and us.*

It is normally up to workers to provide their own food and accommodation, and so a tent and camping equipment are essential. If a farmer does provide board and lodging he will normally deduct the equivalent of two hours' wages from your daily pay packet. If you are planning to leave as soon as the harvest is over, bear in mind that agricultural wages are often not paid until seven to ten days after the harvest finishes (to ensure workers do not leave prematurely). Furthermore the wages may have to be cashed at a local bank, so be prepared to hang around.

In addition to fruit picking there are many other kinds of work which travellers end up doing, from cheese making to haymaking. There may be late autumn work pruning vines and orchards. Poultry farms (especially in the Anjou area) are often looking for chicken-catchers-cum-lorry-loaders who are (not surprisingly) paid fairly well.

The Avignon Region

All manner of fruit is grown in the Rhône Valley in the vicinity of Avignon. Tessa Shaw achieved a long spell of continuous employment in the *départements* of Vaucluse and Ardèche by following the different harvests. In late July she went to the Ile de Barthelasse, which is a 16km-long island in the River Rhône near Avignon which is entirely given over to fruit and vegetable growing. She began by harvesting mange-tout (snow peas), then continued picking peaches, apples and tomatoes throughout August. In September she moved on to a factory in the village of Aubignan where she was employed packing melons, courgettes, peppers and apricots. This job lasted for a month, until the beginning of the grape harvest in nearby Vacqueyras. Once this was finished she moved on to the village of Bedouin which is high on Mont Ventoux, and where the grape harvests are significantly later; her work there took her through to mid-November. Finally, she headed north to Privas in the Ardèche where she picked chestnuts in the frost.

More recently Stuart Bellworthy also looked for work in this area. Having started in Lyon it wasn't until he got to Avignon with its massive fruit distribution centres and the Isle de Barthelasse with its promising sounding street names (Chemin des Vignes, Chemins des Raisins) that he became optimstic:

I spent a whole (very hot!) day wandering around the Isle de Barthelasse, without any luck (though I have never eaten so much fruit in my life free of charge). Just up the road from Camping Etoile (a very cheap campsite near Avignon just on the island) there is a map of the island and a list of all the productuers. *It is worth starting at the north of the island since the farmers nearest Avignon probably get asked for jobs about every ten minutes.*

After I was convinced there were no jobs, I travelled 10km south to Chateaurenard and found a pear-picking job. All the roads to the north of Chateaurenard are lined with farms. The villages of St Remy, Barbentane and Rognons are also good. The pear season lasts from mid-July to early August.

Stuart goes on to recommend visiting the nearby Marché d'International (preferably at about 5am) and asking the farmers for work either on their farms or helping with their market stalls.

Through meeting people at the Koala Bar in Avignon (mentioned above), Dustie Hickey fixed up a job picking olives between early November and late December in St Remy. She says that she would happily do this work again since it was so peaceful, and furthermore you can earn money at it:

We worked at Mas de la Dame, a place where Van Gogh painted. The job involved climbing ladders but as I'm light I would climb right into the trees (best view!) and comb, comb, comb the branches so the olives would fall into the net below. When the tree is cleared, you have to pick out all the twigs and leaves and roll the olives into the crates. It's very satisfying to fill a few crates from one tree (but not at all satisfying when the net turns out to be too small). I was paid F2 a kilo plus two litres of wine a day. It is easy to rent cheap accommodation in St Remy at this time of year. The only problem was transport: although there is a bus to Avignon there is no off-season service south to Les Baux de Provence.

The Loire Valley

Strawberries, apples, pears and many other crops can be found along the River Loire: the towns of Segré, Angers and Saumur are especially recommended. Stephen Febers spent an enjoyable five weeks in the late spring in this area picking strawberries for Jean Leblois (1 rue du Pigeonnier, 49730 Varennes-sur-Loire; 41 51 75 73). The harvest here lasts six to eight weeks from early/mid April, so the best time to contact Monsieur Leblois is early March. He expects applicants to understand French and to be willing to work seven days a week at the peak of the harvest.

In the fruit-picking business, it is unusual to come across an agent willing to mediate between farmers and prospective workers, but one such exists south of the Loire who claims to be able to place up to 1,000 people (preferably rugby players) to harvest melons and apples plus a further 150 (ditto) to pack the fruit. The advertised wage is F5,500 per month, and no accommodation is provided, though it may be that a certain amount of rugby playing will be expected. Applications should be sent to M. Reau, SCA Soldive, 27 Avenue de la Coopér-ation, 86200 Loudun (49 22 40 63/fax 49 22 40 37).

One surprising crop which requires a large number of pickers is mushrooms grown around Saumur. Make enquiries before the harvest begins in early July. Melon farmers who may be looking for pickers in July and August are:

Soldive, Avenue de Ougadougou, 86 Loudun (49 22 40 63).

Monsieur Billon, Route de Richelieu, 86200 Messeme (49 98 09 87).

Monsieur Jean-Jacques Reguilier, Charrière, 86200 La Roche Riganst (49 98 15 38).

Cathy Salt found out from a major cooperative in the Anjou area the name of the largest producer in the area and picked pears and apples for him over a period of seven weeks from early September. The pay was piece work and in order to equal the *SMIC* it was necessary to pick much faster than Cathy could pick.

Castrating Maize

Another source of seasonal farm work consists of castrating maize *(l'écimage),* an expression that calls for some explanation. (Some prefer to call it 'topping'.) A maize field consists of alternate rows of different strains of maize plants, one type growing both male and female flowers and the other producing just male flowers. The job involves moving along the rows of plants which have both male and female flowers and plucking, or castrating, the male flowers to stop the plant fertilising itself. The plant is then fertilised by a male plant from the adjoining row, which results in the production of a bigger and better cob.

Timing is crucial for this job and the work is often over within ten days, having started anytime from the second week of July. Martin and Shirine hitched to St Michel-Escalou near Dax on July 24th only to be told that the maize work had just finished. The height of workers is important since they must be tall enough to reach the flowers, at least five and a half feet tall.

Kate Whatmough found both the sense of urgency and thoroughness that was expected of workers to be the worst aspects of the job:

When we eventually reached the end of a row of maize plants about half a mile long there was nothing more exasperating than to be called back to the beginning by the very strict farm manager to pluck out a flower we had inadvertently overlooked.

Unlike grape pickers, maize castrators have to cope with the intense heat of high summer. This often involves getting up at dawn (5am) to work until noon followed by a three hour break during the hottest hours of the day, with work then continuing from 3pm until sunset at about 9.30pm. As in the *vendange* the pay is almost always *SMIC* but unlike the *vendange* food and accommodation are not provided, so you must have camping gear.

Maize castration is concentrated in the south west of the country and in the Auvergne region, though maize is also grown in the Loire. The following ANPE offices are recommended for this type of work:

2 ave Henri-Farbos, 4000 Mont-de-Marsan (58 46 15 02).

70 rue Blatin, 63000 Clermond-Ferrand (73 37 34 34).

45 rue E. Guichenné, B.P. 1606, 64016 Pau Cedex (59 27 15 18).

Organic Farms

The elusive organic farm organisation Nature et Progrès (BP6, 69921 Oullins Cedex; 72 39 04 36) seems to be alive and kicking, and still publishes a guide *Les bonnes adresses de la bio* which is a directory of organic farmers by *département* with an indication of whether they accept *stagiaires* or volunteers. The cost is F60.

There are many organic farms throughout France run by expatriates or by exiles from the big city. The atmosphere on this kind of farm is often different from that on purely commercial farms, though you will still be expected to work hard. Most temporary workers hear of farms like this by word of mouth *(de bouche à l'oreille)*, but it is always polite to ring or write ahead rather than show up unannounced. The kind of information they are interested in includes your background, age, experience, whether or not you are vegetarian, mode of travel (preferably a bicycle) and of course dates of intended visit.

If you can arrange to swap your labour for room and board you shouldn't have to worry about the red tape. Two Americans staying in Strasbourg, Cindy Roberts and Michael Jordan, phoned the number of a Britanny farmer mentioned in an out-of-date edition of *Work Your Way Around the World* and were offered work immediately. (In the following edition Anton Pinschof asked to be removed since he had been inundated with job-seekers.) Cindy and Michael stayed seven weeks and were treated as members of the family and even given the best room in the house. They were not asked to do very much work but would gladly have done more.

This experience was in complete contrast to the next farmer she visited, notorious for exploiting volunteers and making them work ludicrously long hours for virtually no money. That address has been excluded from this edition.

One address which was brought to our attention in the summer of 1994 is Yves Maillet's farm at le Vieux Jallot, 58240 St Pierre le Moutier (86 37 21 36). He offers accommodation, food and $200 a month to help look after his animals; feedback would be appreciated.

TEACHING

There are so many expatriates living in Paris and throughout France that being a native speaker of English does not cut much ice with prospective employers of English teachers. Without a TEFL qualification, BA or commercial flair (preferably all three) it is very difficult to get a teaching contract. Of course if you can make yourself look ultra-presentable and have an impressive CV, you should ring to make appointments and then tramp round all the possible schools to leave your CV. (As is usual in Europe, there is virtually no hope of success in July and August.)

The technique of making a personal approach to schools in the months preceding the one in which you would like to teach is often successful. On the strength of her RSA Certificate from International House, Fiona Paton had been hoping to find teaching work in the south of France in the summer but quickly discovered that there are very few opportunities outside the academic year. On her way back to England, she disembarked from the train in the picturesque town of Vichy in the Auvergne just long enough to distribute a few self-promotional leaflets to three language schools. She was very surprised to receive a favourable reply from CAVILAM D.L.E. (rue du Parc, BP 164, 03200 Vichy) once she was home, and so returned a few weeks later for a happy year of teaching.

In Paris many schools advertise in the *métro*, or you can look up addresses in the Yellow Pages under *Enseignements Privé de Langues* or *Ecoles de Langues*. A great many schools cater for the business market, so anything relevant in your background should be emphasised. Typical wages are F85-100 per hour. As is increasingly common, schools are often reluctant to take on contract teachers for whom they would be obliged to pay taxes and social security, and so there is a bustling market in freelance teachers who work for themselves and are prepared to teach just a few hours a week for one employer.

Telephone teaching is both lucrative and fun, and therefore hard to fix up. Richard Pitwood describes the advantages of the system:

This is great fun. Everybody tells you their innermost secrets, because of the anonymity, and it's an extremely effective way of teaching/learning English, because the student has to concentrate.

The standard rate of pay for telephone teaching is F40-45 for half an hour plus telephone expenses. The Belgian firm Phone Languages has recently opened an operation in Paris (149 rue de Charonne, 75011 Paris; 1-43 48 70 45) but there are many others.

Partly because of France's proximity to a seemingly inexhaustible supply of willing English teachers, working conditions in France are seldom brilliant. Although Andrew Boyle enjoyed his year teaching English in Lyon and the chance to become integrated into an otherwise impenetrable community, he concluded that even respectable schools treated teachers as their most expendable commodity, a view corroborated by the veteran traveller Jayne Nash who lasted only three months in Le Havre:

Thirty plus hour weeks (not including preparation time), irregular hours at any time between 8am and 8pm with last-minute classes to cover for absent colleagues, and classes of mixed ability, soon took their toll. The money wasn't that good either. I felt my employer cared little for his employees. After three months I found myself under so much stress that I was obliged to leave, although I am normally not someone to shun a challenge or responsibility.

A more realistic possibility is to offset the high cost of living in Paris by doing some tutoring which sometimes shades into au pairing. Language exchanges for room and board are commonplace in Paris and are usually arranged through advertisements (in the places described below in the section on Paris) or by word of mouth. Kathryn Kleypas studied the notice board at the American Church to good effect:

I contacted a family from the notice board and was invited to come over to their home for an interview and to meet the three children to whom I would be teaching English every day. I was not asked if I had any teaching experience, yet was offered the position which involved 18 hours of English teaching/conversation in exchange for room, board and F1,400 per month. My family took me with them to the seaside near Bordeaux in July and to their castle near Limoges during August.

This is a good way for Americans and others to circumvent red tape difficulties as Beth Mayer from New York found in Paris:

I tried to get a job at a school teaching, but they asked for working papers which I didn't have. I checked with several schools who told me that working papers and a university degree were more important than TEFL qualifications. So I placed an ad to teach English and offer editing services (I was an editor in New York City before moving here) and received many responses. I charged F80 per hour but found that after I had spent time going and coming, I earned only F40. It would be better to have the lessons at your apartment if centrally located. I not only 'taught' English but offered English conversation to French people who wanted practice. I met a lot of nice people this way and earned money to boot.

This is most commonly done in Paris though it can work just as easily in other French cities. The usual methods of advertising in newspapers, sticking up photocopied ads in libraries and stores such as Prisunic supermarkets could work. A telephone and answering machine are great assets in the initial stages. Conversation classes with adults are easier than teaching children but tend to pay less well.

Any qualified teacher who wants a year's work in French private or state schools can obtain an information sheet *Teaching Posts in France* from the Cultural Department of the French Embassy at 23 Cromwell Road, London SW7 2EL. University language students who would like to be a part-time English language *assistant* in a French school should contact the Assistants Department of the Central Bureau for Educational Visits and Exchanges.

CHILDCARE

Au pairing has always been a favoured way for young women to learn French, and increasingly for young men too. The pocket money for au pairs in France is linked to the *SMIC* and is currently F1,600 per month (F1,700 in Paris). Au pairs plus should earn F2,200 per month and nannies F4,000. There are dozens of agencies both in Britain (see list in *Childcare* chapter) and in France which arrange placements. CIJ offices and even ANPEs may have a list of families looking for live-in help, and this is the one category of work for which fluent French is unlikely to be a necessity. In Paris, the notice boards described below are always crammed with announcements of live-in positions and so there is little chance of being left jobless if you wait until arrival to look.

Quite a few foreigners are too hasty in arranging what seems at the outset a cushy number and only gradually realise how little they enjoy the company of children and how isolated they are if their family lives in the suburbs (as most do). Unless you actively like small children, it might be better to look for a free room in exchange for minimal babysitting (e.g. 12 hours a week).

Arthur Solovev from Moscow arranged to pick up two American boys (whom he describes as 'gangsters') from their Paris school and look after them until their parents got home. Although it is still more difficult for men than women to find au pair placements, France seems to be streets ahead of Britain in this respect, as Iain Croker reports:

I have had a thoroughly rewarding and enjoyable year as an au pair in France — so much so that I'm going back again in September for another year. Certainly in France there are quite a few male au pairs — four in my village near Fontainebleau alone. In my experience the boys tend to get placed in families with a lot of energetic children or families that have traditionally had a large turn-over of au pairs. After a year in the sticks with four kids I feel I have proved myself and my agency have offered me one of their best placements in Paris, one child and my own apartment. By the way, my agency (Soames International) is great.

Established agencies include the following:

Accueil Familial des Jeunes Etrangers, 23 rue de Cherche-Midi, 75006 Paris (1-42 22 50 34).

L'A.R.C.H.E., 51 rue de Gergovie, 75014 Paris (1-45 45 46 39).

Contacts, 55 rue Nationale, 37000 Tours (47 20 20 57/fax 47 20 68 92).

Euro Pair Services, 13 rue Vavin, 75006 Paris (1-43 29 80 01).

Inter-Séjours, 179 rue de Courcelles, 75017 Paris (1-47 63 06 81).

Séjours Internationaux Linguistiques et Culturels, 32 Rempart de l'Est, 16022 Angoulême Cedex (45 97 41 00).

Soames International, 16 rue du Chateau, BP 28, 77200 Fontainebleau (1-64 22 99 26).

Registration fees are normally fairly steep, often around F700 (even for short-term summer placements) but sometimes over F1,000. By law, families are supposed to make social security payments to the local URSSAF office on the au pair's behalf, though not all do and you might want to enquire about this when applying. Au pairs in or near Paris should receive the *carte orange* (travel pass) which normally costs about £30 a month.

BUSINESS & INDUSTRY

You will normally need impeccable French in order to work in a French office which eliminates the sort of temping jobs you may have had back home. If you are lucky enough to get a job in a French office — as Ben Nakoneczny did through a family connection — you may find yourself benefitting from such perks as a subsidised canteen serving French food and wine. With no contacts, Michael Jordan from St Louis Missouri had no luck when he mounted a job search in his field in Strasbourg which involved cycling round all the bakeries at 2am.

Fluent French speakers can also try for translation jobs. An article in *Transitions Abroad* magazine describes how an American woman placed a typed index card with her credentials in her local *gymnasium* (high school) and was contacted by a publisher of comic books which needed translating into English, a job which lasted over a year.

Fee-paying training and exchange programmes (like the one organised by Interspeak mentioned earlier in the chapter) can provide an opening to employment in French business and industry. Horizon HPL Training Placement Agency was mentioned in the context of its hotel placements but it also runs a one-month computer and French language course in Paris for F5,000 and can make secretarial and marketing placements in Parisian firms which pay next to nothing; all of these could lead to other things.

One interesting scheme is run in the Pyreneen village of Salies de Béarn by an energetic Briton. The Villa Monplaisir Centre (tel/fax 59 38 07 64) is a centre for British 'A' level students where they can stay while having a taste of employment (which is unpaid) and the chance to speak French in local businesses such as the bakery, town hall and various shops. The weekly tariff is £116.

Anyone with secretarial skills and a knowledge of French has a good chance of finding office work, particularly in Paris. The agency Sheila Burgess International has an office in London (4 Cromwell Place, SW7 2JE; 0171-584 6446) as well as Paris (62 rue St Lazare; 1-44 63 02 57) and can often arrange interviews for plausible applicants with both British and French firms. The Union Nationale des Entreprises de Travail Temporaire (UNETT, 22 rue de l'Arcade, 75008 Paris) provided a list of temporary agencies specialising in bilingual secretarial staff:

Bis, 26 rue de Madrid, 75008 Paris (1-42 93 50 44).
Britt France, 10 Boulevard des Capucines, 75002 Paris (1-47 42 06 12).
Elite International, 10 rue Louvois, 75002 Paris (1-42 86 94 82).
Eric Soutou Organisation, 21 Avenue de l'Opéra, 75001 Paris (1-42 61 42 61).
Hôtesse Secretaires, 12 rue Chabanais, 75002 Paris (1-42 96 34 80).
Manpower, 7/9 rue Jacques Bingen, 75017 Paris (1-44 15 40 40).
3T Inter Européenne, 106 Avenue Jean Moulin, 78170 La Celle Saint Cloud (1-30 82 53 00).
Intérim 6, 71 rue Bugeaud, 69006 Lyon (78 24 31 51).

There are a number of British-run building firms (not all of them licensed) active in areas like the Dordogne where many English people build homes. You are more likely to come across building work informally as the American Peter Goldman did:

I was hitching south from Paris when a kind woman stopped near Tours. She was heading to her farm house near Bordeaux where a Dutchman was putting a new roof on the house. I explained that I had some experience in construction and I was hired on the spot. I worked for ten days, received F1,000 plus tons of food, beer and wine and a bed. The Dutchman was happy with my work and took me to Biddary near Bayonne to help him renovate another house. There I made F20 an hour plus all living expenses, learned a lot about European building methods, rural France and met some great people.

It can be profitable to let your fingers do the walking when you are in France: the telephone directory can be an invaluable ally when you are looking for new addresses to contact. Here are a few headings to look under: *Publicité direct* and *Distributeurs en publicité* for jobs handing out leaflets, *Démenagement* for house removals, *Entreprises de nettoyage* for domestic work cleaning houses and *Surveillance* for security work.

VOLUNTARY WORK

France has as wide a range of opportunities for voluntary work as any European country, and anyone who is prepared to earn free board and lodging with a little hard work should consider becoming a volunteer. Projects normally last two or three weeks during the summer and cost between F20 and F120 a day. The leaflet from CIDJ *Chantiers de Travail Volontaire* lists most of the organisations active in France with their general requirements and costs. Many foreign young people join one of these to learn basic French and make French contacts as well as to have fun.

Archaeology

A great many archaeological digs and building restoration projects are carried out each year. The Ministry of Culture (Direction du Patrimoine, Sous-Direction de l'Archéologie, 4 rue d'Aboukir, 75002 Paris; 1-40 16 73 00) compiles a national list of excavations throughout France requiring up to 5,000 volunteers. Most *départements* have *Services Archéologiques* which organise digs. Without relevant experience you will probably be given only menial jobs but many like to share in the satisfaction of seeing progress made.

Anthony Blake describes the dig he joined which the History Department of the University of Le Mans (Route de Laval, 72017 Le Mans Cedex) runs every summer:

Archaeology is hard work. Applicants must be aware of what working 8.30am-noon and 2-6.30pm in baking heat means! That said, I thoroughly enjoyed the working holiday: excellent company (75% French so fine opportunity to practise French), weekends free after noon on Saturday, good lunches in SNCF canteen, evening meals more haphazard as prepared by fellow diggers. Accommodation simple but adequate.

Here is a selection of other digs. Bear in mind that most digs will charge unskilled volunteers for board and lodging, perhaps F40 per day.

Prof. John Collis, Department of Archaeology, Sheffield University, Sheffield S10 2TN (0114-282 6078). Work on pre-Roman and Roman farm settlement in the Clermont-Ferrand region.

Association pour le Developpement de l'Archèologie Urbaine à Chartres, 16 rue du Saint Pierre, 28000 Chartres. (Registration fee F200).

Direction Regionale des Affaires Culturelles, Service Regional de l'Archeologie, 6 rue de la Manufacture, 45000 Orleans (38 78 85 41). Can send a one-page calendar of summer digs *(Liste des Chantiers pour Benevoles)* in the *dèpartements* of Cher, Eure-et-Loir and Indre, with contact addresses.

Labo Anthropologie, UPR 403 du CNRS, Université de Rennes I, Campus de Beaulieu, 35042 Rennes Cedex. Summer digs in Brittany.

Musèe de la Chartreuse, Service Archéologique, 191 rue St-Albin, 59500 Douai (27 96 90 60).

Professor Henry de Lumley, Lab. de Prehistoire, IPH, 1 rue Rene Panhard, 75013 Paris.

Conservation

France takes the preservation of its heritage very seriously and there are numerous groups both local and national engaged in restoring churches, windmills, forts and other historic monuments. Many are set up to accept foreign volunteers, though they tend to charge more than archaeological digs:

APARE, 41 cours Jean Jaurès, 84000 Avignon (90 85 36 72). An umbrella organisation which runs a total of 20 work sites in southern France (and the rest of Europe). Cost of F600 for three weeks.

Club du Vieux Manoir, 10 rue de la Cossonnerie, 75001 Paris (1-45 08 80 40). Board and lodging cost F65 per day. Unusually, their literature is in English.

Les Compagnons du Cap, Pratcoustals, Arphy, 30120 Le Vigan (67 81 82 22). Part work, part holiday restoring an abandoned village in a chestnut forest. F60 per day.

Etudes et Chantiers (UNAREC), 33 rue Campagne Premiere, 75014 Paris (1-45 38 96 26). Environmental workcamps; programme of projects costs F25.

REMPART, 1 rue des Guillemites, 75004 Paris (1-42 71 96 55). Similar to the National Trust in Britain, in charge of 140 endangered monuments around France. Most projects charge F30-40 per day plus F200 for membership and insurance. One recent volunteer had to work just two hours in the morning and one in the afternoon.

La Sabranenque, Centre International, rue de la Tour de l'Oume, 30290 Saint Victor la Coste (66 50 05 05). Approximately F1,300 per fortnight.

The organisation Jeunesse et Réconstruction (10 rue de Trévise, 75009 Paris; 1-47 70 15 88) mentioned above in the section on grape-picking arranges a variety of workcamps *(chantiers)* throughout France to renovate buildings and improve the environment. They are notoriously unreliable at replying to mail but at last report the registration fee was F425. Similarly Concordia together with Solidarités Jeunesses (38 rue du Faubourg Saint Denis, 75010 Paris; 1-48 00 09 05) organise a great many summer workcamps. All workcamp associations in Britain can arrange for you to join camps in France.

Try to be patient if the project you choose turns out to have its drawbacks, since these various organisations depend on voluntary leaders as well as participants. Judy Greene volunteered to work with a conservation organisation (not listed here) and felt herself to be 'personally victimised by the lack of organisation and leadership' or more specifically by one unpleasantly racist individual on her project. Tolerance may be called for, especially if your fellow volunteers lack it.

PARIS

Like all major cities in the developed world, Paris presents thousands of ways to earn your keep, while being difficult to afford from day to day. Unless you are very lucky, you will have to arrive with some money with which to support yourself while you look around. Check notice boards, the weekly property paper *Particular à Particulier* published on Thursdays or (if desperate) use an agency which will cost you at least a month's rent but will help to ensure that you get your deposit of two months' rent back.

Talented musicians should consider joining the army of buskers on the Left Bank on a Friday or Saturday night and graduating to the highly competitive métro. Transit authorities issue licences (which are free of charge) which allow you to perform in prescribed locations. Playing on the trains themselves is not allowed, though many ignore the regulations.

The Grapevine

There are expatriate grapevines all over Paris, very helpful for finding work and accommodation. Most people find their jobs as well as accommodation through one of the city's many notice boards *(panneaux)*. The one in the foyer of the CIDJ at 101 Quai Branly *(métro* Bir-Hakeim) is good for occasional studenty-type jobs such as extras in movies, but sometimes there are adverts for full-time jobs or *soutien scolaire en Anglais* (English tutor). It is worth arriving early to check for new notices (the hours are Monday-Saturday 10am-6pm). Another job which is increasingly advertised at the CIDJ is that of *coursier* or courier. Unlike their counterparts in London, Parisian couriers do not have to take their lives into their hands since they travel by *métro* to the various offices where packages and documents have to be delivered. The pay is quite reasonable and cash-in-hand. When you're at the CIDJ, ask for the leaflet *Recherche d'un Job* which provides a few addresses of useful agencies, employers and information centres in greater Paris.

The other mecca for job and flat-hunters is the American Church at 65 Quai d'Orsay *(métro* Invalides). The notices posted upstairs are the official ones, issued every day, and mainly for au pair jobs and accommodation. The downstairs board is more chaotic and it will take about half an hour to rummage through all the notices. It does no harm to put up your own notice here, since it is free. You will bump into lots of other people studying the board here, and so it is a good place to find someone with whom to share a flat.

Other notice boards include the one at the American Cathedral (23 ave George V; *métro* Alma Marceau), and the two British churches, St Georges at 7 rue August Vacquerie in the 16th *arrondissement* and St Michaels at 5 rue d'Aguesseau in the 8th. The British Council at 9 rue de Constantine has a notice board with some live-in tutoring and au pair jobs, though security is tight and you should go dressed as smartly as possible. Although the notice board at the Alliance Francaise (101 Boulevard Raspail; *métro* Notre Dame des Champs) is for the use of registered students of French, you may be able to persuade a student to look at the adverts for you, many of which are exchanges of room for some babysitting and/or teaching. The notice board is in the annex around the corner at 34 rue de Fleurus.

Arguably the most eccentric bookshop in Europe is Shakespeare and Company at 37 rue de la Boucherie in the fifth *arrondissement* (on the south side of the Seine). It has a small notice board, but is more useful as a place to chat up other expats about work and accommodation. The shop operates as a writer's guest house. If you are prepared to write a short account of yourself, you can stay free for up to a week, assuming there is space. The elderly American expat owner George Whitman still hosts weekly Sunday open house for aspiring *litarati* and also hires English-speaking staff to clean, run errands and work behind the till. When Claire Judge was just 17, she was given a room overlooking Notre Dame in exchange for two hours of work a day.

Most expat places like WH Smith's Bookshop near the Place de la Concorde distribute the free English language newsletter *France-USA Contacts* or *FUSAC* which comes out every other Wednesday. It comprises mainly classified adverts which are best followed up on the day the paper appears. An updated bulletin board can be consulted at FUSAC's office at 3 rue Larochelle (*métro* Edgar-Quinet). An advert in *FUSAC* costs about F100 for 25 words, and can be sent before your arrival (1-45 38 56 57) or in the US to France-Contacts, 104 W 14th St, New York, NY 10011-7314 (212-989-8989).

Another possible source of job and accommodation leads is the weekly free ads paper *J'Annonce* (F10 on Fridays) which will only be of use to people who speak some French. Once you're in Paris, it is a good place to put your own advert, for example for English teaching in the *Petits Cours* section, since all private advertisements are free of charge. Adverts can be sent to *J'Annonce* at 6 rue de La Rosière, 75015 Paris (1-40 59 44 55).

As usual pubs are a good place to pick up job tips. There is a chain of three Guinness-serving bars owned by the same person and with the same kind of clientele: Au Gobelot d'Argent in the rue du Cygne (*métro* Les Halles), Au Caveau de Montpensier (The Cav), 15 rue de Montpensier (*métro* Palais Royal) and Molly Malone's (21 rue Godot-du-Mouroy in the 9th).

Eurodisney

Despite rumours of financial ruin, the enormous complex of Euro Disney 30km east of Paris at Marne-la-Vallée continues to be a major seasonal employer. Although one in ten jobs were shed over the winter of 1993/4, all of these were managerial or administrative. There is an approximate quota of about 1,000 job openings for UK nationals out of a total staff of about 10,000. 'Cast members' (Disneyspeak for workers) are needed to staff the scores of hotels, restaurants, shops and attractions. The majority of jobs are in food and beverage, housekeeping and custodial departments, though one of the best jobs is as a character like Micky Mouse. Some contracts are for the whole season (March to October) while others are for as little as a couple of weeks. Further details are available from Service du Recruitement-Casting, Euro Disney SCA, BP 110, 77777 Marne-la-Vallée Cedex 4 (1-49 31 19 99).

Vicky Nakis describes the way in which she landed her job as a receptionist which lasted for seven months though in retrospect she wishes she had stayed for three or four months:

> *I was in Paris and noticed in the papers that Euro Disney was hiring. So I turned up at the Casting Center at Noisy-le-Grand at Mont d'Est which is on the RER A Line about five stops before Euro Disney. (Follow signs to Place Vendôme then follow signs to the Casting Center.) I filled in an application form (in French) and waited for four hours for an interview. The interview was conducted with three candidates at a time to test team*

spirit. Because I spoke four languages I was given the job of receptionist, but your French doesn't have to be perfect since I met other receptionists whose French wasn't at all good.

For all jobs the well-scrubbed look is required (e.g. no beards), and of course they are looking for the usual friendly, cheerful and outgoing personalities. The monthly gross wage is F6,010 from which deductions would be made for social security (about F1,000). Although Vicky Nakis was allocated accommodation in the staff quarters for which F2,1000 was deducted per month, Euro Disney cannot house all its staff. Whether you will be impressed by the fringe benefits is a matter of individual taste; they consist of discounts on merchandise and in the hotels, free entrance to the theme park itself and the occasional chance to 'meet' the superstars. Because Vicky didn't work inside the park, she missed seeing Michael Jackson and Madonna. The only brush with fame she had was when a famous French singer came to reception and she asked him his name.

Specific Jobs

The job hunt in Paris doesn't get any easier, as Mark Davies described on a post card in the summer of 1994:

Although it has taken me five and a half weeks to find paid employment (plongeur in a creperie) I console myself with the fact that there is high unemployment here at the moment. To give you an example, I turned up as stated on the job notice at 5pm for a dishwashing job, and there were eight other people doing the same, and they were by no means all poor-looking immigrants. The pay for the job I'm doing now is lousy but it pays the rent while I look for something better. But as long as I'm in the Jardin du Luxembourg and the sun is shining I can't complain.

There is a special ANPE in Paris for *Travailleurs Migrants* which may be worth trying for unskilled hourly work. The staff at this office (239 rue Bercy; *métro* Gare de Lyons) are said to be helpful and friendly. This is a better bet than the ordinary ANPEs which can be found in every *arrondissement*. The student employment office known as CROUS *(Centre Régional des Oeuvres Universitaires et Scolaires)* at 39 avenue Georges Bernanos, 75231 Paris (1-40 51 36 00) publishes a booklet *Le CROUS et Moi* to orient newly arrived students in Paris. Their *Service des Emplois Temporaires* is for registered students only.

Stephen Psallidas describes the outcome of pounding the pavements in his job-hunt:

Faced with the prospect of sleeping under the Eiffel Tower to save the few pounds I had left, I went around all the Greek restaurants in the Quartier Huchette in the Latin Quarter (métro St Michel) and found a job in half an hour. I started straightaway, and worked there for five weeks. I wish I could say it was good, but it was a terrible job. I worked 12 or 13 hours every day doing the bar, preparing food, serving, etc. I was paid very poorly — around F180 cash in hand... The only reason I stayed so long was because I was getting two free meals a day and, what with working all day, I didn't spend a centime on my social life since I was continually shattered. So I saved F100 a day (after spending F80 at the youth hostel) but I was going slowly mad.

Sarit Moas from Israel doggedly enquired at all the restaurants and street food stalls until she got a job selling crepes and taffy in the Tuilleries amusement parks.

Although many restaurants insist on work papers and social security numbers, other do not. Pay is usually *SMIC* plus tips and one or two meals a day, although an experienced waiter with excellent French could make over F500 per night). There are many American-style fast food restaurants which employ a majority of non-French staff. Among the best known employers are the Quick chain (3 avenue de Général Galliéni, 93100 Montreuil) and the Chicago Pizza Pie Factory with three locations: 5 rue de Berri, 75008 Paris (*métro* George V; 1-45 62 50 23), 9 Boulevard Edgar Quinet, 75014 Paris (*métro* Edgar-Quinet) and 33 rue Quincompoix, 75004 Paris (métro Les Halles; 1-42 71 52 66). If you write in advance, the most that will happen is that they will write to assure you that you will be offered an interview after arrival in Paris. If you show up, you will be asked to fill out an application form before seeing the manager on duty. If there is a vacancy (as there often is) you could be offered a 45-hour-a-week job at SMIC rates plus tips and one meal a day.

Hostels are always worth trying. Mark Davies particularly recommends A.E.P.P. at 46 rue de Vaugirard, 75006 Paris. The Association pour les Etudiants Protéstants de Paris hires long-stay residents to work on reception, and is generally a good place to meet French students as well as international back-packers (who don't have to be protestant or students, but should be under 26).

Survival

It has been mentioned elsewhere in this book that English churches are often helpful sources of contacts. Jonathan Poulton found himself very short of money in Menton (near Monte Carlo) after discovering that the starting date of his job in a patisserie had been postponed. He wandered into the English church which happened to be next door, explained his situation to the vicar and within five minutes had secured a job as a gardener for one of the congregation. Religious foundations also run many emergency shelters and free hostels throughout France. The only catch according to Dustie Hickey's is that they are almost all for men only, which she considers grossly unfair.

Julian Peachey made use of the Night Shelter in Marseille when he arrived to look for work:

I looked around for likely helpful characters and asked a young man, obviously penniless, where to stay. He told me to go to the Accueil de Nuit in rue Plumier near Vieilleport. This was run by a Catholic order and the routine was very strict: entry between 7.00 and 7.10pm, in bed by 9pm, up at 5am, and out by 6.30am. This did however allow me to recover from my long hitch-hiking journey, without having to spend my emergency fund.

Look up *Foyers/Asiles de Nuit* in the telephone directory or ask a *gendarme* on the beat.

If you would like to survive in rural France, communal living is a possibility. Roberta Wedge enjoyed several months at the 'bleakly beautiful' Le Cun de Larzac Peace Centre (12100 Millau) and says that they need work-for-keep volunteers in the summer to look after visitors, tend the gardens, preserve the fruit, etc. Another Gandhian Community of the Ark is La Borie Noble, Nogaret, La Flayssière, 34650 Roqueredonde. There are dozens of French communes listed in *Diggers and Dreamers* mentioned on page 115.

If you are more into private enterprise, you may wish to follow Tessa Shaw's example. She learned that there were many edible snails to be found along the canal and river banks in the *département* of Vaucluse which she could sell in the market. The snails move about only on still, dank nights: so Tessa would be found between the hours of 2am and 7am scouring the waterside with the help of a torch. She would then keep them in a sack or bin for four or five days until they exuded all the poison in their systems, and then sell them in the market of Carpentras. There is a closed season for snail collecting between April 1st and June 30th.

While you're waiting for something to turn up, it is possible to sleep in parks, railway stations or on beaches, though this is unlikely to be trouble-free. Do not consider spending the night at the Gare de Lyons unless you can produce a current ticket since the patrolling police will not be overgentle when evicting you. T. J. Coles recommends the pebble beach at Nice, though the police regularly arrive at 2.30am shouting *'Debout Debout'*.

Paris hospitals which sometimes pay up to F250 to participants in drug tests include the Institut Aster, 3-5 rue Eugène Millon (45 31 68 90) and Laboratoire Sandoz (47 32 79 17).

Lee Merrick found the Union des Centres de Rencontres Internationales de France (UCRIF, 72 rue Rambuteau, 75001 Paris; 1-4026 57 64) very helpful for accommodation both in Paris and beyond. They have 62 residential centres throughout France, including 15 in Paris, which are about the cheapest hostel accommodation available and largely frequented by young people from overseas.

CORSICA

Although the island of Corsica is officially a French *département,* the inhabitants have more in common with Sardinians than with the mainland French. Corsica is a poor and undeveloped region, but its warm climate does create a few opportunities in farming and tourism for the working traveller. There is a large proportion of Arabs from North Africa who are willing to work hard for low wages, so you will have to be patient if you're going to find an employer.

K. McCausland found the ANPE in Porto Vecchio to be surprisingly helpful, given that there is quite a measure of local animosity to incomers. He was told that there were jobs in tourism and in building and maintenance. However he was so put off by the frequent spectacle of road signs riddled with bullet holes that he didn't pursue the idea of working in Corsica.

Hotel Work

The tourist industry is concentrated in a small number of towns: Ajaccio the capital, Bastia, Bonifacio, Calvi, Ile Rousse and Propriano. Unfortunately these have been the occasional targets of separatists' bombs. Anyone with a knowledge of German would be at an advantage since the level of German tourism in Corsica is very high. Kathryn Halliwell found her job in the hotel Grand Sofitel at Portticio, a resort about 12km down the coast from Ajaccio, by the time-honoured method of asking from door to door. She worked as a chambermaid on a hotel staff of 150, and mentioned that the worst problem faced by the female members of staff was the level of unwelcome attention from local Arab men.

Alison Cooper found the heat to be a more serious impediment to her enjoyment of the summer of 1994 as a Eurocamp courier in Corsica, but managed to have a great season:

I enjoyed this job immensely even if it did get unbearably hot when it's 40°C and you're trying to clean a tent in diret sunlight with a hangover. We had one and a half days off a week on average with a fantastic beach to go and chill out on, or a quick dip in the campsite pool after cleaning. On the whole it was a good summer.

The British tour company Bladon Lines (56-58 Putney High St, London SW15 1SF) recruits hotel staff for their beach hotel in Corsica. The pay is low but the living is free, including flights between London and Corsica and subsidised watersports.

Farm Work

Although Corsica is not as far south as Greece, many sub-tropical fruits such as kiwifruit, clementines and avocadoes thrive. Most of this fruit ripens in mid-November and is picked through December. There is also an important grape harvest which takes place in September/early October.

The best region to try for fruit-picking work is the fertile area on the east coast especially around Bastia and half-way down around Aleria. Vineyards are concentrated along the coast to the north of Calvi, around Ajaccio and Sartene. With the help of the local farming co-operative, Swami veet Sandeha found a job picking grapes in Pianottoli Caldarello, a town between Sartene and Bonifacio. According to Sian Gronow, however, it is very difficult to find work, because of competition from the many Moroccan and Algerian migrant workers:

Although the Moroccans cannot write, they seemed to have addresses of vineyards and clementine farmers. The cooperatives we asked had a pre-arranged work force. I also had the impression that as girls, we would have problems working with the single Moroccan men.

Geoff Skingsley found less traditional farm work near Ghisonaccia during the summer. His was one of the several experimental farms set up along the east coast to grow fruit using new techniques. Although the work itself was not too taxing, the mid-day heat was a problem. To avoid it work began at dawn, and there was a three-hour break in the middle of the day. There were a few other students doing this sort of job nearby, as farmers found that local workers were unwilling to work with the new technology. But Geoff learnt that the real labour shortage existed from late October to mid-December when the clementines, kiwifruit and avocadoes are harvested. He warns that the work is hard — especially picking avocadoes, as they grow on tangled branches.

Germany

Germany has always had a reputation for offering high wages and good job prospects to foreign workers. Undeterred by reports of a German recession, Poles, Yugoslavs and other nationalities including British and Irish people have joined the millions of Turkish *gastarbeiter* (guest workers) who have been in Germany for a generation. Although the recent waves of mostly right-wing violence against foreign workers and asylum seekers have not been directed against young people on working holidays, any foreigner working in Germany at the present time is likely to experience a certain amount of resentment.

The problem is compounded by the huge number of Germans from the former GDR who have flocked to the west in search of affluence and to escape a 17% rate of unemployment which is about twice as high as in western Germany. Surprisingly, there are few reports that Germans from the east take jobs which travellers tend to do, though the accommodation situation has become very tight due to the influx.

Despite all this, there remain many job opportunities for foreigners and students, especially in certain regions such as Bavaria and in fields of employment such as hotels and fast food, nursing and skilled building trades. Anyone who has a reasonable command of German can expect to find decently paid work at some level in Germany.

The Regulations

If you are an EU national you are free to travel to Germany to look for work. However you are still subject to the labyrinthine bureaucracy, as David Hughes discovered when he went to Frankfurt to take up a job as a nurse:

I believe (hope) we've finished our dealings with those German bureaucrats.
Cumbersome is the exact adjective. I'm not sure about why or what we were
doing some of the time. After establishing myself here as a legal worker, I
fully understand the writings of Franz Kafka!

If you intend to work or to stay for more than three months, you will have to
tackle the bureaucracy. (If you don't want to work for more than three months,
don't bother with any of this.) Procedures used to differ from state to state;
however there are now supposed to be national regulations. The first step is to
register with the local authority *(Einwohnermeldeamt)*. Go to the town hall
(Ortsamt or *Rathaus)* to pick up the right form *(Anmeldung)* which will have to
be signed by your landlord. People who are not in rented accommodation will
have problems. One young job-seeker staying at a youth hostel in Berlin described
it, 'I was trapped for a week in a vicious circle of no job — no papers — no
accommodation; without one of these it is very difficult to get the others.'
Take the *Anmeldung* back to the *Ortsamt* in order to pick up a tax card
(Lohnsteuerkarte).

For many jobs (e.g. childcare, food service, etc.) you must also acquire a
Gesundheitszeugnis (health certificate) from the local *Gesundheitsamt* (health
department). Restaurants will be heavily fined if they are caught employing
anyone without it. When you go for the examination, you have to show either
your *Anmeldung* or a job offer and pay a fee of about DM80. You return a week
later, and then your *Gesundheitszeugnis* will be posted. Whereas this works
smoothly for some, Ann Barkett was given the run-around in Munich:

It took three weeks to complete the medical exam and receive the results,
because the doctor required me to meet with her personally for the results.
Her office failed to inform me that the results had not arrived, therefore
causing me to make several unnecessary trips (for which I was billed!)

Only after doing this is it possible to apply for a five-year residence permit
(Aufenthaltsgenehmigung) from the aliens' authority *(Ausländerbehörde)*. Take
all your processed documents, your passport and three photos. David Hughes
offers a word of advice:

On the opening times of offices: absurd, ridiculous, inconvenient and too
bloody early are thoughts that spring to mind. For example the aliens office
in Frankfurt is open Monday, Wednesday and Friday from 7.30am to 1pm;
tough if you're already working. Be prepared for hordes of other hopefuls.
We arrived at 6.20am, queued till 8am and were finished by 8.30am. On a
curiosity note, we had to sign a form saying that if at the end of five years,
we can't speak German, we must leave, which must surely go against the
EC constitution.

Raids on hotels and restaurants are frequent in some places, to clamp down
on people working black *(Schwartzarbeiter)*, including illegal workers from
Eastern Europe and elsewhere. The situation for non-EU nationals who find
employment is confused, and seems to depend on which civil servant you talk
to. Ann Barkett from the US was told contradictory things at every turn when
she wanted to regularise her status as a freelance English teacher in Munich.
After being told by an American colleague that freelance teachers in Bavaria
required a work permit, she went to considerable trouble to apply for a residence
permit in order to obtain a work permit, only to be told by the *Arbeitsamt* that
she didn't need a work permit at all.

CIEE arranges for American students who have studied some German at
college to work for up to three months between May and mid-October. Details
are available by phoning 212-661-1414 ext 1126. American students or recent
graduates in business, engineering or a technical field may wish to spend six
months in Germany with CDS International (330 7th Avenue, New York, NY

10001; 212-760-1400). The first month is spent at an intensive fee-paying language course in Cologne, after which participants undertake a paid internship which they have fixed up previously with the help of the Carl Duisberg Gesellschaft. Longer placements of 12-18 months are also available in the same fields as well as in agriculture.

Australian students may participate in the new SWAP Germany scheme administered by Student Services Australia (PO Box 399, Carlton South, VIC 3053) which allows them to work for up to three months.

German embassies abroad may recommend an English-language booklet published by the *Bundesanstalt für Arbeit* 'Information Booklet (119) for aliens working in the Federal Republic' which covers entry requirements and provisions of labour law among many other topics. It is probably not worth spending DM20 on it, since it does not spell out the practicalities as clearly as one might have hoped. For example there is virtually no separate information for EU nationals. Although it touches on topics such as social security and tax, it is far from comprehensive; for example there is no mention of the tax situation for students (see below). It can be ordered from Auskunfts- u. Beratungsstelle für Auslandtätige u. Auswanderer, Zimmer 202, 2. Stock, Grosse Bleichen 23, 20354 Hamburg.

Tax

You can use a residenced permit to obtain a *Lohnsteuerkarte* (tax card), after which you will be fully legal. Legal workers can expect to lose between 33% and 40% of their gross wages in tax and social security contributions, including a church tax *(Kirchensteuer)* which accounts for 8-9% of income tax, unless you claim an exemption due to atheism (and thereby forego the possibility of ever being married or buried in a German church).

Students taking up a short-term job in the Federal Republic of Germany during their university vacations for not longer than 183 days should be exempt from German income tax, provided they can prove to their German employer that they are enrolled in higher education. Students who are eligible should go the local German tax office before completing their summer contracts and file a claim. They should also make their student status known to prospective employers, for whom student employees are cheaper than non-students.

Anyone who earns less than DM6,360 in a year should not be liable to pay tax in Germany. Emma Forster visited the tax office *(Finanzamt)* in Hamburg after working for two months and was told that she was entitled to all her tax back. When you finish work in Germany, take your *Lohnsteuerkarte* to the tax office and complete a declaration of earnings *(Steuerklärung)* and hope that you are eligible to receive a rebate, which will be transferred to your home bank account.

You will need your processed *Anmeldung* to open a bank account. Anyone who can show a student card will be exempt from bank charges.

German National Employment Service

The *Bundesanstalt für Arbeit* (Regenburgerstr. 104, 90237 Nürnberg) is the Federal Employment Institute. Although the *Bundesanstalt's* monopoly on job-finding in Germany has been broken and private employment agencies have been introduced in the past year or two, these are still strictly controlled and the state agency still dominates employment in Germany. The whole of Germany is covered by the Bundesanstalt's network. There are 184 principal *Arbeitsamter* (employment offices) and a further 646 branch offices. These are all connected by a number of co-ordinating offices which handle both applications and vacancies that cannot be filled locally.

Arbeitsamter will normally refuse to help you unless you have residence papers. If you do, they can be exceedingly helpful, as described by Nick Langley who used the one in Munich at 26 Kapuzinerstrasse near the U-bahn station Goetheplatz:

Germany has one of the most efficient National Employment Services in the world. In Munich there is a massive modern complex which is organised on the basis of different departments handling job vacancies for different work categories such as building and construction, engineering, restaurant work, hotel work, etc. It may be necessary to visit several departments to maximise your chances of a job. Each department has counsellors to handle enquiries, tell you what's on offer and arrange interviews. There is also a microfiche reader listing hundreds of vacancies in the area. I was immediately offered a job at a new Burger King restaurant about to open in the main station.

Unlike Jobcentres, *Arbeitsamter* do not have facilities for drop-in job-seekers. You should make an appointment to meet a counsellor and this can take several weeks to schedule. Not all *Arbeitsamter* are as cooperative as the Munich one. Emma Forster doesn't mince words:

Firstly don't waste your time going to the employment offices. You have to wait hours in order to be laughed out of the place. Our reception was cooler than cool.

However, if you speak German and aren't in a hurry, it's probably worth registering. Look for their weekly publication *Markt und Chance* which lists job vacancies.

It is possible to use the Federal Employment Service from outside Germany. The Zentralstelle für Arbeitsvermittlung (Central Placement Office) has an internationaldepartment *(Auslandsabteilung)* for dealing with applications from abroad. Details and application forms are available from ZAV, Feuerbachstrasse 42-46, 60325 Frankfurt am Main (069-71 11 0; fax: 069-71 11 540). All applications from abroad are handled by this office. Although people of any nationality can apply through the Zentralstelle, only citizens of an EU country are entitled to expect the same treatment as a German. People of other nationalities are accepted only within the framework of special exchange programmes and government-approved schemes such as the one administered by CDS International mentioned above.

There is one exception to this rule. The Zentralstelle has a special department which finds summer jobs for students of any nationality, because this is felt to be mutually beneficial to employers and employees alike. Students who wish to participate in this scheme should contact the Zentralstelle before March. Students must be at least 18 years old, have a good command of German and be available to work for at least two months. Work is available in hotels and restaurants, as chamber staff and kitchen helpers in hospitals, and in agriculture. The Zentralstelle assigns jobs centrally, according to employers' demands and the level of the candidate's spoken German. For example those with fluent German may be found service jobs while those without will be given jobs such as chambermaiding and dishwashing. If you decline the first job offered by the Zentralstelle, you may not be offered another.

The Bundesanstalt also operates mobile temporary employment offices, called *Service-Vermittlung* in addition to permanent *Arbeitsamter*. These are set up as an emergency measure where employers need extra workers immediately for short periods of time. It is, however, worth looking for them at any of the trade exhibitions and wine or beer festivals in which the Germans take such delight.

Other Sources of Work

As mentioned, private employment agencies have recently been permitted to operate. Anyone with office experience and a knowledge of German should look for branches of the Adia, Manpower and Interim chains in the big cities; these will be listed in the *Gelbe Seiten* (Yellow Pages) under *Stellenvermittlungsburo*. A German reader Brigitte Blanka noticed agency advertisements in Bonn and recommends looking out for Persona Service in the major German cities. Emma Forster recommends the agency near the main station in Hamburg: Job-Vermittlung, Kurt-Schumacher allee 2, 2000 Hamburg 1.

To avoid bureaucracy completely, EU nationals with a student card should try the *studentische arbeitsvermittlung* in all German universities. Casual jobs like babysitting and cleaning are registered with the student job service attached to the ASTA students' council.

Nurses looking for 12-month contracts in Germany can try the British agency Forbes Campbell Ltd. (9 Artillery Lane, London E1 7LP; 0171-377 8484).

Most of the main dailies like *Frankfurter Allgemeine Zeitung* carry their job supplements on Saturdays.

If you are looking for labouring or other casual work on the spot, seek out the local Irish bar. For example there are at least four in Berlin and one in Cologne mainly staffed by British and Irish people and meeting places for expat workers.

Accommodation

Flats and apartments are scarce and expensive, and you may find it necessary to go through an agency. *Mitwohnzentralen* are helpful and charge less than many other agencies (some charge two months' rent); in Emma Forster's case the fee charged by the *Mitwohnzentral* in Hamburg was a quarter of a month's rent. There is even a facility for people who are looking for flat-mates. Even here you may not be free of German bureaucracy since some agencies will not take you onto their books without a *Burgschaft*, the name and address of a local referee. If you are chasing a flat through the classifieds of a local paper, be warned that the competition will probably buy the first edition in the wee small hours and not wait until morning to ring potential landlords.

TOURISM AND CATERING

The German tourist industry depends heavily on immigrants and students during the busy summer months. Despite the huge number of (illegal) immigrants from the former Yugoslavia who are often willing to work for exploitative wages, many others do find jobs in hotels and restaurants, especially those which have been raided and are reluctant to break the law.

If you are conducting a door-to-door search of hotels and restaurants in the cities, you will be at an enormous advantage if you speak decent German. But you may be lucky and find a manager who speaks English (as most do) who needs someone behind the scenes to wash dishes, etc. When Robert Lofts worked in a hotel kitchen, he had to phone up his German-speaking brother who was living nearby every time he received a new instruction ('He wants you to peel the cucumbers'). Nidi Rajah from England had her job fixed up by the Zentralstelle:

> *It turned out that my employer relied heavily on foreign student labour and he placed us all in jobs as we arrived according to the fluency of our German.*

As well as trying the Zentralstelle, you can try to fix up a summer job ahead of time by sending off speculative applications. This worked in 1994 for Dean Fisher, an unemployed engineering apprentice, who went to wash dishes in Berchtesgaden on the Austrian border:

> *I spent 2½ months working in a very orderly and efficient kitchen on the top of a mountain in the Kehlsteinhaus (Eagle's Nest) with the most amazing*

view I've ever seen. I actually enjoyed the work even though it was hard going. I met loads of good people and learned a lot of German.

Get hotel addresses from tourist office brochures or, if you know anyone going to Germany on holiday in the spring, ask them to bring back local newspapers.

If your German is shaky and you are finding a door-to-door search isn't producing results, take Emma Forster's advice and concentrate on fast food outlets as she did in Hamburg:

Go in person to any McDonalds or Burger King. We had no trouble getting job offers on the spot, without speaking a word of German. The wages by British standards are high. I get DM11.50 per hour and 20% extra if I do the night shift. We reckon we can save DM2,000 after two months work.

So if you want to save money quickly, selling hamburgers in Hamburg would seem to be the answer.

Munich is estimated to have 2,000 pubs and restaurants (concentrated in the fashionable suburb of Schwabing) and Berlin is similarly well endowed with eateries (try the Kurfürstendamm area). The Munich beer gardens, especially the massive Chinese Tower Biergarten, pay glass collectors and washers-up (most of whom would have lined their jobs up at the beginning of the season) DM100 a day tax free at the height of the season, when people work 14-hour days. Look for adverts in the local press, especially *Abendzeitung* in Munich. Key words to look for on notices and in adverts are *Notkoch und Küchelhilfe gesucht* (relief and kitchen assistant required), *Spüler* (dishwasher), *Kellner, Bedienigung* (waiters/waitresses), *Schenkekellner* (pub type barman); *Büffetier* (barman in a restaurant), *Büffetkräfte* (fast food server), or simply *Services*.

Even untouristy cities like Stuttgart offer many opportunities; 17 year old Julie Wright left her guest house job in the Black Forest after two weeks in search of a better nightlife and was soon employed by the 5-star Steigenberger Hotel (Graf Zeppelin, Arnulf-Klett Platz 7, 70173 Stuttgart), a member of the Steinberger group of hotels.

Be prepared for hard work. In hotels, it is not unusual to work 10 or 12 hours a day and to have only a day or two off a month. The punitive hygiene laws do not help matters. Once you realise that restaurants and hotels are frequently visited by the health department you will appreciate why it is that the head cook orders you to scrub the floors, clean the fat filters regularly, etc. But the very high wages, especially with the Deutsch Mark so strong, make it worthwhile.

Paul Winter has worked several seasons on the lakes near Munich:

I found that it is best to apply around April/May in person if possible. What they usually do is to tell you to come back at the beginning of June and work for a couple of days to see how you get on. As long as you are not a complete idiot they always keep you on until September. Even as late as July I knew of places looking for extra staff but as a rule most places are full by the end of May. I worked for the summer as a barman/waiter earning DM1,600 per month, net. With the tips I got I generally managed to double this. The guy who worked in the kitchens pulled in DM1,200 after his room and board were taken off.

Both Amersee and Starnbergersee can be reached by S-Bahn from Munich. These two lakes are ringed by towns and village which all have hotels and restaurants, popular mainly with German tourists. Paul wrote again in the autumn of 1994 to say that the recession had hit Bavaria and jobs had become not only more scarce but also less well paid. There is continuing competition from students from the old East Germany who tend to get preference.

Other recommended areas to try for a summer job are the Bavarian Alps (along the border with Austria), the shores of Lake Constance, the Bohmer Wald (along the Czech border), the Black Forest (in south-west Germany), and the seaside resorts along the Baltic and North Seas. One employer on the Baltic coast hires a number of general assistants or sports instructors at a coastal campsite/golf and holiday park. The hours are long and you must be able to speak German but the wages are good. Apply in the spring to Camping Wulfener Hals, Gustav Riechey & Sohn, 23769 Wulfen/Fehmarn (04371 4250).

Alpotels (a branch of the agency Jobs in the Alps) carries out aptitude tests on behalf of German hoteliers looking for about 50 English-speaking staff for the summer season. If interested in this scheme, send an s.a.e. to Alpotels, PO Box 388, London SW1X 8LX.

A new organisation Eurotoques (c/o Moet-Hennessy Deutschland, Max-Planckstr. 8, 85609 Aschheim-Dornach; 089-994 21 151; fax 089-9921 190) finds jobs for German-speaking people as kitchen assistants and waiting staff throughout Germany. The catch is that no wage is paid for working nine hours a day, five days a week, for a minimum of three months (at any time of the year); board and lodging are provided.

Winter Resorts

Germany is reported to be a good place to pick up jobs in ski resorts although few British tour companies operate there. Alpotels mentioned above helps in the recruitment of 25 British workers for the winter season in Germany. Two main skiing areas are Garmisch-Partenkirchen (which also has hotels and services for the American Army) on the Austrian border 50 miles southeast of Munich, and the spa resort of Oberstdorf in the mountains south of Kempten.

Most people who work in the area of Garmisch are enthusiastic, thus Brenda O'Shea from Ireland:

I came to Garmisch-Partenkirchen with the intention of staying for six months. That was October 1992 and it's now May 1994, which says everything. Beautiful place full of interesting people.

At one time the US Forces Recreation Camp in Garmisch generated a lot of employment. However the strict labour laws which protect German employees (and by extension EU nationals) mean that the base has stopped hiring local nationals and only hires Americans since they are not subject to the same regulations and are therefore much cheaper to employ. So there is plenty of work for Americans but others will have to try for jobs in German-owned establishments. Amanda Smallwood recommends the Ramada Sporthotel (Am Riess 5, 82467 Garmisch-Partenkirchen; 088 21-75 80) whose seasonal vacancies are mostly in the kitchen or housekeeping departments where the net pay is around DM1,000 after deductions for tax, social insurance and accommodation.

After completing the summer season in Scotland, Isak Maseide from Norway hitched the 2,000km from Oban only to be told the bad news about the new pro-American hiring policy. He was particularly disappointed because he was so well qualified (experience in hotels and restaurants, knowledge of German, French and English, good skiers, etc.). He then went back to the old 'hotel-trot' and was repeatedly told that they wouldn't be hiring until the beginning of the season (December 10-15).

Work on Military Bases

Cutbacks in military spending and the perceived decrease in risk from hostile powers has meant the withdrawal of both American and British troops and resources from military bases in Germany. Many large bases such as the one in Munich have closed. As mentioned above in the context of the US Recreation Camp in Garmisch-Partenkirchen, US Forces facilities are now hiring US citizens exclusively, so much of the following information applies only to them.

US bases are normally self-contained, providing servicemen with all the catering facilities, shops, entertainment and other services they need. Employees are paid in US dollars. Some of the recruitment takes place through Civilian Personnel Offices (CPOs), access to which no longer requires a base pass. Applicants' details are computerised and fed into the Civilian Automated Referral System (CARS) which is a centralised clearing house for vacancies on American bases in Germany. You will improve your chances of being offered a job if you state your willingness to work on any base.

The *Stars and Stripes* is the US Army newspaper and is worth checking for jobs, especially as nannies or au pairs. Ana Güemes from Mexico answered an advert and was hired over the phone by a service family in Beibesheim near Darmstadt. The low pay (US$400 per month) and loss of freedom meant that Ana did not stay long, but it would be easy to move to a better family once you were on a base.

Work on British bases along the Rhine such as Verden, Minden, Münster and Paderborn is now very scarce. The Christian charity TOC H (1 Forest Close, Wendover, Aylesbury, Bucks. HP22 6BT; 0296 623911) runs short-term residential projects including playschemes for the children of British servicemen and work with people in need or with disabilities. About 500 volunteers are taken on annually for periods of between a weekend and three weeks. Their programme in Germany (as well as in the UK and Belgium) comes out on the first Monday of March and September. Cost of participation is about £50 including travel from the UK.

The British Forces Germany Youth Service (BFG Youth Service, Salmond House Training Centre, Rheindahlen Military Complex, BFPO 40; tel/fax 061-47 23 176) recruits young people to work in youth clubs for six weeks in the summer in exchange for free travel and pocket money. Recruitment is undertaken early in the year, so application forms should be requested by early January.

Special Events

Oktoberfest starts each year on the last Saturday in September and lasts a fortnight. They begin to erect the giant tents for the festival about three months ahead so you can begin your enquiries any time in the summer. Some of the hiring is done directly by the breweries, so it is worth contacting the Hofbräuhaus and Löwenbräu for work, as well as pubs, restaurants and hotels. There is also work after it finishes as Brad Allemand from Australia discovered:

> On the Monday after Oktoberfest finished I went around to all of the Beer Halls which were being taken down asking for some work. The first one I went to was Spatenbräu and the boss obliged. Even though my German was almost non-existent, I managed to understand what was needed of me. Many other foreigners were also on the site — English, Australian, Yugoslav, etc.

Brad enjoyed the work, which lasted about six weeks. He worked 7am-5pm five days a week for an hourly rate of DM12.

Here are some other special events which need large numbers of people to set up stands and deal with the maintenance, catering, etc. Some of the major ones are listed below:

March	Frankfurt Trade Fair
April	Hannover Trade Fair
August	International Frankfurt Trade Fair
August	Mainz Wine Festival
August	Wiesbaden Wine Week
August	Rüdesheim Wine Festival
late Sept/early Oct	German Wine Harvest Festival (Neustadt)
late Sept/early Oct	Wiesbaden-Rheingau Wine Festival

late Sept/early Oct	Cannstadt Folk and Beer Festival (Stuttgart)
late Sept/early Oct	October Beer Festival (Munich)
early October	Frankfurt Book Fair

Armin Birrer reported from Hamburg that they hold a fair ('Dom') 3 times a year, for a month after Christmas, Easter and late summer. He helped to dismantle the place at the end of the Easter fair after seeing a 'Worker Wanted' sign on some of the stalls. Opportunities for casual work also exist before the fairs open.

It is possible to combine work with pleasure. Phil New went to Stuttgart primarily for the beer festival but managed to offset his drinking debts by a night's work at the end of the festival dismantling a fun fair ride.

The Frankfurt Book Fair may not offer many casual opportunities, though there is a Fair Employment Office at the City entrance hall 1 to the Fair (Ludwig-Erhard-Anlage 1, W-6000 Frankfurt 1; 069-752339) where you might enquire, if you have a good command of languages and are willing to run messages, etc.

BUSINESS AND INDUSTRY

Germany used to be a mecca for foreigners looking for work in the manufacturing industries. This is no longer the case. Unemployment is very high in the Ruhr Valley, with some of the old traditional industries in crisis. Very high wages are no longer universal, though most production line work pays about DM15-20 an hour.

You generally need to be on the spot to find this sort of job or have contacts. The best advice is simply to head for large industrial towns, such as Stuttgart, Cologne, Düsseldorf, Munich and Hannover, and start asking for work in *Arbeitsamter* and at factory gates. Berlin and Frankfurt have very high unemployment and so are not very hopeful destinations. You should also check the sits vac columns, for example in the *Rheinische Post* in Düsseldorf and *Süddeutsche Zeitung* and *Munchner Merkur* in Munich (particularly the Wednesday and Saturday editions which can be bought the previous evening in stations).

In the wake of reunification, entrepreneurs have had a field day in the old East Germany. But with local unemployment at very high levels, you will almost certainly have to have a contact in order to get a paid job in the former German Democratic Republic, as the American Kathy Merz had:

A month after I left my job Garmisch-Partenkirchen, I went to Reichenbach, East Germany, to visit a penpal and her family for a couple of days. I ended up working in their butcher shop for six months. That certainly was a chance job. I will say that I now know what the word 'work' means and what it means to be tired! I saved every mark I earned as I had room and board and my 'family' paid for everything, from haircuts to movies. My German improved tremendously because no one spoke English, and I am now very familiar with German wursts! I gained so much insight into the everyday life of an East German family and life in an ex-communist country. It was really moving to celebrate the German unification with them and the opening of their second shop.

Building Work

Despite the recession, there is a building boom in Germany, partly to provide new accommodation for Germans travelling east to west, but also to help with the development and modernisation of eastern Germany. It is estimated that there are as many as 50,000 British and Irish building workers in Germany at present, such as bricklayers, carpenters, tilers and plasterers. The German authorities are not keen on this invasion because in many cases foreign tradesmen are not paying tax and are not registered with the authorities. They have recently announced that the number of site inspectors is to be doubled. According to the German construction workers' union IG Bau-Steine-Erden, many British and Irishmen work for a third less than the minimum wage of about DM65. They are planning to cooperate with their counterpart union in Britain, UCATT, to try to solve the problem.

For the time being, the tradition continues of British builders being contracted by Dutch agents mostly in Nijmegen, not all of whom are licensed. In some cases they are flagrantly exploited, as Jason Harris from South Wales reported in 1994:

> *I have recently come back from Germany where I was working for a Netherlands firm as a bricklayer. I would just like to say to other travellers who might be considering this work, that although you are self-employed, they will still take a third of your wages plus 10% for the person measuring up the brick work plus a further 10% as a retainer.*

He soon tired of this arrangement and went to work for a German firm where conditions were much more favourable.

The situation has worsened in the past year and many Britons have ended up being paid a fraction of what they were promised and then dismissed. A typical scenario is that an unemployed labourer sees an ad in the British press (very often the *Sun* or the *Star*) promising high wages, travels to the site to work, is paid a pittance after the first week, a little more at the end of the second (with excuses that compulsory deductions for tax, etc. are being made) and then dismissed at the end of the third week on the pretext of substandard work. Recruiting agents abandon them in a hotel and vanish. An estimated 150 destitute builders have had to be repatriated by the British Embassy. Builders are advised by the relevant UK unions to make sure the contractor has a fixed address with headed paper and to get something in writing.

The fortnightly newspaper *Overseas Jobs Express* carries some ads for job vacancies in the German building trade. It also publishes the following disclaimer:

> *We understand that according to German regulation it is illegal for agencies who are not in possession of a German Labour Leasing or companies who are not registered in Germany to offer work in Germany to British job-seekers. Workers taking up employment in Germany must be employed by the company who will then deduct the individual's tax and insurance.*

Most companies will want you to be registered self-employed with form E101 (see page 82). If you are hired on this basis you are not covered by German health and safety legislation.

Now that indigenous employment agencies are permitted to operate in Germany, the dubious cross-border recruitment may be reduced. Anyone interested in the official line should obtain the leaflet 'Going to Germany as a Self-Employed Person' from the German Embassy which states that it is illegal to work as a self-employed person on German construction sites without being registered at the Chamber of Handicrafts *(Handwerkskammer)* which requires you to show proof that you are properly trained and experienced for the job.

TEACHING

If you enquire at an *Arbeitsamt* about teaching, translation or secretarial work, you will probably be told (truthfully) that there is a surplus of people offering those services. However graduates with a background in economics or business who can speak German do have a chance of finding work in a German city. A TEFL Certificate has less clout than relevant experience, as Kevin Boyd found when he arrived in Munich in September, clutching his brand new RSA/Cambridge Certificate:

I was persuaded by a teaching friend to go to Munich with him to try to get highly paid jobs together. As he spoke some German and had about a year's teaching experience, he got a job straightaway. Every school I went to in Munich just didn't want to know as I couldn't speak German and only had four weeks teaching experience.

If you do intend to look for a teaching job take evidence of any qualifications and some good references *(zeugnisse)* which are essential in Germany. You can always try to arrange private English lessons to augment your income, though you are unlikely to be able to make a living this way. During the four winter months Ann Barkett spent in Munich, she put up flyers for private and group lessons but received no response. She finally answered an ad for a private student whom she taught for a few weeks.

Many secondary schools in Germany (including the former East) employ native English-speaking *Helferen* (assistants), posts normally reserved for students of German who apply through the Central Bureau for Educational Visits & Exchanges (Seymour Mews, London W1H 9PE). Inlingua has over 50 schools in Germany which teach English to adults. However most of its recruitment is done through its Cheltenham office (see *Teaching*). An indigenous organisation to try is the Euro-Schulen-Organisation.

Many commercial institutes employ freelancers, often resident expatriates willing to work just a few hours a week. Working freelance can make the red tape easier for non-EU teachers. This was what Ann Barkett from Georgia hoped to do, but didn't succeed in the end due to an unaccountable change of heart on the part of her employer:

When I sent my resumé around I received a quick response from Berlitz. During my interview, the Director expressed a desperate need for English teachers and enrolled me into the training course which I successfully passed.

After several weeks of tackling German bureaucracy re work permits, Ann phoned Berlitz to say that all was in order. Ann was mystified to be given the cold shoulder with a muttered excuse about troubles with the union. Her fellow trainees (all EU nationals) were all teaching up to 40 hours a week. She was never able to ascertain why one week they were practically begging her to work and then rejected her later.

The reunification of Germany has created some new demand for English in the new *Länder*. So far private language schools do not play a major role in the east, though this may change as integration proceeds. Through university contacts, Catherine Rogers fixed up a job teaching English to unemployed engineers and secretaries in the Dresden area of the former East Germany. Her working conditions were relatively primitive, though there were other compensations:

Accommodation was provided in 'outer Siberia', five miles from the factory where I was teaching. The temperature fell so low that the inside of the window was completely frozen. The wages were very good and I was able to save half my salary. I tried to sort out the red tape but was told by my boss that the local officials were not really geared up for that sort of thing!

The students were extremely helpful and generally thrilled to have a native English speaker. Success was virtually guaranteed if I put them in teams since they were very competitive. The hospitality and kindness were amazing, but I still felt isolated because my German was rather basic and there were no other foreigners around.

Childcare and Domestic

The monthly pocket money for an au pair in Germany is about DM350-400. Some families offer to pay for a monthly travel pass or even your fare home if you have stayed for the promised period of nine months. In return they will expect hard work which usually involves more housework than au pairs normally do.

Commercial au pair agencies have been allowed to operate in Germany since 1991 so the Zentralstelle is no longer involved. Of the six authorised agencies, the principal ones are:

In Via, Karlstr. 40, Postfach 420, 79104 Freiburg (0761-20 02 06). Has branches throughout Germany and one in England (German Catholic Social Centre, House Lioba, 40 Exeter Road, London NW2 4SB).

Verein für Internationale Jugendarbeit, Wesselstrasse 8, 53113 Bonn (0228-69 89 52). The German YWCA has 25 offices in Germany and one in London (39 Craven Road, London W2 3BX; 0171-723 0216).

Au Pair International, Ubierstrasse 94, 53173 Bonn (0228) 95 73 00. A cultural exchange organisation which is also involved in holiday job and internship placements for German young people.

It is possible for non-EU citizens to become au pairs through one of the above organisations provided they are not older than 24. A special au pair visa must be obtained before leaving the home country, a process which takes up to three months.

If you consider your standards of hygiene to be sufficiently high, you might try to find work as a cleaner. The demand for this sort of work is reported to be high in cities such as Mainz, Stuttgart and Munich, and the pay is DM10-15 an hour. The advantage of office cleaning is that the early morning and early evening hours leave plenty of time for other activities including the possibility of a second job. Johannes Sempert, a Munich resident, suggests contacting cleaning firms listed in the *Yellow Pages,* especially in the summer months. Also check notices in supermarkets.

FARM WORK

Farms in Germany tend to be small and highly mechanised: most farm work is done by the owner and his family, with perhaps the help of some locals at busy times. Only on rare occasions are harvesting vacancies registered with the local *Arbeitsamt.* Alan Corrie was treated as quite a novelty by the locals when he worked on a Rhineland farm:

> *The old girls on the farm were unused to having gallivanting seasonal workers pass their way and share their toils. They were a bit wary the first morning, but soon accepted me as a new and curious diversion.*

Grape production is the only branch of agriculture which employs casual workers in any great number. The harvest, which takes place mostly in the west of the country, is one of the latest in Europe, never earlier than October and sometimes lasting until the middle of November. The vast majority of harvesting jobs are taken by East Europeans. Philip O'Hara was not prepared for the new invasion when he set off by bicycle to look for grapes to pick along the River Mosel a couple of years ago:

> *I had to travel 20km from Trier before I found a* Weingut *that hadn't already finished its harvest. When I finally caught the harvest up, I found the place littered with Polish cars and vans. There were hundreds of little Polski Fiat 126s with muscle-bound Poles crammed inside. Believe me when I say that finding work is hard. I was told by many vineyard owners that they had plenty of workers and there was no advantage in employing an Englishman in preference to a Pole. Poles were viewed as being honest, tolerant of poor pay and conditions, strong, friendly, hard-working — it is hard work — and hard-drinking. Strangely enough it seems that Irishmen are viewed the same way here. Since I had an Irish passport, I began to*

boast of my Irishness. That and the bicycle were enough. I worked only with
Polish people on the grape harvest at Leiwen/Mosel.

Wages on the slopes of the Mosel have not risen in the last couple of years;
in some cases they have even declined because of the availability of Eat
European workers. Most farmers pay between DM6 and DM9 per hour plus
free accommodation.

A new source of competition emerged for the 1994 harvest, though it is
unlikely to make a very serious dint in the availability of grape-picking work in
Germany. A British travel company (Moswin Tours, 21 Church St, Oadby,
Leicester LE2 5DB; 0116-271 9922) was organising one-week grape-picking
holidays for people willing to pay nearly £450 for the privilege.

As usual your chances are better if you can visit the vineyards a month or
two before the harvest to fix up work. Ask any German tourist office for a free
leaflet about wine festivals since it includes some sketch maps of all the grape-
growing regions of Germany. The main concentration of vineyards is along the
Rivers Saar, Ruwer, Mosel and Nahe, centred on places familiar from wine
labels like Bernkastel, Bingen, Piesport and Kasel. There are ten other areas,
principally the Rheingau (around Rüdesheim and Eltville), Rheinpfalz (around
Deidesheim, Wachenheim and Bad Dürkheim) and Rheinhessen (around
Oppenheim and Nierstein).

Because the harvest is so late, be prepared for cold weather, as Alan Corrie
explains:

The lateness of the harvest means that the weather can be bad for workers
out in the fields all day. The weather was cold and damp, but the people
warm and friendly and the three half-hour breaks for hot wine, soup and
sandwiches always pleasant. Everyone would be gathered around the wagon
which brought us up into the high fields. At these moments, the clouds
parted, the glinting river with its long ships, the vivid autumnal winefields, the
forested hills and the constant changes in light made the atmosphere idyllic.

Apart from grapes, the most important area for fruit picking is the Altland,
which lies between Stade and Hamburg to the south of the River Elbe and
includes the towns of Steinkirchen, Jork and Horneburg. The main crops are
cherries, which are picked in July and August, and apples in September and
October. Apples and other fruit are grown in an area between Heidelberg and
Darmstadt called the Bergstrasse, and also in the very south of the country,
around Friederichshafen and Ravensburg near Lake Constance. Peter Radomski
recommends the Bodensee area for apple picking: small villages such as Oberdorf,
Eriskirch and Leimau sometimes employ migrant workers.

An account of the 1994 strawberry harvest near Wilhelmshaven in northern
Germany from Kristof Szymczak goes some way to explaining why so few
travellers work on German fruit harvests:

I was strawberry-picking in June/July, and I don't recommend this kind of
work to anybody who isn't desperately short of money. Strawberry picking
for me is really hard work, almost all day under the sun or rain. Of course
it's piece work. The pickers are only from Vietnam and Turkey (already
resident in Germany) and of course Poles like me. During 20 days of work
from 20th June to 10th July I earned about DM800. For travel add living
costs, I spent about a third, so not much left.

Those who wish to volunteer to work on organic farms should contact the
German branch of WWOOF (Willing Workers on Organic Farms) at Stettiner
Str. 3, D-35415 Pohlheim. Membership costs DM30.

VOLUNTARY WORK

Most of the international organisations mentioned in the introductory section
Voluntary Work operate schemes of one sort or another in Germany. Justin

Robinson joined a workcamp to restore an old fortress used by the Nazis as a concentration camp. The green movement in Germany is very strong and many organisations concentrate their efforts on arranging projects to protect the environment or preserve old buildings. For example Internationale Jugendgemeinschaftsdienste (IJGD) organise summer 'eco-camps' and assist with city fringe recreational activities. This organisation was highly praised by a former volunteer Andrew Boyle who wrote:

> *The camp was excellent value both in the nature of the work and in that the group became part of the local community. These camps are an excellent introduction to travelling for 16 to 26 year olds.*

Contact IJGD at Kaiserstrasse 43, 53113 Bonn (228-22 10 02) for details, or Concordia or UNA (Wales) in Britain. An initial fee of about DM140 is charged.

Other German workcamp organisations to try are:

Christlicher Friedensdienst, Rendelerstr. 9-11, 60385 Frankfurt. Tel: (069) 45 90 72. The German branch of Christian Movement for Peace, so initial enquiries should be sent to the local CMP office.

Internationale Begegnung in Gemeinschaftsdiensten (IBG), Schlosserstrasse 28, 70180 Stuttgart. Tel: (0711) 649 11 28. Publish a booklet in English of their projects in both eastern and western Germany. Application fee DM140.

Norddeutsche Jugend im Internationalen Gemeinschaftsdient, Am Vögenteich 13-15, 18057 Rostock. Range of projects in northeastern Germany.

Nothelfergemeinschaft der Freunde e.V., Fuggerstr. 3, 52351 Düren. Tel: (02421) 76569.

Pro International, Aufbauwerk der Jugend in Deutschland, Bahnhofstr. 26A, 35037 Marburg/Lahn. Tel: (06421) 65277. Booklet published in English. Application fee DM100.

Vereinigung Junger Freiwilliger (VJF), Müggelstrasse 22a, 10247 Berlin. Tel: (030) 588 38 14. Most camps are in the former East Germany. Registration fee for applicants who apply directly is DM200.

There are some longer term possibilities as well. Internationale Bund für Sozialarbeit/Jugendsozialwerk (Ludolfusstrasse 2-4, 60487 Frankfurt) takes on young people for a minimum of six months to work in various institutions for the elderly or handicapped. Volunteers are paid pocket money of DM250 per month. Their literature is also published in English.

Survival

At one time medical clinics in Germany such as the Iphar Clinic in Munich and LAB in Neu-Ulm accepted foreign volunteers for their lucrative pharmacological experiments. Unfortunately it is now much more difficult to be accepted because they insist that you speak and read fluent German, so they can be sure you understand and legally agree to any risks involved. Blood donor clinics pay about DM50 and you are allowed to donate every six weeks.

If you do happen to speak German watch out for media market researchers who are sometimes on the lookout for guinea pigs, as Isak Maseide discovered:

> *The different agencies working for TV and movie companies were picking people at random off the streets of Munich when we were there to show them a cut of an episode of a TV series or new film before release. They then interview you to find out what the public thinks. We were accosted by an interviewer just near the Toy Museum and were paid DM10 each for a nice hour in a warm room with plenty of coffee and tea and a rotten German TV series. According to the interviewer, you can make quite a lot of money going from agency to agency. Some pay as much as DM25.*

Finding affordable accommodation in Germany is a challenge and travellers solve this problem in various ways. Dave Bamford slept in the station in Munich for five consecutive nights while conducting his job search. Dave Hewitt managed to find a room in a *Studentenheim* (university residence) in Berlin. International youth camp Kapuzinerhölzl (in den Kirschen, 80992 Munich) is the German equivalent of Tent City in London which costs DM13 per night for bed and breakfast. The maximum stay is five nights.

If you are really in straitened circumstances, you might like to investigate the Bahnhofsmissions (Travellers' Aid) which can be found at most mainline stations. But even these cannot be relied upon as Nicola Hall discovered one cold and hungry night in Munich when she found the Bahnhofmission closed. Station waiting rooms are not recommended either, at least not by Philip O'Hara:

> *I personally don't recommend Berlin Hauptbahnhof as a jolly sleeping experience unless you get your kicks from watching baton-wielding policemen removing the drunks every hour or so through the night, interspersed with said drunks returning to wake you to offer you a drink or try to cadge a fag.*

Greece

Greece has countless attractions: beautiful scenery and climate, friendly and carefree people, memorable wine and food. It is no wonder that so many travellers join the general drift to Greece from Northern Europe in the autumn, and the second migration from Israel and elsewhere after Easter. Many decide to extend their stay in Greece by picking up casual work, such as orange picking, dish-washing or building. Once you become a confirmed Graecophile, working will seem infinitely preferable to spending your remaining travel fund on a ticket home. Greece seems to be the country where travellers are most willing to gamble their last few thousand drachmas on getting a job.

The complicating factor in the last two years has been the influx of Albanians and more recently Serbs and Georgians. Since Albania embraced a form of democracy and opened its borders in 1991, tens of thousands of Albanians have left their country in search of work. It is estimated that 150,000 impoverished east Europeans are working (illegally) in Greece. They have monopolised the vast bulk of casual work on farms, building sites, etc. since they are willing to work for less than half of the standard daily wage and are very hard workers. In many cases, it is impossible for other travellers to compete with them, and this often results in friction between the two groups of job-seekers, although some travellers have managed to get on the 'Albanian grapevine' and have found work alongside them. The Greek authorities are not happy with the situation and in the autumn of 1994 expelled 30,000 illegal Albanians. A further compensating factor for Britons and other nationalities is that Albanians are not always popular in Greece and some employers prefer not to hire them if there is a reasonable alternative.

Casual work is readily available (mainly for women) in bars and tavernas all over Greece, and also in English language schools and private households looking after children. Outside Athens the hiring of itinerant workers to pick fruit, build houses, unload lorries, etc., often on a day-to-day basis, generally takes place in the main café of the town or village, where all the locals congregate to find out what's going on and possibly offer a day's work to willing new arrivals. After you have stayed in one place for a certain length of time, you may not even have to ask door to door for work. Youth hostels as well as cafés are favourite places for local Greek employers to pick up casual labour. You need to strike a balance here: if there are too many eager job-seekers your chances of success will obviously be diminished. Word of mouth and the direct approach are the only effective ways to find work in Greece.

The Regulations

When EU nationals stay in any member country longer than three months, they are supposed to apply for a residence permit at least three weeks before that period expires. To get a residence permit in Greece, take your passport, a letter from your employer and a medical certificate issued by a state hospital to the local police station or, in Athens, to an office of the Aliens Department *(Grafeio Tmimatos Allodapon)*, e.g. 173 Alexandras Avenue (641 1746). The bureaucratic procedures are still fairly sluggish and frustrating and some working travellers continue to find it easier to pop over a border and re-enter on another three-month tourist visa. For example Julian Richards, a British graduate who went to teach English in the town of Veria for the academic year 1993/4 went to the trouble and expense of getting certified and translated copies of his degree certificate in order to obtain a teacher's licence and hence a residence permit; however by the end of his nine-month contract his school had still not got the documents nor had a drachma of his IKA (national health insurance) contributions been paid, which all employers are obliged to do. This situation is not atypical.

The official literature states that even EU nationals who intend to work for periods of less than three months are supposed to report to the police within eight days of arrival in the country. But work in Greece is normally undertaken so sporadically that many decide that it is not worthwhile changing their status from that of tourist. Although most casual jobs are illegal because they are undeclared, the police mostly turn a blind eye, at least to EU citizens.

Non-EU nationals who find employment are supposed to have a 'letter of hire' sent to them in their home countries. In its desire to conform to EU policies, the Greek government has increased the fines for illegal workers to dr200,000 while guilty employers are liable to jail sentences. Yet so much of the work undertaken in Greece (including by Greeks) is done 'black', many casual workers from Canada, Australia, etc. have no problems, in many cases with the full knowledge of the local police. (Of course they will not hesitate to invoke the law if they want to get rid of you as happened to some aggressive Antipodeans in Santorini who were hassling tourists. They were jailed overnight and deported the next day.)

The immigration police seem to target some places and not others. For example an Australian woman worked quite happily for an Athens hostel but was not allowed to work in the café next door (under the same management) since it was often raided by the tourist police. Harvesting areas are sometimes the target of immigration raids, mounted to catch large numbers of illegal East Europeans rather than working holidaymakers. For more high profile and longer-term jobs like English teaching, it seems that most employers will hire outside the EU only if they are desperate, at least according to the American Richard Spacer, who taught English in Corfu until he was fired after the police talked to his employer.

TOURISM

Millions of tourists choose Greece for their annual hols and anyone who looks for work at the beginning of the season (from early May) should be able to find an opening somewhere. A good time to look is just before the Orthodox Easter when the locals are beginning to gear up for the season. If you do fix up a job that early, you will have to be prepared to support yourself until the job starts. In a few cases there is work outside the May to September period. For example Adam Cook's friend Samantha had no trouble getting work as a barmaid in the Lesbos village of Petra in October, provided she was willing to work on a commission-only basis because of the shortage of customers.

You are more likely to find work in places which are isolated from the local culture, in American/European style bars in the cities and resorts, where disco music is played and package tourists willingly pay over the odds for imported Scotch and gin. Anyone with experience or catering qualifications might take advantage of the fact that the Greek tourism industry has a shortage of 'professionals' in this field.

Women travellers will find it much easier than men to land a casual job in a bar or restaurant. As one disgruntled male traveller wrote to us:

In general I would say that if you're a girl you have a 50% better chance of finding work in the tourist industry abroad. In Greece I would say women have a 500% better chance. Every pub I went into on Corfu seemed to have an English barmaid.

Alison Cooper describes the transience she experienced working in the tourist industry:

I spent the summer on the island of Ios doing the typical touristy work: waitressing, touting, dishwashing, etc. It was very common to have worked at four different places in a week due to being sacked for not flirting with your boss, but I had a great time partying all night and sunbathing all day long.

Think of Shirley Valentine. Undoubtedly the motives of some employers in hiring women are less than honourable. If you get bad vibes, move on.

A typical starting wage would be dr3,500 (cash-in-hand) plus tips and two meals for an eight-hour shift (5pm-1am). This is enough to fund quite a good time if you are camping or sharing a cheap room. Bar work is more difficult to find because it is better paid (dr5,000 for a shift) and usually involves cocktail-mixing experience. Hotel work (chambermaiding and cleaning) is not so well paid (say dr600 per hour). Note that foreigners inevitably get paid less than Greeks for the same job, and women are often treated with scant respect as Miss R. Bryant from Weymouth found in Palaiokhora:

The men patronise you, put you down and think you're just a bimbo. As the weeks went on, I had more and more responsibilities in the restaurant but was still treated like dirt (though I think I made the best wages of any holiday worker in town, the equivalent of £18 a day). In the end I told my boss what I thought and walked out.

What I will never get used to is the Greek men flirting with the tourists. They call it kamaki which means 'harpooning'. If an attractive girl came in, the restaurant stopped and the victims never realised it.

(Perhaps another reason she was keen to quit was to get away from a distasteful aspect of her job which was to stand beside the food display outside the front door squeezing the lobsters' eyes to make them move to prove how fresh they were.)

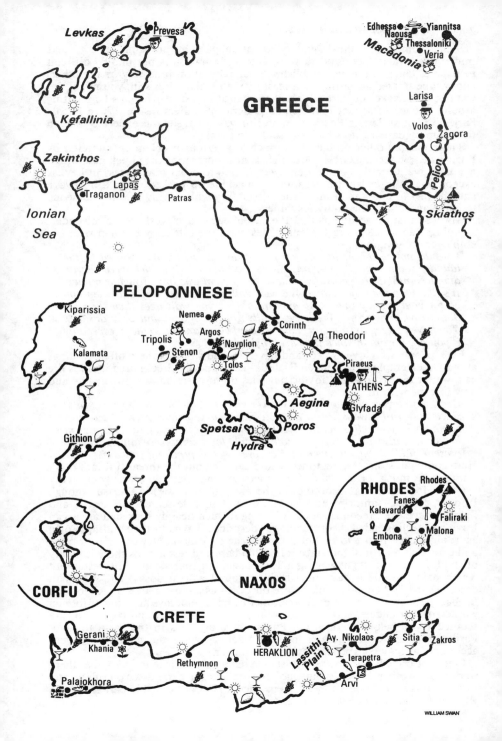

Some women find the legendary attention paid by prowling male Greeks intolerable; others have said this unwanted admiration is not unduly difficult to handle. Once you have established your reputation (one way or the other) you will be treated accordingly, at least by the regulars. But still, you might not want to undertake the sort of job Sharon Inge found in Khania's bars sitting around outside to attract tourists and American soldiers inside. When Nicola Sarjeant's bar at Perissa Beach on Santorini was quiet, she was expected to liven things up by dancing, to which she said 'No thanks'.

There may be other problems. A much less serious problem encountered by English people serving Greek customers is misinterpreting the Greek nod, which is a negative. Camilla Lambert enjoyed her job as a bar manageress in Levkas except when the fridge, freezer and ice machine all packed up in a heatwave and she had to take the brunt of the guests' fury while trying to rouse someone to come and repair the faulty machinery.

Always insist on getting paid at the end of each day's work, so no misunderstandings can arise. Laura O'Connor describes the difficulty she had with her employer on Mykonos:

I would not recommend this job to a fellow traveller. We worked in the laundry room from 11am-7pm, and had all our meals (which were hearty) and accommodation provided. The only problem was in getting our money. It's like blood out of a stone. We were told dr4,000 per day but when you go for your money there's no one around, or you wait ages then they say 'tomorrow, tomorrow'. Well, we finally got our money but only dr3,000. You haven't a leg to stand on. They'll pay if you stand up to them, especially if you are a woman since they are so shocked.

Even people who love Greece and have enjoyed working there offer warnings about Greek employers. Stephen Psallidas (who speaks Greek) describes his life as a waiter on Mykonos as idyllic but goes on to describe the 'down side' and how to cope with it:

Greek employers are the worst I've ever known! You should be very careful since they will always try to rip you off when you first arrive. You must stand up for yourself, since any weakness will be exploited. Greek restaurant bosses are also often very unprofessional, for example requiring you to present 'fiddled' bills to customers or, even worse, pinching your tips.

He recommends threatening to leave and carrying out the threat if things don't improve, as much for the sake of travellers coming after you as for your own.

Corfu, Ios and Paros seem to offer the most job openings in tourism, though Rhodes, Naxos, Santorini and Mykonos, and to a lesser extent Aegina and Spetsai, have been recommended. Working in such heavily touristed areas can leave you feeling jaded. Scott Corcoran describes Kavos in the south of Corfu as a 'nightmare resort town full of northerners drinking Newcastle brown ale and eating chip butties' but since it has 200 bars and restaurants there is plenty of employment. (Scott got work as a 'PR' persuading tourists into 'his' restaurant which paid dr2,000 a day and which he found a 'real doss'.) Jill Weseman describes the 700-bedded Pink Palace on Corfu as a cross between a Club Med for backpackers and an American summer camp. It employs an army of foreign workers as bartenders, cooks, receptionists, etc. but the pay and conditions are reputed to be below average. On Paros, there are jobs in the main town of Parikia and also in the quieter town of Naoussa where the season is shorter, accommodation less expensive and wages higher.

Frequent travellers in the Greek islands reported a change in 1994, that there were more women handing out publicity leaflets for bars, discos, cruises, etc. whereas this used to be a job for men. Nicola Hall noticed this particularly in Kos Town and Hersonisos in Crete.

Safra Wightman was delighted at how easily she found work on Naxos:

Finally I cashed my last travellers cheque and headed for the largest of the Cycladic islands, Naxos, to find a job. The numerous bars, cafès and tavernas seemed quite daunting at first. I decided to be choosy and approach only the places which appealed to me. I strolled the paralia *and a cafè caught my eye. I marched up to a Greek guy standing in the doorway and asked him if he had a job for me. He simply said yes and I started work that evening. The Greeks appreciate a direct approach. They are kind, welcoming, generous people. For working six hours in the evening and an hour's cleaning in the afternoon, I was paid dr4,000 plus food and as much liquid as I could consume.*

Safra went on to recommend going to the favourite haunts of working travellers on Naxos to find out about openings, viz. the Ocean Club, Musique Café, Mike's Bar and Ecstasis.

Foreigners (especially women) may also be hired in tourist resorts to deliver cars for car rental firms or to act as transfer couriers. Xuela Edwards and her companion Nicky Brown went to the package resort of Lindos on Rhodes in April and were offered several jobs on the first day. They worked as 'escorts' on day-trips from the village (which paid £12 per excursion) and also did airport transfers for British tour companies which paid about £15 (whether or not an arriving flight was delayed). They found this work by asking around at those local travel agencies which acted as the headquarters for overseas reps. According to Xuela this work requires that you be 'presentable, reliable, able to work all night and get up very early in the morning'. Another long-time contributor Camilla Lambert was based on the Ionian island of Levkas for five months working for Sunsail (see section *Boats* below) and acted as an occasional freelance guide on the side:

I also earned money driving tourists round the island in a hired jeep, as many had forgotten their driving licences and I knew which roads were passable and where the cheapest tavernas were. It cost me about £30 a day to rent a 4-wheel drive vehicle so if you take three passengers and they pay £15 each you make a profit while getting away from base.

If men are finding it difficult to find a service job, they may find taverna-owners willing to hire them as washers-up or roof menders. Some men are needed to build, paint or clean villas and hotels. In populous resorts, men are hired to unload trucks of supplies (crates of soft drinks, Retsina, etc.) for the cafés.

Seasonal jobs can be arranged from the UK. Mark Warner (George House, First Floor, 61/65 Kensington Church St, London W8 4BA) run several holiday clubs in Greece which require British staff who are paid from £35 to £150 per week depending on the position, in addition to all expenses. Best Travel Ltd (31 Topsfield Parade, Crouch End, London N8 8PT) hire up to 100 reps and other jobs to work a full season for Grecian Holidays.

Hostels

The competition for business among hostels and cheap pensions is so intense that many hostel owners employ travellers to entice/bully new arrivals into staying at their hostel. In exchange for meeting the relevant boat, train or bus, 'runners' receive a bed, a pitiful basic sum (normally dr1,500-2000) and a small commission for every 'catch.' The system of 'hustling' or 'touting' is well established in Athens (especially among the hostels around Omonia Square) and to some extent on the islands, but is not necessarily to be recommended. Leah White spent some time 'doing the hostels' when she first went to Athens and describes the competition as cut-throat:

Sometimes there are as many as 30 hostels vying for custom at Athens

*station, not to mention further competition and much animosity from taxi
drivers (who want to earn a commission from hotels). Working conditions
vary among the hostels and you soon learn which are the bad ones. You
always get free accommodation (shared) and occasional perks in the form
of free beers and cheap food.*

Kenneth Corcoran managed to save dr50,000 as a runner while Isak Maseide
saved half of a flight to London in four weeks of hard work and no social life.

If you are looking for this work, it is easier making enquiries at the station
where the runners congregate rather than going from hostel to hostel. During
Isak Maseide's stint as a runner, several hotels tried to bribe him to defect.
According to Isak, 'if you vaguely resemble the conscientious hard-working type,
you have a job, since so many runners have to be replaced every week due to
the sheer uselessness and proneness to alcoholic binges so often seen in northern
Europeans visiting Mediterranean countries.'

Many enjoy the hostel atmosphere and the camaraderie among hostel workers
(at least the ones who do not take the job too seriously), and they regard the job
as a useful stop-gap while travel plans are formulated, often based on the advice
of fellow travellers. Anyone who sticks at it for any length of time may find
themselves 'promoted' to reception; in this business a fortnight might qualify
you for the honour of being a long-term employee.

A great many hostels offer a free bed, pocket money (e.g. dr4,000 a week) and
in some cases meals to people who will spend a few hours a day cleaning. This
work is easy-come, easy-go, and is seldom secure even when you want it to be.
The popular and cheap Festos Youth & Student Guest House near Syntagma
Square in Athens (18 Filellinon St; 323 2455) has a notice for staff posted
permanently. The owner Mr Theo Consolas also advertises in the UK, inviting
applicants to write to him for details at Consolas Travel, 100 Eolou St, Athens
10559 (325 4931). As well as working in the upstairs bar, Heather McCulloch
worked in the Consolas travel agency, dodging traffic in the stifling heat to
deliver and collect tickets. However she was pleased with the wage (paid after
an unpaid trial week) of dr10,000 a day plus board and lodging. Mr. Consolas
also owns the Hotel Pension Consolas in Heraklion, Crete and the Hotel Pension
Piccadilly on Paros.

Selling & Enterprise

When taking advantage of the opportunities afforded by tourism, you need
not confine yourself to hotels, restaurant and cafés. Mandy Blumenthal funded
her island-hopping by selling 500 pairs of sunglasses brought from England. If
you have any handicraft skills like making jewellery, the tourist areas of Greece
could provide a lucrative market for your wares. Safra Wightman was very glad
she had remembered to take her scissors to Naxos where she was able to market
her training as a hair dresser. If you are arriving from Asia, you can stock up
on cheap Eastern jewellery as Kristen Moen did. She found Corfu a very
successful market for Indian, Nepali, Thai and Chinese jewellery.

You may try to sell your product to souvenir shops, set up an independent
market stall or sell on the streets. If you choose the latter, make sure that it is
allowed, since the police in busy resorts have been cracking down on this as
Nicola Hall reported from Crete in the summer of 1994:

*We came across a young lad who had been making friendship bangles and
hair pieces and street trading in Hersonisos (on the coast east of Heraklion).
It is now illegal to sell on the street here, as it is in Malia, the next town
along. The police give you three warnings and then fine you dr60,000 and
if you can't pay they put you in jail for 22 days where all you are given is*

bread and water. He was paid to look out for the cops and, if they came, to clear up the stuff and run with it.

Anyone who can paint portraits may be in for a bonanza. Street artists in the main resorts charge £10 for a 15-minute portrait and can expect to do four in an evening. You can also try to sell paintings of restaurants, banks, etc. to the establishment concerned. There is often work to be had painting signs and notice boards (primarily at the beginning of the season) or decorating the walls and doors of tourist places themselves. This can be quite well paid if you are good at it and get a good reputation.

A more original way of exploiting a market was found by Michael Jenkins, also on Corfu. With a friend he would chat up holidaymakers about to try parascending, take photographs of any who seemed at all interested and arrange to meet them again in the evening at no obligation. Michael and his partner took turns going into Corfu town on their rented motorbike to get the pictures developed at a commercial developer. Most people bought the pictures for dr1,200 which meant Michael had a very lucrative summer.

Grimly Corridor is another traveller who has combined ingenuity and exploitation of the market, this time in Crete. He found a stand of bamboo, and perfected making Pan-pipes from them. He attracted the attention of potential customers (mostly American tourists) by playing a simple tune and then improvised the myth of Pan. A surprising number of tourists could not resist parting with £5 for such an unusual souvenir.

More conventional forms of busking have also proved successful, and many travellers have eked out an existence by playing music.

Building and Manual Work

If women have the advantage in getting bar and restaurant jobs, men often succeed at finding building and labouring jobs which are usually much better paid (and so they should be, considering how much harder the work is). Also, building work is available year-round unlike bar and restaurant work. It is best to travel to sites on Rhodes, Santorini, Crete, etc. where new hotels and apartments are being built. Ask restaurant proprietors or simply keep your eyes open for work in progress as Tony Davies-Patrick did:

I noticed a huge number of unfinished houses outside Heraklion. The first building site I walked past I asked through sign language if they needed any extra workers and was surprised when they turned around and asked me to start the next day. The pay wasn't good but it paid for my extravagant eating and drinking at the Cottage Pub (opposite Camp Heraklion), an Irish bar which is a great place to get info on jobs.

Incidentally, these shells of uncompleted houses proliferate in Greece and are an excellent source of free accommodation. Ben Nakoneczny squatted in this way quite frequently, and found that no one minded as long as the house was left as it was found (which also helps the reputation of squatters for future travellers).

The standard labouring wage for an eight-hour shift is dr5,000. Greek builders are not renowned for their safety-consciousness and the work can be dangerous. Most Greek building-site workers pay IKA (national insurance) but foreigners are unlikely to be covered.

Trained builders are in greater demand than mere labourers, and bricklayers, plumbers and electricians can often find work out of season in areas where hotels are being built or renovated. But fit men can find unskilled manual work in the most surprising places as Ben Nakoneczny found a few year ago in Palaiokhora, a mecca for working travellers:

I only worked one day in Palaiokhora, which was a job of a quite extraordinary nature. It was arranged in the kafeneon through an intermediary since my employer spoke no English. He ascertained that I would accept dr2,000 for six hours work, of which only two hours would be heavy, and we duly drove off in his truck. I was no closer to finding out the exact nature of my work when we stopped off at his house in town and loaded up with huge slabs of marble before riding out into the Cretan countryside. Eventually we arrived at a mountainside cemetery, at which point I realised I was being paid to help construct a marble tomb!

Anyone with a knowledge of engine repairs could do worse than approach one of the dozens of jeep and motorbike hire companies in any tourist resort in Greece.

Boating

Yachting holiday companies are a possible source of jobs, which can be fixed up either ahead of time or on the spot. Camilla Lambert greatly enjoyed her season with the sailing holiday operator Sunsail (see *Tourism* chapter) which started in April with a two-week refit of the clubhouse and scrubbing and painting the boats. In the past people have found work by visiting skippering brokers and yacht agencies around Piraeus. English companies such as Camper & Nicholson prefer to hire English speakers, as do many local firms.

On islands where there is a lot of yachting traffic, you might find a job living on a boat. Mary Falls frequented Popeye's bar in Rhodes Town and soon found a half day's work polishing the brass of a boat. Someone who happened to notice how industriously she worked invited her to stay on his boat, working in exchange for her keep. After that she was taken on as the cook while the boat cruised the Turkish coast. The numerous cruise ships which ply the Aegean Sea are occasionally looking for personnel to replace people who have left their jobs in the ship's restaurants, bars or in the entertainment programme. Phone numbers of the relevant companies can be obtained from travel agents or found in the Yellow Pages under *Krouazieres*.

AGRICULTURE

Working in the English-speaking environment of tourism is not for everyone and certainly does not conform to Ben Nakoneczny's philosophy of travel:

If you are to work abroad it is preferable to be employed in a capacity which allows an insight into the people of the country you are visiting. To serve English tourists bottled beer in a western-style bar is merely to experience the company of those travellers who cling to what they know, unprepared to risk the unfamiliarity of an alien culture. I believe that the best way of breaking cultural boundaries is to work outside the tourist areas, probably in agriculture.

Unfortunately these days you might end up deserting an English-speaking environment only to find yourself in an Albanian one. A man writing in 1994 who signed himself Damon Das (read it backwards) described the contrast between his two visits to Crete in search of harvesting work:

This winter I started my search for work, as before, in Khania. I arrived at the square in town where the trucks pull in to pick up workers. From my previous experience, I expected to find work clearing the groves and repairing and laying olive nets in preparation for the harvest. But my first day was a nightmare. Instead of the camaraderie of all the nationalities looking for work, I found Albanians and a few Georgians. Every truck that pulled in was mobbed by hordes of people, leaving yours truly out in the cold. After

*half an hour of watching the manic maelstrom I moved on to look around
the building sites but to no avail. The following day I got to the Square very
very early and got arrested by the immigration police (but being a Brit they
soon let me go). After this I gave up on Khania and went inland to Fournes.
But I found the same again — loads of Albanians just hanging around
waiting for the harvest to start.*

But for the reasons mentioned in the first few paragraphs of this chapter, work
is still available. Jane McNally worked for a farmer on the Peloponnese in 1994
and reported that the demand for workers exceeded the supply of Albanians
there. As with openings in the tourist industry, opportunities to work in rural
areas can arise in an impromptu manner. For example Edward Peters and his
wife were doing some nude sunbathing on an isolated Peloponnesian beach
when they were approached by an old Greek. Contrary to their first assumption
that he was having a 'perv', he wanted to offer them work on his orange farm
near Skala.

Truck drivers in rural areas are a useful source of tips on job openings, as
Peter Radomski from Poland found during his stint of apricot picking and
general maintenance work near Corinth.

Assuming you have had no luck at the café or youth hostel, you can go into
the countryside as Tim Gunn recommends:

*The best way to get work is to approach a farmer when his fruit looks ripe
and use sign language to find out if he will employ you. Ascertain wages
and accommodation in the same way because there is very little chance of
his speaking anything other than Greek.*

Jane McNally suggests mastering the following few words: *kopse* (cut), *sheera*
(drill/row), *ilea* (olives), *thermo keepio* (greenhouse), *kafasi* (crate). (Do not try
to use a conventional phrase book which will specialise in questions like 'Excuse
me, does Yorkshire pudding come with my roast beef?' or 'I'm going to be sick'
rather than 'Do you need help in your fields?') Another way of communicating
across a language barrier is to ask a friendly bilingual local to write out in Greek
a simple request for work and then, like Bill Garfield, 'put it under farmers'
noses' in any of the cafés they visit early in the morning. According to Bill, you
will be able to recognise the farmers' cafés by the Datsun pick-ups parked
between 6 and 7am.

Sometimes, there is a well known meeting place, where farmers arrive very
early in the morning to collect enough workers for that day's work. Khania Gate
in Heraklion (described below) is the best known example. The disadvantages
of this day-to-day employment are that accommodation will not be offered by
the farmer and budgeting will be impossible due to the unpredictability of work.
The advantage is its complete flexibility. An average wage for a day's work
(typically 7am-1.30pm) should be dr4,000-5,000 plus some wine and lunch,
though in areas flooded with economic refugees, you will have to haggle to get
a wage of dr3,000.

Organic farming is not widely practised in Greece, though a farm in Rhodes
is an exception. The owner, Mr. Panayotis Passalis (Stavros Kallas, Theologos
85106, Rhodes) wants to use his olives as income to subsidise his idea of making
an international community composed of people concerned with health and
nutrition, preferably with a knowledge of natural crafts like pottery and spinning,
alternative energy, bee-keeping, etc. The work, which is varied, is for six hours
a day. Whereas Mr. A. J. Hubbard enthused about the hospitality shown to him,
Susan Brush from Newcastle expressed reservations (after leaving prematurely).
She found it increasingly frustrating that only one point of view was tolerated
plus the conversation turned too frequently to the subject of sex. She was
concerned that inexperienced (female) travellers might feel uneasy.

The Peloponnesian Peninsula

Orange groves abound between Corinth and Argos and south to Tolo. Picking oranges can be heavy and tiring, but is generally thought to be easier than other picking jobs. The season runs from late November to late February, with the crop at its peak between mid-December and mid-January. The harvest can be badly hit by frost and other calamities. The centre of orange picking on the Peloponnese is Navplion though the nearby towns of Tolo and Drepano are also recommended because the accommodation is likely to be cheaper and better than in Navplion. There is an infamous bar in Navplion (formerly called Harry's) where most of the hiring goes on.

Many orange-pickers have commented on the amount of friction between locals and itinerant workers, and between East Europeans and young travellers. When Martin and Shirine were there, they were told that a large group of Albanians had just been deported leaving the farmers with a sudden shortage of workers, so they were offering above average wages. Martin and Shirine were offered jobs in Argos train station with the promise of dr5,000 a day plus food and accommodation. Unfortunately they had made other plans and couldn't accept.

In Tolo there are contractors who hire on a daily basis. Again, cafés are the best places to fix up work. In Drepano the hiring café is the one painted blue in a corner of the square where countless trucks and vans congregate every morning. Another village to try is Inaxos about 4km outside Argos where the hiring café is Café Pancho.

The orange-picking wages are either a fixed daily rate starting at dr4,000 or dr4 a kilo. The piece work rate is good if the oranges are big, while a flat daily rate is preferable if the oranges are small or if you are asked to pick from the tops of the trees. If being paid piece work rates, it is advisable for the group you're in to keep track of how many boxes are filled. Also one person should go with the truck to the factory where the oranges are weighed, so there will be no arguments about earnings. Be prepared to lose two days a week to rain and much more if there is a frost.

When the work in the orange harvest begins to drop off at the end of February, you can either try to hang on (oranges are picked as late as May in good years) or move on to other crops. Many people head off to the mountains between Argos and Tripolis or north to Nemea to pick olives, though this can be erratic. In the autumn it is not unusual to be offered just a day or two's work clearing olive fields of brambles as Martin and Shirine were in Olympia or longer term work picking as Peter Goldman from Ohio was near Pirgos (though he declined because the wages were too low for the amount of work expected).

Wayne Meyer has followed the fruit and vegetable harvests around the Peloponnese and has provided a selective timetable:

April	— potato picking around Kalamata
May/June	— apricot picking around Navplion and elsewhere for about 1½ months
	— loading apricots is very well paid but very hard work
May	— cherry picking between Argos and Tripolis (Stadhiou, Rizais)
June	— pear picking in same area
October	— apple picking from the middle of the month, also around the villages of Stadhiou and Rizais
	— raisin grape picking from early October around Nemea or outside Tripolis in the village of Stenon
	— wine grape picking in the latter part of the month

Another harvest which should be added to the list is watermelons which are picked in the north-west of the Peloponnese in June/July, though again there will be competition from gypsies as Julian Peachey found:

One café outside a town called Kiparissia, was used by gypsies wanting to pick melons. I was on my own by this time and worked with them. They were rather proud of their strength and the speed of their work, and I must say I spent the hardest working days of my life there. You had to pass enormous melons, like giant medicine balls, along a chain of people, very fast; if you were too slow to turn around and catch the melon, it would smash in your face or chest.

The gypsies invited me to eat with them one afternoon when they were very drunk, so I accepted. I came into their camp, ate cooked vegetables, drank wine and ate barbecued hedgehog, freshly killed and prepared in front of me. I was too polite to refuse, and they were really quite nice, tasting vaguely like chicken.

More recently Jane McNally earned dr5,000 a day doing back-breaking melon weeding around Kiparissia alongside a gang of Romanians. She claims there is plenty of work in this area for men during the melon harvest in June, but women are not accepted by the farmers. In addition to Kiparissia, Lapas west of Patras is another place to try for watermelon picking and greenhouse work, and Tragano for the tomato harvest.

If you arrive in Greece in May you might try the village of Kalloni in the fertile area south of Athens. The Kafeneon Maria is reputed to be the place where employers go in the mornings in search of workers.

Edward Peters gladly accepted the invitation to work for the orange farmer mentioned above and earned a generous dr500 an hour. His wife and he saved a record £250 in 12 days. Inevitably there were drawbacks, viz. Yannis's wandering hands and the complete absence of concern for the environment. This area between Githion and Skala offers many agricultural possibilities both in late summer and during the winter for the olive and orange harvests. Apparently Britons have a good reputation among local farmers.

Crete

The largest of the Greek islands is able to provide a huge number of travellers with work, from the bananas in Arvi on the south coast (the most northerly commercial banana plantations in the world) to the potato harvest around Ayios Georgios in the Lassithi Plain in August. Most of the work though is with grapes and olives, and there is related work loading and processing fruit, vegetables and olives. The olive harvest normally begins in late November but can be delayed if the rains are late. In the old days, the villagers waited for the ripe olives to fall by themselves into nets beneath but nowadays the trees are beaten with sticks and branches are shaken to dislodge the olives. A pair of pickers can strip about five trees in a day. Whereas the older generation still tends the olive groves, most young Greeks are not prepared to do the hard work in cold weather and jobs for travellers proliferate.

Men can find jobs in olive processing plants as Scott Corcoran did in December 1993:

I eventually got a job at an olive oil processing shed in the village of Kallithea (5km southwest of Heraklion). This involved working 16 hours a day (8am till midnight) carrying sacks of olives and processing them in the factory. I was paid dr8,000 a day and was given free room and board. By Christmas I had had enough and moved on.

Most villages operate a cooperative olive press so it is worth asking in any village café, particularly along the south coast.

The two areas which absorb the most pickers are around the two largest cities, Heraklion and Khania. There are two ways of trying to find work: either wait to be picked up by a farmer at a central collection point in town or go into the villages where your chances are better of being taken on for the whole month-long harvest and of being offered meals and accommodation. Note however Damon Das's discouraging account of the situation he encountered at the main hiring square in Khania at the beginning of this section.

As throughout Greece, the grape harvests of Crete are a major employer. Andrew Owen thinks that grape-picking is the best summer job on Crete:

If you head a few kilometres south of Heraklion you will hit valley after valley of grapes all waiting to be picked in mid-August. The easiest way to fix up a job is to drink coffee or beer in the village tavernas and wait to be approached for work. If this doesn't pay off go around the farms asking farmers. Don't be disheartened: one valley may be completely picked before the next one has even been started. I worked in a small town called Voutes, along with about 20 others. A standard daily rate is paid to pickers, dippers, hangers and donkey-loaders and as little more to porters. The social life after work more than made up for a hard day's work. After working on the grapes I had saved enough to travel extensively in Turkey for three weeks.

Scott Corcoran chose the other technique, of staying in Heraklion (at the youth hostel on Veronus St, which is a good source of information on work) and going to the Khaniaporta early each morning, the ancient city gate on the western edge of the capital which serves as a collection point for labour. Scott and his brother Kenneth both found fairly regular work this way from August until October when the work dried up. They normally earned dr5,000 a day, though Kenneth warns that you have to be prepared to do almost any job for arrogant bosses.

Other crops to consider are oranges which are picked from the beginning of December for up to six months. Before the Albanian invasion, Paul Bridgland landed a dr5,000-a-day job picking oranges in the area of Platanius or Gerani near Khania within 24 hours of arriving in Khania.

There are extensive hothouses for tomato-growing where the wages are reputed to be quite good, for example in Palaiokhora from April to June and in the village of Stomio on the south coast. It seems that there is still plenty of work in the greenhouses and at the cucumber pickling factory in Ierapetra. Try the area around Sitia and Ayios Nikolaos and the remote village of Zakros in the extreme east.

Other Islands

Crete is not the only island where harvesting work is available and you may have to contend with less competition on other islands. Adam Cook's destination in October was the charming village of Petra in northern Lesbos, an island which Adam says has 11 million olive trees:

I found the job hunt quite difficult probably because my enthusiasm for work was waning and I didn't really push that hard. I did eventually find work with a man called George, digging holes around his olive trees to help catch the rains when they came. This paid dr9,000 for six hours or so. If we'd hung on, there was a fairly solid rumour of work beating and shaking the harvest in for dr18,000 a day.

Since Adam wasn't able to stay long enough, he never found out whether or not this improbably high wage really was paid for the olive harvest.

Fruit (e.g. strawberries) is grown on Naxos, for example, and grapes are grown throughout the country, especially on the Ionian Islands (Zakinthos, Levkas, etc.) and on Rhodes. The villages of Embona, Kalavarda and Fanes on the west side of Rhodes have been recommended for grape-picking in September and olive picking from November. On the less fertile west side of the island try the villages of Malona and Massari in the same months. For some reason there seem to be no opportunities in the orange harvest on Rhodes; Xuela Edwards made extensive enquiries between January and March and drew a complete blank.

Harvests in Northern Greece

Although much of northern Greece is rugged and forbidding, some of it is very fertile and an area not to be neglected. The area west of Thessaloniki, encompassing the market towns of Veria and Yiannitsa, is a major peach growing area, centred on the villages of Makrohoria, Diavato, Kavasila, Kasmena and Stavros all near Veria. The harvest gets started in mid-July but peaks after August 1st. Your chances of arranging accommodation with the farmers are much higher if you arrive before the urgent picking begins. Philip Longwe (a Zambian then living in Bulgaria) was very well treated by his peach farmer, who provided not only a bed and bedding but an occasional kilo of beef, cooking oil, etc.

People are also needed to pick tomatoes in the village of Kavasila. A good worker who can stand the sun can make a lot as piece work rates are paid. Yiannitsa 50km northwest of Thessaloniki is the centre of a rich agricultural area and anyone arriving in July or August might be able to find work picking tobacco. Further west there is apple and pear picking in September/October around the towns of Skedra and Edhessa. Ian Brooks also found work in the region of Macedonia:

I have worked in Greece for about eight months and found this the best work of all. I worked for a farmer in Rodohori near Naoussa. Cherries start June 10-15 and last two weeks; apples start September 6-12 and also last a fortnight. In addition to our wages and full board and lodging, the farmers would often take us to the taverna and pay the bill.

At the risk of repeating what has gone before, this is another place where there is stiff competition for work. Ian Govan wrote from Makrohoria at the end of July 1993:

The whole of Macedonia is swarming with illegal Albanians who are willing to work for dr2,000 a day — and they are good workers. We're the only non-Albanian workers here. We've managed to haggle our way up to dr3,000 a day but there aren't many employers who will go above that. Luckily the Albanians are thought to cause trouble here (theft, fighting, etc.) and are not liked or trusted by the Greeks. The English have a good record here so we're very popular with the locals. As well as having steady jobs, we also get the odd jobs which helps us save a bit more.

Another region to try is the Pelion peninsula south of Volos. This area is very fertile and green with apple trees, pears, walnuts and blackberries fruiting in September. Most of the apple picking is centred on Zagora, though work can be found in the much smaller town of Makrirakhi.

OTHER WORK

It is sometimes worth checking the Situations Vacant column of the English daily *Athens News* (3 Christou Lada, 10237 Athens; 1-333 3404/fax 322 3786). Adverts range from the distinctly dodgy ('Smart-looking girls required for cooperation in luxury bar') to the legitimate ('Wanted an English teacher for a school of foreign languages'), though most are for au pair jobs in private households. Obviously these jobs may not be the most desirable in the world as Vaughan Temby discovered: he left his 'hideous valet/houseboy job' after just two days. You could also try placing your own advertisement in the column 'Lessons' or 'Situations Wanted'. The advertising rate is about £5 for 15 words.

Employment Agencies

Several agencies in Athens place foreigners in various kinds of temporary job throughout Greece, mainly as au pairs, or as hotel, bar or restaurant staff. Normally agencies charge a registration fee of dr10,000-15,000 (which does not guarantee a suitable job) and some pay travel expenses from Athens. None will be willing to assign a job before you arrive. Jane McNally visited the agencies in search of work recently and offers the following warnings:

I've come across some very dodgy agencies which ask for applicants' passports and hold them as security while they go off on a wild goose chase for a job. They have also been known to promise the same job on an island to more than one person. Never pay an agency fee before you leave for the job. If they are unwilling to negotiate taking the money out of your first month's salary, do a vanishing act. Instead of leaving your passport, leave some less important document (e.g. an old student or medical card). Women should never accept a job outside Athens unless they have enough money to flee if they have to. Agencies sometimes send girls to seemingly safe waitressing jobs which turn out to be as 'company girls' in sleazy bars.

One of the longest established agencies is Pioneer Tours (Working Holidays Department), 11 Nikis St, Off Syntagma Square, 10557 Athens (322 4321) who charge a non-refundable fee of £20. Another one to try is Apan Express (91-93 Academis St, Athens; 364 1130). The Intertom Agency (24-26 Halkokondili St, 10432 Athens; 523 9470) has not been heard from recently but its past advertisements have offered 'jobs for any nationality in Athens, country or islands, in offices, hotels, restaurants, bars, discos and factories'. Miss G. Morton was distinctly unhappy with the service she received. Although she had rung the agency several times from England and explained that she was coming with a male companion, it was not until they showed up at the agency that she was told that she could not be employed if Ian accompanied her. All of this seemed so suspicious that they turned around and went home.

Childcare

Adverts appear in the *Athens News,* usually placed by well-off families in the wealthy suburbs of Athens. The Galentinas European Childcare Consultancy (PO Box 51181, Kifissia, 14510 Athens; 808 1005) has emerged in the last couple of years as the most respectable agency. It keeps detailed dossiers on vacancies, most of which are for a year, providing information about the children and the household, e.g. 'single ship-owning mother travels a lot' or 'summer on islands and yacht'. Among employers in this category a high percentage speak fluent English. Many employers have domestic staff, so au pairs do not normally have to do as much cleaning, etc. as in other countries. The Greek attitude to privacy differs from the British one, and in some cases the au pair is expected to share a room with one of the children. The going rate for ful-time au pairs in Athens is dr68,000 a month, while full-charge nannies can earn twice that. Some employers offer free outgoing flights and health insurance to long-term au pairs/ nannies. There is a limited number of summer positions available.

The YWCA at 11 Amerikis (362 6180) runs an occasional referral and placement service for young women looking for work in the greater Athens area.

Au pair and mother's help positions may of course be booked through agencies in Britain such as BJ International Services (49 Lower Church St, Croydon CR0 1XH; 0181-681 8285). Julie Richards tried using several other UK agencies but was disappointed that they expected nannying experience. She decided to go to Athens in any case and was offered five jobs in the first few days. The main advantage of waiting until you get to Greece is that you can meet your prospective family first. It is far better for both parties if you can chat over a cup of coffee and bargain in a leisurely fashion for wages, time off, duties, etc.

Teaching English

There are literally thousands of private language schools called *frontisteria* throughout Greece, which create a huge demand for native English speaker teachers. This is one job for which there will be no competition from Albanians. Standards at *frontisteria* vary from indifferent to excellent, but the run-of-the-mill variety is usually a reasonable place to work for nine months. By no means all of the foreign teachers hired by *frontisteria* hold a TEFL qualification, though all but the most dodgy schools will expect to see a university degree (which is a government requirement for a teacher's licence).

The majority of jobs are in towns and cities in mainland Greece. Athens has such a large expatriate community that most of the large central schools are able to hire well qualified staff locally. But this is not the case in Edessa, Larisa, Preveza or any of numerous towns which the tourist to Greece is unlikely to have heard of. The basic salary (net of tax and insurance) falls in the range of dr100,000-125,000 per month, which can be increased substantially by compulsory bonuses (typically dr60,000) if you stay till the end of your contract. Be prepared for long hours by normal English teaching standards, often 30 or more hours per week.

Chains of schools are always worth approaching with your CV. Try for example Stratigakis Schools of Foreign Languages (6 George Street, Canningos Square, 10677 Athens; 361 1496/361 2858; fax 361 3251); the Omiros Association (52 Academias St, 10679 Athens; 362 2887; fax 362 1833) with 120 branches throughout Greece; and the smaller but expanding Hambakis Schools (1 Filellinon St, Syntagma Square, 10557 Athens) which caters for 2,000 students at its four branches in Athens.

Fortunately there are several active teacher recruitment agencies which specialise in Greece with offices in Greece and/or Britain. These agencies are looking for people with at least a BA and preferably TEFL qualifications and/or experience (depending on the client *frontisterion's* requirements). Complaints about a lack of back-up are occasionally heard, so do not expect to be nannied along after placement. The following undertake to match EU teachers with *frontisteria* and do not charge teachers a fee:

Teachers in Greece (TIG), Taxilou St 79, Zographou, 15771 Athens. Tel: 779 2587. Fax: 777 6722. UK address: 53 Talbot Road, London W2. Tel: 0171-243 8260. Back-up address: 13 Mill Hams St, Christchurch, Dorset. This agency which has been in business for twelve years is run by Carol Skinner who comes to London every summer to carry out interviews.

English Studies Advisory Centre (ESAC), 22 Belestinou St, 11523 Athens. Tel: 691 0462. Fax: 649 4618. Has mainly nine-month jobs but also some summer positions as well. Applicants should enclose CV, recent photo, phone number and international reply coupon. Andrew Boyle (who had no TEFL background) answered one of ESAC's adverts in the *Guardian* and secured a job in Tripolis after one telephone call.

English Teachers for Greece (ETFG), 160 Littlehampton Road, Worthing, West Sussex BN13 1QT. Tel: (01903) 218638/766029.

Kkais Educational Services, Asopou 6, 35100 Lamia. Tel/fax: (231) 21028. Recruits qualified staff for more than 150 private language schools. Michael Kkais sometimes interviews potential candidates in the UK during July and August but accepts CVs after that (enclose five IRCs). He also places students as live-in children's companions and English tutors for the summer or for a year off.

Britannia Teacher Services, Ipierou 33, Athens. Tel: 821 6285. Recruits teachers with an English-related BA for *frontisteria* mainly in Athens. The majority of their client teachers are interviewed in Athens.

Jane McNally started travelling and working in Greece in 1992 and wrote from a school in Macedonia in April 1994 with some advice:

> *Most English speakers find work in private English schools, It can be difficult to find work by just knocking on school doors. Most school owners recruit their staff through agents two or three months in advance of the new term. If you want to bring a partner check first with your employer in case you are expected to share a flat or even a room with another teacher. All my colleagues and myself have had discipline problems in the classroom. Be prepared for employers that range from nutty to demented!*

By the time Jamie Masters decided to go to Crete to teach English, it was too late to register with the agencies. He arrived in Heraklion in October:

> *I advertised (in Greek) in the Cretan newspapers, no joy. I lowered my sights and started knocking on doors of* frontisteria. *I was put onto some guy called Saridakis who ran an English-language bookshop and went to see him. Turned out he was some kind of lynch-pin in the* frontisterion *business and in fact I got my first job through him. Simultaneously I went to something which roughly translates as the 'Council for owners of frontisteria' and was given a list of schools which were looking for people. The list, it turned out, was pretty much out of date. But I had insisted on leaving my name with the Council (they certainly didn't offer) and that's how I found my second job.*

If you are looking for a more informal arrangement, many Greek families are looking for live-in tutors for their children. The rich Athens suburbs of Kifissia and Politia are full of families who can afford to provide private English lessons for their offspring. The suburbs of Pangrati and Filothei are also well-heeled as is the more central suburb of Kolonaki.

Private lessons, at least in the provinces, are easy to find. The going rate is dr2,000-3,000 an hour. Most employed teachers do at least three or four hours a week — more than enough to cover their Retsina bill (according to Loraine Christensen who taught in Kastoria in northern Greece for a number of years).

Voluntary Work

European Conservation Volunteers in Greece (ECVG, 15 Omirou St, 14562 Kifissia, Athens) is an organisation which concerns itself primarily with architectural preservation, especially in remote areas, rather than environmental conservation. A typical project is the restoration of a traditional village on Mount Pelion, where the streets around the village square need recobbling. Registration in Britain is either through UNA (Wales) for a fee of £75 plus food, or through the British Trust for Conservation Volunteers for an inclusive fee of £115.

Sporting types may wish to volunteer their services to help row a 170-oared trireme, a reconstruction of a ship used by the ancient Greeks now berthed at Poros. Anyone who is 'physically fit, with a sense of humour and appreciation of history' is welcome to apply, provided they are not taller than 6 foot 2 inches and are prepared to contribute £175 to cover expenses. Fitness tests in New York are usually compulsory for American volunteers. Further information is available from the Trireme Trust c/o Pyrton Halt House, Watlington, Oxford OX9 5AN or in the USA, 803 South Main St, Geneva, NY 14456.

Friends of the Ionian Ltd (21A Stanbridge Road, Putney, London SW15 1DX) hires up to 30 voluntary wildlife guides to accompany British school groups around the Ionian islands (Kefallinia, Zakinthos and Levkas). Applicants must have an appropriate background in environmental science.

Cyprus

Although the Cypriot economy like the Greek relies heavily on tourism and agriculture which can normally be counted on to provide work for travellers, the very strict immigration regulations make it difficult.

The Regulations

Cyprus is not a member of the EU and takes a very dim view of foreigners working illegally. The regulations stipulate that for both paid and unpaid work, a permit must be obtained by the employer in advance from the Department of Aliens and Immigration, Ministry of the Interior, D. Severis Avenue, Nicosia (02-300 3138/fax 449221). Even permits for au pairs are not usually granted and voluntary and youth exchange organisations have virtually no programmes in Cyprus.

However there have been more reports from working travellers in Cyprus (including Turkish Cyprus) for this edition than for previous ones, so it is a destination which is worth considering. One recent correspondent Karen Holman from Nottingham has been working legally as a barmaid for two years. Work permits must be applied for by your employer while you are out of the country, and will be granted for an initial three months only for jobs which a Cypriot national won't or can't do (and very few Cypriot women are prepared to work behind a bar). Other documents which will be required are a police clearance certificate and HIV test.

Employers who want to hire English-speaking staff are likely to tell you that you don't need a work permit for temporary work and many foreigners accept work on this basis. However it should be stressed that the penalties are strict; you risk a fine of up to £500 and a five or ten-year ban from the country. Until recently the risk to employers was negligible. However Rhona Stannage was told that proposed legislation was going to increase the penalties on employers who hired foreigners without papers and that from 1994, fewer employers would be prepared to take the risk. The reason she was given was that the tourist industry had been hit by the European recession causing local unemployment to escalate.

Cyprus is one country where the regulations are enforced. The Immigration Police have very sharp eyes and ears and frequently visit cafés and bars likely to employ foreigners. Two of Tom Parker's friends working at back street bars in the old town of Limassol had to impersonate a customer whenever the police visited. A Briton called Dave who was helping to renovate a yacht in Larnaca boatyard was discovered by immigration after three days and was forced to leave town. Yet the same man went on to work a season as a drinks waiter in Protaras (he had had the foresight to bring a pair of black trousers and white shirt) and was not troubled by immigration once. It seems that the authorities concentrate their efforts in May (which is when the resort of Ayia Napa was purged in 1993) and are less inclined to bother you once the season gets busy.

Tourist visas expire after three months but may be renewed if you can show enough money to support yourself. It might be easier to cross the border (to Greece or Israel) and return to Cyprus when your tourist visa will be renewed. You cannot cross between Greek and Turkish Cyprus for longer than one day.

The Tourist Industry

As in Greece, women are at a great advantage when looking for work in cafés, bars and restaurants, but they should exercise caution according to Karen Holman:

In my two years there I heard stories about Cypriot employers expecting more of their barmaids than just bar work. I worked in two pubs and I would say that both bosses employed me with an ulterior motive. I was lucky — both of them were shy. By the time they realised I wasn't going to be their girlfriend, they had found me to be a good worker and were used to me being around. Many employers will sack the girls, or threaten to report them for stealing. If you're legal, your work permit is valid for that job only, so if you leave the job, you have to leave the country.

Just such a serious case of exploitation and harassment was recently reported in the British press. A 23 year old trainee lawyer who had met her employer on a previous holiday found herself working 15 hours a day without a day off in temperatures of over 100°. The final straw came when the manager made advances which she declined which prompted her employer to hit her. She instantly quit and was paid C£40 for 15 days work. She had no recourse because she had no work permit.

Rhona Stannage was much luckier: her boss (whom she met in a novel way) was gay. In the supermarket in Protaras she and her husband Stuart introduced themselves to a man whose trolley was so full of bottles, they reckoned he must run a restaurant. He practically offered Rhona a job on the spot as waitress and cleaner, and offered Stuart a cooking job two days later.

Tom Parker arrived in Limassol in April 1993 and started the search along the seafront, with little success.

The same evening we headed for the tourist area and were soon told that we would stand a better chance if we bought a drink for the manager before asking about jobs. The only concrete result was that we got very drunk. No job opportunities (they told us we were too early). The next day we concentrated on the small cafés in the back streets of the old town. Here my two companions (both girls) were offered jobs in separate cafés. The kitchen job paid £13 a day and the waiting job £16, both plus tips. They both also worked in a bar in the evening, sitting round talking to the mainly local customers and being bought drinks for which the customer was charged £6.50 whether it was water or vodka and they earned a commission of £1 per drink, in addition to the evening fee of £13.

Outdoor Work

Because he was male, Tom Parker did not find a restaurant job. But on the advice of his guest house landlady he found two weeks of (backbreaking) weeding work with a landscape gardener, which paid £20 a day.

There is a lot of casual day work in the Larnaca boatyard mentioned above which pays about £15 per day. However security has been very strict since terrorists murdered a boatful of Israelis about ten years ago and even stricter since the president decided to keep his boat there, and you are obliged to leave your passport with a guard at the gate of the harbour (this is how immigration caught Dave mentioned above). Apparently if you have been promised a position as a crew member you are exempt from the work permit requirements. Try putting up a notice in the Globe Bar or asking a member to put up a notice for you in the private Marina Bar.

Moving away from the tourist resorts, there is a lot of grape-picking which can stretch from August to October. Olives are also picked in the autumn. There are two strawberry harvests a year, one in May/June and another in November/December. Oranges are picked for up to three months around Limassol. Some years ago, Robert Mallakee had no trouble finding miscellaneous agricultural work in Cyprus. By chatting with the owner of a café he was soon put in touch with a peasant farmer in Piyi (in the interior of the island) whom he helped with the haymaking. He was paid only a pittance in addition to food and accommodation but hoped this would lead to better things. Later in June he moved on to Paphos in the south west where he and a friend rented a flat very cheaply and worked for the last two weeks of the melon harvest which starts in mid-May. The pay was much better but the work was extremely hard and hot because the melons were grown under plastic. Women's wages are lower than men's. Men interested in labouring work should look for new tourist developments in resorts like Ayia Napa on the south-east coast. Arrange to be paid daily or weekly rather than monthly, since it can be difficult to extract earned money.

The cost of living in Cyprus is high. For example it took Rhona and Stuart a long time to find a cheaper alternative to their £13-a-day apartment.

Turkish Cyprus

As is well known, Cyprus is a divided island. The southern part is the Republic of Cyprus, a member of the British Commonwealth. The north, occupied by Turkey since the intervention of 1974, is called the Turkish Republic of Northern Cyprus (Kibris). It is not recognised by any country except Turkey. This is the first edition which has included a section on northern Cyprus, thanks to a very encouraging report from Eric Mackness. He sums up the job situation as excellent:

There are a lot of opportunities here. It is a very small place (population 170,000) and job vacancies become known as soon as they exist. Most opportunities lie in the catering trade and are open to men and women. The wages are poor by British standards, say between £80 and £130 per month (with a few exceptions) in addition to food and accommodation. This can often be supplemented with tips. But the cost of living is low and life is so relaxed, like Greece was 20 or 25 years ago.

Eric was (is?) working at a restaurant called Rita-on-the-Rocks in the village of Lapta 10km from the capital Kyrenia (Girne in Turkish). He arranged this before he left Coventry by writing directly after seeing it mentioned briefly on a BBC travel programme.

Other jobs can be found in hotels and pensions and on boats such as the one run by Bicen Tours which employs about six English people on the boat as well as on land (leading tours, bike hire, etc.). There is a sizeable English-speaking community and a number of restaurants and bars are owned by expats. Many of these can be found advertising in the English-language paper *Cyprus Today* and many employ at least one foreigner to communicate with the tourists.

The authorities seem refreshingly unconcerned about the red tape, whatever your nationality. The only requirement is that you have to leave Cyprus every three months to renew your tourist visa; this entails a two-hour catamaran trip to mainland Turkey at a cost of about £15. Note that a stamp from TRNC (the Turkish Republic of Northern Cyprus) could make future visits to Greece difficult. At entry you can request that the stamp be put on a separate form.

Italy

Italy is a remarkably welcoming country. Once Italians accept you, they will go out of their way to find you a place in their communities, without any emphasis on the barriers of nationality. Once you get a toehold, you will find that a friendly network of contacts and possible employers will quickly develop. Without contacts, if only a sympathetic landlady at your pension, it is virtually impossible to find work.

Some travellers mistakenly expect Italy to be poor and backward in some respects. They are surprised, especially in the north, to discover that the cost of living is considerably higher than in other Mediterranean countries. They find the best dressed and most sophisticated people in the world. With an unemployment rate over 10% (not to mention British and American dress sense), it is going to take time to find a job. The situation for casual job-seekers has been made more difficult by the arrival of Albanians and refugees from the old Yugoslavia.

The Regulations

Unfortunately there are more red tape hassles in Italy than there are in other EU countries. Matters have been made worse by legislation intended to prevent an influx of refugees from eastern Europe. Many job-seekers have found employers reluctant to consider hiring them because of the bureaucratic hurdles which must be jumped. The 'Notes for British Citizens Wishing to Visit Italy' (last issued June 1994) available from the Consular Section of the British

Embassy in Rome (Via XX Settembre 80a, 00187 Rome) do not go into much detail about the red tape, and the leaflet 'General Information Regarding Living and Working in Italy' issued by the Italian Consulate in London contains even fewer hard facts. Be prepared to be given the run-around and for delays in the processing.

If you arrive with the intention of working, you must first apply to the police *(questura)* for a *Ricevuta di Segnalazione di Soggiorno* which allows you to stay for up to three months looking for work. Upon production of this document and a letter from an employer, you must go back to the police to obtain a residence permit — *Permesso di Soggiorno.* Then in some cases you will be asked to apply for a *Libretto di Lavoro* (work registration card) from the town hall or *Municipio,* although this should not be necessary for EU nationals. If you want to open a bank account for example a further and, if desired, (for opening a bank account, etc.), you need to register at the registry office *(Ufficio Anagrafe)*; in Rome the address is Via Luigi Petroselli 50.

Even farmers eager to hire people for a very temporary period will ask to see your papers, as Xuela Edwards found when she looked for grape-picking work in the Chianti region:

> *Several vineyard owners were keen to take us on but insisted we get the correct papers. As EC citizens we were entitled to work and so set out to get our papers. We were told to apply for a* Libretto di Lavoro *from the Town Hall on the Piazza del Campo in Siena. When we found the right office they said we needed a* Permesso di Soggiorno *first and directed us to another part of Siena. On application we were told that it would take 60 days to come through, by which time of course the grape harvest would be over. We did hear that it was possible to get a* Permesso *by queuing all day in Rome; take a couple of passport photos and a packed lunch.*

Once the paperwork has been dealt with, your employer will have to pay contributions on your behalf which can be very substantial in Italy. As usual, all of this should be more straightforward for EU nationals than in fact it is. When Ian McArthur tried to get a *libretto di lavoro* he was treated little better than an illegal immigrant (but nevertheless has embarked on a 'lifelong love affair with Italy'). Roberta Wedge who taught English for a year in Bari recalls the red tape:

> *I had to visit three different government offices about eight times in total. Not exactly the free movement of labour! My health card arrived six months after the wheels were set in motion.*

Work permits for non-EU nationals will be issued only to people outside Italy and only for jobs where the Provincial Office of the Ministry of Labour is satisfied that no Italian can do the job. The *Autorizzazione al Lavoro* must then be presented at the Italian Embassy in the applicant's home country. In other words, they are virtually impossible to obtain except for elite jobs.

Do not be too discouraged by the regulations and the red tape since there is a great deal of unofficial, cash-in-hand work or *lavoro nero* available in Italy. Even reputable au pair agencies encourage their au pairs to tell the authorities that they are in Italy for cultural reasons, not for work. Before Dominic Fitzgibbon left his home in Australia he decided he wanted to live in Italy for a year and arrived in Rome in the spring. He spent six weeks unsuccessfully looking for a job which used up a large proportion of his travel fund. But the landlady of the flat he was renting off the magnificent Piazza Navona took a shine to him, and arranged for him to work for one of her friends who owned a 3-star hotel as a night porter, although he had 'no work permit and practically no Italian'.

Remember that medical expenses can be crippling if you're not covered by the Italian Medical Health Scheme (USL). If your employer is not paying contributions, you might want to take out your own insurance at an office of SAI, one of the major Italian insurance companies.

FINDING WORK

If you can't speak a word of Italian, you will be at a distinct disadvantage. Provided you can afford it and are sufficiently interested, you should consider studying a little Italian before you set off on your travels or enrolling in one of the many short Italian language courses offered in most Italian cities. Italian is one of the easiest languages to learn, especially if you already have some knowledge of a Latin-based language.

However your inability to speak Italian need not be an absolute barrier, as Ian Moody found when he got a job as a door-to-door salesman of English books and language courses, without himself knowing any Italian. His technique was more amusing in retrospect than it was successful:

I was given the spiel in phonetic Italian and told to learn it off by heart before knocking on the doors of middle class, professional Italians in various northern Italian towns. Reeling off the sales pitch parrot-fashion was okay until they asked a question which I couldn't make head nor tail of. I found it was often easier to run away. So it was extremely difficult to make many sales. For those who persevered at the door, sales were often promised just to get rid of the rep. Still the working conditions were good, mainly because it was permanently sunny. And you were able to meet people (even if you couldn't actually understand a word they were saying).

This sort of work is still available as Mr. P. G. Penn recently reported. After graduation he wanted to work abroad and learn a language for six months and landed a job as a travelling book salesman:

Having submitted my CV I was accepted for a one-month trial period. I flew to Rome and immediately received bad vibes when I learned that of the 17 English-speaking people hired in the previous six months only two remained. The other two guys in my group had become very stressed and seemed permanently tired, a fate which did not escape me. The work was 8am-9pm Monday to Friday with a half-day on Saturday. We had no time to learn the language, since the sales talk had pre-programmed answers to questions. This was what ultimately led me to leave. Sales work is difficult but this was demanding too much, whilst denying personal freedom and time.

Anyone who is not put off by that description might like to contact a company which actively recruits English-speaking sales people to join small groups travelling throughout Italy to sell language courses and reference books to business people. Mercury Enterprises (Italia) in Bergamo take on people who need not speak Italian but are eager to learn. Sales training is given. Payment is on a commission basis after the basic weekly wage, accommodation and travel expenses are paid. Interested people should write to Mercury Enterprises, c/o 13 Castle Hill Avenue, Folkestone, Kent CT20 2TD, enclosing a CV and photo. Another firm advertising for sales staff in 1994 was Cultural Contact, 35 Musard Road, London W6/Via Nino Bixio 95, 18038 San Remo.

Although you should not neglect scouring the newspapers for job adverts, you may be disappointed. Ian Abbott noticed in Roman newspapers that there were more adverts placed by *stranieri* (foreigners) asking for work than there were situations vacant. And when Stephen Venner replied to ads in a Florence paper which an Italian-speaking friend had translated for him, he found that in practice the adverts were impossible to follow up because the advertisers wouldn't answer their phones or were vague and noncommittal. After being told many times to come back in a few days, he fixed up a job delivering leaflets to houses in Pistoia near Florence. The pay was related to the number of leaflets delivered and turned out to be not enough to live on, and neither did it leave time to do another job.

The first free-ads papers in Europe were published in Italy in 1977. *Second-amano* (meaning Second Hand) is published in ten regional editions covering the industrialised north of the country.

The Employment Service

Officially, all foreign job-seekers are obliged to register with the government employment service. (As in several other European countries, private employment agencies are prohibited.) Unless you are fluent in Italian, the state employment service *(Ufficio di Collocamento)* is unlikely to be much use to you. Although they usually have jobs available for short periods, it is essential to visit them regularly (preferably every day) to make your presence felt. The employment offices in the smaller towns might be more helpful than the ones in the main cities being less accustomed to foreign job-seekers. For example before the summer season, the ones in seaside resorts often have lists of hotel and restaurant jobs.

Contacts

Contacts are even more important in Italy than in other countries. Many of the people we have heard from who have worked in Italy (apart from TEFL teachers, au pairs, etc.) have got their work through friends. They may not necessarily have had the friends or contacts when they arrived, but they formed friendships while they were there as visitors. Louise Rollett, for example, first went out as a paying guest to a town near Bologna (an arrangement made through the Experiment in International Living, see page 19), and then extended her stay on a work-for-keep basis as an English tutor. Dustie Hickey went for treatment to a doctor in Milan who immediately offered to pay her L20,000 an hour to tutor his children in English.

In Rome try the notice boards in the following locations: the English language Lion Bookshop at Via Del Babuino 181, the Church of England on the same street and the student travel agency CTS (Centro Turistico Studentesco) at Via Genova 16. Two publications are also recommended: the fortnightly newspaper *Wanted in Rome* for the expatriate community, in which there are notices for au pairs, etc., and *Porta Portese* which is roughly equivalent to *Exchange & Mart* but includes adverts for jobs (bars, teaching, etc.) and cheap accommodation. Language school notice boards are always worth checking; at the *Centro di Lingua & Cultura Italiana per Stranieri* where Dustie Hickie took cheap Italian lessons in Milan, there was a good notice board with adverts for au pairs, dog-walkers, etc. Dustie got a cleaning job this way which paid L8,000 an hour.

Laurence Koe had collected the addresses of many of his pupils at a summer school where he had worked on the south coast of England. The first one he looked up was in Como and the family promptly invited him to stay until he found work (an invitation which made him marvel at the contrast with English habits of hospitality). One of the daughters had the idea of asking the local radio station to employ Laurence, mainly for novelty value. She accompanied Laurence to the station and stood in for him at the interview, inventing freely about his past history as a DJ. They put him on a jointly presented afternoon music programme and his task seemed to be to adjudicate the correct English pronunciation of song titles. No wage was paid, but it was good experience and good fun. Also he became very well known in the town, a kind of celebrity, and felt that

he was giving something to the community instead of just taking. He would let it slip on the radio that he was there to teach English and opportunities began to present themselves.

Even with contacts you are not guaranteed of finding work as Edward Peters found one summer:

After travelling through Eastern Europe and Austria, we had hoped to find something in Italy; but three sets of contacts were unable to find us anything — perhaps because it was August (national holidays) or perhaps because we were too busy enjoying ourselves in Milan, Rome and Ischia.

TOURISM

Italy's tourist industry employs between 6% and 7% of the Italian workforce and does not seem to have many openings for non-Italians. Perhaps this is partly because most tourists from outside Italy head for the major cities — Florence, Rome, Venice, Pisa and so on — where there are thousands of locals available to do the jobs. It is also difficult to find work with a UK tour company, since there are severe legal restrictions on the hiring of non-Italian staff.

There are cheering exceptions however. As mentioned above, an Australian traveller found a job in a hotel in Rome:

After six weeks of no luck I told my landlady that perhaps I would head off to Greece. She said I was far too nice to look for dishwashing work and told me about a friend who needed help running his seasonal hotel off Piazza Barberini. Within 20 minutes I was behind the counter having the telephone system explained to me and was told I would be paid L1,100,000 a month for six nights a week as a night porter. After praying the telephone wouldn't ring for the first few weeks, everything settled down. It's quiet, a little boring, but allows me to read and study Italian, more than the few key words related to the hotel trade I knew before. My boss is even going to lend me a TV to help me improve my Italian. I now know how lucky I was to find my place and this job.

As throughout the world, backpackers' haunts often employ travellers for short periods. Jill Weseman recommends trying the Pension Il Nido (a.k.a. Fawlty Towers) at Via Magenta 39 (5th floor) near the Termini Station in Rome where she noticed several Antipodeans working in reception, maintenance and cleaning. (Bruce Fawlty doesn't have quite the same ring as Basil.)

One reader who thoroughly enjoyed a season working in an Italian city is Carolyn Edwards who was hired by Contiki (see page 101) as a general cleaning assistant at their stopover site (a haunted villa) in Florence for clients on 18-35 tours of Europe. The company operates as an 'art and cultural association' to get round the Italian regulations, and this suited Carolyn who found that she loved standing in front of 53 people talking about the local sites. When the season with Contiki finished in October she got a job in an American-style bar in Florence called the Red Garter. She worked here for four months with barely enough Italian to get by. Unlike many people in jobs like this she was legal, at least for three days of the week, when she netted the equivalent of £29 for five hours work. If she worked any extra evenings, she was paid L50,000 cash (which she says certainly beats £2.91 in London before tax).

Although less well known than the seaside resorts of other Mediterranean countries, there may be seaside possibilities for foreign job-seekers, especially in the resorts near Venice, as an Italian reader Lara Giavi confirms. She is familiar with two holiday regions: the Lake Garda resorts like Desenzano, Malcesine, Sirmione and Riva del Garda; and the seaside resorts near Venice like Lido di Jesolo (which she says is a great resort for young people), Bibione,

Lignano, Caorle and Chioggiaa, all of which are more popular with German and Austrian tourists than Britons so a knowledge of German would be a good selling point. Lara disagrees that there are few opportunities for foreigners in catering, bars and hotels in Italy, though she admits that a knowledge of Italian is necessary in most cases, apart from the job of *donna ai piani* (chambermaid).

The seaside resorts are full of people (including Italians) working black and not being paid the going wage, overtime or holiday pay, but earning plenty of tips. She provides an indication of what a legally employed waiter should be paid after tax and contributions: L1,100,000-1,300,000 per month plus an end-of-season bonus of about L400,000, with a monthly deduction of just L50,000 for board and lodging. She acknowledges that it is difficult enough for an Italian to find an employer who pays by the book, but thinks that travellers looking for a 'working holiday experience' who don't mind about the money should certainly pursue this possibility.

EU nationals can try using official channels to find work at the beginning of the season (mid-May), i.e. the *Ufficio di Collocamento* and the local *Associazione Albergatori* (hotels association) which should know of vacancies among its members. Legal hotel workers will also have to obtain a *Libretto sanitario* after having a free medical check-up at the local *Ufficio Igiene*.

The relatively low unemployment in the Veneto region makes it a better bet than some of the other tourist regions of Italy such as the Adriatic coastal resorts of Rimini and Pescara and the Italian Riviera (Portofino, San Remo, etc.), though it may be worth trying resorts on Lake Maggiore like Stresa and Cannero. Michael Cullen worked in three hotels around Como and Bellagio and found 'a nice friendly and warm atmosphere, despite the heat and long hours'. High unemployment together with a huge population of migrant workers from poor countries in the south of Italy means that it is probably not worth trying the resorts south of Naples, viz. Capri, Sorrento and Amalfi. Even in flourishing resorts like Rimini, there seems to be nearly enough locals and Italian students to fill the jobs in hotels, bars and on the beach. As Stephen Venner observed, 'Although prospects appeared to be good in Rimini, café and hotel owners were unwilling to take on foreigners because of the paperwork,' which reinforces the points about red tape made above.

If you don't get a job in a hotel, you might get work servicing holiday flats or gardening. If you plan far enough in advance (and speak some Italian) you might get a job as a campsite courier with one of the major British camping holiday organisers such as Canvas Holidays (see the chapter on *Tourism*). Catherine Dawes enjoyed this job near Albenga on the Italian Riviera — 'a fairly uninspiring part of Italy' — even more than she did her previous summer's work on a French campsite. She reports that the Italians seemed to be more relaxed than the French, especially under high season pressure, and would always go out of their way to help her when she was trying to translate tourists' problems to the mechanic or the doctor.

You can also try Italian-run campsites which have a large staff to man the on-site restaurants, bars and shops. Stephen Venner noticed that the two main campsites in Rome (the Tiber and the Flamignio) take on English help before the season begins (i.e. March).

Any EU national aged 18-27 with a vocational qualification in Leisure and Tourism (but not a university degree) should investigate the EU-funded Petra schemes. In 1994 they were offering attractive summer packages of one month's language tuition in Florence followed by three months' work experience in the Italian tourist industry for a mere £100. Details are available from ProEuropa (Europa House, Sharpham Drive, Totnes, Devon TQ9 5HE; 0803 864526).

Winter Resorts

On-the-spot opportunities are probably more numerous in the winter resorts of the Alps, Dolomites and Apennines (see list on page 107). Many of the jobs are part-time and not very well paid, but provide time for skiing and in many cases a free pass to the ski-lifts for the season. According to *Working in Ski Resorts Europe*, Sauze d'Oulx and Courmayeur are the best resorts for job hunting. Although Cortina is probably the most famous, it has a high percentage of year-round workers, and is too sophisticated and expensive. Sauze d'Oulx is particularly recommended because it hosts so many British holidaymakers that every bar and shop in the resort likes to hire an English speaker. Cathy Salt describes her and her partner's success:

> Upon arrival at Sauze d'Oulx on 14th November, we found we were much too early for on-the-spot jobs. The place was practically dead. Only a few bars were open. Fortunately an English guy working in a bar informed us that the carpenter was looking for help. Jon was able to get four weeks work with him, sanding down and varnishing, also enabling him to be on the spot for other work that would come up. The same day I found a babysitting job for a shop owner's son, but I wouldn't start until 5th December. We were both fortunate in finding this since we came up on a Thursday and have since found out that the weekend is a much better time to look because the ski shops and restaurants are open.

Such stories are counterbalanced by the inevitable failures: Susanna Macmillan gave up her job hunt in the Italian Alps after two weeks when she had to admit that her non-existent Italian and just passable French were not getting her anywhere.

PGL Ski Holidays (Alton Court, Penyard Lane, Ross-on-Wye, Herefordshire HR9 5NR) and Skibound Holidays (Olivier House, 18 Marine Parade, Brighton, East Sussex BN2 1TL) offer reps' jobs and instructor positions to BASI-qualified skiers. Your fare to the resort will be paid and you will earn between £70 and £120 per week. As in other alpine resorts there are also jobs for chalet girls, though not as many as in neighbouring countries due to the very strict regulations which govern chalets in Italy.

In Italy, you are more likely to find a job in a small family run bar or hotel than in one of the big concerns. The large hotels usually recruit their staff in southern Italy and then move them en masse from the sea to the mountains in the autumn.

AU PAIRS

One possible way of visiting the Italian seaside, mountains or countryside without actually having to slave in a hotel kitchen is to become an au pair or mother's help. Most Italian families in the class which can afford au pairs go to the coast or to the mountains in the summer and naturally take their helpers with them. There are also quite a few summer-only jobs in this capacity, and a huge demand for experienced nannies. The average monthly wage for au pairs is L300,000-350,000 with mother's helps earning at least another L100,000.

The majority of European au pair agencies deal with Italy, so you should have no trouble arranging a job or, rather a placement for 'cultural reasons' (to satisfy the bureaucracy). In Britain Au Pairs-Italy (46 The Rise, Sevenoaks, Kent TN13 1RJ) has been specialising in Italy since 1975 and has a large number of established clients throughout the country. The agency frequently revises and publishes a list of actual vacancies which helps you to choose a suitable location and family, e.g. 'Mother's help for boy 11 and girl 8 until end August, urgent! — *Palermo*' or 'Au Pair for girl 3, baby due end March — *Rome*'. There is an optional services charge of £20 which covers the cost of translations where necessary, information about insurance, addresses of other au pairs in your region and post-placement advice. Dustie Hickey was pleased with her placement as an au pair in Rimini through Au Pairs Italy, and received quite a lot of information about her family before departure. She was surprised to discover that she had to work *fewer* hours than the ones specified in the contract drawn up by the agency.

Another agency in the UK which specialises in Italy is the English-Italian Agency (69 Woodside, Wimbledon SW9 7AF; 0181-946 5728) which does not charge for making placements in Italy via its partner in Turin (The English Agency, Via Pigafetta 48, 10129 Turin; tel/fax 11-597372).

You can of course work directly with an Italian agency, since most of them will speak English. You will then have to pay the local registration fee which in most cases will be more expensive than going through a UK agency. For example the Rome agency Intermediate (Via Bramante 13, 00153 Rome; tel/fax 6-574 7444) charges applicants who are still abroad L200,000 (more than £80) or L100,000 if they are already in Italy.

Agencies are usually strongest in their own region. Two Bologna agencies which make placements in northern and central Italy are Au Pair International (Via S. Stefano 32, 40125 Bologna; 51-267575) and the recently opened Easy Travel — Giovani in Europa (Via Borgonuovo 9/b, 40125 Bologna; tel/fax 51-223983). ARCE (Via XX Settembre 2/44, 16121 Genoa; 10-583020) is a long established agency which makes placements free of charge throughout the country.

If you are already in Rome and want to tap into the au pair grapevine, the San Silvestro Church in Piazza San Silvestro is a favourite meeting place for English-speaking au pairs.

TEACHING

Hundreds of language schools around Italy employ native English speakers. Unfortunately for the ordinary traveller, the vast majority of the jobs require some basic qualification in Teaching English as a Foreign Language. Xuela Edwards arrived with a friend who is a qualified English teacher at the right time (September) and reported that the language schools were flooded with teachers and just being able to speak English was not enough. This view has to be set against P.G. Penn's experience. After he left his selling job, he went to Turin to find TEFL work and after putting in some effort he succeeded without any experience whatsoever.

Doing an introductory TEFL course at home simplifies the job search, especially since many of the training organisations feed their 'graduates' to Italian schools. But not everyone who does a TEFL course is handed a job on a platter. After doing the Linguarama TEFL course in England, Bruce Nairne and Sue Ratcliffe set off to find work:

Rather unimaginatively we packed our bags and made for Italy in the middle of the summer holidays when there was no teaching work at all. Nevertheless we utilised the Yellow Pages in the SIP office (the equivalent of British Telecom) in Syracuse, Sicily and proceeded to make 30 speculative applications, specifying our status as graduates who had completed a short course in TEFL. By the end of September we had received four job offers without so much as an interview.

Unfortunately the jobs in Bari which they chose to accept fell through at the last moment. This is not so unusual since many schools wait until their enrolment figures are finalised before signing teachers' contracts. So Bruce and Sue once again resorted to looking up *Scuole di Lingua* in the Yellow Pages, this time in Milan railway station where they managed to secure the interest of three or four establishments for part-time work. This is the normal way to get started as a teacher if you wait until you arrive in Italy, and may involve dashing between institutes to scrape together enough hours to live on. Mr. Penn recommends Turin over the more glamorous cities of Milan and Rome where there are just as many language schools but fewer aspiring teachers.

Without any TEFL training whatsoever, the job hunt will be an uphill struggle as Laurence Koe discovered in both Como and Lecco. He visited all the language schools, some of them three times, and was always told he needed a TEFL qualification or that he was there at the wrong time (October). After three weeks of making the rounds he was asked to stand in for an absent teacher on one occasion, and this was enough to secure him further part-time work. After a few more weeks he found work teaching an evening class of adults. He began to attend the weekly English club (a good source of contacts and leads) and was offered a few thousand lire to answer questions on the plot after English film shows.

Similarly Natalia de Cuba could not persuade any of the language schools in the northern town of Rovereto where she was based to hire her without qualifications. So she decided to enrol in the RSA/Cambridge Certificate course run by International House in Rome (Accademia Britannica, Viale Manzoni 57, 00185 Rome). She found the month-long course strenuous but not terribly difficult, and worth the fee (which now stands at L2,400,000). Job offers come into the Accademia from all over Italy and no one seems to have a problem getting a job immediately after the course (which everyone passed). Natalia went back to a teaching job in Rovereto where she was paid L900,000 for 18 hours of fairly enjoyable teaching a week. This in fact is well above the average of L15,000-20,000 per hour net. Teachers in Italy should not expect their accommodation to be paid for, but schools generally help their staff to find something reasonably priced.

Agencies may be of some assistance. Connor Language Services (Via M. Macchi 42, 20214 Milan; 2-669 87016) maintains a register of teachers with at least a university degree and an RSA or Trinity Certificate. Applicants should send their CV, photo and covering letter to this agency which supplies teachers to client schools throughout Italy. The placement service is free to teachers. Many of their client schools turn to the Register when they have urgent vacancies especially in September and October but also throughout the year.

There are several Italian-based chains of language schools which you might try. Recruitment is normally carried out by the individual schools, but the administrative addresses given here will send a list of addresses. For example the British Schools Group (Via Lucullo 14, 00187 Rome; 6-488 0333) has about 65 member schools. Other chains include Oxford Schools with 19 schools in northern Italy (Via Battisti 31/35, Mirano 30035; tel/fax 41-430513), Oxford Institutes, Wall Street Institutes (with 46 schools), British Colleges with four schools in southern Italy (Via Luigi Rizzo 18, 95131 Catania) and British Institutes with 50 affiliated schools (Via Marghera 45, 20149 Milan; 2-480 11149).

Another possibility is to set up as a freelance tutor, though a knowledge of Italian is even more of an asset here than it is for jobs in schools. You can post notices in supermarkets, tobacconists, primary and secondary schools, etc. It may be worth advertising in a free paper which cost Dustie Hickey (for example) L27,000 for four editions of the local free paper in Rimini. Soon she had several private pupils who paid her £8-10 per hour to be taught in her idle afternoons as an au pair. As long as you have access to some premises, you can try to arrange both individual and group lessons, and undercut the language institutes significantly. The going wage for qualified private tutors is L30,000-40,000 an hour in Rome, less elsewhere. The ever-enterprising Laurence Koe presented himself to a classroom teacher who asked her class of 12 and 13 years olds if they would like to learn English from a native. They all said Yes and paid Laurence the equivalent of 50p each for a class after school. With no TEFL background, Dustie Hickey ended up tutoring a Milanese doctor who had treated her for a head wound. Whereas she charged him L20,000 an hour, she charged a younger less prosperous woman who wanted conversation practice L15,000, which seemed fair in view of the fact that the woman invited her to stay and eat a meal after the lesson.

As in other European countries, summer camps for unaccompanied young people usually offer English as well as a range of sports. One organisation which advertises in the UK for 'enthusiastic, adaptable cheerful lovers of children' to teach English and organise activities is Summer Camps, Via Matteotti 34, 18038 San Remo, Liguria (tel/fax 184-506070). The promised wage is between £600 and £720 for a two-month work period, plus board and lodging and insurance. They also advertise for actors to participate on 'hard-working theatre tours'.

AGRICULTURE

Italy does not have the tradition of hiring large numbers of foreign young people for its harvests. With the arrival of so many Albanians and East Europeans, the situation has become even less promising. Seasonal jobs in the grape and olive harvests are reserved and carefully regulated among locals and other Italian unemployed. However if you have local friends and contacts or if you speak some Italian it is worth trying to participate in one of the autumn harvests which by most accounts are thoroughly enjoyable. Wages are also reputed to be relatively good. In northern Italy you can earn up to L9,000 an hour, though south of Rome you would probably earn less. Typically, people working on a harvest work eight hours a day with no days off.

Several people have succeeded in finding a place on the grape harvest *(vend-emmia)*. Italy was called *Oenotria* by the ancient Greeks meaning 'the land of wine' and it remains the biggest producer of wine in the world. Today there are no regions of Italy which are without vineyards. Xuela Edwards and Nicky Brown made enquiries at vineyards in the Chianti region and met several growers who were keen to pay them the equivalent of £30 a day for the three weeks of the harvest. Although there seemed to be no prejudice against women pickers, the employers did insist that they obtain the proper papers which, as reported above in the section *Red Tape*, turned out to be impracticable.

Once you are in a fruit-growing area, a good place to look for work is the warehouse run by the local cooperative where all the local farmers sell their produce to the public. There may even be a list of farmers who are looking for pickers. Natalia de Cuba found her job picking apples and grapes this way, by going to the *Società Agricultura Vallagarina* in Rovereto in the region of Trentino, a major agricultural area.

The style of grape-picking is reputed to be easier than in France since the plants are trained upwards onto wire frames, rather than allowed to droop to the ground, so that pickers reach up with a clipper and catch the bunch of grapes in a funnel-type object, which is less strenuous than having to bend double for hours at a stretch. The worst problems that Natalia de Cuba encountered were stained hands (which could be avoided by wearing rubber gloves) and bee stings (which apparently can be soothed with grated potato, bound in place and left as long as possible). Accommodation can also be a problem since it is not normally provided by farmers. The good aspects of a harvesting job in Italy are described by Natalia de Cuba in glowing terms:

Apple picking is great on the ground. The ladders require much more concentration (beware of drinking too much wine!) and are considered a man's job. Lunch with the family was included — pasta, salad, wine and a shot of grappa. It was delicious and friendly, as all the pickers — many of them family members — ate together and gossiped and joked. There is always plenty of opportunity to chat while working, especially if you are assigned the job of sorting the fruit. The Italian pickers really do sing opera in the orchards.

The valley of the River Adige in Trentino is one of those famous destinations for migrant workers. The most prolific apple-growing area is around the town of Cles in the Val di Non in the Alto Adige north of Trento. Whereas some travellers find the work situation bleak (such as Kristof Szymczak from Poland who described the area as a tower of babel and didn't find a willing orchard owner), others recommend it. Amanda Bridle spent seven weeks in the autumn of 1994 earning L8,800 an hour sorting apples while the pickers (all male) earned L9,500. She says most farmers offer accommodation.

Tomatoes are supposed to be a well-paid picking crop in Italy. Also there may be seasonal agricultural work in the strawberry harvests of Emilia Romagna. Cherries are grown around Vignola (just west of Bologna) and are also picked in June. The Valtellina area, near the Swiss border, is another area with a multitude of orchards.

VOLUNTARY WORK

Many Italian organisations arrange summer work projects which are as disparate as selling recyclable materials to finance development projects in the Third World, restoring old convents and preventing forest fires. Mani Tese (Via Cavenaghi 4, 20149 Milan) and Emmaus Italia (Via La Luna 1, 52020 Pergine Valdarno, Arezzo) are of the first kind, while the major workcamps organisations like Service Civil International and Christian Movement for Peace carry out, among many others, the latter. Mani Tesi's summer projects include study and discussion of development issues for which a basic knowledge of Italian is needed.

The Italian equivalent of the RSPB is LIPU (Lega Italiana Protezione Uccelli, Vicolo San Tiburzio 5, 43100 Parma; 521-233414) publishes a list (in Italian only) of their programme of summer working holidays. Camps last one or two weeks and cost from L400,000 per week. The same is true of the Italian branch of the Worldwide Fund for Nature (WWF Italia, Via Dontello, 5/B, 20131 Milan) which publishes an annual list of *campi* in magazine form, in Italian only.

There are also archaeological camps which volunteers can join. Gruppi Archeologici d'Italia (Via Tacito 41, 00193 Rome) organise excavations throughout the country, many of which use voluntary labour. Unusually for Italy, their information is available in English. They usually charge between L500,000 and L600,000 for participating in a two-week project. If you would rather restore old buildings for a utilitarian purpose contact the Italian branch of International Building Companions (Soci Construttori, Via Cesare Battisti 3, 20071 Casalpusterlengo, MI).

Malta

Although small in area (30km by 15km), Malta has much of interest for the traveller. Work permits are required and are very difficult to get, as Philip Dray, an EFL teacher from Ireland, discovered:

> *I tried many times to get a teaching job in Malta but was thwarted by the paranoia surrounding work permits. The annoying thing is that there is a shortage of teachers. However these vacancies are normally filled by 18 year olds with just A levels. My advice is if you're thinking of working in Malta, forget it.*

In 1992 BUNAC (see page 22) introduced a new work scheme in Malta for registered catering students to work in resort hotels for six months, or occasionally three. The scheme has been set up with the cooperation of the student and youth travel organisation NSTS (220 St Paul St, Valletta).

Tourism plays such a large part in the island's economy that it may be possible to get a job on the spot. Try cafés, bars, hotels and shops in Sliema, Bugibba and beach resorts in the south. Wages are far from high.

If you would like to extend your stay on the island as cheaply as possible you should contact the Malta Youth Hostels Association. In exchange for 21 hours of work a week you will receive free accommodation and breakfast. The work will either be maintenance, decorating or hostels administration. (MYHA is not a member of the International Federation of Youth Hostels.) Naturally they are looking for people interested in the development of Malta rather than freeloaders. If interested, send your details and three international reply coupons to the MYHA, 17 Triq Tal-Borg, Pawla, Malta PLA 06; 356-693957) at least three months before your proposed visit and specify your preferred dates. They will help you obtain a work permit. You can work for as many two-week periods as you like, up to a maximum of three months. On arrival you will be required to pay a good faith deposit.

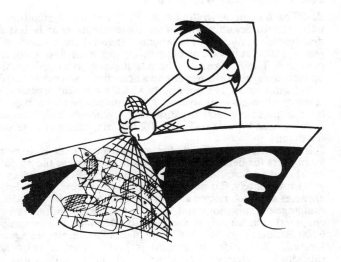

Scandinavia

January 1994 saw a great improvement in the chances for Europeans to find work in the countries of Scandinavia. Until that date the only country which posed few problems to the European job-seeker was the EU member state Denmark. Effective from 1994, most countries in EFTA (the European Free Trade Association) signed the European Economic Area (EEA) Agreement permitting the free movement of goods, services and people among the 12 members of the European Union and the four Scandinavian members of the EEA, Finland, Iceland, Norway and Sweden. EEA citizens are now entitled to enter any Scandinavian country for up to three months to look for work. When they find a job and get a 'Confirmation of Employment' from their employer, they can then apply to the police for a residence permit which, in the case of open-ended (i.e. permanent) jobs, will be for five years; otherwise it will be for the duration of the job. From January 1995, Sweden and Finland will become fully-fledged EU members.

At the time of writing it was too early to tell how quickly the various countries would adapt to the new relaxation of immigration rules and whether the job hunt on the ground has been noticeably improved. All reports on this subject will be welcome for the next edition.

This will probably make the employment prospects of non-EEA nationals even gloomier than they were. In order to work legally, North Americans and others will have to obtain work permits before leaving home, which is well-nigh impossible. The American-Scandinavian Foundation (Exchange Division, 725 Park Avenue, New York, NY 10021) places about 30 American trainees aged

21-30 each summer in the fields of engineering, agriculture, horticulture, chemistry, etc. in Scandinavia. Work assignments usually last 8 to 12 weeks. The deadline for applications is January 1st and there is a non-refundable application fee of $50. Trainees are paid the going wage and accommodation is usually provided. The ASF can also help 'self-placed trainees', i.e. those who have fixed up their own job or traineeship in a Scandinavian country, to fix up a work permit.

Voluntary work is a possibility and the relevant organisations are listed in the country chapters. Involvement Volunteers Inc (see page 141) hope soon to have in place two new organisations Involvement Volunteers Scandinavia and Involvement Volunteers Finland & Estonia; write to the headquarters in Australia for details.

It is occasionally possible for young women over 18 to be placed with families as au pairs for between 6 and 12 months. Because the au pair system is not well developed in Scandinavia, do not expect a British agency to be able to place you immediately. To have any chance of success, it is advisable to give several agencies as much notice as possible or, better yet, make direct contact with the exchange organisations and agencies in most Scandinavian capitals (see country chapters). The au pair agency Exis in Denmark (Rebslagergade 3, Postbox 291, 6400 Sønderborg; 74 42 97 49) places candidates in Denmark, Norway and Iceland. The fee for placement is kr700. The au pair agencies listed in the introductory chapter *Childcare* which have links with Scandinavia include Solihull and the South-Eastern Au Pair Bureaus.

One of the features which unifies these countries is that the cost of living and of travel is very high. Woden Teachout hitch-hiking as the best way to keep down the expense:

> *As far as transport goes, I hitched all over Norway and Sweden without incident, except for one ominous truck driver who told me leeringly that he himself was virtuous, but he had friends who were not so reliable. My other experiences with truck drivers have been universally positive. I got rides very quickly since I was something of a curiosity. In five months I didn't see another soul hitching.*

Watch out for the mosquitoes in summer and the short daylight hours in winter.

Busking, begging and street-selling are illegal in many places, however prosecutions are rare. As long as you are not causing a nuisance or blocking traffic you should be left alone by the authorities but will attract the attention of many passers-by for whom busking is a novelty.

The cost of alcohol, particularly spirits, is uniformly high throughout Scandinavia (apart from Denmark) and in some areas like the Faroe Islands unobtainable. Whether this will change when Scandinavia becomes part of the EU remains to be seen. Sweden and Finland have agreed to deregulate their state alcohol monopolies which may bring down prices. Furthermore Scandinavians will be able for the first time to go on duty-free shopping trips to Denmark (just as Danes went shopping in Germany when their country first joined the EU), so travellers may no longer be able to sell their duty-frees at a handsome profit.

Denmark

On the plus side, Denmark has the highest average wage of any EU country; on the negative, unemployment is currently very high at around 13%. The number of Danish students spotted picking grapes in France leads to the conclusion that there is a shortage of holiday jobs in Denmark. However it is an undeniably rich country and there are opportunities. Employers are obliged to pay an extra 12.5% holiday pay *(feriepenge)*.

WILLIAM SWAN

Work exists on farms and in factories, offices and hotels: the main problem is persuading an employer to take you on in preference to a Danish speaker. In an interview at the labour exchange Elfed Guyatt was told that without speaking Danish his chances of getting work were poor and indeed he couldn't find a job.

Many travellers recommend the youth information centre in Copenhagen called Use It Touristinformation, which can be found at Rådhusstraede 13, 1466 Copenhagen K (33 15 65 18). They publish a leaflet called *Working and Residence in Denmark* which was updated in 1994 and explains the procedure for registration as a foreign worker. The leaflet maintains that a job-seeker who is having trouble making use of the telephone directory *(fagbogen)* can ask staff at Use It for help, but note that they cannot themselves offer or arrange employment. However they can give advice on cheap accommodation. Wherever you are in Denmark, try the local labour exchange or AF *(Arbejdsformidlingen)*; a list of addresses can be obtained from the State Employment Service *Arbejdsmarkedsstyrelsen* (AMS, Blegdamsvej 56, Postbox 2722, 2100 Copenhagen Ø; 35 28 81 00).

It is possible to place a free advertisement in English or Danish in the twice-weekly Copenhagen paper *Den Bla Avis* (meaning The Blue Paper), a member of the Free Ads Paper International Association. If you know a Danish speaker, check adverts in the Sunday editions of *Berlingske Tidende* and *Politiken* newspapers. Advertisements in English are accepted by these papers.

The Regulations

EU nationals who intend to stay longer than three months should apply for a residence permit at least a fortnight before that time is up, to the *Direktoratet for Udlaendinge* (Aliens Department) in Copenhagen (Ryesgade 53, 2100 Copenhagen Ø; 31 39 31 00) or from the local police in other towns. The residence permit will be granted after you provide a passport, two photos and a confirmation of employment which indicates that your salary is enough to support you and that you are a member of an authorised unemployment fund *(arbejdsløshedskammer)*.

The minute you find employment, even if it is going to be very temporary, apply for a tax card *(skattekort)* from the *Skatteforvaltning* (Gyldenløvesgade 15, 1639 Copenhagen V) and give it to the employer the same day. Without one, you will be taxed at a punitive 60%. If you do end up overpaying, you won't have a chance of getting a rebate until six months after the calendar year in which you worked. The office is open Monday to Friday 10am-2pm plus 4-5pm on Thursday. Less urgent is a personal registration number *(personnummer)* which you are supposed to apply for within five days of finding a place to live (other than a hostel or hotel). This entitles you to use the Danish health service and is available from the Folkeregistret which in Copenhagen is at Dahlerupsgade 6.

People from outside the EU will find it tough, though not impossible. Potential sources of work whose addresses are included in books like this one receive loads of letters from East Europeans whom they cannot help, as Joanne Patrick describes:

> *We worked at a tropical plant nursery near Faaborg. One year my farmer's brother got in trouble with the police because they had illegally employed Eastern Europeans doing black work. Now his wife doesn't even reply to the letters because a couple of years back some Polish people turned up on her doorstep having thought that all they needed for a work permit was her reply to their letter.*

The Cities

Copenhagen, the commercial and industrial centre of the country, is as good a place as any to look for work. It is also the centre of the tourist industry, so it is worth looking for jobs door to door in hotels and restaurants. Many of the large hotels have personnel offices at the rear of the hotel which should be visited frequently until a vacancy comes up. Some job-seekers may have to call only once, as in the case of the Dutch traveller Mirjam Koppelaars:

> *My Norwegian friend Elise and I rather liked Copenhagen but realised that money was going quick again and decided to try to find some work. After filling in an application form and having a very brief interview at the Sheraton, we both got offered jobs as chambermaids starting the next day. To get a permit, we only needed an address. The next five weeks I cleaned 16 rooms and 16 bathrooms a day in a very funny uniform. We earned kr60, an hour. Although I had to pay over half in tax, I was able to save for more travels.*

Fast food restaurants, such as Burger King and McDonalds, which have a considerable turnover of unskilled foreign staff are also recommended.

The Jobcenter in Copenhagen is at Kultorvet 17 (33 93 43 53). Also the *Arbejdsformidlingen* at Svanevej 22, 2400 NV Copenhagen (31 87 50 88) may be able to assist EU nationals to find temporary work, especially those with a sought-after skill and a knowledge of Danish. It may also be worth asking for unskilled work in warehouses, canteens, etc. at private employment agencies *(vikarbureaux)* such as Adia Interim. Adia has offices at Amagertorv 7, 1160 Copenhagen K; Vestergade 48, 5000 Odense; Køgevej 64, 2630 Taastrup; and Frederiksgade 31, 8000 Aarhus. Manpower also has an office in Copenhagen.

In Denmark the morning newspapers are not delivered by school children as in Britain and North America. Work starts at between 3 and 4am, and a knowledge of Danish is not required. Ian Clegg found this a useful way of earning some money while conducting a job hunt during the day, though he says the job is much easier if you have invested in a second-hand bicycle. To get a job as an *omdeler* or 'paper boy/girl', visit one of the distribution offices of A/S Bladkompagniet, for example the one at Tomsgardsvej 32.

Martyn Rutter used an agency which specialised in supplying cleaners and dishwashers to hotels in Copenhagen, but we haven't had any recent confirmation that they are still active (Royal Service Appointments, 28B Norregade, 1165 Copenhagen). In general, cleaning and dishwashing work is normally available.

Agriculture

Farming plays an important part in the Danish economy and farm work is arguably the easiest door by which to enter the working life of Denmark. The main crops are tomatoes (picked throughout the summer), strawberries (picked in June and July), cherries (picked in July and August) and apples (picked in September and October).

The island of Fyn has been recommended over the years for fruit-picking work, especially the area around Faaborg, most recently from a Polish traveller, Kristof Szymczak:

> *Yes it's true that Fyn is the best fruit-picking part of Denmark. I started seeking work in July. I tried so many places, and always received the same answer, 'I am sorry, We don't need a helper.' Finally I met the most friendly family in the world and they helped me find a job. I picked flowers for about two weeks.*

No doubt most of Kristof's difficulty in finding a job was due to the fact that he did not have the good fortune to be born in an EU country. But times are harder for all job-seekers. The number of strawberry plantings are on the decrease since Danish growers can't complete with the cheap fruit exported from Eastern Europe. For example the famous strawberry farm Orbaekgard in the village of Orbaek which for many years provided employment to hundreds of itinerant workers no longer grows strawberries.

Here are a couple of strawberry farms to try, though don't count on receiving a reply to a written application:

Anders Ploug-Sorensen, Broholm, Tastebjerggyden 13, Horne, 5600 Faaborg (09 60 10 28).

Birkholm Frugt & Baer ApS, Hornelandeveg 2D, 5600 Faaborg (62 60 22 62).

Alstrup Frugtplantage, Alstrupveg 1, Alstrup, 8305 Samsø (86 59 13 38/fax 86 59 31 38).

Fruit pickers are normally paid reasonably good piece rates, for example kr5 per kilo (before tax). As with all harvesting, you can't be sure of making a quick fortune due to the unpredictability of starting dates and hours. The farmers know one another and can direct you to one of their colleagues with vacancies. Joanne Patrick and Steven Conneely arrived at Broholm listed above at the beginning of June and were lucky to go straight into a 37-40 hour-a-week job at Anders Ploug-Sorensen's brother's nursery. They received kr60 an hour from which 30% was deducted for tax (equivalent to a net wage of more than £4.50). One difficulty was that they were paid monthly. Before they got to Fyn they were offered work at the farm on Samsø listed above, where the strawberry season begins about the middle of June and lasts for four or five weeks.

Bjorne Knutsen who owns Birkholm Frugt & Baer describes the farm's requirements:

We require about 12 people for the start of the strawberry season which is usually around the 20th of June and lasts until the end of July. The working day starts at 6am and finishes about midday. the rate of pay is kr4-5 for each kilo of strawberries picked. There are camping facilities at our farm which we provide free of charge.

Anyone who is determined to work on a Danish farm and has the time to plan ahead could place an advertisement in *Landsbladet,* a farming journal, which is published by Landboforeningernes at Vester Farimagsgade 6, 1606 Copenhagen V. Gary Tennant spent £8 on such an advert (cheap by Danish standards) and was immediately successful (see page 113). He was paid about £400 a month after tax, living expenses and Danish lessons since the latter were provided free by the commune.

Another possibility is to contact VHH (the Danish equivalent of WWOOF) to obtain a list of their 25-30 member farmers, most of whom speak English. In return for three or four hours of work per day, you get free food and lodging (sometimes just a place to pitch your tent). Always phone or write before arriving and don't plan to stay more than three days unless you have made a prior arrangement. The list can be obtained only after sending £5/US$10/kr50 to Inga Nielsen, Asenvej 35, 9881 Bindslev.

VHH cooperates with Kollektiv Koordinering, the Danish Communes Association (Ko Koo, Radhusstraede 13, 1466 Copenhagen; 33 15 52 53) which may be able to help people who want to become a guest on one of Denmark's many communities. For example the Svanholm Collective (Svanholm Gods, 4050 Skibby; 42 32 16 70) has a continuous stream of foreign working guests. Gary Tennant contacted some communes:

I had arranged a place for three months with a group on one farm which promised much: work and life with young intelligent socialistically-minded, even smoking, ecologists. One problem was the fact that, being hippies, they could not pay much at all. But they were prepared to train me in milking, and the work would no doubt have been lighter than on the farm I ended up on.

As usual it is best to find out as much as you can about what you're letting yourself in for. David Anderson made private arrangements to work on an organic farm on Mors in the north of Jutland. He regretted his haste in deciding to take the job:

> *I arrived at the doorstep with the equivalent of £10. The owner was a strict vegetarian (all home-grown) and expected me to be the same. And there was no hot water. I was the only staff to pick the fruit and vegetables plus I had to help him build a greenhouse in the shape of a pyramid since he was convinced pyramids have some special power. When I received my pay for the first three weeks, I left and headed straight for the McDonald's in Esbjerg.*

Unlike most organic farms, this one paid a wage of about £50 a week, but this was not nearly enough to make up for the culture shock David was experiencing in the 'back of beyond,' as he no doubt described it to his fellow diners at McDonald's.

Voluntary Work

You can arrange to spend a few weeks during the summer on a voluntary workcamp in Denmark by applying through the organisations mentioned in the chapter on *Voluntary Work* (CMP, IVS and UNA) or, only if you are already in Denmark, Mellemfolkeligt Samvirke, Mejlgade 49, 8000 Aarhus. MS organise between 20 and 30 summer workcamps in Greenland as well as Denmark proper, which last two or three weeks. The main objective of these camps, which carry out projects such as building playgrounds, conservation work, etc., is to bring participants into contact with the social problems found in every society. The Greenland camps have, for example, renovated a Viking village. After paying the participation fee of kr885, everything is provided except travel expenses.

Another association for social voluntary service is the Danish branch of Emmaus International known as the Swallows of Denmark. Two-week work-camps are held in July to raise money for projects in India and Bangladesh by collecting saleable goods. More information (in English) is available from U-landsforeningen Svalerne, Osterbrogade 49, 2100 Copenhagen Ø (35 26 17 47).

'Tvind of Denmark' runs 40 residential schools of different types all over Denmark. Volunteers work for a year or more, helping to run active programmes covering academic studies, sports, arts, study trips, etc. No teaching qualifications are necessary but commitment to helping young people, many of whom have behavioural problems, is essential. Travel expenses are paid plus about kr1,000 a month in addition to free meals and accommodation. For more information contact Anna Jorgensen, Red House School, Buxton, Norwich NR10 5PF.

Finland

Finland actively encourages trainees to come to Finland for short-term paid work. The International Trainee Exchange programme in Finland is administered by CIMO, the Centre for International Mobility (PO Box 343, 00531 Helsinki, Finland; 0-7747 7877/fax 7747 7064). British students and graduates who want on-the-job training in their field (agriculture, tourism, social work, teaching, etc.) lasting one month or longer — the norm is a few months between May and August — should request an application form from the Vocational & Technical Education Department of the Central Bureau (Seymour Mews House, London

W1H 9PE). Applications for summer positions must be in to CIMO by the end of February. This programme is open to people from outside Europe, for whom the red tape is relatively straightforward. Readers in other ocuntries should write to CIMO for their list of cooperating organisations in 13 countries. Work and residence permits are granted for an initial three months but may be extended in Finland for the whole training period. (Immigration queries should be addressed to the Office for Aliens Affairs, Ministry of the Interior, PO Box 92, 00531 Helsinki; 90 160 2784).

To qualify to become a trainee, you must have studied for at least one year, preferably with a year's related experience as well, in a subject such as commerce, economics, agriculture, forestry or tourism, since the majority of placements are technical, agricultural, horticultural or as assistant language teachers. Despite the designation 'trainee', wages are on a par with local Finnish wages for the same work.

Family Stays

Another of CIMO's programmes is the Family Programme. Participants live with a Finnish family for one to three months in the summer or for longer periods up to 12 months starting at any time of the year, helping on their farm or in their home and teaching them English. Anyone who is aged 18-23 and who can speak English, German or French is eligible. Placements on farms are given primarily to young people who have had farming experience. Without an agricultural background, you are more likely to be placed with a city family, many of whom spend at least part of the summer holiday in the country. The school term for Finnish students begins in mid-August so most summer placements come to an end at that time.

The host families' principal motivation for participating in the programme is to improve their English, though it can't be a deterring factor that they also get five hours work from you a day, in their garden or house, including looking after their children. The arrangement is a sophisticated version of the au pair arrangement but is open to men as well as women. Teaching English usually involves no more than just talking. Most Finns have a good knowledge of English.

In addition to free room and board, you will be paid pocket money of between FIM1,000 and FIM2,000 per month (£130-260). Bob Seymour enjoyed the Finnish Family Programme immensely:

> The location of my family in the forests of northern Finland was so idyllic and the atmosphere so congenial that I refused to accept the pocket money, since I reckoned it to be payment enough that I could live there free for two months.

Application forms for Britons are available from the Vocational & Technical Education Department of the Central Bureau and should be submitted by March for summer placement. Readers in other countries should write to CIMO for their list of cooperating organisations in 13 countries.

The Finnish Youth Cooperation Alliance (Allianssi) is a non-profit youth exchange organisation which has a small number of Finnish families looking for au pairs (girls only at present) for 6-12 months or (in a handful of cases) three months in the summer. The pocket money is FIM1,100 for about 30 hours of work a week. Write to Allianssi for details: Olympiastadion, Eteläkaarre, 00250 Helsinki (348 2422/348 24312; fax 491290).

Casual Work

Those who do not qualify as international trainees will find it more difficult to find work, since Finland has been badly hit by recession. However there are areas of employment which have occasional labour shortages, such as the flower nurseries around Helsinki, language tutoring and the 500 hotels included in the Tourist Board's list of hotels, especially in resorts like Hämeenlinna and Lahti.

Some time ago, Natasha Fox fixed up her own work with private families: *I found work as a nanny in Finland simply by placing advertisement cards in a few playgroups. The best area to place them if you are in Helsinki, is Westend Espoo, the most affluent area of the capital. My job paid £110 a week for working Monday to Friday 8am-4pm.*

If you have Finnish friends, ask them to translate newspaper advertisements for you. Helsingin Sanomat, *Finland's daily newspaper, has several vacancies for domestic positions each day. It's certainly worth ringing up and asking if they would like an English speaker for the children's benefit. (Since so many Finnish parents want their children to learn English, this often works.) If you advertise yourself, try to write in Finnish; it shows you aren't an arrogant foreigner. You probably won't have to speak a word of it in the job.*

Here is the advert I put up:
Haluaisitko vaihtaa vapaale', lasten hoidon lomassa? Iloinen, vastuullinen Englandtilais-tytto antaa sinulle mahdollisuuden! Olen vapaa useimpina päivinä/iltoina.

This translates as, 'How would you like a break from the kids? Responsible cheerful English girl will give you the chance! I am free most days and evenings.'

There is no reason why male readers could not advertise themselves likewise. In fact anyone could try this technique for any kind of job, especially teaching English. The going rate for tutoring is up to FIM150 (£20) an hour. Of the Scandinavian countries, Finland is the only one in which language schools occasionally advertise for teachers in the British educational press. One of the key English teaching organisations in Finland is the Federation of Finnish British Societies (Puistokatu 1 b A, 00140 Helsinki). There are 26 Finn-Brit societies and clubs throughout the country, ten of which employ native speaker teachers, usually for a period of nine months. Applications should be sent by the end of February and interviews are held in London in April.

On a more frivolous note, busking might be one way of stretching your travel fund, especially outside Helsinki. According to a correspondent in Finland, buskers are an unfamiliar sight which means that they attract great crowds and a lot of money can be made. He goes on to say that collecting empty bottles, both alcoholic and non-alcoholic, can be profitable.

Workcamps

The coordinating workcamp organisation in Helsinki is called KVT (Rauhanasema, Veturitori, 00520 Helsinki), though applications should be sent in the first instance to IVS. They organise about 15 summer camps each year. Allianssi mentioned above has just joined the international network of workcamp organisations and sends volunteers sent by their counterparts in other countries to about 20 camps in Finland.

An Eastern Orthodox monastery (Valamo Monastery, 79850 Uusi-Valamo; 72-61911) recruits volunteers to work in the gardens, kitchens, etc. in exchange for free board and lodging.

Iceland

Iceland has a tiny population of about 250,000. After years of having virtually no unemployment, Icelanders have had to face the fact that their economy is more fragile than they thought. The official line is that there are no job opportunities for foreigners at the present time, and this seems to be borne out by many travellers' exhaustive but unsuccessful job searches in Iceland.

Of the five countries which joined the European Economic Area in 1994, Iceland is the only one which is not on the brink of joining the Economic Union in the near future. However its EEA status means that European Union nationals are permitted to look for work on the usual terms.

Even tourists to Iceland may be asked to show a return ticket and sufficient funds to maintain themselves throughout their stay. If you are planning to take advantage of the new freedom to go to Iceland to look for work, take plenty of money to cover the notoriously high cost of living, e.g. £7 for a bottle of wine and £2 for a cup of coffee or a loaf of bread. Accommodation is of course also very expensive. One way of solving the problem is to arrange to live with a family in exchange for minimal duties (housekeeping, English conversation, etc.) Check the adverts in the main national daily *Morgunbladid*. The only au pair agency we know of which offers a realistic hope of placing au pairs in Iceland is Exis in Denmark (see chapter introduction) who say that au pairs receive free flights from Europe and pocket money of kr2,000 per month.

THE FISHING INDUSTRY

The fishing industry is fairly labour intensive, employing 14% of the working population directly and many more indirectly. Fish products account for three-quarters of the country's exports. It is a seasonal industry and the busiest season coincides with the long dark winter. The demarcation of jobs seems to be strictly adhered to according to sex: men go to sea or do the heavy lifting and loading in the factories and women do the processing.

There seems little hope of getting taken on a trawler these days, as Tim Wetherall described after a fruitless search for work:

I was in Reykjavik for three weeks in October/November and failed to find work of any kind. Maybe I was unlucky but I don't think so. I'm normally pretty good at finding work when I need it but couldn't manage to pull it off in Iceland. I was ideally looking for work aboard a trawler but then realised that experienced Icelandic trawlermen were unemployed. Years ago casual labour was available to many foreigners aboard trawlers but now Icelandic people are very keen to get taken on because of the excellent money to be earned (around £3,000 per month). A resident Englishman told me that in order to get work on a trawler these days you need to marry the skipper's daughter. I couldn't get a job in a fish factory either. One consolation is that the people of Iceland are very friendly.

Fish Processing

Processing work is not popular and not particularly well paid which has in the past resulted in occasional recruitment drives abroad. Advertisements would be placed in foreign papers and interviews would be carried out for six or eight-month contracts including free flights. For both this edition and the previous one, we have not heard from anyone who has been to work in Iceland, so most of what follows may have little relevance to the job-seeker in the mid-1990s.

There are various tasks to be done in a fish-processing plant including sorting, cleaning, filleting, weighing, deworming and packaging. The worst job is in the *Klevi* or freezer where the temperature is around -43°C (-45°F). The work of packing and shifting boxes of fish would not be too bad were it not for the intense cold. Without proper gear including fur-lined boots and gloves, a balaclava and layers of sheepskin, this work is unendurable. In the rest of the factory the temperature is 10°C-16°C (50°F-62°F). Another undesirable job is hanging up fish to be wind-dried, which is done only occasionally.

It takes weeks of practice before you can fillet and pack fish expertly. Standards are usually very high and if the supervisor finds more than two bones or worms, the whole case will be returned to you to be checked again. Since pay is normally according to performance, your earnings will increase as your technique improves, but the wages will not be wonderful in view of the high cost of living. Debbie Mathieson described her work at a small factory in Hnfisdal as 'not really difficult, but mind-blowingly boring'. At the then exchange rate, she earned £150 from which she had to buy her food but not accommodation. One of the compensating features of the job for Debbie was that she was eligible for a tax rebate at the end of her contract which amounted to several hundred pounds.

There is little conventional social life in the fishing villages of northern Iceland, though many are so prosperous that they offer facilities which would be unheard of in a village their size elsewhere. The five dark months of winter, when villages are cut off from their neighbours, can be depressing. Vicki Matchett signed a six-month contract with a factory in the village of Vopnafjörd in north-east Iceland and describes the life:

> *Fishing villages usually have about 800 inhabitants with almost no social life, no pubs, not even any wildlife, and the weather between December and May made sightseeing risky. For the sake of saving £1,000 I'm not sure it's worth vegetating for six months. I must admit I spent most of my spare time reading travel journals to remind myself that civilisation still existed.*

Other

Agriculture is a major enterprise in Iceland, but farms are principally family concerns and employ few outsiders. Sheep rearing is the only economically feasible form of farming as few crops grow in the short summer months. Hay-making is an important summer job; much of the grass is cut by scythe as tractors cannot work the steep slopes, particularly in the narrow valleys where many of the farms are located. However this work is mainly done by school children.

Other work outside the primary sectors of fishing and farming is very limited. The municipal employment office in Reykjavik can be found at Borgatuni 1. Alafoss (PO Box 404, 121 Reykjavik; 666300), a company just outside Reykjavik which weaves carpets and the famous Icelandic lopi wool, sometimes employs foreign workers and provides living quarters. There may be casual work available in the Reykjavik docks; it is a matter of turning up in the morning and seeing if anyone is needed. The pay is reasonable and fringe benefits are considerable.

Icelandic Nature Conservation Volunteers (SJA, PO Box 8468, 128 Reykjavik) run a summer programme of projects at eight locations throughout Iceland lasting from between one and ten days, which are open to everyone. Transport from Reykjavik is usually provided free (including to the remote Vestmannaeyjar Islands), as is the food and accommodation in huts or (weather permitting) tents. Recent projects have been mainly involved with building paths and steps in national parks such as Jökulsárgljúfur National Park. You can fix up some of these ahead of time through the International Development Unit of the British Trust for Conservation Volunteers (36 St. Mary's St, Wallingford, Oxfordshire OX10 0EU), which arranges two to three week volunteer tours of Iceland. The cost is £380-£420 including flights.

Norway

After years of escalating intolerance of foreigners working in their country, the Norwegian authorities are now coming to terms with the fact that citizens of any EEA country can come to look for work. As mentioned at the beginning of the chapter *Scandinavia,* any EU/EFTA national may enter Norway for up to three months to look for work. Once they succeed they must apply to the police for a residence permit *(oppholdstillatelse)* on a specified form. All of this should mean that one reader's experience of sending a 'blizzard of mail to find work in Norway without a smidgen of luck' may not be typical in future.

The Europa Service of the *Arbeidsformidlingen* (Employment Service) distributes a useful English-language leaflet 'Looking for Work in Norway'; request a copy from the Euroadviser, Øvre Slottsgate 11 (Postboks 420 Sentrum), 0103 Oslo (22 42 41 41). A new temporary work unit operates from the same address (22 4260 00). Also private agencies place people in temporary jobs. Look up *Vikarutleie* in the Yellow Pages or look for names like Manpower, Top Temp and Norsk Personnel in city centres. Also check ads in the main daily paper *Aften Posten* or try placing one yourself.

As throughout Scandinavia, wages are high in Norway, though the high cost of living makes it difficult to save. Almost no jobs pay less than 50 Norwegian kroner (nearly £5) per hour. Travellers have commented on how friendly and generous Norwegian people are. Because buskers are a relative novelty, earnings can be remarkably high. Mary Hall plucked up the courage to do some busking in Bergen on her newly acquired penny whistle. Although she knew only two songs, she made £15 in 15 minutes, mostly due to the fact that her audience was drunk.

Tourism

A reasonable number of English-speaking tourists visit Norway each summer, so there are some openings for English-speaking staff. You can also try winter resorts like Lillehammer, Nordseter, Susjoen, Gausdal or Voss. For either season, you can try to get something fixed up ahead of time by writing to hotels listed in the accommodation brochure available from the Norwegian Tourist Office, Charles House, 5-11 Lower Regent St, London SW1Y 4LR (send a 50p stamp), in which hundreds of hotels are listed. There is a greater density of hotels in the south of Norway including beach resorts along the south coast around Kristiansand, and inland from the fjords north of Bergen (Geilo, Gol, Vaga, Lillehammer, and in the Hardanger region generally). Remember that even in the height of summer, the mountainous areas can be very chilly.

The starting net monthly wage of an unskilled hotel worker is kr7,500-8,000 with a deduction of between kr500 and kr1,000 for board and lodging. Some hotels pay considerably more. Wages are lower outside the big cities, but the work may be more pleasant.

Norwegian youth hostels have a steady demand for unskilled domestic staff who are willing to accept little more than a living wage. You can also try approaching the Youth Hostels central office as Dennis Bricault did:

I wrote to several IYHF national offices to offer my services as a volunteer and specified some of my talents (kitchen, maintenance, painting, cleaning, etc.). The Norwegian and the German organisations were the most accommodating.

The Norwegian Hiking Association take on some people to be caretakers at their network of mountain huts, though the only foreigner we have heard of who did this job was studying at the University of Oslo and therefore was on the spot.

Neil Tallantyre, who spent several winter seasons in Lillehammer, found that there is quite a demand for British workers. He has been amazed at the resourcefulness of travellers who have extended their time in ski resorts (primarily to ski), by doing odd jobs like snow clearing and car-cleaning (for kr75), waitressing, DJing (especially common since the British are thought to know their way around the music scene), au pairing and English teaching. One traveller who happened upon a short-term opportunity for teaching is David Moor:

> *I saw an advert in a supermarket in Lillehammer for a native English speaker to teach for a month and jumped at the chance, although I had gone there for a skiing holiday. I'd intended to stay in the hostel or a cheap hotel but was finding Norway expensive, and was lucky that another teacher was able to put me up and feed me. I was just working for keep, but only teaching three days a week, so I had lots of spare time.*

Woden Teachout describes one intriguing avenue you might pursue:

> *The other opportunity I know of is something I nearly did. There is a very posh cruise during the summer months called the Hurtigruten. It sails up the coast to the Arctic Circle, touring the fjords under the midnight sun. Because it is such a luxury liner they need a lot of staff to pander to the passengers. I called the offices and asked if they needed help; they said to meet the boat in Bergen at the docks and ask the captain. I did this on three successive days and none of the captains wanted help. But they didn't laugh at me (as I'd expected) and in fact were quite encouraging, saying that chances were I'd get something within the week. I imagine the trick is to catch them quite early in the season. I don't know what the wages were but the trip is supposed to be so spectacular that it would be worth doing one 14-day run for nothing. Ask as early in the season as possible.*

Norwegian Farm Working Guest Programme

Atlantis, the Norwegian Foundation for Youth Exchange, at Rolf Hofmosgt. 18, 0655 Oslo (22 67 00 43) runs an excellent programme which allows people aged between 18 and 30 of any nationality to spend between one and three months in rural Norway. The only requirement is that they speak English. They wrote in 1994 to say that there is a shortage of applicants, especially from North America and Australia.

Farm guests receive full board and lodging plus pocket money of at least kr500 a week (£48) for a maximum of 35 hours of work. The idea is that you participate in the daily life, both work and leisure, of the family: haymaking, weeding, milking, berry-picking, painting, house-cleaning, babysitting, etc.

After receiving the official application form you must send off a reference, two smiling photos, a medical certificate confirming that you are in good health and a registration fee of kr830 (approximately £80). Anyone applying directly to Atlantis should address their request to Ingeborg Sutterud, the Inbound Manager. British applicants can apply through Concordia and Americans to Interexchange (Att; Ms. P. Santorielli, 161 Sixth Avenue, New York, NY 10013; 212-924-0446). Atlantis will try to take into account your preferences: proximity to a friend, whether you are willing to go to a family who speaks no English or to a family living in the far north of Norway, etc. There are about 400 places (for all nationalities), so try to apply at least three months before your desired date of arrival. If they are unable to place you, all but kr130 will be refunded. Applying through Concordia increases your chances of acceptance.

Robert Olsen enjoyed his farm stay so much that he went back to the same family another summer:

> *The work consisted of picking fruit and weeds (the fruit tasted better). The working day started at 8am and continued till 4pm, when we stopped for*

the main meal of the day. After that we were free to swim in the sea, borrow
a bike to go into town or whatever. I was made to feel very much at home
in somebody else's home. The farmer and his daughter were members of a
folk dance music band, which was great to listen to. Now and then they
entrusted me to look after the house while they went off to play at festivals.
Such holidays as these are perhaps the most economical and most memorable possible.

Outdoor Work

One of the best areas to head for is the strawberry growing area around Lier,
accessible by bus from Drammen. According to a Norwegian news report, the
majority of the harvesters are foreign, since wages are notoriously bad. Kristin
Moen and her Italian friend Maurizio were given jobs at the first farm phoned,
but earned only kr120 between them after $2\frac{1}{2}$ hours, and then quit. The strawberry
season here reaches its peak in early July.

Further north the harvest is a little later. For example in Steinkjer (north of
Trondheim), it goes from mid-July to August. Wages are a little higher here
since the fruit is smaller, and accommodation may be available, unlike in the
south where you normally have to provide a tent. Nordfjord, south of Romsdal,
is also a possibility. The raspberry harvest starts at the beginning of August at
Andebu near Tansberg. Potatoes and other vegetables are harvested in early
September; try the village of Loen, in the Romsdal area and inland around
Hamar.

The steep hillsides on either side of the many fjords support abundant wild
blueberries. It is possible to freelance as a berry picker and then sell the fruit to
the local produce and jam co-operatives. In Lapland it is not permitted to pick
certain berries in certain seasons, since only native Lapps have the right, so
make local enquiries first. Autumn brings wild mushrooms — Norway has about
2,500 varieties. In some of the larger towns, there are weekend mushroom
controls where you can have what you have picked checked.

Au Pairs

The situation is promising for the au pair of any nationality (provided she
speaks some English) who aspires to work in Norway, though the red tape is
still considerable. Atlantis runs a programme for incoming au pairs (the only
one in Norway) who must be aged 18-30 and willing to stay between ten months
and two years. The first step is to write to the foundation for an information
sheet and application forms. Atlantis charges no registration fee. Au pairs from
an EEA country can obtain the residence permit fter arrival. When a family has
been found for someone from outside Western Europe, the agency in Norway
obtains an agreement of which four copies are forwarded to the au pair, together
with an invitation letter. These must be presented to the Norwegian Embassy
in the applicant's home country, together with an original birth certificate. At
least three months should be allowed for these procedures. Upon arrival in
Norway you must register with the local police within a week.

The pocket money in Norway is set by law at kr2,300 per month, which
sounds generous until you realise that it will probably be taxed at 30%. The
majority of families are in and around Oslo, Bergen or the other cities in southern
Norway, although applicants are invited to indicate a preference of north, south,
east or west on their initial application. Virtually all employers will be able to
communicate in English.

A few UK au pair agencies have vacancies in Norway, including Pre-Select
(924 Stratford Road, Springfield, Birmingham B11 4BT; 0121-702 2100).

Voluntary Work

The Nansen Internasjonale Center for disturbed teenagers near Oslo will sponsor foreign volunteers to get work permits. They require leaders to motivate and lead residents and to join in domestic and farm activities. All volunteers should have some experience of working with young people, be at least 22, and prepared to stay for at least one year. The centre also requires a limited number of volunteers for six weeks in the summer, to work with Norwegian children on holiday. Applicants who need work permits must be prepared to wait between three and six months for it to be processed. Volunteers receive kr500 (£45) per week in addition to basic board and lodging. Send an IRC for details to Nansen Internasjonale Center, Barnegarden Breivold, Nesset, 1400 Ski; 09-94 67 91.

The workcamp organisation in Norway is called Internasjonal Dugnad at Langes Gate 6, 0165 Oslo 1 (22-11 31 23/fax 22-20 71 19). If you're in Norway and want to spend two or three weeks volunteering, for example at a peace centre or an experimental farm, contact them; otherwise apply through the Service Civil International/IVS branch in your own country.

Sweden

Until Sweden joined the European Union the only chance for finding legal work in Sweden was as a participant in a special summer scheme which allowed foreign people to undertake vacation employment between the 15th of May and 15th October, provided they could find an employer before entering Sweden. This scheme is now of interest only to students and others from outside Western Europe. When applying to your local Swedish Embassy for the permit, you must submit a written offer of work on form AMS PF 1704, at least two months before your proposed arrival. Queries should be addressed to Statens Invandrarverk, Box 6113, 60006 Norrköping (15 60 00). General information and addresses of local employment offices may be obtained from the employment service *Arbetsmarknadsstyrelen,* 17199 Solna (08-730 60 00). Since 1993 private employment agencies have been allowed to operate in Sweden.

Casual Work

State handouts are so generous in Sweden that very few natives are willing to undertake hard work like dishwashing or fruit picking for a few kroner an hour. Now that the red tape has been simplified for EU nationals, it should be easier to find casual work.

Even without the benefit of having the right stamp in your passport, there are possibilities, as the American Woden Teachout discovered:

In southern Sweden I did the cleaning lady's tour of Swedish mansions. I found the first job through a couple who picked me up hitch-hiking and who contacted a friend of theirs. There are a great number of large country houses in Skane, and the Swedes who live in them find it no luxury to pay for household help. All the families I worked for were the acme of repsectability, and a neat appearance in probably very important. So I had several weeks of sweeping out from behind stoves, washing windows, and generally helping with the spring clean. Housework has never been my great speciality, but the living was easy since the relics of Swedish gentry are both rich and hospitable. I had my own room, four-course meals under the evening sun and they took me merrily along to celebrate midsummer, or on outings to the beach or theatre. Plus I was paid the equivalent of $4 an hour.

Several years ago Elfed Guyatt from Wales chanced his luck by looking for work after arrival in Sweden and soon found work as a barman in both Malmö and Lund. In Malmö he worked as a barman in a sports club where the pay was negligible but he was given all the beer and food he wanted plus accommodation shared with one of the club members. Lund was also a good place to look for work and shared accommodation through the student grapevine.

It may be worth trying to find work in hotels, usually in the kitchen. Your best bets are the large hotels in Stockholm and Göteborg. Elsewhere you might try areas where tourism is well established. Try the Sunshine Coast of western Sweden including the seaside resorts between Malmö and Göteborg, especially Hölsingborg, Varberg and Falkenberg. Other popular holiday centres with a large number of hotels include Orebro, Västeras, Are, Ostersund, Jönköping and Linköping. The chances of fixing up a hotel job in advance are remote. After writing to dozens of Scandinavian hotels, Dennis Bricault's conclusion was 'Forget Sweden!'.

If you are interested in outdoor work, try the southern counties, especially Skane, where a wide variety of crop is grown. Woden Teachout found morning work at a strawberry farm near Skane:

> *Strawberry picking jobs are incredibly easy to come by. Our motley crew consisted of six spindly Swedish teenagers, most of whom quit over the course of the harvest, myself and a carload of Polish students. We worked from 7am till lunch and could make up to $3.50 an hour if we worked fast.*

With wages like that, it is obvious why few Swedes would want to accept such jobs.

There are also vacancies in the market gardening sector, but no centralised means by which to find a job. Peas, cucumbers, spinach and many other vegetables are grown under contract to canneries and if you can't find work in the fields, you might find it in the processing plants. In the eastern part of Skane there is specialised fruit growing: apples, pears, plums, cherries, strawberries and raspberries. The islands of Oland and Gotland are also very fertile and you might find a farming family short of a helper.

If you can't find an employer willing to take you on, you could consider freelancing as a berry picker. Wild strawberries, blueberries and raspberries can be found in the forests of Sweden from June till September and might be successfully sold at weekend street markets, in youth hostels, etc. In the late summer there are mushrooms and loganberries to pick, though you should be knowledgeable about which mushrooms are edible before trying to market them and also be sensitive about local laws which protect the livelihood of Laplanders. Be warned that forested areas in Sweden are commonly mosquito-ridden, so be prepared. Either remain fully clothed at all times (despite the summer heat) or apply liberal lashings of a powerful repellant.

Au Pairs

One Swedish au pair agency which has been advertising recently is Eurojob Au Pair, Jarpgatan 11, 58237 Linköping (13-13 07 34). IRCA International/ Sprakcenter (PO Box 293, 29123 Kristianstad; tel/fax 44-12 22 63) mainly arranges au pair placements abroad for Swedes, but also makes a few family placements in Sweden.

Au pairs are subject to the same regulations as all other foreign employees so non-EU nationals must obtain a work permit before leaving their home country. Once you arrive, it is worth checking university notice boards for baby-sitting openings. The same social class which employed Woden Teachout as a cleaner is often willing to hire live-in childcare. In fact the last family for whom Woden cleaned gave her free room and board in exchange for acting as a companion to their ten year old daughter.

Teaching

Casual work teaching English is rarely available. The Folk University of Sweden runs an adult English language programme in many towns throughout the country. Most of the teachers are recruited in Britain. At one time a university degree was sufficient to get a one or two year contract, but these days an EFL qualification is expected. The institutes in small towns may not insist on advanced qualifications. The rate of pay is kr110 an hour, though one quarter of this disappears in tax. Contact International Language Services for details (Salisbury School of English, 36 Fowlers Road, Salisbury, Wiltshire SP1 2QU; 01722 331011). They also run a summer employment scheme for which teachers are needed between June and August, though these posts are normally filled by contract teachers already in Sweden.

Voluntary Work

The main workcamps organiser in Sweden is Internationella Arbetslag (IAL), Barnangsgatan 23, 11641 Stockholm which is the Swedish branch of SCI. It is essential to apply through your local branch of Service Civil International (IVS in Britain).

Every summer there is a massive flea market in Stockholm organised to raise money for the Third World. Drivers, promotion workers and general assistants are needed to work on a voluntary basis.

The busy and flexible commune of Stärnsund (Stifelsen Stärnsund, 77070 Langshyttan; 225-80001) operates a working guest programme.

Survival

Many items in Sweden are very expensive such as cigarette papers which some travellers have profited from selling. If you are very short of money, you can try railways station cafés between 6am and 9am when they get rid of the food left over from the previous day (because of the very strict regulations governing food hygiene). If the food isn't free it will be very cheap. Another tip is to visit one of the many restaurants offering cheap buffet meals (less than £5); it becomes an even better bargain if you share subsequent helpings with one or two of your friends. The words *Extra pris* on food in shops means that it has been discounted (by as much as 50%) for being damaged or close to its sell-by date.

Collecting discarded bottles and cans can be a fairly profitable way to earn some money anywhere in the country. The carnivals which take place in July and August are recommended as prime targets for bottle-collecting; Elfed Guyatt earned around £50 a day during three days in Norrköping. British and American souvenirs are trendy, so you can make up to 500% profit by selling such things at local weekend markets. Medals, caps, books, etc. are worth stocking up on at home for possible sale in Sweden.

Spain & Portugal

The decade of the 1980s was one of unprecedented economic growth in Spain as business and industry forged ahead in anticipation of gaining full European Community status in 1992. Although unemployment remains the highest in the EU (24% in 1994), the demand for foreign labour, particularly in English language teaching, persists. Spain's tourist industry continues to absorb thousands of foreign young people in a temporary and part-time capacity. Otherwise there is not much job mobility at present, due to a legal requirement that anyone (employer or employee) who signs a contract must pay compensation if he or she breaks the contract.

Do not imagine that it will be easy to find work in Spain nor that the living will be cheap while you look. After hitching successfully around Europe, Martin and Shirine found that the lifts dried up as soon as they crossed the Spanish border, and everything was more expensive. For example campsites were the same price as youth hostels and all food items in supermarkets seemed to cost the equivalent of one pound, whether it was a tin of tuna or a bag of carrots.

The Regulations in Spain

The procedures for regularising your status are similar to those in other EU countries. Those who intend to stay more than three months must apply for a residence card *(Tarjeta de Residencia)* within 30 days of arrival. Application should be made to a regional police headquarters *(Comisaría de Policía)* or a Foreigners' Registration Office *(Oficina de Extranjería)* which in Madrid is at

Los Madrazo 9. The documents necessary for the *residencia* are a contract of employment, three photos and a passport. This information is confirmed both in the hand-outs from the Labour Counsellor's Office of the Spanish Embassy (20 Peel St, London W8 7PD) and in 'Settling in Spain' (revised February 1994) from the British Consulate-General in Spain (c/ Marqués de la Ensenada 16-2°, 28004 Madrid).

The red tape for which Spain is famous does not stop at residence cards. One contributor was working for an expat British bar owner on the Costa del Sol when a Social Security woman turned up saying that he had not yet applied for his *residencia* as he should have and the landlord hadn't done 'this and that'.

The rules for non-EU citizens have not changed and those who find a legitimate job (e.g. teaching English, working for a tour company) will have to go through the complex rigamarole as before. You must obtain a *visado especial* from the Spanish Embassy in your country of residence after submitting a copy of your contract, medical certificate in duplicate and authenticated copies of your qualifications. In some cases a further document is needed, an *antecedente penale* (police certificate). Invariably the Spanish authorities take months to process this and when the visa (normally Type A which is for one specific job) is finally issued, it must be collected in your home country.

The strict rules make it almost impossible for people from outside Western Europe to pick up casual work as Ana Güemes from Mexico found:

Although we Latin Americans speak Spanish, I insist in saying that Spain is one of the hardest countries to find a job in. Everywhere you go they ask to see your identity card because of the problems they have with Moroccans.

That being said, Ana did make friends with the daughters of a vineyard owner and picked grapes in exchange for free food, wine and tours of the area.

Americans, Canadians, Australians, etc. do sometimes find paid work as monitors in children's camps, tutors at language schools and in private households, touts for bars and discos. When their tourist visas are about to expire, they usually follow the example of others who simply cross into France or Portugal to extend their tourist visa for a further three months on their return to Spain.

The official minimum wage is just over pta50,000 per month. The Spanish employment service *(Oficinas de Empleo)* has a monopoly on job-finding, so private employment agencies are banned.

TEACHING ENGLISH

The Olympics in Barcelona, Expo 92 in Seville and Madrid as the 1992 City of Culture prodded Spanish schools and businesses into a frenzy of English language learning. Few job interviews would have omitted the question, 'Can you speak English?'. It seems that the market has now peaked and the boom in English is over, apart from in the specific area of teaching children as young as pre-school (for which a knowledge of Spanish is virtually essential, not to mention songs and games).

There are of course thousands of foreigners still teaching English in language institutes from the Basque north (where there is a surprisingly high concentration) to the Balearic and Canary Islands. The entries for language schools occupy 20 pages of the Madrid Yellow Pages. But the days are gone when any native speaker of English without a TEFL background could reasonably expect to be hired by a language academy.

Job Hunting on-the-Spot

Most teaching jobs in Spain are found on the spot and, with increasing competition, it is necessary to exert yourself to land a decent job. Most people

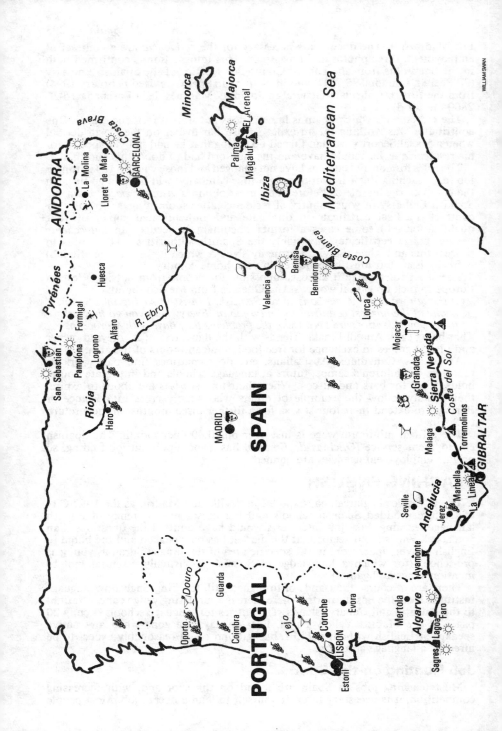

WILLIAM SWAN

simply use the usual method of consulting the Yellow Pages *(Las Paginas Amarillas)* and pounding the pavements of the place where they are staying. The best time to look is at the beginning of September, after the summer holidays are ended and before most terms begin on October 1st. Spanish students sign up for English classes during September and into early October. Consequently the academies do not know how many classes they will offer nor how many teachers they will need until quite late. It can become a war of nerves; anyone who is willing and can afford to stay on has an increasingly good chance of becoming established.

Kevin Boyd didn't decide to go to Spain until mid-October. Although he had previously failed to get work in Munich and Bologna, even with an RSA/ Cambridge Certificate, he landed a job with a good school in Valencia at that unpromising time of year.

Ben Hockley from Australia recommends trying Wall Street Institutes. This chain of 11 schools (eight of which are in Madrid) is reputed to have a high staff turnover, partly because the pay is at the lower end of the spectrum. Ben had no trouble fixing up a job with them on his second visit to Madrid; the first time he had no luck job-hunting because he had no TEFL qualification and no Spanish. Try also Berlitz, whose Madrid branch (Gran Via 80-4, 28013 Madrid) recruits EFL teachers who have a degree but not necessarily any teaching experience or qualifications.

Some people end up having to withdraw from the fray. After going a certain distance, the American George Kelly gave up his job-hunt in Madrid:

In September of last year, I spent about two weeks in Madrid looking for an English teaching job. I contacted about 40 schools and had received only one firm offer when I left Spain on September 21st. Many schools told me that they would contact me if they ended up needing teachers, and I believe at least a few of them would have called me.

His situation was no doubt made more difficult by the fact that Spain had just entered fully into the European Community and so being an American was a much greater disadvantage than it had been previously.

Other sources of job vacancy information include the Madrid daily *El Pais* which usually has a few relevant classifieds under the heading *Trabajo — Idiomas.* Also try *Segundamano,* Madrid's free ads paper which comes out Monday, Wednesday and Friday. (It is possible to place an ad from wherever there is a sister paper; in Britain this is *LOOT,* 24 Kilburn High Rd, London NW6 5UJ.)

Turner Bookshop (C/ Génova 3 & 5) has a very active notice board with notices for teaching jobs, schools, language exchanges and flats for rent. Unfortunately the board is put up only between November and August, and is cleared on a bi-weekly basis to avoid congestion.

In Advance

Anyone with an EFL component on their CV might try to fix up work ahead of time. A list of the 350 member schools of the national federation of English language schools (FECEI) can be obtained from the Spanish Labour Office (20 Peel St, London W8 7PD; 0171-221 0098), together with an outline of Spanish immigration regulations and a one-page handout 'Teaching English as a Foreign Language.' The book *Teaching English Abroad* (published by Vacation-Work) has about 100 address of language schools which welcome applications from prospective teachers.

Qualified applicants might want to make use of a recruitment agency, whether a general one or one which specialises in Spain such as English Educational Services (Alcalá 20-2°, 28014 Madrid; 532 9734/531 4783; fax 531 5298). The owner Richard Harrison recommends that candidates with a degree and RSA Certificate come to Spain in early September and contact his agency on arrival.

For voluntary work as an English assistant on summer language/sports camps, try Relaciones Culturales, the youth exchange organisation at Calle Ferraz 82, 28008 Madrid (541 71 03/fax 559 1181), which also places native speakers with Spanish families who want to practise their English in exchange for providing room and board. Some years ago, Noel Kirkpatrick found them very helpful in finding students for him to teach and a family with whom to live one summer.

Kursolan S.A. (c/ Maria de Molina 32, 28006 Madrid; 1-561 3100/8) run two summer camps outside Madrid for which they need 30-40 counsellors-cum-teachers, preferably with camp experience. Similarly the Technical College in Zaragoza (C/ Maria Lostal No. 22, 50008 Zaragoza; 976-227909) runs summer courses in the Pyrenees for which it hires sports monitors and EFL teachers. Vigvatten Natur Klubb (Apartado 3253, 01002 Vitoria Gasteiz) also have summer positions at sports camps in the Basque country, Pyrenees and Sierra de Urbion (near the town of Soria), which pay £150 for a fortnight.

Conditions of Work

Salaries are not high in Spain and have not increased significantly since 1990. Net salaries are in the range pta90,000-135,000 per month with a steady average in the middle of that scale. Compulsory social security payments of 8% will be deducted. Tax deductions are paid in arrears and do not normally affect teachers on nine-month contracts. A full-time contract normally consists of 25 contact hours, which can feel gruelling, especially if the teacher has to travel around a big city like Madrid.

One of the worst problems in the classroom is the difficulty in motivating students. Many are children or teenagers whose parents enrol them in classes in order to improve their performance in school exams. David Bourne echoes this complaint after completing a nine-month contract in Gijón:

> *I have found it very hard work trying to inject life into a class of bored ten year olds, particularly when the course books provided are equally uninteresting. The children themselves would much rather be outside playing football. So you spend most of the lesson trying (unsuccessfully in my case) trying to keep them quiet.*

Despite this he still sums up his job in Spain as exhilarating.

Private Tutoring

As usual, private tutoring pays much better than contract teaching because there is no middle man. The going rate for teaching individuals is about pta1,500. Freelance rates in Madrid are as much as twice that but travelling time has to be taken into consideration.

It is difficult to start up without contacts and a good knowledge of Spanish; and when you do get started it is difficult to earn a stable income due to the frequency with which pupils cancel. Getting private lessons is a marketing exercise and you will have to explore all the avenues which seem appropriate to your circumstances. Obviously you can advertise on the notice boards mentioned above as well as at universities, corner shops and wherever else you think there is a market. Send neat notices to local state schools asking them to pin it up broadcasting your willingness to ensure the children's linguistic future.

Many contract teachers engage in some private teaching as well, though this is risky as Stuart Britton, who was last heard from teaching for inlingua in the untouristy north of Gran Canaria, discovered:

> *The only negative experience working here has been a cutting off of my*

private tutoring at home by the academy where I work. Through spying, I believe, they heard I had been teaching outside the academy. If I am found out again I was told my contract would be stopped. So it knocked my chance of earning extra money on the side.

He found this restriction particularly frustrating in the quiet months of August and September, but otherwise was much happier teaching in this peaceful backwater than he was in either northern Spain or Mexico.

TEEMING TOURISM

Spain hosts a staggering 40 million visitors a year and is by far the most popular destination for British tourists. Of the top ten package holiday destinations for Britons in 1994, five are Spanish: Majorca, Tenerife, Ibiza, Menorca and the Costa Blanca. There is a vague rumour that a Spanish Euro Disney is being considered for the site of EXPO 92 in Seville which, as in France, would provide an enormous amount of temporary employment.

Although not quite so booming as they were in the late 1980s the coastal resorts continue to draw hordes of tourists, especially Lloret de Mar, Calella (Costa Brava), Benidorm (Costa Blanca), Torremolinos, Benalmadena, Fuengirola (Costa del Sol), Mojacar (Costa de Almeria) and Ibiza and Palma (Majorca). The proverbial British tourist in Spain is not looking for undiscovered villages but wants to have the familiar comforts of home along with the Mediterranean sunshine. The Spanish tourist industry has recognised this preference for a long time and has employed large numbers of English-speaking young people to make the tourists feel at home. It is always worth checking the English language press for the sits vac column: the papers listed below carry occasional adverts for cleaners, live-in babysitters, chefs, bar staff, etc. Simon Bond recommends the free English language paper he came across in Benalmadena, the *Sur*. It is usually not very expensive to place your own advert.

If you can arrange to visit the Spanish coast in March before most of the budget travellers arrive, you should have a good chance of fixing up a job for the season. The resorts then go dead until late May when the season gets properly underway and there may be jobs available. If you are heading for the Canary Islands, the high season for British package tourists is November to March. Bear in mind that while working in these environments you will barely get a glimpse of genuine Spanish culture.

Year-round resorts like Tenerife, Gran Canaria and Lanzarote afford a range of casual work. Nick Crivich, who worked a season as a rep in Tenerife for a subsidiary of Thomson, observed that there were ample opportunities for bar staff, DJs, beach party ticket sellers, timeshare salesmen, etc. in these places and on the islands. Magaluf on Majorca is another busy resort full of English bars like Prince Williams where you can enquire about local jobs. At one time there were many jobs in the tourist industry of Ibiza but recent reports indicate that the only thing available is for young women dancing in clubs.

People have successfully found (or created) jobs in highly imaginative ways. One of the most striking examples is a 19-year-old Finnish student who wrote to the address on a Spanish wine label and was astonished to be invited to act as a guide around their winery for the summer. Tommy Karske returned home 'knowing a lot about wine and believing that anything is possible'. Tradespeople, mechanics, handymen and gardeners usually have no trouble finding work inside the expatriate community in any resort.

A more conventional form of employment is with a British tour company such as Canvas Holidays, Eurocamp, Keycamp Holidays, etc. (see *Tourism* chapter). Haven France & Spain (Northney Marina, Northney Road, Hayling

Island, Hants. PO11 0NH) needs Spanish-speaking couriers and children's staff to work at mobile home and tent parks from early May to the end of September. And don't ignore the possibility of winter work with a British tour company in a Pyreneen ski resort either in the Spanish province of Huesca or in the principality of Andorra.

Odd Jobs and Touting

There is a job which is peculiar to the Spanish resorts and which allows a great many working travellers to earn their keep for the season. The job is known variously as 'PRing', 'propping' or 'blagging', that is to entice/bully tourists to patronise a certain bar or disco. Ian Govan from Glasgow thinks that previous descriptions in this book have not done it justice, since he found it an excellent way to spend the season in Lloret de Mar:

> *There are literally hundreds of British props and a fair number of Commonwealth and other European nationals. I worked as a prop for over a dozen bars in three months and by the end I was earning up to pta80,000 a month with free beer to boot. Be warned that saving is virtually impossible, but you will have one hell of a social life, and will soon enjoy the job and the challenges which arise as you try to match the experienced props and develop your own routine. The highest compliment is when the old hands start using your lines. It's pure unadulterated showbiz.*

New people are usually taken on on a drinks-only basis for one or two sessions and, after proving they are effective at drawing in customers, begin to earn a wage, possibly pta2,000-3,000 a night. When you first arrive, try to get a toe-hold by working at one of the less sought-after places. You must decide whether to work as a 'bar-prop' or a 'disco-prop'. According to Ian the former is much more fun (though worse paid) while the latter involves 'dressing snazzily, being multilingual and shady-looking, as liable to sell you heroin as give you a free ticket to a disco'. The authorities normally turn a blind eye to this activity provided props don't hand out leaflets or stickers in the road, don't drink or prop ostentatiously when the police are in the vicinity, don't upset the locals and stick to the opening hours. The hours of work are usually midnight onwards, as late as 7am.

In 1994 Rikke Bogensberger from Denmark came across even higher wages for propping, in the resort of Calella about an hour's train journey north of Barcelona. This resort is popular with Swedish, German and Dutch tourists, both backpackers and older people, though Britons are beginning to discover it. Rikke made pta10,000 a week though much of that went on his accommodation. He claims that it is extremely easy to get this work or bar work in Calella.

After leaving Lloret de Mar (which Alison Cooper describes as a 'nightmare resort') she moved to the much smaller resort of Estartit where she managed to get a job as a dishwasher in a restaurant. She worked from 6pm-2am every day for £75 a week:

> *Although it was backbreaking work, it certainly was a laugh. I worked with three Moroccans and one Spaniard, and we all had to communicate by sign language and by drawing pictures. In September my Spanish boss gave me a lift to Perpignan and invited me back to work anytime. I was pleased to feel appreciated.*

Time-share touting is another of those jobs which some find objectionable but others recommend. Nicola Sarjeant (with joint Canadian/British nationality) had little choice but to give it a go in Gran Canaria when her money was running out, and concluded it had its redeeming features. Although Euro-legislation introduced in the 1990s has limited the kinds of selling techniques used, time share developments (or 'holiday ownership' companies which is the new euphemism) continue to market their properties, and the job of OPC ('Offsite Personal Contact') is still around. Nicola describes her job:

> We spoke to an OPC who told us we would be able to get a job and one month's free rent in an apartment. It sounded too good to be true but it wasn't. There are six or seven companies in Puerto Rico and Playa del Ingles which pay between pta5,000 and pta9,000 per couple. We made on average (working together) pta75,000 in cash per week. Admittedly it can be quite frustrating as you are paid only when you send a couple on a tour of the resort. (British couples are the most difficult as virtually everyone in England has heard about the 'evils' of time-share.) The job is not for everyone since you have to be fairly aggressive and also prepared to face a lot of rejection. However the pay as well as the freedom of the job make up for this. There were few (if any) problems with the police; at worst they ask to see your passport and write a denuncio, which is no more than a warning.
>
> We also worked briefly as OPCs in Tenerife, which is much more difficult than in Gran Canaria, though the rates were correspondingly higher. We are at present [summer 1993] working in Alcudia, Mallorca also as OPCs. It is very lucrative here at the moment, because there is not as much competition from other OPCs. I must stress that in order to make decent money, one must speak a foreign language, though not perfectly: the best is German with French as a close second.

It is still possible to get a job as an OPC simply by showing up in the island resorts in the winter and asking around. Sometimes the time-share company will pay for your accommodation for a fortnight or a month or even reimburse your flight after they've seen whether you're any good. No one should expect to make a lot of money at the beginning, nor should they be too cavalier about the police. The *guardia civil* can come down very hard on anyone openly working the streets.

Exploiting the Tourist Market

As in all areas of heavy tourism, selling your handicrafts and busking should prove to be profitable. Martin and Shirine's money-making scheme in Benalmadena are typical: while she made money on the promenade making hairwraps each evening, he plied the English bars with a bag of rune stones and some well-placed rhetoric.

If your skills are literary, rather than manual or musical, you should try to sell an article to one of the many English language magazines and newspapers which thrive on tourism and resident expatriates. Get hold of, for example, the *Costa Blanca News* (Apartado 95, 03500 Benidorm, Alicante; 965 85 5286), *Lookout* (Puebla Lucia, Fuengirola, 07012 Malaga; 52-46 09 50) which issues detailed editorial guidelines, the *Majorca Daily Bulletin* (Calle San Felio 17, Apartado 304, Palma; 71-21 61 10) and the monthly *Canary Island Gazette* in Tenerife (22-33 51 62), and see what type of article would suit (probably articles about hitch-hiking would go over less well in this market than articles about yacht cruising). One enterprising writer whose yacht had foundered off the Portuguese coast earned £30 by writing about the disaster.

Barcelona has been especially recommended for busking. Although there will be plenty of foreign buskers already installed, the majority of passers-by give a small amount to anyone who is any good, which results in decent earnings after a couple of hours.

Sailing

Acorn Venture (137 Worcester Road, Hagley, Stourbridge, West Midlands DY9 0NW) need RYA qualified windsurfing and sailing instructors, BCU qualified kayak instructors and SPSA qualified climbing instructors for their activity centre on the coast north of Barcelona, for the season May to September. Similarly Rob Hastings Adventure Ltd (25 Southcourt Avenue, Leighton Buzzard, Beds. LU7 7QD) recruits sports instrucotrs for an activity centre in the Spanish Pyrenees during the school holidays.

There are many yachts moored along the Costa del Sol and all along the south coast. It should be possible to get work cleaning, painting or even guarding these luxury craft. There are also crewing possibilities as Peter Goldman discovered:

In Alicante I was taking a day off from hitching and was engrossed in the sunset when I noticed some folks coming off a sailboat. I asked them if they needed crew and they said they did. I hinted that I had little experience (really none) but they said that was no problem and I was on. We sailed around Spain including Ibiza and settled in Palma de Majorca. There were five of us and we decided we would look for work in Palma and live on the boat, but we soon discovered that Palma is a terrible place to look for work in January/February.

AGRICULTURE

Reports of people finding harvesting work in Spain are less common than in Greece, but they do filter through every so often. Traditionally there is an excess of cheap immigrant labour from North Africa and landless Spanish workers especially from Andalucia to pick the massive amounts of oranges, olives, grapes, and latterly avocadoes and winter strawberries. In places where migrant pickers congregate, the Caritas charity often sets up a temporary food stall or even arranges basic accommodation. This would certainly be a good place to find out about the best ways of getting hired.

A standard arrangement is to work in a semi-freelance capacity and earn on a percentage basis; for example you get 40% of the price at market of the olives or almonds that you have picked, while the patron gets 60%. This is what Brendan Barker did near Granada. He had hitched to an organic farm (whose address he had noticed on a card displayed in a health food shop in Brixton!) and worked happily there on a work-for-keep arrangement for six months, while picking olives at a neighbouring farm in his free time. He describes the job as 'not particularly hard work but a little boring' and was told of a local superstition which claimed that having olive trees on your land means that you have been cursed by God.

Another reader who enjoyed an informal spell of work in the country was Ana Güemes from Mexico. She made friends in a local bar with a vineyard's family and arranged to help with the harvest in the village of Villasandino near Burgos (200km north of Madrid) just for the food and drink and fun of it.

A variation on the theme of crop share picking has been heard of in Majorca where a traveller was invited by a farmer to help with the almond harvest in September. In lieu of wages he was allowed to keep half the nuts he had shaken from the trees to sell in the local market.

There are more conventional harvests, too, where travellers can be paid by the hour or the crate. The shortage of pickers willing to stay until the end of the season was sufficient in 1993 to prompt an expat New Zealander in Pamplona to negotiate jobs with Spanish growers and to advertise them in Britain. He claimed to be in a position to fill 350 vacancies for pickers and packers from the beginning of May till October. The wage range was £120-210 plus accommodation for a 50 or 60 hour week. At the time of writing, he was not replying to requests for updates, but it might be worth trying Working Holidays, c/o Kerry Scott, C/ Kaleberri 1, Berriozar, 31013 Pamplona (fax 48-30 15 10).

Another new discovery for this edition is the strawberry harvest from Easter to June around Huelva on the southwest coast of Spain. Dozens of strawberry farms are located around the village of Moguer (from which half of Columbus's sailors came), plus Cartaya and Lepe. The usual struggle to find work pertains; newcomers must go to the hiring café at 6am each morning until a farmer picks them up. Then there is the usual struggle to earn decent money. It is possible to earn £50 a day in the latter part of the season, though £30 would be the average for a practised picker and £10 for a beginner who is not yet used to bending double in the broiling sun.

When the strawberry harvest finishes in June, the apricots in the area are ready for harvesting. Elsewhere try the Lorca area for pepper picking in early November followed by artichoke picking. You might also try the famous wine-making region of Spain, the Rioja Alta which is centred on Logrono, Haro, Cenicero and Fuenmayor. The local councils in some of these towns along the River Ebro have been known to allow migrant grape-pickers to camp free of charge in a public space.

The organic farming movement *(Coordinadora d'Agricultura Ecològica)* in Spain can supply a list of about 50 farms which accept people to work in exchange for board and lodging. They stress that some of the member farmers want to hear only from people whose main interest is organic farming, not learning Spanish. To receive a copy of the list send an international reply coupon to C.A.E., Apt de Correus 2580, 08080 Barcelona.

Sunseed Trust (PO Box 2000, Cambridge CB3 0JF (01480-411784) has a small simple research centre near Almeria in southern Spain, in Europe's most arid region. The work involves helping with research into new ways to reclaim desert, purifying water and cooking with solar power, trying new composts, as well as the usual conservation tasks of maintaining terraces, footpaths, etc. Working visitors work 24 hours a week, and pay £48 in the winter and £57 in the summer for accommodation and vegetarian food. There is a £20 administration fee as well, even if you drop in on the offchance of finding a vacancy (Sunseed Desert Technology. Apdo, 9, Sorbas, 04270 Almeria). Bela Lal found conditions too rigorous for her taste and thought that the literature should have given a more accurate picture:

The centre is very remote and conditions are extremely basic; for example there are no mains services for gas, water or electricity. Potential volunteers will have to contend with holes-in-the-ground toilets and grey bed linen. Perhaps more important, this project is really for those with a deep-rooted interest in desertification. Those with a casual interest in conservation such as myself may find themselves out of their depth. The atmosphere is extremely communal and 'happy' which means that solitary types will have a hard time. Having said this, the surrounding valley is beautiful and rugged.

The information being sent out by Sunseed in 1994 does mention the low-tech nature of the facilities, e.g. the necessity of taking turns doing the chores like pumping and fetching water. (They do warn that there will be no white lab coats, but perhaps they should also mention the shortage of bright white sheets.)

AU PAIRS

Gone are the days when all the live-in positions in Spain were taken by Irish girls because of their Catholicism (so that it is said that the aristocracy of Spain regularly used such expressions as 'Begorra', at least according to Maura Laverty's amusing book about being a governess in Spain in the 1920s and 30s called *No More Than Human*).

The pocket money for au pairs at present is pta24,000 a month. Demi pairs earn pta15,000 and au pairs plus (who work 40 hours instead of 30, some of which may be tutoring the children in English) earn pta40,000.

Several au pair agencies in Spain are associated with language schools such as Centros Europeos Galve (Calle Principe 12-6°A, 28012 Madrid) which promises to help people already in Spain. Agencies are not confined to the big cities. For example Agencia Intercambios Culturales y Au Pair (C/ San Joaquin 17, 07003 Palma de Mallorca; 71-75 51 24) places au pairs in Majorca (as well as Madrid, Seville, Valencia and Alicante). The Canary Islands Bureau (Urb. Santiago B.4, 5° dcha, 38005 Santa Cruz de Tenerife) has families in the Canary Islands. The hundreds of private language schools can often prove a good source of local families looking for an English-speaking live-in helper. For example the O'Neill School of English (Ibarluce 20, Galdacano, 48960 Vizcaya; 4-56 49 17) recruits summer and year-long au pairs for Spanish families in the Bilbao area where the weekly pocket money is pta7,500.

One of the most energetic agencies is GIC (Gestión de Intercambios Culturales, Avda. Barón de Cárcer 48, Oficina 7P, Edificio Galerías, 46001 Valencia; 96-394 43 19). You can also try Relaciones Culturales Internacionales (address above), which is a non-profit club allied to the Ministry of Culture and the Ministry of Education, though they are not very reliable about answering correspondence. They charge an annual subscription fee of about £30 to join their club, which entitles you to make use of their broad range of services for the year, including one or more au pair placements.

Non-EU nationals who wish to work as au pairs should apply for a student visa before leaving their country of residence. Officially the Embassy requires both an offer of employment from the family and a letter from the school where the au pair is enrolled to study Spanish but in fact only the former is required, since the authorities recognise that it is usually impracticable for au pairs to enrol in classes before arrival in Spain.

VOLUNTARY WORK

The major workcamp organisations recruit for archaeological, conservation and other projects in Spain. The coordinating workcamp organisation in Spain is the Instituto de la Juventud (José Ortega y Gasset 71, 28006 Madrid; 401 66 52) whom you can approach independently as well as through a partner organisation in your own country. This address is also the Spanish Youth Hostels headquarters.

The owner of a 15th century farmhouse called Can Volta on the Costa Brava invites individuals and couples to come for short or long stays and exchange 14 hours of work a week for free rent. Jobs include gardening, painting and general upkeep. Working guests must pay a security deposit of pta30,000 and expect to spend about the same amount on food and entertainment. Details are available from Gary Angel, Can Volta, Calle Mayor 1, Calabruig, Bascara, 17483 Gerona (72-56 05 33).

Gibraltar

Gibraltar is an anomaly, an accident of history. It is a tiny British enclave on the Spanish coast with the same currency, the same institutions, etc. as the UK. Until as recently as 1982, Gibraltar was inaccessible from Spain. Hostility towards Spaniards persists and fuels the Independent Gibraltar Campaign, which is ludicrous in a place less than three square miles with a working population of just 12,000.

A further anomaly was created in 1993 when the Gibraltar Government decided to withdraw the automatic right of Britons to live and work on the Rock, in response to a rising unemployment rate of 10% and a perceived anxiety that the number of job-seeking Britons was rising. But because Gibraltar is a part of the European Union, it is obliged to allow other EU nationals to enter to look for work. It is only Britons who are affected by the change which came into effect July 1st 1993 and who are now supposed to obtain a work permit from the Employment & Training Board before they can legally take up a job. To get a work permit, the prospective employer must do the following: prove that no Gibraltarian or other resident is available to fill the vacancy, undertake to repatriate the worker if necessary and show that suitable accommodation has been found. Needless to say, not many employers are willing to jump through these hoops for the sake of legally employing a temporary waitress or labourer.

It seems that the new regulations have not decimated job opportunities for new arrivals as anticipated in some quarters, as reported by Mark Hurley in June 1994;

> At this time of year there are quite a few jobs around, but as for work permits, forget it. You can't get a job without a work permit and can't get a permit before you have a job (catch 22). But working without one is quite easy, since not many employers ask for one. The situation is not half as bad as the Employment Board says. I recommend bypassing them completely (since they will just make you angry and frustrated and make you think you shouldn't have come to this god-forsaken place). Start at one end of Gibraltar and work through asking at all the bars and restaurants, which should only take about two or three days. You will have a very good chance of work if you look tidy and sell yourself.

If you do find an employer who is willing to help you regularise your status, you must first obtain a Terms of Engagement form from the Employment & Training Board (Duke of Kent House, Line Wall Road; 42995) and apply to them for a work permit. To get a tax code you take the Terms of Engagement to the Income Tax Office (St Jago's Office Block, 331 Main St). (To apply for a tax rebate, fill out a tax return, a leaving form and produce your P7A form.) Next an ID card can be applied for at the Immigration Office in the Treasury Building.

Job Prospects

Gibraltar has always been a mecca for working travellers who, in the past, have found seemingly endless possibilities to work in construction, bars and cafés. The winding down of the defence presence in Gibraltar has meant a significant decrease in the amount of work around and is partly responsible for the climbing unemployment rate. But there are still 365 bars and restaurants in Gib (or so it is said) and in many cases not much competition from Gibraltarians for serving jobs.

Out of those hundreds of drinking holes, Andrew Giles recommends Charlie's Tavern as a good source of job information. Charlie's is the one favoured by the owners and crews of boats which are moored in Marina Bay. Also try his other Marina Bay recommendation, the Admiral Collingwood pub opposite Safeways. Other pubs which have recently offered work to travellers are Cool Blues Café, Half Way to Heaven and the Breadbin.

Even Adam Cook, who complained of the shortage of work in 'that litter-strewn blob of all that's undesirably British', managed to find a little yacht-varnishing work, and then was taken on to help redecorate a restaurant, before his big break came and he was taken on as paid crew back to England.

Another disappointed visitor to Gibraltar was Brigitte Blanka, who came away convinced that 'if you can find a job in Gibraltar, you can find work anywhere in the world'. She and her friend had several jobs while they were there (January to June) until they were most driven back to Germany by low wages and unbearably hot weather. In fact Brigitte found a job the day after arriving from Morocco. Bianca's Bistro in Marina Bay is reputed to be the busiest restaurant in Gibraltar and has a constant turnover of staff (mostly female). With only one day off in three weeks, Brigitte decided to try for a better job which took a disheartening four weeks to find. Some say that February/March is the best time to look since that is when the daytrippers from the Costa del Sol begin to arrive.

One source of work is the Burger King (formerly Wimpy's) which employed Andrew Giles, though he doesn't wax lyrical about it:

> Burger King always seem to be advertising for staff. It's not the best job in the world, and you'll more than likely get treated as an imbecile but, as I kept saying to myself, you earn money and you get local contacts. Actually, working there led me to finding out about my present job as chef in the Admiral Collingwood pub.

Accommodation

There are neither campsites nor youth hostels on the Rock and free camping is completely prohibited on the beaches. Camper vans are not even permitted in after midnight. The cheapest accommodation we have heard of is at the TOC H hostel.

It is so difficult to find cheap accommodation in Gibraltar, that many working travellers head for La Linea, the town in Spain just across the border. Initially they look for a cheap pension and then graduate to a flat, provided they and their flatmates can raise the £500 or so needed for a deposit. Nicola Sarjeant's word for La Linea is 'scummy'. No one — except perhaps for drug addicts and prostitutes — has a good word to say about it. Andrew Giles endured constant harrassment and two muggings before he decided to move to Gib. Although Mark Hurley was paying just £45 a week for a three-bedroom flat in La Linea, he got out of the place as soon as he found an affordable room in a shared flat in Gib.

One solution to the high cost of accommodation in Gibraltar is to live on a yacht or a barge in Scotts Yard, nicknamed the Graveyard since none of the boats ever leaves. Quite a few of the owners here take in travellers for a small rent and sometimes it is even possible to rent a whole boat. If you can prove to a boat owner that you are trustworthy, you may even be able to stay free of charge while doing some boat-sitting. Sheppards Marina is where most of the yacht work is carried out, whereas Marina Bay (near Scotts Yard) is where the long distance yachts are moored. A good source of information on jobs and lodgings in the marinas is the newsagents next door to Bianca's Bar in the New Marina and to a lesser extent the Star Bar or Aragon Pub in central Gibraltar. A notice board worth using is located in Sheppards Marina equipment shop at the Old Marina.

In bars in La Linea, you will no doubt hear about a number of unsavoury scams such as approaching cars queuing to enter Gibraltar and selling them a phony entry card or smuggling cigarettes from Gib and selling them in Spain. According to Mark Hurley, if you ask any school boy in Gib what he wants to do when he grows up he will say 'be a smuggler'. Ben Hockley noticed that as soon as the female border guard on the Spanish side knocked off work at 9pm, hundreds of Spanish women would walk across the border fat with cartons under their skirts to make a profit of about £50 a trip. It is convincing proof that the single Europe without border controls is infinitely more civilized.

Opportunities for fixing up a crewing position on a yacht are abundant; see the chapter *Working a Passage*. It took Mirjam Koppelaars a week to hitch-hike from her home in Holland to Gibraltar but only a couple of hours to arrange to crew on a 40-foot transatlantic yacht. If you want to arrange a free lift by land, frequent the Pig & Whistle and Rodolfo's Bar where long-distance lorry drivers congregate. According to Andrew Giles they are unlikely to offer a lift to a complete stranger.

Portugal

Portugal has always been considered a virtual desert by travellers looking for work. The mailbag for this book for several editions running has had barely a whisper about work opportunities in Portugal. The few who have found work have often found that the wages were appallingly low, which simply reflected the underdevelopment of Portugal's economy. Yet Portugal entered the 1990s with one of the fastest growing economies in Europe and with a modest unemployment rate of less than 6% which is predicted to remain steady.

There is a long and vigorous tradition of English people settling in Portugal, and the links between the two countries are strong. There are large numbers of expatriates around Lisbon and on the Algarve coast, many of whom are retired. English-speaking travellers might expect to find odd jobs in this community, and there are some possibilities. But the friendly relations between foreigners and locals mean that the former are quite happy to employ the latter for such jobs.

Ask expatriates for help and advice. Probably the best idea is to scan the advertisements in the weekly *Anglo-Portuguese News* (Apartado 113, 2765 Estoril; 244 3115). You can of course place your own advert in this paper, though the rates are fairly expensive. Also check *The News* (PO Box 13, 8400 Lagoa; fax 82-341201) which covers the Algarve and is published fortnightly. It has a large English language classified section in which you can place a 12-word advert free of charge. The other English language publication worth trying is the monthly *Madeira Island Bulletin* (Apt. 4621, 9008 Funchal, Madeira). You can always try to contribute a story to these publications.

The Regulations

Portugal has always had comparatively liberal immigration policies, possibly because it has never been rich enough to attract a lot of foreign job-seekers. Like other EU countries, it stipulates that foreign workers from EU countries should obtain a residence permit if they are staying more than three months. But the regulations say that seasonal workers who will be working for less than eight months do not require a residence permit, which simplifies the red tape for anyone working a season in the tourist industry for example. To apply for a residence permit, you need among other things a letter of confirmation and duration of employment from your employer.

The Consular Section of the British Embassy in Portugal (Rua da Estrela 4, 1200 Lisbon; 1-395 40 82/3) distributes information on employment and on taking up residence in Portugal (updated March 1994) which goes into more detail than the information from the Consulate-General in London.

Non-EU nationals must provide the usual battery of documents before they can be granted a residence visa, from a document showing that the Ministry of Labour *(Ministerio do Trabalho)* has approved the job to a medical certificate in Portuguese. After arrival the non-EU applicant must take the contract of employment to the *Serviço de Estrangeiros e Fronteiras* (Aliens Office) in Lisbon at Avenida António Augusto Aguiar 20 (1-523324/523395) or in Oporto,

Coimbra, Faro, Madeira and the Azores. The final stage is to take a letter of good conduct provided by the applicant's own embassy to the police for the work and residence permit. There are stories of non-Europeans arranging a residence permit after finding a job on arrival, but this is difficult.

Tourism

As in Italy, the Portuguese are protective of their tourist industry and this has been formalised in law. For example if you have an English guide on a tour coach, you are obliged to carry a Portuguese one too. But of course there are British tour companies which may hire you as a courier or rep, and property companies which want English-speaking time-share sales people (see the relevant section in *Spain* on the job of OPC). Another possibility is a chain of donut cafés in and around Lisbon whose expatriate owner, according to a rumour Heather McCulloch heard, employs a number of foreigners

Any EU national aged 18-27 with a vocational qualification in Leisure and Tourism or Marketing (but not a university degree) should investigate the EU-funded Petra schemes. In 1994 they were offering attractive packages of one month's language tuition in Devon followed by three months' work experience in marketing or tourism in Portugal in the autumn, for a mere £100. Details are available from ProEuropa (Europa House, Sharpham Drive, Totnes, Devon TQ9 5HE; 0803 864526).

Another possibility is the Novastor Hostel & Recreation Centre in Porches near Lagoa on the Algarve which is open from 1st July to 15th September. Dave Stokes stumbled upon it by chance when he was down to his last £5, and was hired immediately as a cook for three months.

On the whole it was a lot of fun, although the work can be long and hard. In the kitchen I did a 10+ hour stint in stifling heat and primitive conditions, and all for £18 a week plus a share of the tips, but there's also plenty of opportunity to play hard.

The management has sent a recent assurance that the long hours have been eliminated, and people now work for a maximum of eight hours a day for a bed, food and pocket money.

Occasionally a traveller who arrives with the intention of staying in Portugal for just a few weeks finds a bar on the Algarve willing to hire them and they stay on for a season. Entertainers and watersports instructors will have a better chance than unskilled people.

The bull ring does not offer much scope to working travellers, but it is has been known for an English person to work in it. Virginia Montesol (her ring name) went to Spain, made contacts, moved on to Portugal and for two years fought as a *Rejoneador* in the Portuguese bullrings. In Portugal the bullfighter is usually on a horse and the bull is not killed. Virginia was an amateur and therefore was not paid but stayed free with a country family; the qualifications are to be an excellent rider with nerves of steel.

Teaching

The market for English tuition is more buoyant than anywhere in Europe, especially in the teaching of young children and especially in the north. Apart from in the main cities of Lisbon and Oporto, both of which have British Council offices, jobs crop up in historic provincial centres such as Coimbra (where there is also a British Council) and Braga and in small seaside towns like Aveiro and Póvoa do Varzim. The RSA/Cambridge Certificate is widely requested by schools, but a number of schools (especially those advertising vacancies in June, July and August) seem willing to consider anyone with a BA plus a promising CV and photo.

Most teachers in Portugal have either answered adverts in the educational press or are working for International House, which has ten affiliated schools in Portugal. One of the most well-established groups of schools is the Cambridge School group (Avenida da Liberdade 173, 1200 Lisbon; 1-352 74 74) which every year imports up to 100 teachers.

The consensus seems to be that wages are low, but have been improving at a favourable rate in view of the cost of living. On the positive side, working conditions are generally relaxed. The normal salary range is 130,000-160,000 escudos per month gross, and higher in Lisbon. Some schools pay lower salaries but subsidise or pay for flights and accommodation. Teachers being paid on an hourly basis should expect to earn between 1,300 and 1,500 escudos an hour and possibly up to 2,000 escudos.

Business

If you know some Portuguese, you might find an opening in an office; without a knowledge of the language, chances are remote. For temporary office or manual vacancies, try Manpower in Lisbon at Praça José Fontana 9c (1-352 54 55) and also in Oporto (2-200 24 26), Albufeira on the Algarve (89-58 81 13) and in the Azores (96-62 98 30). Three other Lisbon employment agencies are listed by the British Consulate:

José Joaquim Calvo, Rua Marques da Silva, 46-1°, 1100 Lisbon (1-355 46 65).
SELGEC, Rua Alexandre Herculano 39-1°, 1200 Lisbon (1-54 35 05).
SELMARK Marketing, Rua do Salitre, 175-3°, 1200 Lisbon (1-387 71 00).
The British-Portuguese Chamber of Commerce (Rua da Estrela 8, 1200 Lisbon and Rua Sá da Bandeira, 784-2°-E/F, 4000 Oporto) may be able to offer general advice to people seeking jobs in commerce.

Agriculture

Although it is the fifth largest wine producer in the world, we have never heard of any traveller picking grapes. The farms are generally so small, and the farmers so poor, that hiring extra help is simply not done. In the words of the General Director of the Ministry of Agriculture in the late 80s, 'Due to the heterogeneity of the specie's distribution whose maturation is since May to November and due the small dimension of the farms, we employ the local handwork'.

Voluntary and Au Pair

There isn't a strong voluntary movement in Portugal and what organisations there are seem loath to send details. In all cases applications should be sent through a partner organisation in the applicant's own country, for example Concordia and UNA (Wales) in the UK. Here are the principal organisations which need volunteers during the summer:

Instituto da Juventude, Av. da Liberdade No. 194, 1200 Lisbon (1-315 1955; fax 315 1960). The Ministry of Youth is the most reliable of the organisations and the largest, recruiting 750 volunteers to work on conservation and restoration projects.

ATEJ (Associacao de Turismo Estudantil e Juvenil), PO Box 4586, 4009 Oporto (Rua Joaquim Antonio Aguiar No. 255, 4300 Oporto). Places volunteers on farms, archaeological digs, projects with handicapped, etc. Also places au pairs.

Companheiros Construtores, Rua Pedro Monteiro 3-1, 3000 Coimbra (39-71 67 47). Needs up to 200 volunteers to work on three to four week projects in the poorest parts of Portugal to do construction work, agricultural jobs and help with underprivileged people. Inclusive fee $200.

International Friendship League, Apartado 36, 2890 Alcochete. Tel: 234 1082. As of several years ago, the IFL was arranging live-in English tutoring placements and voluntary workcamps in the summer. Membership costs 20,000 escudos.

Turicoop, Rua Pascoal-Melo, 15-1°DTO, 1100 Lisbon. Tel: 531804. Another organisation for which confirmation was not forthcoming. They used to arrange workcamps to protect nature, carry out archaeological digs, etc. and arrange au pair stays in Portugal.

Au pairing is not very common in Portugal, and very few placements are made by UK agencies to Portugal. The weekly pocket money is by far the lowest in Europe. Manpower listed above may be able to assist. Summer openings are most likely to occur in the school holidays between the end of July and end of September.

Switzerland & Austria

With an incredibly low unemployment rate and a high proprotion of foreign workers, Switzerland would seem to be the working traveller's nirvana. But one of the reasons Switzerland is able to preserve such a low figure is that the state imposes strict work permit requirements on all foreigners. This together with the very high cost of living while you are job-hunting and the (deserved) Swiss reputation for hard work discourage many travellers. But people who have spent time working in Switzerland and have come to know the Swiss have nothing but compliments. According to Tony Mason who picked grapes four seasons running and worked as a builder:

The Swiss are a genuinely friendly and hospitable people and we are often invited to local homes for meals and on outings to the mountains. Hitching here is excellent and also a valuable source of potential employers. I can't say enough good things about the Swiss.

The Regulations in Switzerland

On the other hand, the Swiss have often been accused of xenophobia (fear and loathing of foreigners) and their immigration policies are designed to make life difficult for foreign workers, although they depend on them in large measure to keep their economy flourishing. They have refrained from ratifying the European Economic Area Agreement, and have obtained an exemption from the free exchange of labour within Europe until 1998.

In Switzerland, there is no separate document for working. A residence permit

(Aufenthaltsbewilligung or *autorisation de séjour)* covers both the right of abode and employment. Employers are entitled to a certain number of *Permis* A or *Saisonbewilligung* which are valid for up to nine months in one year. Rules and quotas vary from canton to canton. Official regulations require that the permit be posted to an address outside the country, though it is sometimes possible to obtain one on-the-spot. One significant advantage of the Swiss system is that there is no requirement for the work permit to be applied for or picked up in your home country. There are about 100,000 *saisonniers* or *Permis* A holders at present, the vast majority of whom are from southern Europe. *Permis* B and C are for more permanent work and very difficult to get. One way of acquiring a *Permis* B without being subject to the strict quotas is to become a cross-border commuter *(frontalier/Grenzganger)* which refers to people who work in Switzerland but live in France or Germany within 10km of the Swiss border.

Although the official literature does not mention it, readers have written to say that they have obtained four-month permits. These do not seem to be so strictly limited, though the fee which the employer must pay is much higher. Unfortunately Australians and New Zealanders are not eligible for permits and with reports of four or five policemen posted in ski resorts simply to check visas, the chances of working black are decreasing. According to Mary Hall who worked as a nanny at a hotel in Wengen, everyone in Wengen had a permit. Her employer had no trouble obtaining the four-month permit for her (though he never did pay for it as he promised). After picking it up from the hotel, she nipped across the border into Italy so that she could have the compulsory chest X-ray on crossing the border back into Switzerland.

With a residence permit you become eligible for the state insurance scheme, for the minimum wage (approximately £800 a month) and the excellent legal tribunal for foreign workers which arbitrates in disputes over working conditions, pay and dismissals. Accident insurance is compulsory for all foreign workers and the employer pays the bulk of the premium, though foreign workers should take out their own health insurance. One advantage of having a residence permit is that in certain resort areas it entitles the holder to a *Carte d'Indigène* or 'red card' available from the *Controle de l'Habitant/Fremdenpolizei* (Aliens Police). The card may allow you to travel on public transpsort at a subsidised local rate, and also to buy a cheap seasonal ski pass.

A reciprocal Swiss/UK trainee exchange agreement began in 1989 which allows up to 400 young Britons to gain work experience in Switzerland for up to 18 months after completing their studies. Permits for temporary trainee placements *(stagiaires)* can be obtained from BIGA (Sektion Auswanderung und Stagiaires, Monbijoustrasse 43, 3003 Bern; 31-322 29 03). Information in the first instance should be requested from the Overseas Labour Service of the Department of Employment, W5, Moorfoot, Sheffield S1 4PQ.

Casual Work

In many cases the local supply of labour is so clearly inadequate (in the building trade, tourism, fruit picking, etc.) that there are many people working without the benefits of a residence permit, willing to run the risk of exploitation and occasionally even deportation. There are frequent purges, especially at the beginning of the summer and winter seasons, and possible fines of SFr3,000 for an employer caught employing people black. You are probably more inconspicuous working in the cities, but law enforcement tends to be stricter there. One contributor was working in a village outside Lausanne, building a house across from a policeman who never raised the matter of permits after they had let him win at ping pong.

Although Switzerland doesn't go so far as to demand that buskers get a work permit, Leda Meredith was surprised to find that the city of Bern (a 'goldmine for buskers') publishes a leaflet about when and where busking is permitted. Merchants keep a supply and will not hesitate to give you one if you transgress.

TOURISM

It has been said that the Swiss invented tourism. Certainly their hotels and tourism courses are still the training ground and model for hoteliers worldwide. For the hotels and catering industry, a rapid short-term injection of labour is an economic necessity both for the summer and winter season — June/July to September and December to April.

Swiss hotels are very efficient and tend to be impersonal, since you will be one in an endless stream of seasonal workers from many countries. The very intense attitude to work among the Swiss means that hours are long (often longer than stipulated in the contract): a typical working week would consist of at least five nine-hour days working split shifts.

Whether humble or palatial, the Swiss hotel or restaurant in which you find a job will probably insist on very high standards of cleanliness and productivity. After working at an independent hostel and then a 3-star restaurant in Interlaken, Kathy Russell from Australia concluded that 'the Swiss are very picky to work for, so a good temperament is needed'.

On the other hand, the majority are *korrekt*, i.e. scrupulous about keeping track of your overtime and pay you handsomely at the end of your contract. Alison May summarised her summer at the Novotel-Zürich-Airport: 'On balance, the wages were good but we really had to earn them'. The 1994 gross *(brutto)* monthly wage for a 42-hour week is SFr2,500, about half of which is lost in deductions for board and lodging, tax and insurance (with slight cantonal variations).

Steve Rout sums up the joys of working in a Swiss resort:

In my opinion Switzerland can't be recommended too highly, especially in the winter. If you are lucky, you will get fit and healthy, learn a new language, earn plenty of money, and make some great friends, all in one of the most beautiful areas of the world.

The Job Hunt

Provided you have a reasonable CV and a knowledge of languages (preferably German), a speculative job hunt in advance is worthwhile. For example Katherine Jenkins wrote to several Swiss hotels in August/September and was gratified to have a choice of three definite contracts for the winter season. Eighteen-year old Kate Billington also wrote (in the relevant language) to about 20 hotels taken from a hotel directory and was offered a contract for the period mid-April to early July by the Hotel Beau Rivage in Thun. Two hotel groups worth trying are Fassbind Hotels, Via Basilea 28, 6903 Lugano and Park Hotels Waldhaus, 7018 Flims-Waldhaus.

The Swiss Hoteliers' Association has a department called Hotel Job SHV which runs a placement scheme (in German-speaking Switzerland only) for registered EU students from the age of 18 who are willing to spend three to four months doing an unskilled job in a Swiss hotel or restaurant between June and September. Excellent knowledge of the German language is essential to apply for a job. Member hotels issue a standard contract on which salary and deductions are carefully itemised. From the gross salary of SFr2,500, the basic deduction for board and lodging (for any job) is SFr810 and a further 12-15% is taken off for taxes and insurance. Tips for waiting staff can bring net earnings back up to the gross. Application forms are available from the Swiss Hoteliers' Association,

WILLIAM SWAN

GERMANY

Garmisch

Mayrhofen

Innsbruck

Tyrol

AUSTRIA

Oberstdorf

Lech

St. Anton

Vorarlberg

Brand

Davos Platz

St. Moritz

Lake of
Constance

St. Gallen

LIECHTENSTEIN

ZURICH

ZUG

Lucerne

SWITZERLAND

ITALY

Lugano

TICINO

St. Gotthard

Grindelwald

Interlaken

Kandersteg

Crans Montana

Sierre

Saas-Fee

Thun

Sion

VALAIS

Zermatt

BASEL

JURA

Delemont

Rhone River

Saxon

Thyon

La Chaux de Fonds

Kerzers

BERN

Murten

Martigny

Verbier

Neuchatel

Leysin

Aigle

Montreux

Champery

Vevey

Pully

Lausanne

VAUD

Lake Geneva

Cote Lake

GENEVA

Coppet

FRANCE

Monbijoustrasse 130, 3001 Bern; 31-370 43 33. The deadline for applications is 20th April and there is an upfront registration fee of SFr50.

Quite a few British travel companies and camping holiday operators are active in Switzerland such as Mark Warner, Canvas and Eurocamp. Venture Abroad (Richmond House, High St, Cranleigh, Surrey GU6 8RF) hire 'carefully chosen British students' to meet and guide youth groups around Gstaad, Grindelwald, Interlaken and several other places. The Swiss Travel Service Ltd (Bridge House, 55-59 High Road, Broxbourne, Herts. EN10 7DT; 01992 456143) hires about 25 resort reps and tour guides who are talented linguists. Most ski tour operators mount big operations in Switzerland, such as Crystal Holidays and Ski Total (see page 104). The main disadvantage of being hired outside Switzerland is that the wages will be on a British scale rather than on the much more lucrative Swiss one.

The Swiss organisation Village Camps S.A. advertises widely its desire to recruit people over 21 as general counsellors, EFL teachers, sports instructors and nurses on its summer and winter camps in Leysin, Saas Fee, Saas Grund, Anzere, Fiesch, Les Collons, La Tzoumas and Morgins on the principle that 'staff want to enjoy Switzerland as tourists at little or no cost' (i.e. low wages and no necessity of getting a work permit). In exchange for working fairly long hours, counsellors and domestic staff receive free room and board, insurance and an 'expense allowance' of SFr275 for 10 days and SFr325 for 14 days. The minimum period of work is just four weeks. Application forms are available from Village Camps, c/o Chalet Seneca, 1854 Leysin (25-34 23 38/fax 34 25 73).

The Jobs in the Alps Agency (PO Box 388, London SW1X 8LX) places waiters, waitresses, chamber staff, kitchen assistants and porters in Swiss hotels, cafés and restaurants in Swiss resorts, 200 in winter, 150 in summer (see page 105). The Alpine Agency run by Jacqueline Ecoeur (C.P. 22, 1981 Vex; 27-27 29 22) is a temporary job agency which places British people in a similar range of seasonal jobs plus au pairs.

Summer language and sports camps abound in Switzerland. Susanna Macmillan hitch-hiked from Italy to Crans Montana in the Swiss Alps in the autumn and within three days had arranged a job as a *monitrice* at the International School there. The job, which was to teach English and sports, came with room and board plus the low sum of SFr850 per month. (Perhaps one reason the job was so easy to get was because of the 60-hour weeks and compulsory overtime with no compensation.)

Most people go out and fix up their jobs in person, as recommended in the section on *Winter Resorts*. Steve Rout, a resort expert, has always found this to be the most satisfactory way to find work. He recommends looking in Les Portes de Soleil at Champery, Les Crosets as well as the major resorts of Leysin, Verbier, Thyon and Crans Montana. This valley is a major road and rail route and is ideal for concentrated job hunting. Another area which has been recommended is the Jura between La Chaux-de-Fonds and Delémont.

Surprisingly, tourist offices may be of use. Susanna Macmillan reported that the tourist office in Crans Montana issued photocopied lists of 'Jobs Available' and were advertising for summer staff in March. Always check notice boards and adverts in local papers like *L'Est Vaudois* for the Montreux region or *Le Nouvelliste* in the Rhone Valley.

Like most people, Andrew Winwood found the job hunt tough going:

All in all I asked in over 200 places for ski-season work, but eventually could have counted 10-12 possibilities. Going on that rate, it would be possible to get work after asking at 50 or 60 places, but of course the 'Grand Law of Sod' would prevail. As far as I can see, it's a simple case of ask, ask, ask and ask again until you get work. It was costing me about £80 a week to

*live in Switzerland, so I couldn't let up until I definitely had a way of getting
the money back.*

Although job-hunting on the spot works for some, there is no guarantee of
success. The most promising time to introduce yourself to potential employers
is April/May for the summer and September/October for the winter. November
is a bad time to arrive since most of the hotels are closed and the owners away
on holiday. When David Loveless arrived in Verbier in mid-November, he
declined an invitation to add his name to the bottom of eight sheets of people
waiting for jobs. After moving on to Crans Montana, David soon found work
at the Hotel de l'Etrier as a *chasseur* (messenger/odd jobs man).

Rob Jefferson had no luck whatsoever and describes his discouraging experiences job-hunting in Swiss resorts:

*We arrived in Grindelwald in mid-December, and stayed in the youth hostel
(along with 11 others all looking for work). After ten days, only one of the
hostellers had found work, and so we left for Saas Fee with half-promises
of work from seven hotels of the many we'd phoned. We were flatly refused
by six but the seventh promised Sonja my girlfriend a job as a waitress if
the pre-contracted waiter did not show up the next day. Sonja is very
attractive, speaks near perfect English and good German. We had been
around about 70 hotels in all and it took a late arrival for her to get a job.
If this was the case for her, what about me? No chance.*

The Club Vagabond in Leysin (25-34 13 21), which has frequently been
mentioned by travellers as an international meeting place for foreign workers,
was in danger of being turned into time share apartments a year or two ago but
has found a new owner who plans to maintain the same atmosphere. It is a
favourite destination for Australians and New Zealanders in search of work,
some of whom end up working in the Club itself. While looking for work, Club
Vagabond is also the cheapest place to stay in Leysin.

Another recommended meeting place with American overtones is Balmer's
Gasthaus in Interlaken (Hauptstrasse 23-25, 3800 Interlaken; 36-22 19 61) whose
staff is almost entirely English-speaking. They say that they do not have any
specific requirements when looking for staff other than that the person must be
a 'people person.' They also offer the usual hostel arrangement of giving free
room and board to those who do a few hours of work a day. The owner Erich
Balmer is willing to advise on local job openings in Interlaken.

Anyone who has connections with the Scout movement might be interested
in Andrew Green's three-month job in Kandersteg at the Scout Centre where
everybody speaks English and does the whole gamut of jobs from sports instructor
to toilet cleaner. The staff aren't paid but they eat, sleep and ski free of charge.

AGRICULTURE

Swiss Farm Organisation

One report estimated that nearly one-third of farm hands employed during
the summer are foreigners (mainly Portuguese). Young people who are more
interested in rural experiences than in money may wish to do a stint on a
Swiss farm. The Landdienst-Zentralstelle/Service Agrigole (Central Office for
Voluntary Farm Work) located at Mühlegasse 13 (Postfach 728), 8025 Zürich
(1-261 44 88; fax 1-261 44 32) fixes up farm placements for a minimum of three
weeks for young people from Western Europe who know some German or
French. (This scheme used to be open to all nationalities but the Aliens Police
now limit participants to European nationals.) Workers are called 'volunteers'
and can work for up to two months without a work permit. They must pay a
good faith bond of SFr50.

Most places in German-speaking Switzerland are available from the beginning of March to the end of October and in the French part from March to June and mid-August to the end of October, though there are a few places in the winter too. Each canton has a farm placement representative who liaises with the Zürich headquarters. Usually about 50 British young people are placed, though there is no strict quota. It is also possible to apply through Concordia for an administration fee of £25, preferably at least a month before you wish to work.

Despite Switzerland's reputation as an advanced nation, there are still thousands of small family farms, especially in the German-speaking cantons, where traditional farming methods are practised. Part of the reason for this is that not many mechanical threshers or harvesters can function on near vertical slopes (neither can every human harvester for that matter).

The hours are long, the work is hard and much depends on the volunteer's relationship with the family. Most people who have worked on a Swiss farm report that they are treated like one of the family, which means both that they are up by 6 or 7am and working till 9pm alongside the farmer and that they are invited to accompany the family on any excursions, such as the weekly visit to the market to sell the farm-produced cheeses. The arrangement is similar in many way to the au pair arrangement; in fact young women who get placed on a Swiss farm may be asked to do more chores inside the house than out. Gillian Forsyth found the life lonely on her isolated farm and she had few chances to improve her French since she was often alone in the house with the baby or in the fields with the goats.

Ruth McCarthy gives an idea of the range of tasks to do on the farm, and a taste of village life:

> *The work on my farm in the Jura included cleaning out cow stalls, hay making, grass cutting, poultry feeding, manure spreading, vegetable amd fruit-picking, wood cutting, earth moving, corn threshing and also house-work, cooking and looking after the children. The food was very wholesome and all produced on the farm: cheeses, fresh milk, home-made jam, fresh fruit, etc. The church bells struck throughout the day and peeled at 6am and 9pm to open and close each day. As well as church bells the sound of cow bells was also present so that it was quite noisy at times. There was little night life unless you went to a gasthof bar in the village. Anyway it's probably better to get a good night's sleep.*

In addition to the good farm food and comfortable bed, you will be paid SFr20 per day worked. Necessary qualifications for participating in this scheme are that you be between 17 and 30 and that you have a basic grounding in French or German. On these small Swiss farms, English is rarely spoken and many farmers speak a dialect which some find incomprehensible.

Unofficial Work

Much of Swiss agriculture consists of dairy and cereal farming. Fruit and vegetables are grown in a few regions of the country especially along the Rhone Valley from Montreux to Sion. Tobacco is grown around Bern and picked in August. Cherries are picked from the end of June until the beginning of August, and plums, apples and pears are picked in September/October. You might find some harvesting work in any of the following:

Cherries	Bern, Aargau, Basel, Zug
Strawberries	Upper Rhone Valley
Peaches	Upper Rhone Valley, Ticino (Italian border), Vaud
Apricots	Valais, Upper Rhone Valley
Pears	Valais
Apples	Bern, Thurgau, Valais, Zürich, Vaud (around Aigle)

Tomatoes	Bern, Vaud, Valais
Lettuces	Ticino
Tobacco	Ticino, Rhone Valley/Montreux
Hazelnuts	throughout Switzerland

The area along the River Rhone between Martigny and Saxon in Valais has been recommended for agricultural work. Visit the local markets and make enquiries. Farmers around Martigny growing tomatoes, carrots and other crops may require casual workers.

Although Glen Mitchell was discouraged to find that New Zealanders cannot get work permits for Switzerland, he decided to try his luck in the tobacco-growing region around Bern:

I headed into the countryside between the towns of Murten and Kerzers at the end of July. The very first farmer I asked sent me up the road to his neighbour who offered me six weeks work picking tobacco leaves and told me I could start the next day. I was given a room in the farmer's house and excellent food. I enjoyed the company of a very nice Swiss family, was able to add a lot to my extremely limited German vocabulary and learn all about the work attitudes of the Swiss (the hours were from 7am to 7pm). The pay was SFr1,200. I was lucky to arrive at the start of the tobacco season (1st August) and to find work within half an hour.

Grimly Corridor also had a lucky experience. While drinking in a bar in the Jura, he fell into conversation with a farmer who knew enough English to convey his request. He wanted someone to help him on his small farm (13 cows, 10 horses) until the snows fell. Grimly was delighted to accept and was soon driving a tractor, ploughing fields, looking after the cows, etc. for SFr50 a day.

Paul Barton arranged to work for the same farmer he'd worked for through the Landdienst-Zentralstelle. He was given a work permit and paid nearly three times his previous summer's wage. He was also expected to do twice as much work, which was impossible when he'd already been working 16 hours a day. For his own amusement he kept track of the number of hours worked and counted up to a staggering 1,250 in ten weeks before returning home for some essential rest and relaxation.

One group of farmers who may have a more balanced outlook form the organic farming organisation of Switzerland. For details of working-for-keep in one of these send an IRC to the new WWOOF coordinator: Thomas Schwager, Postfach 615, 9001 St. Gallen (tel/fax 71-23 24 15).

Grape-Picking

Like every country in Europe south of Scotland, Switzerland produces wine. The main area is in the Vaud north of Lake Geneva, but also in Valais around Sion and Sierre, where the harvest begins on October 6th, give or take a day or two, with surprising regularity. Steven King wrote during the *vendange* from the Vaud village of Féchy to say that British pickers are still toiling away in the fields of the Vaud despite the presence of East Europeans some of whom can earn in ten days the equivalent of five months wages at home.

Valerie Birtwistle recommends the Swiss *vendange*:

I had a marvellous time at the Cretegny farm in Bougy-Villars. The owners were extremely kind and friendly, the food was first-class, the wine was plentiful and we were paid a very generous £140 for 7½ days of work.

Vineyards are found along the north shores of Lake Geneva on either side of Lausanne. One district is known as La Cote, between Coppet and Morges west of Lausanne, and the other is the Lavaux, a remarkably beautiful region of vineyards, rising up the hillside along the 25km between Pully on the outskirts of Lausanne and the tourist city of Montreux. The vineyards, enclosed within low stone walls, slope so steeply that all the work must be done by hand, and the job of portering is recommended only for the very fit. The harvest here is later than in France (early to mid-October) when the weather is beginning to get cold and rainy (the latter curtails work). Also the harvest is shorter (a week to ten days), because of the lower density of grapes per hectare.

Despite these disadvantages, many grape pickers prefer the Swiss *vendange* to the French. The pay is considerably higher than in the French harvest, usually SFr70-100 a day in addition to room and board. The accommodation and food are generally of a higher standard, and everyone seems to enjoy the festive atmosphere of the Swiss harvest.

If you can get hold of some names and addresses, write to the farmers (in French) well in advance to give them a chance to get you a four-month permit. It is also possible to find work on the spot as Rizla Plus did:

I arrived in Lausanne on the 16th of October. Heading east I cycled as far as Chexbres before being offered work. I was in the fields the next day and eating delicious Vaudois specialities, drinking lashings of wine and sleeping in a hotel. At the end of ten days (with seven and a half days worked) I was paid a hefty SFr530, had made lots of friends, improved my French to incredible levels and gained important knowledge about where to go for the winter.

Without a permit you should look for farms which someone has just left, leaving the *vigneron* desperate for pickers. Dave Bamford had also heard about the glories of the Swiss *vendange* and, after completing the harvest in France, headed for Geneva and Lausanne. Perhaps because he lacked a bicycle, he had no luck. He next tried some vineyards in the Zürich region but found there that farmers hire the same people every year, generally family members.

BUILDING

There are far fewer Swiss nationals working as building labourers than foreigners. There is a building boom in Geneva at present but throughout the country there are many buildings being reroofed or expanded. Tony Mason did some roofing work a few years ago for which he was paid SFr15 an hour in addition to cellar accommodation. Apparently this is considered to be cheap labour and yet it funded Tony's first trip to America.

In addition to building improvement in residential areas, resorts have a continual demand for painters and builders out of season. Much of the construction work is done by Portuguese, Spanish and Italian workers. Ask them for advice or visit timber yards or estate agents *(agences immobilieres)*.

In winter you may be able to find occasional work chopping firewood or mending roofs. A special opportunity for odd jobbers is afforded by the Swiss law that prohibits snow on roofs from reaching more than two metres depth. Apparently casual labourers are needed at the giant vegetable market in Zürich (near the football stadium). The wage for shifting heavy sacks of produce is £8 an hour. It will probably be necessary to sleep at the market since farmers start arriving long before dawn breaks.

AU PAIR and VOLUNTARY WORK

For those interested in a domestic position with a Swiss family there are rules laid down by each Swiss canton, so there are variations. You must be a female between the ages of 17 and 29 (18 in Geneva) from Western Europe or North America, stay for a minimum of one year and up to 18 months, obtain a proper work permit and attend a minimum of three hours a week of language classes in Zürich, four in Geneva. Families in Zürich pay half the language school fees of SFr60-100 per month but au pairs in Geneva have to bear the whole cost of SFr130.

Au pairs in Switzerland work for a maximum of 30 hours per week, plus babysitting once or twice a week. The monthly salary varies among cantons and is, for example, a minimum of SFr620 for 20 year olds (SFr690 for 21 year olds) in Geneva, and SFr570-680 in Zürich. In addition, the au pair gets a four or five week paid holiday plus SFr18 for days off (to cover food).

There are two major au pair agencies: Verein der Freundinnen Junger Mädchen (FJM), Zähringerstrasse 36, 8001 Zürich (1-252 38 40) whose registration fee is SFr50 plus a further SFr100 when a family has been found. In French this organisation is called Amies de la Jeune Fille (rue du Simplon 2, 1006 Lausanne; 21-616 29 88). The other agency is Pro Filia which has seven branches including 51 rue de Carouge, 1205 Geneva; 22-329 84 62, for the French-speaking part, and Beckenhofstr. 16, 8035 Zürich; 1-363 55 01, for the German part. Other private agencies do operate, for example Swiss-O-Pair run by Ettie Moesker (Case Postale 295, CH-1233 Geneva; 22-757 59 14) who makes placements in both French and German-speaking Switzerland also places girls with families in the French border zone of Geneva which means that they are not subject to the work permit and other restrictions.

Although it is hard to imagine the necessity, several of the international workcamp organisations operate in Switzerland to do conservation work or building on behalf of the underprivileged. For example the German organisation IBG (Schlosserstrasse 28, 70180 Stuttgart) sends volunteers to a project renovating footpaths in the mountains near the Simplon Pass in late August. Another organisation based in St. Gallen uses German-speaking volunteers on its environmental protection projects, mostly in the Zermatt and St. Gotthard areas; contact Internationale Umweltschutz Korps, Postfach 1, 9101 Herisau for further details of their summer workcamps. Genossenschaft Campo Cortoi (6647 Mergoscia) needs volunteers in its reconstruction of an old alpine settlement. The cost of joining the camp for one week is SFr100, and for two weeks SFr180.

Austria

Since the implementation of the European Economic Area (EEA) Agreement on January 1st 1994, citizens of the EU plus Scandinavia have been able to work in Austria with minimal formalities. In June 1994, two-thirds of Austrians voted in favour of joining the European Union and from January 1995, Austria will be a full member of the EU. Many employers who in the past have been desperately short of labour during the tourist seasons will be delighted that the restrictive immigration policies have been abolished, as will European jobseekers. The arrival of refugees and others from Eastern Europe has been a complicating factor, but on the whole the job hunt in Austria should be easier than it has been for many years.

According to a handout from the Austrian Embassy in London called 'Entry Regulations... for EEA Citizens,' EU nationals have six months (rather than the usual three) to look for an employer willing to support their application for a residence permit. The sheet also claims that the eight state-run regional employment offices *(Arbeitmarktservice)* are no longer a relevant contact because all vacancies will be registered with EURES, the European Employment Service (see page 83). However once you are in Austria, you should see what they can come up with. For example some offices have a special department for seasonal work in the hospitality industry *(Sonderteil: Saisonstellen im Hotel und Gastewerbe)* which publishes lists of winter vacancies in September. There are no private employment agencies in Austria.

It is too early to predict how much of an impact the changes will have on job-seekers from outside the EU. As usual, they are officially supposed to obtain a work permit before departing from their home country which, as usual, is virtually impossible for casual and seasonal work. Au pairs from outside the EU must still obtain both a work and residence permit *(Beschäftigungsbewilligung)* though this can be applied for inside Austria for a fee.

If working legally, you can expect to have up to 16% of your gross wage deducted for contributions to the compulsory Health and Social Security Scheme (except for au pairs).

THE JOB HUNT

Competition for unskilled jobs is intense, particularly from the thousands of East Europeans who have flooded into Austria in the past five years. According to a report in *The Times* of London which appeared during the 1994 ski season:
> *Hard-working immigrants from former Yugoslavia are taking over chalet jobs and freezing out the ski bums. This season in St Anton in the Austrian Tyrol the large immigrant population, particularly of Slovenians and Croatians, has taken up the skiing jobs. Hotels and bars have found a pool of ideal employees who work hard to maintain their relatives back home.*

Ian McArthur encountered the same thing in Vienna where he worked as a cleaner in a bar:
> *I worked 25 hours a week and was paid £4 an hour cash-in-hand. I had the opportunity, had I stayed longer, to work as a bartender which required a basic knowledge of German. I was paid every day, which permitted me a carefree disregard for financial prudence. This is common practice among illegal workers in Vienna, many of whom are Czechs and Yugoslavs (who are notoriously badly paid). I heard of openings for life models at art colleges, restaurant work and English teaching.*

Tourism

There is no shortage of hotels to which you can apply either for the summer or the winter season. Get a list from the local tourist office. The largest concertration is in the Tyrol though there are also many in the Vorarlberg region in western Austria. Wages in hotels and restaurants are low compared to Switzerland, starting at AS4,500 a month plus free room and board. A good wage before deductions is about AS11,000. So many foreigners work on a casual basis that exploitation is rife and there are many stories of people being treated shabbily, for example being fired after an injury.

If you want to improve your chances of finding work in a ski resort, you could consider joining the annual trip to Club Habitat in Kirchberg organised by Top Deck Travel (131-135 Earls Court Road, London SW5 9RH; 0171-370 4555) in December. During the three weeks of the trip, participants are given German lessons and lectures on job opportunities and red tape at a cost of nearly £400 which includes travel and half-board accommodation.

The main winter resorts to try are St Anton, Kitzbühel, Mayrhofen, St. Johann-im-Pongau which is a popular destination for British holidaymakers creating a demand for English-speaking staff, St. Johann in Tyrol, Lech and Söll. Once you are in a resort like St Anton or Brand which, during the season, has to accommodate and service thousands of holidaymakers, it should be easy to find an opening. Try puting an ad in the *Tiroler Tageszeitung* newspaper. Camilla

Lambert found a live-in job this way with a family whose father coaches the Austrian ski team. Several years before this, she prearranged a job in a hotel in Brand after talking to a woman from York who had worked there, but says that there are plenty of on-the-spot opportunities:

> *It is easy to find out about jobs in hotels, shops, as an au pair, in specialist areas like the 'skiverleih' (ski hire) as a technician or just working on the drag-lifts. If you arrived without a job, it would probably be best to target one or two villages where there are a lot of guesthouses and hotels. Ask in the Tourist Information first, but I found the bus driver who whizzed up and down the valley every day a good source of info, as were most of the bar staff in the various cafès and the 'British' pub. I was offered several positions for the coming winter.*

Camilla went on to work near Innsbruck as a high-season ski rep for Ski Partners (Friary House, Colston St, Bristol BS1 5AP) whose only requirement is that applicants be fluent in German.

Pubs, clubs and discos should not be overlooked since many of them regularly hire foreigners. Karin Huber, a native of Zell am See, reckons there are plenty of openings for foreigners, especially in the winter, since she found herself the only Austrian working in a club. The best time to arrive is late November.

Asking door to door is the most effective way though it is by no means guaranteed to succeed as Carolyn Edwards discovered in January:

> *We arrived in Söll on a Sunday and things looked very quiet. They were. It took me only two days to try everywhere in Söll with no luck. So I started on day trips to other resorts with no luck. The reps told me that the tour companies had brought very few people because of the bad snow conditions.*

The ski season in the Innsbruck region could be a better bet since the Stubai Glacier normally ensures snow from early December until the end of April.

To avoid all this you could try to fix up a job with a British tour operator beforehand; because Austria is a very popular destination for British skiers, there is a large choice, for example Bladon Lines, Crystal Holidays and Ski Total (see introductory chapter *Tourism: Winter Resorts.* The UK company PGL Ski Europe (45c High St, Hampton Wick, Kingston upon Thames, Surrey KT1 4DG) hires ski instructors for winter as well as sports instructors for their summer programme. Another possibility for the summer season is Travelbound (Olivier House, 18 Marine Parade, Brighton, East Sussex BN2 1TL) which hires people to work in hotels in Austria; no qualifications are required.

English Teaching

As in Germany, the market for EFL in Austrian cities is primarily for business English, particularly in-company. Most private language institutes such as SPIDI (Lothringer Strasse 12, 1031 Vienna) depend on freelance part-time teachers drawn from the sizeable resident international community because they prefer to hire people for a minimum of two years. The hourly rate at reputable institutes starts at AS200, which is none-too-generous when the high cost of living in Vienna is taken into account.

Berlitz is well represented with four separate premises in Vienna alone. Inlingua also has operations in Vienna and Linz. According to an American teacher-traveller Richard Spacer, who taught privately in Vienna for two months, the manager of inlingua in Vienna was very welcoming and informed him that the two-week methods course was offered to promising teachers free of charge. Richard earned AS200 per hour cash-in-hand.

Summer camps might provide some scope to the EFL teacher. Village Camps (c/o Chalet Seneca, 1854 Leysin, Switzerland; 25-342338) run a language summer camp at Zell-am-See. Language monitors over 21 and teachers over 23 are needed from the end of June to mid-August. Some experience of teaching children and a knowledge of a second European language are the basic requirements. Room and board, insurance and a weekly allowance of approximately £75 and £200 respectively are offered.

Another organisation active in this field is Mini-Schools & English Language Day Camp (Postfach 160, 1220 Vienna; 1-22 77 17).

The organisation Young Austria (Osterreichisches Jugendferienwerk, Alpenstrasse 108a, A-5020 Salzburg; 662-257580) recruit about 30 teachers and monitors over the age of 21 to work at summer language and sports camps near Salzburg. For about three or four hours of each day of the three-week camp, 10 to 19 year old children receive English tuition from teachers (who must have teaching experience). Monitors help the teachers with the social and outdoor programme as well as with the lessons. Teachers receive about AS5,800 for a three-week camp and monitors receive AS4,800 along with board and lodging and a lump sum payment of AS2,000 for travel expenses. Applications should be in by the end of February since compulsory interviews and briefing are held in London in the spring. Once Young Austria have enough staff, they do not reply to enquirers.

Au Pairs

Austria, together with Switzerland, was one of the first countries to host au pairs so there is a well-developed tradition and two well-established and respectable agencies which between them place over 500 au pairs in Austria each year. Most of the families live in Vienna and Salzburg. The two agencies are Okista (Garnisongasse 7, 1090 Vienna; 222-40148/225) and Auslands-Sozialdienst (Johannesgasse 16, 1010 Vienna; 222-512 9795), both of whom are accustomed to dealing with direct applications from abroad. Both charge an upfront registration fee of AS500-600. A private agent, Irmhild Spitzer (Sparkassenplatz 1, 7th Floor, 4040 Linz; 732-237814) may have a better choice of families in the Linz area. The pocket money of AS700-750 per week differs very little from family to family.

It should be possible to find babysitting work if you are based in a resort. Ask for permission in the big hotels to put up a notice. The going rate is about AS80 an hour.

Voluntary Work

The work done on workcamps normally takes place outdoors, e.g. laying out hiking paths, helping at peace or other festivals, etc. Contact IVS in the UK or, if in Austria, SCI at Schottengasse 3a/1/59, 1010 Vienna.

The Austrian organisation Osterreichischer Bauorden (Postfach 149, Hörnesgasse 3, 1031 Vienna) recruits about 150 volunteers for their projects in July and August. Tasks include building old people's homes, constructing sports facilities for underprivileged children, etc. Some knowledge of German is preferred, and a fee of DM110 is required.

Eastern Europe

Political change in Eastern and Central Europe provoked revolutions in many spheres. English has largely replaced Russian as the first foreign language taught in Polish, Hungarian, Czech and Slovak schools, and there is still a shortage of qualified English teachers and a tremendous need for native speakers. However the air of desperation has receded and there is now a concerted effort on the part of the national ministries of education to create an all-graduate teaching profession where there is less room than there was for untrained and inexperienced volunteers. It is no longer easy to walk into a job and, for the most part, the recruiting agencies all now require a TEFL background for Poland, Hungary, Slovakia and the Czech Republic. With each passing month, the number of Westerners flocking to Prague, Budapest and Warsaw has increased astronomically, to the point where the market for English teaching has become saturated. The opportunities for native speakers which exist now in these countries tend to be in the less attractive cities and provincial towns.

The land of opportunity now lies in Russia, the Baltic states of Latvia, Lithuania and Estonia and the other newly independent states of the old Soviet Union which are at least a couple of years behind and where the English teaching situation is more fluid. Almost any native speaker can arrange some kind of teaching, often on a private basis, but with no guarantee of earning a living wage from it.

In fact the supply of trained and experienced EFL teachers willing to accept the low salaries and working conditions offered throughout Eastern Europe does not meet the demand. In the words of an expert recruiter writing in September

1994, 'Let's face it: working in Eastern and Central Europe is not as sexy as it was three years ago.' So, at least for the next few years, eager but unqualified volunteers will find some opportunities both in private language institutes and in the state systems. While travelling around Hungary and the Czech Republic in the early autumn of 1994, Jill Weseman noticed ads for native speaker teachers in the papers and on public notice boards all the time.

Most teachers have to contend with three major problems: low pay, a shortage of accommodation and red tape. In most cases, a foreign teacher's salary is barely enough to live on; so private teaching on the side and/or a private income are the only ways to keep afloat, especially when there is high inflation. Fewer employers are supplying accommodation and you may have to join the fray looking for accommodation on the 'open market' (so-called). Volunteers who teach in a remote area, especially in Bulgaria or Romania, often find that it is difficult to purchase food staples because the local people are self-sufficient in these items and therefore they are not available in shops. And of course there may be a dire shortage of books and teaching materials. If you intend to teach outside the main centres, it is a good idea to carry your own supply of teaching aids and supplementary material, for example illustrated magazines, old comic books, travel brochures and photos of your home and neighbourhood. While tutoring adolescent girls in Russia, Hannah Start decided against using glossy fashion magazines since the pupils were so dazzled by the pictures that they didn't bother with the text; Hannah recommends using *The Big Issue* instead.

Finding a Teaching Job

Only a small proportion of the population can afford courses offered by private language schools. Therefore many foreigners teach in state schools where there is a guaranteed salary, access to state health insurance, a long-term contract (which makes it easier to obtain a work permit) and a light teaching load after exams are over in late May. Private schools offer less financial and job security though they usually pay better.

There are several approaches to finding a teaching job. Many of the native speaker teachers working in Eastern Europe at present are under the auspices of a British or American agency such as GAP, VSO and the Peace Corps which were quick to set up teaching programmes. As planned however some of these are being phased out, for example the Peace Corps is withdrawing its teachers from Hungary in 1995.

Here are the main organisations based in the UK which continue to recruit teachers for more than one country in the region:

Brit-Pol Health Care Foundation, Gerrard House, Suite 14, Worthing Road, East Preston, West Sussex BN16 1AW (01903 859222). This organisation sends English language assistants (aged 20-25) and EFL teachers to summer camps in Poland, Slovakia, Hungary and the Ukraine.

Central Bureau for Educational Visits and Exchanges, Seymour Mews, London W1H 9PE (0171-725 9411). Selects sixth formers, undergraduates and teachers to work at various UNESCO-sponsored holiday language camps in Poland, Hungary and Russia during July and August. The deadline for applications is early February.

East European Partnership, Carlton House, 27A Carlton Drive, London SW15 2BS (0181-780 2841/fax 780 9592). An initiative of VSO which annually sends 150 qualified volunteers, including teachers, to a range of postings in education, health and social welfare and business. Volunteers are requested by governments and ministries in Albania, Bulgaria, the Czech Republic, Estonia, Hungary, Latvia, Lithuania, Slovakia, Macedonia, Romania and Russia. Teaching posts are mainly in secondary schools, teacher training colleges and universities. Applicants should have a degree in English, modern languages or the humanities, TEFL and/or PGCE with a minimum of two-years' classroom experience. Salaries are based on local equivalent plus many perks are offered (e.g. flights, accommodation, training and insurance).

Teaching Abroad, 46 Beech View, Angmering, Sussex BN16 4DE (01903 249888/ 502595; fax: 785779). Young people recruited to teach conversational English for the summer or during the academic year in Moldavia, the Ukraine and Russia (Moscow, Kursk, Siberia and Magnetogorsk in the Urals). No TEFL background required. Package costs £545 for the Ukraine, £645 for Moldavia and £545-795 for Russia which includes return travel, a local salary and accommodation, but not insurance and visas.

Students for Central & Eastern Europe Inc, SFCEE, Suite 1720, 3421 M St NW, Washington, DC 20007 (202-625-1901; fax 333-1147). Student-run non-profit organisation which runs teaching programmes including summer language camps in the Czech Republic, Slovakia, Poland and Bulgaria. Teaching experience is not an absolute requirement; processing fee is $20.

Soros English Language Programme, 888 Seventh Avenue, Suite 1901, New York, NY 10106. The powerful American-based Soros Foundation has sent hundreds of English teachers to the region.

Americans should try to obtain the free leaflet 'Teaching English in Eastern Europe' from the Citizens Democracy Corps (2021 K St NW, Suite 215, Washington, DC 20006; 800-394-1945 or 202-872-0933) which lists organisations of interest to potential volunteers, especially to Russia and the Baltic States. It also operates a Volunteer Registry, though it is not known how effective this is.

If you intend to look for work after arrival, be sure to take a reasonable sum of money. The police in many areas have little patience with penniless foreigners who arrive expecting to find a job straightaway. British Council offices in the main cities keep a list of English language teaching centres and normally have a notice board on which job ads are posted.

Freelance

Once you have a work base, the supply of private teaching is seemingly infinite. The pay for private lessons can be excellent compared to wages offered by schools. A small notice placed on a prominent university notice board or in a daily newspaper would certainly produce results. Sometimes notices are posted in less likely places: Hannah Start says that in the Russian city of Yaroslavl, locals pin notices to trees, as the equivalent of the news agent notice board.

What Paul Winter noticed while travelling in the Czech Republic in 1994 is typical of the region:

Local papers in Pilsen are full of adverts for teachers. many are from families offering accommodation, meals and pocket money in return for a few lessons a week. The same is also true of Prague, though it is full of Americans looking for such work. Being able to speak some Czech is useful, but I have met several people who found work simply by sitting in a busy café in the centre of town and making it obvious that they were English and available.

Pilsen (as in Pilsener) is the Anglicised version of Plzen in the west of the country.

CZECH & SLOVAK REPUBLICS

The Velvet Revolution of 1989 was followed by the Velvet Divorce in 1993 which saw the separation of the two republics and many changes in the organisations which place English teachers. In addition to the recruitment organisations mentioned above (especially SFCEE which used to be called Students for Czechoslovakia), the main recruitment agency abroad is Education for Democracy with offices in the US and Canada:

EFD/USA, PO Box 40514, Mobile, AL 36640-0514 (205-434-3889/434-3890; fax 434-3731).

EFD/Canada, 174 Browning Ave, Toronto M4K 1W5 (416-463-3745).

Initial requests for an information package should be accompanied by a stamped envelope. Applicants must have either experience or a certificate in English language teaching. EFD stresses that applicants must be completely flexible about the starting date and destination, and have access to at least $1,500. The minimum commitment is for five months and there is a $50 application processing fee. They send out preparatory information which, according to one recent volunteer, stressed two points in particular, that teachers should not teach in pubs, and should not become personally involved with their students.

The major contact for work in state schools in both republics is the Academic Information Agencies (AIAs) in Prague and Bratislava. Britons can obtain the Czech AIA's standard information sheet and application form directly from them (Dum zahranicních sluzeb, Senovázné námesti 26, 111 21 Prague 1, Czech Republic; 2-24 22 9698/fax 24 22 9697 or from the Cultural Attaché at the Czech Embassy (26 Kensington Palace Gardens, London W8 4QY; 0171-243 1115). They recruit qualified teachers of EFL for teaching posts from September to June at primary and secondary schools. The qualifications they are looking for are a B.Ed./PGCE, BA/MA in English or Applied Linguistics, TEFL/TESL course and previous experience in EFL teaching. The salary is approximately 6,000 crowns per month and low-cost accommodation is arranged by the schools. The closing date for applications is the end of April.

The Slovak AIA (Hviezdoslavovo námesti 14, PO Box 108, 810 00 Bratislava 1; 7-333010/333762/fax 332195) largely depends on EFD in North America for its supply of volunteer teachers. The Slovak AIA maintains no formal links with other Anglophone countries so prospective teachers in the UK, Ireland, Australia, etc. should contact them indpendently. Volunteers pay for their own transport and are paid a monthly pre-tax salary of £85/$130, given free accommodation and help with the work permit process.

The private sector has passed out of its infancy and is now developing quickly. There is a high turnover of teachers especially at the cowboy end of the market. Most of the recruitment takes place locally, often via notice boards at the British Council and adverts. The British Council in Bratislava (Panská 17, 81101 Bratislava) opened its own teaching operation in October 1993, and has a very helpful English Teaching Resource Centre which keeps a list of English language schools *(Anglicky Jazyk)* in the area. The Yellow Pages are also a good source of addresses.

Monthly wages range from 4,000-6,000 crowns and are very slow to rise. Writing from Prague, Vera Paulsen reported that an average net wage for 19 contact hours per week was 4,400 crowns. Some schools withhold up to a quarter for tax and health insurance. A full-time salary should be adequate to live on by local standards but will not allow you to save anything, unless you take on lots of private tutoring.

Two other US organisations which may be able to help are:

Foundation for a Civil Society, Masaryk Fellowship Program, 1270 Avenue of the Americas, Suite 609, New York, NY 10020 (212-332-2890). One-month summer placements in Czech and Slovak Republics for people with teaching experience.

InterExchange, 161 6th Ave, New York, NY 10013 (212-924-0446). Placements in the Czech Republic for a fee of $200.

The Regulations

There are separate procedures for the Czech and Slovak Republics. As of August 1994 you need to obtain a Temporary Residence Permit from the Czech Embassy in your country of residence. For this you need to submit a work permit (or written promise of work), notarised proof of an address and a document proving you have no criminal record. All these must be in the Czech language; consular staff or your employer will assist. The Consul in London (0171-243 7943) charges a fee of £5 and requests that applications be sent in at least two months before departure.

Although people do still teach without worrying about any red tape, schools can be fined for hiring teachers black.

HUNGARY

The EFL boom in Hungary continues unabated with a concerted effort to attract native teachers both to the private and public sectors. For some reason the invasion of foreigners, particularly Americans, has not been so overwhelming as in Prague. But like Prague, Budapest has a glut of teachers and the opportunities that do exist now both for qualified EFL teachers and for native speaker teaching assistants in state schools are mostly in the provinces.

The English Teachers' Association of Hungary (Dózsa György út 104. II. 15, 1068 Budapest (1-132-8688/fax 131-9376) is part of the Ministry of Education and tries to help schools all over Hungary to find qualified English teachers. This is the way Brian Komyathy, who describes himself as a New York suburbanite, fixed up his job at a vocational school of economics, foreign trade and banking in Szolnok in central Hungary:

> *I found out after the fact that my query to the English Teachers' Association was forwarded (along with 24 others) to my current employer. They selected eight finalists whom they contacted, and when the dust settled, I was seen to have gone the distance. The eight Hungarian teachers of English here liked my credentials. I was rather surprised at how effortlessly I was able to arrange the job considering my lack of any previous teaching experience, only a BA in East European and Russian studies. Apparently the department (who have all been to Russia) thought I might have had some common experiences and would fit in as one of the gang, so to speak.*

Efforts are also being made in the private sector to coordinate the recruitment of teachers for language schools throughout the country. The Hungarian Chamber of Language Schools has established both an accreditation scheme which will give the stamp of approval to quality schools and also a database of job vacancies. About half of the 45 member schools have been accredited at present. Although the database of mostly qualified teachers is not much used, this may change in the future. Address enquiries to the Hungarian Chamber of Language Schools (Nyelviskolák Kamarája, Ráth György u 24, 1122 Budapest; tel/fax 1-155-4664); they request a registration fee of $30.

A programme called Teach Hungary (175 High St, Suite 433, Belfast, Maine 04915; tel/fax 207-338-6852) places up to 100 teaching assistants per year in Hungarian state schools and, with the withdrawal of the Peace Corps in 1994/5, is set to increase. Participants (who need not be qualified TEFL teachers and can be of any nationality) receive a very detailed and helpful handbook to guide them through the complicated red tape and also to attune culturally to Hungary. The contract is for one year and confers a salary of about $250 a month.

Summer schools employ native speakers of English as monitors and teachers. Recruitment is carried out by the Central Bureau for Educational Visits and

Exchanges. Volunteers must pay for their own transport and insurance which will be about £250.

Salaries for teachers vary, but most earn between 25,000 and 35,000 forints (net) a month for teaching 20-25 hours a week. The gross hourly rate at commercial centres is normally in the range 600-1,000 forints, up to half of which could be lost in tax. (Inflation in Hungary is running at about 20%.)

The Aaron Nanny & Au Pair Agency (Suite C, The Courtyard, Stanley Road, Tunbridge Wells, Kent TN1 2RJ; 01892 546601) can make placements with Hungarian families primarily to teach English to the children but also to undertake the usual au pair duties; the advertised weekly wage of £30 (around 5,000 forints) represents a good wage by Hungarian standards.

The Regulations

Hungarian bureaucracy gets stickier by the moment. The following description of the requirements was kindly provided by Lesley Davis, the Director of Teach Hungary mentioned above, in October 1994. For the work permit, the employer needs a copy of education diplomas and a doctor's letter, both of which have been notarised and officially translated. (The Central Translation Office in Budapest charges a small fee.) Foreign employees cannot legally be paid without a labour permit and can be deported if more than three months elapses without a labour permit.

The labour permit must then be sent with your passport, fee ($15 at present), two photos and an s.a.e. to the Hungarian Embassy in your country in order to obtain a work visa. (If you are already in Hungary, the documents will have to be sent by registered post.) Work visas are valid for one month, in which time you and your employer must apply to the local police station for a residency permit (now a stamp in your passport) for a fee of 3,000 forints valid for one year and extendable. You can also get a multiple-entry visa (for 3,000 forints) which allows you to travel freely in and out of Hungary. In Budapest there are often lengthy queues outside the processing office on Izabella utca.

The medical tests required have been a matter of controversy lately and are not standard throughout Hungary. In some counties a doctor's statement of good health is enough. But in other cases a prospective worker must be tested for VD, HIV, leprosy (!), cholera, etc. which involves a great deal of time and expense (about $70) and has prompted such an outcry from the expat community that the system may be modified in due course. At the moment it's best to get an HIV test done before arrival, though in some places in Hungary the test is free if you have an ISIC student card.

POLAND

Prospects for teachers in provincial Poland, especially western Poland, remain promising. While Warsaw and the historic university cities of Wrocław, Kraków, Poznań and Gdańsk are flooded with native speaker teachers, lesser known provincial centres and industrial towns are better bets. There is a trend for schools to open in the suburbs rather than in the city centre, where staff vacancies are more likely to occur. As in the other East European countries, there are possibilities in both state and private schools. State schools and many other institutions have organised English lessons at the end of the working day, so anyone with initiative can create a job for him or herself with hours and a location to suit.

Semesters begin in October and February, and the best time to arrive is a month or two beforehand. After arrival, try to establish some contacts, possibly by visiting the English department at the university. When you fix up interviews with private language schools, it is often useful to have an interpreter present, since even the directors of such schools do not always speak much English. If you base yourself in Warsaw and wish to advertise your availability for private English tuition, try placing a notice just to the right of the main gate of Warsaw University or in one of the main dailies, *Gazeta Wyborcza* or *Zycie Warszawy*.

The current average net monthly salary in Poland is about US$120-130 (2,500,000-3,000,000 złoties). Rent-free accommodation remains an integral part of the usual contract, which involves a teaching load of 18 hours. As long as teachers have free housing and fairly ascetic inclinations, this is just about enough to scrape by on, though almost all foreigners (like Polish teachers of English) supplement their basic income by working in the private sector. The going rate for private teaching, either individual tutorials (which are very popular) or in private language schools is 150,000-180,000 złoties (£4-5) an hour, depending on the town and local supply of teachers.

Fixing up a Job

The principal organisations mentioned in the introduction to the chapter are very active in Poland, e.g. the East European Partnership, the Peace Corps and the Soros Foundation (whose English Teaching Program in Poland is administered by the Batory Foundation, 9 Flory St, 00-586 Warsaw). SFCEE (Students for Central & Eastern Europe) mentioned above has recently expanded from the Czech and Slovak Republics to Poland. The organisation which places untrained volunteers, Teaching Abroad, is planning to extend to Poland in 1995/6.

The organisation Teachers for Poland places about 50 volunteers a year for a minimum of one semester, mostly in liceums and technical schools. The primary target group are retired school teachers from Britain but Teachers for Poland does also accept younger people with a TEFL qualification and four years of teaching experience. Interested applicants should contact Teachers for Poland, Hereford Education Centre, Blackfriars St, Hereford HR4 9HS; 01432 353363; fax: 276969.

A better bet for getting in touch with state schools which need staff is to contact the Language Methodology Advisory Centre (JODM) in Wałbrzych (Att: Rajmund Matuszkiewicz, JODM, ul. Kombatantów 20, 58-302 Walbrzych; tel/fax 78694) which has set up a network of communication between native speaker teachers (preferably qualified ones) and state secondary schools and teacher training colleges. Applications sent to JODM are copied and sent to schools which have indicated their need for native speaker teachers, after which it is up to the schools to respond individually.

Virtually every institute of higher education has a Foreign Language Department *(Studium Jezyków Obcych)*, many of which employ native speakers. One such is Lingua in Czestochowa which employs up to 15 foreign teachers, who should preferably have a TEFL/TESOL Certificate. The 1994/5 gross monthly salary was 7,500,000 złoties.

Summer Camps

Holiday language camps are popular among Polish secondary school students and many employ native speakers as monitors. For example UNESCO-sponsored camps are held in several locations in Poland; recruitment of teachers and monitors takes place through the Central Bureau for Educational Visits and Exchanges (Seymour Mews House, Seymour Mews, London W1H 9PE). Typically, ten experienced teachers are employed along with ten assistants who are sixth-formers or university students. Tanya Kotecha enjoyed her summer in Poland:

As a sixth former I spent one month teaching English to Poles in Nowy
Sacz in southern Poland. At the end of the camp (in a boarding school), there
were visits to Warsaw, Kraków and Auschwitz. The food and accommodation
were provided free and there were weekly trips to places of local interest
including a bee farm. All I paid was the cost of the air fare.

Group travel and insurance cost £250.

Other organisations to try for summer camp teaching are:

Anglo-Polish Academic Association, 93 Victoria Road, Leeds LS6 1DR (0113-
275 8121; fax 234 0365). Volunteer lektors teach people from universities and
schools, and families at summer centres. 45 hours of teaching over three
weeks. Send large s.a.e. and £2.50 for info pack.

Program, ul. Fredry 7, pok. 22-26, 61-701 Poznań (61-536 972/fax 089 740).
12-14 EFl tutors and activity supervisors needed.

Szansa, Prywatny Zakkad Oswiatowy, ul. Lubowska 6a, 60-433 Poznań (61-
488 176).

The Regulations

Visa procedures in Poland would be straightforward were it not for the
difficulty in many cases of getting a letter from landlords to confirm your
accommodation, due to the fact that they do not wish to declare tenants for tax
reasons. Before writing your address on any official form, try to find out as
much as possible about this situation, preferably with the help of a bilingual
local. If you are lucky enough to have accommodation provided by your school,
it is a simple matter of taking letters from your employer and landlord to the
local foreigners' registration office *(Urzad Miejski).*

RUSSIA & THE CIS

The potential for English teaching in the vast Commonwealth of Independent
States is unimaginable. At present the English-teaching situation is as chaotic as
the Russian economy. Educational institutes are suffering such serious financial
hardships that they can't attract local teachers let alone Western ones. The
British Council in Moscow has a one-page handout 'Teaching in Russia' which
doesn't mince words about the lack of rewards facing the prospective teacher.

The experiences of Bruce Collier from the west coast of the US belie this
rather gloomy picture:

*Upon my arrival in Moscow I had no intention of working, but found it
easy to live off my salary and even save money while residing in my own
flat. There was no bureaucratic nonsense as right now, and probably for the
forseeable future, the place is in a kind of anarchy or 'anything goes' mode.
I learned about the teaching job quite by accident, really. Out of curiosity I
took the metro to Moscow State University to have a look around. I poked
my head into what turned out to be an intermediate level English class and
later struck up a conversation with the professor. He asked me how long I
was staying in Moscow and soon afterwards I was teaching Conversational
English 101 two days a week. I negotiated my pay in hard currency, either
US dollars or German marks.*

In fact any institute of higher education is a very good place to start making
contacts. Almost every young Russian wants to learn English to maximise his
or her chances of getting into business. Many Russian institutes are eager to
establish links and exchanges with their counterparts in Britain and North
America but so far the practical problems have discouraged many large-scale
programmes from becoming established. Britons have had the advantage in the
past since British English and British text books prevailed. However in 1994

the Russian Ministry of Education declared that the standard would now be American English, though this can hardly be changed overnight. This has not prevented the Central Bureau in London from recently setting up a placement scheme for voluntary language assistants in Russian schools and institutes.

There are several American schemes including the Teaching Intern Program run by Project Harmony (6 Irasville Common, Waitsfield, VT 05673; 802-496-4545/fax 496-4548). In 1994/5 they placed teachers in Moscow, St Petersburg, Petrozavodsk, Pskov, Cheboksari and Tomsk in Russia as well as in other former Soviet Republics. Recent college graduates and teachers spend from six months to a year teaching classes in host schools and institutions, and normally live with a family. The fee for participants is $1,650 which includes all travel and visa costs.

There is also a fast-expanding private sector in language teaching. In Moscow, Polyglot (124 prospekt Mira, k.14, kv.6, Moscow 129164; tel/fax 95-282 7632) is one of the biggest and is always looking for staff. The Sunny School (PO Box 23, 125057 Moscow (95-151-2500/fax 198-0287) is looking to hire university-educated Americans and Britons with some teaching experience. The British Council in Moscow (c/o Mailing Section, 10 Spring Gardens, London SW1A 2BN) sends a standard letter to people enquiring about teaching in Moscow listing the following schools:

Intense Language Business Centre, ulitsa Gilyarovskogo 31/2, PO Box (a/ya) 38, Moscow 125183 (284 8264/281 5022).
Maria Language School (404 6993).
Moscow School (376 8826/fax 292 6511.
Cicero/RISC 123 9078/126 9641.
International Education Centre, Kutuzovski prospekt 22, school N 56, Moscow (243 6845/fax 457 0473).
Language Link School, BKC London-Moscow, kashirskoe shosse 54, Moscow 115409 (329 5384/fax 327 1114).
Breitner Language School, Sakharova prospekt, school N. 1284 (m. Turgenev-skaya) (955 4340/fax 955 4300).

Many teaching jobs will pay only in roubles — the equivalent of about $75 per month is standard — which makes life much harder when it comes to renting accommodation. Finding a place to live is one of the most difficult logistical problems which faces new arrivals in Russian cities. Bruce Collier recommends the Traveler's Guesthouse in Moscow (95-971-4059) as a temporary solution to the problem. Many teachers lodge with landladies, of whom there is no shortage considering how many widows there are trying to make ends meet on vanishingly small pensions. It is preferable to have a comfortable financial cushion since salaries are often paid a month or two late, especially in state schools.

The organisation Teaching Abroad charges language assistants £545 and £645 respectively for placements in the two republics of the Ukraine and Moldavia, where you can teach at a summer camp or for a longer period. Teaching Abroad's literature makes it all sound very appealing:

> *Say you have a small group of children for a couple of hours on a sunny afternoon in Moldavia. You may decide to take them for a walk in the town where you can help them develop their powers of description. You may decide to play them a tape from your local radio station back home. You may decide to talk about some articles in the* Daily Mail, New Musical Express *or the* Sunday Times, *about politics, Peter Pan, hip hop, Fireman Sam, cookery or football; or you could take some pictures or prose or a song and discuss different words and expressions.*

It is also possible to arrange a voluntary teaching position in Moldavia (otherwise known as Moldova) independently. In October 1994 the National

Didactic Centre (CND Ltd, 18 Moscow Avenue, ap. 4, Kishinau 277045, Moldova; 0442-23-24-58/fax 32-18-17) sent the following information:

> *We manage English courses in various educational institutions throughout the country, ranging from kindergartens to science universities. We regularly require English-speaking people to assist on the teaching of our courses. All applicants of good general education and character would be considered for our posts. They will be paid in the form of board and lodging with a local family.*

Anyone who enters the republic of Moldavia independently at present has to buy a visa at the border for $100.

Freelance

Virtually any native speaker of English who plans to spend some time in the region can find pupils to teach privately. Hannah Start spent six months in the beautiful and historic town of Yaroslavl (250km northeast of Moscow) as a student of Russian and found it easy to find private pupils. She decided to accept only high school pupils to diminish the risk of crime; apparently if you are teaching in your own accommodation, it is wise to refrain from displaying any expensive Western items. Hannah was paid the rouble equivalent of $7-10. After the term was over at Moscow University, Bruce Collier took on a few private pupils to teach at his flat, mostly in the evenings, and lived quite comfortably. Note that it may be possible to offset the cost of rent with language tuition. Anyone who can claim to teach business English will be paid premium rates.

One disadvantage of having no institutional employer is that it will be difficult to extend your visa. A one-year multiple entry visa has been introduced but it costs nearly £500 and is very difficult to obtain.

Ukraine

The Ukraine is a republic with a serious shortage of English teachers and many other things too if the advice from one of the placement organisations is anything to go by: the first item on the list of suggested gifts to pack is a stainless steel potato peeler. Several emigré organisations in the US recruit volunteer teachers warning that teachers do not live particularly well in the Ukraine:

Ukrainian National Association, Inc, PO Box 17a, 30 Montgomery St, Jersey City, NJ 07303 (201-451-2200/fax 451 2093). Sponsors an English-teaching programme for volunteers who stay for at least four weeks between May and August. Applicants from the US, Canada and Europe must pay a non-refundable application fee of $25.

Ukrainian-American Educational Exchange Association Inc, PO Box 116, Castle Creek, NY 13744 (tel/fax 607-648-2224). Volunteers receive a local teacher's salary equivalent to about $5 a month, plus free accommodation and meals if staying with a host family, otherwise not. Programme fee is $530.

An organisation based in the Ukraine which does the same thing for native English speakers of all nationalities is Mir-V-Mig, PO Box 1085, 310168 Kharkov (fax 572-227614).

The Baltics

An organisation in Latvia is very enthusiastic to recruit English-speaking volunteers for its summer programme. The International Exchange Center (2 Republic Square, LV-1010 Riga; fax 3718 830257) needs over 100 volunteers for at least a month to work as leaders and sports instructors at children's camps on the Baltic Sea, the Black Sea (Crimea) and in Russia. No special qualifications are required and a tourist visa will suffice. It is possible to apply direct to the IEC (registration fee US$50).

A similar organisation in Lithuania is Minta (Perkuno al. 4, 3000 Kaunas, Lithuania; 3707-202560/fax 208321) which places up to 50 foreigners as group leaders and conversation assistants at summer language camps on the Baltic coast. Volunteers can be of any nationality but must be over the age of 20; the placement fee is $65. Both Minta and the IEC also arrange au pair placements (see below).

Qualified EFL teachers can become Volunteers for Latvia through the Latvian National Council in Great Britain (53 Gocdhard Way, West Wickham, Kent BR4 0ER). Two American organisations send volunteer teachers to the Baltic states on short contracts: American Latvian Association (400 Hurley Ave, Rockville, MD 20850) and the American Professional Partnership for Lithuanian Education (PO Box 1370, W Hartford, CT 06119). Project Harmony in Vermont mentioned above send teaching interns to Latvia and Lithuania as well as the central Asian republics of Uzbekistan, Kyrghyzia and Kazakhstan.

THE REST OF EASTERN EUROPE

Bulgaria

Teaching positions in Bulgaria are organised by the Ministry of Education & Science precluding the possibility of signing a private contract (at least officially). We have heard of no private language schools in Bulgaria. Specialist foreign language secondary schools in Bulgaria are being provided with native speaker teachers on one-year renewable contracts starting in September by the Central Bureau on behalf of the British Council and the Bulgarian Ministry of Education. Americans should try SFCEE mentioned above which has expanded its teacher placement operations to Bulgaria.

The Union of Free Students of Bulgaria (c/o 99 Haberdasher St, London N1 6EH) send undergraduates and graduates to teach conversational English at August summer schools in Bulgaria. The usual arrangement pertains: volunteers must pay for their own travel but free accommodation and pocket money are paid.

Romania

Predictably the demand for English is now enormous but the country is virtually bankrupt with few resources to divert into EFL, one of the countless unfortunate legacies of the ruinous Ceausescu regime. The demand that exists is in the state sector, where there is a handful of English medium secondary schools. The voluntary organisation Teaching Abroad (see above) sends a considerable number of volunteer teachers to Romania.

Anyone prepared to travel to Romania and teach on an entirely voluntary basis would probably be able to find a niche. Paul Converse from Oregon spent the summer travelling around Romania:

I doubt that anyone could make any money teaching English but they would certainly get a free place to live and food and appreciation. When I was in Felenc, the entire village wanted me to stay and teach English.

Foreigners involved in education may be eligible to obtain an 'AVIZ,' a card which allows them to pay for accommodation and travel in local currency rather than hard currency.

According to a contact of Paul's who has been an English teacher in Cluj for 25 years, a small salary in local currency might be paid. Mr. Busca recommends that prospective teachers contact Romanian universities direct as well as the

British Council in Bucharest and the Ministry of Education (Strada Berthelot 30, 70749 Bucharest).

VOLUNTARY WORK

The opening up of Eastern Europe is a double-edged sword. On the one hand, there has been a dramatic increase in the number of contacts between voluntary groups in east and west and a recognition of the urgent need to expand programmes to help disadvantaged communities and to try to reverse some of the environmental crimes of the past decades. On the other hand, the decentralisation of power at every level means that the old state-run voluntary organisations are either disintegrating or have lost all government subsidies.

The main workcamp organisations in Britain (IVS, CMP and UNA Wales) and in the US (SCI-USA, VFP and CIEE) can provide up-to-date details of projects and camps in all the countries of the region including some of the newly independent states of the old USSR. In many cases the projects are a pretext for bringing together young people from East and West in an effort to dismantle prejudice on both sides. Often discussion sessions and excursions are a major part of the three or four week workcamps and some volunteers have been surprised to find that their experiences are more like a holiday, with very little work expected. The people of Eastern Europe are repeatedly praised for their generosity and hospitality.

Some preparation is recommended by all the recruiting organisations and participants are encouraged to get some workcamp experience closer to home first and to attend orientations. There is normally a registration fee of £70-85. The national workcamp partners (listed below) normally handle the travel and insurance arrangements once you arrive in their country. The language in which camps are conducted is usually English. Projects vary from excavating the ancient capital of Bulgaria to organising sport for gypsy children in Slovenia. Many projects, especially in the former Soviet Union, concern themselves with the reconstruction of ancient churches and other buildings which fell into ruin under Communism. There is also a high proportion of much-needed environmental workcamps.

Applications for workcamps should be sent through the partner organisation in the applicant's own country. Readers who do not know the addresses of the workcamps organisers in their countries may contact the following addresses:

Bulgaria — Youth Alliance for Development (MAR), PO Box MAR, 1387 Sofia.

Czech Republic — INEX Centrum, Senovázne námesti 24, 116 47 Prague 1. Also: Klub Mladych Cestovatelu (KMC, Karolíny Svetlé 30, 110 00 Prague 1.

Hungary — UNIO, Nepszinhaz ut. 24, 1081 Budapest. Also: Service Civil International, Olasiget ut. 28, 1103 Budapest.

Latvia — Latvian Student Centre, Elisabetes 45/47, Room 514, 1010 Riga. The IEC mentioned above also arranges workcamps.

Lithuania — Centre of Stu⁻ ⸱ ₊t Activities, K Donelaidio 73, 113, Kaunas 3006. Minta mentioned above also arranges workcamps for up to 500 foreign volunteers for a fee of $35.

Poland — Foundation for International Youth Exchange (FIYE), ul. Kosynierów 22, 04641 Warsaw.

Slovakia — INEX, Prazská 11, 81104 Bratislava.

Slovenia — MOST, Breg 12, 61000 Ljubljana. They wish to stress that the war does not affect Slovenia.

Youth Voluntary Service (Bol. Komsomolski per. 7/8, 103982 Moscow) which still tries to coordinate workcamps throughout the CIS seems, by all accounts, to be dying a slow death. Organisations in the various republics may organise workcamps independently, such as the Cooperation Project in Siberia (PO Box 52, 665718 Bratsk 18) which publishes its programme in English and the Belarusian ATM (Association of International Youth Work, 10a Oktyabrskaya St, PO Box 64, 220119 Minsk) which recently broke away from the state-run organisation and organises 13 work and study camps, many of which are concerned with the aftermath of Chernobyl. While the CIS is experiencing such disastrous socio-economic and organisational problems, anyone interested in volunteering there would be advised to keep abreast of developments through a local workcamp organisation.

The only country to have an active organic movement is Hungary. The president of the Hungarian Association of Organic Growers (Biokultúra Association, Rezeda u. 3, Budapest 1204) gives the contact address for prospective farmworkers as Ifjúsági Iroda/WWOOF, Gödöllö ATE, 2103 Práter Károly u 1; 28-310 200/fax 310 804). They may be able to find placements for volunteers on organic farms and gardens in Hungary. Work can include weeding, animal husbandry and helping with the harvest. Participants receive food, lodging and experience but no pocket money in exchange for eight to ten hours of work a day for a minimum of one or two weeks between April and October.

Hungary is also the only Eastern Bloc country to host groups of volunteers from the British Trust for Conservation Volunteers. They have four summer projects which cost between £125 and £155 including ones to guard nesting colonies of wetland birds and to restore a peat bog. There are indigenous organisations concerned with conservation in some of the other countries, for example the Brontosaurus Movement (Bubenská 6, 170 00 Prague 7, Czech Republic).

The Romania Information Centre (Southampton University, Southampton, Hants. SO9 5NH) maintains a database of voluntary organisations active in Romania and a list of volunteers looking for positions. There are far fewer voluntary vacancies than there were two or three years ago, and now they are all for people with the appropriate skills such as therapists (physio, occupational or play), teachers (occasionally TEFL), nurses and nursery nurses.

Voluntary organisations working with helping displaced persons inside the former Yugoslavia do sometimes take on foreign volunteers. Two Croatian organisations which are involved in providing services for refugees (especially children) are Pakrac, Strossmajerovo 63, 43550 Pakrac, Croatia; and Suncokret, Marusevacka 8, 41000 Zagreb. The latter recruits volunteers through IVS North (21 Otley Road, leeds LS6 3AA; 0113 230 4600). Needless to say the situation in the refugee camps is chaotic and there is an element of risk involved for volunteers.

There is a severe shortage of labour in some rural areas and urban dwellers in the CIS often work on the land in exchange for much needed produce. Anyone who has contacts might be able to arrange this independently during the summer. A Canadian writing in the travel magazine *Great Expeditions* described what he found in Estonia:

If you are looking for farmwork, you simply go to the farms and try to communicate your intent. Your main problem will be explaining why you would want to share their humble lives. The main farmwork takes place in the summer: June is hay cutting month (when it stays light until 11pm) before it is stacked, dried and moved to the barn. Most work is still done by hand. Then later in the summer potatoes have to be picked before the rainy season sets it.

OTHER OPPORTUNITIES

People based in the cities of Eastern Europe are taking advantage of the new entrepreneurial spirit to take up more conventional forms of employment. Many companies advertise in the English papers for computer programmers, English proofreaders, English language radio station personnel, etc. Bruce Collier warns that sub-editing English translations of technical books can be tedious in the extreme:

In Moscow there was quite a bit of work proofreading translated Russian-to-English legal and medical documents. Don't apply for these unless you really know what you are doing. The jobs are very demanding, detail-oriented and very technical. Remember you're travelling the world for the cultural experience and to have fun. If you wanted to hole yourself up in a room all day looking at papers you could've stayed at home. But if you must, contact the Russian State Bureau of Information.

If you want something fixed up ahead of time write to Teaching Abroad's sister organisation Business Abroad (46 Beech View, Angmering, Sussex BN16 4DE) which places students in unpaid positions in new firms in Romania, Moldavia and Ukraine. The East European Partnership (address above) has launched a new recruitment drive for people who can serve as business advisers. Another option is to contact human rights groups in one's home country which might have an office or a programme in your destination country. There are even recruitment agencies emerging which place skilled people from the west in jobs in the east, for example Altonwest Ltd (PO Box 717, Head Post Office, Moscow 101 000) which maintains a database of tradesmen and professionals willing to work in Russia.

The American Slavic Student Internship Service & Training Corporation (ASSIST) offers a variety of position in Russia, quoting a generous inflation-linked salary (in roubles). Placements in publishing, business, education, etc. are open to students of Russian, international relations and related subjects. Internship programme fees range from $1,900 for one month to $6,900 inclusive for a one-year placement. Details from 399 Ringwood Road, Freeville, NY 13068 (tel/fax 607-539-6145).

The newly formed democracies of Eastern Europe are all targeting tourism as a means of aiding their economies and are encouraging foreign tour operators to develop resorts, etc. which in time may have large staff requirements. Already ski tour operators like Ski Ardmore (11-15 High St, Marlow, Bucks. SL7 1AU) and Crystal Holidays (The Courtyard, Arlington Road, Surbiton, Surrey KT6 6BW) are recruiting reps, ski leaders and chalet staff for resorts in Bulgaria and Romania.

Young people in east European capitals are so eager to embrace western culture that American-style restaurants have sprung up everywhere. In Moscow at least they even hire English speakers, as attested by Bruce Collier whose British wife Sharon was hired by La Cantina Restaurant on Tverskaya near the Intourist Hotel and Red Square:

There are more and more Western businesses opening in Moscow all the time and the opportunities should continue to grow. This is especially true of the restaurant and entertainment industries. My wife was steered to a job as a waitress in, of all places, a Mexican restaurant (a joint Russian-Irish venture). Her job provided discounted meals (and the standard was equal to that of any Western country) and paid dollar wages.

Of course as more and more Russians attain a working knowledge of English, there will be fewer jobs for foreigners in this sector.

Such jobs will be heard about by word-of-mouth or possibly advertised in the English-language papers mentioned earlier in the chapter. Turn-over of foreign students is high so if you are staying for a while your chances are reasonable. The trendy area of Moscow is on New Arbat; try the American-style Sports Bar. Irish pubs like Rosie O'Grady's (at Ulnanenka 9) are where expats, including workers, gather. Musicians will find a flourishing jazz and rock music scene; according to Bruce there is even some country-and-western music around.

If you are looking for some casual work, ask discreetly around the universities or among expatriates teaching English. Your services as anything from a disc jockey to a freelance copy editor may be in demand. English-language papers like *Prognosis Weekly* (Arabská 683, 16000 Prague) which was started by a group of Californians in 1991 pay about 1,000 crowns for a full-length feature from a freelancer. They also advertise for people to help with the distribution of the paper (whose free classified ads can be generally useful in the job/house/friend search).

Marta Eleniak started as a volunteer in Warsaw teaching English in a primary school and within a year listed her various paid activities as assistant to the Vice-President of a consulting firm, translator and teacher at a real estate agency, UK representative of a Polish musician and exportor of paragliders. She concludes that 'England seems so sleepy in comparison'. Obviously there are many niches which keen foreigners willing to stay for a while can fill.

Au Pairs

There are possibilities for au pairing, almost always with an element of providing English conversation practice for the family. For example the International Exchange Center in Riga (Latvia) and Minta in Kaunas (Lithuania) both place young people in families for an academic year. The latter says it needs up to 300 au pairs who receive an improbably high rate of pocket money of £200 a month.

The Sussex-based organisation Teaching Abroad now organises three month homestays in two cities in Russia (Moscow and Magnitogorsk) with informal English teaching in exchange for full room and board. The cost including travel is £600.

Two British agencies to try for family placements in Hungary are Aaron Employment Agency (Suite C, The Courtyard, Stanley Road, Tunbridge Wells, Kent TN1 2RJ) and Bunters Agency (17 Cooper St, Macclesfield, Cheshire SK11 7LH). A Budapest agency which does make placements of foreign girls in the city, mostly in expatriate families, is Avalon 92, Erzsébet Krt. 15, 1/19, 1073 Budapest.

There are au pair agencies in most Eastern European capitals, but they are primarily concerned with the placement of their nationals in the rest of Europe. For example in three years of operation, the 5-Star Agency of Croatia (Trakoscanska 51b, 42 000 Varazdin) has been asked just once to try to place a British au pair (who was studying Serbo-Croat).

Work Your Way
Worldwide

Australia

After suffering the severest recession since 1930, the Australian economy has been picking up since 1993. The unemployment rate is falling and now stands at 9.5%. But even at the height of the recession, there were plenty of travellers' jobs around, since the vast majority of unemployed Australians do not want to do this kind of work. This is the conclusion to which a longstanding contributor to *Work Your Way Around the World*, Armin Birrer, came when he worked as recruiting officer at a vineyard in northern Victoria:

> *Local unemployment was very high, and yet I had severe problems getting pickers. Most of the unemployed didn't want to pick grapes because it is too hard for them. Plus lots of them don't think it's worthwhile to go off the dole for three to four weeks and then wait to go back on again. I came to the conclusion in Mildura that I can always find some work even if unemployment rises to 20%, if I go to where the work is. People who can work hard and don't make trouble are always in demand.*

Those same people are probably the ones who arrive with just a few pounds after having travelled across Asia or the States and earn enough in a few months to fund further months of travel. This is not too difficult in a country where unskilled workers are generally paid $10-$12 an hour.

First-time visitors to Australia are often surprised by the degree to which that far-off continent is an imitation of Britain. Despite their reputation as 'pommy-bashers', most Australians take for granted a strong link with Britain, and this may be one reason why British travellers are so often welcomed as prospective employees. On the other hand, employers who have seen round-the-world travellers come and go do not generally want to hire a mere tourist and it is a good idea at interviews to say that you are in Australia for an 'indefinite period' or even that you intend to apply for residency. Job adverts in Darwin have recently been specifying 'No visas' and some employers have made it policy not to hire people on working holiday visas since they are so fed up with travellers leaving after a short time.

The kinds of job you are likely to get in the rural areas are of a very different nature from city jobs. Contrary to popular belief kangaroos do not hop around downtown Sydney or Adelaide and you will have to penetrate into the interior to discover Australia's more exotic features. It is worth thinking about the pros and cons of each milieu (city vs. country). While some experienced travellers declare that Sydney and Melbourne are the only places you can work on a steady basis at reasonably good wages, others advise heading out of the city as soon as you've seen the Opera and the harbour. Farm work often comes with accommodation whereas city rents (a minimum of $100 a week for two sharing a small flat) can eat into your wages, as can the social life.

Working Holiday Visas

British, Irish, Canadian, Dutch and Japanese people between the ages of 18 and 30 and without children are eligible to apply for a working holiday visa (visa class 417). More than 25,000 are granted to Britons alone each year. The visa is meant for people intending to use any money they earn in Australia to supplement their holiday funds. Working full-time for more than three months is not permitted. Although applicants older than 25 are eligible to apply, their applications are scrutinised more closely and they must prove that their stay in Australia will be of benefit not only to them but to Australia. It also helps if they can give a convincing account of why they waited until after their early 20s to travel in Australia (e.g. they were in higher education, looking after an ailing parent, etc.)

The visa is valid for 12 months and normally expires 13 months after the date of issue, which is why the High Commission in London (Australia House, Strand, London WC2B 4LA; 0171 379 4334) advises applicants to apply no more than a month before their proposed departure date. The visa is not renewable either in Australia or at home. People in northern Britain can apply to the Australian Consulate in Manchester (Chatsworth House, Lever St, Manchester M1 2DL; 0161-228 1344). Britons can also apply at Australian Consulates outside the UK: Dublin, Bangkok, San Francisco and Beijing have all been recommended for their speed and leniency.

The first step is to get the working holiday information sheet and application form 147 from the High Commission's mailing house *Australian Outlook*, 3 Buckhurst Road, Bexhill-on-Sea, East Sussex TN40 1QF (01424 223111), enclosing an A4 stamped addressed envelope (47p stamp). The non-refundable processing fee in the UK is the sterling equivalent of A$150 (at present £71). The second step is to get as much money in the bank as possible. Each application is assessed on its own merits, but the most important requirement is a healthy bank balance. The amount currently recommended is £2,000 from which the cost of the airfare may come. Exceptions are sometimes made if you can supplement your more meagre savings with an official letter of guarantee from a bank manager who has been persuaded a large sum will be coming your way or if you have a letter of support from an Australian citizen who will put funds of £2,000 at your disposal if necessary. If you have borrowed a large sum to bump up your balance, rather than saved steadily over a period of time, be prepared to provide a plausible explanation for this. Outside London you can apply in person and may even get the visa over the counter. In other cases it will take between ten days and three weeks to process by post (autumn is the busiest time). They advise you not to make a firm flight booking until your visa comes through (though this is often impracticable since the best air fares must be booked months in advance).

One advantage of the working holiday visa is that the immigration authorities at your point of entry will not expect to see a return ticket. Although they are always entitled to refuse entry to anyone who has insufficient funds, they are unlikely to do so if you have a working holiday visa.

The discretionary machinations of Australian consular services are sometimes difficult to fathom especially in the case of applicants over 25. After working for a year in Dutch nurseries, Dermot Campbell from Northern Ireland decided to go to Australia:

> *I visited the Embassy one week before my 29th birthday. I was intending to apply for a six-month visitor visa but they told me the maximum was three months unless I got a working holiday visa (which I had assumed was a virtual impossibility for someone my age). The bloke almost jumped over the counter and gave it to me when I told him I'd studied horticulture. I also typed out lots of addresses of people I'd met over the years (most of whom I don't even remember).*

Not all geriatric applicants are greeted so warmly. Carl Griffith from Bristol decided to wait until he got to New Zealand to apply, so as not to waste months of the visa's validity en route:

> *I was 29 when I left on my round-the-world trip and ended up applying for the Australian working holiday visa in Wellington. Because of my age I was given an extra sheet of three or four questions to answer. I answered them as best I could but less than 24 hours later (and £65 poorer) I was told my application had failed. No real reasons given. I later applied for a visitor visa in Auckland and was told that if I had applied there they would have interviewed me instead of asking for written answers. I'm sure I would have fared better in that situation.*

The 13-month validity from the date of issue is a real problem for the many travellers who spend months en route, often in Asia. It is now possible to present yourself to an immigration office several months before expiry and ask for the time you have spent in transit to be credited to the end of your visa, for a fee of $200 (the same fee charged for extending a visitor visa). Again, the decision is at the discretion of the officer dealing with the case.

Some people worry that if their application for a working holiday visa is turned down for some reason, they won't be granted a tourist visa. But the High Commission maintains that this is an unfounded anxiety.

Although it is not widely known, other nationalities may also successfully apply for a working holiday visa. For example Frank Schiller showed up for an interview at the Australian Embassy in Bonn, 'neatly attired, clean shaven and smooth talking' and was issued with a working holiday visa. More recently Ben Hockley's Spanish girlfriend got one without difficulty (and even with imperfect English and youth unemployment running at 45% in some places, she managed to find well-paid work whenever and wherever she wanted).

Obtaining a resident's visa (for permanent migration) is, predictably, much more difficult, though not impossible if you have a skill in short supply or a close relative in Australia. The Application for Migration package including application form 48 explains the points system and is available from the High

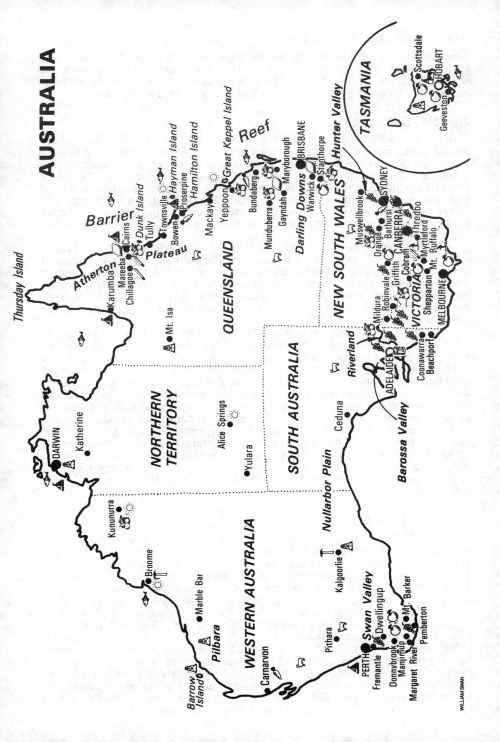

Commission for a fee of £6. Rhona Stannage was very surprised to learn that three states in Australia recognise a Scottish law degree and considered the seven-month wait and the fee of £250 for a resident's visa worthwhile, although she and her husband were really interested only in a working holiday.

Special Schemes

BUNAC (16 Bowling Green Lane, London EC1R 0BD) features Australia as one of its destination countries. Anyone who is eligible for the working holiday visa may choose to join the BUNAC Work Australia package which costs £1,200-1,500 from London or £1,000-1,200 from California. This includes the return flight (departing from the UK in July and September only), orientation on arrival and back-up from Student Services Australia (PO Box 399, Carlton South, VIC 3053). Canadian students and recent graduates can participate in the SWAP programme whereby students qualify for visas lasting six months; ask at any office of Travel Cuts.

WTN Programs (World Travellers Network, 3 Orwell St, Potts Point, Sydney NSW 2011; 02-357 4425) offers people with the working holiday visa support and guidance on job-finding after arrival, as well as other services such as airport pick-up and message forwarding. The programme fee is £125. Details in Europe are available from Travel Active Programmes (PO Box 107, 5800 AC Venray, Netherlands; 04780 88074; fax 11577). They also have a representative in the US whose address is available from WTN Sydney.

CIEE (205 E 42nd St, New York, NY 10017) run a working programme to Australia on similar terms as the working holiday scheme for UK students. The quota of 100 may increase in the next few years.

The Involvement Volunteers Association Inc keeps a register of volunteer placements in all states of Australia and can also help with some paid itinerant work on farms for individuals from the UK and the Netherlands. Recent placements include assisting zoology research in Queensland, acting as wardens at bird observatories in Western Australia and Victoria, and working at a zoo and reptile park in South Australia. The programme fee of A$400 includes collection from Melbourne Airport and an orientation and back-up service for up to 12 months. All travel costs are extra though discounts on coaches, scuba diving courses, etc. are arranged. Some living costs are free, others are extra. Details from Involvement Volunteers, PO Box 218, Port Melbourne, VIC 3207 (tel/fax 03-646 5504) or from contact addresses abroad (see page 141).

Unofficial Work

Those who don't qualify because of advanced age or the wrong passport should not despair. Even though in 1993 the Immigration Minister ordered the tax authorities to cooperate with the Immigration Department in order to track down illegal workers, the clampdown is still a lot less dramatic than in the US. Employers seldom ask to see the stamp in your passport and a 'no worries' attitude continues to prevail. As Tommy Karske from Finland found:

I found out that employers never asked for a visa, indeed, they preferred it if you didn't use it, thus avoiding lots of paper-work. Secondly, pay was better and no tax was deducted.

The necessity of employees producing a tax file number (see below) has meant that fewer employers are quite as blasé about the rules as this. Also the CES (national employment service) now normally enquire about your status before offering assistance and, worse, the immigration authorities are beginning to enforce the rules. Armin Birrer described a clampdown near Mundubbera in Queensland on one of the biggest citrus farms in the state:

I heard from a couple of Swedes that they got away by running off the farm into the hills. The breath of the immigration people wasn't good enough to chase them long. To work on the biggest farm is sometimes more risky; the tactics of the immigration people include ringing up the farm office and asking for the names on the payroll to be read out. If they hear lots of foreign names they may decide it's worth travelling the long distance to the farm. The most dangerous time is near the beginning and end of the season, but not the very beginning and very end when there aren't many workers around. If the immigration officials don't catch a reasonable number of offenders, they get into trouble themselves for all the fuss.

Similar stories have emerged from the tomato-growing area around Bowen in Queensland in October (the peak picking season), from the large fruit-picking camps at Shepparton and Mildura in Victoria (where raids are an annual event resulting in a large number of deportations) and from Donnybrook and Carnarvon in Western Australia. Some areas were raided for the first time in the early 1990s such as Griffith, Kununurra and Broome, which had hitherto been considered too out-of-the-way and therefore too expensive for immigration to bother. It is hard to understand the official attitude, for it can hardly be said that these illegal workers are taking employment away from Australians. During certain harvests, the farmers are desperate for labour and put out appeals over the radio and on the notice boards of backpackers' hostels. Without a working holiday visa you might decide to steer clear of farms where you are relatively exposed, and find work inside the relatively safe and anonymous walls of the urban jungle or on smaller family farms where the immigration people are unlikely to bother you. Marcus Scrace, who didn't have a work visa, made it a rule never to work alongside Swedes, since in his experience it was Swedes who got caught most often. Stephen Psallidas urges discretion after an Australian guy working with him in Bowen 'dobbed in' (Australian for informed on) two English girls who had foolishly let it be known that they had no work visas. Immigration officials arrived and deported them.

Tax

In 1988 tax file numbers were introduced for the first time and this has had repercussions for foreign workers. All people in employment in Australia are now obliged to apply for a 9-digit tax file number. If you refuse to divulge it to an employer within 28 days (which is your legal right), you are automatically taxed at the top rate of 49% and furthermore arouse suspicion about whether or not you are entitled to work. Therefore it is greatly to your advantage to obtain one.

Foreigners are eligible to apply for a tax file number at a post office or tax office. Processing normally takes between four and six weeks. You require two strong documents (i.e. passport, original or certified copy of your birth certificate, bank statement with local address) or three weak documents (driving licence with photo, proof of payment of an electricity, gas or phone bill). It seems that having a working holiday visa stamped in your passport is not a prerequisite, as Lucy Slater discovered when she got one in Kalgoorlie:

I filled in a form and told no lies and got one without any trouble whatsoever. I found I had only one identifying document, i.e. my passport, and needed another. So I simply opened a bank account and then used my bank pass book. On the form they ask you why you want a tax code and I said that the bank wanted it. (The bank had asked if I had one but said it wasn't really important.) After taking this to the post office, I received my number.

We have heard of several cases of people being deported for inventing tax file numbers (but giving their real names).

The ultimate tax liability for non-residents of Australia is 29% of all earnings (up to $20,700). Non-residents are not eligible for the personal allowance of $5,400 nor for concessionary tax rates (for example residents who work north of the 26th parallel and those who work in the fruit and vegetable industries pay only 15% tax). There is some confusion about the definition of 'resident'. Although the length of the visit does not in itself determine residency status, as a general rule, a person whose intended visit to Australia is less than six months cannot be regarded as a resident. According to information from the Australian Taxation Office (including the new leaflet *Visiting Australia? Tax help for working tourists and backpackers*), an overseas visitor whose usual place of abode is outside Australia and who does not intend to take up residence, would be treated as a non-resident even if he or she did stay longer than six months. Therefore a person who is in Australia on a working holiday will always be treated as a non-resident.

On the basis that temporary visits can turn into longer-term ones, many working holidaymakers tick the box for 'resident' on all employment declaration forms, which allows them the possibility of applying for a tax rebate should they decide to leave the country at some unspecified future date. Assuming you have claimed resident's status, you should obtain a Group Certificate (statement of earnings and tax deducted) after you leave each job, arranging to have it posted on to you if necessary. If you have earned less than your personal allowance during the tax year (starting June 30th), you could be eligible for a rebate.

As the end of the tax year approaches, get a tax pack from a newsagent or pay a tax agent to make the application for you, preferably in July when the tax office is overstretched. (Returns must be lodged by October 31st.) At the end of Fiona Cox's six-month stint in catering, she spent $80 and ten minutes with Income Tax Professionals in Sydney and three weeks later received $1,000. Normally rebates are processed within four or five weeks. Home Tax Advisers in Sydney (02-747 5999) charge a fee of $50 and promise refund cheques in as little as a fortnight. If you have not called yourself a resident from the beginning, you should not apply for a rebate, since in that case you may actually owe the tax office some money. Dawn Smith was billed over $1,000 after returning home to Worcester.

If you have problems or queries about your tax position in Sydney, personal callers may visit the Tax Office at 100 Market St (02-224 0990).

THE JOB HUNT

Although everybody finds some kind of job in the end, it isn't always easy. You are likely to encounter a surprising degree of competition from others on working holidays, many of whom are chasing the same kinds of job. According to a magazine article, a company which operates tours of Sydney Harbour received 50 replies to an advertisement for waiting staff and a receptionist, 42 of which were from Poms. The glut of travelling workers is especially bad before Christmas. In addition to asking potential employers directly (which is the method used by about one third of successful job-seekers in Australia), there are four main ways of finding work: Commonwealth Employment Service (Jobcentres), private employment agencies, newspaper advertisements and notice boards.

The CES

Despite its name, the Commonwealth Employment Service or CES is not solely for the benefit of Commonwealth visitors; it happens to be the name for Australian job centres. Like job centres anywhere the CES post job details which have been registered with them. The card should give the name and address of the employer, the number of helpers required, the approximate duration of employment, accommodation if any, pay and conditions. In most cases you will have access to a free telephone for arranging job interviews and you can also collect a copy of the *Harvest Table* (see *Fruit Picking* section below). In times of acute labour shortages for specific harvests, the city CESs sometimes supply a bus or train ticket to your work destination, so enquire about this if it seems a possibility.

In times of high unemployment it is not too surprising to learn that the state employment service treats working holidaymakers as second class citizens. If making telephone enquiries from afar, politely but persistently ask specific questions about local prospects to find out if it's worth travelling to that area. Foreign visitors without working visas are advised to stay away from the CES.

Some CESs have separate departments or even separate addresses which specialise in casual work or in jobs in the hospitality industry; look for branches called Templine which specialise in temporary office jobs. Competition for casual jobs registered with the CES, such as an afternoon in a warehouse or a few days of making sandwiches, varies from place to place, but there will always be a hard core of travellers attracted by the prospect of instant cash. Do not put too much faith in these places. Rhona Stannage and husband Stuart (who both arrived with extensive restaurant experience) registered with the hospitality section of the Darwin CES in June 1994 and were not contacted with any job details until September.

Will Barnett had better luck with the CES in Darwin when he looked for labouring work there in May at the beginning of the dry season:

At 6am on Monday I headed down to the CES office where I joined a queue of 20 rough-looking Aussies, some of whom had slept the night outside the door. Fortunately Darwin has a special department for casual labourers, as it has a very high transient population. After waiting four hours, I was offered a job unloading 10kg boxes of frozen prawns off a trawler. The following morning I went back to the CES and at 10.30 was called out of the waiting area apparently because I looked a reliable type. This time the job (as handyman) lasted two weeks.

This sounds fairly civilised compared to the crush which sometimes develops at the casuals department in Sydney (10 Quay St, Haymarket; 02-201 1166). People start arriving about 6am for the 6.30am opening. As soon as the doors open, men and women sign their names and list their skills. Those who go in every day and stay on the list shouldn't have to wait more than a week for some work; and if they have skills in demand they may well succeed on their first visit. While Lucy Slater described the staff in one CES as 'rude and totally unhelpful,' J. Jordan was delighted to be given a voucher for travel to a farm near Dareton NSW (worth over $100) by an overworked employee in the same office.

Descriptions of CESs around the country range from 'hit and miss' to 'hopeless and depressing'. Despite travellers' complaints, the majority of CES staff are friendly and sympathetic. Stephen Psallidas's description of the Cairns CES on Lake Street is valid for the vast majority of offices: 'with friendly and helpful staff, and not many jobs on the board.'

Diane Elliott was disgusted not to be allowed to register for general clerical work through the Adelaide CES because she could not type 50 words a minute. In general, suburban offices especially in well-heeled suburbs may prove more useful than the over-used central city office. After deciding that the downtown Sydney CES was too impersonal and depressing, he visited a few smaller ones and found that they had more genuine vacancies and were able to offer more valuable advice. Lucy Slater (minus a working visa) was very chuffed to be offered a permanent switchboard job she had seen up on the board at the CES in the Warringah Mall, North Manly, Sydney. A complete list of all metropolitan and country CES offices can be found in the Commonwealth Government section in the front of any phone book.

Private Employment Agencies

Private agencies are not as widespread as in Britain. Still, they are a good potential source of jobs for travellers, especially those who have some office skills, computer, data processing or financial experience. A surprising number positively encourage UK people on working holidays either by contacting hostel managers or even visiting hostels regularly to sign up likely temporary workers. The offered wages are good too: $12 an hour for clerical work and $13.50 for secretarial.

An ability to type is virtually essential, at least in Stephen Psallidas's experience:

I went round the temping offices, but alas. Despite my extensive experience with computers, well-prepared CV, shirt and tie, etc. I had no luck. All of them required at least 60 words a minute typing for any office work. I would recommend anyone to take a short typing course before coming over since there is plenty of work.

Major agencies include Drake, Bligh, Ecco, Swift, Adia and ACOM. Most agencies do not occupy the equivalent of high street premises, and you will often find yourself in some obscure office block. You should make an appointment to register. Since the majority of city job-seekers stay in Sydney, here are a few agencies to try:

ECCO Personnel, Suite 4, Level 6, 109 Pitt St, Sydney 2000 (02-221 5200). Have four branches in Sydney including two industrial sections, plus offices in Brisbane, Canberra and Melbourne.

Bligh Appointments, 9th Floor, 425 George St, Sydney 2000 (02-235 3699). They trawl the YHA and other hostels every week.

ACOM Personnel, 303 Pitt St, Sydney 2000 (02-264 2124). Temps must have a minimum of two years' office experience.

Adia, Level 2, 280 George St, Sydney 2000 (02-231 6622). Word processor operators and others who register in Sydney can also work in other states.

Most agencies won't let you sign up unless there is a fair chance of work, though according to a report from Debbie Harrison sent in August 1994 this shouldn't be a problem:

I'm a secretary by trade and am currently doing temp work in Sydney. There is a major shortage of temp secretaries at the moment, so if you've got decent skills, you're practically guaranteed work. The agency I work for is Drake International who have been really good to me. And I know they have a number of Brits on their books. They have the added benefit of having offices all over the world, so if you're travelling on, they'll give you what they call a Career Passport to introduce you to other offices. The pay is good and the work is generally very easy.

In Sydney and Melbourne, the agencies almost always ask about your visa status. Carolyn Edwards side-stepped the issue with one agency by saying she had just moved into a flat and couldn't locate it and another time claiming that she had left it in a safety deposit box in Queensland and was arranging for it to be sent. After she had proved herself a reliable worker and was getting called back by companies, the agency seemed conveniently to forget about her claims. The two temp agencies in Kalgoorlie for whom Lucy Slater worked didn't even ask to see her passport. They were more interested in whether or not she could drive since most secretarial work there is with the mines and involves driving a company car between sites.

Some agencies specialise in certain kinds of work for example work on stations and farms, in tourist resorts or as nannies and au pairs (see section near end of this chapter).

Newspaper Advertisements

In the major cities, get hold of the excellent free booklets *For Backpackers by Backpackers* which carry advertisements and features of interest to job-seekers in their sections on 'Finding Work'.

The main dailies have job supplements once or twice a week, for example on Wednesday and Saturday in the *Sydney Morning Herald,* the *West Australian* (Perth), *Adelaide Advertiser* or the *Courier-Mail* (Brisbane). The Monday Job Market in the Melbourne *Age* is particularly worthwhile. Remember that these wide-circulation papers generate a lot of competition for jobs. Try to buy the paper the preceding evening so you can start your job at the crack of dawn. For example the *Herald* in Sydney goes on sale about 2am from outlets in Taylor Square (Darlinghurst) and near Kings Cross Station.

Ken Smith was so dismayed by the level of competition that he decided to check out the more local papers:

Any jobs that are advertised in the Sydney Morning Herald *are normally so flooded with replies that your chances are minimal. I replied to a bar vacancy along with 119 other people and was very honoured to make it to the final selection stages. I then started looking through the smaller papers and replied to an advertisement for labourer/factory cleaner. In this case, four people applied for two jobs and I soon was working from 7am to 3.30pm with the prospect of daily overtime and Saturday work if I proved myself a good worker. Soon I was taking home just under $500 a week. The work (which was often very physical) was for an engineering firm in Botany Bay which designed and manufactured abattoirs.*

The range of jobs advertised in the newspaper can be discouraging. Sarah Snell describes the choice in the Darwin paper:

Jobs that were advertised included cooking on prawn trawlers (and I gathered through various accounts that this may have included rather more demanding activities than merely preparing meals for the hardy crew), jillarooing (the female counterpart of the jackaroo, who is a kind of cowboy on sheep and cattle stations in the outback), training as a croupier for a new casino, and nude modelling for aspiring life artists at the local college.

Meanwhile the 'Casual Work Available' columns in other cities can carry an equally umpromising range of opportunities including 'promoting art' (i.e. selling prints door-to-door), delivering junk mail for a pittance, telephone sales and working as a film extra (where you will be required to pay a registration fee with little immediate prospect of work). Furthermore all these jobs are gone by 6am.

However it is worth persevering since there will also be adverts for bar and restaurant jobs (especially under the specific heading 'Positions Vacant — Hospitality Industry'), for work on guest ranches, for factory jobs and so on. Posts for live-in child-carers are sometimes advertised in daily papers; check under the 'Situations Vacant — Domestic and Rural' column (though almost all the jobs are urban not rural).

If you think you might be a successful door-to-door salesman, the newspaper is the place to look. Unless you're prepared to exaggerate the virtues of your product you might last no longer than Simon Whalley from Hull did after answering an advert in the *West Australian,* for salesmen of paintings, i.e. two hours. Adam Jones found this work more congenial and managed to make about

$400 a week by selling an average of seven paintings an evening. Ben Hockley and his Spanish girlfriend fixed up a job over the phone from Adelaide selling T-shirts door-to-door in Brisbane. They made a lot of money and saw quite a bit of Queensland in one month.

Perennial advertisers for fund raisers include Greenpeace in all the major cities and in Sydney the Australian Quadriplegic Association (Suite 204, 2nd Floor, 64-67 Kippax St, Surry Hills, NSW 2010; 02-281 8214/6). Fiona Cox answered their ad and ended up having the 'most humiliating day of her life.' She earned an agreed cut of the donations collected which in her case turned out to be $20 instead of the advertised $40-100.

You can steal a march by placing your own advert, e.g. 'Pommie labour willing to undertake any job. Call F.R.E. Spirit.' This technique requires a fixed address and a phone number.

Hostels and Notice Boards

Youth hostels and backpackers' lodges everywhere are a goldmine of information for people working their way around the world. And nowhere are they better than in Australia. Some hostel managers go so far as to run their own informal job-finding service and try to put backpackers in touch with local employers. The disadvantage of basing yourself in a big city hostel is that it is always a struggle to get messages from possible employers.

You may find employment in the hostels themselves of course. Stephen Psallidas describes the proliferation of work, especially on the 'Route' between Sydney and Cairns:

I've met loads of people working in backpackers' hostels. Typically you work two hours a day in exchange for your bed and a meal. Work may be cleaning, driving the minibus, reception, etc. and is always on an informal basis so there are no worries about visas, etc. I will be jumping on the bandwagon myself soon. I'll be completely shattered from picking tomatoes so I'm going to 'work' in a hostel in Mission Beach, where the owners invited me to work when I stayed there earlier. I'm going to rest up in a beautiful place before continuing my travels, and not spend any of my hard-earned dollars.

Another one to try along the Queensland coast is the Federal Guesthouse in Bundaberg (071-533711), as recommended by Andrew Smith.

There are about 140 YHA hostels where employment can sometimes be found on a casual basis, especially at busy periods. In the low season, people are employed as relief managers. Enquiries can be made either directly to the Hostel Manager, or to the following YHA state offices:

Queensland: 154 Roma St, Brisbane 4000 (07-236 1680).
New South Wales: 422 Kent St, Sydney 2000 (02-261 1111).
Victoria: 205 King St, Melbourne 3000 (03-670 7991).
Tasmania: 1st Floor, 28 Criterion St, Hobart 7000 (002-34 9617).
South Australia: 38 Sturt St, Adelaide 5000 (08-231 4219).
Western Australia: 236 William St, Northbridge, WA 6003 (09-227 5122).
Northern Territory: Darwin YHA, 69a Mitchell St, Darwin, NT 0800 (089-81 3995).

One of the most successful groups of non-YHA hostels is Backpackers Resorts of Australia which is especially strong in New South Wales and Queensland. A booklet listing their 122 Australian hostels is widely available after arrival or can be obtained from overseas by sending A$5 to BRA, PO Box 1000, Byron Bay, NSW 2481. Almost all BRA hostels have notice boards advertising jobs, flats, car shares, etc. and all charge $10-15 a night for a dorm bed. On the other hand, hostels are full of your main competition for available work. Andrew

Owen was discouraged to find that every backpackers' hostel seemed to be populated almost entirely with Brits on working holidays. Also be a little suspicious of claims such as 'Plenty of farm work available for guests' since this may just be a marketing ploy.

Most Sydney hostels are well clued up on the local job scene, especially in the two main backpackers' areas, Kings Cross (which is becoming increasingly sleazy) and Glebe. One that is recommended is Pat's Place with the promising description 'Sydney's Working Holiday Hostel' (209 Bridge Road, Glebe, NSW 2037; 02-660 0998) which is run by an Englishwoman who is well versed in the range of employment available and who intends in the future to offer self-contained flats to working/travelling couples. Another pleasant area in which to be based is the beach suburb of Coogee (pronounced Cudjee) for example at Coogee Beach Backpackers, 94 Beach St, Coogee, NSW 2034) which is regularly contacted for casual workers. The same is true of two other Coogee Beach hostels, Aaronbrook Lodge at 116 Brook St, and Aegean Backpackers at 40 Coogee Bay Road. In Kings Cross, the Pink House at 6-8 Barncleuth Square (02-358 1689) says that it can offer work to anyone, provided they are willing to undertake selling work, for example of flowers for a 40-50% commission. Their advert in the most recent issue of *For Backpackers by Backpackers* (which is an excellent source of hostel information) promises $20-80 for four hours' work.

In Melbourne, check out Enfield House Backpackers, 2 Enfield St, St Kilda. In Adelaide, try Rucksackers International at 257 Gilles Street which tries its best to direct travellers to relevant agencies and seasonal fruit picking as well as to jobs at show time and during the Adelaide Grand Prix (see *Special Events* below). In Perth, one of the best places to head is Cheviot Lodge, 30 Bulwer St, Northbridge (09-227 6817) which Mary Bell heartily recommends:

Joe and Diane Lunn, the managers of Cheviot Lodge, get work for residents. Apparently Joe gets rung up each evening with a long list of jobs and gives his residents first chance. Then he rings up other hostels with any left-over work. While I was there all the residents had been found work. Furthermore it is the cleanest and best hostel I have ever stayed in and excellent value.

THE OUTBACK

Most of Australia's area is sparsely populated, scorched land which is known loosely as the outback. Beyond the rich farming and grazing land surrounding the largest cities, there are immense properties supporting thousands of animals and acres of crops. Many of these stations (farms) are so remote that flying is the only practical means of access, though having a vehicle can be a great help in an outback job search. Sandra Gray describes the drawbacks of spending time on a station:

Be warned! Station life can be severely boring after a while. I managed to land myself on one in the Northern Territory with very little else to do but watch the grass grow. If you have to save a lot of money quickly station work is the way to do it since there's nothing to spend it on. But make sure the place is within reasonable distance of a town or at least a roadhouse, so you have somewhere to go to let off steam occasionally.

Despite the large flocks and herds, it is usually possible for one or two experienced stockmen to take care of the animals unaided. Your chances of getting a job as a station assistant (a jackaroo or jillaroo) will be improved if you have had experience with sheep, riding or any farming or mechanical experience, but it is not essential.

Shearing is out of the question for the uninitiated but the post of roustabout (the first rung on the ladder to becoming a shearer) is open to the inexperienced.

Roustabouts fetch, carry, sweep and trim stained bits from the fleeces. Check adverts under the heading 'Stock and Land' for shearing team recruitment. David Hughes got a job as a 'mulesing contractor's catcher', having answered an advert in the agricultural press. It is easy to see from his description why there might be a shortage of catchers:

> *The job I was involved in was 'mulesing'; to prevent blowfly infestation, the lambs have the fleshy area around their sacrums removed. At the same time, the boys are 'marked' (i.e. castrated — I even saw this done with teeth, but I suspect this was more for my pommie eyes) and de-tailed. It's a bloody procedure and perhaps not for the faint-hearted (though I'm a vegetarian!) The mulesing itself is a fairly skilled operation, but the contractor needs a catcher or two to catch the lambs and put them in the frame to hold them. You may be paid about 30 cents per lamb or more usually $7-10 per hour. The lambs can vary in size from the cute little springy things to some virtually indistinguishable from their parents. Meals are usually provided, i.e. a pie and flavoured milk.*

In Western Australia there are far more casual jobs on farms than on stations. Busy times in WA's wheatlands are April to June when the seeding takes place. One traveller who got a job as 'Sheila of all trades' on a small wheat and sheep farm (3,500 acres!) near Pithara, got paid about $200 a week in addition to room and board. On a bigger farm, it can be quite a challenge to keep the piles of 'tucker' appearing for meals and 'smokos' (coffee breaks).

Some city-based employment agencies deal with jobs in outback areas, primarily farming, station and roadhouse work. In Western Australia try Pollitt's (251 Adelaide Terrace, 15th Floor, Perth 6000) who say that tractor drivers are paid $8-10 an hour for 12-14 hour days, seven days a week at seeding time (April to June). Housekeeping, nannying and cooking positions are available for two or three months at a time throughout the year. The standard wage is $200 a week after board, most of which can be saved. For work in roadhouses and outback hotels, there is lots of work in kitchens, restaurants and shops, but experience is essential to earn the going wage of $300 a week after board.

Look for adverts in the publication *Queensland Country Life, Land* or other farming papers. Station work is easiest to find in the Northern Territory and western Queensland in February/March when station managers hire their seasonal helpers.

Although you may not be forced to eat witchetty grubs for tea, there are some obvious disadvantages to life in the outback, viz. the isolation, the heat and to some extent the dangers. Even if you have had experience of living in the rural areas of Europe, it may be hard to adjust to life in the outback. Lots of towns have nothing more than a post office and small shop combined, a hotel (pub) and petrol pump. The sun's heat must not be underestimated. It is important to cover your head with a cowboy hat or a towel and to carry a large water bottle with you. Droughts are not uncommon in the outback. On Tricia Clancy's guest ranch near Sofala NSW, where it hadn't rained for a year and a half, both guests and staff were permitted to have one shower a week (in spite of the terrible heat and dust) and this water had to be recycled for laundry.

Finally there is the ever-present hazard of spiders and snakes which Tricia describes:

> *The hay barn attracted mice and the mice attracted snakes, so whenever we entered the barn we had to make a loud rumpus to frighten them away. Huntsmen spiders proliferated. These great tarantula-like creatures were not poisonous, however it was still frightening when they emerged from behind the picture frames in the evenings.*

Once you get into the habit of checking inside your boots and behind logs for snakes, and under the loo seat for redback spiders, the dangers are minimised. The outback is often a rough male-dominated world, and not suited to fragile personalities.

Conservation Volunteers

Several organisations give visitors a chance to experience the Australian countryside or bush. The main conservation organisation in Australia, the Australian Trust for Conservation Volunteers, is well geared to place volunteers from overseas, though it charges for the privilege. The ATCV is a non-profit organisation which undertakes conservation projects such as tree planting, erosion and salinity control, seed collection from indigenous plants, building and maintaining bush walking tracks, etc. Overseas volunteers are welcome to become involved in these 'conservation tasks' by booking the 'Echidna Package'. This package includes transport within Australia, food and accommodation for an initial period of six weeks at a cost of $720. Further details are available from the ATCV National Head Office, Box 423, Ballarat, VIC 3350 (053-327490) or from their official overseas representative WTN Programs (mentioned above) who charge £475 for the six-week package.

There is also a very active WWOOF organisation in Australia. The headquarters of Willing Workers on Organic Farms are at Mt Murrindal Cooperative, Buchan, VIC 3885; 051-550218. There are about 400 member farms included on the Australian Worklist, all looking for short or long term voluntary help. The network is especially well developed in Tasmania. The list can be obtained by sending £13 to the above address (sterling cheques are acceptable). This fee includes accident insurance. It should be noted that WWOOF has recently been having trouble with the Department of Immigration and wishes to stress that farm stays are for volunteers to train in organic farming and enjoy a cultural exchange.

Before becoming a Long Term volunteer with ATCV, Susan Gray joined WWOOF Australia and worked on several farms on a work-for-keep basis.

They are all growing food organically and usually in beautiful countryside. Most are very keen to show you around and show off their home region to you. The work was as hard as you wanted it to be, but about four hours of work were expected. I usually did more as I enjoyed it, and I learned a lot from those experiences.

Interesting research projects take place throughout Australia and some may be willing to include volunteers. Anne Wakeford (who has a background in marine biology and much experience of boats) joined a series of projects which she thinks might well take on other volunteers, whatever their training. It might be worth trying the Heron Island Research Station (Great Barrier Reef, via Gladstone, QLD 4680) which has been known to offer free accommodation in exchange for about four hours or work a day. The Australian Institute of Marine Science in Townsville (PMB 3, Townsville Mail Centre, QLD 4810) conducts a Research Experience Program for people with a science background who are qualified scuba divers (with a minimum of 15 hours diving experience). Volunteers assist on research trips to the Great Barrier Reef. For other possibilities enquire at the relevant departments of James Cook University or the University of Queensland at St Lucia (Brisbane).

Moving from the Pacific to the Indian Ocean, Anne fixed up a place in the remote Cape Range National Park in Western Australia by visiting CALM (the Conservation & Land Management Department) in Perth.

FRUIT PICKING

Of course there is more to Australia than urban sprawl and outback. There are areas throughout the country which are well-watered and therefore grow fruit and vegetables in abundance: grapes around Adelaide and in the Hunter Valley of New South Wales, tropical fruit on the Queensland coast, apples in the southwest part of Western Australia and in Tasmania, etc. Although fruit farms may be more fertile than the outback, the same considerations as to isolation, heat and dangers from the fauna hold true. The standard hours for a fruit picker working in the heat are approximately 6am-6pm with two or three hours off in the middle of the day.

Just as in Europe and North America, there are professional pickers who follow the harvests around the continent, though it may be possible to spend seven or eight months in one region such as the valley of the Murray River. So if you find yourself falling behind your fellow-workers during the first few days of the harvest, you should console yourself that you are competing with years of experience.

The CES publishes a useful little 'Harvest Table', though it is by no means comprehensive. For example it lists only 11 crop areas for the state of New South Wales. In the major growing regions, the CES may also supply a leaflet setting out the rates of pay. Such a list may also be available from local packing sheds, setting out the 'award' i.e. union-negotiated wages. Different methods of calculating the pay are used in different areas, but quite often the hourly rate for casuals is higher than for full-time employees, say $9 an hour.

Harvest seasons are often diverse: crops ripen first in Queensland and finish in Tasmania as you move further away from the equator. Even the two major grape harvests take place consecutively rather than simultaneously. For easy reference, we have included tables showing crops, regions and times of harvest (omitting grapes which appear on a separate chart) for the most important fruit-growing states of New South Wales, Victoria, Western Australia and Queensland.

You should not give up hope of a harvesting job just because the local CES makes discouraging noises over the phone. As a rule they will not go out of their way to volunteer information. If you ask, 'Are there any vacancies?' they will reply in the negative, even if they have filled ten jobs that morning. You have to ask specific questions to get the whole picture, for example 'Have you had any vacancies recently?' 'Do you have a list of farmers in the area who normally employ seasonal workers?' or 'Is there any particular campsite which pickers stay at?' For example the CES in Orange (centre of a rich agricultural region) told Armin Birrer that the apple harvest was over. Undeterred, he visited a few orchards, talked to pickers and before long had found two full months of work which took him up until the first snowfall in early June.

Quite often farmers will offer a shack or caravan for little or no money. Not all fruit farmers can supply accommodation, however, so serious job-seekers carry a tent. It also helps to have your own transport, first to find a vacancy and then for shopping, banking, socialising, etc. The ideal solution to both problems would be to have a camper van; prices start at $3,000 at the active secondhand markets, especially in Cairns and Darwin. Failing that you will have to rely on hitch-hiking. The CES 'Harvest Table' gives an indication of whether accommodation is provided by farmers and whether you will need your own transport.

Women on their own tend to encounter resistance among farmers (known as 'blockies'). Many of the growers are of Italian or Greek descent and the old Mediterranean sexism creeps in. Certain jobs such as cutting apricots and work in the shed generally are considered 'women's work' and with these jobs it is usually impossible to earn the big money. Louisa Fitzgerald was disgusted by the blatant discrimination:

I was all ready to go and pick fruit down in Victoria, but when I phoned the farm to check if work was still available and they discovered I was a girl intending to go alone, they said unless I was accompanied by a male,

I couldn't pick fruit! It seems that under union rules, females are not allowed to lift over a certain weight which means that for fruit picking a man has to be with you to lift weights — typically chauvinist I'd say!

The Grape Harvest

Australian wines have made a startling impact on the rest of the world as the volume, quality and consumption increases each year. Regardless of their quality, the important fact for itinerant workers is that there is a large quantity of grapes to be picked (by women as well as men).

The main centres for grape-picking are the Mildura region of Victoria, the Riverland of South Australia (between Renmark and Waikerie) and the Hunter Valley of New South Wales (around Pokolbin and Muswellbrook), though they are grown in every state including Tasmania. Detailed tables are set out below. The harvests usually get under way some time in February and last through March or into April. Earnings can be impressive: Raymond Oliver made $2,200 during the five or six week harvest near Mildura.

Many grape varieties are grown in Australia and all demand different styles of picking which (like any fruit-picking) take some time to master before you can earn the big money. The amount you can earn depends on the condition of the vines, the type of grape, whether you have tough enough hands to pull the grapes off (which is much faster than cutting with a knife or snips), whether you have a hard-working partner (which is faster and less demoralising than picking on your own), how fit you are and of course how competitive (or desperate for money) you are.

Normally they start with sultanas and currants moving through different grape types as the wineries demand. Picking for a winery is easiest; it doesn't matter too much if the grapes are squashed or there are a few leaves left in (a blockie would have a fit if he read that). Picking for drying means the grapes shouldn't be squashed and picking for market (i.e. table grapes) demands extreme care and is usually paid as wages or at a higher rate per box.

You will be paid by tin, by bucket (25% more) or by weight. The fairest way to pick is by weight. The idea that you can pick as long as you want or take a break in the afternoon is a misconception. The only time you are likely to get a break in the afternoon is when it is too hot to leave the grapes out in the sun. Around Perth it might be 36°C (97°F) which can be a determining factor when you are deciding whether or not to persevere with the work. Pickers often resort to hosing each other down before they can face the afternoon.

Certainly the demand for pickers is intense in many regions. After deciding that the Sydney employment scene was unremittingly grim, Henry Pearce phoned some CES offices in mid-February and decided that Griffith in New South Wales was the best bet. When he arrived, he was delighted to see that the job board was full of grape-picking jobs. He was hustled into the harvest office, allocated to a farmer and driven to a farm in the region, where he began work the next morning. It paid the going rate of 60-70 cents a bucket and by working ten hours a day, he could manage 90 buckets.

Across the River Murray the situation is the same around Mildura in Victoria, the grape capital of the area. Armin Birrer reported from the town of Cardross that, despite high local unemployment, 300 picking jobs were advertised in the local papers and on roadside signs. This is the area that the CES in Melbourne is most likely to send you if you arrive in January/February. Although Caroline Perry had to wait for a month, she was eventually sent to work for an Italian grape-grower:

The owner met us at the bus station as promised and took us to our accommodation on the farm. We were dumbfounded when we saw where we had to live: it was worse than a shed with rats and cockroaches. The dunny was a tin shed with no lights and so we worried about redback spiders.

It was very tough work, which killed your back and arms before you got used to it. We could work whatever hours we liked, but because we needed the money we worked from 7am-7pm, seven days a week. We usually managed 150-200 buckets a day which isn't bad since the crop was poor that year and we were inexperienced. We were paid a very low 38 cents a bucket.

After describing all these privations Caroline goes on to say that they had a good time and that the employer treated them well. Not only does she recommend carrying a tent (if only to repel rats), but she recommends ringing her employer if you need work in the area in the summer: Joe Blefari, PO Box 152, Nichol's Point, VIC 3502 (050-212671). He is well connected with local farmers and so if he is full will know who may need pickers.

Grape Harvests

South Australia	Dates of Harvest
Clare-Watervale	Feb-Apr
Barossa Valley	Feb-Apr
Adelaide and Southern Vales	Feb-Mar
Coonawarra	Feb-Apr
Langhorne Creek	Feb-Apr
Riverland (Waikerie, Berri, Loxton, Renmark)	Feb-Apr
New South Wales	
Orchard Hills	late Jan-mid March
Camden	early Feb-mid March
Wedderburn	mid Feb-mid March
Nolong	late Feb-April
Orange	March-April
Mudgee	late Feb-April
Hunter Valley (Pokolbin, Bulga, Denman-Broke, Muswellbrook)	early Feb-March
Murrumbidgee Irrigation area (Griffith, Leeton)	mid Feb-Mar
Dareton	Jan-April
Curlwaa	Mar-April
Buronga	Feb-June
Mid-Murray (Koraleigh, Goodnight)	late Feb-April
Corowa	Feb-Mar
Victoria	
Goulburn Valley	Feb-Mar
Swan Hill	Feb-Mar
Lilydale	Feb-Mar
Mildura/Robinvale	Feb-Mar
Great Western-Avoca	Feb-Mar
Drumborg	Feb-Mar
Glenrowan-Milawa	Feb-Mar
Rutherglen	Feb-Mar
Western Australia	
Swan Valley (near Perth)	Feb-Apr
Margaret River	Feb-Apr
Mount Barker	Feb-Apr

An unusual way of finding out about vacancies locally was discovered by Michel Falardeau from Quebec:

When I got off the train in Mildura, I went in to the park since I had seen two people who looked like grape pickers. I asked them if there was work around. One of the guys told me he could help me out and invited me to join them for a drink. After more than one had been consumed I began to get apprehensive, but decided to stick around. At the end of the afternoon he showed me some kind of mission for homeless people, where it was possible to stay free and fill out an application form for work. The management made some telephone calls and the next day drove me to a farm where I worked for two weeks.

The CES offices should be willing to direct you to the areas where prompt employment is most likely. They may even be prepared to fund your travel cost, though you will have to be very persuasive to succeed. Designated CES offices have special harvest services, such as the Adelaide Hills Harvest Service based at the Payneham Job Centre in an Adelaide suburb. Other CES offices are not as helpful. Martin Goff travelled to the Hunter Valley where he had heard they needed grape-pickers and the landlord of the pub gave him a list of the vineyard owners in the region, something the CES had not done.

Grape-picking isn't for everyone but most seem to enjoy the experience. Usually a degree of camaraderie develops between pickers and blockies and hassles about weights, buckets, etc. are more in the nature of a game. If you are lucky enough to find a friendly employer, there may even be an end-of-harvest party or barbecue.

It is more difficult to find work as a cellar-hand, but the pay is better. This is not surprising considering the long shifts, the claustrophobia and the danger of suffocation from the noxious fumes given off inside the vats. Apply at least two months before the harvest begins.

The Apple Harvest

Although apple-picking is notoriously slow going for the beginner, you can usually pick up enough speed within a few days to make it rewarding. In harvests where the conditions seem at the outset to be unattractive, it is not hard to get work especially when it is the time of year (normally February to May) when students return to college and the weather is getting colder.

Many travellers have fared well in the Western Australian harvest which takes place around Donnybrook and Pemberton. (The apple orchards around Manjimup have been badly hit by disease.) Hourly wages are generally reasonable. Farmers ring the associate YHA hostel in Donnybrook (Brook Lodge; 097-311520) throughout the year but especially between November and May, with the peak of the apple harvest falling in the autumn. The manager runs a list system which you sign on arrival if you want work and usually your name gets to the top within a few days (though it took Andrew Smith two and a half weeks, which prompted him to recommend arriving with a good book). Unusually, Andrew was paid an hourly wage of just $8. Pemberton has an official Youth Hostel which also helps guests to find seasonal fruit-picking work at most times of the year. This area has been a target for immigration raids, but farmers continue to employ foreign holidaymakers.

As well as a long and riveting novel, warm clothes will also come in handy as Armin Birrer discovered one chilly autumn:

The only problem with the south of WA is that the wet season starts in May which lasts till August. And as the season progresses it gets colder and colder and more and more miserable. It's very hard work when you get wet and

*cold every day, and the trees give you a nice shower when they're wet. I had
to buy a heater for my van mostly for drying wet clothes.*

Tasmania is not known as the 'Apple Island' for its shape alone. The harvest
takes place between February and April, though other fruit harvests start at the
beginning of the summer. The work is available in the Huon region around
Cygnet and Geeveston not far south of Hobart. Fruit pickers can find out about
possibilities from the CES in Hobart at 175 Collins St. (002-20 5774) or at
'Balfes Hill' Cygnet Youth Hostel (Cradoc Road, Cradoc; 002-95 1551).

When Victor Philpott and Hannah Watts from Essex picked apples in Franklin
just north of Geeveston, they earned $130 between them on a good day, which
they considered fairly good for unathletic and unfit people. They also found the
local farmers very cooperative when it came to sorting out their tax position.

OTHER HARVESTS

From asparagus to zucchini there is an abundance of crops to be picked from
one end of Australia to the other, and the energetic itinerant picker can do very
nicely. Australia has such an enormous agricultural economy that there will
always be jobs. Gordon Mitchell from Aberdeen is just one Briton who has
worked out a profitable route:

*I've been picking fruit in Australia for a few years. I make the best money
between November and April/May, starting at Young NSW picking cherries.
When they finish I do the smaller cherry harvest in Orange NSW, then on
to Shepparton Victoria in early January for the pear picking. When the
sultanas start in Mildura in early February I do them, though most people
stay in Shepparton to finish the pears and apples. This takes me to early or
mid-March when the apples start in Orange and finish in late April or early
May. Sometimes it's very hectic but that's when the picking is good.*

Tobacco and Hops

There are two major areas of tobacco growing: the Atherton Tablelands in
northern Queensland and around Myrtleford in the interior of Victoria. The 20
degrees in latitude which separate these two harvests mean that they take place
at completely different times. The Queensland harvest goes from late September/
early October till Christmas, while the Victorian harvest lasts from late January
to March.

The places to head for in Queensland for tobacco work are Mareeba, Dimbulah
and Chillagoe. Emma Dunnage from Cardiff worked in Mareeba for six weeks
and was paid $9.50 an hour, though some other farms were paying $12. She
warns that tobacco picking is only for the thick-skinned, literally as well as
figuratively:

*Beware. The tobacco plant and the chemicals they put on them are not at
all good for your health. The nicotine eats your skin especially your cuticles.
I'd like to warn any would-be female tobacco pickers: you have really got
to be tough. After the farmer told us we had the job he asked us for sex for
more pay. We made it completely clear that if he was going to harass us,
we would leave right there and then. He said sorry, but he thought all
'pommie sheilas' would do it.*

A less serious problem was the irregularity of the work. The tobacco does not
ripen evenly and the harvesting machinery often breaks down.

Despite the enormous quantities of beer consumed in Australia, most of the
hops are produced in a few areas of Tasmania, around New Norfolk inland from
Hobart, around Scottsdale and in the Devonport area. Jayne Nash helped with
the hop harvest near Scottsdale in northeast Tasmania from mid-March to early

April, which is as long as the harvest lasts. She worked in the shed on a hop stripping machine (where most of the women were employed) while others worked on tractors. Accommodation was not provided, though they stayed in an acquaintance's caravan for $10 a week. Most of their co-workers were locals of all ages who seemed to get by just working on the hops followed by the apples each year. The work was hard but very well paid: they earned $1,000 in 18 days.

Queensland

As you travel north the produce, like the weather, gets more tropical so that citrus, pineapples, bananas and mangoes grow in profusion in the north, while stone fruits, apples and potatoes grow in the Darling Downs, 220km inland from Brisbane. In the tropics there are not always definite harvest seasons since crops grow year round. A good clue to the available work can be deduced from the excessively large artificial fruits by the roadside, for example the big pineapple near Nambour.

The prying eyes of immigration are everywhere along the Queensland coast and anyone whose papers are not in order must be careful. In November 1993 the Immigration Department coordinated early morning raids on farms from Bundaberg in the south to Tully in the north, which caught a large number of fruit pickers working illegally, all of whom were told to leave the country.

About 400km north of Brisbane, the agricultural and rum-producing centre of Bundaberg absorbs a great many travelling workers. The two hostels, Federal Guest House (071-533711) and City Centre Backpackers both on Bourbong St help residents to arrange work and provide transport to neighbouring farms. Rita Hoek from the Netherlands had to wait a few days for work but reckons it was worth it:

I started with a few days of picking snowpeas and a few days of picking zucchinis. After that they found me a job in the packing shed of a tomato grower where I worked for three months. Although working in a packing shed is not as physical as picking, don't underestimate the conditions you're working in. Usually a shed turns out to be a tin oven and doing nothing but sorting thousands of tomatoes is really mind-numbing if not mind-breaking.

According to Rita, the hourly wage in 1993/4 was $7 after tax. When the weather is good expect to work ten hours a day, but when it rains you may work only two hours.

The town of Bowen, centre of a fruit and vegetable-growing region (especially tomatoes) 600km south of Cairns, is by far the best known destination for aspiring pickers. Julian Graham spent part of his working holiday in Australia as manager of Barnacles Backpackers in Bowen, which sounds an excellent place to find out about work:

Part of my duties consisted of finding work for travellers at the many local farms. All sorts of picking and packing is available and Bowen is a superb place to recover considerable funds. My girlfriend and I arrived broke and left with enough money to fly to Tasmania for the Sydney-Hobart race and finance a month's travelling in Tas. Anyone arriving in Bowen should do themselves a favour and go straight to Barnacles where they will find you work (May-December) and make you more welcome than anywhere else in the town by a large margin.

Picking and packing work is normally paid hourly — $9 for men and (in sexist Queensland) $8 for women. It is possible to double that if contract picking. Tomatoes are paid piece work, about $1 a bucket; inexperienced pickers can pick 100-120 buckets a day while the pros can do twice that. Stephen Psallidas saved $5,000 in five and a half months of tomato picking. A good time to arrive is the end of August. If the backpackers' hostels in Bowen are full, accommodation is limited so having a tent is an advantage.

The farm areas are mostly out-of-town and so a means of transport such as a hired bicycle is a great asset. The farmers usually provide a minibus once the picking really gets going, which costs $2 from Bowen. If you're job-hunting farm-to-farm, go out on the Bootooloo or Collinsville Roads or to the Delta or Euri Creek areas. Some names provided by Stephen Psallidas to look up in the phone book are Wright, Price, Fisher, Morgan, Todd, Collyer and Eatough. Apparently the tail end of the harvest in November can be a good time to show up, when lots of seasonal workers are beginning to drift south. If the farmers are desperate enough, they pay premium rates sometimes even double.

Caroline Perry got off the harvest-workers' minibus at the last stop called Climate Capital Packers (PO Box 908, Bowen 4805; 077-852296), a packing shed for four of the largest farms in the area. She got a job packing peppers, rock melons and pumpkins and earned $3,274 net in two and a half months. Her high weekly earnings of $350-400 were partly due to the fact that she was paid double time whenever she worked more than 42 hours a week. Weekly pay cheques were paid directly into a bank account (Caroline recommends the ANZ Bank.)

Heading north, vegetables are picked around Ayr south of Townsville between July and September. Henry Pearce recommends staying at the Silverlink Caravan Park in Ayr, whose owners gave him a list of farmers and where all new arrivals looking for work found it within a couple of days, picking squash, zucchini, cucumbers, peppers, pumpkins and rock melons. Apparently locals prefer to work on the better paid sugar cane harvest which takes place over the same period. Frank Schiller saved a cool $1,400 after four weeks of capsicum-picking near Ayr. Among their recreations, the pickers went dancing in Ayr 'where they've got both kinds of music — Country and Western.'

Cardwell, Innisfail and Tully offer work in banana and sometimes sugar plantations. Farmers around Tully also organise transport between town and the properties. Try asking in the Bilyana hostel just south of Tully. Henry Pearce describes his gruelling job as a banana cutter in October:

The bananas all grew together on a single stem which could weigh up to 60kg. The farmer cut into the trunk to weaken it and, once I had pulled the fruit down onto my shoulder, he cut the stem and I staggered off to place them on a 'nearby' trailer. The work was physically shattering and the presence of large frogs and rats inside the bunch (thankfully no snakes) jumping out at the last minute didn't do anything to increase my enjoyment. We were paid $8 an hour and worked an eight hour day, five days a week which was standard for the area.

Working with Queensland fruits seems to be an activity fraught with danger. If you decide to pick pineapples, you have to wear long-sleeved shirts and jeans (despite the sizzling heat between January and April) as protection from the prickles and spines. Caroline Perry advises anyone who packs rock melons to wear gloves; otherwise the abrasive skin rips your hands to shreds. Worst of all apparently is that lovely fruit, the mango, as Julian Graham explains:

One in three pickers is allergic to the sap contained in mangoes, and in some cases contact with the fruit produces an extreme reaction. Having sent pickers out to the fields and seen at first hand the state they come back in I feel duty-bound to warn people that they may be that unfortunate one in three. One girl's face and limbs became so swollen she had to fly home where it took several injections of steroids to cure her. Remarkably, the hospital at Bowen proved completely incompetent in dealing with this problem and offered no remedy at all. Having spoken to many farmers, it became evident that if the sap squirts into your eyes, serious damage can occur.

Still, if you don't react badly, mango picking can be less strenuous than other harvests since the mangoes are picked off the ground after the trees have been shaken. Whereas the four-week mango harvest around Bowen starts in November, the harvest in the Atherton Tablelands (around Mareeba) starts in early to mid-December.

Southern Queensland is also a good destination. Henry Pearce found work in the citrus harvests around Gayndah in April/May, which was well paid but unreliable. Potatoes and onions are harvested in the Lockyer Valley in the Darling Downs. The harvest around Gatton lasts from August to November, although problems caused by the increasing saltiness of the soil have been cutting yields. Head for the Tenthill Caravan Park near Gatton (074-627200) where it is possible to rent a tent for just $30 a week or a caravan for $75 (plus a $75 bond), and where the owner knows about local opportunities. In most cases you will have to have your own transport. Potato picking is paid piece work, from $18 a bin. If you start at sunrise it is possible for a dedicated novice to pick six bins by noon, though many travellers find this work too hard to tolerate. Contract jobs with local growers of lettuce, etc. are also available but will probably pay no more than $8 an hour.

New South Wales

Two other harvests are the cotton harvest in the extreme north of New South Wales and the onion harvest around Griffith. Richard Edwards discovered that the possibilities for cotton workers around Wee Waa were extensive year-round but especially in October/November which is the cotton-chipping season. Richard earned $600 a week.

Of all the many picking jobs which Henry Pearce found, the best money was earned working on onions around Griffith, where he and his girlfriend saved an impressive $5,000 in ten weeks between early January and March. For a short time Henry was paid $11 a bin and could manage 17 bins a day, alongside a clan of Turks who return every year. However, mostly he was paid the agreed rate of $50 a day (however long the day) but the reliability of work made up for the low pay. You have to be lucky to find work in this harvest particularly if you don't have your own transport. Ask at all the onion-packing sheds in Griffith.

Victoria

The summer fruit harvests in northern Victoria annually attract many participants on working holidays. The best time to arrive is early February and work should continue until the end of March. The Northern Victoria Fruitgrowers' Association Ltd. actively recruits pickers and can be contacted at PO Box 394, Shepparton, VIC 3630 (21 Nixon St, Shepparton; 058-21 5844), while the Victorian Peach and Apricot Growers' Association is at 21 Station St (PO Box 39), Cobram, VIC 3644. Although there is some work in January, this is usually booked up by Australian students and others. Victorian farmers are noted for providing accommodation more often than elsewhere, though anyone with camping gear will be placed more easily.

Work is also available nearer Melbourne for example at the market gardens in the Dandenongs and weeding tomatoes in November/December.

Although harvesting work is often not hard to *get*, some find it hard to make any money. According to Jane Thomas, the pear crates may have looked quite small but were virtually unfillable and she and her companion began to suspect that they had false bottoms. Jane had not realised how hard the work would be physically, and decided at the end of a week, when she'd earned only a pittance, that she was not cut out for it. Perhaps more typical is Andrew Walford's experience of progressing fairly quickly to four or five bins a day at a rate of $16 a bin for strip-picking.

South Australia

Another good place to head as summer approaches is Waikerie (SA) in the Riverland region. As in the case of the grape harvest, most people seem to stay at the local campsite. One of the biggest employers in the area, according to Andrew Owen, is Lester Twigden, most of whose casuals pick rock melons for a reasonably good hourly wage. After picking apples in WA, Andrew Smith arrived in Riverland but found that he was too late for the grapes and too early for oranges. He recommends the Backpackers Hostel in Berri for job information and a good social life.

Western Australia

The area around Donnybrook is not just good for apple-picking: vegetables are extensively grown creating jobs in the fields and packing sheds. Armin Birrer packed onions around Manjimup just long enough to remind himself how much he dislikes indoor work, especially in dusty and smelly conditions. More appealing is the orange harvest around Harvey (north of Bunbury) which starts in June.

There are over 100 vegetable and banana plantations around the cities of Geraldton and Carnarvon north of Perth, many of which are very short of pickers in the winter when they are busy supplying the markets of Perth. The tomato harvest lasts from early August until mid-November, with the month of September being the easiest time to find work. The banana harvest starts in October, but there is casual work available anytime between April and November, most of which pays $8-9 an hour. This is such a well known area for casual workers that immigration raids are not unknown.

Agricultural development around Kununurra in the extreme north of the state continues apace, and every traveller passing through seems to stop to consider the possibility of working in the banana, melon or vegetable harvests. Travellers are regularly hired during the first part of 'The Dry' (the dry season lasts from May to July). If you can't fix up work through the Youth Hostel or the Backpackers Resort hostel, ring some of the following farms: Pacific Seeds (681172), Desert Seeds (682471), Bloecker (681305), Ord River Coop (682255), Ord River Bananas (681481) and Top Bananas (682418).

INDUSTRY

Canneries and Factories

As in other countries, Australian canning factories take on large numbers of casual staff during the harvest. Several contributors have in the past recommended the Golden Circle Cannery near the Bindha Railway Station in Brisbane as a promising employer. During the pineapple season (mid-February to early April) it is a good idea to show up at the canteen early in the morning and look conspicuously eager. R. Howe describes the job:

> *Working conditions were appalling: hot, smelly and, above all, noisy which made conversation impossible. Without earplugs the thunder of machinery was physically painful.*

Factory jobs are occasionally advertised in newspapers or you may hear about openings from other working travellers. City employment agencies like Drake

Crop	New South Wales	Dates of Harvest
Strawberries	Glenorie & Campbelltown	Sep-Dec
Cherries	Orange	Nov-Jan
	Young	Oct-Dec
Peaches & Nectarines	Glenorie	Oct-Jan
	Campbelltown	Nov-Jan
	Orange	Feb-Mar
	Bathurst	Jan-Mar
	Leeton & Griffith, Forbes	Feb-Apr
	Young	Feb-Mar
Plums	Glenorie	Nov-Jan
	Orange	Jan-Mar
	Young	Jan-Mar
Apricots	Leeton & Griffith	Dec-Jan
	Kurrajong	Nov
Apples & Pears	Oakland, Glenorie & Bilpin	Jan-Apr
	Armidale	Feb-May
	Orange	Feb-May
	Bathurst	Mar-May
	Forbes	Feb-Apr
	Batlow	Feb-May
	Griffith & Leeton	Jan-Apr
	Young	Mar-Apr
Oranges (Valencia)	Outer Sydney	Sep-Feb
	Riverina, Mid-Murray	Sep-Mar
	Narromine	Sep-Feb
Lemons	Outer Sydney, Riverina, Mid-Murray, Coomealla	Jul-Oct
Grapefruits	Mid-Murray	Nov-Apr
	Curlwaa	Jun-Feb
Asparagus	Dubbo, Bathurst, Cowra	Sep-Dec
Wheat	Narrabri, Walgett	Nov-Dec
Cotton	Warren & Nevertire, Wee Waa	Nov-Mar
Onions	Griffith	Nov-Mar

Crop	South Australia	Dates of Harvest
Apricots	Riverland (Waikerie, Barmera, Berri, Loxton, Renmark)	Dec-Jan
Peaches	Riverland	Jan-Feb
Pumpkins & Oranges	Riverland	May-Jul

Industrial are a good bet. Ken Smith took the unusual step of visiting factories in Sydney door-to-door:

There are huge industrial estates all over Sydney and really some of them have staff turnovers that are almost daily. My advice would be to get a 336 bus from Circular Quay, get off at Matraville or Botany Bay and just walk around the factories asking if they have any vacancies.

Crop	Victoria	Dates of Harvest
Pears & Peaches	Shepparton, Ardmona, Tatura Kyabram Invergordon, Cobram	Jan-Mar
Tomatoes	Shepparton, Ardmona, Tatura Kyabram Echuca, Tongala Rochester Swan Hill Elmore	Jan-Apr
Tobacco	Ovens & Kiewa Valley	Feb-Apr
Potatoes	Warragul, Neerim	Feb-May
Cherries	Wonga Park, Silvan, Warburton	Nov-Dec
Berries	Silvan, Wandin, Monbulk, Macclesfield, Hoddles Creek, Daylesford	Nov-Feb
Apples & Pears	Myrtleford	Mar-May
	Goulburn Valley	Jan-Apr
	Mornington Peninsula	Mar-May

Crop	Western Australia	Dates of Harvest
Apples & Pears	Manjimup, Pemberton, Balingup, Donnybrook,	Mar-Jun
Oranges	Bindoon, Lower Chittering	Aug-Sept
	Harvey	Jun-Jul
Lemons & Grapefruit	Bindoon, Lower Chittering	Nov-Feb
Apricots, Peaches & Plums	Kalamunda, Walliston, Pickering Brook	Dec-Mar
Tomatoes, vegetables	Carnarvon, Geraldton	Aug-Nov
Bananas	Carnarvon	Oct
Melons, Bananas, etc.	Kununurra/Lake Argyle	May-Oct

Crop	Queensland	Dates of Harvest
Bananas	Tully	October
Tomatoes	Bowen	Aug-Nov
Peaches & Plums	Stanthorpe	Dec-Mar
Watermelons	Bundaberg	Nov-Dec
Potatoes	Lockyer Valley	Oct-Dec
Onions	Lockyer Valley	Sep-Oct
Pineapples	Nambour, Maryborough, Bundaberg, Yeppoon	Jan-Apr
Apples	Stanthorpe	Feb-Mar
Citrus	Gayndah, Mundubbera	May-Sep
Strawberries	Redlands	Jul-Nov
Mangoes	Bowen	Nov-Dec
	Mareeba	Dec-Jan
Pumpkins	Ayr	May-Nov
Courgettes	Mackay	Aug-Sep

Overall Sydney is a wonderfully cosmopolitan place. Of the 23 people who workied for the engineering firm I worked for only three were Anglo-Australians. The rest were Indians, Fijians, Indians and several Chinese who had left China after the Tiananmen Square massacre.

The wages can be very good for tedious jobs and even when they're not, the basic wage is often augmented with awards (compulsory bonuses), for example a 20% award for being a casual worker.

If you are really desperate there is a large meat factory in Merinda north of Bowen in Queensland where it may be possible to get work in the meat-packing sheds by turning up at the factory gates at 6am.

Mining

The mining industry of Australia has recovered somewhat from the recession but offers few casual jobs these days. However rumours still float around that very highly paid work is sometimes available in the iron ore mines and offshore oil industry of northern Western Australia. Armin Birrer was told that 'fronting up' in the mining and shipping towns of Dampier, Karratha and Port Hedland could bring results (i.e. a job paying $65,000 a year) to people willing to sit around waiting for a vacancy.

Gold mining continues to flourish, and union membership is seldom a pre-requisite of employment. The gold mining town of Kalgoorlie in Western Australia is a place recommended for year-round employment by several readers including Lucy Slater:

I know everyone tells you not to hitch but we found that people who gave us lifts between Perth and Kalgoorlie were mines of information with ideas of companies to try, people to ask for, etc. Through a hitching contact my boyfriend got a job in the gold mines which paid $12 an hour. The work was hard going but the hours were long and so there was a lot of money to be made. There seemed to be quite a lot of work going, which did not surprise me since the place is a hellhole. The red dust gets everywhere, it's hot, loads of flies and is quite dead.

After travelling workers (male) become known by the people at the mines, they may be offered work on surveys and with drilling crews as unskilled assistants, known variously as TAs, offsiders and fieldies. This work takes you right into the outback to places like Norseman and Leonora. A driving licence is virtually essential and can easily be acquired (see *Driving* below). Jeremy Pack describes his job:

As an offsider, I have been going off into the bush with a walkie talkie, axe, tape measure and stakes, while the boss stays behind his instrument making sure my pegs are in straight. Sometimes we camp out in the really nowhere bush.

To find such a job you must visit or phone all the mines, drilling and survey companies in the *Yellow Pages,* though the CES does provide a list. Spending time in the pubs is a good way of meeting the right people. For jobs in the remote bush, payment of $500 a week in addition to free pub or caravan accommodation is not uncommon. Otherwise you will have to find your own accommodation, probably in the Kalgoorlie campsite favoured by working travellers.

It is possible to find opals by 'noodling', i.e. sifting through the slag heaps around Coober Pedy. Anne Wakeford had a go and found seven opals in two days of careful searching, one of which was worth $100. Other recommended places are Mintabe and Andamooka, which are on Aboriginal land in remote South Australia, but can be visited after purchasing a permit from the police in Marla.

You might also find a job in areas related to mining. For example there is a firm called Inchcape whose headquarters are at 50 Murray Road, Welshpool, WA 6106 (a suburb of Perth) which occasionally takes on temporary staff (09-458 7999). The work involves the preparation of rock samples for chemical analysis, a job which is reported to be dirty and monotonous. Some laboratory work is occasionally available too. The pay is about $9-10 an hour. It is also worth trying others in this chain of laboratories, in Kalgoorlie, Adelaide, Brisbane, Cairns, Townsville and Burnie (Tas).

Construction and Labouring

Darwin has always been a mecca for drifters, deportees and drop-outs looking for labouring work, though there are fewer job adverts in the Territory's papers than a few years ago. As the rains recede in May, the human deluge begins and competition for jobs through the CES and elsewhere is intense. It is better to be around at the end of the Wet (April) to fix something up beforehand.

There is also some work in Broome. Dan Ould was offered three jobs without even trying, and he believes that there will be lots of construction work for the forseeable future. Anyone considering going there to look for work should take a tent since there is a dire shortage of budget accommodation. Even people who have been working there for some time live in their vans or tents.

If you do happen to get a building job in Australia, you may benefit from some of the interesting perks which the strong unions have negotiated. Workers on buildings over eight storeys high earn a height allowance, even if their work keeps them firmly on the ground. Try ringing furniture removal firms from the Sydney Yellow Pages, e.g. United and TransCity.

Tradesmen of all descriptions usually find it easy to get work in Australia, especially if they bring their papers and tools. A lavish new waterfront development in Townsville is being built as well as a new Queensland resort called Laguna Quays south of Proserpine and various marinas, hotels, roads, houses and airports in the island, all of which are worth trying.

Driving

Several travellers have found it possible to get driving jobs after they have gone to the trouble of acquiring an Australian licence especially the 'B' class licence which permits you to drive trucks. Dan Ould wasn't worried about failing the test:

The test mainly involves driving a truck around the block while the examiner gazes out of the window. If you don't crash you've passed. But the process of taking a few lessons and the test will cost several hundred dollars, worth it in my view since it opens up lots of job opportunities.

Dan liked Broome so much that he was tempted to investigate driving a taxi for Chinatown Taxis who seemed to have a chronic shortage of drivers. Later, in the South Australian town of Ceduna on the Nullarbor highway, he heard of more driving jobs, mainly because so many locals had lost their licences for drunk driving.

An ability to drive can be a handy asset in the cities too, since papers like the Melbourne *Age* are full of adverts for furniture removers, drivers and cab mates (called 'jockeys' in Victoria). Stephen Psallidas observed that there seemed to be more bicycle and motorcycle couriers in Sydney than cars, so you might investigate possibilities.

TOURISM AND CATERING

This category of employment might include anything from cooking on prawn trawlers out of Darwin (read the fine print), to acting as a temporary warden in a Tasmanian youth hostel. You might find yourself serving beer at a roadhouse along the nearly uninhabited road through the Australian north-west or serving at an eat-as-much-as-you-can Sizzlers salad bar in the big cities. Casual employees make up 60% of the 140,000 workforce employed in the hospitality industry.

Casual catering wages both in the cities and in remote areas are high compared to the equivalent British wage. The casual rate for waiting staff is $9-10 an hour, with weekend loadings. Unfortunately these were cut in 1993 by the Industrial Relations Commission to time and a half on Saturdays and time and three-quarters on Sundays and holidays. Partly because of this convention of paying high wages in the hotel and catering industry, Australians are not in the habit of tipping much.

Standards tend to be fairly high especially in popular tourist haunts, as Stephen Psallidas found when he approached a hospitality employment agency in Cairns called the Black and White Brigade:

> *I was in Cairns in April and thought I'd have little trouble getting work. But though I had a visa and experience I had no references, having worked as a waiter in Greece, where they wouldn't know a reference if one walked up and said 'Hi, I'm a reference', so I was doomed from the start. The Black and White Brigade told me that if I'd had references they could have given me work immediately. Curses.*

Anyone with experience as a cook or chef will probably find themselves in great demand. *Work Your Way* correspondents report that they have been paid $750 (net) a fortnight as a chef for the Australian army in Sydney and $400 a week plus a free flat as a cook at a motel in Kununurra. One tourist area which is not normally inundated with backpacking job-seekers is the stretch of Victorian coast between Dromana and Portsea on the Mornington Peninsula near Melbourne. The best time for looking is late November/early December though most jobs start after Christmas.

If exploring Australia is your target rather than earning high wages, it is worth trying to exchange your labour for the chance to join an otherwise unaffordable tour. For example camping tour operators in Kakadu and Litchfield Park have been known to do this; try Northern Explorer and Billy Can Tours. Several holiday cruises depart from Cairns to tour the islands en route to Thursday Island, and take on general staff to clean, cook and serve the guests. Anne Wakeford worked long hours on the *Atlantic Clipper* in exchange for the chance to snorkel and tour the islands in her (limited) time off during the six-day trip. If she had been able to stay for more than one trip, she would have been paid a wage. Also make enquiries of the *Queen of the Isles* and the *Nole Buxton*.

Queensland

Because of Queensland's attractions for all visitors to Australia, the competition for jobs comes mostly from travellers, who are more interested in having a good time than in earning a high wage. The pay is generally so low in seasonal jobs in the Queensland tourist industry that the work does not appeal to many Australians, since they can earn nearly as much on the dole. When employers need to fill a vacancy, they tend to hire whomever is handy that day, rather than sift through applications. For example if you phone from Sydney to enquire about possibilities, the advice will normally be to come and see.

If you want a live-in position, you should try the coastal resorts such as Surfers Paradise and Noosa Heads and islands all along the Queensland coast where the season lasts from March, after the cyclones, until Christmas. If Cairns is choc-a-bloc with job-seekers try the huge resort of Palm Cove just north of the city.

Be warned that Queensland employers are notorious for laying off their staff at a moment's notice without compensation, holiday pay, etc. Emma Dunnage was disillusioned with one of the six backpackers hostels on Magnetic Island where she worked for ten weeks as a catamaran instructor-cum-general dogsbody. She was paid $100 a week, half of what most of the other staff were getting. In fact there is an 'Offshore Islands Award' for workers in isolated places which is a minimum of $350 a week in addition to board and lodging, though it seems that it is often ignored.

Tourist facilities along the coast and the Great Barrier Reef as far north as Port Douglas are being developed at an alarming rate, especially with an eye to the Japanese market. Anyone who has travelled in Japan or who has a smattering of Japanese might have the edge over the competition (unless the competition happens to be a Japanese working holiday maker of whom there are many in Cairns and elsewhere). James Blackman, who hadn't studied any Oriental languages, describes how he got his job at a resort in the Whitsunday Islands:

> I had no luck finding work in Airlie Beach, partly because I bumped into two other people looking for work in this small resort town. The next day I went to Hamilton Island to search for work. I went to practically every establishment and was turned away. However I persevered and the second last place gave me a job as a kitchen hand in a restaurant which was on the beach front. Lots of different people staffed the resort and most were quite friendly, always asking, 'How're ya going?' (which does not mean 'Which bus are you taking to Brisbane?'). I spent ten weeks there earning about $150-200 per five-day week.

James also noticed that working holiday visas were expected on these resort islands.

One of the larger employers is the dive industry. Although not many visitors would have the qualifications which got Ian Mudge a job as Dive Master on *Nimrod III* operating out of Cookstown (i.e. qualified mechanical engineer, diver and student of Japanese), his assessment of opportunities for mere mortals is heartening:

> Anyone wishing to try their luck as a hostess could do no worse than to approach all the dive operators with live-aboard boats such as Mike Ball Water Sports in Townsville, Down Under Dive, etc. 'Hosties' make beds, clean cabins and generally tidy up. Culinary skills and an ability to speak Japanese would be definite pluses. A non-diver would almost certainly be able to fix up some free dive lessons and thus obtain their basic Open Water Diver qualification while being paid to do so. Normally females only are considered for hostie jobs.

Many of the small islands along the Barrier Reef such as Brampton Island, Great Keppel Island, Dunk Island and Fitzroy Island are completely given over to tourist complexes. The first three are owned by Australian Airlines who recruit staff through their Personnel Department on Dunk Island (off Mission Beach). You might make initial enquiries at CES offices on the mainland for example in Prosperpine, Cannonvale, Mackay or Townsville, though normally you will have to visit an island in person (and therefore pay for the ferry).

Caroline Perry was fairly confident that a commercial resort like Surfers Paradise would offer opportunities to work:

> Jobwise we didn't have much luck in Surfers. We went to every hotel, filling in forms and just waiting for the phone to ring. We both got work in Movie World where they seem to like employing backpackers. Warner Brothers Movie World is similar to Disney World, with lots of coffee shops and restaurants that need staff. I got a job cooking burgers in 'Gotham City' but the pay wasn't that good, especially since we had to spend so much on travel from our backpackers' hostel in town. There is such a high turnover of staff, you are nearly guaranteed a job.

The address of Movie World is Pacific Highway, Oxenford 4210 (075-733999). Similar attractions to try along the Gold Coast are Sea World (Sea World Drive, Main Beach, PO Box 190, Surfers Paradise; 075-882222), Dreamworld (075-733300), Wet 'n' Wild (075-532277) and Jupiters Casino (Conrad Jupiters, Broadbeach Island, Broadbeach 4218; 075-921133).

Ski Resorts

Another holiday area to consider is the Australian Alps where ski resorts are expanding and gaining in popularity. Jindabyne (NSW) on the edge of Kosciusko National Park and Thredbo are the ski job capitals, though Mount Buller, Falls Creek, Baw Baw and Hotham in the state of Victoria are relatively developed ski centres too. The best time to look is a couple of weeks before the season opens which in Jindabyne is usually around the 11th of June. The CES offices in Wangaratta and Cooma can advise, though most successful job-seekers use the walk-in-and-ask method. In 'Jindy' try the Brumby Bar, Aspen Hotel, Kookaburra Lodge or any of the dozens of other hotels and pubs.

Denise Crofts went straight from a waitressing job in Kings Cross Sydney to the large Hotel Arlberg in Mount Hotham, where she had a terrific season, since that year the resort had the best snow it had had in a decade. She recommends trying for work at all of the tourist establishments like the Jack Frost Restaurant, the General Store & Bistro Tavern, BJs, Herbies, etc. There is considerable staff turn-over mid-season, though obviously May/June is a better time to look.

Henry Pearce's experiences looking for work were not so positive, despite heavy radio advertising by the CES:

When we hitched to Cooma on June 2nd, we enquired about the progress of the applications we had sent in April. We were told that there had been 4,000 applications and two vacancies for bar staff to date. We carried on up to Thredbo and half-heartedly asked around a few chalets and hotels and it seemed most of them had already fixed up their basic requirements. We were told of several definite posts available once the snow fell. In Jindabyne we were hired to work at the 'highest restaurant in Australia' (at the top of the ski lift) for $12 an hour. But accommodation was uniformly expensive in Jindabyne ($100+ a week) as is the cost of lift passes and ski hire.

Anyone qualified as a ski instructor should attend the hiring clinics which are held in the big resorts before the season gets underway.

If you are already in Tasmania, you could try for work at the ski resorts in that state, Mount Field and Ben Lomond.

Cities

Jobs in catering can usually be found in the major cities, especially Sydney and Melbourne. Just as in London, restaurant jobs in Australian cities seldom provide accommodation, so you will have to find rented accommodation, which is not too difficult in any of the big cities. Meals, however, are normally provided. Outside ordinary restaurants and cafés, catering jobs crop up in cricket grounds, theatres, yacht clubs and (in Sydney) on harbour cruises.

Although there is very little unionism in tourist and service industries, award wages are high both in 5-star hotels and fast food restaurant like Fast Eddy's in Melbourne and Perth. Carole Knight who runs the Working Holiday Hostel in Glebe (Sydney) wrote in 1994 to say that the demand for hotel and waiting staff is increasing as Asian tourism picks up after the recession: 'People who speak Japanese usually get a job within three hours of landing in Australia.' Function work is usually easy to come by via specialist agencies provided you can claim to have silver service experience. It is worth applying to catering companies as

Fiona Cox did in Sydney, though she was not impressed with the wage of $7.40 an hour (weekly take-home pay of $200).

Small family-run establishments are not normally a good bet, but this is where Louisa Fitzgerald worked (though not for long):

Make sure you get the wages you deserve as many bosses will do their best to pay you as little as possible, as I found out when I worked in a sandwich bar in Marrickville, a western suburb of Sydney. I quit because I wasn't satisfied with my wage, a flat rate of $115 a week no matter how many hours I was expected to work! Don't be deceived by what may sound a good deal, e.g. tax-free cash-in-hand wages (which usually applies to small businesses such as cafès and sandwich bars).

The best opportunities for bar and waiting staff in Perth are in the city centre, Fremantle and Northbridge, the area around William and James Streets. Rhona Stannage and her husband Stuart Blackwell arrived in Perth in November 1993 and, having had chalet experience in the French Alps and restaurant experience in Cyprus en route, were in a strong position to find hospitality work:

Since there were lots of adverts in the newspapers for bar/restaurant staff we didn't go door-knocking, but we did meet a Canadian guy who had been in Perth one week and who had immediately found work in Northbridge just by asking around in the restaurants, bars and nightclubs. We both got jobs fairly quickly — me within a week and Stuart a couple of weeks later. (I put my relative success down to the usual sexism in the hospitality trade since we have virtually the same experience.) I'm working in an Irish pub called Rosie O'Gradys (they prefer Irish accents but stretched a point when it came to my Scottish one). I would also recommend the 'traditional British pub' the Moon and Sixpence in the City, since they seem to have only Poms and no Aussies working there.

Rhona was also offered a job at the Burswood Resort Casino which often needs staff willing to work shifts (it is open 24 hours). To attract 'permanent' staff, they pay twice the going wage and offer their staff lots of perks such as free meals and a staff gym.

The preference for females is even stronger in places like Kalgoorlie where waitresses are sometimes known by the offensive name 'skimpies' (after their uniforms). Partly because Darwin has such a small population (60,000), tourist bars and restaurants rely heavily on transients for their staff. As well as being easier to find work than in Sydney or Melbourne, the cost of accommodation is substantially less.

Special Events

As always, special events such as test matches and race meetings are a possible source of employment. If you happen to be in Melbourne in late October or early November for the Melbourne Cup (held on the first Tuesday of November which is a public holiday in Victoria), your chances of finding casual work escalate remarkably. An army of sweepers and cleaners is recruited to go through the whole course clearing the huge piles of debris left by 15,000 race-goers. Hotels, restaurants and bars become frantically busy in the period leading up to the Cup, and private catering firms are also often desperate for staff. An application to a firm like Rowlands (which also operates in Sydney) or O'Brien in September or October is quite likely to turn up some casual work. All the major cities have important horse races. Rowena Caverly was hired for the Darwin Cup Races 'mainly to check that none of the Lady Members had passed out in the loos'.

Another major event in Australia's sporting calendar is the Adelaide Grand

Prix, also held in early November. Ask at your hostel or at likely looking companies (e.g. Spotless Catering).

Travelling fairs are very popular and have frequent vacancies. Richard Davies joined the Melbourne Show in September and was paid $100 a day tax-free (to work 12-14 hours). It travels from Adelaide to Melbourne, Sydney and on up the Gold Coast staying a week or ten days. Ask at the local tourist office.

With so many crowded city beaches, you might have expected good opportunities for pedlars of cold drinks, etc. as described in the chapter *Enterprise.* But choose your beach carefully, since beach inspectors are bound to object. This happened to two readers who tried to sell fruit on Bondi Beach but were thrown off after just 20 minutes.

The Interior

Ayers Rock is a place of pilgrimage for 200,000 visitors a year. The nearest facilities are in the resort village of Yulara about 20km north of the Rock. Opened in 1984, it is now the fourth largest settlement in the Northern Territory and a good place to look for a job. Although the resort has a long waiting list of job-seekers, many people have moved on before they reach the top of the list. Yulara employs about 500 people and the turnover rate for catering and cleaning staff is said to be about six weeks. Staff accommodation is available.

Alice Springs is a very popular tourist destination because of Ayers Rock. One traveller who stayed at one of the many backpackers' lodges reported that 8 out of the 12 women staying there were working as waitresses or bar staff. (Some enterprising travellers have made a little money by collecting the $5 Aboriginal Territory passes from returning visitors to Ayers Rock and selling them in hostels for half that.) Tourist towns like Alice also have plenty of openings for shop assistants and many stores are regularly forced to hire transients. Ally Green and Martin Spiers put in an appearance at the weekly hiring session at the K-Mart Store and had no trouble fixing up work in the housewares and gardening departments, since it was coming up to Christmas. The casual rates they were paid were higher than the regular wages.

Similarly Andrew Walford found occasional work at Lucas Supermarket in Coober Pedy (opal capital of Australia in the South Australian outback). Kununurra and Broome are other places worth trying for tourist work in the Dry (May to October). Broome hosts a big festival in early September just prior to the monsoon (when travel becomes hazardous and uncomfortable) which is a good time to try.

As a general rule the lower the wage the higher the staff turnover. However low wages are not the only reason for people staying a short time at any one job. Working at a road station can be a very lonely business. A typical station consists of a shop, a petrol pump and a bar, and they occur every couple of hundred miles along the seemingly endless straight highways through the Australian desert. The more remote the place (and these are often the ones that are unbearably hot) the more likely there will be a vacancy. If you see a job going in Marble Bar, for example, remind yourself that it is arguably the world's hottest inhabited town with summer temperatures of 50°C-52°C (122°F-126°F).

The Australian Pub

Until the early 1970s, pubs were licensed only from 5pm to 6pm, which resulted in some fairly barbaric drinking habits known as the 'six o'clock swill.' Now that the licensing hours are more civilised (from about 10am-10pm on weekdays and until midnight on Friday and Saturday) many Australian pubs or 'hotels' are now quite genteel establishments where the staff are treated courteously. An increasing number are becoming trendy and yuppified. But there still is a strong preference for hiring women rather than men. The tradition in male-dominated pubs of heavy drinking and barmaid-taunting continues, so you should be prepared for this sometimes irritating (though almost always good-natured) treatment. You may get especially tired of hearing sporting comparisons between Australia and Britain.

Standards of service are high and many hotel managers will be looking for some experience or training. Only those desperate for staff will be willing to train. Even if you have had experience of working in a British pub, it may take you some time to master the technique of pouring Australian lager properly. There is a bewildering array of beer glasses ranging from the 115ml small beer of Tasmania to the 575ml pint of New South Wales with middies, schooners, pots and butchers falling in between. Names and measures vary from state to state.

The local pub is always a good place to find out about local opportunities, from the 'Animal Bar' where fishermen drink in Karumba Queensland to the 'Snake Pit' where fruit pickers congregate on a Friday night in Waikerie SA.

CHILDCARE

Nanny agencies exist in Australia and might be of interest to working holiday makers. The long established Dial-an-Angel agency has branches in most cities and is recommended by Rowena Caverly who managed to find a succession of very short-term jobs through them.

There are also au pair agencies which place European and Asian women in live-in positions normally for a minimum of three months, not all of which require childcare experience. Try for example the AuPaire Connection (PO Box 686, Balgowlah, NSW 2093; 02-451 9537) which advises that the demand for au pairs exceeds supply in the period April to August, when some families will pay higher wages than the basic $100-120 per week. Another possibility is Au Pair Australia (6 Wilford St, Corrimal, NSW 2518; 042-846412) which places au pairs in Sydney, Melbourne and the country. Others can be found in the *Yellow Pages* under the heading 'Domestic Services'.

Most agencies will expect to interview applicants and check their references before placement. As in America, a driving licence is a valuable asset. As well as long term posts, holiday positions for the summer (December-February) and for the ski season (July-September) are available.

Julia Stanton was pleased with the way her agency in Melbourne helped her. Not only did the Australian Au Pair Connection (404 Glenferrie Road, Kooyong, Victoria 3144; 03-824 8857) find her a family the day after she arrived in Australia, but they showed similar alacrity the following week when she left that job because of the long hours. Her next job was much better because it allowed her every weekend off and paid $150 a week live-in.

Anyone considering a childcare position may be interested in Rowena Caverly's experiences:

> *I look after a 15-month old boy at a permaculture farm set in a rainforest. The job is teaching me new skills daily, such as how to persuade a baby that the Huntsman Spider on the wall really does not want to play. Summer is on its way and my next task will be to teach him to toddle heavily to scare off snakes. Otherwise I forsee a nasty situation developing and my money would not necessarily be on the baby as the victim.*

FISHING

It is sometimes possible to get work on prawn fishing vessels out of Broome, Darwin, Cairns, Townsville, Bowen or even Karumba on the Gulf of Carpentaria.

Stephen Psallidas noticed lots of trawler and yachting jobs in the *Cairns Post* (especially on Wednesday and Saturday) and in the CES. You can either try to get work with one of the big companies like Raptis or Toros in Queensland, or on smaller privately-owned boats. Fishing trips from Queensland tend to be day trips.

The main jobs assigned to male deckhands are net-mending and prawn-sorting. Work is especially demanding during the banana prawn season of March/April, since banana prawns travel in huge schools which are caught in one fell swoop, requiring immediate attention. Women are taken on as cooks. They should make it quite clear before leaving harbour whether or not they wish to be counted among the recreational facilities of the boat, since numerous stories are told of the unfair pressures placed on women crew members at sea, though Anne Wakeford encountered no problems of this kind when she went out on a small fishing boat from Darwin. The most that some women have had to complain about is that they were expected not only to cook but to help sort out sea snakes and jelly fish from the catch. Men are not immune to problems, of course: if the skipper takes a dislike to any of his crew, he can simply leave them stranded on an island or beach.

Ian Mudge, who worked on a diving boat in northern Queensland, heard terrible things about prawn trawler work and thinks that it would be safer for a woman to work in a Kings Cross brothel than to sign up on one. He also thinks that the general working conditions are very unsafe, though he does admit that the money can be excellent.

Naturally, skippers operating out of the main fishing ports (like Port Lincoln SA, Eden NSW and Lakes Entrance VIC) prefer to recruit experienced deckhands. If after enquiring at all the fishing offices and after making yourself a familiar sight at the wharfs (e.g. the Pig Pen in Cairns) you still have had no luck, you might consider going along to the net shed (there is a large one in Townsville) and volunteering to work unpaid for a few days, learning how to mend nets. Then if an opening on a boat does crop up, you will be the first to be considered for the job.

The prawn fishing season in Darwin starts on April 15th and continues through till Christmas. Any traveller who goes down to the docks at the beginning of the season has a good chance of being taken on for a one or two week trip, even without experience. Catches are much less than they used to be and most deckhands these days prefer to take a wage of a couple of hundred dollars a week as opposed to taking a share of the profits. The work of sorting and loading prawns is tedious but not too unpleasant except when the spines stick into your hands. Alternatively you may find work on the quayside unloading prawn trawlers or other vessels. The *Northern Territory News* gives details of ships in port or expected, which could provide clues.

If you don't manage to join a crew, try for work in the fish-processing plants. For example the Bundaberg fishing fleet keeps three processing plants supplied, especially with scallops. The CES harvesting booklet includes prawning and scalloping on the coast of Western Australia around Carnarvon. The season lasts from March to October and accommodation is available in caravan parks. The rock lobster season around Geraldton WA also starts in March but lasts only three months. Katherine Berlanny noticed that the CES in Fremantle was looking for crayfish-shellers to work locally. Sometimes you see advertisements for oyster openers, a skill worth cultivating if only for your own consumption. Scallop-splitting is another favourite among casual workers, e.g. around Bicheno on the east coast of Tasmania, though the quantities have been drastically curtailed recently by overfishing.

Conclusion

Ian Fleming sums up what many working travellers have observed about Australians:

The opinion that we formed regarding Australian employers is that they are hard but fair. They demand a good day's work for a fair day's pay, and if you do not measure up to their expectations they will have no hesitation in telling you so. But generally we found that the British worker is held in quite high esteem in Australia. I also found the Aussies to be much more friendly and helpful than anticipated and very easy to socialise with (in spite of the fact that I was nicknamed 'P.B.' for Pommy Bastard).

Most people are struck by what a good standard of living can be enjoyed for not very much money. As Gawain Paling put it so graphically, 'If you're poor in Britain it's the pits; if you're poor in Australia you can have a nice comfortable life'. There is a marvellous range of jobs even if you are unlikely to repeat Sandra Grey's coup of being paid $50 for three hours 'work' testing a sunscreen on her lily-white back, or Jane Thomas's bizarre jobs, one in a sex change clinic, the other in a morgue typing up the labels for dismembered parts of bodies.

Even after several setbacks with bosses and jobs, Louise Fitzgerald concludes:

To anybody not sure about going, I'd say, go, you'd be stupid not to. Australia is a wonderful country and the Australians are great people, even if the males do have a tendency to be chauvinists. If you prove to them you're as good as they are, they tend to like you for it!

New Zealand

New Zealand is a charmingly rural country where 3.2 million human beings are substantially outnumbered by sheep. Travellers have found hitch-hiking easy, the youth hostels congenial, camping idyllic (when it's dry) and the natives very hospitable. If wages are lower than in Australia, life is comparatively cheap. Unemployment (mid-1994) fell to 8.4%, the lowest in four years, so the economy is looking less shaky than it has been in recent years.

Although there is an official minimum weekly wage for people over 20, many travelling workers end up earning a lot less plus subsidised or free accommodation. After looking at the wages and likely hours available in the fruit-growing far north and the ski resort of Queenstown, Henry Pearce decided to change his air ticket and return to Australia where he knew he could earn much more. This is a country where it is better to take enough money to enjoy travelling, and perhaps supplement your travel fund with some cash-in-hand work, odd jobs or work-for-keep arrangements. Camping on beaches, fields and in woodlands is generally permitted. In addition to official youth hostels, there is a wealth of budget accommodation, where you can often learn of local opportunities for casual work, particularly the ubiquitous fruit-picking.

Now that the six-year recession is over, there should be less resentment of foreigners working. Yet in areas of high unemployment outside the cities, a certain amount of tact should be exercised if you wish to undertake a working holiday in New Zealand.

The Regulations

New Zealand deserves its national reputation for friendliness to visitors. Tourists from the UK need no visa to stay for up to six months, while Americans,

Canadians and Europeans can stay for three visa-free months. According to the High Commission literature (available from the New Zealand Immigration Service, 3rd Floor, New Zealand House, 80 Haymarket, London SW1Y 4TE; 0171-973 0366/fax 973 0370) when you enter the country you may be asked to show an onward ticket and about NZ$1,000 per month of your proposed stay (unless you have pre-paid accommodation or a New Zealand backer who has undertaken to support you). In practice, respectable-looking travellers are unlikely to be quizzed at entry.

The immigration authorities are not so easygoing when it comes to *working* visitors. However a new scheme was introduced in 1993 called the UK Citizens' Working Holiday Scheme whereby a maximum of 500 Britons aged 18-30 are granted permission to work in New Zealand for up to 12 months from your date of arrival. The allocation begins on May 1st so the timing of your application is crucial. The New Zealand Immigration Service starts to send out application forms in March, and any applications received after that will be opened on May 1st. If more than 500 suitable applications have been received by the end of May (as is very likely), 500 will be selected at random, and the scheme closed for that year. If the quota has not been filled by the end of May, then a further selection takes place at the end of June. If you apply after the scheme is full, your application will be returned to you, and you can try again the following April/May. To apply you need the form, your passport, the fee of £50, evidence of a return ticket and evidence of NZ$4,200 (about £1,700).

A possible alternative for those who have contacts in New Zealand and can obtain a firm offer of employment before leaving the UK is to apply for a temporary work visa (the same non-refundable fee of £50 applies). Your New Zealand sponsor must be prepared to prove to the Immigration Service that it is necessary to hire a foreigner rather than an unemployed New Zealander. The leaflet 'Getting a Work Visa' available from the New Zealand Immigration Service goes into more detail. The work visa does not in itself entitle you to work, but does make it easier to obtain a work permit after arrival.

It is also possible to apply for a work permit at one of the seven Immigration Service offices in New Zealand even if you arrived in the country as a visitor and landed a job. To be considered for a work permit you must have a written job offer from a prospective employer confirming that the position offered is temporary, a full description of the position, salary, evidence that you are suitably qualified (originals or certified copies of work references, qualification certificates, etc.) and evidence that the employer has made every effort to recruit local people (proof of advertising, vacancy lodged with Employment Service, etc.) As usual there are no hard and fast rules and no guarantee of success, as Ken Smith (a native New Zealander) found when he worked alongside foreigners at Franz Josef resort;

> There was a northern Irish girl working there who had been granted a work permit to work as a waitress. She was assured of the job over the phone having told them that her application for a work permit was being processed (which it wasn't) and when assured of the job she promptly set about applying for a work permit before arriving at the hotel. The work permit was granted three months later, a week or so before she was due to move on, so she was quite annoyed because it cost over NZ$100. On a previous occasion working at the same resort I remember an English fellow who was working as a barman. His application for a work permit was flatly refused, so I guess it depends on 'Do you feel lucky?'

Deborah Porter's application was successful but she encountered problems in Auckland, which is the most popular destination for many itinerant workers, (including Maori people, Samoans and other Pacific Islanders):

The queues at the city's Department of Labour were such that in order to get an interview you had to start queuing at 5am to have any chance of being seen that day. Someone suggested I try the local Department of Labour on the North Shore, and there I was seen straightaway. I paid my fee (very steep and non-refundable if declined) and was told to come back the next afternoon to see if I'd been granted one. Luckily for me, it had, but it was specific to that job and that employer and stated clearly when it expired.

During eight enjoyable months of working as a 'rousie' (sheep shearers' assistant), waitress and office worker, Gina Farmer found that New Zealand employers were less concerned to see a work permit than a tax number:

To obtain a tax (IRD) number you simply go to an Inland Revenue Department and ask for one! You will then be given a form to be filled in after which they take it away. A few minutes later (just when you think they have called the police), they return with your official IRD number. The only thing which is an advantage when applying is to have an address that you can use in the country. It couldn't be simpler, and you are now able to get almost any job. Then, having paid all your taxes, when you come to leave the country, go and get a tax claim form and apply for a refund.

Having an IRD number also means that you are taxed at a much lower rate than otherwise.

Carolyn Edwards had an IRD number left over from a visit to New Zealand four years before, and when she returned in early 1994 to look for work as a temporary secretary, simply told the agencies that she had dual nationality, and this was never queried.

Not all working travellers are so lucky, however. As in Australia, the immigration authorities have begun to pay unwelcome visits to large fruit farms looking for illegal workers. For example during a single week in April, the New Zealand Immigration Service in Hamilton applied to the courts to deport 90 people found working illegally in the Te Puke/Bay of Plenty area. There is no question that overseas workers are needed for the work, since the same office issued work permits to foreigners for the same work at the same time. But they have obviously decided to police the situation and not to turn a blind eye to irregularities. One possible reason for this is pressure from the unions in the Napier area (where unemployment is high), which made the Immigration Service both crack down on illegals and also become more reluctant to issue work permits.

Student Exchanges

GAP Activity Projects send a number of school leavers to New Zealand departing September and January. All placements are in schools, mostly boarding schools, where the work is assisting with the teaching of English, sports and other extramural activities.

American students are eligible to apply for a six-month work permit from CIEE (fee $160) to work between April 1st and October 31st. Also Travel CUTS in Canada administer a similar work abroad scheme for Canadian students. All visas expire at the end of October. The point of allowing foreigners to work only during the New Zealand winter is in order to prevent competition with New Zealand students seeking holiday jobs during the summer. Most students find work in catering, retailing, farming, etc. using advice from the cooperating organisation Student Travel Services (STS) in Auckland.

CASUAL WORK

Because New Zealand has a very limited industrial base, most temporary work is in agriculture and tourism. As in Australia hostels are the best source of job

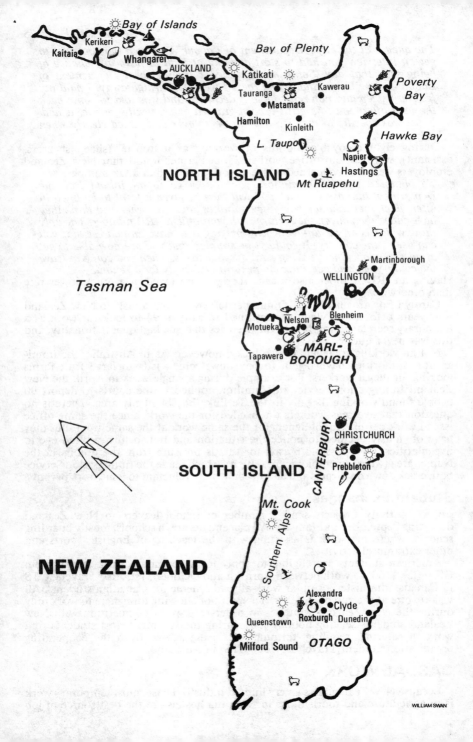

Bay of Islands

Kerikeri

Kaitaia

Whangarei

AUCKLAND

Katikati

Bay of Plenty

Tauranga

Kawerau

Poverty Bay

Matamata

Hamilton

Kinleith

Hawke Bay

L. Taupo

Napier

NORTH ISLAND

Hastings

Mt Ruapehu

Tasman Sea

Martinborough

WELLINGTON

Nelson

Blenheim

Motueka

MARL-BOROUGH

Tapawera

CANTERBURY

CHRISTCHURCH

SOUTH ISLAND

Prebbleton

Mt. Cook

NEW ZEALAND

Southern Alps

Alexandra

Clyde

Queenstown

Roxburgh

Dunedin

Milford Sound

OTAGO

WILLIAM SWAN

information, most of which will be with local farmers. Farmers have been known to visit the local youth hostel or backpackers' lodge looking for seasonal workers as Ian Fleming observed:

> *During our travels around the North and South Islands, the opportunity to work presented itself on several occasions. While staying in the Kerikeri Youth Hostel, we discovered that the local farmers would regularly come into the hostel to seek employees for the day or longer. (This was in July, which is out-of-season.) My advice to any person looking for farm work would be to get up early as the farmers are often in the hostel by 8.30am.*

Alternatively local farmers cooperate with hostel wardens who collate information about job vacancies.

Other farmers circulate notices around youth hostels, for example, 'Orchard Work Available January to March; apply Tauranga Hostel' so always check the hostel board.

Fruit Picking

The climate of New Zealand lends itself to fruit-growing of many kinds including citrus fruits and kiwifruit. The recession particularly affected agriculture causing instability in the work available and wages paid. For example in 1991 Fiona Cox found work in the far north not picking but throwing away half a million kiwifruit for pig feed. But the situation is improving and travellers can once again hope to find paid casual farmwork.

There is a growing trade in fruits and vegetables from roadside stalls and direct from the farmers' properties, so you should keep your eyes open while travelling along country roads where you might even see signs posted 'Pickers Wanted'. Anne Willcocks noticed an organic farm in Central Otago with a large roadside stall:

> *I ended up working there picking fruit and vegetables, and running the stall, living with the family and getting $100 a week for six weeks plus a $200 bonus for staying over the Easter weekend. That replenished my funds, let me rest up from travelling and meant I could afford luxuries like a plane ride over Mount Cook — wonderful!*

Just turning up in towns and asking around is a safe bet for work while the season is on. Below are some general guidelines as to what areas to head for in the appropriate seasons. Motueka/Nelson, Tauranga, Hawke's Bay and Kerikeri seem to be favourites among travellers.

The demand for workers is also very great in the Nelson/Motueka area, which is a great area for travellers for its beaches as well as jobs. Many foreign travellers are hired for the apple harvest, and also at the apple packing and processing works in Stoke, just outside Nelson. The union is strong here and they have succeeded in making it obligatory for farmers to provide accommodation other than just a campsite; some charge will be made though often the deduction is negligible. Orchard workers must join the union. The negotiated rate is about $25 per bin; the average picker fills three to four bins a day, though star pickers like Frank Schiller manage between six and eight and a half bins a day.

The tobacco harvest is another labour intensive activity in the area which takes place in late summer (January to March). If you're willing to work hard you can earn a considerable sum, especially if you stay until the end of the season and get the farmer's generous bonus.

Most farmers are able to provide some kind of shack or cottage accommodation (known as a 'bach' in the North Island, a 'crib' in the South), though the spring and summer weather is suitable for camping provided you have a good waterproof tent. Farmers often provide fresh fruit and vegetables, milk and sometimes lamb.

Another excellent area for finding work is the Bay of Plenty where the majority

Place	Crop	Season
Nelson/Motueka	tobacco	Jan/Feb/Mar
Nelson/Blenheim/Motueka	apples (also pears & peaches)	Feb/Mar/Apr
Wairau Valley (Marlborough area)	cherries, grapes	Dec
Nelson/Tapawera	raspberries	Dec
Kerikeri (Bay of Islands)	peaches, apricots	Dec/Jan
	citrus packing	Oct/Nov
	kiwifruit	late Apr
Northland (peninsula north of Auckland	kiwifruit	May
	strawberries	mid-Oct
Paiumhhue (just south of Auckland)	kiwifruit	May
Poverty Bay (Gisborne)	kiwifruit	May
Tauranga/Te Puke (Bay of Plenty)	citrus	Oct/Nov
	kiwifruit	May-Jul
Clive/Napier (Hawke's Bay)	apples, pears & grapes	late Feb/Apr
	pruning work	Jun
Martinborough (north of Wellington in the Wairarapa area)	grapes	Mar
Central Otago (Alexandra & Roxburgh)	plums, apricots	Jan/Feb
	apples & pears	Mar/Apr
Christchurch area	peaches	Mar
	apples, berries & mixed fruit	Jan-May
	potatoes	Jan-Mar
Hastings	tomatoes	
	apples	
Albany	tulips	Jul-Oct

of New Zealand's kiwifruit is grown. The tiny community of Te Puke swells in number from 6,000 to 10,000 for the duration of the picking and packing season (May-August). A couple of years ago Richard Edwards found work picking, packing and pruning the fruit and was paid an average of $300 a week. The harvest traditionally commences on the 1st of May — though it is wise to arrive a week or two earlier than this — and lasts up to 12 weeks. Rates of pay (either by the bucket or by the hour — called 'award rate' as in Australia) are higher for this crop than for most.

Local students are not available for autumn harvests such as apples and pears in the Hawke's Bay area, so you may be able to pick up casual work in the apple orchards around Napier. Craig Ashworth arrived in late February and found that there was lots of no-questions-asked apple picking work around. He found it tough at first but was eventually earning about $500 for five days of work. There is also pruning work in the area in June.

As mentioned above, the far north of the country, which specialises in citrus growing since it is the hottest part of New Zealand, is another favourite. In addition to the fruit picking work, there are several major packing sheds which employ a large number of casual workers in November/December. Contract pruning can be more lucrative than picking. Kiwifruit pickers normally work in gangs of ten and are paid piece work, while kiwifruit packers and citrus pickers are paid by the hour. Any of the hostels in Kaitaia and Kerikeri will be able to advise. Armin Birrer picked fruit from October to January and reports:

> *There is work in Kerikeri almost year round. The best way is to hire a bicycle and ask from orchard to orchard. Usually you have to work for various orchards at the same time since farmers can't afford to put too much fruit on the market at once.*

Fiona Cox found that it was difficult in this area to earn much though the work was certainly hard:

> *Our first day's work in Kerikeri was strawberry picking, backbreaking work in the hot sun which took days to recover from. For 7½ hours we got $30 and came away hot, sweaty and very pissed off.*

Agriculture

To state the obvious, there is a great deal of sheep and dairy farming in New Zealand. Wages on sheep stations are not likely to be high, perhaps $250 a week in addition to room and board. The International Agricultural Exchange Association offers six to nine month placements in New Zealand to trained agriculturalists, which will cost well over £2,000.

The Saturday edition of the *New Zealand Herald* and the *Waikato Times* in Hamilton are recommended for people looking for work on the land. Philippa Andrews noticed that there were almost daily adverts for milkers in the latter paper between July and Christmas. Usually experience is required.

Gina Farmer describes her job as a 'rousie':

> *Some of the jobs I have done in New Zealand have not been at all easy. For example, as a rousie, you get up at 4am, are working by 5am and don't stop until 5pm, with no guarantee of a day off until it rains so much that the sheep get wet. If you work with a slow gang where the average number of sheep shorn is about 250 a day per shearer then life can be quite fun. However if you land with a gang where the average is 350 and you have to look after two shearers, then life get decidedly tough. So anybody considering this sort of job would be wise to make some enquiries first. Whatever the case this is not a job for the faint-hearted.*

At least Gina was decently paid for all this hard work: $9 an hour on top of board and lodging.

Willing Workers on Organic Farms or WWOOF is active in New Zealand and has a rapidly expanding fix-it-yourself list of about 450 farms and smallholdings which welcome volunteers in exchange for food and accommodation. The list can be obtained from Andrew and Jane Strange, PO Box 1172, Nelson (025-345711), for a fee of £8/US$12/NZ$20. In fact the informal exchange of labour for food and lodging is widespread in country areas. Craig Ashworth describes the pros and cons:

> *I met some marvellous characters and stayed in some wonderful isolated places. A great way to see places and folk off the beaten track. But beware of being used as cheap labour in some unscrupulous places. Also a lot of the WWOOF farmers are quite wacky.*

Craig found that his WWOOF hosts often had leads for paid work and was able through WWOOF contacts to fix up a job on a market garden in Kerikeri and another on an angorra goat farm in Whangarei. One unusual WWOOF host is a travel company for cyclists which describes itself as a truly organic bike shop, Bicycle Tour Services, PO Box 91-296, One Fort Lane, Auckland.

Tourism

Despite the recent recession, tourism in New Zealand continues to flourish. Openings for hotel and catering staff proliferate. Waiters and waitresses are usually paid $7-8 an hour, though in 1994 one correspondent earned only $6 an hour working evenings at a private members' club, but it was cash-in-hand. Remember that tips in New Zealand are virtually non-existent. On the plus side, restaurant kitchens tend to be more relaxed places than they are in Europe.

There are many adventurous forms of the tourist industry. You might get taken on by a camping tour operator as a cook; perhaps you could find a job on a yacht; or if you're a skier, you should try one of the ski resorts. The main ski resorts in the Southern Alps are Coronet Peak and the Remarkables (serviced by the holiday town of Queenstown), Mount Hutt and Treble Cone (with access from Wanaka), all on the South Island. On the North Island try Mount Ruapehu a semi-active volcano (especially the Chateau Resort Hotel) and nearby Lake Taupo. The ski season lasts roughly from April to October.

The lakeside resort of Queenstown is particularly brimming with opportunities. It is a town whose economy is booming due to tourism and whose population is largely young and transient. The central town notice board in the pedestrian mall often carries adverts for waitresses, kitchen help, etc., as do the boards in the Queenstown Youth Hostel and backpacker haunts. One of the favourite drinking establishments for itinerant workers is Eichardts Hotel, while a popular eatery (which also sometimes hires working holidaymakers) is the Cow pizzeria in Cow Lane. One of the perks of being a worker and therefore an honorary resident (instead of a 'loopy', the local term for tourist), is that often workers can get discounts on local activities like rafting. On the other hand, the town's popularity means that there are often more people (including New Zealanders) looking for work than there are jobs, so it might be advisable to try more out-of-the-way tourist areas. Mike Tunnicliffe landed a job as dishwasher at the hotel at Milford Sound and says that one stands a better chance of obtaining casual work in remote underpopulated places on the tourist trail (of which there are many in New Zealand).

This view is corroborated in the experience of New Zealander Ken Smith:

It is accepted practice to phone the resort hotels and ask if they have any immediate vacancies. Good resorts to phone are Milford Sound, Fox Glacier, Franz Josef and Mount Cook. The THC chain of hotels specialise in high-class hotels in remote and scenic locations.

Fishing

Fishing is a profitable business for New Zealand and fishermen can be found in most coastal towns. Nelson is one of the important centres for fishing and fish processing, and one of the largest processing operations is called Sealords where you might get a job (though it's a long shot) filleting, freezing and packing fish in the block freezer. If you can, try to get taken on instead as a 'wharfie,' transferring the fish from the boats to the chiller, since the pay will be better. Go down to the docks before 6am to see if any casual work is available.

The oyster season runs from April to December and oyster shelling work is available especially in Whangerei on the North Island and also Kerikeri. Fiona Cox enjoyed this work far more than fruit picking:

We found work the day after we arrived in Whangarei in December and worked for the three weeks of the Christmas rush. We phoned about four fisheries, none of which asked about visas. We were paid $7.90 an hour and we even got a gumboot allowance! Loads of overtime and in terms of perks and fairness to the workers, it was one of the best places I've worked in, even if we did work in a bloody cold disco. Managed to save enough money to do some touring in the North Island.

Business and Industry

New Zealand is not one of the advanced industrial nations of the world, but there are of course factories which require unskilled workers. Your fellow employees are likely to be Maori and also Pacific Islanders, especially Samoans, who come in large numbers to find work. Check the Saturday and Wednesday editions of the *New Zealand Herald* which carry adverts for labourers, clerks, waiters, drivers, receptionists, etc. Inevitably there are plenty of job advertisements in the papers for salesmen (especially of computers). Beware of advertisements such as the following which may at first sound appealing: 'A Working Holiday — Young People 17-25. See Rotorua, Bay of Islands, the Southern Alps, etc. while earning money and having fun. Must be able to join our friendly team immediately.' These invariably refer to sales jobs and apparently have a history of delayed payments or even of leaving members of their 'friendly team' stranded.

Experienced secretaries are in constant demand in Auckland and Wellington, though temp agencies like Alfred Marks will want to be reassured that you have a legal right to work in the country. Carolyn Edwards has done this twice (with a four-year gap), most recently in Auckland:

> *For temping in Auckland I was earning $11-12 an hour minus 78 cents holiday money. This normally worked out to be $60 a day after tax for a 40-hour week. One of my contracts was with Air New Zealand in Queen St. If I had gone straight to them, I would have been able to join their temporary staff (on six to twelve month contracts) and earn $14 an hour. Something to remember for next time.*

Agencies which Carolyn has tried in Auckland include Alpha Personnel (Suite 2, Level 3, 27 Gilles Ave, Newmarket) and Kelly Recruitment (ASB Chambers, 4th Floor, 138 Queen St), and Lampen, Kelleher and Paxus in Wellington.

Without secretarial skills, try market research (which Mike Tunnicliffe enjoyed doing in Auckland) and labouring agencies, though these have been badly hit by the economic downturn. As usual hostels may be able to help, for example in Wellington the Beethoven House Hostel (89 Brougham St, Mt. Victoria, Wellington) or Rosemere Budget & Backpackers Lodge at 6 McDonald Crescent (04-384 3041) which occasionally refers people to labouring, driving or cleaning jobs.

You may be able to make a profit by selling Reebok training shoes or sports/sailing equipment at the largest sports store in New Zealand, the Sports Bazaar (538 Karangahape Road, Corner Gundry St, Auckland). Backpackers can also save money by buying new or used equipment and selling it at the end of their stay, which is cheaper than hiring.

United States

The great American Dream has beckoned countless people who have left their homelands in eager pursuit of the economic miracle. Whether Latin Americans fleeing poverty at home or East Europeans seeking a brave new world, generations of foreigners have become part of the American population which is often described as a 'melting pot'. But the tide has changed to a trickle. Although the unemployment rate has been falling (to 6.4% at present), the authorities do all in their power to keep out people who come to their country to look for work.

Despite the wide open spaces and warm hospitality so often associated with America, their official policies are discouraging for the traveller who plans to pick up some casual work along the way. The choice of the word 'alien' in official use to describe foreigners may not be intentionally symbolic, however it does convey the suspicion with which non-Americans are treated by the authorities. It is very difficult to get permission to work. Even applications for tourist visas should contain proof of means of support and documentary evidence that the applicant will be returning home. On the face of it, it is all or nothing: either your status is as a tourist who is categorically forbidden to work, or you are an immigrant who must offer a whole range of advanced qualifications and connections. But as we have found in so many other countries, there are some special provisions and exceptions to the rule.

The most important exception to the gloomy generalisation is the special work visa available through the British Universities North America Club or BUNAC (16 Bowling Green Lane, London EC1R 0BD; 0171-251 3472) or through the Irish Student Travel Service for Irish citizens (USIT, 19 Aston Quay, Dublin

2). BUNAC's programmes are described in detail since they are one of the few organisations which can arrange for large numbers of people to work legitimately in the USA. This is because they are authorised by the US Information Agency to give out J-1 exchange visas. A large part of BUNAC's programme consists of placing young people on summer camps, as does another major recruiter of young British people for summer work, Camp America (see below). Other possibilities include joining the one-year Au Pair in America Programme (see section on Childcare below). For a brief list of approved exchanges and internship programmes in the US, send an s.a.e. to the Educational Advisory Service of the Fulbright Commission, 62 Doughty St, London WC1N 2LS.

The other side of the coin is the possibility of working without permission, which carries a number of risks and penalties to be carefully considered beforehand. As described below, the laws are always changing in order to tighten up on black work. The missing link between you and a whole world of employment prospects is a social security number to which you will not be legally entitled unless you have a recognised work visa. We have heard rumours for getting round this problem, and we have been told of some types of employment where legalities hardly seem to matter. We shall be examining these in due course, but first we shall look at the legal ways.

VISAS

Most British citizens no longer need to apply for a tourist visa in advance. Tourists can wait until arrival to obtain a visa-waiver (I-96) which is valid for one entry to the US. However for those planning trips for more than 90 days, it is advisable to obtain the Visitor (B) Visa in advance which entitles you to a maximum stay of six months, though the immigration officer on entry may give you less. Note that the US Embassy does not issue visitor visas to those who are eligible for the visa-waiver. Individuals entering through the visa-free travel scheme or with a visitor visa are prohibited from engaging in paid or unpaid employment in the US.

The Visa Branch of the US Embassy (5 Upper Grosvenor St, London W1A 2JB) can send a brief outline of the non-immigrant visas available. The visa of most interest to the readers of this book is the J-1 which is available to participants of government-authorised programmes, known as Exchange Visitor Programmes (EVP). The J-1 visa is a valuable and coveted addition to any passport since it entitles the holder to take legal paid employment. You cannot apply for the J-1 without form IAP-66 and you cannot get form IAP-66 without going through a recognised Exchange Visitor Programme (like BUNAC and Camp America) which have sponsoring organisations in the US.

For Australians, STA Travel's SWAP Department (PO Box 399, Carlton South, Melbourne 3053) arranges group packages for full-time students aged 18-29 to work in the US between 1st November and 19th March. Applicants must have access to support funds of at least A$2,000 in addition to the cost of the programme (which includes flights to Los Angeles and back-up services) starting at A$2,100. The working visa cannot be extended past mid-March (which makes it tricky for people working in ski resorts) but participants can stay on for an extra month on a tourist visa.

The programmes are allowed to exist because of their educational value. These exchanges and their quotas are reviewed regularly by the government, though with constant lobbying and proof from employers of staff shortages, the quotas have been increasing. Still it is important that the arrangement not be abused (e.g. participants breaking the terms of the programme, or even worse, breaking the law) since this will damage the reputation of the entire programme.

Apart from the J-1 visa available to people on approved EVPs, there are two possible visas to consider. The Q visa, introduced in 1991, is the 'International Cultural Exchange Visa' (affectionately dubbed the 'Disney' visa, since it was introduced partly in response to their lobbying). After working at Disney World on a Q visa, Paul Binfield concluded that the main difference between the J-1 and the Q-1 was that the latter obliges you to pay more tax. If you find a job in which it can be argued that you will be providing practical training or sharing the history, culture and traditions of your country with Americans (e.g. Morris dancing teacher), you might be eligible to work legally for up to 15 months. This must be applied for by the prospective employer in the US and approved in advance by an office of the Immigration and Naturalization Service.

The other possibility is the B-1 'Voluntary Service' visa. Applications must be sponsored by a charitable or religious organisation which undertakes not to pay you but may remimburse you for incidental expenses. Applicants must do work of a traditional charitable nature.

In addition, the H-1B 'Temporary Worker' visa is available for 'prearranged professional or highly skilled jobs' for which there are no suitably qualified Americans. All the paperwork is carried out by the American employer. The H-3 'Industrial Trainee' visa is the other possibility. Applicants must indicate in detail the breakdown between classroom and on-the-job time, and why equivalent training is not available in his or her own country. H-visas are rarely relevant to the average traveller.

Internship is the American term for traineeship, providing a chance to get some experience in your career interest as part of your academic course. The book *Internships* published by Peterson's Guides (address below) lists intern positions which are paid or unpaid, can last for the summer, for a semester or for a year. The book offers general advice (including a section called 'Foreign Applicants for US Internships') and specific listings organised according to field of interest, e.g. Advertising, Museums, Radio, Social Services, Law, etc. This annually revised book is available in the UK from Vacation-Work for £19.95 plus £2.50 postage.

Several organisations in the UK arrange for students and in some cases graduates to undertake internships in the US. The most important is the Council on International Educational Exchange (CIEE, 33 Seymour Place, London W1H 6AT; 0171-706 3008) which helps between 450 and 600 full-time students to arrange sandwich placements in the US lasting up to one year. You (often with the help of an academic adviser) must find the job which has to be related to your course of study, though CIEE offers practical advice on sending speculative applications to US employers. Those who qualify get a J-1 visa. The programme fee is £125 or £150 depending on the length of the internship. Applicants in France should apply to CIEE (1 place de l'Odéon, 75006 Paris; 1-44 41 74 74) and in Germany to CIEE (Thomas Mann Strasse 33, 5300 Bonn).

While studying for a leisure and recreational management degree at Thames Valley University, Neil Hibberd arranged a CIEE internship at a Colorado ski resort:

> *The Council's policy is that they need a letter from the employer before giving you the visa. I first went out to Colorado in August. The Steamboat Ski Corporation gave me a written job offer as a lift operator on the condition that I could obtain a work visa. I returned to the UK, obtained the visa through the CIEE and went back to Steamboat in October. Travelling twice to the States and paying for the work visa and insurance came to £650, which exhausted my savings. Looking back on the process, I see that there should be an easier way to obtain such a placement.*

The Central Bureau (Seymour Mews, London W1H 9PE; 0171-725 9537) administers a Career Development Programme for British nationals aged 19-35 with relevant qualifications and/or at least one year of work experience in a very broad range of careers from chemistry to horse racing. Individuals must arrange their own work placement, though the Central Bureau can provide some assistance. The fee for participants is £55 while the US employer must pay a $1,000 processing fee.

It is exceedingly difficult to get an immigrant visa or 'green card' (actually it's pink) which allows foreigners to live and work in the US as 'resident aliens'. Nearly all the permanent resident visas which are issued each year are given to close relations of American citizens. Money and love are not the only reasons to marry, though this course of action is too drastic for most. If you can find an employer unable to find an American qualified to do the job and have $800-$1,000 for legal fees, you might have a chance.

Arrival

If you have a visa, a return ticket and look tidy and confident, chances are you will whizz through immigration. But American immigration is so notoriously tough and unpleasant that it is worth describing some of the techniques used by readers to avoid possible catastrophe. If you are sure that you will not want to stay longer than 90 days, you can sign the visa waiver form at entry. One reader wrote to say that she had trouble crossing back from Mexico with a visa waiver; however the official word is that you can cross borders as long as the crossing takes place within 90 days of your return ticket from North America to Europe.

Whichever method you choose, be prepared for a gruelling inquisition when you first arrive. It is probably better to ask for a relatively short stay since the authorities are bound to be suspicious of someone who says he or she plans to be a tourist for five months. Whatever you do, don't confess that you hope to find work. Dress as smartly as possible. Ian McArthur got six months at JFK with $1 and the phone number of a friend of a friend, probably because he'd put on a suit and placed his rucksack inside a cheap but respectable looking suitcase. But don't count on having Ian's luck.

If you are taken away to be interviewed, expect to have your luggage minutely examined. Be prepared to explain anything in your luggage which an average sightseeing tourist would be unlikely to have, such as smart clothes (for possible interviews). Better still, don't pack anything which could be incriminating such as letters from an American referring to jobs or interviews, or even a copy of this book. Having written proof that you have a full-time job to return to, property ties or a guaranteed place in higher education in the UK are also an asset. It can be helpful to provide them with a travel itinerary, a list of places and people you want to see in your capacity of tourist.

Although having a return or onward ticket is no guarantee that you will not be hassled, it helps your case. Many travellers recommend entering the US on a short-term return ticket which can be extended after arrival, for instance with Kuwait Airways or Virgin Atlantic. (If you do choose this option, make sure before you buy a ticket that the date can be changed without an excessive penalty.) If you don't have much money or an onward ticket, it is a good idea to have the names of Americans willing to put you up or a letter from a friend, undertaking to put you up and support you for a month or so. Laurence Koe had asked his grandmother to type up a list of all their family connections on the continent which he showed to the suspicious immigration officer at Hawaii Airport, accompanying it with a touching story of how it had been his boyhood dream to encircle the globe.

Rilda Maxwell wants to stress the importance of being adequately prepared for a possible ordeal:

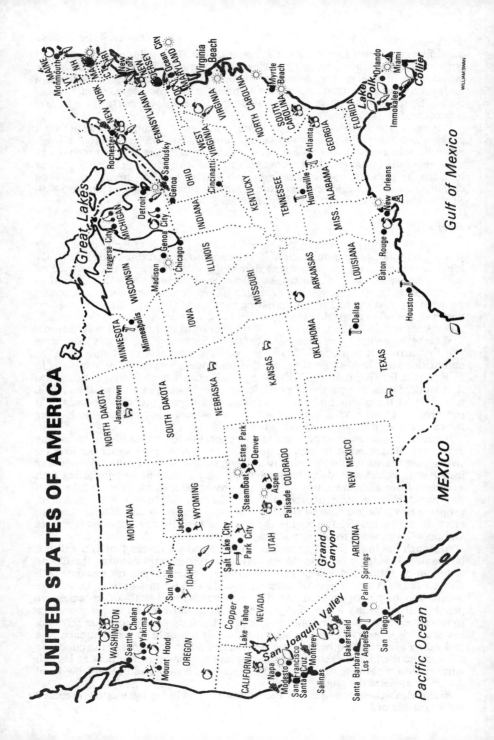

People (especially if they are black, travelling alone or staying more than three months) should have at hand the following:
1) at least $500 for every month of their proposed stay plus credit cards. Don't lie, since you have to count the money out in front of them.
2) names, addresses and telephone numbers (work and home) of your contacts or hosts. If they are suspicious, they won't hesitate to ring the numbers. Have several numbers in case the first people are away or out. Otherwise you'll be stuck at Immigration until they get an answer.
3) be prepared for your luggage and handbag to be thoroughly searched. They read letters, go through your diary and address book with a fine tooth comb. A CV and reference are a give-away, so be sure to send these on ahead if you think that you'll need them. Don't leave anything to chance.

Steve King has an innovative suggestion for proving how wealthy you are. Many British building societies are now affiliated to the 'Link' system, which entitles card holders to withdraw money from over 20,000 cash dispensers in the US. Get friends and family to lend you money for a few days, bring the passbook up to date and then return the money. The card and healthy balance in the account can be paraded before the eyes of any curious immigration officers. Despite taking all these precautions you may still be unlucky enough to get only a couple of weeks permission to stay.

The length of time given seems to be completely random. Marcus Scrace has entered the US three times: the first time he asked for two months and was given three; the second time his request was for three weeks and they gave him two; and the last time he asked for two weeks and was given six months! Jane Roberts adopted a coy approach. She did not fill out the part of the form about proposed length of stay. When she was pulled over and asked why she had left it blank, she confidently gave them a detailed (though fictitious) itinerary and list of contacts (also fictitious) and asked them what period of time they would recommend. With the tables so flatteringly turned, she was given 90 days although she had with her only $280.

Visa Extensions

It is possible though time-consuming to extend your tourist visa. Before your permitted time is up, ask the local office of the Immigration and Naturalization Service for the form entitled 'Application for Issuance or Extension of Permit to Re-enter the United States.' To get a renewal you will have to show adequate means of support and have a reason for wishing to prolong your stay. Merely saying you wish to travel longer may work, or you might claim that your parents are arriving soon and you wish to show them around. If you do this more than once, it's best to apply to a different immigration office. (Note that it is almost always a waste of time to ring INS offices since you will spend hours listening to irrelevant recorded messages.)

Alternatively you can slip over the Canadian or Mexican border and recross the border and hope that the immigration officer on your return will automatically extend your stay. Paul Donut recommends one border crossing in particular:
The border crossing at Point Roberts near Vancouver is a good one. It is on a peninsula and once crossed you can't go anywhere except back into Canada. The US Immigration officials accept that people cross purely to visit the bars and seem to give everyone a six-month visa without asking too many questions. The last time I crossed I actually had to ask for the stamp and card (as a souvenir) as they just weren't interested. By contrast the Canadian crossing on the Pacific Highway is very strict. The officer I encountered checked everything in great detail: money, plane ticket, where

I had been, where I was going, etc. I believe strongly that being polite and friendly to the border guards pays dividends.

If you overstay, you can 'lose' the immigration card showing your date of entry from your passport. In most cases it is only the airline which looks at your passport on your way out and they don't care. The best plan is to exit by land to Mexico or Canada where there is no US immigration control. If trying to reenter the States without a valid visa, try to arrive in a car full of Americans. US citizens do not normally show any documentation at these borders, so if you have overstayed put on your all-American clean cut look, get some chewing gum, smile confidently and hope the word passport does not crop up.

BUNAC

The Exchange Visitor Programme with the most scope and flexibility is undoubtedly the one run by BUNAC. BUNAC administers three basic programmes in the US: one is the 'Work America Programme' which allows full-time university students to do any summer job they are able to find; the second is 'BUNACAMP Counsellors' which is open to anyone over 19½ interested in working on a summer camp as a counsellor; the third is 'KAMP' (Kitchen & Maintenance Programme) which is open to students who want to work at a summer camp in a catering and maintenance capacity. All participants must join the BUNAC Club (£4), travel on BUNAC flights between June and October and purchase compulsory insurance (about £85). BUNAC runs its own loan scheme.

It is worth contacting BUNAC headquarters or your local club branch (in most universities) for their detailed brochures setting out the various and potentially confusing procedures as clearly as possible. There is no easy way of circumventing the red tape and accompanying uncertainty though BUNAC are very experienced at guiding applicants as gently as possible through the process.

Work America Programme. There are around 4,000 places on the Work America Programme. Once you are accepted on to the Programme and obtain your J-1 visa, there is considerable flexibility, i.e. you can travel to the place of your choice in the States and look for any job. But the process of collecting the evidence necessary for participation is complicated and the earlier you start (preferably by early April) the better your chances. In addition to the programme fee of £81 and the flight cost (£379), you must submit:
(a) evidence of full time student status (university, HND, 2-year BTEC, NVQ4/5 or in the gap year with a confirmed university place for the following autumn).
(b) either i) a definite offer of employment in the USA plus proof that you have purchased $500 in American dollar travellers cheques or ii) a letter of sponsorship from a responsible American — preferably a relative — who promises in writing to bail you out in a financial emergency, plus supporting funds of $700, or iii) a vague letter of support from America plus $700 and proof of access to a further $700.

If you choose either of the latter methods you do not have to worry about finding a job until you arrive in the States and, just like finding jobs in any other country, it is much easier if you present yourself in person to prospective employers. BUNAC participants who go to the States without a prearranged job (40% of the total on the programme) take anything from two days to two weeks to find a job. Avoid filling out application forms if there is no immediate vacancy, except at temping agencies which are usually a good bet. The cost of living in America remains low: BUNACers who are not given free room and board with their jobs paid on average $50 a week for a place to live. It should be possible to save enough to fund at least a month of travelling around North America and even have some left over.

If you have no obliging friends or relatives residing in the USA to sponsor you, the only other way is to fix up a job ahead of time by writing to prospective employers. Over half of the BUNACers who are successful with this method use BUNAC's own Job Directory made available to Club members early in the year with a later supplement sent upon request. This is a very useful listing of employers who know about the programme and who have hired British students before.

To widen your scope, you might also look at an annually revised book called *Summer Jobs USA* published each December in the States by Peterson's Guides (202 Carnegie Center, Princeton, NJ 08543) and distributed in Britain by Vacation Work at £10.95. Each employer's entry indicates whether applications from foreign students are encouraged. The categories for each state cover specific job listings in business and industry, summer camps and summer theatres, resorts, ranches, restaurants and lodgings, commercial attractions, as well as in government for which only American citizens are eligible.

BUNACAMP Counsellors. Summer camp work is described in detail in the following section. BUNAC is one of the two biggest counsellor placement organisations in the field, sending between 3,000 and 4,000 people aged between $19\frac{1}{2}$ and 35 as counsellors at children's camps in their programme known as BUNACAMP Counsellors. The registration fee of £59 includes camp placement, return flight and land transport to camp and pocket money of $370-$430 (depending on age) for the whole nine-week period. The fact that you do not have to raise the money for the flight is a great attraction for many; the camp which decides to hire you advances the amount from your wages to BUNAC who in turn put it towards your flight. Interviews, which are compulsory, are held in university towns throughout Britain between November and May.

KAMP. Summer camps provide more scope for employment than just counselling. The Kitchen and Maintenance Programme, otherwise known as KAMP, is open only to students including those at the end of their gap year who are given ancillary (which normally means menial) jobs in the kitchen, laundry or maintenance department, for which they will be advanced their air fare and paid more than the counsellors, i.e. at least $500 for the nine-week period of work. The registration fee is £69.

SUMMER CAMPS

Summer camps are uniquely American in atmosphere, even if the idea has spread to Europe. Almost every American kid is at some point sent to summer camp for a week or more to participate in outdoor activities and sports, arts and crafts and generally having a wholesome experience. The type of camp varies from plush sports camps for the very rich to more or less charitable camps for the handicapped or underprivileged.

It is estimated that summer camps employ nearly a third of a million people. Thousands of 'counsellors' are needed each summer to be in charge of a cabinful of youngsters and to instruct or supervise some activity, from the ordinary (swimming and boating) to the esoteric (puppet-making and ham radio). Several summer camp organisations are authorised to issue J-1 visas, primarily Camp America and BUNAC, but some smaller ones are also mentioned below. The American Camping Association (5000 State Road, 67 North, Martinsville, IN 46151-7902) publishes a *Guide to Accredited Camps* which lists 2,000+ camp for $18.95 (including airmail postage), though this is superfluous if you go through one of the placement organisations.

After camp finishes, counsellors have up to six weeks' free time and normally return on organised flights between late August and the end of September. Camp counselling regularly wins enthusiastic fans and is worth considering if you enjoy children (even the rambunctious American variety who might sue you if you shout at them) and don't mind hard work. As Hannah Start concluded after a summer at an expensive camp, primarily for Jewish kids, in upstate New York, 'If you can survive the bugs and the kids, Bunacamp is a healthy, rewarding way to spend the summer.' Some camps are staffed almost entirely by young people from overseas, which can be useful if you are looking for a post-camp travelling companion. Others have a reasonable proportion of American employees, in which case there is a good chance that you will be invited to visit their homes when camp finishes. In Hannah's view, whatever happens at camp is compensated by the amazing travel opportunities afterwards.

If the idea of working at a remote lakeside or mountain location appeals to you but the 24-hour-a-day responsibility for keeping children entertained and well-behaved does not, you might be interested in a behind-the-scenes job in the kitchen or maintenance. Camp directors often find it difficult to attract Americans to do these jobs, partly because the wages are low, and both BUNAC and Camp America can arrange this for UK students.

Bear in mind that your enjoyment of a summer camp job will be largely determined by the standard of facilities at the camp and its proximity to interesting places to visit on your days off. Where you end up will be potluck, unless you are able to make an informed choice, for example by attending one of the recruitment fairs held in the new year by Camp America. Many impose strict rules, such as no alcohol (apparently Irish and Australian counsellors, true to their reputations, are the most likely to be fined for drinking at camp.)

Camp America

Camp America (Dept. WW, 37A Queen's Gate, London SW7 5HR; 0171-581 7373/fax 581-7377) is a major camp counsellor recruitment organisation in Britain, with 7,000 positions available annually. (The decrease from the 1990 peak of 8,500 is probably due to the fact that the recession in the US has forced many American students to take camp jobs instead of finding more lucrative summer employment.)

The counsellor's flight is paid for by Camp America and then deducted from his or her wages. You must take out Camp America's health insurance policy of £105 as soon as you are offered a place. There are some differences between BUNACAMP and Camp America. The main one is that 18-year olds are accepted, although they receive less pocket money than older people. There is a registration fee of £50 which must be paid in two instalments. When you complete your nine weeks of work you will receive $150-450 pocket money depending on your age and position in the camp. In some cases, grateful parents leave tips for the counsellors which can more than double your earnings.

Despite some initial anxiety, Mark Welfare enjoyed his counselling job arranged through Camp America:

Although I applied in January I didn't hear that I was definitely going until three weeks before departure, when I was just about to start my A-level exams. But it all worked out and I spent a very enjoyable summer working with handicapped and problem children at a camp in the Appalachian mountains of Pennsylvania. For me the Camp America scheme was ideal. I had never been away from home and it was a very easy introduction to travelling since flight, insurance, visa and job are all arranged for you.

One way to avoid the last-minute uncertainty is to try to attend one of Camp

America's recruitment fairs in London, Manchester and Edinburgh in February, which is what Colin Rothwell did:

> *At the recruitment fair at Manchester Poly, you could actually meet the camp directors from all over the States and find out more about particular camps. If you are lucky, like me and a thousand others, you can sign a contract on the spot. Then you leave all the 'dirty work' to Camp America and wait until they call you to the airport in June sometime.*

Camp America also offers two other summer programmes: Campower for students who would like to work in the kitchen/maintenance areas at camp and the International Family Companion Programme for students aged 18-24 who would like to spend ten weeks looking after children in American homes (see *Childcare* section below). The pocket money for nine weeks on Campower and ten weeks with families is $350/$400 respectively.

Other Summer Camp Organisations

There are a few other Exchange Visitor Programmes which deal exclusively with jobs in summer camps:

Camp Counselors USA (CCUSA), 154A Heath Road, Twickenham TW1 4BN (0181-744 9060; fax 744 9252). Also 27 Woodside Gardens, Musselburgh, Scotland EH21 7LJ; 0131-665 5843). They place over 2,000 counsellors aged 18–30 from 25 countries including 400 from the UK and a large number from Australia, New Zealand, Eastern Europe, etc. The pocket money of up to $900 for the nine weeks is generally higher and they are meant to offer a good service as reported by Melissa Stephens:

> *I thoroughly enjoyed my camp experience and appreciated the supportive network that CCUSA provided. We had someone come to see us during the summer to see how we were going. I loved being part of a caring camp and took away many friendships when camp ended.*

The US headquarters are at 420 Florence St, Palo Alto, CA 94301. The Australian office is at Shop 3A, Cumberland St, The Rocks, Sydney, NSW 2000; and the New Zealand one is at 33 Brillian St (PO Box 25-115) St Heliers, Auckland. The deadline for applications is April 1st.

International Counselor Exchange Program (ICEP), 38 W 88th St, New York, NY 10024 (212-787-7706). Also regional office at 12528-A South Truro Ave, Hawthorne, CA 90250 (310-973-8067). Place several hundred foreign counsellors aged 20-30 with relevant experience. Applications must be in by 15th April.

Many organisations in the rest of Europe send young people to the USA as camp counsellors; for example Travel Active Programmes in the Netherlands (PO Box 107, 5800 AC Venray) have up to 1,000 places for counsellors. Readers on the Continent should enquire of their national youth exchange organisation for details.

CASUAL WORK

A law stipulates that all employers must physically examine documents of prospective employees within three working days, proving that they are either a US citizen or an authorised alien (see *Documents* below). All US employers are obliged to complete an I-9 form which verifies the employee's right to work. Employers who are discovered by the Immigration and Naturalization Service (INS) to be hiring illegal aliens are subject to huge fines. Yet it is estimated that there are up to 200,000 British workers living and working illegally in California alone (a state which has been particularly hard hit by recent defence cuts causing soaring unemployment). The law is unenforceable in seasonal industries such as fruit growing and resort tourism where it is still not uncommon for more than half of all employees to be illegal. Farmers and restaurateurs have claimed that they would be put out of business if they didn't hire casual workers without permits. In the autumn of 1994 a US cross-party commission on immigration called for tighter controls in the five states which house the highest number of immigrants. California is leading the way in cracking down on illegal immigrants. A new state law requires that all applicants for a driver's licence (considered an essential piece of ID) must prove that they are in the country legally. The INS has just published a proposal (highly controversial) to create a national database to fight illegal immigration.

Those who are caught working illegally run the risk of being deported, prohibited from travelling to the US for five years and in some cases for good. If your place of work is raided and you are caught, you will be detained while your case is being 'processed', which can take up to three weeks. If you are 'in-status' (which means your tourist visa has not expired) you are given the option of departing voluntarily. If not, you will be automatically deported.

The law seems to be more strictly enforced in areas which are traditional strongholds for 'wetbacks', illegal workers from Mexico and the rest of Latin America, such as California, Texas and Florida. Several years ago, Iain Kemble spent 11 lucrative weeks packing oranges in southern Florida. When he returned at the end of the year hoping to be hired again by the boss who had promised him a job, he was turned away, because the INS had visited the farms in the area putting a stop to cash-in-hand work.

On the other hand, when the authorities are targeting illegal hispanic workers, they may not notice others, as Jan Christensen from Denmark found when he worked in southern Florida on and off for two years, in which time he had no run-ins with the INS:

I arrived in southern Florida very low on cash. So I was very pleased to be offered a job on the second farm I went to and started the same day. No one seemed to care about my status. After about two weeks I was asked by the manager to fill out an employment form which had me worried for a while. I managed to avoid the question about the form for three more weeks until the manager finally cornered me. So I laid down the cards. Apparently he couldn't care less about permits. He was only bothered that I had tried to take him for a ride, and not told him the truth right away. I ended up working there for about six months, without paying tax and earning an average of $500 a week cash-in-hand.

In areas less accustomed to migrant workers, immigration checks are scarcely an issue. Matt Tomlinson from Sheffield found this to be the case in Philadelphia:

I got a great job canvassing for an environmental group. I had no hassle over my lack of documentation. I said it was in the post and they forgot to check. Another staple is restaurant work. I'm now working in a pizzeria which pays the minimum wage of $4.25 cash-in-hand no questions asked. Most other restaurants are the same in terms of laxity, especially take-aways. My friends and I have never had to spend more than a day looking for a job.

Eamon Nolan tells a similar story about New Orleans:

New Orleans employers accept your invented social security number and show less than a passing interest in seeing your green card. You simply say you haven't got it with you today or you had it stolen.

Always act as though you have a perfect right to work. In many cases it is prudent to keep up this pretence with your fellow workers as well as your employer, at least until you know them better. Even menial jobs are taken seriously and harmless jokes or confidences to your work mates often result in your speedy departure.

Documents

Every American can reel off his social security number by heart. J-1 visa holders normally receive theirs within three weeks. Others have managed to get a number for the purposes of banking but it will normally be stamped 'Not Valid for Employment'. This is reputed to work in some states and not others, for example in Florida but not New York.

Some travellers have managed to get away with inventing a nine digit number (3-2-4) with the first three digits taken from the holder's home town zip code. Others have 'borrowed' an American friend's number, especially if they're out of the country, or out of work, since if social security payments are deducted, they will benefit someone. If the false number is traced, the friend can claim that he lost his card and never suspected that some miscreant would find and use it. Be sure that any foreigner caught by the authorities will be deported.

One of the easiest ways for the authorities to realise you are working illegally is when the Internal Revenue Service processes your W-4 form which all employees must fill out when they start work. Some wily travellers recommend using a false name on the W-4 in case the INS and Internal Revenue compare notes. The danger of being caught out is greatest at the end of the tax year (December 31st). Although students should be exempt from state and city income taxes (but not normally federal tax which is 15%), these are normally withheld at source. If you think you might have overpaid, ask your exmployer to send a W-2 form (statement of earnings, equivalent to a P45) to your home address. This will not arrive until the end of the tax year. In January request a non-resident tax form (104ONR) and a *Tax Guide for Aliens* from a US Embassy or Consulate and file your claim accordingly.

Hostels

Occasionally notices of casual jobs appear on the bulletin boards of youth hostels and backpackers' haunts, such as the New Orleans International Hostel at Marquette House, 2253 Carondelet St, New Orleans, the Washington DC YHA Hostel on the corner of 11th and K Streets, and Boston International YHA Hostel, 12 Hemenway St, Boston (which enforces the seven-day maximum stay). Carolyn Edwards had a discouraging time looking for work in Hawaii, but came across plenty of travellers spending four hours a day cleaning in hostels in exchange for bed and board. Richard Davies was given free accommodation and paid $10 an hour to clean toilets at his Los Angeles hostel which allowed him time to look for other work.

Employment in your hostel is always worth asking about since many operate an informal work-for-keep system. After giving up a depressing job hunt in California, Jane Roberts phoned some hostels on her proposed route and was not only offered a job by one in Flagstaff, Arizona, she was even advanced her flight. Ask at privately owned travellers' lodges in the Grand Canyon area; according to Iona and Steve Dwyer they pay $4-6 per hour in addition to allowing you to stay free in beautiful surroundings. The most often-recommended accommodation in the congenial university town of Flagstaff is the Motel de Beau behind the station.

Mark Horobin patronised a different sort of hostel when he found himself skint in California:

> Males who line up in the early afternoon outside the San Diego Rescue Mission on 12th and Market Streets have a good chance of being given a bed and meals for three days. If you need a longer stay you may consider signing up as a helper as I did, but to do this you'll have to explain your reason (claiming to be an ex-alcoholic goes over well) and attend a

compulsory daily Bible study session. If you are accepted you work about four hours a day. Later I stayed at the Prince of Peace Monastery in Oceanside.

Drive-Aways

The term 'drive-away' applies to the widespread practice of delivering private cars within North America. Prosperous Americans and Canadians and also companies are prepared to pay several hundred dollars to delivery firms such as Auto American Transport Inc, Auto Driveaway Company of America and Driveaway Service who agree to arrange delivery of the car to a different city, usually because the car-owner wants his or her car available at their holiday destination but doesn't want to drive it personally. The companies find drivers (an estimated three-quarters of whom are not American), arrange insurance and arbitrate in the event of mishaps. You get free use of a car (subject to mileage and time restrictions) and pay for all gas after the first tankful and tolls on the interstates. Usually a deadline and mileage limit are fixed, though these are often flexible and checks lax. When there is a shortage of drivers you may even get a fee; Michael McDonnell was paid $150 on his first of many deliveries which was from Orlando to Ottawa. A good time to be travelling east to west or north to south (e.g. Chicago to Phoenix) is September/October when a lot of older people head to a warmer climate. On the other hand, when there is a shortage of vehicles (e.g. leaving New York in the summer), you will be lucky to get a car on any terms.

The only requirements are that you be over 21 and have a driving licence (preferably an International Driving Permit). Look up 'Automobile Transporters and Driveaway Companies' in the *Yellow Pages* of any big city or ring a national toll-free number such as Auto American Transport (1-800 CAR SHIP), All American (1-800-942-0001), American International Delivery (1-800-248-0079) or Rent-a-Car Florida (1-800-GO ALAMO). An alternative to the *Yellow Pages* is to ask at a travel information centre for car rental agencies which arrange delivery of rental cars to the places where there is a seasonal demand, for example to Florida or to ski resorts in the winter. The colloquial expression for these cars is 'deadheads'.

If no company has what you want, then try to leave a number where they can reach you, or arrange to phone the most promising ones daily. If you actually call in to register with the company, they are more likely to take you seriously. When establishing your criteria, try not to be too fussy. The greater your flexibility of destination, the quicker you'll be out of town. If you want to go coast to coast, it's probably worth waiting for a through vehicle; but if you have plenty of time and people and places to visit en route, you can piece together shorter runs which will eventually bring you to your destination. Carl Griffiths's company (Auto Driveaway) offered to photocopy the forms so that he could present them to subsequent offices.

If you are travelling with one or more people, you can save money by splitting the cost of the gas. The company allows you to take co-drivers and/or passengers provided they register for insurance purposes. This precludes the picking-up of hitch-hikers, so if you start alone, you should stay that way.

The type of vehicle you are assigned to drive can make a significant difference to the overall cost. Since you are paying for gas, the more fuel-efficient the car, the cheaper your trip will be. You should therefore try to find a modest sized car. This is difficult at the best of times in the United States but even harder among the kind of people who pay to have their cars moved for them. In fact you may not be able to avoid a Cadillac.

Eventually a company will have something going in the right direction and summon you to their office where you are told the details of pick-up, drop-off, time and distance restrictions. You may have to produce two passport size photos, a returnable cash deposit ($250-$350) and your thumb prints. You will be given two copies of the way-bill, an insurance claim form and a notice informing you of the FBI's penalties for delay, diversion and other atrocities. Make sure the company is ICC bonded. You will be expected to nominate a final destination where your deposit can be returned to you. But if you change your mind, you may have to make alternative arrangements; in Carl Griffiths' case, his $350 deposit was sent to his home address in Bristol.

Few agencies store cars themselves so you will need to get a bus to the car's home. When you are introduced to the vehicle, check through a list of existing damage with the owner (or agent) and fill out a 'Condition Report'. Be very thorough, since otherwise you may be held liable for existing damage or faults. If you do have mechanical problems on the road, you pay for any repairs costing less than a specified sum (perhaps $75), which you reclaim from the recipient of the vehicle. For more expensive work you should call the owner (collect) and discuss how he will arrange payment for the repairs. Ten minutes spent checking and going for a short test ride can save an awful lot later. Even if you know nothing about cars, you should be able to check the lights, oil, battery, brakes, and seat belts and also look for rust. If you do know some elementary mechanics, look for a worn fan belt and a leaky radiator which can cause serious problems during your trip. You should point out to the owner/agent anything you are unhappy about. Also check that there is a full tank of petrol, pointing out this requirement on the way-bill if necessary.

Andrew Vincent thinks you should be clued up before deciding:

It's important to have some knowledge of American cars before committing yourself to anything. For example, a 1987 Pontiac Grand Prix would be a great car to deliver. A 1984 Pontiac Grand Prix bears no resemblance to the later model and is expensive to run. You're expected to drive about 400 miles a day, which can be daunting if you're on your own. I delivered a car from San Francisco to Birmingham, Alabama, two days ahead of schedule and was given a $40 tip by the owner, so occasionally you can get back more than just your deposit.

This system is ideal for travellers who can't face the prospect of a three-day bus ride and yet are short of both money and the courage to hitch-hike. Two sisters from Scotland, Fiona and Alison Cox, travelled 2,000 miles (Washington to Boulder) in six days and spent just $100 on petrol. They concluded that this is a 'fantastic and cheap way to travel, cruising down the freeways at the frustratingly slow speed of 65mph.' Michael McDonnell and his son enjoyed drive-aways so much that they did nothing else for their month's holiday.

THE JOB HUNT

It is more difficult to lead a hand-to-mouth existence in North America than elsewhere. Whereas in Europe it is possible to pick up a little work here and there, live on a pittance and get by okay, in North America such a lifestyle puts you at risk of going on the streets where you are vulnerable to what one reader describes as 'the geeks and weirdos of this cutthroat society'. Finding suitable accommodation should be a priority especially in a place where you can't stay long-term at the youth hostel. Adda Macchich was driven out of Boston because she found it was difficult to rent a room without undergoing a credit check and proving that she had a job (and concluded that this explains why there are large numbers of homeless people begging everywhere).

You should not go to the States in search of work without enough money to support yourself for several months and preferably enough for an old car (normally available for about $1,000). Even in cities, a car is a great asset from the start when you may be house-hunting and job-hunting. Another invaluable acquisition is a telephone. There is no quicker way to develop a lifelong phobia for public telephones than having to conduct a job search from one.

As in any place, job-seekers will rely on newspaper adverts for leads. However this tends to be less productive than walking in and asking. Similarly, placing your own advert in order to prearrange a job is not recommended since the chances of attracting undesirables are high. Kev Vincent flew all the way to Hawaii supposedly to work on the farm of the woman who had answered his advert, only to find that she had two fruit trees and was proposing to charge him $150 a month for a cupboard off the garage. Pre-arranging a job from so far away is always a danger as Lee Morton found when he arranged a position as a trainee groom in California through an agency in England. Although the house and setting were beautiful, he lasted only a couple of days because the woman for whom he was working was so unreasonably demanding.

Word of mouth and personal contact are particularly important in the States. According to Tony Mason it's not what you know but who you know that counts. Again and again we have heard from travellers who have been offered some casual work while hitching or chatting to local residents. Many of these jobs have been in building, landscape gardening, furniture removal, etc.

Other jobs are less conventional. Paul Donut didn't have to look too hard for work in the capital of Louisiana, but the opportunities that presented themselves were distinctly unappealing:

> *When I arrived in Baton Rouge I looked up a friend of a friend who I was told might be able to help me find work. She did. She found me a job escorting customers from a bar called the Chimes at the gates of Louisiana State University to their cars, as many of them had been mugged on this short but perilous journey. After considering this job for about 30 seconds, I declined it. (The murder rate in Baton Rouge is second only to that of Washington DC.) The only other job opportunity to arise was helping out on an alligator farm which I wasn't sure would be any safer than protecting people from mugging.*

TOURISM AND CATERING

Labour demands in summer resorts sometimes reach crisis proportions especially along the eastern seaboard. However the majority of catering staff are paid the minimum wage of $4.25 an hour, and some are paid less. Because tipping is so generous, employers can get away with offering derisory wages (e.g. $6 for an evening shift, $45 for a week). In fact the legal minimum hourly wage for tipped employees is $2.13. This is clearly exploitative, but some people who lack a visa do submit to it. An average weekly take in tips for a full-time waiter/ waitress might be $120 with possibilities of earning twice that. Bar staff earn much more in tips, as much as $200 a night (but note that bar staff have to be the legal drinking age of 21). Apparently a British accent helps, except in the case of Jane Thomas who was accused of putting it on to attract a higher tip! Even if you don't get a job as a barman or 'waitperson', busboys (tableclearers) are usually given a proportion of tips by the waiter whom they are helping, typically 10%. Jobs which do not earn tips (like dishwashing) usually earn a reasonable hourly wage, as much as $6.50 when restaurants are desperate.

The majority of food-related jobs are in fast food establishments where labour is not unionised. It is always worth enquiring at the local Kentucky Fried Chicken, McDonalds or Pizza Hut for jobs, since there is a very high turnover of staff. These major chains will invariably ask to see your social security card but, if they are pushed for staff, may not insist on more than reassurance. Try to carry out your search before local college students finish their term, usually in May. The two main disadvantages of working in this kind of job are the lack of accommodation (some are even stingy about the food) and the unreliability of working hours, making it difficult to save. If you want more hours, keep pestering the manager to give you some. One British traveller says:

> *Fast food restaurants offer a great chance to settle into a place. You won't make great money but they're always looking for people, and you'll get to find out what's happening in a place.*

At the other end of the tourism spectrum, the hotel trade is not easy to get into because of the number of people intending to make 'hospitality vending' their career. Liam Lynch tried six or seven plush hotels in downtown Seattle and got the definite impression that the management were not looking for bearded round-the-world latter-day hippies. British nationals aged 19 to 35 beginning a career in the hotel and food service industry or students studying a hotel/catering course with relevant work experience who want to train for up to 18 months in the US should write to the Central Bureau for information about the Hospitality and Tourism Exchange (0171-725 9437).

We have been told that plenty of Brits find work in Los Angeles and also in the cafés of Greenwich Village New York, though you'll have to serve a great many generous tippers before you'll be able to afford accommodation in Manhattan. As an aside, Jane Thomas solved this problem by getting on a house-sitting circuit via contacts. Through a friend she met various people who were only too glad to have a nice reliable English girl live in their houses while they were away on holiday, to discourage burglars, water the plants, etc. One of the places she stayed in was a luxury apartment overlooking Central Park. The incongruity of passing the commissionaire every morning arrayed in the tacky orange uniform of Burger Heaven (where she had finally got a job after much searching and exaggeration of her experience) struck her as highly amusing. The more people she got to know, the more offers of accommodation came her way, including some of pure hospitality.

Live-in jobs are probably preferable, and are often available to British students whose terms allow them to stay beyond Labor Day, the first Monday in September, when American students must resume their studies. After working a season at a large resort in Wisconsin, Timothy Payne concluded:

> *Without doubt the best jobs in the USA are to be found in the resorts, simply because they pay a reasonable wage as well as providing free food and accommodation. Since many resorts are located in remote spots, it is possible to save most of your wages and tips, and also enjoy free use of the resort's facilities. Whatever job you end up with you should have a good time due to the large number of students working there.*

New Orleans is repeatedly described as a casual workers' paradise. Any of the cheap travellers' hotels (for example along Charles St or Prytania St) should be able to recommend places to try or offer work themselves. After fleeing from a boring job in Arizona, Jane Roberts headed for New Orleans in time for the Jazz Festival at the end of April:

> *After 15 minutes of desperate job-hunting I landed a job in a restaurant in the French Quarter. The following day I moved my pack into the apartment above and began work over the Festival. When it ended, business dropped. I was told I could carry on working, but only for tips. No customers meant no tips, so I left.*

In most cases the wages are $4-5 an hour in addition to free accommodation. After having a hard time looking for work in Florida, Steve and Iona Dwyer moved on to New Orleans:

Our luck changed for the better when we decided to stay in the Prytania Inn about a mile outside the French Quarter. Our German boss likes to employ travellers since he thinks that they are able to turn their hand to varied tasks. While Iona went from serving breakfast to sanding and painting, I was a general dogsbody and did such diverse jobs as unblocking toilets and making beds. There are five separate buildings and the work never stops.

The address off Charles St is 1415 Prytania St, New Orleans, LA 70130 (504-566-1515).

Seaside Resorts

Popular resorts are often a sure bet, especially if you arrive in mid-August (when American students begin to leave jobs), or in April/May (before they arrive). Katherine Smith, who got her J-1 visa through BUNAC, describes the range of jobs she found in Ocean City, a popular seaside resort in Maryland which absorbs a large number of Britons:

I decided to spend my summer in Ocean Beach because I knew the job scene would be favourable. I found a job as a waitress in a steak restaurant and another full-time job as a reservations clerk in a hotel by approaching employers on an informal basis and enquiring about possible job vacancies. In my case this was very fruitful and I found two relatively well-paid jobs which I enjoyed very much. Other jobs available included fairground attendant, fast food sales assistant, lifeguard, kitchen assistant, chambermaid and every other possible type of work associated with a busy oceanside town. Ocean City was packed with foreign workers. As far as I know, none had any trouble finding work; anyone could have obtained half a dozen jobs. Obviously the employers are used to a high turnover of workers, especially if the job is boring. So it's not difficult to walk out of a job on a day's notice and into another one. It really was a great place to spend the summer. I would recommend a holiday resort to anyone wishing to work hard but to have a really wild time.

According to Andrew Boyle, there seemed to be more BUNACers in Ocean City than natives and in fact he noticed considerable tension and a 'clash of ideologies' between the party-loving young workers and the older year-round residents. In fact a lot of young foreigners go to resorts like this simply to party and anyone who is willing to work really hard stands out and is usually treated better.

Wildwood New Jersey near Atlantic City is another mecca for holiday job-seekers. A very high percentage of the people working in the fast-food outlets, ice cream parlours, slot machine arcades and fun piers are UK students especially from Scotland and Northern Ireland. As long as you arrive by the Memorial Day weekend (the last one in May) there is every chance of finding work. The New Zealander Ken Smith heard about Wildwood when he was working on a farm in Northern Ireland and found it just as easy to find a job as he had been told:

I was just strolling along the boardwalk when I stopped for an ice cream at a store and was offered a job by its owner. The pay is just $5 an hour but by working 80+ hours a week, it soon adds up. The most hours I worked in a day was 19, and then was told to be back the next day at 8.30am. The other workers told me the boss ripped them off but I must say he always paid me in full.

Apparently the Harbour Bar is the place to go to find out about job possibilities and also cheap accommodation (which is easy to find in Wildwood). Ken Smith shared an apartment for $50 a week. On days when the boardwalk is rained out, you can eat cheap buffet meals at the casinos in Atlantic City. Ken made enough that season to pay for nearly two months of 'quality trvelling' throughout New England as well as paying for his airfares and insurance.

The tourism and catering business is not known for its generous treatment of its employees and America is no exception. Adda Maccich described working conditions at a 4-star hotel on Cape Cod as terrible:

I found a waitressing job despite my non-existent work visa and made-up social security number. Off-duty staff were not allowed anywhere within the hotel grounds (including the beach). The accommodation turned out to be some three miles away without any public transport. I had to hitch a ride with my fellow workers every morning for the 6am start. A lot of the staff were Jamaicans brought over for the season. Staff were expected to walk long distances with a huge tray piled up with dishes held in one hand. Afraid of injury, I reduced the load as much as possible, but soon my colleagues complained and I was fired without notice and asked to move out of the housing unit the following morning.

Other resorts to try are Virginia Beach (Virginia), Myrtle Beach (South Carolina) and Atlantic Beach (North Carolina). David Hewitt found work at a specialised kind of restaurant largely on the strength of his knowledge of kosher food gained while working on a kibbutz. He worked in Jewish hotels in Miami Beach and later in the Catskill Mountains north of New York. Earnings over Passover were spectacular.

Boats

For a yachting job, Florida is the best place to look. Innumerable pleasure craft and also fishing boats depart from the Florida Keys (at the southern tip of the state) bound for the Caribbean, especially between Christmas and Easter. You might also try for work on a cruise ship (see section on *The Caribbean*). There is usually plenty of bar and kitchen work in the Keys, though according to Kev Vincent, this is the second largest gay centre in North America, and many of the jobs had certain conditions attached. The area is swamped by tens of thousands of students during their spring breaks, so accommodation is almost impossible to find in March and early April.

Tim Pask describes his experiences in Huntingdon Beach, California:

My first job was in a boat broker's yard. I found this job after days of walking around the area asking in every shop, garage, restaurant and marina. My work involved cleaning all the boats which were on display as well as any minor maintenance jobs. I held this job for a period of two months earning $5 an hour which was around the going rate. The job suited me perfectly as I was able to stay in the local hostel cheaply. The boat yard was situated next to the beach, so I was able to earn whilst developing an enviable tan. From then on I accepted work which came my way even though I was not actually looking for it. I would pick up odd day jobs which included roofing, cleaning, and kitchen work, often heard about at my hostel.

In Los Angeles most travellers stay in hostels in Venice Beach like Jim's Hostel. Casual work is plentiful in the shops along the beach. Nautically-minded travellers may be able to find work in nearby Marina Delrey which is the largest pleasure boat marina in the world with 4,000 slips.

Ski Resorts

There is plenty of winter work in ski resorts, especially in Colorado, between December and the 'Mud Season' in May. Aspen, Vail and Steamboat Springs Colorado have all been recommended. The best time to arrive is October/ November. Jobs are available as lift operators, restaurant workers, ticket clerks, basket check (like left luggage for skiers) assistants, etc. The main problem in big resorts (especially Vail) is a lack of employee accommodation. Unless you arrive in August/September, you will have to be very lucky to find a room of any kind. Check adverts in the local papers for example in Stamboat the *Steamboat Pilot* and *Steamboat Today*. You should also be aware that immigration raids are frequent, which makes employers reluctant to hire people without papers even when desperate for staff. This danger is less likely at small out-of-the-way resorts like Purgatory or Crested Butte in Colorado but then of course there will be fewer jobs. The local Chamber of Commerce can give you the addresses of most local businesses, for example the Steamboat Springs Chamber Resort Association (PO Box 77448, Steamboat Springs, CO 80444).

Condominiums or 'condos' are sometimes a good bet for casual employment. Hotels aren't a big feature of American resorts (though the two principal ones at Steamboat, the Sheraton and the Ptarmigan Inn, hire large numbers of non-local workers). Resort companies like Mountain Resorts and the Steamboat Ski and Resort Corporation hire chambermaids, maintenance men, drivers, etc. It is common for one company to own all the facilities and control all employment in one resort, and in some cases provide accommodation to all staff. If you're just looking for occasional work, chopping wood in late autumn is a simple way of making a quick profit and contracts for clearing snow from roofs are sometimes available.

Neil Hibberd worked a season as a ski lift operator for the Steamboat Corporation on a J-1 visa fixed up through CIEE (described at the beginning of the chapter). According to Neil the Corporation offers subsidised rental accommodation to its employees who pay about $200 a month in rent.

Aspen is one of the wealthiest resorts and supports a large transient working population. When you arrive, visit the Cooper Street Pier bar and listen for foreign accents. Unfortunately wages are very low in this setting; one worker reported that he saved less than $100 a month after room and board, ski pass and equipment rental. This figure would have more than doubled if he had been able to stay until the end of the season and had been able to collect his share of the season's tips. For a list of major American ski resorts see the end of the section on Winter Resorts in the introductory chapter *Tourism*.

Amusement Parks

Although British people are acquainted with fun fairs and theme parks, they will be amazed at the grand scale on which many American amusement parks and carnivals operate, sometimes employing up to 3,000 summer assistants to work on the rides and games, food service, parking lot and maintenance, warehouse, wardrobe and security.

The opportunities afforded to young people looking for summer work by just one of these enormous commercial complexes are enormous and dwarf Butlins and PGL entirely. But if such immense enterprises intimidate you, you should consider the small-scale possibilities of travelling carnivals and fun fairs which may need a few assistants to set up, operate and dismantle game stands and rides.

Since the keynote of American business is to encourage competition and provide incentives, many of these carnival operators let you take home a cut of the profits on your particular stall, and these can be very high. The trouble is that a lot depends on the type of concession you are allotted in the first place. Whether you get rich or not, you will certainly experience a uniquely American way of life and meet some authentic American characters. Chris Daniels got a job through the BUNAC job directory with a small travelling fair in the mid-West:

The convoy of trucks made an impressive sight, taking 'all the fun of the fair' from one sleepy town to another linked by miles of straight, often deserted roads. The romance of this nomadic lifestyle could not unfortunately offset the harsh realities of working 18 solid hours whenever we moved on to the next town, permanently dirty truck accommodation and a low fixed wage.

The other employees were a strange mixture: the fellow who ran a ride called the 'Tilt & Whirl' was called 'Rosebud' and was something out of the days of the Wild West (or at least out of a Saturday night TV Western); he chewed tobacco incessantly and spoke with an almost unintelligible drawl. The fair was owned by one man, an elderly gentleman, patriot and entrepreneur with the frontier spirit which had built it up from scratch.

There was less romance and more dirt at the fun fair which employed another BUNACer, Robert Lofts. Although his fair was advertised as a travelling fair, in fact it travelled only about 20 miles around the outskirts of the Detroit conurbation. No accommodation of any kind was provided and employees were half expected to sleep behind their stalls as unpaid night watchmen. With no washing or cooking facilities, this arrangement soon became unbearable and Robert set off for new worlds to conquer. BUNAC does try to warn 'reserved' or 'highly sensitive' individuals who may not be able to cope with the 'cowboy-like lifestyle'.

The International Staffing Department of Walt Disney's EPCOT Center (PO Box 10,090, Lake Buena Vista, Florida 32830-0090) prefer to rely on the word of mouth network rather than have their six month or one year vacancies for young people to represent the culture and customs of Britain widely publicised. Anyone applying will probably have to wait at least six months until there is space at one of the two annual recruiting presentations which Disney organises in Britain. Paul Binfield from Kent describes the process of being hired by Disney as 'a long and patient' one:

I initially wrote to Disney in October and started my contract in January, 15 months later. It was the most enjoyable year of my life, experiencing so many excellent things and making the best friends from all over the world. The pros far outweigh the cons, though some people did hate the work. Disney are a strict company with many rules which are vigorously enforced. The work in merchandising or the pub/restauarant is taken extremely seriously and sometimes it can be hard to manufacture a big cheesy Disney smile. There are dress codes (for example men have to be clean shaven every day), and verbal and written warnings for matters which would be considered very trivial in Britain, and indeed terminations (which is a very nasty word for being fired). If you go with the right attitude it can be great fun.

OTHER POPULAR JOBS

Selling

By reputation, anyway, American salesmen are a hardbitten lot. Some travellers have found that their foreign charm makes selling surprisingly effortless. ('Are you really English? I just love that accent.') Americans are not as suspicious of salesmen as other nationalities and you may be pleasantly surprised by the tolerance with which you are received on the doorstep and, even more, by the high earnings which are possible. If you have the stomach for time-share selling in Florida, you can do very well apparently (although the legal status of approaching people in the street is tricky in some municipalities). In some cases you may need a permit for door-to-door selling which your employer might expect you to pay for. It is also not unknown for companies to run compulsory training courses which are not necessarily free.

Advertisements for salesmen, especially of magazine subscriptions and cleaning products, proliferate in local papers. Many employers will not be too concerned if your visa is not in order as long as you inspire them with faith in your selling ability.

For general comments on the pros and cons (sic) of selling, see the chapter *Business and Industry*. You may find telephone work less off-putting than door-to-door salesmanship, but it will also be less lucrative. On the other hand, if you want to experience the hard edge of selling, why not tackle a job which forces you to rely solely on commission? Grimly Corridor (who is arguably a born salesman) answered a newspaper advert in Kansas and was soon selling cleaning products during the day and being housed in Holiday Inn-style hotels at night. After a couple of weeks in Kansas, the team of salesmen was moved on (at the company's expense of course) to Chicago. Grimly thinks that at least some of his success was due to the Cockney accent and manner which he assumed. Also he had gained some experience of American salesmanship in Portland Maine where he had worked as a telephone canvasser selling subscriptions to the local newspaper; he managed about six or eight leads at $5 each per evening.

Fishing and Hunting

Fishing off the coast of Alaska and fish-canning are classic money-spinning summer jobs in the US. But it seems that in the past few years the salmon industry has been devastated by a change in taste away from tinned salmon. Whether this crisis is passing or permanent remains to be seen. In case there is a salmon revival, here is the lowdown on what seasonal jobs there might be. In any case, do some ringing around before making the expensive trip to Alaska.

The first halibut are caught over a 24-hour period in early May and this opens the fishing season. It is easier to pin down job openings then than later at the peak salmon season of July/August. Some novices frequent the docks in places like Kodiak, Ketchikan, Homer and Petersburg in Alaska, Astoria and Newport in Oregon, etc. and try to volunteer to work in exchange for their keep on their first fishing trip. After that they will have earned a place on the boat and will be able to share in the profits. Without lots of stamina and some mechanical aptitude, it will be very difficult to persuade a skipper to take on inexperienced crew.

Not only is the job extremely gruelling and often dangerous, but the redneck society of the rest of the crew may not be to your taste. Shooting birds and even whales for fun is commonplace and fishing methods which destroy all manner of marine life are regularly used even if forbidden by law. It has forced more than one hardened traveller to leave before the end of the season and turned others into vegetarians. No doubt all join Greenpeace the minute they get home.

Finding work in an Alaskan fish processing plant may not be quite as difficult, though it will take a lot of patience and initiative. You must go to each cannery and put in an application (before the salmon run begins in the beginning of July for the Kenai area). After that, it is a question of waiting, preferably outside the canneries every day, to see if they are hiring. The big hiring days are when the fishermen come in. When there are openings, the right number of people will be picked from the waiting crowd, more or less at random, which can be very frustrating. A lot of people give up and leave, so the longer you wait the better your chances. The salmon run at different times during the summer, depending on the area of Alaska. The farther west you go in Alaska, the earlier the run is; for instance it takes place in August on the Panhandle.

Kenai south of Anchorage has a large number of processing factories and hires hundreds of workers during the latter half of June; try Kenai Packers and

Columbia Wards Fisheries. Canneries and freezing plants occasionally provide food and accommodation but it is much more usual for cannery workers to camp.

David Irvine caught a standby flight to Anchorage in mid-July hoping to get a fishing job. After looking into the situation, he decided against fishing and tried hunting lodges instead. He got a list of recognised guides from the Alaska Department of Fish & Game and began phoning. Partly because of the difficulty of talking to the hunters (who are often out in the bush) this method did not work. Although the tourist season was already underway, a job was advertised in *The Anchorage Times* for a lodge assistant which David had the good fortune to get. He worked at a fly-in fly-out lodge in the Alaskan interior for two months, landscaping and doing maintenance work for the benefit of the JR clones and German millionaires who patronised the lodge. He had the impression that women cooks were in considerable demand at other lodges.

David also gained experience of 'moose-packing' which means lugging the shot game (often weighing over 100lbs) out of the bush. Because the carcases attract bears, it is dangerous to do this job unarmed. By the end of September it had started to snow so David collected his meagre wages ($25 a day) and left.

Childcare and Domestic Work

The US Government includes au pair placement programmes on its list of Exchange Visitor Programmes. These allow thousands of young Europeans with childcare experience to work for American families for exactly one year on a J-1 visa.

The basic requirements are that you be between 18 and 25, speak English, have Western European nationality, have childcare experience, be a non-smoker and a car driver/learner. In fact many applicants have discovered at interview that childcare experience is interpreted fairly loosely to include babysitting. The majority of candidates are young women though men with relevant experience (e.g. sole care of children under five) may be placed. (It is still not unusual to have about two blokes out of 200 au pairs.)

The job entails working 40-45 hours a week (including babysitting) with one and a half days off per week plus one complete weekend off a month. You will have to put down a deposit (the sterling equivalent of $500) as a pledge that you won't leave before completing your one-year contract. Successful applicants receive free return flights from one of many European cities, orientations and follow-up. The time lag between applying and flying is usually about two months. A community counsellor is assigned to all au pairs. Her role is to advise on any problems and organise meetings with the European au pairs in your area.

The fixed amount of pocket money for au pairs is $100 a week which has not changed in five years. This is considerably less than an American nanny would expect, though still a reasonable wage on top of room, board and perks. An additional $300 is paid by the host family to cover the cost of educational courses (up to four hours a week). Au pairs are at liberty to travel for a month after their contract is over but no visa extension is available beyond that. There may be fewer liberties in the preceding 12 months as Michelle Frances discovered:

> *My host family began to insist on knowing where I was in my spare time, whom I was going out with, where I would be staying that night and, worst of all, a curfew of midnight. At 20 I decided that I was quite old enough to know when to go to bed and as long as my work wasn't suffering it was up to me what I did in my spare time. After lengthy discussions with my host family and counsellor I was basically told that I would have to get used to it. I'm afraid to say that I couldn't tolerate such an invasion on my privacy and returned to the UK after two months in America.*
>
> *Of the many other au pairs in Seattle, my position was considered not*

too bad. One girl had a curfew of 10.30pm, another had to do all the housework, cooking and cleaning for four children and parents, and another had to hoover the carpet in stripes like mowing a lawn and fold all the towels and underwear in a particular way. Obviously these are exceptions but as it is really difficult to get to know somebody by just a telephone call or two, it's much better to ask as many day-to-day questions as possible. I would advise anybody considering embarking on such a trip to establish exactly what will be expected of them, how many nights babysitting at weekends, restrictions on social life, use of the car, how private are the living arrangements, etc.

The American Institute for Foreign Study or AIFS (37 Queens Gate, London SW7 5HR) run the Au Pair in America programme which is by far the largest of the placement organisations, sending over 3,000 participants a year. It has representatives in all the countries of Western Europe and agent/interviewers throughout Britain. Brochures and application forms can be requested on free-fone 0800 413116.

Other active au pair Exchange Visitor Programmes are the Experiment in International Living (EIL Ltd, 'Otesaga', West Malvern Rd, Malvern, Worcs. WR14 1DX; 01684 562577), AuPairCare Cultural Exchange (101 Lorna Road, Hove, Sussex BN3 3EL; 01273 220261) and EF Au Pair (74 Roupell St, London SE1 8SS; 0171-401 8004).

The requirements of the ten-week International Family Companion Programme starting in late June, also administered by AIFS, are less rigorous, apart from the requirement that you be a student. A genuine interest in and positive attitude to children will suffice for this programme. A driving licence is not absolutely essential. Like camp counsellors, family companions get a free flight and then a lump sum payment at the end of the summer of $400. There are about 400 places altogether.

Many British women who want to work for families may not qualify for or may not want to join one of the approved programmes. In recent decades thousands of young Europeans have gone to the States to work as nannies or au pairs, virtually all of them on tourist visas. They should tread carefully, especially in view of all the recent publicity surrounding high-profile Washington politicians who have been caught employing illegal house staff as nannies, cleaners, etc. (As far as we can ascertain, nannies are not eligible for the Q visa as was orginally hoped by agencies and others.)

It should be possible to fix up a job working with a family after arrival in the States, though the penalties for working illegally described earlier in this chapter apply equally. There are many job notices for au pairs and nannies on hostel notice boards (especially in San Francisco) and in big city dailies. After finding it impossible to get a job without a social security card in Houston, Ana Maria Guĕmes from Mexico started reading the ads and soon had a live-in job as a babysitter.

After having been in California for a while, Paul Young decided to try to market himself as an informal butler, willing to drive and cook in a household. After advertising in the rich county of San Anselmo, he received a disappointing response, mostly from disabled people offering $100 a week. He chose the most lucrative position paying $320 a week cash-in-hand, but was far from thrilled with his choice. His employer sounds the worst kind of snobbish spoiled American; even the dog was horrible and, in Paul's view, needed (and probably got!) a psychiatrist. He concludes that a sane wealthy American is a contradiction in terms, and recommends checking out the situation carefully before committing yourself.

Medical

Nurse shortages are chronic in the US and qualified nurses might like to investigate possibilities through a specialist UK agency. For people with a more casual interest in medicine, there is the possibility of testing new drugs as well as donating blood.

While putting off his return from California to the West Midlands as long as possible, Mark Horobin sold plasma in San Diego and Oceanside. He says that you can give a pint twice a week and be paid between $10 and $16 for it. He did it for six consecutive weeks and claims it didn't affect him adversely.

When Lindsay Watt arrived in the US, he intended to sustain himself with conventional kinds of employment. But almost immediately he discovered that the longish-stay male travellers staying at the International Students Center in New York City (895 Amsterdam Ave; 212-666-3619) were all earning money solely through medical studies. All that is needed is a social security number (including ones stamped 'Not Valid for Work'). In 1994 most studies were paying $100 a day and since most are in-house you spend nothing on food, accommodation or entertainment. On the three studies in which Lindsay participated, he earned $300 in five days in New York, $475 for four days in Philadelphia and $3,000 for a month in West Palm Beach (Florida). Together these funded a tour of South America. The best he ever heard of was a three-day study in Baltimore which paid $800. (It must have involved some fairly unpleasant tests, such as a spinal tap.) There are Drug Research Centers in many American cities especially Massachusetts, New York, New Jersey, Pennsylvania, Maryland and Florida. Women are seldom accepted unless they are sterile.

Manual Work

Cash-in-hand work can be found, especially as a loader with removal firms (wages of up to $12 an hour have been reported), as security guards and in construction (especially for those with skills). Since houses throughout the States are wood-framed, carpenters can do well. It is common practice to pay employees as 'contract labour', which leaves them with the responsibility of paying taxes, social security, etc.; this is a definite advantage if your papers are not in order. Even if you can't find work building new houses, you can offer your painting or maintenance skills to any householder, preferably one whose house is looking the worse for wear.

Surprisingly, building work is not the exclusive domain of male travellers. Mandy Blumenthal, an intrepid traveller who contributed to *Work Your Way* throughout the 1980s, did a fortnight's construction work in California before moving on to become the cook on a diving boat. Mandy thinks that being British is a definite advantage throughout the States: 'If anything goes wrong tell them it's typically English and they'll love it.'

Recently, the USA has had more than its fair share of natural disasters which always create a lot of urgent work. While Paul Donut was in Florida he came across this phenomenon:

> I was told of the devastation caused by Hurricane Andrew and of the armies of workers down in Homestead. Apparently the place was in such a mess that the officials there just didn't care about work permits, etc. Later in Toronto I met up with some Brits who were going down to Des Moines Iowa to look for work after the floods of 1993. I received a note from one of them about a week later saying there was so much work they would be there for months.

This doesn't always succeed however. After the forest fires which swept through Santa Monica California, rumours spread (like wildfire!) that there was a huge demand for building workers. In Britain, the *Sun* newspaper printed an article saying that they were crying out for skilled builders, and soon large numbers of unemployed British builders had booked flights to California, including bricklayers (although brick is not used in the area). They all congregated in the expat pub in Santa Monica (the Old King's Head) only to be told that there was no work to speak of, since builders from other states had already arrived and the work was spoken for.

Rumours continue to circulate in the 1990s of money to be made in the offshore oil industry of Lafayette, Galveston, Freeport and Corpus Christi on the Gulf of Mexico. It might be worthwhile for people with catering or mechanical skills to approach marine catering companies for rig work, galley handwork, etc. The pay would be minimum wage; but with 84-hour weeks and all living expenses paid, significant sums could be saved.

A more definite but offbeat suggestion has been proffered by Mark Kinder who wrote from rural Maryland:

After spending the summer on the Camp America programme, a friend and I decided to do a parachute jump. Once you have made about ten jumps, the instructors expect you to learn how to pack parachutes, which takes about five hours to learn. Once you have learnt how to pack you get paid $5 per chute cash and with a bit of practice can pack three or four chutes an hour which is good money. I would say that 90% of parachute centres in the US pay people cash for packing the chutes but you generally have to be a skydiver to do the job. It is definitely a fun way of earning money. Skydivers are very friendly people and are thrilled to meet foreigners, so they will often offer a place to stay. If not, you can always camp at the parachute centre.

A list of the 275 parachute centres in the US can be obtained from the national association USPA, 1440 Duke St, Alexandria, VA 22314.

Private labouring agencies can be a useful source of instant money to anyone with a legitimate visa and a social security number. It is normally essential to be at the agency office by 6am to offer yourself as day labour. Nineteen-old Nicola Smith worked through an agency in Dallas called Industrial Force which was desperate for workers (including ones with invented social security numbers) to work as cleaners and in fast food restaurants.

AGRICULTURE

Like everything else in America, many farms (often agribusinesses rather than farms) tend to be on the grand scale, especially in California and the Midwest. This means that the phenomenon of cycling along a country road, finding the farmer in his field and being asked to start work in an adjoining field is virtually unknown in the US. Furthermore it could be dangerous, since anyone wandering up a farmer's driveway would be suspected of being a trespasser and liable to be threatened with a vicious dog or a gun.

In many important agricultural areas, much of the fruit and vegetable harvesting has been traditionally done by gangs of illegal Mexicans or legal Chicanos (naturalised Americans of Spanish descent) for notoriously low wages. It is very common for an agent to contract a whole gang, so that there may be no room for individuals and pairs of travellers.

A gentler form of agriculture is practised on organic farms which flourish in many corners of the USA. Unfortunately working for keep on a farm counts as employment for the purposes of Immigration. One major WWOOF style group (North East Workers on Organic Farms, Box 608, Belchertown, Massachusetts 01007) wrote to say that because of visa difficulties, they no longer place international workers. Their apprentice placement service is for US citizens, as are various internships listed in the free booklet *Educational & Training Opportunities in Sustainable Agriculture* available from the Alternative Farming Systems Information Center, USDA, National Agricultural Library, Room 304, 10301 Baltimore Boulevard, Beltsville, MD 20705-2351. In theory the long-established organisation Friends of the Trees Society (PO Box 1064, Tonasket, WA 98855; 509-485-2705) provides a networking service for international travellers, though the director Michael Pilarski is not a brilliant correspondent. The WWOOF International Handbook published by WWOOF Australia lists a number of communes and alternative farms which accept working guests (send £8/US$15 to WWOOF, Mount Murrindal Coop, Buchan, VIC 3885, Australia).

In the world of conventional agriculture, there is scope for finding work. While working at parachute centres in rural Delaware and Maryland, Mark Kinder from Blackpool found that farm work was easy to come by on an intermittent basis, with an hourly wage of $4-6 in addition to free caravan accommodation. In every state in the Union (except perhaps Nevada, Montana and Alaska) there is some fruit or vegetable being picked throughout the summer months. Below is a chart setting out the times of summer harvests which may need temporary helpers. In a country as vast and as agriculturally diverse as the US, this is bound to be a mere selection.

Both in large scale harvests and on small family farms there is a chance that no one will be concerned about your legal status. This is what Jan Christensen from Denmark found when he looked for summer farmwork in Minnesota:

> *The farmers seemed to have a very relaxed attitude towards permits. The best places to look are along route 210 just off Interstate 94 at Fergus Falls which is a rich farm area with good employment prospects from April/May till mid-October. But it's best to have some experience in tractor driving and combine harvester work. If you try to bluff, you will find yourself on the road PDQ. I found that my farmer expected me to know just about everything about farming and had no time to train me.*

Fruit pickers congregate in the counties of Yakima, Chelan, Douglas and Okanogan in Washington State. Another example of a large-scale harvest is the peach harvest in Western Colorado around Palisade. A few thousand pickers are suddenly needed for the second fortnight in August. Similarly the three-week cherry harvest around Traverse City Michigan in late June/early July employs large numbers of non-locals.

California and Florida are the leading states for agricultural production, especially citrus, plums, avocadoes, apricots and grapes. Most of these are grown along the Central Valley particularly the San Joaquin Valley around Fresno. The work is notoriously poorly paid. Kev Vincent fared better in the Salinas Valley on the California coast, which is a huge vegetable growing area, again predominantly Spanish-speaking. The Farm Labor Office in Greenfield directed him to a job cutting broccoli which is extremely fast and hard and very well paid, then on to the pepper harvest which was easier work but less lucrative.

California's successful rival in the production of vegetables and fruit is Florida whose citrus groves yield nearly 70% of all US citrus production. All citrus fruit in the state is picked by hand and massive numbers of itinerant pickers or local casuals must be enlisted over the winter and spring, when the Florida climate is at its most pleasant.

Florida Harvests

Citrus production is greatest in the central counties of Lake and Polk, inland from Tampa and north past Orlando, where more than 25 million boxes of fruit are picked annually. The surrounding counties of Marion, Volusia, Orange,

	May	June	July	August	September	October
Alabama	potatoes, tomatoes					
Arizona	carrots, lettuce		cotton			
Arkansas			peaches			
California	cherries		peaches, broccoli, peppers		grapes, apples	
Colorado			cherries	apricots, peaches	peas, apples	
Florida	(winter: citrus and most vegetables)				cucumbers	
Georgia		peaches		peanuts		
Idaho			cherries	onions	apples, potatoes, sugar beets	
Illinois	asparagus (April) corn detassling					
Indiana		corn detassling		tomatoes, corn		
Iowa	asparagus	corn detassling beans				
Kentucky	strawberries			tobacco		
Louisiana	strawberries					sugar cane
Maine	asparagus (April)			blueberry-raking		apples
Maryland	strawberries, cabbages					
Michigan		strawberries	cherries	haying	peaches	apples
Minnesota					beet root, potatoes	
Missouri				peaches	apples	
Montana			cherries		sugar beets, potatoes	
New Hampshire					apples	
New Jersey		strawberries	cranberries	blueberries		apples
New York		strawberries, peas, cherries			apples	
North Carolina			tobacco			
North Dakota		sugar beets				
Pennsylvania					peaches, apples, grapes	
Ohio			field vegetables			
Oklahoma	wheat cutting		corn detassling			
Oregon	strawberries, cherries		peaches		apples, nuts, hops	
South Carolina		peaches				
South Dakota			wheat	hay, potatoes		
Utah		cherries		apricots	apples, sugar beets, potatoes	
Vermont					apples	
Virginia			tobacco	apples, peaches		
Washington		cherries	berries, hops		apples	
Wisconsin			lettuce, onions, peppers			
Wyoming						sugar beets

Hillsborough, Hardee, De Soto, Highlands, Indian River and St. Lucie are also major producers. Another good area is around Arcadia in De Soto County.

The harvest season for all citrus crops broadly lasts from mid-October until early July, exactly opposite from the usual summer harvesting season. As far as individual crops are concerned, oranges normally start up in November and peak in January, February and March with another peak in May with the late Valencia orange crop.

Buses drive into large local towns at around 6 o'clock in the morning and anybody who wants to pick fruit that day can get on and be driven to that contractor's grove. Ask around in bars what the form is as regards buses, rates of pay and good groves. To them you are nothing more than a box number in a given row and so, with luck, visas won't be a problem, unless there are rumours of an impending immigration raid.

Wages are based on piece rates, the basic unit being a bin or box. You determine your own work level and nobody rushes you. Pay is given out by the day or by the week if you want, and it is cash in hand. Steve and Iona Dwyer were distinctly unimpressed with the earning potential of picking oranges in Florida:

> *We got ourselves a car in Florida which became very necessary during our jaunt. I would say that unless you are almost broke don't bother with the orange harvest. The Hispanics have kept the wages very low. When we were there the rate was $7 per half-ton bin. For one and half days we toiled in sweltering heat to earn $60 between us.*

The speed at which you can fill boxes is heavily dependent upon your ability to place your ladder cleverly. A lot of time is wasted moving around ladders from branch to branch and this means fewer boxes filled and hence less money earned. A good picker can clear half a tree from one position — as a novice you will not be able to do so. So the best thing to do is to buy a bottle of wine and a packet of cigarettes and offer them to one of the 'winos', probably lying underneath a tree, in exchange for a lesson in placing ladders. These guys know more about picking than anybody.

An alternative method operates in the groves which supply juice factories. In this case you knock the fruit from five or six trees onto the ground, pick them up and fill a big sack which is dumped into giant bins.

Picking is organised by the foreman assigning each picker or pair of pickers a row of trees to clear. Once he realises a particular picker is keen, he or she should be given the better rows.

The picking season is divided into early, middle and late. Early picking means selecting the ripe fruit which is slow and hence badly paid. Much the same applies to late picking when one takes what is left on the trees. Middle picking starts up when the fruit demand is high and involves virtual stripping of the fruit. This is the best paid part of the season. The price being paid per box varies per week, per grove and per fruit type. The only way to make the most of the grove variation in price is to have your own car and drive around a few groves and offer yourself for work at the best paid grove or the one that looks fullest in fruit. Sometimes you may have to drive 30 miles to work. Many people do this, though the majority rely on the labour buses.

Iain Kemble headed for a small town 15 miles inland from Boynton Beach which is so far south it is a little out of the way of migrant gangs. All the picking was done by an extended family of local blacks, but foreigners were employed in the packing shed at slightly more than minimum wage.

Although citrus is the most important crop in Florida, the state also produces a whole range of vegetables. Southern Florida is the only place in the nation where vegetables can be grown between December and March (e.g. tomatoes, peppers, cucumbers). The best areas are Collier County centred around Naples on the Gulf of Mexico and the area around Homestead south of Miami. The September cucumber harvest is reputed to be the best paid work in the area ($100 a day) but the work is incredibly hard and most travellers barely survive their first day. Apparently cabbages and watermelons are none too easy either.

A lot of the produce is designed for markets outside Florida and there are dozens of packing houses in these two areas which employ thousands of seasonal workers. Contact the Southwest Florida Growers Association in Immokalee Florida for more details of times and locations of harvests and job availability in the packing factories. Despite a significant presence of itinerant Mexicans, there is a shortage of labour since the President of the Growers Association was quoted in an interview:

Our survival depends on a few factors. We have to be assured of the land; water is critical, and labour. You've got to have the people to pick a crop. There's nothing worse than watching a field rot.

Try the growers in and around Route 31 near Arcadia, such as McBee Ltd., Chastiens Farms, Singletary Farms and Hatton Desoto Farms.

In Jan Christensen's opinion, work is more lucrative around Homestead, and he should know since he has worked three winter seasons there:

I worked with green beans and potatoes. Expect to work 80 hours a week, and the work is hard. The pay was $6-7 an hour. Best of all, most farms provide free housing. Of course it's best to have a car. I got my first job on the day I arrived.

The bean season runs from November 1st till April and the potatoes from New Years to the middle of May, so the best time to arrive is October. The farms and packing houses are easy to locate near Homestead along US 1 from Miami. Jan recommends trying F & T Farm (on the road to the Everglades National Park), John Alger Farms on Farm Life Road and Hilson and Son on US 1. Also there is a massive farmers' market on the same highway which employs more than 2,000 people in the season.

The Apple Harvest of Maine

In the early autumn, the local newspaper in south central Maine (around the town of Monmouth) is full of apple picker ads in the 'Help Wanted' columns. The season lasts two months, starting in early September and continuing until the first deep frost near the end of October. Roger Brown enjoyed his stint of working for Chick Orchards of Monmouth and has the following observations about the apple harvest.

Pickers start out at the minimum wage, but graduate to piece work per bushel as soon as their speed reaches a certain level. Rates of pay are standard among orchards, as is the custom of paying a bonus to people who complete the harvest for one grower. Hours are flexible, though people who put in 70 hours a week are preferred. Crews are formed by the orchard foremen according to speed of picking; the French Canadian professional crews are a sight to behold and they earn well over $100 a day right from the beginning.

Like the citrus-picking in Florida, a lot depends on the placement of the ladder. At first it is a very awkward business but after a while, you begin to forget that the ladder isn't a part of you. As well as speed, skill is important. Bruising of apples is not tolerated and the crew leaders shout up to you 'advice' such as 'we want to sell apples not cider'. But once you get a little fitter and master the techniques, apple picking in Maine can be enjoyable. Roger comments:

Standing on top of an apple tree in the bright sunshine and chatting away to a colleague became a very pleasant way of passing the time. It was good too that the apple-picking season falls during the 'season of mists and mellow fruitfulness'. You get to the top of an apple tree on the top of a hill in Maine and the whole world seems to unroll at your feet. Beyond the white wooden church and steeple of Monmouth, ranges of hills can be seen in the distance creating a rainbow of colours with the bright leaves of the autumnal maples.

Roger enjoyed his experiences in the USA so much that he has since emigrated and is now a journalist turned real estate agent.

VOLUNTARY WORK

The Council on International Educational Exchange publishes *Volunteer! The Comprehensive Guide to Voluntary Service in the US and Abroad* which includes a wide selection of organisations looking for volunteers (available from CIEE's Publications Department, 205 E 42nd St, New York, NY 10017; $8.95 plus postage). Be warned that many American voluntary organisations have religious affiliations which are more obtrusive than they would be in Europe.

The three main workcamp organisations in the US (see page 140) have incoming programmes too. For example Volunteers for Peace place about 500 foreign volunteers on 40-50 workcamps in the US. CIEE accepts around 200 individuals from abroad over the age of 18 to participate in its international voluntary service projects. In the past, volunteers have been placed on environmental projects in Yosemite National Park, the Golden Gate National Seashore and northern Idaho's Kaniksu National Forest, assisted with urban renovation and preservation of historic landmarks in New York and New Jersey, and worked with disabled children and adults on their summer holidays. Prospective volunteers must register through a workcamp organisation in their own country.

Voluntary opportunities in the US range from the intensely urban to the decidedly rural. In the former category, you can build houses in deprived areas with Habitat for Humanity (Global Village, 12 Habitat St, Americus, GA 31709; 1-800-HABITAT ext 547) or work for the Winant Clayton Volunteers (109 East 50th St, New York, NY 10022). Clayton volunteers work on summer playschemes and with HIV/Aids sufferers, the homeless and in drug and psychiatric rehabilitation centres, mainly in Manhattan. British volunteers are recruited to work from mid-June to mid-September; contact WCV, 38 Newark St, London E1 2AA. The Habitat for Humanity office in Greater Miami uses up to 250 volunteers a day at a site in Dade Country which was flattened by Hurricane Andrew. Short-stay volunteers pay $10 a day for their keep, which is waived for longer-stay volunteers. Details are available from the Workcamps Director, PO Box 560994, Miami, FL 33256-0994 (305-670-2224).

Working outside the big cities is an attractive prospect. For example the US Forest Service organises workcamps to maintain trails, campsites and wildlife; volunteers should apply to the regional headquarters, e.g. PO Box 7669, Missoula, MT 59807 for Montana, Idaho and the Dakotas, and PO Box 3623, Portland, OR 97208 for Oregon and Washington. The Heritage Resource Management department of the US Forest Service operates a volunteer programme to conduct archaeological surveys, record oral histories, etc. The Volunteer Coordinator's office is in Modoc National Forest (800 West 12th St, Alturas, CA 96101; 916-233-5811). He sends out application forms, tries to match volunteers with appropriate vacancies and assists with obtaining a J-1 visa. The 1995 programme hopes to place 50 volunteers for at least four to six weeks during which time they will receive free housing and up to $90 a week.

Archaeological digs which need volunteers are listed in the *Archaeological Fieldwork Opportunities Bulletin* (see *Voluntary* chapter for details). Volunteers are also needed to work for a minimum of eight or ten weeks with Sioux Indian children in isolated reservation communities and summer camps; details from the Sioux YMCAs, PO Box 218, Dupree, South Dakota 57623.

Volunteers (including Europeans) are recruited by the American Hiking Society to work in the wilderness. The AHS sends out volunteers on two week 'Volunteer Vacations' to build and maintain trails, etc., from the Green Mountain National Forest of Vermont to Haleakala National Park in Hawaii. Volunteers should be fit and experienced backpackers capable of walking ten miles a day with ease. Camping accommodation is arranged and food is provided. There is a registration fee of $50. For further information contact the AHS, PO Box 20160, Washington, DC 20041-2160 (703-319-0084). The AHS also publishes a potentially useful booklet in November called *Helping Out in the Outdoors: A Directory of Volunteer Work and Internships on America's Public Lands* which costs $10 overseas.

A new organisation has been established called Backcountry Volunteers, run by the former director of AHS's volunteer programme. Details of current projects may be obtained by writing to Kay Beebe, PO Box 86, North Scituate, Massachusetts 02060 (617-545-7019). The administrative fee for joining a project is $40.

The Appalachian Mountain Club, Route 16, PO Box 298, Gorham, New Hampshire 03581 (603-466-2721 or 413-443-0011) publishes a newsletter of Volunteer Trail Opportunities which charge volunteers $35-95 for a week-long working trip. It may also be worth trying the Student Conservation Association (PO Box 550, Charlestown, NH 03603; 603-543-1700) which places volunteers in national parks for a minimum of 12 weeks and pays them a 'meals stipend' of $50-90 a week.

A travel club in the UK advertises placements on environmental projects in the US: the Frontier Club at 58 Manchester St, Heywood, Manchester OL10 1DL charges a joining fee of £14 in order to receive details. Since it is possible to contact US conservation organisations directly, readers may decide against this route. (No reports have been received from participants, so feedback would be welcome.)

Involvement Corps Inc of Los Angeles (in association with the Australian-based organisation Involvement Volunteers) arranges volunteer placements in the USA particularly California and Hawaii. Volunteer placements range from assisting staff involved in social service or in environmental projects e.g. protecting endangered species. Details are available from 15515 Sunset Boulevard, Suite 108, Pacific Palisades, CA 90272 (tel/fax 310-459-1022). After careful consideration, Catherine Brewin decided to pay the registration fee (now about US$350) and was soon working on a short-term project in Los Angeles, digging ditches, mixing cement and sledgehammering concrete at a Presbyterian Conference Centre. After a fortnight she flew on to her second IV project in Hawaii which she enjoyed less, but both were interesting.

CONCLUSION

This chapter has only scratched the surface, but we hope that it has sparked a few new ideas for your trans-American trip. Together with reading Jack Kerouac's *On The Road,* you should be all set. It also helps if you have a cousin or acquaintance living in the US who is willing to guide you through your first few days. As one of our less intrepid correspondents recalls:

When we first arrived in the States we went immediately to visit the parents of a friend. I'd never met them before but they made us welcome. A good thing too, because America seemed so strange to me and expensive, that I just wanted to get on the first plane back. I think it was because everything seemed so big and in advance of us. I was used to being in more 'backward' places (i.e. Ghana and Scotland) and America was much more complicated.

There is no denying that it is preferable to qualify for an Exchange Visitor Programme like BUNAC or Au Pair in America. One of the advantages is that they choose a comprehensive insurance policy for you. If you go on your own, make sure you have purchased enough insurance cover since medical care is astronomically expensive in the US.

You must balance caution with a spirit of adventure, accepting and even revelling in the bizarre. When you learn that it is possible to get a night's lodging at a rescue mission or Salvation Army hostel, you need not shy away. You might have an experience similar to Benjamin Fry's in Alaska:

> *I stayed in another rescue mission in Anchorage and there witnessed an amazing spectacle: a tearful Indian or perhaps Eskimo confessing his sins in his native language. We were also fed — revolting food but free.*

You may end up in some unlikely situations, but some of them may also lead to a few days of work helping a trucker with his deliveries, joining an impromptu pop group to perform at private parties, gardening on a Californian commune, building solar houses, and so on. If you aren't lucky enough to have the appropriate visa, you should grasp every opportunity (even if it looks like a nettle at first) to earn a few dollars, taking advantage of offers of genuine hospitality.

If you do conduct a proper on-the-spot job hunt, the two most useful tools you can have are a car and a phone, tools which are synonymous with the American way of life. It also helps to have not only a tidy but a conservative appearance. But even without these, you should be able to get some kind of job which will introduce you to the striking cultural differences between Europe and America and which will provide you with some capital with which to explore this amazing country.

Canada

Countries like Canada which are favoured with a high standard of living and a reputation for unlimited job opportunities have traditionally attracted many travellers and emigrants. But, alas, it is not easy to work in Canada, both because of strictly enforced 'Canada-only' immigration policies and high unemployment. However Canadians are hospitable and eager for visitors to like their country. Even the immigration officer who deported one of our contributors expressed regret that the offender had not had a chance to see more of Canada.

RED TAPE

British citizens require only a valid passport to enter Canada. Normally on arrival they will be given permission to stay for 90 days as tourists, though a request for six months is sometimes granted, especially if sufficient funds and a return ticket can be shown. David and Greeba Hughes were stamped in for six months without being asked to show either of these but they were asked if they had any Canadian contacts (which they did). But don't count on breezing through. Although Canadian Immigration is reputed to be less savage than its American counterpart, many young travellers without much money have been given a rough ride.

To work legally in Canada, you must obtain an Employment Authorisation before you leave home. The Canadian government allows a certain number of British students to work temporarily in Canada. The quotas are allocated on the basis of reciprocal agreements between Canada and the UK and can fluctuate from year to year. Interested students should obtain the general leaflet 'Student Temporary Employment in Canada' by sending an s.a.e. to the Canadian High Commission (Immigration Section, Macdonald House, 38 Grosvenor St, London W1X 0AA; 0171-629 9492); the premium line Immigration Info number is 0891-616644. All participants in the official work exchanges must be British citizens aged 18-30 years and must have proof that they will be returning to a tertiary level course on their return to Britain.

Students who already have a job offer from a Canadian employer may be eligible for 'Programme A'. They can apply directly to the High Commission in London for an employment authorisation (reference 1102) which will be valid for a maximum of 12 months and which is not transferable to any other job.

The other and more flexible possibility is to obtain an unspecified employment authorisation which is available only through BUNAC (16 Bowling Green Lane, London EC1R 0BD; 0171-251 3472). Their 'Work Canada' programme offers about 1,100 students (including gap students with a university place and finalists with proof that they will return to the UK) the chance to go to Canada for up to six months and take whatever jobs they can find. The only requirements are that applicants have C$1,000 in Canadian funds (or $600 plus either a letter of sponsorship from a Canadian relative or a job offer) and a return ticket. It is no longer compulsory to have a medical examination with a designated doctor unless you want to work in childcare or healthcare. The programme fee is £79, and compulsory insurance £90. Participants can travel independently or on a BUNAC flight (costing approximately £370). Places are allocated on a first come, first served basis so early application is advantageous (from December). Departure for Canada must be between the beginning of February and the end of August (which precludes working the winter season in a ski resort).

Certain special categories of work may be eligible for authorisation, such as nannies who are in great demand but must be qualified (see *Childcare* section below) or for the tobacco harvest (see *Farm Work* below). There is also a category of work permits for voluntary work which takes about a month to process if you have found a placement through a recognised organisation.

Americans do not require a passport to visit Canada (only proof of US citizenship if requested) but they are not allowed to enter in order to look for work. Like all foreign nationals, they must fix up a job (before arrival) which has been approved by the employer's local Canada Employment Centre. The one difference is that they can apply for employment authorisation at the port of entry rather than having to apply through a Canadian consulate in the US.

Australians should write to the Canadian Consulate General, Immigration Office, Level 5, Quay West, 111 Harrington St, Sydney, NSW 2000 (02-364 3050) to request an application form for a working holiday visa which is an open employment authorisation valid for a year from the date of issue, available to young people (not necessarily students) aged 18-25. Applicants must prove that they have access to $4,000 and have no criminal record. Applications open on January 1st each year and close as soon as the quota of about 4,000 is filled, which is usually in the spring. Processing normally takes 12 weeks.

Special Schemes

BUNAC produces its own Canadian Job Directory for members (13% of participants got jobs though it in 1994). Most of the jobs listed are in hotels and tourist attractions in the Rockies which is a beautiful part of the world in which to spend a summer. British university students have an edge over their Canadian counterparts in this sphere of employment since they don't have to return to their studies until mid to late September rather than the beginning of September.

Additionally, the BUNACAMP Counsellors programme (see *USA* chapter) places students as counsellors in a variety of summer camps throughout Canada.

CIEE in New York operates a student work exchange in Canada. US college and university students may accept employment between May 1st and October 31st.

For Australians, STA Travel's SWAP Department (PO Box 399, Carlton South, Melbourne 3053) arranges group and individual packages (for those eligible for the working holiday visa described above) which include flights to Vancouver, visa costs and support services from about $2,000.

All participants of approved student schemes benefit from orientations and back-up from the Canadian Federation of Students' SWAP offices in Toronto and Vancouver. They even oraganise pub outings and excursions for participants, as well as advising on nitty-gritty issues like tax. Students on work exchanges receive the same tax exemption as Canadian students, provided they earn at least 90% of their total annual income (including educational grants) in Canada and that the amount earned will not exceed $3,000. Overpayers should request that their employers send a T4 statement of earnings at the end of the tax year (end of December) and then file an income tax return.

The Council on International Educational Exchange (CIEE, 33 Seymour Place, London W1H 6AT; 0171-706 3008) arranges for students to undertake internships in Canada lasting up to one year. Interns must find their own jobs in their field of study, often with advice from their tutors. Those who qualify get an employment authorisation as with BUNAC. The programme fee is £125.

CASUAL WORK

The lack of an employment authorisation or Social Insurance Number (the SIN is comparable to the American social security number) is a perpetual thorn in the sides of itinerant workers. Without them, you will have to steer clear of official bodies such as Canada Employment Centres, tax offices, etc. and many employers will be unwilling to consider you.

Ana Maria Guëmes from Mexico recommends looking for catering work in the big cities, where so many residents speak with foreign accents that you are taken for a resident if you act like one:

> It took me a week to find my job as waitress at a restaurant in the Yorkdale Shopping Centre in suburban Toronto, which was displaying a 'Help Wanted' sign. It is important to be confident when looking for a job and talking about previous experience, implying that you have been living in Canada for several years. I put the names of people I hardly knew on the application form as referees (my landlord, my friend's boss) and used a friend's social insurance number changed by a digit. I told them I had just left another restaurant in Toronto, a name I'd chosen at random from the Yellow Pages. I was there for seven months and left with a letter of reference and plenty of money to continue my travels in Europe.

If you decide to work without proper authorisation, you should be aware that you are breaking a law which is taken seriously in Canada with a very real danger of deportation. If you are working in a job known to hire large numbers of foreigners (e.g.tree-planting and fruit-picking in BC), there is a chance that the area will be raided by immigration control. Raymond Oliver could hardly believe their efficiency: at 10am he gave his BC employer a made-up SIN, at noon a phone call came to say it was fake and at 11am the next day an immigration officer arrived to tell him he had to leave the country within a fortnight. If you cannot fund your own departure, you will either be given a 'departure notice' which allows you to travel to the US or deported and prohibited from returning for a prescribed period. If you are caught and want legal advice, contact the nearest legal aid lawyer whose services are free.

Prospective employers seldom ask to check the actual SIN card but will certainly ask for the number. Numbers which are issued to foreign workers begin with a 9, though this might prompt an employer to ask to see proof that your status is legitimate. Some employers are more sympathetic than others, for example in the booming construction industry of Vancouver as Paul Donut describes:

> *Within a month of arriving I had permanent work on one of the many construction sites. After my first week, the foreman asked me for my SIN number. I hold him that I didn't have it with me, expecting the worst. Instead he took me to one side and said so long as it starts with the numbers 721 and has nine digits, he didn't care what number I gave him. I learned later that hardly anyone uses their real numbers including the Canadian workers who avoid paying tax and also collect welfare.*

Paul also worked for a farmer in the Niagara region of Ontario and had the impression that fruit-growers in the area were more interested in whether or not prospective workers had transport to the farm than whether they had working papers.

On the other hand we have heard of a skilled baker from Manchester who kept telling employers his number was in the post, and was dismissed every couple of months when they became suspicious. Obliging employers might be prepared to pay your wages to a workmate who will hand over the cash, so that your name stays out of the books. A variation is to work under a Canadian friend's name and number and ask him or her to cash your pay cheques for you.

Anyone on shaky legal ground should keep a very low profile. It is rumoured that it is not difficult for people without permits to find winter work in ski resorts in the Rockies but not on the slopes. Brigitte Albrech worked as a tree planter in Prince George BC using a SIN number given to her by her employer. But because she was German and a woman she was such a novelty that the authorities somehow heard of her (after she had been working for three months) and sent her a request in writing to leave within six weeks or face a court hearing.

Wages are fairly good in Canada with statutory minimum wages, e.g. $6.70 per hour in Ontario ($6.25 for students) and $5 to $6 in most of the other provinces. Last year the average BUNAC participant earned the minimum wage, with an average weekly wage of $235 and average accommodation cost of $50 per week.

Iain Kemble earned well in excess of the average when he got a few days work ferrying buckets of cement to a crew of fence-builders in Alberta. Because this was a government contract (to prevent animals from being killed on the Icefield Parkway between Banff and Jasper), the wage was excellent. Iain concluded that after earning $450 in five days, he must have been the best paid illegal worker in the Banff Youth Hostel.

THE JOB HUNT

The job hunt is tougher in Canada than almost anywhere else. Whereas it took BUNACers an average of $3\frac{1}{2}$ days to find their own job in the US, it took them a discouraging $7\frac{1}{2}$ days in Canada. After reading BUNAC's Work Canada Orientation Notes, it seems puzzling that anyone would subject themselves to such misery:

> *Job-hunting is never easy but hard slog will definitely pay off. Remember you'll feel alone, lost, homesick and everything else, and in hot and humid weather. Work at it with high energy day after day. Look presentable, be eager to please, be positive and cheerful, even if the responses are negative or the employers rude. Try again and again.*

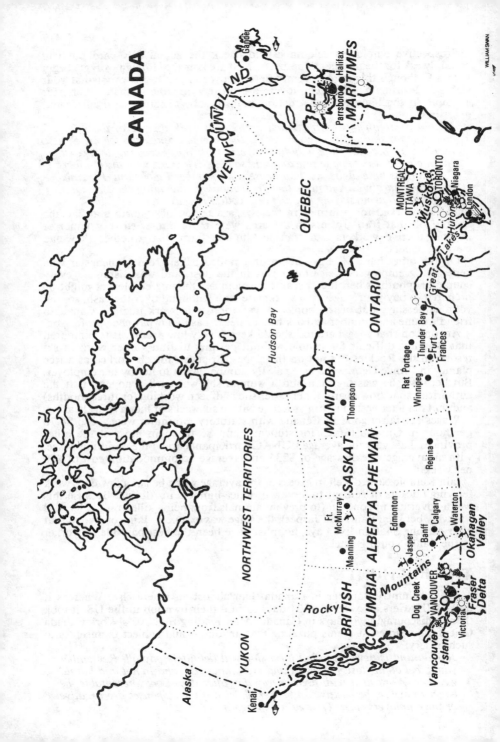

Unfortunately these doom-laden predictions are borne out by readers of this book like Adda Macchich:

> _I decided to settle in Ottawa last February and spent five weeks looking for work, with no luck. I filled out about 50 applications; the answer was invariably 'leave it with me; we'll get back to you' and they never did. You never even get to see the manager. I returned to Canada in June, hoping things had improved as the summer approached. I went to Niagara Falls expecting as many summer jobs as in Cape Cod but was disappointed at the total absence of Help Wanted signs or ads in the local paper, so I returned to Toronto. Spent a whole month on an unsuccessful job hunt, constantly being asked to submit resumes for menial jobs in restaurants and cafés and tramping from one end of town to the other merely to fill out more forms. The only available jobs were those paid on commission, which were advertised everywhere._

Just as Adda was about to give up and fly back to London she stumbled across a commission-only ice cream vending job which was open to virtually anyone willing to man a stationary or bicycle-powered ice cream unit. At first the money wasn't very good but as the season picked up so did the sales. The most lucrative areas are around the base of the CN Tower, the Skydome and Harbourfront. On average, Adda earned between $20 and $60 daily and on good days $100+. The best times are during Caribana the annual Caribbean festival at the end of July (when she made $200 in a single afternoon) and over the Labour Day weekend at the beginning of September. The contact number Adda provided is 695-8601, but you could simply ask the vendors for the name and number of their boss.

Where to Look

As ever, youth hostel notice boards are recommended for information on jobs. To take just one example the Youth Hostel on Jericho Beach in Vancouver allows many travellers to stay free of charge in exchange for doing anything from maintenance to dishwashing. Vancouver is generally recommended for work, though David Hughes didn't have much luck:

> _I've advertised my services as an English teacher to the huge Chinese population, emphasising my teaching experience in Taiwan. No replies. I've also registered with a movie-extras agency which services the expanding film industry here. The deal is you pay $40 to register and they guarantee work. This isn't as good as it sounds, since if you don't get work in the initial two years, your membership is automatically extended. No replies._

But David was not too downcast since his wife Greeba had taken over some friends' sandwich selling business in their absence, accommodation was no problem (he says you can rent an apartment on the seedy side of town for $300) and he was continually impressed by the mixture of natural and manmade splendour on the Canadian west coast.

In addition to Vancouver, the best cities to look for work are Toronto, Calgary and Edmonton. It is little wonder that Adda Maccich (quoted above) found so few opportunities in Niagara Falls, since the town's mayor recently declared it an economic disaster zone with one of the highest rates of unemployment in the country.

Newspapers are also worth scouring. Ana Guëmes got one of her two waitressing jobs from the _Toronto Sun_ while Vancouver's papers (the _Vancouver Sun_, _Province_ and _Westender_) and the _Calgary Herald_ contain job adverts, especially for dishwashers, waiting and bar staff.

The Rocky Mountain resorts of Banff, Jasper, Lake Louise, Sunshine Mountain and Waterton are among the best places to try both summer and winter. Banff seems to absorb the largest number of foreign workers as catering and chamber staff, trail-cutters, etc. It is an expensive town in which to job-hunt but if you are prepared to walk you can find free campsites out of town and up the mountain-sides. The huge Banff Springs Hotel alone employs 750 people. One traveller to Western Canada reported:

> *While on holiday in Banff, I met a lot of Australians and Britons staying at the youth hostel. All of them were just on holiday visas, and all of them had found work in the height of the tourist season. I was offered hotel work. There is a lot of work to be had in Canada and men in particular would have no trouble supporting themselves. Canadians are very warm towards foreigners and employers are generally prepared to risk hiring casuals 'black' if they can't get through the red tape. Wages are very good for this type of work.*

Travelling further west you eventually come to the charming city of Victoria on Vancouver Island. Several readers have recommended the job of pedicab driving for which the only requirements seem to be a driving licence and a returnable bond. As with the ice cream vending jobs described above, drivers are virtually self-employed and no one checks documents.

Other popular holiday areas are the Muskoka District of Ontario centred on the town of Huntsville (comparable to England's Lake District) and the shores of the Great Lakes, particularly Lake Huron. Since most of the holiday job recruitment in Ontario is done through Canadian universities, and the resorts are so widely scattered that asking door to door is impracticable, it is advisable to concentrate your efforts in the west.

There are jobs for sales staff wherever you go in Canada. Tanufa Kotecha joined BUNAC's Work Canada programme and quickly learned that Canadian selling techniques are just as aggressive as American ones:

> *I landed a job within a week in Toronto working in a French Canadian clothing store. In my store as soon as a customer walked in, they had to be greeted by a 'sales associate' within 15 seconds! The North American way of selling is pushy and upfront, but it does get results. One must have confidence to sell.*

Almost all shop jobs of this kind pay minimum wage.

Selling in a shop is too high profile for people without permits, but door-to-door and telephone selling are possible and once again your British accent should work in your favour as it did for Helen Welch in Barrie Ontario when she was hired to persuade people to buy photographic portraits of themselves. This was working well until the last day of May when a freak tornado hit Barrie and the people whom she had been telephoning suddenly didn't have any walls left on which to hang their pictures. So she was forced to move to Toronto in her quest for a roof over her head.

University Towns

Living in a university town and becoming involved in the life of a university often leads to a range of casual work opportunities. Canadian students tend to hold part-time jobs and you may inherit this type of job when they leave university or temporarily while they go away for the vacations. Student Employment Centers may be of use to people with work permits.

Ann Sommerville stayed in Canada for four years altogether, mostly in the industrial city of Hamilton (near Niagara Falls) where McMaster University is located. She pieced together a living from a large variety of casual jobs, including part-time waitressing and washing up, bar work in the campus bar, babysitting and occasional house cleaning (which was easy to get through private advertising), essay typing (especially in December and March as terms draw to an end), and assisting at academic conferences, e.g. working a slide projector, manning a bookstall.

Universities can be found in the following Ontario towns: Toronto (2), Hamilton, St. Catharines, Waterloo (2), London, Windsor, Kingston, Peterborough, Ottawa, Sudbury and Thunder Bay as well as in the capitals and the biggest cities in all the other provinces.

Tree-Planting

The archetype of the working Canadian is the lumberjack. Nowadays there are fewer jobs for tree-choppers than tree-planters which, in these environmentally-conscious times, is an ideologically sound job to have. In areas which have been logged or burnt, forestry officials are encouraging massive reafforestation and every March planting contractors begin to recruit crews for the season which begins in April. The payment is piece work (30-40 cents a tree in British Columbia, a little less in Alberta and Ontario) and novices can usually earn $100 a day after a few weeks' practice. In some cases 'rookies' are earning $200 a day by the end of the season. A deduction is made for camp expenses, normally about $20 a day. You will need a waterproof tent and work clothes including boots and waterproofs. Many firms do not lend out the equipment, so the cost of shovels and bags (which are expensive) are deducted from your wages.

Prince George is an important centre for tree-planting. While travelling in Mexico on annual leave from her job in Germany, Brigitte Albrech met up with a van full of French Canadians who were heading for Prince George to plant trees, and decided to follow them rather than return to her job. She provided the names of three companies: Bugbusters, Folklore and Triple A.

Chris Harrington planted trees and recommends picking up a copy of a magazine called *Screef* in outdoor stores in British Columbia in early March. (The word screef refers to the removal of loose debris with your boot or shovel.) The magazine lists tree-planting companies and gives some job information. But with rising local unemployment, jobs are scarcer than they used to be as Chris discovered when he returned the next year:

> *This time I met many disappointed Canadians who couldn't find work, a situation which is likely to worsen in the future. Without a work visa it's practically impossible. I didn't have one but fortunately had Canadian friends who went to a lot of trouble to help me. Otherwise I would have had to find someone willing to let me use their name and number (the two have to match when fed into a company computer).*

Dates are uncertain due to weather. There is a spring and a summer season with two to four weeks in between. Some BC contractors start as early as late March and finish in August, though Chris's job didn't begin until early May. Around Fort Frances and Thunder Bay in Ontario, the season is shorter, late April until the first week of July.

Although Brigitte Albrech agrees that the work is hard and the hours long, she greatly enjoyed the team spirit and solved a few problems she didn't know she had. Chris Harrington paints a fairly negative picture (while concluding that he had a great time):

> *Tree-planting itself consists of a ten-hour day starting about 6am, though overtime is available to masochists. This is awful work, make no mistake. The job is monotonous and weather conditions can be appalling (snow in June!). This coupled with the bugs can lead you to question your sanity. One of the worst aspects is 'down time' which occurs regularly between contracts, where you will find yourself hanging around expensive motels with no idea when and if you will be working again. How much you earn depends on how well you can motivate yourself. Not easy when you hate*

*the job, it's been raining for a week, you are half way up a near vertical
mountain and you've got bags full of trees which you can't find a suitable
planting spot for.*

Kevin Vincent and his brother both got jobs in the Slocan Valley in BC and
disagree that tree-planting is one of the most miserable jobs in the world, which
may have something to do with the fact that, in his first season, Kev's brother
saved $2,750 after expenses in just two months:

*Tree planting is a job which can become a traveller's dream. It is a hard
job, but not as hard as people say, no harder than construction work or
heavy farm work. The food is great (sometimes outrageous) and camp life
is very sociable with people playing music, etc. Whole families with babysitters come along. The money is good, there's no doubt about that. If camping
out in Canada's forests and living a real healthy lifestyle for three or four
months appeals, plus earning top wages, this is for you.*

FRUIT PICKING

British Columbia

The fruit-growing industry of Western Canada takes place in decidedly more
congenial surroundings. The beautiful Okanagan Valley of British Columbia is
tucked away between two mountain ranges in the interior of British Columbia
and supports 26,000 acres of orchards. The Valley stretches north from the
American border at Osoyoos for over 200km to Armstrong. Cherries, peaches,
plums, pears, apricots, grapes and apples are all grown in the Valley, with a
concentration of soft fruits in the south and hard fruits (apples, pears) in the
north. All of these must be picked by hand. The harvesting dates vary slightly
from area to area, possibly as much as a fortnight or so earlier in Osoyoos than
in Armstrong. The harvests in Kelowna, a town approximately in the centre of
the Valley take place at the following times:

Species of Fruit	*Approximate starting date*	*Approximate duration*
cherries	June 22	through July
pricots	mid-July	approx. 3 weeks
Vee peaches	August 5	2 or 3 weeks
Elberta peaches	August 28	,,
Red haven peaches	late July	,,
Prune plums	mid-August	
Bartlet pears	August 12	Sep/early Oct
Anjou pears	late September	October
Macintosh apples	early September	3-4 weeks
Spartan apples	late September	,,
Newton apples	late October/November	,,
Winesap apples	late October	,,
Golden delicious apples	September	,,
Red delicious apples	,,	,,
Rome beauty apples	,,	,,

The best source of information on fruit-picking generally is the Agricultural
Employment Service or AES with offices in Penticton, Kelowna and Armstrong.
The AES issues bulletins throughout the summer which can be consulted in any
AES office or Canada Employment Centre in the region. Unfortunately you
have to have legal status to make use of them. As has been mentioned, immi-
gration raids are frequent and merciless in this area, because it attracts so many

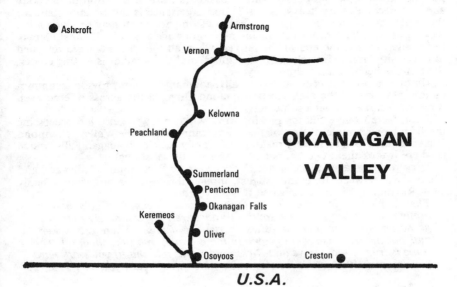

illegal workers. Of course students with employment authorisation may want to consider trying for a job in the Okanagan, so here is more detailed information about the harvests.

At the Okanagan offices of the AES, picking jobs are assigned on a first come first served basis (all things being equal) and so it is important to arrive at the office early in the day. Sometimes 100 hopeful job-seekers have gathered at the door of the AES by 7am. When the AES is less busy, the job-seekers are required to register, giving their name, social insurance number and contact address. Some attempt is made to screen applicants to avoid sending out a picker who has caused trouble elsewhere.

Iain Kemble recommends avoiding the AES and instead hanging around the local fruit packing shed which all the farmers in the area visit at least once a day and asking for work as they arrive. Professional migrant pickers (many of whom are from Quebec) begin with the cherries in the south of the valley and move up the valley to pick only the peak cherries. Then they come south again to work the apricots in the same way and so on.

Almost all fruit-picking is paid piece work. For example recently the rate for cherries was $1.80 a pail and people picked four or five an hour, which is lucrative though gruelling in temperatures of 35†C. Raymond Oliver says that in order to make a lot of money you can't be afraid of heights, though most picking of soft fruit can be done from an 8ft ladder. The rate when he was there was $18 a bin. A friend of his picked for 11 solid hours and earned $140. The majority of wages are paid directly into a bank account, which is a further difficulty for casual workers without proper papers.

Apples are the Okanagan's most famous export product. There is continuous picking of one variety or another from mid-August to the end of October. Apple-picking can be slow and poorly paid. A basket is worn at the front of the body and this becomes very heavy as it fills up. Experience is not so important for the apple harvest, though if you confess to having none you may be given a job picking up windfalls for the provincial minimum wage of $6 ($5.50 for students). Especially towards the end of the harvest when all the students have returned to university (approximately mid-September) and the weather is getting colder, the farmers begin to take almost anyone.

Although most pickers do not live locally, not many farmers provide accommodation. Not one of the orchardists Raymond Oliver came across offered even camping facilities, though some do.

If you have trouble finding picking work you can try to get a job processing the fruit, for example at one of the many canneries in the Valley. Raymond Oliver found a job at a factory making fruit candy bars in Okanagan Falls (which is where it took them two hours to discover his illegal status).

Berry picking takes place nearer Vancouver in Richmond, Chilliwack and Abbotsford between June and August, though this work is notoriously badly paid. Raymond Oliver investigated this harvest too:

> *There's plenty of ground crops (strawberries, blackberries, blueberries) around Abbotsford one hour south of Vancouver. Unfortunately there was no accommodation and campsites charge $16 a night. There are pickers' huts but the Indians seem to come in large groups and take them all. The same is true of Aldergrove and Richmond. I was told that if you work hard you can pick 100lb of blueberries a day which would earn you only $33.*

Ontario

The micro-climate in the fertile Niagara region bordering Lake Ontario is excellent for growing peaches, pears, plums, grapes (mostly for wine) and cherries. But it has already been pointed out that Niagara is an employment black spot, and it will be difficult to get a decent job, even though there is no shortage of fruit needing to be picked. To meet farmers, it is a good idea to go to the Saturday farmers' market (around the corner from the Manpower Centre on Main Street in Niagara Falls). Paul Donut had a compelling reason to stay in the area because he wanted to stay with a girl he knew:

> *Even here in Niagara I managed to find work. I called around all the local farms listed in the phone book and got a job picking cherries. The pay was dismal as the harvest was poor (most of the time was wasted throwing out the bad ones and being paid only for the baskets we filled with good cherries. However the farm was beautiful, my workmates, all Caribbean, were great fun. The peach harvest was somewhat better and after a couple of months I had enough money to look around for better paying work.*

Paul says he could have found a better-paid job if he had had transport from town to the farm, but since he didn't he had to accept work with the only farmer who would pick him up.

Elsewhere in the province there is a major tomato harvest in south-western Ontario, centred around Chatham and Leamington, which starts in mid-August and lasts for six to eight weeks. Other fruit and vegetable harvests take place around the province, especially in the counties bordering Lake Erie. The best source of information on these is the leaflet *Seasonal Agricultural Employment in Ontario* available from one of the 24 Agricultural Employment Services offices throughout Ontario. There are also separate leaflets *Work in Ontario's Tomato Harvest* and *Pick Ontario's Fruit Crops* designed to attract seasonal workers from outside the local areas. End-of-season bonuses are commonly paid. Below is a chart of harvests based on the above leaflets.

Crop	Part of Ontario	Dates of Harvest
Asparagus	Chatham, Aylmer, Tillsonburg, Delhi, Simcoe, Alliston	early May to mid-June
Strawberries	Chatham, Simcoe, St. Catharines, Hamilton, Cobourg, Trenton	early June to mid-July
Cucumbers	Windsor, Leamington, Chatham, Aylmer	mid-June to mid-Aug
Cherries (sweet)	Chatham, Niagara Falls, St. Catharines, Hamilton	early July
Cherries (tart)	Chatham, Simcoe, St. Catharines, Hamilton	late July
Raspberries	St. Catharines, Hamilton, Cobourg	mid-July to mid-Aug
Plums	St. Catharines, Hamilton	Aug/Sept
Peaches	Windsor, Leamington, Chatham, Simcoe, St. Catharines, Hamilton	mid-Aug to end Sept
Tomatoes	Windsor, Leamington, Chatham, Simcoe, Picton	mid-Aug to end Sept
Pears	Leamington, St. Catharines, Hamiton	early Sept to mid-Oct
Apples	Leamington, Simcoe, Hamilton, Owen Sound, Cobourg, Trenton, Picton	early Sept to end Oct
Grapes	Niagara Falls, St. Catharines, Hamilton	mid-Sept to end Oct

In addition to the important tobacco harvest described below, another seasonal agricultural job which needs to be done on Southern Ontario farms is detassling seed corn. During three or four weeks in July, about 5,000 people are needed for this work in the Chatham area. Busloads of students are brought in from cities 60 miles away, so if you were on the spot you would have a good chance. As in the tobacco-growing area, local unemployment is high in this county. Local people on the dole are required to register with the Kent & Area AES in Chatham (615 Grand Avenue West; 519-354-8722), so you will have competition from more than just students.

The Ontario Ministry of Labour has brought harvesting wages into line with all other jobs, i.e. $6.70 an hour for adults and $6.25 for students under 18. A maximum of $74 a week may be deducted for providing food and accommodation.

The Maritimes

High unemployment in some Maritime areas has driven many locals west in search of employment. However if you are travelling in the Maritime Provinces in August/September, you might try to find paid work picking or 'raking' blueberries in the Nova Scotia towns of Parrsboro, Minudie, Amherst or Pugwash and elsewhere. Earlier in the summer (i.e. mid-June to mid-July), strawberry picking is available. In the autumn you can also look for work picking apples. Head for the Bay of Fundy coast of Nova Scotia around Annapolis Royal, Bridgetown and Middleton. If you're lucky, fruit picking wages will be paid cash-in-hand.

Another seasonal job which you can try for is fish processing as described by Stephen Boss, himself a Nova Scotian:

I am financing my round-the-world travels by working in a fish plant during the herring season (mid to late August until the end of September). This job consists of cutting open herring for the roe which is inspected and collected by Japanese technicians to be made into caviare. Cutters make good money. I was successful working for Sullivan's Fisheries and I. Deveau Fisheries both in the town of Meteghan.

OTHER FARM WORK

If you are interested in working your way from farm to farm or homestead and want to meet Canadians, you might consider volunteering for WWOOF-Canada (Willing Workers on Organic Farms). For a membership fee of C$25 (cash) and two international reply coupons, John Vanden Heuvel (RR2, S18, C9, Nelson, BC V1L 5P5) will send a list of more than 100 farms across Canada to prospective volunteers, along with a description of the farms. All volunteers must have valid tourist visas.

Anyone with a background in agriculture might profit by placing an advert in small town newspapers as an enterprising Australian Mark Newton did. While waiting for his job to start at the Biting Fly Institute in Winnipeg, Mark put an advert in the *Stonewall Argus*, a small town north of Winnipeg and fixed up two weeks of work with a pig farmer.

Tobacco

The other harvest in Ontario which has also been traditionally assisted by migrant workers is the tobacco harvest in Southern Ontario. But times are tough for tobacco farmers (due to anti-smoking campaigning) and many have been forced to replant tomatoes. Yet the demand for pickers continues to be sufficiently great that it warrants a separate government quota of foreign temporary workers. Recruitment of British, French and Belgian male students is done through Canadien National (subsidiary of Canadian National Railways), 1 rue Scribe, 75009 Paris (1-47 42 76 50/ fax 47 42 24 39). The inclusive cost of the programme (including the flight from London in late July, returning late September) is F4,570 (approximately £550). Karl Beringhs from Belgium was keen to sign up but was rejected because his claim to student status was not accepted, i.e. a student card bought at the University of Cairo. (Yet he met someone in Paris who was accepted on the basis of a fake made-in-Thailand ISIC card, after persuading them that his university was closed for the summer.)

Work commences on or about the 1st of August until the third week of September (depending on the first frost) in the area surrounding the city of London, i.e. Tillsonburg, Aylmer, Delhi (pronounced 'Dell-high') and Strathroy. Although the work is not as strenuous as it was before mechanical pickers were introduced, the hours make it a hard job: seven to ten hours a day for six and sometimes seven days a week. Pay will be approximately $68 per kiln or $6.70 per hour, whichever is higher. A deduction of $2 per meal is made unless the picker remains until the end of the harvest, in which case the deduction is waived.

One tobacco picker, Tim Kelly, describes a typical day of picking:

We would be up at 5.45am every day for breakfast and start work by 6.30. After our one hour lunch break we worked until the kiln was full of leaves, usually around 5pm. Often after supper we were asked to help empty a kiln, which takes another hour of hard work. The picking (known as 'priming') was a very tiring job, and the first few days were by far the worst. Nearly every morning we got soaked from dew off the leaves. During the rest of the day we got bitten by mosquitoes, scratched, bruised, as well as covered in black sticky nicotine tar which accumulates on skin and clothing.

Ontario is not the only place where tobacco is grown in Canada. There are about 80 tobacco farms in the small island province of Prince Edward Island in eastern Canada. While hitching around the region in May, Iain Kemble learned that there had been urgent messages on the radio asking for 800 tobacco planters. He pretended to the lady in the Montague Employment Centre that he had a work permit and was promptly assigned to one of many local farmers of Belgian extraction. He worked in the massive greenhouses from 7am to 8pm bending over a conveyor belt picking out plants at the appropriate stage of maturity. For this back-breaking work, he was paid considerably more than the minimum wage. Good meals and bunkhouse accommodation were provided for $40 a week. The season lasted about a month until late June. He felt relatively safe from the prying eyes of immigration, but did hear of some Swedish planters who had been raided a few years before.

CHILDCARE

Live-in nannies and mothers' helps are in great demand in Canadian cities. However domestic employment in Canada is governed by a number of carefully formulated and strictly enforced regulations. A detailed leaflet about the 'Live-in Caregiver Program' may be obtained from the Canadian High Commission, though any agency which deals with Canada should be well informed and will guide you through the various stages of the process. There is now a requirement that nannies must either have had at least six months full-time training as a child-care worker or one year's full-time paid employment as a care-giver, six months of which must have been with the same employer. The other main requirement is that the nanny must live with her employers and commit herself to stay for at least one year.

If you are eligible and have found an employer (probably through an agency such as Childcare in Canada, 40 Kingsley Court, Welwyn Garden City, Herts. AL7 4HZ; 01707 391001), you can apply for an employment authorisation for Canada valid for one year and renewable once. There is a handling fee of £60 for the permit. (After that it is possible to apply for 'landed residency'.) The procedure for getting an authorisation usually takes three to four months and will include a very strict medical examination by an appointed private doctor who will charge £100-120. The authorisation will be valid for one employer, though it can be changed within Canada as long as your subsequent job is as a live-in child-carer.

Working as a nanny or mother's help in Canada has more status attached to it than au pairing in Europe, and the conditions of work reflect this. The federal government sets out guidelines for hours, time off, holidays, minimum salary and deductions. Nannies earn $650-850 net per month for a standard 44 hour week; overtime such as babysitting is paid accordingly. Deductions from the gross salary include income tax (some of which may be reclaimable), unemployment insurance and pension.

City newspapers are full of ads for nannies and babysitters. Several readers have fixed up informal jobs, including Miss T. P. Lye, a student from Malaysia, who was in Toronto several years ago:

After looking through the classifieds in the Toronto Star, *I called up several numbers for nannying. Most were unwilling to employ me without papers but I found one job, nannying and housekeeping for $175 a week. As I didn't pay taxes and paid $60-75 for rent, this rather high wage allowed me to save a considerable amount.*

The job wasn't bad; when the kids were at school, I had hours to myself to potter around, do some cleaning, preparing dinner, reading and watching TV. It was my childcare experience and my love of kids that got me the job: I am a rotten cook and a fairly pedestrian housekeeper, but the family put up with all that because the kids liked me. For anyone who is interested in nannying abroad, the wages are really high in Canada and the US. I would say get as much local experience as possible. The rest is up to your natural charm.

VOLUNTARY WORK

Some interesting practical community projects are organised by Frontiers Foundation (2615 Danforth Avenue, Suite 203, Toronto, Ontario M4C 1L6; fax 416-690-3934) in low income communities in Canada, which tend to be native communities in isolated northern areas. Some of the projects (known as Operation Beaver) consist of helping the local people to build houses or community centres. Others take place on wilderness camps for native children. Project locations have such picturesque names as Dog Creek, Rat Portage and Goose Bay. Whatever the project Frontiers Foundation will pay all food, travel and insurance expenses within Canada. A modest living allowance will be paid if you stay beyond the minimum period of three months. The accepted volunteer only needs to fund a return flight to Toronto and get the appropriate volunteer visa. Send three IRCs for an information pack and application form.

The work itself does not occupy all of your time and energies. According to Sarah King, there was time left over to participate in some quintessentially Canadian backwoods activities:

One of the great benefits about being a guest worker was that our activities became a focal point for the community. We played volleyball, helped break in wild horses, watched bears, made wild berry pies and rose-hip jelly, went camping, hunting, fishing and swimming, baked porcupine packed in clay, ate a delicacy of sweet and sour beaver tail, and all took up jogging around a local basketball park.

Another contributor recently stumbled (or rather strode) across a different way to experience the Canadian bush. Obbe Verwer from Amsterdam spent part of the summer of 1994 hiking in British Columbia:

After enjoying my visits to a couple of farms listed by WWOOF, I went on by myself to Vancouver Island. I set off to hike through the rainforest along the Clayoquot Valley Witness Trail. When I came to the trailhead, I met the trail boss who was working with a group of volunteers to build boardwalks at both ends of the trails. This was to enable more people to walk part of the trail which is important because this valley has to be saved from clearcut logging. I decided to join them. All the wood to build the boardwalk had to be carried into the trail, steps, stringers, nails and tools. We worked till 4pm, but it was not strict at all. Sometimes it was pretty hard, but it was fun. The forest impressed me more and more. The big trees, the berries, the mushrooms and the silence in the mist. It was just amazing. It was very satisfying to be helping to save this forest.

The Western Canada Wilderness Committee can be contacted at 20 Water St, Vancouver, BC V6B 1A4; 1-800 661 WILD. Volunteers should bear in mind that while working in rainforests one is bound to get wet. The WCWC also needs people to work in roadside kiosks, selling T-shirts, etc. for fund-raising. These volunteers should expect a certain amount of hostility from local loggers.

The workcamp movement in Canada seems to be in a certain amount of disarray. The Canadian Bureau for International Education (85 Albert St, 14th Floor, Ottawa, Ontario K1P 6A4) who used to organise workcamps for international volunteers are in the process of handing over operations to the Canadian Federation of Students; ask UK workcamp organisers for details.

Latin America

Most Latin American nations do not need unskilled workers from abroad to perform the menial tasks associated with agriculture and industry. For every such job, there are several dozen natives willing to work for a pittance, and gringos (white westerners) will not be considered for such work. People who are bilingual in Spanish may find opportunities in the cities, especially bilingual secretaries. Because Britain has few colonial ties with Central and South America, there is a general cultural and economic orientation towards Uncle Sam which means that Americans tend to occupy many jobs rather than Britons. Apart from voluntary opportunities, the main sphere of employment in which foreign travellers have any prospect of gaining acceptance is the teaching of the English language.

TEACHING

Spanning 75 degrees of latitude, the mammoth continent of South America together with the Caribbean islands and the eight countries of Central America, offer a surprising range of teaching opportunities. All but Brazil have a majority of Spanish speakers and, as in Spain itself, there is a great demand for English teaching, from dusty towns on the Yucatan Peninsula of Mexico to Punta Arenas at the southern extremity of the continent, south of the Falkland Islands.

The countries of most interest to the travelling teacher are Mexico, Colombia, Peru, Venezuela, Chile and Portuguese-speaking Brazil. Despite high levels of economic and often political uncertainty, demand for English language tuition continues to increase in the various kinds of institution engaged in promoting English, from elite cultural centres supported by the British and American governments to technical centres, from prestigious bilingual secondary schools to backstreet commercial institutes. Experience is not always essential to land a teaching job on-the-spot.

The Job Hunt

David Hewitt from Yorkshire describes the ease with which he found work in Brazil:

I easily found a job as an English teacher without any experience. I was even teaching the owner of the school which says something about the standard of teaching in Brazil. I was making about $3 an hour which is very good money when you consider that most people receive the minimum wage of about $30 a month. Towards the end of my time, after I had learnt some Portuguese, I started taking private students which pays much better wages.

In a land where baseball is a passion and US television enormously popular, American (and also Canadian) job-seekers have a distinct advantage. The whole continent is culturally and economically oriented towards the States and there is a decided preference for the American accent and for American teaching materials and course books. The California based chain of language schools ELS International (see page 120) has affiliated schools in Argentina (Av. Belgrano 624, 8° Piso, 1092 Capital Federal, Buenos Aires), Brazil (Av. Santo Amaro 3454, 04556 Brooklin, Sao Paulo; and Rua Paula Frassinetti 94, Rio Comprido, 20261-170 Rio de Janeiro) and Lima (14-419733) where the Academic Director wishes to be contacted only after applicants are in Peru.

Britons interested in teaching in South America should request details from the Central Bureau for Educational Visits & Exchanges of the 'Language Assistants' programme whereby people are placed in local secondary schools in nine Latin American countries for a year. Applicants must be aged 20-30 with at least 'A' level Spanish and preferably a degree in modern languages. Application forms are available from October; the deadline is December of the preceding year.

But if you are looking for more casual teaching work after arrival, it will be a matter of asking around and knocking on enough doors. There is less competition (although fewer jobs) in the smaller cities, off the beaten track. Try to charm the receptionist, librarian or English language officer at the British Council, Bi-National Center (the American counterpart of the British Council) or any other institute which might have relevant contacts or a useful notice board. Check adverts in the English language press such as Mexico City's *The News*, the *Buenos Aires Herald* or the Caracas *Daily Journal*. English language bookshops are another possible source of teaching leads, for example the English Book Centre in Guayaquil (Ecuador), Libreria Rodriguez in Buenos Aires or Barreiro y Ramos in Montevideo (Uruguay). Ask in expatriate bars and restaurants, check out any building claiming to be an 'English School' however dubious-looking, and in larger cities try deciphering the telephone directory for schools or agencies which might be able to use your services.

The crucial factor in becoming accepted as an English teacher at a locally-run language school may not be your qualifications or your accent as much as your appearance. You must look as neat and well-dressed as teachers are expected to look.

Travellers working their way around the world are more likely to find hourly jobs in local private tutorial colleges on subsistence wages (perhaps US$2 an hour) than in prestigious establishments. However if you have a good education, are carrying all your references and diplomas and are prepared to stay for an academic year, it may be possible to fix up a relatively lucrative contract.

Red Tape

Work permit requirements are usually ignored by most travellers though the school which employs you or other teachers will be able to offer advice. In some countries there is little problem; for example one contributor simply paid US$90 for a two-year visa for Bolivia. For jobs in certain countries it may be possible to apply for a work permit from a neighbouring country once you have fixed up the job. But in most cases the application procedure will be too long-winded or, worse, doomed to failure. You are unlikely to be refused employment on the grounds of lacking a permit. In some countries not even the language institute directors can get permits for themselves. As is true in so much of the developing world, the authorities do not go out of their way to clamp down on this wholesale disregard of work permit regulations in the English teaching field, since they are aware of the long-term economic benefits.

Mexico

The enormous demand for English teaching in Mexico has increased with the coming of the free trade agreement with the US. Companies of all descriptions provide language classes for their employees during all the waking hours of the week but especially in the early morning and at weekends. Roberta Wedge even managed to persuade a 'sleek head honcho in the state ferry service' that he needed private tuition during the siesta and that busy executives and other interested employees of a local company needed English lessons at the same time of day.

Demand is not confined to the big cities but exists in the remotest towns, at least one of which must remain nameless in order to preserve Roberta Wedge's dreams:

After doing a 'taster' ESL course in Vancouver, I set out for Nicaragua with a bus ticket to San Diego and $500 — no guide book, no travelling companion, no Spanish. On the way I fell in love with a town in Mexico (not for worlds would I reveal its name — I want to keep it in a pristine timewarp so I can hope to return) and decided to stay. I found a job by looking up all the language schools in the phonebook and walking around the city to find them. The problem was that many small businesses were not on the phone. So I kept my eye out for English school signs. I had semi-memorised a little speech in Spanish, 'I am a Canadian teacher of English. I love your town very much and want to work here. This is my CV...' Within two days I had a job at a one-man school.

David Brown managed to pre-arrange a teaching job in Mexico (by writing to an address mentioned in a previous edition of *Work Your Way Around the World*) and his experiences at the Culturlingua Language Center (Plaza Jardinadas, Local 24 y 25, Zamora, Michoacàn) were entirely positive:

Zamora is a down-to-earth agricultural centre very much off the beaten track. I wrote to them enclosing a brief CV and was offered a job even before leaving the UK. The school is always looking for teachers and will consider anyone who is a fluent English speaker and is not painfully shy. I teach five hours a day, five days a week and receive a room in an apartment, an hour of Spanish tuition every day and the equivalent of about £130 a month. You are never going to save money with this job, but it's enough to live comfortably and to pay for the odd weekend trip around the state of Michoacàn, one of the most beautiful in Mexico. Actually living in the community, plus the daily conversations with the students, provides a fascinating insight into the Mexican way of life.

The city of Monterrey held out no appeal for Paul Donut when he was given the chance to teach there:

A woman on the bus from Monterrey to Mazatlan gave me her phone number and said if I would teach her English, I could stay with her family in Monterrey and she would get me at least two paying students too. But even the prospect of a free bed and meals plus private students couldn't entice me back to a smog-ridden industrial city when I was heading for the Mexican Pacific Coast.

Mexico City is a thousand times more polluted, yet offers the best prospects for language teachers, some of which are advertised in the English language newspaper *The News*. Rupert Baker answered an advert and was invited to attend a disconcertingly informal interview at a restaurant (to which he still wore his tie). He ended up working for six months. More recently Michael Tunison contacted half a dozen major teaching organisations from the Yellow Pages and was interviewed by Berlitz and Harron Hall. Both offered tentative positions based more on his native speaking than his American university degree and journalism background. The starting wage at both schools was the peso equivalent of US$400 per month which seemed typical of the large chains. He later heard of less publicised opportunities to make $700 in institutes specialising in executive language training.

The red tape situation in Mexico is bound to cause headaches. Teachers have to provide a CV in Spanish, notarised TEFL and university certificates which have been certified by a Mexican consulate and, if you are already in Mexico, a valid tourist visa. People do teach on tourist visas which will have to be renewed every 90 days either by proving at a local government office that you have enough funds to support yourself or (more inconveniently) by leaving the country and recrossing the border to get a further 90 days.

Bolivia

Even the poorest of Latin American nations offers possibilities to EFL teachers. For example Judith Twycross received three job offers within a week of arriving in Bolivia's second city Cochabamba. If you have a good standard of education, are carrying all your references and diplomas and are prepared to stay for an academic year, it is possible to fix up a relatively lucrative contract. Judith timed her arrival in Cochabamba so as to be a couple of weeks before the beginning of the winter term. With the advantage of a year's teaching experience in Spain and France and a good knowledge of Spanish, she soon found employment:

I took with me a letter of introduction and a CV both in Spanish plus a photocopy of my degree certificate. These I photocopied and delivered by hand to the directors of schools and institutes in Cochabamba. I got a list of schools from the Yellow Pages (which you could borrow at a hotel, photocopying kiosk, tourist information office, etc.). I told everyone I met what I was trying to do and received help and advice from hotel managers, taxi drivers and people I stopped on the street to ask for directions.

Chile

Unlike the economy of most other South American nations, Chile's economy is flourishing. In the 1990s it has been achieving a remarkable ten percent rate of growth and unemployment is less than 5%. To quote from an article in the *Independent*, 'If you're young and educated but disappointed by unemployment in Britain... consider Chile, where it's still 1985.'

The market for English language teaching is very healthy, although short-term casual teaching is not well paid. Non-contractual work usually pays no more than 2,000 pesos per hour and often less. Private clients will pay more if you can find them. If you do not find them through personal contacts, it will be necessary to advertise. The best results are obtained by putting a small ad in *El Mercurio,* the leading quality daily. Other newspapers such as *La Epoca* and *La Tercera* have classified ads sections which will cost slightly less than *El Mercurio.* The free ads paper is called *El Rastro.* A useful option is to put up a small ad in a supermarket like Almac or Jumbo.

If you want to do more than just a few hours of casual teaching each week, many Institutes will insist that you obtain an official work permit from the *Extranjeria.* These are valid for one year in the first instance and, all being well, can be changed into a *visacion de residencia* which allows an unlimited stay. To get a list of the documents you need in addition to a contract of employment, go to the State *Intendencia,* which includes an *Extranjeria* section, on Moneda in the city centre just west of Plaza de la Constitucion.

Edwin Hunt, who is now permanently resident in Santiago, lists the following schools which would be worth trying after arrival in the capital:

Berlitz, Padre Mariano 305, Providencia, Santiago (02-236 1557/223 5818). Also Moneda 1160.

British English Centre, Dr. Manuel Barros Borgono 79, Providencia, Santiago (02-496165).

Concord Chile Inc., Nueva York 57, Of. 501, Central Santiago (02-724363).

ELADI José M. Infante 927, Providencia, Santiago (02-251 8111).

Fischer English Institute, Cirujano Guzman 49, Providencia, Santiago (02-490765).

John Kennedy Language Institute, Avenida Ejercito 20, Central Santiago (02-696 1851).

L.I.C.S.A. (Lang International Co. S.A.), Pedro de Valdivia 478, Providencia, Santiago (02-233 5056/233 0270).

Linguatec, Los Leones 439, Santiago (02-233 4356/233 2390). Also Huerfanos 757, Oficina 308, Central Santiago (02-399843).

Tronwell Apoquindo 4499, 3er Piso, Las Condes, Santiago (02-246 1040).

Peru

Lima is potentially one of the most lively EFL centres on the continent, as well as being one of the most stressful and dangerous in which to live. At present low wages and the difficulty of obtaining working papers mean that very few professional teachers can be attracted to the private EFL sector, so there is plenty of scope for casual teachers willing to accept $2 an hour. Many schools are located in the well-to-do port area of Miraflores, where a door-to-door search for work might succeed.

Venezuela

Even though the oil boom is fading to some extent, there is still a thriving market for English tuition. Proximity to the US and the volume of business which is done with *El Norte* mean a strong preference for American accents and teaching materials. Check adverts in Caracas' only English language daily, the *Daily Journal.* Wages average 350 bolivars per hour, though private tutors can charge up to twice that. In 1993 Kumar Tandon from New York state was offered a combined work/study contract by Centro Venezolano Americano (Av. José Marti, Edif. CVA, Urbanización Las Mercedes, Apartado 61715 del Este, Caracas 1060-A) but never took it up because he was worried that not enough contractual details were put in writing before he left home.

Most people work on tourist visas which are valid for two months but extendable to six. Work permits are available only if the employer has obtained approval from the appropriate Ministry and sent the necessary papers to a Venezuelan consulate in the teacher's country of residence. Getting a work visa *(transeunte)* is possible within the country but for a fee and probably only if you have the right contacts.

Central America

If you keep your ears open as you travel throughout this region, you may come across opportunities to teach English, especially if you are prepared to do so as a volunteer. After his stint in Zamora Mexico, David Brown from Fife travelled south, and was offered a teaching post at a secretarial college in the lovely old colonial town of Antigua in Guatemala, which he was unable to take up:

> *The salary was pitiful, but Antigua would be an enjoyable place to hang out, with its high number of cake shops and indigenous markets. There are always people wanting to learn English there to enable them to make the most of the 'gringo trail'.*

The English language bookshop in Antigua (Casa Andinista, 4a Calle Oriente No. 5 A), run by an energetic expat Briton Mike Shawcross, is a good point of contact. He can be found in Dona Luisa's restaurant opposite the bookshop most evenings.

Costa Rica is the wealthiest country in Central America and there are plenty of private language academies in the capital San José. In early 1994 part of the campaign platform of the new president was to provide native English speakers in all public schools. As a consequence, the organisation WorldTeach (Institute for International Development, 1 Eliot St, Harvard, Cambridge MA 02138-5705; 617-495-5527) is sending up to 200 volunteer teachers to the country. The application deadline is September 1st for a departure date in early February; the programme fee is $3,575.

VOLUNTARY WORK

Short-term voluntary work projects are surprisingly scarce for such a vast continent, and the few workcamp opportunities that exist are exclusively for Spanish-speakers. It is sometimes worth approaching the Embassy of your destination country. At the least they could give you the address of the National Federation of Voluntary Organisations, assuming there is one. In some cases there may even be a central register which attempts to match volunteers with vacancies, such as the one run by the Nicaragua/US Friendship Office (225 Pennsylvania Ave, SE, 3rd Floor, Washington, DC 20003) which charges a programme fee of $300. When one traveller enquired at the Anglo-Chilean Society via the Chilean Embassy in London, she was put in touch with an orphanage in Santiago looking for self-funding volunteers.

Among the voluntary organisations active in several Latin American countries are:

American Friends Service Committee, 1501 Cherry St, Philadelphia, Pennsylvania 19102-1479, USA (215-241-7000). A Quaker organisation which recruits Spanish-speaking volunteers aged 18-26 to work for seven weeks in the summer mostly on building or teaching projects in Mexico (programme fee $750 plus travel expenses) and Cuba ($300/500).

Amigos de las Americas, 5618 Star Lane, Houston, Texas 77057 (800-213-7796). Runs a training programme for more than 500 volunteers from the age of 16 for one or two months to work mostly in community health projects in Mexico, Costa Rica, the Dominican Republic, Brazil, Ecuador and Paraguay. The fee for participation is $2,355-2,995 including travel from the US. All volunteers must have studied Spanish and undergo several months of training, though it is possible to do this by correspondence.

Interfaith Task Force on Central America, (PO Box 3843, La Mesa, CA 92044-3843). Publishes a booklet *Travel Programs in Central America* for $8. It also sponsors community projects in Central America.

Interns for Peace, 165 E 56th St, New York, NY 10022 (212-319-4545). Run a programme to express solidarity with peace organisations in Nicaragua, Panama, Ecuador, Bolivia, etc. Placements last from two months.

Alliances Abroad, 2525 Arapahoe Ave, Suite E4-288, Boulder, CO 80302 (303-494-4164). Sends American students to Ecuador, Chile and Uruguay for three, six or nine months to live with local families and do some voluntary work as an English teacher, in a children's home, the tourist industry, etc. Fees range from $2,700 to $3,700.

Latin Link, Whitefield House 186 Kennington Park Road, London SE11 4BT (0171-582 4952). Run Short Term Experience Projects (STEP) in Argentina, Bolivia, Brazil, Ecuador, Nicaragua and possibly Peru, for committed Christians only.

As you travel throughout the region you are bound to come across various charitable and voluntary organisations running orphanages, environmental projects and so on, some of which may be able to make temporary use of a willing volunteer. A good place in Mexico City to learn about voluntary opportunities throughout Central America is the Quaker-run hostel Casa de los Amigos which will accommodate casual travellers especially if they are involved in political work.

Casa Guatemala is an orphanage which relies on travellers to carry out maintenance, cooking, building, organic gardening, teaching the children English, etc. in exchange for board and lodging. They can use as many as 100 volunteers a year preferably for a minimum of three months. The orphanage office in Guatemala City is at 14th Calle 10-63, Zona 1 (25517) while the orphanage itself is about five hours north of Guatemala City, a 10 minute boat ride from the El Relleno Bridge over the Rio Dulce which is off the Atlantic Highway on the road to the Petén region. The director is Angelina de Galdamez (319408).

There are a few famous communes in South America which passers-by are welcome to stay at free of charge if they join in the work, for example Atlantis, Telecom, Icononzo, Tolima, Colombia, whose members place a lot of emphasis on 'deep self-exploration' and who warn prospective American volunteers (especially the 'overeducated, know-everything' variety) that Atlantis is 'fiercely opposed to North American politics, culture and ideology.'

Archaeological digs may be open to passing volunteers. The *Programme de Antropologicos Para el Ecuador* (c/o Presley Norton, PO Box 8717, Quito, Ecuador) sometimes allows people to stay at this project on the Ecuadorean coast free of charge in exchange for basic cleaning chores. They also run an animal programme *(Hogar de Fauna Sivistre).*

Conservation

An increasing number of organisations, both indigenous and foreign-sponsored, are involved in environmental projects throughout the continent. Many can be pre-arranged though all charge a fee which is often equivalent to the price of a holiday:

Artemis Cloudforest Preserve, Apdo 937, 2050 San Pedro, Montes de Oca, Costa Rica. Volunteers are needed to build trails and plant trees. They must stay for at least a month and pay $100 a week towards expenses.

Caribbean Conservation Corporation, PO Box 2866, Gainesville, Florida

32602-2866, USA. Runs a sea turtle monitoring programme in Costa Rica using volunteer helpers.

Nicaragua Solidarity Campaign, 129 Seven Sisters Road, London N7 7OG. In cooperation with the Environmental Network for Nicaragua, NSC organise month-long summer and Christmas brigades to assist agricultural cooperatives and environmental organisations in Nicaragua. The cost is £1,100 which includes air fares to and from Managua and all other expenses.

Coral Cay Conservation Ltd, 154 Clapham Park Road, London SW4 7DE (0171-498 6248). Mount monthly expeditions to Belize which use teams of fee-paying divers to conduct marine surveys. The cost of participation is £1,725 for four weeks, £2,675 for eight weeks and £3,300 for 12 weeks, inclusive of travel, accommodation, food and most diving equipment. The minimum qualification is BSAC Novice Diver or equivalent.

Conservation International/Eco-Escuela de Espanol, 1015 18th St NW, Suite 1000, Washington, DC 20036 (202-973-2264). A joint project with the community of San Andrés in the Petén district of Guatemala, known for its tropical forests and Mayan ruins. Students engage in conservation and development work while studying Spanish for four hours a day, all for less than $100 a week.

One World Work Force, PO Box 3188, La Mesa, CA 91944-3188 (619-270-5438). Send volunteers to assist scientists at three wildlife projects along the Pacific coast of Mexico. The cost is $450-470 per week.

OTHER OPPORTUNITIES

Apart from teaching, the only paid work available in Latin America tends to be for bilingual professionals. CIEE runs a working holiday programme in Costa Rica which enables American students who have intermediate level Spanish to look for casual work between 1st June and 1st October in hotels, offices and the service industries generally. The wages quoted in the recent brochure were $52 a week for a hotel receptionist, $38 for an English instructor and $65 plus board for a kitchen manager.

Journey Latin America (16 Devonshire Road, Chiswick, London W4 2HH) needs tour leaders who can speak Spanish or Portuguese and who are familiar with the company's routes in Latin America. Foreign guides are occasionally hired by expatriate or even local tour operators. For example in the Tambopata jungle region of southeast Peru, there are two possibilities. The Tambopata Reserve Society (c/o J. Forrest, 64 Belsize Park, London NW3 4EH) has a resident naturalist programme whereby volunteers over the age of 20 are given free room and board for three months while acting as guides. The Tambopata Jungle Lodge (PO Box 454, Cusco, Peru; 084-225701/fax 238911; Director Tom Hendrickson) takes on guides who should speak some Spanish. Andrew James was there in the summer of 1994 and reports:

> We lived in a jungle camp consisting of wooden lodges a four-hour boat trip up the Tambopata River from Puerto Maldonado. I was one of three English guides who took visitors of all nationalities in groups of about five on dawn walks to explore the rainforest and see the amazing plant life and the occasional animal. I was there for three months and was paid $150 a month for working 20 days a month with the other ten days free to do research, live it up in Puerta Maldonado (a town straight out of the Wild West) or visit the old Inca city of Cusco.

Bilingual secretaries who can produce letters in proper English are in demand from commerce and law firms. Americans should find out if there is a local American Chamber of Commerce, as there is in Caracas. Translators, particularly of scientific, medical and technical papers tend to be well paid by universities and large industrial concerns. Both types of vacancy are advertised in English language newspapers, which may themselves need proofreaders and editors or know of companies which do. In many large cities there is a sizeable English-speaking expatriate community, predominantly involved in international commerce. The bars and restaurants that they frequent are good job-hunting grounds: not only might you hear about opportunities for temporary work in business, but you could obtain work serving in the establishment itself.

Tourism is booming in Venezuela and many expat-style bars and clubs employ foreigners. Margarita Island in the Caribbean has dozens of places catering to package holiday makers; try 4th of May Avenue and Santiago Marino Avenue, particularly between June and September and again December to March. Time-share companies also need OPCs, preferably with a knowledge of more than one language. In Caracas most foreign establishments are on the wealthy east side of the city in the Palos Grandes/Altamira area.

Mexico is another country in which travellers have been approached to work not as waiters or bar staff, but as hosts, entertainers and touts. While travelling in Mexico, Paul Donut was not expecting to work:

I stopped at Creèl, a very small town in the Sierra Madre Mountains of north-west Mexico. It is about halfway through the Copper Canyon and looks like a town from a wild west movie. I was very surprised to find about a dozen travellers trying to entice people to stay at a group of small hotels known collectively as Margueritta's. In return for ambushing incoming trains, Margueritta (the owner) gave the travellers a free place to sleep and three excellent meals a day. I had a bit of luck here as I went to stay at a smaller place up the street. While we were on a tour the next day with the Irish manager, I was offered a job as tour guide, guest recruiter, wood cutter and general helper at the pension. I stayed for about a month, in a clean room with free meals and received a commission of $2 for everyone I brought back from the train. I would definitely recommend staying in Creèl and going to the hotels for work. You won't make a fortune, but you should be able to stay here for free in return for some light duties.

Information on where and when to look for yachts in Mexico which may be needing crew is contained in the chapter *Working a Passage*. You might be able to find day work on boats in some of these harbours before the yachts set sail or perhaps an opportunity to boat-sit as Anne Wakeford did in Puerto Vallarta. She recommends asking boat owners to radio your request for work to their fellow yachtsmen in the morning. She also noticed that there might be work further south helping boats to navigate the locks of the Panama Canal.

The Caribbean

The Caribbean is far too expensive to explore unless you do more than sip rum punch by the beach. A host of Britons, Australians, South Africans, etc. are exchanging their labour, mostly on yachts, in order to see this exotic part of the world.

JOBS AFLOAT

Perhaps the easiest jobs to find are those working on the countless charter yachts and cruise ships which ply the Caribbean each winter and spring. From November until May the Caribbean becomes a hive of marine activity. Christmas, since it marks the start of the main tourist season, is a particularly good time to look for work. The main requirement for being hired is an outgoing personality more than qualifications or experience. Hours are long and wages are minimal, but most do it for the fun. Board and lodging are always free and in certain jobs tips can be high. It would not be unusual to work for a wage of $50 a month and then earn $700 in tips.

Cruise Ships

For general information about cruise ship work see *Working a Passage*. Contracts are normally for six to nine months and the hours of work are long, often 14 hours a day, seven days a week living aboard the passenger ship with all onboard facilities provided by the ship owner. Most cruise ships active in the Caribbean contract their staff from Florida-based personnel agencies (known as concessionaires), some of which liaise with UK agencies. All workers aboard passenger ships require a C1/D1 seaman's visa issued by the United States Embassy which is only given through an employer or agency presenting a confirmed letter of appointment.

A long established cruise company which recruits its own staff is Windjammer Barefoot Cruises (Box 120, Miami Beach, FL 33139; 305-672-6453). The largest cruise line in the world is Royal Caribbean Cruise Lines (RCCL, 1050 Caribbean Way, Miami, FL 33132) which has a recorded Job Hotline on 305-530-0471. Similarly Premier Cruise Lines (400 Challenger Road, Cape Canaveral, FL 32920; 407-783-5061) hire some of their staff direct. They specialise in family cruises, so anyone with extensive experience of looking after and amusing children has a chance of being hired.

Concessionaires specialise in different services, for example Greyhound Leisure Services (8052 NW 14th St, Miami, FL 33126) provide staff for gift shops, while Carberra NV and Zerbone Cruise Ship Catering Services (both in Suite 700, 100 South Biscayne Boulevard, Miami, FL 33131) place bar and catering staff.

Yachts

The lack of a work permit can be a definite hindrance in the search for work with a charter company. Yacht charter companies such as Nicholson Yacht Charters in English Harbour (Antigua) and Caribbean Sailing Yachts in St. Vincent are unwilling to publicise vacancies, both because they have enough speculative enquiries on the spot and also they are forbidden by their respective island governments from hiring anyone without the proper working papers. However once you are on the spot, you will soon hear of vacancies, and there may even be a broker who matches up crew with boats, for example Captain and Crews in St. Thomas (US Virgin Islands)

None of this affected contributors such as Tim Pask and Mirjam Koppelaars. Tim arrived in Boston in August on the look-out for work and soon found day work on a large power boat. After a few weeks he was taken on as a deckhand/ steward on a 72ft luxury charter yacht bound for the Virgin Islands:

My starting pay was $150 per week, all food and accommodation included. Tips were extra when on charter and could be as much as $400 each. It was very hard work and included long hours, keeping the boat clean, being involved in all aspects of sailing the yacht, maintaining the engine and serving meals and drinks to the guests.

As far as advice for finding work, I suggest simply walking along the docks and asking skippers. This may seem rather awkward at times but it certainly is the best way. If the skipper or owner is unable to offer a position as crew he may well need an extra pair of hands to help out with varnishing, etc. Try to find out when and where boat shows are being held as people are always in a rush to get their boats looking first class. Quite often finding

day work such as this can prove financially more rewarding. One can always
try the numerous crewing agencies, but usually a fee is required.

After crewing across the Atlantic Mirjam Koppelaars (from the Netherlands) found that persistence was definitely required when trying to find a crew position in the Caribbean:

When our yacht arrived in English Harbour in Antigua, everybody started
looking for a job. One got a job on British Steel *(once sailed by Chay Blyth)*
due to an affair with the captain; one found a job on a boat we had met in
Las Palmas (yes, the sailing world is small); one gave up and flew to the
States. I walked to Nicholson Yacht Charters every morning asking for a
job, and asked around the docks of English, Falmouth and Catamaran
Harbours. This way I found a job for two months as stewardess/deckhand
on a 60ft charter yacht.

Like Tim, Mirjam often earned more in tips than she did in wages (which were $800 a month in her case). She warns that there were lots of stories of crew not being paid their promised wages, often because of disagreements between owners and captains. From Antigua, Mirjam was offered a job as delivery crew on a yacht headed for Grenada, from where she got a lift with a 36ft trimaran to Isla Margarita in Venezuela (mentioned above). She concludes that her marvellous experiences were all 'part of being in the right place at the right time (and some lucky stars!)'.

JOBS ON LAND

BUNAC run a Work Jamaica programme which allows about 30 students to spend up to four months between 1st June and 1st October working at whatever job they can fix up in Jamaica. Red tape is minimal compared to the Work America and Work Canada programmes described above, but costs are considerably higher, i.e. £950 (including air fares) and wages lower, which probably accounts for the fact that there is not always a full take-up rate of the places available. The deadline for applications is April 30th. Andrew Owen hugely enjoyed participating in Work Jamaica, despite being paid a nearly non-existent wage:

Despite the high cost it is an experience not to be missed. I worked in the
kitchens of a large hotel in Montego Bay where I received £10 a week for
six days work (9am-4pm). I was provided with three excellent meals a day
from the restaurant and my own room 20 yards from the white sand palm
beach — PARADISE!

The choice of job seems to be either in the resorts along the north coast, which offer the advantage of food and accommodation, or in the capital Kingston where the range of jobs tends to be more interesting (e.g. working on the newspaper, radio station, at the Red Stripe Brewery, etc.) but you have to find your own accommodation (many stay in the university halls of residence) and access to Caribbean beaches is not so easy.

People find work in night clubs and hotels where British staff are considered chic. The Cayman Islands are meant to be one of the best places to look for this sort of work, with over 1,500 Americans alone working there. Construction work may also be available on Grand Cayman; ask around at bars. Suzie Keywood from Surrey found work as a bartender at 'Big Daddy's Lounge' in Grand Cayman. Without a 'Gainful Occupation Licence' or work permit (difficult to obtain with hundreds of locals after the same jobs) you should not take for granted that you will be treated fairly. There are plenty of horror stories in circulation concerning maltreatment by employers, such as failure to pay wages and to honour agreements to provide a homeward flight. Keep your beach-scepticism handy, and don't hesitate to cut your losses and run, if you sense you're on to a bad deal.

There are some opportunities for voluntary service. The Bermuda Biological Station for Research Inc. (17 Biological Lane, St. George's, GE01 Bermuda) accepts students throughout the year to help scientists carry out their research and to do various jobs around the station in exchange for room and board. Work/study volunteers from around the world are chosen on the basis of their academic and technical backgrounds. Summer is the peak period (applications must be in by February); otherwise apply at least four months in advance.

The West Indies Travel Group comprises a few Americans who decided to live and work in the British West Indies, and ended up on the undeveloped island of Providenciales in the Turks & Caicos Islands. They have recently published a book describing how to go about setting up.this, including information about work permits. The book costs $25, and it is available from Jacquie Manning, 397 Wise Road, Cheshire, CT 06410, USA.

With the recent upheavals in Cuba, there may be more opportunities in that beleaguered country in the future. The Cuba Solidarity Campaign (Red Rose Club, 129 Seven Sisters Road, London N7 7QG; 0171-263 6452) runs a work/study scheme every year in which volunteers undertake mainly building work and citrus fruit picking for three weeks in September/October. Applicants should be sympathetic to the Cuban Revolution and have been involved in recent political work. The cost of participation is about £600. The American Friends Service Committee (address above) organises month-long study-work projects in Cuba each July.

Africa

It is difficult to generalise about countries as different from each other as Morocco, Uganda and South Africa; however, we have not discovered enough employment opportunities in these countries to warrant separate treatment. The red tape can be truly daunting in emergent Africa, and discouraging both in industrialised Southern Africa and Mediterranean Africa.

While travelling throughout Africa, be prepared for contradictions and aggravations. One traveller recommends carrying an official-looking list of addresses (whether invented or not), particularly of voluntary organisations, to show to suspicious immigration authorities. If you are given a job, you may be able to get a work permit though this is not always necessary.

You must also be prepared to cope with some decidedly uncomfortable conditions, whether you are staying in a cockroach-infested (yet still overpriced) hotel in Alexandria while scraping together some money from English teaching; or enjoying the ten-hour truck ride into the Okavango Swamps of Botswana to look for work in the tourist bars and restaurants. As one contributor commented about this journey, 'it's an ordeal guaranteed to make you question whether working your way around some parts of the world is worth it after all.'

TEACHING

What makes much of Africa different from Latin America and Asia (vis-à-vis English teaching) is that English is the medium of instruction in state schools in many ex-colonies of Britain including Ghana, Nigeria, Kenya, Zambia,

Zimbabwe and Malawi. As in the Indian subcontinent, the majority of English teachers in these countries are locals. Still there is some demand for native speakers in secondary schools, especially in Zimbabwe and Kenya.

Africa is not a promising destination for the so-called teacher-traveller. The majority of foreign teachers in Africa are on one or two year contracts fixed up in their home country. Because a high proportion of opportunities is in secondary schools rather than private institutes, a teaching certificate is often a prerequisite. Missionary societies have played a very dominant role in Africa's modern history, so many teachers are recruited through religious organisations, though even here some of the major organisations like Christians Abroad and the Volunteer Missionary Movement are being asked to supply far fewer English teachers than previously.

Furthermore, conditions can be very tough and many teachers in rural Africa often find themselves struggling to cope at all. Whether it is the hassle experienced by women teachers in Muslim North Africa or the loneliness of life in a rural West African village, problems proliferate. Anyone who has fixed up a contract should try to gather as much up-to-date information as possible before departure, preferably by talking to people who have just been there. Otherwise local customs can come as a shock, for example finding yourself being bowed to (as Malawians do to anyone in a superior job). A certain amount of deprivation is almost inevitable; for example teachers, especially volunteers, can seldom afford to shop in the pricey expatriate stores and so will have to be content with the local diet, typically a staple cereal such as millet usually made into a kind of stodgy porridge, plus some cooked greens, tinned fish or meat and fruit.

Finding a Job

The United States Information Agency (USIA) has English Language Programs at its Bi-National Centers in 20 African countries; a list of addresses is available from USIA, English Language Programs Division, 301 4th St W, Washington, DC 20547. Normally they hire people who are already resident in the country. For example the Director of the American Language Center in Cameroon (PO Box 4045, Douala) wrote to say that the Center is inundated weekly with applications for employment from the US and 'it is absolutely impossible to recruit teachers from abroad'.

On the other hand, if teachers (British as well as American) are prepared to travel to an African capital for an interview, they may well get taken on. Denise Bouthillier, Director of the English Language Program at the *American Cultural Center* in Libreville writes in a more encouraging vein:

Work in an American Cultural Center is a great way to start off. I myself did it five years ago and am now running a programme. It allows a person to work in Africa but also provides up-to-date material which teachers in the national programmes are often forced to go without. Classes are small and the hours are not too heavy but can usually be increased depending on the capabilities of the teacher. We also do outside programmes in specialised institutions and thus give teachers experience in ESP (hotels, oil companies, Ministries). People with degrees in EFL are very much in demand.

The following organisations are involved with placing volunteer teachers in Africa:

Africa Venture Ltd, 10 Market Place, Devizes, Wilts. SN10 1HT (01380 729009; fax 720060). Places school leavers aged 18 or 19 in East African schools (primarily in Kenya) as assistant teachers normally for one term. The four-month package includes an in-country orientation course, allowances during the work attachment and an organised safari at the end. The 1994 participation fee was £1,540 plus air fares.

Daneford Trust, 18 Cheverell House, Pritchards Road, London E2 9BN (0171-729 1928). Educational charity which sends students and school-leavers (who must be from inner city areas) to Zimbabwe and Botswana for a minimum of three months. Volunteers must raise at least £2,000 towards costs.

Link Africa, 11/12 Trumpington St, Cambridge CB2 1QA (0223 322983; fax 323244). Education development charity with two programmes in Lesotho, Uganda and South Africa: school teaching projects for graduates with a degree, and teacher training programmes for qualified teachers and graduates with teaching experience.

Schools Partnership Worldwide, Westminster School, 17 Dean's Yard, London SW1P 3PB (0171-976 8070). Places school leavers for six to ten months in secondary schools in Tanzania, Zimbabwe and Namibia.

WorldTeach, Harvard Institute for International Development, 1 Eliot St, Cambridge MA 02138 (617-495-5527; fax 495-1239). Sends volunteers from the US, Canada and the UK to teach English and other subjects in Namibia and South Africa. Volunteers pay about $4,200 for airfare, health insurance, training, orientation and field support. Housing and a small stipend are provided.

Other opportunities crop up in the most obscure places. For example any EU national is entitled to work in Réunion, a *département* of France between Madagascar and Mauritius. It is reported that the standard rate for freelance native English teachers is F110 per hour. It is possible to advertise your services free of charge in two weekly papers, *Quotidien* and *SIR*.

Egypt

Respectable and dubious language teaching centres flourish side by side in the streets of Cairo and to a lesser extent Alexandria. Teaching jobs are not hard to come by, especially if you have an RSA/Cambridge Certificate (and if you are thinking of doing the course, Cairo is one of the cheapest places to do it.) Many parents enrol their children to do intensive language courses in the summer, so this is a good time to look for an opening (assuming you can tolerate the heat).

While the Australian Kate Ferguson was in Egypt, she was handed a leaflet advertising jobs with the International Languages Institute (ILLI) in central Cairo:

> *I went there to make some initial enquiries and it was not the dodgy exploitative business that I expected. Instead it was quite professional in its appearance. I also got the impression that the Institute was nearly always looking for teachers. The pay was 10 Egyptian pounds an hour. Training, accommodation, medical care and a one-year work permit were all promised free of charge.*

The address to apply to in person is ILLI, 34 Talaat Harb St (5th Floor), Cairo; 748 355/392 7244.

The British Council in Cairo has a list of English medium schools in Cairo plus a short list of TEFL establishments including several with insufficient addresses (e.g. The International Centre for Idioms, Behind Wimpy Bar, Dokki). There are several other listings in Dokki including the London Business Institute and the British Broadcast College.

Jobs can be found not only in the centre but in the leafy prosperous residential districts like Heliopolis, Mardi or Zamalek. These are also the best areas to look for private clients as Ian McArthur found:

> *In Cairo I sought to work as a private English tutor. I made a small poster, written in English and Arabic, with the help of my hotel owner. I drew the framework of a Union Jack at the top, got 100 photocopies and then meticulously coloured in the flags. The investment cost me £3. I put the*

posters up around Cairo, concentrating on affluent residential and business districts. I ended up teaching several Egyptian businessmen, who were difficult to teach since they hated being told what to do.

Kenya

Kenya has had a chronic shortage of secondary school teachers for some time, mostly in Western Province. Although legislation has made it harder for unqualified teachers to find jobs, it may still be possible to fix up a teaching job by asking in the villages, preferably before terms begin in September, January and April. Be prepared to produce your CV, diplomas and official-looking references. Basic accommodation and a monthly salary (local rates) may be provided, though not all schools can afford to pay it, especially non-government self-help *Harrambee* schools. For information about work permits, contact the Principal Immigration Officer, Department of Immigration, PO Box 30191, Nairobi, though it is the usual story of employers having to file the application and proving that no Kenyans can do the job, while you are out of the country.

School leavers should consider the programme offered by Africa Venture (see above).

Zimbabwe

The expanding educational system of Zimbabwe also needs more teachers than are available. Recruitment of qualified teachers takes place through Zimbabwe Embassies abroad (e.g. three year contracts through the High Commission in London), through personal contacts or on the spot. If while travelling you find a school willing to hire you, a work permit can be obtained without too much difficulty. While travelling through Africa, Stephen Psallidas met at least four English teachers on one-year contracts earning local wages.

Martin Goff was lucky enough to fix up a teaching job in Zimbabwe through contacts at his own school. He was paid the equivalent of £150 per month. With a university degree, he would have been paid two and a half times as much. He supplemented the basic wage with teaching in adult night schools, which have been set up as part of the government's policy to make education available to everyone. He concluded:

Zimbabwe is a beautiful country; the people are 95% very friendly and $4\frac{1}{2}$% friendly, and they seem eternally pleased to see you. My time out there was easily the best of my life, and it was only a booked plane ticket that made me leave.

Morocco

English is gaining ground despite Morocco being a Francophone country. Outside the state system there is a continuing demand for native speakers. The British Council in Rabat can supply a list of 18 schools, which includes its own teaching centre and ten American Language Centers. The biggest employs more than 50 teachers on a part-time basis (1 Place de la Fraternité, Casablanca 21000; 2-277765/275270). A British-oriented school in Casablanca which recruits qualified EFL teachers is the British and Professional English Centre (74 rue Jean Jaurès; tel/fax 2-296861).

TOURISM

Once again travellers' hostels are one of the few providers of casual work in the developing nations of the African continent. It is something that many independent trans-Africa travellers do for the odd week, which is a very nice way to have a break without having to pay for it. While cycling through Africa, Mary Hall stopped at a backpackers hostel in Malawi where she was even offered a permanent job, but the road called. Two places in Malawi that have been mentioned as being sympathetic to working travellers are Dougle's Hostel in Blantyre and Abdul's in Nhkata Bay on Lake Malawi. The latter offers one of the cheapest diving courses in the world; Iona Dwyer got a basic Open Water I qualification after investing just £65.

Tourism is well established both on the Mediterranean coast of Africa and in the countries of East and Southern Africa where game parks are the major attraction. (Opportunities in South Africa are discussed separately below.) It is possible to find work in hotels and bars in resort areas; try the so-called trendy establishments rather than humble locally-staffed ones.

A few British tour operators need reps and support staff for resorts like Monastir in Tunisia or Agadir, Morocco. Try for example the Panorama Holiday Group (29 Queens Road, Brighton BN1 3YN) who need a handful of French-speaking reps in Tunisia.

K. McCausland reports on what he found in Morocco one winter:

Agadir is a serious winter hotspot for European tourists and as such there are lots of opportunities in hotels, bars and discos. A little further north on the coast is a beautiful and friendly town called Essaouira. It's the only place where we were offered work and were sorry to have to turn it down. It's rapidly making a name for itself among travellers with a big windsurfing fraternity and a service industry starting to gear up. My girlfriend was offered a job as a receptionist in one of the several new hotels being built. Wages are considerably lower than in Europe, but as the cost of living is extremely low, it's not such a problem.

Purveyors of overpriced carpets in Morocco try to enlist the help of travellers whom they loosely employ to lure high-spending tourists into the shops. You approach a stranger and pretend to want advice on which carpet to buy yourself, and hope that the tourist will follow suit; most 'plants' find that they can't stomach this charade for long.

Anyone with a diver's certificate might be able to find work at Red Sea resorts like Sharm el Sheikh and Ras Muhammad. The British firm Emperor Divers (22 High St, Sutton, Ely, Cambs. CB6 2RB) employs diving instructors for at least a year in Egypt. You can sometimes get free lessons in exchange for filling air tanks for a sub-aqua club. It is possible to be taken on by an Egyptian operator (especially in the high season December/January); however the norm is to be paid no wage and just earn a percentage of the take.

The Nile cruise business is booming and it may be possible to find a job as Ana Güemes discovered:

In Aswan I met a guy from Texas who had found a job on the cruises that sail between Luxor and Aswan just by offering his services personally. The main reason he was hired as an office aid was that he spoke some French. I was so excited about the possibility of getting this kind of experience that in spite of the temperature being 48†C in the shade and my clothing not the best, I visited some of the cruise offices. Bad business, lack of knowledge of German, difficulty in getting a permit and a strictly male staff were the most common answers I got.

Note that tourists in Egypt have been targetted by terrorist groups in the past two years. Britons might like to contact the special Egypt advice line set up by the Foreign Office for the current situation 0171-839 1010.

Suitably connected people might be able to run their own safaris, something Jennifer McKibben observed in Kenya:

Some entrepreneurial travellers used to make money by hiring a jeep and taking holidaymakers on mini expeditions. This would either be to places inaccessible by public transport or would undercut the travel agencies on standard trips. They found customers by placing notices in the youth hostel and cheap hotels.

In her whole year of volunteer nursing in Uganda, Mary Hall met only one foreigner who had found work on the spot and without a work permit. This woman was asked to manage a tourist lodge in the middle of nowhere and jumped at the chance since it was such a beautiful nowhere.

Longer term possibilities are available with the overland companies like Truck Africa (37 Ranelagh Gardens Mansions, Fulham, London SW6 3UQ), Africa Explored (Rose Cottage, Summerleaze, Magor, Newport, Gwent NP9 3DE) and some of the others mentioned in the section *Overland Tours* on page 48. For courier work, applicants are required to have first-hand knowledge of travel in Africa or must be willing to train for three months with no guarantee of work. Requirements vary but normally expedition leaders must be at least 23 and be diesel mechanics.

The organisation Wind Sand and Stars (2 Arkwright Road, Hampstead, London NW3 6AD) takes on overland tour leaders for short periods to conduct scientific field work with youth groups in Egypt. Applicants must have travel experience, knowledge of first aid and preferably an acquaintance with Arabic.

OPPORTUNITIES IN SOUTH AFRICA

With the political changes of the 1990s, the Republic of South Africa has become a much more attractive destination for the travelling community. The transition to black majority rule has not resulted in the 'brain drain' which some anticipated, although there are openings for people with skills and experience (especially in computing, engineering, electricians, etc.). Check adverts in the Monday edition of the main dailies, the *Argus* in Cape Town, and the *Star* and *Citizen* in Johannesburg. Temporary employment agencies such as the long-established Kelly Girl might be willing to register likely candidates whom they are persuaded plan to settle in South Africa. German-speakers in Jo'burg should try the German Employment Agency on Jorissenst. in Braamfontein.

The most important difference for job-seekers is that hiring policies now practise affirmative action and there is a concerted effort to redistribute labour. That means that it is very difficult for a white foreigner to get a work permit for a job which a local person could do. Furthermore local black people are willing to work for very low wages. After arriving in Cape Town by bicycle, Mary Hall advertised her nursing experience in the newspaper nd fixed up a live-in job looking after an elderly man. After two weeks, her employer realised that a black person could do the same work for a third of the price and Mary got the boot. By then she had decided that South Africa was too nice a country to strain herself to get a job.

Red Tape

Not surprisingly, the new government has tightened up on foreign workers as it endeavours to find jobs for its own citizens (the rate of unemployment currently stands at 40%). It is still not too difficult to extend a three-month tourist visa: one Australian we heard of got an extension without an outgoing ticket but with a promise to hitch-hike out of the country. Be sure to do this about two weeks before the expiry date.

Work permits are not as easy to obtain, though it is possible. You need a letter from an employer and proof that the job has been advertised. The main difficulty is that you must deposit a security bond of R6,000 into a bank account.

This will be returned to you (in rands of course) only when you leave the country. According to Brigitte Albrech, there is a certain amount of flexibility in the system, and she recommends approaching Home Affairs offices in smaller towns and suburbs like Wineberg (Cape Town). As mentioned below, key tourist places are regularly raided by the Department of Home Affairs, and employers caught employing foreigners without permits are fined heavily (e.g. R20,000). Deportations are not uncommon. One UK contributor who was sharing a flat with a Bangladeshi ice cream seller, had their front door nearly broken down by immigration officials who dragged the hapless Bangladeshi off to jail before deporting him two days later. (Our contributor claims that his South African accent was sorely tested that day.)

Tourism

Yet, many travellers do wish to extend their stay by undertaking casual work. Cape Town is the tourist capital of South Africa including for backpackers: there are now about nine youth hostels in the city. The Backpack is recommended by Brigitte Albrech for its notice board and Oak Lodge on Breda Street by Steve and Iona Dwyer who say that you can earn a week's rent by doing two days of painting.

Everyone who has looked for a tourist job in Cape Town recommends Seapoint, a beach suburb lined with cafés, ice cream kiosks, snack bars and other places which have high staff turnovers. (Ice cream is also sold from cycle carts; find out whom to contact for work by asking the sellers.) Also try using the door-to-door approach in the flashy new Waterfront development, Camps Bay and the beaches along the Garden Route. People who can speak more than one language may find that hotels will not only hire them (e.g. Hotel Peninsula, Seapoint) but will help them to obtain a work permit. Bear in mind that these high-profile tourist meccas have been the target of immigration raids, so casual workers might prefer more discreet places. Suburban fast food restaurants such as Spur, Mike's Kitchen and St. Elmo's are often hiring, though the first two are liable to pay only commission. Suburbs to concentrate on are Observatory, Rondebosch, Wineberg and Plumstead.

The best time to look for catering work is in early December, which is when a contributor called Steve arrived. He managed to find a waiter's job the day after he arrived, though he wasn't very impressed with the wages. He was paid only R3.50 an hour, but tripled this with tips, earning R80-100 for an eight or ten hour shirt. Since he was paying only R350 a month for a room in a shared flat, this turned out to be enough to save, but only $500 in 14 weeks.

Brigitte Albrech managed to get a job in her career field with the South African Tourism Board, but expressed her view that anyone could find a job in the tourist industry. She recommends explaining to prospective employers that you arrived on holiday but are now considering permanent residency. She also suggests that people who want to be tour guides should head for the Oudtshoorn region where ostrich farms often need linguists for the summer season. The local Backpackers Resort hostel (the Oasis) should be able to advise.

Although Johannesburg is frequently described as a 'dump', there are job possibilities there, for example in the Yeoville area of town where bars, restaurants and travellers' hostels like Rocky Street Backpackers on Regent St and the Pink House are located. Try also the Backpackers Ritz which takes on long-term residents at favourable rates. According to Iona Dwyer, Tekweini Backpackers in the Morningside area of Durban employs foreigners for free rent and a small wage (which soon gets swallowed up in the happy hour at Bonkers, the local pub). If you stay any length of time in one place, you may be asked to act as relief manager as regularly occurs at Sani-Lodge in the Drakkensberg near

Himeville. Steve from South Shields did this for a couple of weeks at a campsite in the Transkei.

Selling

Tiring of his job as waiter at a Greek restaurant in Cape Town, Steve answered an ad (posted up in hostels) for sales people. He was accepted to sell dodgy paintings door-to-door which he (like so many others who have done this job in various countries) described as a nightmare. (Perhaps he wouldn't have loathed it so much if he had earned as much as a couple of Israelis he met who were making R10,000 a month each.) He also heard of a company in Stellenbosch called Duplex (02231-98173) which organised sales tours in different areas of South Africa, selling gadgets and household goods on a 20% commission.

He also came across money-making opportunities in the markets of Cape Town:

I've met several travellers selling arts and crafts items or doing hair-wraps in Greenmarket Square and St. George's Mall. In the latter you don't even need a licence; just turn up before 8am and pay R5 for a patch of ground. In the Greenmarket Square market you have to work for a stall-holder.

Farm Work

The provinces of the Northern Transvaal, the Orange Free State and the Cape are rich agricultural areas where extra help may be needed at harvest time. The rural economy of South Africa is dominated by Afrikaaners, though most of them speak at least a little English. Generally speaking the slog work of fruit and vegetable picking will be done by local black labourers, but anyone with a background in agriculture might find an opening.

The towns of Stellenbosch and Paarl to the east and north of Cape Town respectively are the centres of South Africa's wine industry. Around Stellenbosch picking begins in late January/early February and lasts for four or five weeks. Further inland (e.g. around Worcester) it starts a few weeks later, and continues well into March. If you find a farmer willing to put you up and give you work, the problem of work permits is unlikely to arise.

Boats and Fishing

Work may be available in the boatyards of Cape Town and other places, especially doing the dogsbody jobs of sanding and painting. Activity peaks before the Cape-to-Rio yacht race in the winter.

Of the many fishing ports around South Africa's coastline, Plettenberg Bay is the only one which has been recommended for casual work on fishing boats. Karen Heinink and her friend Mark ended up in 'Plett' because the last lift they had hitched put them down there:

Mark got up one morning at 5am and went down to the beach where the boats leave to catch squid. He was instantly given some tackle and bait, and was told to board. He was paid according to the number of crates he could fill. A lot of money can be made when the fish are running well, but if not you at least catch a few fish for supper.

Apparently late November/early December is the main squid season in Plettenberg Bay, though it varies from year to year depending on the route the fish take and climatic conditions.

BUSINESS & INDUSTRY

If you are interested in joining a business in Africa (especially if you have a technical or managerial skill) you should contact the Commercial Section of the embassy of the country which interests you for information about job prospects. If you are on the spot, the expatriate community may be willing to offer advice or even more practical assistance.

Other work opportunities in Africa include translating business documents from and into French, German or English, depending on the particular country's position and trade. You could put an ad in the paper or visit firms. When Jayne Nash travelled in East Africa, she noticed many temporary employment agencies in Nairobi and Harare, some with familiar names like Alfred Marks and Brook Street. She reckons accountants and secretaries would have no trouble finding working.

Egypt is the capital of the Arab world's film industry, and many of the films require Western extras, often to play drunken, drug-taking, promiscuous degenerates. This pays around E£30-45 (£6-9). Budget hostels such as the Oxford in Talaat Harb St and the Hotel des Roses are often visited by people looking for extras. Katherine Berlanny and a friend were approached and asked if they wanted to be extras in a television soap opera. During their one day of employment, they had to play guests at a dinner party which involved some chandelier-swinging on the part of the stars. They could have had more work but had to catch a train to Aswan.

According to Ian McArthur, Western models are also required for TV commercials in Cairo:

> *Models are normally recruited through the agencies listed in the Yellow Pages (which fortunately has an English language version). A portfolio is an advantage though not essential and a smart outfit is useful if only to create a good impression. I was offered this work at the Hotel Oxford (well-known for its long-term residents) but was told to come back the following day three times in a row, and lost patience. The pay is supposed to be high (£20-25 a day) and can involve several consecutive days shooting, although it tends to be sporadic.*

The Black Market

In most countries the black market in currency is no longer as worthwhile as it once was. The best bets are Malawi and Ethiopia where most people exchange at hostels and get about 75% more than the bank rate. Small gains of about 10% can be made in Zimbabwe and Tanzania, though rip-offs are commonplace especially in the latter. Asian shopkeepers and traders are usually reliable. Do not consider black market exchanges in Kenya where it is not unusual to be offered less than the bank rate.

You may also encounter a black market in consumer goods such as T-shirts, sneakers and jeans, though it is probably not worth stocking up on these things because people-in-the-know (like overland couriers) have this trade sewn up. Brendan Barker came across a few possibilities during his brief stay in Morocco:

> *Alcohol and English/American cigarettes can be sold (discreetly) in Tangiers to one of the many guides and touts. My made-in-the-USA bandana was frequently asked for as a gift, trade or for cash, as was a pin badge of a guitar I bought in Madrid. I wish I'd bought a bag of them, since I could have traded them for lots of things. Even my scummy T-shirt advertising a Mexican restaurant was open to trading offers. So basically anything European or unavailable is fairly good trading currency.*

Travellers in Egypt have benefitted from selling whisky as Ian McArthur reports:

> *Another potential moneyspinner is to sell duty-free whisky. In the first month of their stay in Egypt, foreigners are entitled to three bottles of duty-free spirits or wine to be paid for in hard currency at Egypt Free Shops (for*

example at Cairo Airport or on Arab League St in Mohandiseen). The best buy is Johnny Walker Black Label which can be sold in a bar at two or three times its cost price.

VOLUNTARY WORK

Africa is still very reliant on aid agencies and voluntary assistance. The large majority of volunteers in Africa are trained teachers, doctors, nurses, agricultural and technical specialists who have committed themselves to work with an international organisation like VSO and Skillshare Africa (3 Belvoir St, Leicester LE1 6SL) for at least two years.

It may be possible to offer your services on a voluntary basis to any hospital, school or mission you come across in your travels, though success is not guaranteed. Travellers who have found themselves in the vicinity of a famine crisis have often expressed shock when their offer of help has been turned down. Passers-by cannot easily be incorporated into ongoing aid projects, but it is always worth asking the local OXFAM or Save the Children Fund representative.

If you have a useful skill and the addresses of some suitable projects, you are well on the way to fixing something up. Mary Hall had both, so wrote to a mission clinic in Uganda offering her services as a nurse:

There wasn't a doctor so it has to have been the most stressful thing I've ever done. After a couple of weeks I was helping to run the clinic, see and examine patients, prescribe drugs and set up a teaching programme for the unqualified Ugandan nurses. There's an incredible need for any form of medical worker in Africa but especially in Uganda where HIV and AIDS are an increasing problem.

We had no running water, intermittent electricity and a lack of such niceties as cheese and chocolate. Obviously adaptability has to be one of the main qualities. Initially I worked on my visitor's visa which wasn't a problem, but when it became apparent that I would be staying for !onger, the clinic applied for a work permit for me. Quite an expensive venture (£100) and I think very difficult without a local sponsor. The local bishop wrote a beautiful letter on my behalf, so I got one.

A white person is considered to be the be-all and end-all of everyone's problems, and I found it difficult to live with this image. I'd like to say that the novelty of having a white foreigner around wore off but it never did. Stare, stare and stare again, never a moment to yourself. Still it was a fantastic experience. I've learnt an awful lot, and don't think I could ever do nursing in Britain again. My whole idea of Africa and aid in particular has been turned on its head. Idealism at an end.

Workcamps

The kind of short term voluntary work available to unqualified people is generally confined to workcamps which operate in many African countries. Most of the projects have to do with rural development. Normally you have to finance your own travel and pay a not insignificant registration fee to cover food and lodging for the three to six week duration of the camp. Camps are sometimes arranged in winter as well as summer. The work consists of building, installing water supplies, conservation or assisting in homes for disabled or underprivileged children and adults. The national headquarters are often good sources of local information, though not by post.

If you want to arrange a place on an African workcamp before leaving home, you may have to prove to an international organisation that you have enough relevant experience. The 1994 *Projects Directory* from UNA Wales contained information on workcamps in 11 African countries from Morocco to Uganda. The workcamp movement is particularly well developed in North Africa especially Morocco which has a number of regional organisations creating green spaces, building communal facilities. For example Chantiers Sociaux Marocains (BP 456, Rabat, Morocco; 07-791370) places about 300 volunteers who apply directly or through one of CSM's cooperating partners. The main language at camps in Morocco is French.

French is also the second language of Tunisia, and you may well be the only English speaker on a workcamp organised by the *Tunisian Association of Voluntary Work*, ATAV, Maison du RCD, Boulevard 9 Avril, Tunis, Tunisia (264899). Some of their projects are concerned with the restoration and maintenance of historical monuments, of which Tunisia has a great many splendid examples.

To find out about the range of workcamps in Africa, it is a good idea to buy the international list of projects from a sending organisation in your own country. Sometimes even they find it hard to extract an answer from their counterparts in developing nations, so there is little point in listing them here. If European organisations have to operate on a shoestring, African ones survive on a broken sandal strap and even when international reply coupons are sent, replies are rare. If you decide to try to joi   )ject once you are in an African capital like Nairobi, Accra, Freetown or Maseru, it should not be hard to track down a coordinating office. Ask at the YMCA or in prominent churches.

American applicants should also be aware of Operation Crossroads Africa Inc (475 Riverside Drive, Suite 242, New York, NY 10115-0050; 212-870-2106) which runs various seven-week projects from late June in rural Africa; the cost of participation and travel is $3,500. Canadians should explore the possibilities through Canadian Crossroads International, 31 Madison Avenue, Toronto, Ontario M5R 2S2. World Horizons International (PO Box 662, Bethlehem, CT 06751) sends high school and college students from the US and Canada to Gaborone (capital of Botswana) and Namibia for six weeks during the summer. The cost of participation is $4,200. Alliances Abroad (2525 Arapahoe Ave, Suite E4-288, Boulder, CO 80302) send American students to Ghana for three, six, nine or twelve months to live with local families and do some voluntary work in a children's home, the tourist industry, etc. Fees begin at $2,500.

Other Opportunities

Missionary societies still play a large part in Africa and organisations like the Volunteer Missionary Movement (Comboni House, London Road, Sunningdale, Ascot, Berkshire SL5 0JX) recruit qualified technical and professional people for two year stints in Africa (particularly Zimbabwe, Kenya and Uganda).

There are other voluntary organisations based in Africa in addition to workcamps associations. Sierra Leone has several projects which are worth investigating. Pa Santigie Conteh Farmers' Association/PASACOFAAS (5a City Road, Wellington, PMB 686, Freetown; fax 022-224439) which sends volunteers to some 26 villages in the Northern Province to build, teach and tend the land. The project is having financial problems so the director requests that £10 be sent for the application form and further information.

For the majority of African countries, family farming on a subsistence (or lower) level is practised. Two voluntary organisations in Ghana work to help farmers. The Rainbow Relief Foundation (PO Box 673, Kaneshie-Accra) organises workcamps to help with community farms. Also, Ebenezer Nortey-Mensah has recently set up a group affiliated to WWOOF and wants to place volunteers (who need not have special skills) on traditional farms in Ghana to help with the weeding by hoe and cutlass [sic] and the harvesting of food and cash crops like maize and cassava. He is also keen to host volunteers who can repair bicycles for his new workshop. Details are available from PO Box 154, Trade Fair Site, La-Accra (fax 021-772737).

Throughout Africa there are a great many volunteer workers with VSO, the Peace Corps, Canada's CUSO, etc. in hospitals, schools and agricultural projects who are sometimes willing to put up travellers. Probably the more remote and cut-off the volunteers are, the more welcoming they will be, but be careful not to abuse or presume on this kind of hospitality. Always offer to pay, or go armed with treats.

Contacts are a great help here. Your path will be made smoother if you can procure an introduction from a church or family friend. Catherine Young spent a summer trying to set up a play group in a Nigerian village where a friend's father was setting up a medical clinic. But people have succeeded without contacts. One traveller we heard of went to Cape Town Central Library and looked through the 'green directory' which lists hundreds of environmental agencies. He then fixed up some voluntary work on a cheetah reserve near Johannesberg, where he was given free board and lodging but no wages. There is a myriad of plant and wildlife studies being carried out throughout Africa and you might be fortunate enough to become attached to one of these.

Frontier Conservation Expeditions (77 Leonard St, London EC2A 4QS; 0171-613 2422) give volunteers the chance to take part in environmental research and conservation projects in Tanzania and Uganda. Frontier projects run in ten-week phases during which volunteer research assistants can make a practical contribution to scientific and other research whilst visiting some of the most remote, beautiful and largely unexplored areas of the world. Each expedition is self-funded and volunteers must make a contribution of between £1,800 and £2,800. Detailed information on how to raise funds is provided to prospective volunteers.

Clare Ansell enjoyed her time in Tanzania so much that she joined the London office after her expedition:

I joined Frontier as a paying volunteer in October 1990 and then stayed on for an extra three months as unpaid staff managing a field camp in the Coastal Forests and later returned to work as UK Coordinator in the London office. Frontier offers great opportunities to those who want to make the most of them. I've learned a fantastic amount about the practicalities of the conservation world and personally collected a new species of toad! Scientific training isn't necessary. Interest and determination are what matter.

Israel

Most people associate working in Israel with staying on a kibbutz or a moshav. Although there are other working opportunities, including a few in a Palestinian rather than Jewish context, these are by far the most popular ways of having a prolonged visit in Israel, and one which many thousands of British people take advantage of every year plus many more from all over the world. Although the numbers fell off a few years ago, the advancing peace process has made the country a more attractive destination than ever before. Although not everyone enjoys the work they end up doing in Israel (especially if they are there in winter and have been expecting hot sun), they all agree that it is an excellent country in which to meet working travellers and therefore a good place to begin their travels.

The Regulations

Having previously had one of the most lenient immigration policies in the world, the Israel Interior Ministry has now tightened up on working travellers. It is now obligatory to obtain a B4 Volunteer Visa (at a cost of $20) within 15 days of joining a kibbutz, archaeological dig, etc. If you arrange something after you arrive in Israel or through official channels (e.g. the volunteer offices in Tel Aviv), it is fairly straightforward obtaining the visa, but may be difficult if you fix up something informally. If you stay more than three months, you must renew the B4 at a cost of $40.

It is much more difficult to obtain a work permit and virtually impossible for the kind of casual work most travellers do in Israel. People do work on tourist visas which have to be renewed every three months. Some people cross into Egypt and get a new visa on returning. (If you are counting on receiving some wages owed to fund the trip, be warned that wages are often slow to come and you might find yourself trapped with a visa due to expire and no money to make the trip.) Others move onto a moshav and let the volunteer leader get the visa. Be careful not to let your visa expire, especially in Eilat. According to Rupert McDonald, 'people were being chucked out left, right and centre and police cruised the Peace Café every 15 minutes'. Contrary to what some people believe, a deportation order does not arrive with a free flight ticket.

On arrival, you may be asked to show enough funds to support yourself, which is when a pre-arranged letter of invitation from a kibbutz or moshav organisation can be very handy. All visitors must be prepared for an unpleasant time both entering and leaving the country, with sometimes vicious interrogations, especially if you have been wandering around the country for a long period. Security measures are draconian and your luggage may be subjected to painstaking searches by X-ray, chemical analysis, etc. before you are allowed to board a plane. (A copy of a kibbutz certificate and a letter from your home country addressed to you at your kibbutz/moshav will smooth your passage out of the country.)

KIBBUTZIM and MOSHAVIM

Everyone has some idea of what a kibbutz is: it is a communal society in which all the means of production are owned and shared by the community as a whole. This idea appeals to many young people who flock to the 270 kibbutzim of Israel to volunteer their services and participate in this ideal community based on equality. In fact late twentieth-century pressures mean that some of the founding principles have been abandoned and the economy of kibbutzim is increasingly based on tourism and light industry rather than agriculture. In other ways, the reality may not live up to the ideals; for an alternative view of kibbutz culture, send an s.a.e. to the London Friends of Palestine (21 Collingham Road, London SW5 0NU) for their leaflet 'The Kibbutz: Who Benefits, Who Suffers?'

In return for their labour volunteers receive free room and board and a small amount of pocket money. Most enjoy their stay, and find that some kibbutzim make considerable efforts to welcome volunteers. For example the majority of kibbutzim try to provide one organised sight-seeing tour per month for volunteers.

If the kibbutz is broadly based on a socialist model, the moshav is on a capitalist model, with members owning their own machinery and houses, though the produce is marketed cooperatively. The kind of experience the volunteer has on a moshav is very different and usually more demanding. Although the term 'volunteer' is used of moshavim, a wage is paid (normally about 1,000 shekels (£220) a month, which allows a frugal person to save enough to fund further travels — normally in Egypt — especially if an end-of-season bonus is paid. Paul Bridgland's travelling fund went from 20 agorots (about enough for a box of matches) to $1,000 during the three months he worked on Moshav Pharan.

On both kibbutzim and moshavim, it is a good idea to take along a few personal objects such as posters or a cassette recorder to humanise your life. Other valuable assets are an alarm clock since the working day gets underway as early as 4am to cheat the noonday sun and plenty of mosquito repellant. If you want to get rid of anything when you leave, you may be able to make a profit by selling it.

Arranging a Job in Advance

There are two possibilities for fixing up a place on a kibbutz or moshav: application may be made through an organisation in your own country or you may wait until you get to Israel. The demand for volunteers fluctuates according to many factors including national politics, the point in the agricultural calendar when you arrive, competition from new Jewish settlers (especially from Russia) and so on. If you wait until you arrive in Israel, especially in the summer months, there may be a delay before you can be placed, though it has to be said that delays are also possible for people who have gone to the trouble of pre-registering.

There is no doubt that making contact with an organisation in advance will give you a certain peace of mind, especially if you do not have much money. Advance registration is certainly recommended for any traveller who lacks confidence or whose circumstances are unusual such as the determined 56-year old Maureen Dambach-Sinclair who wrote such stroppy letters from her home in South Africa to the Volunteer Center in Tel Aviv about their discrimination on the grounds of age that they eventually gave her a chance. She ended up having a marvellous stay on a kibbutz and was invited back the next year by the volunteer leader.

In Britain the main kibbutz placement organisation is Kibbutz Representatives at 1A Accommodation Road, London NW11 8ED (0181-458 9235/fax 455 7930). To register with them you must be between the ages of 18 and 32, be able to stay for a minimum of eight weeks, attend an interview in London or Manchester, provide a medical report and pay the fee of £45. Processing takes three to five weeks (longer in summer). If successful, you are then given a letter of introduction to the kibbutz office in Tel Aviv which is meant to give you placement priority. You are also given a guarantee of a B4 volunteer visa once you reach your kibbutz. For most of the year you can either fix up your travel to Israel independently, buy your ticket through the travel desk at Kibbutz Representatives or join a small group where travel arrangements are made for you. From June to August, it is compulsory to book your travel through KR. Purchasing your insurance in the UK is compulsory year round. KR's policy costs from £32-£80 depending on length of stay.

American applicants should contact the Kibbutz Aliyah Desk (110 East 59th St, 4th Floor, New York, NY; 212-318-6130/fax 832-2597) in order to be referred to their local representative. The requirements are the same as above and the non-refundable registration fee is $95. There are several other programmes besides straight volunteering, including Kibbutz Ulpan, which means spending half the day learning Hebrew.

There are two commercial kibbutz and moshav holiday organisers in Britain: *Project 67,* 10 Hatton Garden, London EC1N 8AH (0171-831 7626).
Transonic Travel, 68 Camden High St, London NW1 0LT (0171-0077/fax 388 7545).

These act as travel agencies which have specialist kibbutz and moshav programmes. If you book with them, you are also urged to participate in their travel arrangements though this is not compulsory. For example the 1994 price of Project 67's package was £285-295 for kibbutz placement and £240-250 for moshavim, which includes an open return flight to Tel Aviv and administration, but not insurance. A further enticement is that they offer a back-up service from Project Tel Aviv (78 Ben Yehuda St, entrance from 18 Mapu St), where luggage can be stored, mail collected, etc. Transonic charges a registration fee of £35 and return flights start at £200. Compulsory insurance of £35 covers up to a year.

Nes Ammim Village in northwest Galilee is one of the very few Christian moshavim in Israel, which welcomes 'card-carrying Christians' to work for at least a year in this community whose main activity is rose-growing. Details of their annual Work and Information programme for young European students and other volunteer requirements are available from Peter Jennings, 49 The Coverdales, Barking, Essex IG11 7JY.

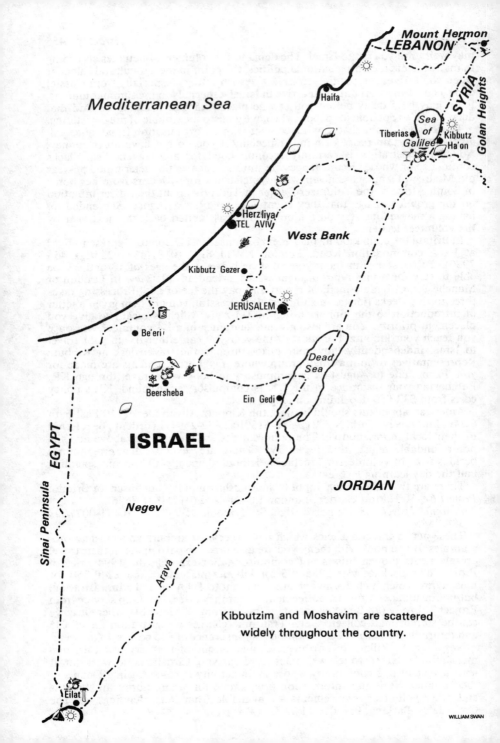

Mount Hermon
LEBANON

Mediterranean Sea

SYRIA

Haifa

Sea of Galilee

Tiberias

Kibbutz Ha'on

Golan Heights

Herzliya
TEL AVIV

West Bank

Kibbutz Gezer

JERUSALEM

Be'eri

Dead Sea

Beersheba

Ein Gedi

ISRAEL

EGYPT

Sinai Peninsula

Negev

JORDAN

Arava

Eilat

Kibbutzim and Moshavim are scattered
widely throughout the country.

WILLIAM SWAN

Arranging a Job on the Spot

A number of offices in Tel Aviv are able to place volunteers who simply show up, particularly between October and May. However they do give priority to people with letters of introduction from sending agencies, and it has not been unknown for willing volunteers (especially British ones for the reason outlined below) to wait up to a month for a place on a kibbutz and a fortnight for a place on a moshav.

The two main kibbutz movements Takam and Artzi united their volunteer departments, so there is now one volunteer placement office for kibbutzim: the Kibbutz Program Center, Volunteer Department, 124 Hayarkon St (POB 3167), Tel Aviv 63573; 03-522 1325 or 524 6156 (fax 523 9966). The opening hours are Sunday to Thursday 8am-2pm. Bear in mind that if you arrive during religious holidays, all offices will be closed.

It must be stressed that registration is not cheap. To apply through the Kibbutz Program Center, you must take your passport, medical certificate, insurance policy (which must show that your insurer has an Israeli representative), an airline ticket out of Israel, two passport photos and registration fee of $50. They now also want to see proof of funds ($250), though if there is a shortage of volunteers they are unlikely to be strict about this. Comprehensive insurance cover is compulsory, so if your policy is not sufficient, you will have to buy one for $35. A returnable deposit of 100 shekels is payable to guarantee that you stay for the minimum period of two months.

There are several moshav placement offices and agents which you will soon hear about in any of the Tel Aviv hostels. Try to get detailed instructions before setting off to find a certain address, since these offices tend to be hard to locate. Although we have not heard from the Moshav Volunteers Center at 17 Shivtei-Israel St, Jaffa (03-582 0953) for this edition, it may still be active. To reach this office from the Central Bus Station, take bus number 44 and get off at the seventh stop (54 Shderot Yerushalaim-Jaffa), turn back and then left to Yehuda Hayamit St, left to Shivtei-Israel St. The opening hours are Sunday to Thursday 9.30am-3pm.

Another moshav (and kibbutz) agent who is frequently mentioned is Meira who has recently moved to the first floor of 73 Ben Yehuda St (03-523 7369/ fax 524 1604); the entrance to the building is behind the restaurant). J. Hains describes this office as 'extremely efficient and friendly' and claims that Meira offers a 'brilliant service'. The Project 67 Tel Aviv office near the corner of Ben Yehuda and Mapu Streets (in the basement of a building which is hard to find) will place new arrivals if there are vacancies, as there often are in winter.

One problem is mentioned repeatedly by Britons seeking placement (even ones who have gone to the trouble of registering in advance through Kibbutz Representatives, etc.), that they are discriminated against (women as well as men) on account of their reputation for drunkenness and rowdiness. Alison Cooper describes her experiences at the Project 67 office in Tel Aviv:

The agencies in Tel Aviv were most unhelpful when I said I was English. Unfortunately the reputation of the drunken, lazy, violent, English yob does go against you. After being told repeatedly that they couldn't help me, I was quite disheartened. The next day I returned in the company of three South Africans from my hostel. The change in attitude at the agency was amazing: they couldn't have been more helpful. They assumed at first that I was South African too and placed all four of us at the same moshav. When they saw from my form that I was British they rechecked several times with the moshav to see if that was a problem. Luckily the farmer didn't care if I was English or from the moon.

If you are clued up when you visit the agencies, it is possible to request a certain kind of kibbutz or moshav (big or small, politically left or centre, well established or new) and in a certain location, though much depends on the individual volunteer leader and conditions change frequently. The vast majority are located on the fertile lands of central and northern Israel. It is best to be prepared for the climate; for example the north can be cold and rainy in winter, whereas the West Bank can be one of the hottest and driest places in the world. One possible source of information on kibbutzim and kibbutz placements is the re-activated International Communes Desk at Yad Tabenkin Study Centre, Efal P.O., Ramat-Efal 52960.

Moshav farmers themselves seem far less concerned than the agencies about the nationality of their workers. Mark Horobin's solution to being discriminated against in Tel Aviv was to go out into the countryside and approach moshav farmers directly. He says that the ones who had work available were generally willing to sign up new workers for a minimum of three months. It is not too difficult to arrange independently to change from one kibbutz or moshav to another. If you happen to be passing a kibbutz or moshav, it is an accepted practice to walk in and ask the volunteers what your chances are. Make sure you get a letter of recommendation from your last kibbutz to prove that you did not leave under a cloud.

Life on a Kibbutz

Kibbutzim are not the holiday camps which some people expect them to be. The average working week in many cases has increased from 36 to 48 hours, though the pocket money has also increased to 160-200 shekels (£35-40) a month. Many kibbutzim give an extra three days off per month to allow their volunteers to travel (since travel is difficult on the sabbath when there is no public transport). Hours may be reduced in the hot summer, for example 4-6am and 7-10am and extended at busy times. You are entitled to a day off for every six hours of overtime you put in.

Jimmy Hill describes the variety of jobs he did in just two months at a small kibbutz south of Jericho: 'dining hall duties, baby house, chopping date trees, a lot of gardening, working in a vineyard, electrician, turkey chaser and guest house cleaner'. New volunteers are often assigned the undesirable jobs though most volunteer organisers are willing to transfer a dissatisfied volunteer to a different job. Catherine Revell claims that if you are assertive and show willingness to work hard, you can find yourself doing more interesting work; among the jobs she did on three different kibbutzim were kitchen manager, shepherdess and a sculptor's assistant. One unexpected hazard in the fields is the wildlife. The only job John Mallon was reluctant to do was to carry bunches of bananas since they housed rats and spiders. And although in most respects Deborah Hunter's kibbutz was no Garden of Eden, she recalls several shrieks and hasty descents of the ladder when volunteers encountered snakes in the fruit trees.

Facilities can differ radically from one kibbutz to the next as Kevin Boyd discovered when he moved from a kibbutz 2km from the Gaza Strip fence to another one recommended by a woman he had met:

> My first kibbutz was very poor. Our rooms consisted of two pre-fab concrete huts with very thin plastic walls which meant that there was very little privacy in the rooms. The volunteer leader was unnecessarily harsh and was always throwing people off the kibbutz for being drunk or late for work. After ten days I decided to go to Kibbutz Giniger, one of the oldest and richest in Israel. The people were very nice and welcoming and the accommodation consisted of small houses with their own kitchen and bathroom.

Although his second kibbutz had a swimming pool, barbecues, volunteers' pub, etc., these were all closed for the winter, and Kevin was made to feel that by arriving in the autumn, he had come just as the party was over. He was told that the best time to join a kibbutz is March, so that you can be well established by the time the hordes arrive in May/June.

Meeting people is the central theme of kibbutz volunteer life and everyone agrees that the social life on kibbutzim is never dull. Some have compared the atmosphere to that of a Club 18-30 holiday. The fact that some kibbutzim administer an HIV test and hand out free condoms reinforces this image. The party atmosphere has prompted some volunteers to concludethat the prejudice against Brits is justified; however Bela Lal is not one of them:

> *In my experience of Kibbutz Afek near Haifa and others I visited, the reputation of Britons is often unfair. Certainly a small number are lager louts but the majority respect the kibbutz and its members, thus ensuring that friction is kept to an absolute minimum. It must be said that alcohol fuels many romantic episodes between female volunteers and the few male kibbutzniks who frequent the kibbutz pub on Friday nights, which are usually unwise and prove to be little more than fodder for gossip.*

It is difficult to get to know the kibbutzniks, especially if you are there for the minimum stay. If you happen to be around for a Jewish festival, you should be able to join in some of the celebrations. Most kibbutzim still take their volunteers on a trip as a reward for good behaviour and hard work. The kibbutz trip was definitely the highlight for Paul Bridgland:

> *The kibbutz took us all on a three-day holiday to the south, gave us decent food, free beer and meals out. They were generous. We went sightseeing, snorkelling and hired out boats, one of which ended up being rammed through the side of another at high speed on account of the free beers.*

Most of the necessities of life are provided by the kibbutz including stationery, tea, coffee, basic toiletries and cigarettes, though perks differ and have been generalling shrinking as wages rise. The non-profit kibbutz shops and bars sell most items cheaply.

Bela Lal is one of the many volunteers who found the communal lifestyle to bring a feeling of relaxation and inner harmony, though she says that after you have been there a few months you begin to tire of the menial nature of the work, the boss's attitude and to feel that all that can be gained from the experience has been gained. Kevin Vincent, who stayed on various kibbutzim during his four years in Israel, sums up the experience this way:

> *Many people love the kibbutz life, a few hate it, but only a handful will disagree that when it comes to a tranquil, easy, relaxed, uncomplicated way of living, a kibbutz is hard to beat. With no money worries, no commitments, no cooking and washing chores and a very short working day, I found the lifestyle therapeutic, a real rest from the normal western rat-race. Add the sporting facilities, the chance to meet people from many different countries and walks of life, it adds up to a very worthwhile experience.*

Life on a Moshav

Life is very different on a moshav. As Alison Cooper says, 'getting up at 5am every day, working approximately 75 hours a week for a pittance, and doing your own cooking and washing is bloody hard work.' And there is no wild social life to compensate. On a moshav, you must be prepared for what Vaughan Temby calls the 'usual sweat and tears' kind of hard work, as elaborated by Paul Bridgland:

> *I'd heard so many horror stories about moshavs and they all proved to be true. Moshavs are horrible places, soulless and depressing. They are solely work camps. You are there to work and that is it. I shared a broken down*

old shack with a weirdo from Blackburn. Moshavs are incredibly dull places. Apart from the bar on a Friday night, there is nowhere to spend your money so they are good places to save money. We started the day picking tomatoes and peppers at 6.30am, had up to an hour and a half off for lunch and continued picking until sunset. Sunset seems a reasonable time to stop work but no, we'd leave the fields with our trailer bulging with vegetables to do a couple of hours in the packing sheds. For the last month of my stay we were working seven days a week, 12-13 hours a day, all for the princely sum of 3.5 shekels an hour and 5 shekels overtime. I left the moshav with $1,000.

Moshavim differ as much from each other as kibbutzim do, so other reports are not nearly as negative. Paul Kington found himself working with cows in the Golan region in December, where it was cold and windy and he was the only volunteer. But he wasn't complaining since the work was easy, he had his own heated flat, the people were friendly and he had lots of time to explore some of the best scenery he had very seen. He also had a generous boss who paid him a third more than the going rate plus a bonus. The high season for most moshavim is November to April, so spring is when you are most likely to receive a bonus of up to two months' wages.

A few moshav volunteers live with the *moshavnikit* (moshav farmer) but most are housed in spartanly furnished volunteers' houses where they are responsible for buying and cooking their own food. Some moshav volunteers recommend keeping your wages in the moshav safe including one volunteer who had 500 shekels (the equivalent of 120 hours of labour) stolen from her room. Volunteers may have access only to the moshav shop where prices may be inflated and choice minimal. Living on a moshav has the potential for giving a better insight into Israeli life than staying on a kibbutz, though the quality of the experience is at the total discretion of your employer. You have more chance of meeting and experiencing the hospitality of local Arabs than you do on a kibbutz.

Alison Cooper describes the difficulty she encountered fraternising with another ethnic group while she worked on a moshav in the Arava region:

A high percentage of male workers from Thailand are employed on one or two year contracts. The moshav I worked on employed about 100 Thais. Unfortunately the Thais did not mix well with the 50 other volunteers of all nationalities. Women couldn't talk to them without giving them the wrong idea. On a Friday night you had 100 drunken, sexually frustrated Thais on the loose and it wasn't very safe to walk home by yourself.

An alternative point of view was expressed by Laura O'Connor who saw the Thai presence as a good way of making contact with people from a country you might want to visit.

TOURISM

The best places for finding work in tourism are Eilat, Tel Aviv, Herzliya (a wealthy resort north of Tel Aviv), and to a lesser extent Haifa and Jerusalem. There is a plethora of cheap hostels around Israel, almost all of whom employ two or three travellers to spend a few hours a day cleaning or manning the desk in exchange for a free bed and some meals. If you prove yourself a hard worker, you may be moved to a better job or even paid some pocket money. Heather McCulloch worked for her hostel near Lake Galilee:

I took the ferry to Israel and almost immediately landed a job in a pension. I worked as a runner/tout before switching to manning reception, which must be the most relaxing job I've ever had. I received free accommodation, one felafal and 20 shekels a day, which was standard for the Tiberias area. Runners/touts received the same but the work was much tougher.

Competition was fierce, as was the bus station manager who threatened in hysterical Hebrew to call the police and get everyone deported.

The Youth Hostel Association of Israel (PO Box 1075, 3 Dorot Rishonim, Jerusalem (02-252706/fax 250676) can send a list of about 30 hostels around the country which may be in a position to offer free accommodation, meals and pocket money in exchange for six hours of work a day.

Casual work in cafés, restaurants, bars and hotels is also easy to find. As in Greece, these jobs are much easier to get if you're female. The pay is usually low and sometimes non-existent, but you will get free food and drink, and tips. There is no accepted minimum and, as throughout Israel, the price of a day's work has to be negotiated. Most working travellers also recommend collecting your wages (and paying your own hostel bills) on a daily basis to prevent aggravation later. The places that do pay wages on a monthly basis tend to make pay-day about the tenth of the month, so that is a good time to look for a job because lots of people move on after collecting their wages.

Jobs in fast-food restaurants are bound to increase since in 1993/4 McDonald's and Kentucky Fried Chicken opened their first outlets in Tel Aviv, and Burger King intends to open 51 branches in Israel in the next five years.

Eilat

Eilat is the main holiday resort on the Gulf of Aqaba, with several large seafront hotels, numerous smaller establishments and more being built. Virtually all aspects of Israeli culture have been killed off, but it is still an established haven for the working traveller despite a general tightening of immigration rules. The foreign tourist season lasts from late October to March. (Israelis do take their holidays in the extreme heat of the summer but most workers then will be expected to speak Hebrew.) There is such a ready supply of workers desperate for any excuse to stay on that some employers try to get away with murder, as Laura O'Connor describes:

When in November it begins to get cold in the rest of Israel, there is a mass migration to Eilat which is a mega tourist trap. We are our own worst enemy since there are so many travellers looking for jobs that employers can be right bastards.

An additional problem for women is the level of hassle they must endure from male tourists from various countries who are attracted to Eilat on account of its thriving escort business.

The rendezvous point for hopeful workers (mostly men) in Eilat is still the Peace Café on the edge of town. If you hang around the 'Wall' (preferably arriving by 6am), there's a good chance of being picked up and given a day's labouring. A spontaneous union system operates whereby any employer offering less than the accepted norm is laughed at. The going hourly rate for café work is about 10 shekels while casual construction work pays 10-15 shekels. Once you've proved yourself a decent worker, you may get longer term jobs or employers choosing you ahead of the competition, which is what happened to Bill Garfield:

The Jews respect hard work and it will pay off with offers of further work. When you are sitting on the wall outside the Peace Café with 20 other guys, feeling like a prostitute, it is nice when a previous employer singles you out for a job because you have proved yourself.

Inevitably, women work in tourist-related places. Make the rounds of the hotel personnel managers as early in the season as possible. The Tourist Center near the Youth Hostel has lots of bars, restaurants and sandwich bars worth trying. Laura O'Connor describes the range of jobs she did in two months in Eilat:

I had a variety of jobs: sold tickets for a boat cruise and handed out fliers

for a restaurant (both for two days), waitressed in a fish restaurant for a
week (had to leave as the chef would let me stay in the staff apartment only
for sex), worked in Luna Park amusement park and cleaned in my hostel
(Fawlty Towers).

Another possibility is bakeries, one of which is near the Peace Café, where
workers are hired for a night shift on a first-come first-hired basis.

Seve   ellers warn of the 'Eilat Trap' in which penniless travellers are
sometimes caught, unable to extract owed wages from their employer and unable
to leave before their visa expires. Like all international resorts, Eilat is expensive,
and many people end up sleeping on the beach, where every precaution must
be taken to safeguard belongings. Julian Peachey, who lived in a tent for four
months until a car ran over it, describes the scene:

> *In the winter there were literally thousands of travellers living (not all in*
> *tents) on the beach. The council made a feeble attempt to move them, but*
> *they never managed it. We formed quite a close-knit community, sharing*
> *meals and going out together.*

Eilat is also an important yachting and diving centre. Vacancies are sometimes
posted on the gates to the Marina, but work as crew or kitchen staff, cleaners or
au pairs is usually found by asking boat to boat. According to Xuela Edwards,
the atmosphere among working travellers is friendly and a 'welcome relief from
the rougher Peace Café crowd'.

One of the best paid jobs in the Eilat area has nothing to do with tourism.
There are a few hard-to-track-down private farms inland from Eilat which
depend on a steady stream of transients for their labour force and which pay
good wages. Melon planting begins in early November and lasts till mid-
December, while the fruit is picked in the months of March, April and May.
The current hourly wage is about 8 shekels, and camping is permitted on the
farms. At the busiest times, travellers are bussed in from Eilat to pick and pack
melons, tomatoes and zucchini.

Tel Aviv

Although not as easy to find as in Eilat, there is plenty of work in Tel Aviv,
mostly for women in bars, restaurants and beach cafés. It is a common practice
for cafés not to pay any wages and to expect their staff to exist on tips, which
are enough to live on providing the restaurant is sufficiently popular. Try to
have a private conversation with the staff before taking a tips-only job.

Many of the dozens of hostels are good sources of job information or jobs
themselves such as the Hotel Josef at 15 Bograshov St which receives daily
phone calls from employers needing workers for dishwashing, construction, au
pairing and even sometimes film work. Hostels along Hayarkon St are worth
trying such as the House Hostel, the Riviera Hotel and the Gordon Hostel
(corner of Gordon St). Also try the Star Hostel, the Number One Hostel, Top
Hostel, Momo's and the Traveller's Hostel on Ben Yehuda St and the Green
House Hostel. Cafés along the seafront such as Cherry's Café offer a good chance
to earn high tips. This is also a good area for buskers and traders as is Nachalat
Binyamin on Tuesday and Friday afternoons.

Male travellers can also find work as Peter Goldman reports:

> *In Tel Aviv, the work situation is thriving as usual. I stayed in the Shanbo*
> *Hostel (Hebrew for 'sleep here') and after a few weeks I was offered the*
> *night desk position. This consisted of sitting at the desk from midnight until*
> *8am every other night and letting all the dishwashers in from the late shift.*
> *They would usually bring in beers from their restaurants, so I spent the last*
> *four hours of my shift drinking with them, before going to my day job in*
> *the boatyard.*

I got this work after managing to meet the guy in charge of the boatyard.
It had rained for two weeks straight so they were way behind on their
projects; I told them I knew a little carpentry and I started that moment.

As in Eilat, people sleep on the beach. According to Safra Wightman, it is
safer to tuck yourself against a well to avoid being disturbed by the tractor which
turns the sand at 3am. She goes on to recommend two travellers' meeting places
where if you don't find a job, at least you can eat cheaply: the Gypsy near the
Marina for a cheap breakfast and MASH near the corner of Dizengoff and Ben
Yehuda Streets.

Jerusalem

Jerusalem is also reported to be a good centre for hotel and bar work, and
girls may be offered jobs while wandering round the bazaars. Work is much
easier to find in the Jewish rather than the Arab areas, though hostels in the Old
City do employ people on a free-bed basis. Buskers should head for Ben Yehuda
St, the crowded pedestrian precinct in the New City.

Some good sources of information on jobs in Jerusalem are the King George
Hotel, Ritchie's Pizza Shop (also on King George St) with a good notice board,
the New Swedish Hostel at 29 David St and the Lemon Tree Hostel also in the
Old City, and finally the Palm and the Fiasel, both Christian hostels. Also check
out the notice board in the Goldsmith Building which houses the overseas
students union just outside the campus.

The English language *Jerusalem Post* (Jerusalem Post Building, Romena,
Jerusalem 91000) carries job adverts especially on Fridays for English secretaries,
au pairs, etc.

Like buskers, sellers of handicrafts report good profits in Jerusalem. Home-
made jewellery is popular. David Stokes had mastered macramé (a surprisingly
easy skill) and earned his way by selling on the streets of Jerusalem, while Leda
Meredith sold woven string bracelets on Ben Yehuda St for 3 shekels each. Also
try the evening market around the base of the main bank where it is possible to
rent a stand for a modest sum. Some shopkeepers hire English speaking assistants
to help them sell their wares to tourists.

OTHER PAID WORK

Cleaning in private houses throughout Israel can be a lucrative proposition,
though it takes time to build up a clientele. Steven Hendry recommends placing
advertisements on lamp posts, in shop windows or in the newspaper. You may
be able to persuade your hostel to let you use their phone number in the
advertisement; otherwise you'll have to rent a flat and install a phone. After
persevering at this, Stephen was earning $4 an hour, well above the average
wage in Israel. Religious Jews want to set their house in order for Passover in
April and so this is a particularly busy and profitable time for a house cleaner.
Catherine Revell was paid 10 shekels an hour a few years ago, and was grateful
to the Hotel Josef in Tel Aviv for helping her to fix this up. (As a comparison,
Safra Wightman, a trained hair dresser, earned 3 shekels at a salon in Tel Aviv.
When she complained, her boss offered her a job in a gym, which she claims
are often associated with brothels in Israel.)

Teaching English is virtually impossible to fix up since the market is flooded.
Anyone with secretarial skills may be able to temp though work normally takes
quite a while to come along. Manpower in Tel Aviv are reputed to be helpful
and do not require a knowledge of Hebrew. They will even arrange work permits
for you. Rates of pay for people with secretarial skills vary between 10 and 15
shekels an hour before tax.

Male visitors may wish to investigate the possibility of donating to a sperm bank; Israeli hospitals are rumoured to pay up to £30.

Many foreign movies and American television programmes are made in Israel, especially around Tel Aviv, Jaffa and Eilat. Several Tel Aviv hostels carry advertisements for film or TV extras. Katherine Berlanny followed up an advert and became a 'crowd artist' in an Agatha Christie movie. More recently Xuela Edwards describes what she found in Eilat where a dodgy US cop show was being filmed:

There were lots of opportunities for work as an extra which pays 50 shekels a day plus a free breakfast. To find this work, you had to turn up at Eva's office, beneath the Neptune Hotel at 4pm and join the crowd. The selection process was pretty humiliating, but endured by everyone in town on the off-chance. New faces may well get work on the first attempt but you can't rely on getting work because they are reluctant to use the same people too often.

Au Pairing

Live-in childcare is absolutely booming and any plausible candidate will have no trouble finding a job. It is a good idea to meet several families if possible and choose the one with whom you feel most comfortable. Hours are long (up to ten a day) but wages are relatively high, averaging $500-700 a month. You should be prepared to learn how to keep a kosher kitchen.

The two longest established agencies are Au Pair International in a suburb of Tel Aviv (2 Desler St, Bnei Brak 51507; tel/fax 03-619 0423) and Star Au Pairs (16 Michal St, POB 26571, Tel Aviv 63261; 03-201195/fax 291748). Another one which has been advertising recently is Shlomi Meiri, 24 Tabenkin St, Tel Aviv 69353, who requests that applicants be at least 19 with childcare experience; anyone interested should send a CV and two photos. Most families are looking for a minimum commitment of one year, though there are a few six-month placements. Shreen Imam wrote to Star Au Pairs before leaving her home in South Africa and was pleased with the service:

The director Mr David Star fetched me from the airport and the same day I got a family after a short interview. I was given the chance to choose a suitable family. After a trial week, the agency contacted me with the names of other au pairs in the area. After my first pay cheque the agency helped me to open a bank account. Altogether I am happy in Israel.

Their specifications are odd (to say the least), e.g. 'we are interested in a slim worker as the employers are not interested in fat girls, and they prefer non-Jewish girls, non-smokers and not beautiful.' They charge a US$150 service fee. Their literature claims that after fulfilling a one-year contract, mothers' helps may be eligible for a free return flight to their home country; however Au Pair International says that families are no longer willing to pay for airline tickets.

VOLUNTARY WORK

Several organisations can use voluntary assistance for Palestinian projects. The Universities Educational Fund for Palestinian Refugees or Unipal (63 Holbrook Road, Cambridge CB1 4SX; tel/fax 01223 211864) sends volunteers to work on short-term projects during July and August in the Israeli-occupied West Bank and Gaza Strip as well as with Palestinian communities in Israel and Jordan. Most projects involve teaching English or work with children for which relevant qualifications or experience is needed. Interviews are held in April.

The World University Service (20 Compton Terrace, London N1 2UN; 0171-226 6747) processes applications from prospective British volunteers wishing to participate in international summer work camps run by the Palestinian Bir Zeit

University near Ramallah in the West Bank. A registration fee of approximately £60 covers food, accommodation and trips to other areas of the West Bank and Gaza strip. Volunteers will experience incredible Arab hospitality but must realise that, despite the peace process, large parts of the Occupied Territories are still under Israeli military occupation and conditions can be difficult.

The London Friends of Palestine (21 Collingham Road, London SW5 0NU) may be able to advise on further summer openings in the region. Americans who wish to spend three weeks doing community service on army bases or hospitals should request information from Volunteers for Israel (330 W 42nd St, Suite 1818, NY 10036-6092).

Archaeology

The Israel Antiquities Authority (PO Box 586, Jerusalem 91004; 02-292607/fax 292628) oversees a large number of excavations — many on Old Testament sites — and volunteers are needed to do the mundane work of digging and sifting. As of late 1994 they have decided not to publish their annual free list of archaeological excavations in Israel any more, however it might be worth contacting them for the names and addresses of digs looking for volunteers. In the majority of cases, volunteers must pay a daily fee of about $25 to cover food and accommodation (often on a nearby kibbutz) plus a registration fee of $25-75. For example the excavation of the ancient port site of Yavneh Yam carried out by the Department of Classical Studies at Tel Aviv University (fax 03-640 9457) charges volunteers $400 for a fortnight, which is the minimum stay.

Camps generally last two weeks and provide an excellent opportunity to live in a unique landscape. Most take place during university holidays between May and September when temperatures soar. Emergency surveys of sites threatened with building or demolition often need volunteers at short notice and for these there is a chance that volunteers will not have to pay so much for food and lodging. Ring the Israel Antiquities Authority in the Rockefeller Museum Building or look for adverts of other rescue digs on hostel notice boards or at the Moshav and Kibbutz Volunteer Centers in Tel Aviv.

Jennifer McKibben, who worked on a kibbutz, in an Eilat hotel and on a dig in the Negev desert, waxed most enthusiastic about the latter experience:

Actually the work was often enjoyable but not usually before the sun had risen (it gets incredibly cold at nights in the desert). It did seem madness at times when a Land-rover would take a team of us out to an unremarkable spot in the desert marked only by a wooden peg, and tells us to start digging. I think the romance of excavations quickly fades once the blisters begin to appear and that long term camps are suitable only for the initiated or fanatic.

However despite the difficulties I really enjoyed the camp. Group relations were good — there were people of all nationalities — and there was normally a camp fire going with a couple of musicians. It was wonderful just to spend time in such a beautiful desert, to go off wandering over footprintless dunes, over great red hills to look and see no sign of civilisation. More practically, it was a cheap way to eat well for a couple of weeks, see another area and extend one's all-too-short stay in Israel.

Asia

For a continent as vast as Asia, this chapter may seem disproportionately short. That is simply because there are not many kinds of work open to the traveller in developing countries, as has already been noted in the chapters on Africa and Latin America. Third World economies struggle to support their own populations and can rarely accommodate novelty-seeking foreigners. The main exception is Japan — a country with a 'Western' economy and an unemployment rate of 3% — which can pay high wages to foreign language teachers. Another possibility is Singapore where people with a professional skill may find work. For example the American Matthew Goodman fixed up seven interviews at architectural firms in Singapore on the basis of his bachelors degree in interior design, and landed two freelance design jobs.

Having made your fortune in an industrialised country, whether as a designer in Singapore, an English teacher in Japan, a chambermaid in Switzerland or a tomato picker in Australia, you should be able to finance many months of leisurely travel in the inexpensive countries of Asia. In most of Asia it is better to concentrate on travelling for its own sake rather than for the sake of working. However, described below are a number of ways to boost your budget between enjoying the beaches of Turkey and the temples of Thailand.

TEACHING

Although the English language is not a universal passport to employment, it can certainly be put to good use in many Asian countries especially Japan,

Taiwan, Hong Kong, Korea, Thailand and Turkey. There are thousands of people of all ages eager for tuition in English and native English speakers with a university degree or just a degree of enthusiasm are cashing in. This is also true on the Indian sub-continent but there the educated classes speak fluent English and therefore foreign English speakers are not much in demand. Serious teachers should always seek the advice of the British Council.

Outside the major cities, paid teaching jobs are rare. If you do end up working for a small locally run school, do not expect to find many teaching materials. You are likely to spend your evenings cutting up magazines and writing stories for the next day's lessons. Off the beaten track, it may be possible to arrange with locals, especially the local teacher, to stay with a family in exchange for conversation lessons. Stuart Tappin travelled around South-East Asia doing this:

> *In Asia I managed to spend a lot of time living with people in return for teaching English. The more remote the towns are from tourist routes the better, for example Bali is no good. I spent a week in Palembang (Sumatra) living with an English teacher and his family. You teach and they give you their (very good) hospitality. I did the same in Thailand. During the three months that I lived in Kanchanaburi (not far west of Bangkok) my only daily expense was a few baht for a newspaper.*

In addition to the information which follows on finding work with language schools in specific countries, it is also worth considering setting up as a private English teacher. Working as a self-employed freelance tutor is more lucrative but hard to set up until you have been settled in one place for a while and have decent premises from which to work. Steven Hendry, a long-time travelling Scot who has taught in Japan and Thailand, describes the steps to take:

> *Be in town for at least a few months and get access to a telephone. Make up a little advertisement (half in English, half the local language) and plaster it all over town as quickly as possible, in universities, colleges, coffee shops, etc.*

Japan

Teaching English in Japan is one of the classic jobs for working travellers. The demand for language tuition is very strong, although it has been diminishing in the past three years. Schools which once accepted anyone with fluency are now becoming more selective, and the competition for jobs is fierce. It is not uncommon now for hopeful teachers to spend several weeks job-hunting in Japan and end up with nothing but a large debt. Julie Fast from the US describes the drastic changes which she has witnessed:

> *In 1990 when I arrived in Tokyo, there were so many high paying jobs, prospective teachers (experienced or non-experienced) could pick and choose their work. This is no longer the case in Tokyo. I feel I should underline that sentence and write it in capital letters. Things are simply not as they were. When I first started managing a children's English school, I had a hard time finding a good teacher. Now teachers call me looking for work.*

But many people persevere because of the potential earnings. The wage is among the highest of any job mentioned in this book, normally at least £12 an hour. This must be set against the notoriously high cost of living in Japan which swallows up much of the high wages. Many people who have spent time in the Far East shy away from working in Japan since a monumental struggle lasting several months is normally required before enough teaching hours can be lined up to make saving possible. They prefer to teach in neighbouring countries where there are fewer initial hassles. But there is no denying that once you have established yourself as a teacher in Japan, the rewards (mainly financial) are great. Steven Hendry, who spent ten months supporting himself by teaching (and he still saved £1,000), stresses that 'Japan is no kindergarten; it's very hard work. But if you get in, the reward is worth it.'

There are hundreds of English schools in Tokyo alone, with many more in other Japanese cities. A great many of these are willing to hire native speakers of English with no teaching qualification, though almost all expect teachers to have a university degree and some teaching experience. Apart from a few schools (including the most prestigious ones) who advertise and conduct interviews abroad, most schools recruit their teachers within Japan. The most common means of recruitment is by advertising in newspapers, especially the English language *Japan Times* on Mondays, and also *Kansai Time Out* magazine. With over 9 million Japanese adults learning English at any one time, it is not surprising that advertisements abound.

In order to shine over the competition, a number of practical steps should be taken when presenting yourself to a potential employer. These should be taken even more seriously than when trying for teaching work elsewhere in the world, if only because travelling to an interview in Tokyo is a major undertaking, often taking several hours and costing £10; so it would be a shame to blow your chances because of a simple oversight.

Dress as impeccably and conservatively as possible, and carry a respectable briefcase. Inside you should have any education certificates you have earned, preferably the originals since schools are catching on that forgery is a widespread practice. (If you apply for a working visa, you must have the original.) Also have a typed resumé which does not err on the side of modesty. Steven Hendry suggests converting 'travelling for two years' to 'studying Asian cultures and languages' and describing a period of unemployment as 'a chance to do some voluntary teaching with racial minorities'. Apparently these are never checked. Be prepared at the interview to take a little test or do a demonstration lesson.

Speaking slowly and clearly is another key to success, as Steven Hendry discovered:

> *If you don't speak slowly, you won't get a job. With my photocopied degree and my thick Glasgow accent, I was given a job in preference to a highly qualified Londoner with a nice English accent, on the basis they couldn't understand his speech, since he hadn't learned to slow it down. In the main, Japanese people can't distinguish between the Queen's English and Scouse or a Sydney drawl.*

Anyone arriving in Japan cold should go straight to one of the dozens of 'gaijin houses', cheap hostels for foreigners, which are listed in the glossy monthly *The Tokyo Journal*. (*Gaijin* means literally 'outside person'.) Popular gaijin houses like Okuba House (1-11-32 Hyakunin-cho, Shinjuku-ku; 3361-2348) and the English House Ryokan (2-23-8 Nishi-Ikebukuro, Toshima-ku; 3988-1743) will be full of new or nearly new arrivals chasing teaching jobs.

Because the rental of flats in Tokyo is virtually prohibitive in cost (for example a six month deposit is standard), some foreign teachers stay in gaijin houses throughout their working stay. Sometimes the manager will allow you to use the house phone as a contact number. The longer you stay, the more likely you are to inherit the pupils from teachers who are leaving.

Japanese people of all ages eagerly sign up for lessons, especially evening classes, which are given on the school premises, in town halls or at their place of work; for many it is an excuse to socialise, and the atmosphere in these so-called 'conversation lounges' or 'voice rooms' can be relaxed and pleasant for students and teachers alike (although unsatisfactory for serious English teachers).

Most foreigners enter Japan on a tourist visa (90 days for Britons and Americans) and then begin the job hunt. The best times are just before April and August. The key to obtaining a work visa is to have a sponsor in Japan.

Schools will be unwilling to sponsor their teachers unless they are persuaded that they are an ongoing proposition. If you do get hired by a school or company, your employer has to take your CV (resumé), educational certificates, etc. to the Immigration Office for processing within six weeks. Officially you are not supposed to work until this process is complete, but most schools seem to get you working straightaway. Once your visa is confirmed, you must leave the country and apply to a Japanese Embassy abroad for your tourist visa to be changed. You can do this in 48 hours in Seoul. Some schools will pay your air fare to Seoul; others won't.

Although TEFL training is not necessary, the government of Japan will not give work permits to anyone without a university degree. Others never bother with a work permit (though this is illegal) and periodically renew their tourist visa. This has become more difficult since the introduction of steep fines on both employers and illegal aliens. A third visa option is a 'cultural visa' which helps your job prospects. To qualify for this you must be able to prove that you are studying something Japanese, e.g. flower arranging, Shiatsu massage, martial arts or the Japanese language (though if you opt for the latter, the visa authorities may well pose their questions in Japanese).

Australians, New Zealanders and Canadians are eligible for a working holiday visa valid for six months in the first instance but extendable in the home country for a maximum of two years. Because schools do not have to sponsor them for a work visa, they are eminently employable. Australians can participate in the SWAP programme either as part of a group with departures in November/ December or individually at any time of the year. Further details including costs (from $1,800 in 1994) are available in Australia from SSA/SWAP, PO Box 399, Carlton South, Melbourne, Vic 3053 (03-348 1777) and in Canada from any Travel CUTS Office. The Tokyo office of CIEE acts as a support office for foreign students teaching English.

If you want to arrange a teaching job in advance, the best bet is the government's JET (Japan Exchange & Teaching) Programme. Anyone with a BA who is in principle under 35 and from the US, UK, Ireland, Canada, Australia or New Zealand (plus France and Germany) is eligible to apply. In Britain the programme (which accepts approximately 350 teachers annually) is administered by the Council on International Educational Exchange, 33 Seymour Place, London W1H 6AT (0171-224 8896); applications (from British passport holders only) are due by early December for one-year placements beginning mid to late July. Americans, who make up about half of the total of JET participants, should contact their nearest Japanese Consulate or the Embassy in Washington (2520 Massachusetts Avenue NW, DC 20008; 202-939-6700). The salary is 3,760,000 yen (about £22,000) a year in addition to a free return air ticket if you complete your contract.

Nearly half of JET teachers renew their contract for a second year. In the opinion of Mark Elliott, the JET programme is much more about meeting people and enjoying Japan than it is about teaching. Mark went on to edit a guide to help retiring JET participants *JET and Beyond* which can be bought by anyone; details from AJET (Association for Japan Exchange and Teaching, AJET Drop Box, c/o CLAIR, 4F Nissaykojimachi Bldg, 3-3-6 Kudan Machi, Chiyoda-ku, Tokyo 102).

A number of private organisations also recruit graduates abroad, and most pay about 250,000 yen per month. Most will prohibit lucrative private work (between 2,000 and 5,000 yen an hour, and sometimes much higher). The following organisations hire abroad:

Nova Intercultural Institute, The Atrium Court, Apex Plaza, Reading RG1 1AX
   (01734 560546). The Nova Group has 120 schools in many parts of Japan,

for which their offices abroad recruit throughout the year. US office is 2 Oliver St, Suite 7, Boston, MA 02110.

International Office for Asia of the YMCA, 909 4th Avenue, Seattle, Washington 98104 (206-382-5008). Sends university graduates resident in North America to Japan for two years (and Taiwan for one) to teach English in community-based YMCAs. Round-trip air fare provided and salary range of 250,000-350,000 yen.

AEON Intercultural USA, 9301 Wilshire Boulevard, Suite 202, Beverly Hills, CA 90210 (310-550-0940). Recruits throughout the US and places American teachers in their nearly 200 branch schools in Japan.

James English School, 2429 Middleton Beach Road, Middleton, Wisconsin 53562 (608-238-0712). American applicants must be interviewed in Wisconsin.

Institutes in Japan which recruit on a large scale include:

ASA Community Salon, Toyota Building, No. 10, 3-62-7 Sendagaya, Shibuya-ku, Tokyo 151 (03-3796 4488).

ECC Foreign Language Institute, Shikata Building 1F, 4-43 Nakazaki-Nishi, 2 chome, Kita-ku, Osaka 530 (06-359-0531). Teachers for over 100 schools.

International Education Services, Rose Hikawa Building, 22-14 Higashi 2-chome, Shibuya-ku, Tokyo 150 (03-3498 7101). One year contracts to teach government and company employees.

English Club Language Schools, Naritaya Building, 2nd Floor, 1-3-2 Tsukagoshi, Warabi City, Saitama 335 (048-432 7444). Looking for enthusiastic, friendly and fun graduates willing to commit themselves for two years.

Many language schools never need to advertise and yet are hiring constantly. A couple of the major chains to look out for are Bi-Lingual Language Institutes, Kent Schools and Success English Clubs.

Hong Kong

The Hong Kong brain drain sparked by the coming return to Chinese rule has caused even more locals to sit up and pay attention to their English lessons. A knowledge of English improves their chances of emigration. Therefore it is another good centre for prospective English teachers, especially Britons who need no work visa. The *South China Morning Post,* especially the bumper Saturday edition, is the best source of jobs in private institutes. The majority of adverts state that experience is not necessary. Also there are columns of language schools in the *Yellow Pages.* Other travellers staying at the infamous Travellers Hostel on the 16th floor of Chung King Mansions (40 Nathan Road, Kowloon) will be able to advise. Although grotty and depressing, the hostel is cheap (from HK$50 for a dorm bed) and has a notice board.

Most schools ask you to sign a three-month contract, which in Hong Kong counts as a long stay; after that you are free to leave anytime after giving a fortnight's notice. The main disadvantage of teaching in Hong Kong is the low hourly wage, from HK$50 (£4). A decent starting wage is HK$60 though you can make HK$100-200 by going private and teaching one-to-one. Teachers on low wages end up working long hours six days a week to be able to support themselves. Since jobs abound at the lower end of the scale, do not accept the first offer you receive. As a first move, trawl the language schools listed in the papers and register with as many as possible. Shopping around can pay off. Always try to collect your wages at frequent intervals since some schools have been negligent in this regard.

Leslie Platt returned to Hong Kong reconciled to supporting himself by teaching English until a more permanent job materialised. He encountered the problems which often beset casual language teachers. The first school was so vague about when pupils were going to show up that he soon moved on to one of the four branches of the Hong Kong English Club, where he was horrified to be confronted with a classful of 7 and 8 year olds whose main ambition was to torment the teacher, especially when he tried to conduct a sing-song. Don't count on much sympathy from your employer who is very likely to be more interested in his profits than your loss of control. One shocked teacher related that she was told if she did resort to corporal punishment, not to hit them where the bruise would show!

Nineteen year old Martyn Owens had no trouble rounding up work and emphatically declares that anybody can teach English in Hong Kong. He recommends the Hong Kong English Club (Ground Floor, 176B Nathan Road, Tsim Tsa Tsui, Kowloon; 03-722 6061) which has several branches around Hong Kong.

People without British nationality will have more problems and may want to investigate some of the many unlicensed schools, for example in the suburb of Mongkok. Brett Muir from New Zealand decided that the wages in language schools were so low that he would try to break into the much more lucrative private tuition market, mostly providing housewives and businessmen with conversation practice:

> *My best recommendation is to hire a paging device, which is really cheap to hire per month, and write an attractive looking advertisement for placing in the letter boxes of the ritzy apartment estates in Mid Levels, Jardines Lookout, Causeway Bay, etc. Although the gates are locked, the maids go in and out every few minutes so you just walk in with them to post your photocopied ads. In this way you are always on the phone and open yourself to much higher pay.*

Taiwan

With one stroke of the legislative pen in April 1992, the Taiwanese government pulled the plug on the casual English teaching scene. Of all the countries of the world, Taiwan used to be the one in which native speakers could most easily find work and earn large sums of money. But the crackdown on foreigners working for short periods, which coincided with a decline in the Taiwanese economy, means that the number of opportunities has been cut drastically. Many of the hundreds of private language institutes or *buhsibans* (a large number of which were undoubtedly cowboy operations), which had crammed high school students for university entrance examinations and generally serviced the seemingly insatiable demand for English conversation and English tuition for a decade, have been forced to close, which appears to have been the main intention of the new law. As a side effect, language schools have been visited by the police and people found to be working illegally have been deported.

But it is not all a case of doom and gloom. North American graduates can fix up a one-year job ahead of time with the Overseas Service Corps of the YMCA (909 4th Avenue, Seattle, WA 98104). The pay is NT$13,000 for the first six months, rising to NT$15,000. There are some well-established legal language schools which are prepared to sponsor foreign teachers for the residence visa and working permit. Due to the considerable paperwork involved, schools in Taiwan will consider sponsoring teachers for residence visas only if they are willing to work for an extended period of time, usually a minimum of one year. As in Japan, residence visas are given only to university graduates who have the original of their certificate (or a certified copy). Other visa requirements include an HIV test and a Chinese guarantor.

Most two-month visitor visas are non-extendable within Taiwan. Renewal is possible outside Taiwan (typically hong Kong), but have a good story prepared about why you want to stay in Taiwan so long. If you claim to be studying

Chinese, expect a spot test in Mandarin. Legally, foreign students are permitted to work up to 12 hours a week during term and full-time in the holidays, though this is rarely enforced.

The American accent is invariably preferred, though many Taiwanese can't really distinguish among various English accents. As well as checking adverts in the *South China Post,* check notice boards at travellers' hostels and the Mandarin Training Center of Taiwan Normal University on Hoping East Road in the student lounge on the sixth floor.

Other possible sources of employment are the following chains of schools:

Hess, 83 Po Ai Road, 2F, Taipei (02-382 5442 ext 152). Hires 200 people to teach children's classes in nine cities in Taiwan.

ELSI, 12 Kuling St, Taipei (02-321 9005). Have six schools in Taipei, and two in other cities.

GRAM English Institute, 7th Floor, 216 Tun Hwa South Road, Sec. 1, Taipei (02-741 0970). Hire exclusively by local interviews for their 44 centres.

The majority of schools pay NT$400 per hour, though higher wages are possible. Lee Coleman was offered NT$800 to teach businessmen. Private pupils are prone to cancel at short notice, so most teachers try to extract one month's fees in advance.

Not everyone wants to stay in Taipei where the air pollution is second only to that of Mexico City. Jobs are also available in the other cities of Taiwan such as Kaohsiung, Taichung and Tainan, where they pay higher rates.   The tax rate for foreigners in Taiwan is 20% and legal schools are obliged to withhold this. If a teacher can establish residency, i.e. has stayed in the country for more than 183 days in one calendar year, a rebate can be obtained of all but 6%. So try to arrive before mid-June.

Korea

Prospects for casual teachers in South Korea are good. Competition for jobs is less acute than in Japan since Korea is often overlooked by working travellers and wages are lower with a decent hourly wage of 20,000 won (though some teachers earn as must as 25,000 or 30,000 won per private class). There is a definite bias in favour of American accents, partly because so many young Koreans want to study in the US. According to the American Coral Grossman, language institutes not only advertise in the English language *Korean Times* and *Korean Herald* but they actively recruit around the American military bases (Yongsan and Hannam Village). If you do get a job it shouldn't be too strenuous since it will consist of conversation classes, with no emphasis on formal grammar.

Job prospects are best at *hogwons* (language schools) in the Chongro district of Seoul and also in Pusan. But there are possibilities in other cities. For example the American franchise chain ELSI has a major operation in Korea, including five institutes in different cities and affiliated ECC Language Institutes in Seoul and throughout the country. Ask the California headquarters (see page 120) for their 40-page booklet *Teaching English in Korea.* The minimum qualifications are 'nativelike fluency in English, a BA and a positive attitude' which could earn you 900,000-1,015,000 won per month. The correct address to which completed applications should be sent is Recruitment Officer, ELS International, PO Box 7927, Tacoma, WA 98407.

Another useful contact is the Korea Services Group (147-7 Bum Jeon Dong, Jin-ku, Pusan 614-060) which recruits 100 teachers on behalf of about 40 employers in Korea. On a smaller scale, Top Language School (34-1, 2-Ga, Chung Ang-Dong, Chon Ju City) hires 50 teachers at its five franchise schools.

For new arrivals, a good place to pick up information is the Daewan Yogwan (hostel), Dangju-dong, Chongro-gu in the centre of Seoul. Private tutoring normally requires travelling to the clients though in Seoul this is less stressful than in Japan since the stops are announced in English. Coral Grossman was clearly enjoying her experiences in Korea:

> *The people are extremely friendly and I have received many perks, where my students have invited me along to visit other places and restaurants. I would stay away from universities as there have been several riots because of GATT.*

Most teachers who just turn up work unofficially. Immigration hands out 90 day permits to most nationalities on arrival, and these can be extended. The Immigration Office is opposite Chong Dong Church at the back of Toksu Palace in the centre of Seoul. If you do arrange a contract, work permits may be obtained only outside Korea. Processing takes up to two months and requires a university degree certificate.

China

China is more eager than ever to import English teachers, mostly for academic institutes in the provinces. Many English teaching posts in the provinces cannot be filled and Chinese institutions turn to foreign voluntary organisations like VSO and Christians Abroad (see *Voluntary Work* chapter) to fill the vacancies. The requirements for these two year posts are not stringent, and in return teachers get free air fares, a local salary and other perks. According to one source, VSO can fill only two-thirds of its teaching vacancies in China.

Most official recruitment is filtered through the Chinese Education Association for International Exchange (CEAIE) in the capital (37 Damucang Hutong, Beijing 100816; 1-602-0731/fax 601 6156) which is a non-governmental organisation with 23 local branches in major cities and extensive contacts with institutes of higher education throughout China who wish to invite native speaker teachers. Contracts are for one year in the first instance. Depending on experience and qualifications, teachers are designated either as foreign teachers (FTs) or foreign experts (FEs). The latter usually requires a post-graduate degree and confers much more status as well as a higher salary, a return air fare, holiday pay and other benefits. FTs earn about 800 Yuan a month in addition to board and lodging while foreign experts are paid upwards of 1,600 Yuan. Most foreign teachers are expected to teach between 14 and 16 hours a week, which sounds a light load until you find yourself with classes of up to 150 students.

CEAIE cooperates with Chinese Embassies in the West. In Britain contact the Chinese Embassy's Education Section, 5-13 Birch Grove, Acton, London W3 9SW (0181-993 0279/fax 993 2215) and in the US request an application form from the Chinese Embassy at 2300 Connecticut Avenue NW, Washington, DC 20008 (the Education Office telephone number is 202-328-2563 and fax 234-2582). The Education Section in London screens applications for positions mainly as FTs but also as FEs. Late winter and spring is the best time to be making enquiries for one-year contracts starting in September. The Embassy interviews prospective teachers at a selection of British universities. Successful interviewees are given the addresses of the institutes to which they can then apply directly with an application form, CV and two references.

To facilitate central recruitment, it is hoped that an independent agency called 'Teaching in China' (TIC) can be set up in Beijing to strengthen links between hiring institutions and university careers services overseas and individual applicants, starting with Britain. The agency will be responsible for the acceptance of applications and subsequent placements. In the meantime the State Bureau of Foreign Experts (SBFE), Friendship Hotel, 3 Bai Shi Qiao Road, 100873 Beijing (1-849 888 ext 83500/fax 831 5832) attempts to coordinate the selection of FTs and FEs, though applications sent directly to them do not always receive a reply.

Travellers in China have been approached and invited to teach English as Rachel Starling discovered:

> *Whilst travelling extensively in China, I was offered several opportunities to teach English. If you want a place just ask at all the colleges, as it is likely that one school or college will require someone.*

It has even been known for job-seeking teachers to stand in Beijing Railway Station with a placard to that effect. But it is not necessary to go to such lengths to meet Chinese people looking for language tuition. Try attending an 'English Corner', scheduled meetings often in public parks where people gather to practice English conversation. The job will be much easier to get than the visa. For a working visa, it is necessary to leave the country.

Two US-based placement programmes to consider are the eight-week Shanghai Summer Teaching Program from WorldTeach (Harvard Institute for International Development, 1 Eliot St, Cambridge, MA 02138-5705) which costs about $3,500, and the China Teaching Program at Western Washington University, Old Main 530, Bellingham, WA 98225-9047 (206-650-3753).

Thailand

Bangkok is a good bet for the casual teacher, although standards are creeping up and the RSA/Cambridge Certificate is preferred by most reputable schools. Although jobs are easy to come by, the main problem seems to be the low wages, usually about 150 baht (less than £4) per hour for a part-time teacher in Bangkok which is just enough to live on (flats are about 3,000 baht per month with at least two months rent upfront). Contract teachers (i.e. full-time ones) usually start on 15,000 baht a month with first refusal of overtime. Outside Bangkok, wages are less.

The best place to start a speculative job hunt is Siam Square where numerous schools and the British Council are located. The noisy Khao San Road is lined with budget accommodation (where a room costs B50-80), many with notice boards offering teaching work and populated with other foreigners (known as *farangs*) well acquainted with the possibilities. But Vaughan Temby who recently taught in Bangkok advises against staying in this area:

> *I would recommend the Peachy Guest House (10 Phra Athit Road, Banglamphu; 281-6471). The overwhelming majority of people who stay here are working or looking for work. Most are teachers and it seemed as if opportunities, information and advice were endless.*

People in the know will also be able to warn you of the dubious schools which are known to exploit their teachers. There is such a high turnover of staff at many schools that there are bound to be vacancies somewhere for a new arrival who takes the trouble to present a professional image. As usual, it may be necessary to start with part-time and occasional work with several employers, aiming to build up 20-30 hours in the same area to minimise travelling in the appalling traffic.

Consult the adverts in the *Bangkok Post*. The best times to look for work in private schools are mid-March to mid-May and October when students are on holiday from state schools and eager to receive extra tuition. The worst time to look is January/February. Walk around and ask in each school. Men with long hair, ponytails or earrings will be out-of-luck; as throughout Asia, smartness is essential.

After finding a cheap hotel in Bangkok Laurence Koe plotted his strategy on a city map of Bangkok, after looking up language schools in the *Yellow Pages*, (though it can be difficult to find the Yellow Pages and when you do they may be several years out of date). He could visit only a couple a day, since getting around Bangkok is so time-consuming. He made telephone contact first, and all of them showed some degree of interest. Soon he landed a job, mostly teaching one-to-one, sometimes at the school, sometimes in the students' houses. Although house calls paid more, a lot of time was wasted in travelling.

Try any of the private language schools such as:

English & Computer College (ECC), 430/17-20 Chula Soi 64, Siam Square, Bangkok 10330 (02-255-1856). Reputable school with 13 branches in Bangkok, one in Chiang Mai and one in Hadyai. Average monthly wage 15,000 baht. Sometimes offer work doing voice-overs on tape (300 baht an hour) and helping to made videos (which Vaughan Temby says are worthy of John Cleese).

Siam Computer & Language School Head Office, 471/19 Ratcha Withi Road, Victory Monument, Ket Ratcha Tevi, Bangkok 10400 (02-247 2345). Have about a dozen branches in Bangkok. High turnover of part-time staff.

American University Alumni Center, 179 Rajadamri Road, Bangkok 10330 (02-252-8170). May be moving soon. Americans preferred.

inlingua School of Languages, 7th Floor, Central Chidlom Tower, 22 Ploenchit Road, Pathumwan, Bangkok 10330 (02-254-7028).

CIC Language Centre, 43/26 Pracharat Bumpen Road, Huaykwang, Bangkok 10310. Recently paid Vaughan Temby B100 an hour (with unlimited hours) and provided free food and accommodation.

English for Busy People (EBP), 268 Siam Square, Soi 3, Rama I Road, Patumwan, Bangkok (02-254 8486). Rigid lesson plans.

Oxford English Centre, 424/7-8 Siam Square, Soi 11, 10330 Bangkok (02-252 9378/254 2194). Administer a grammar test at interview.

Officially you need a work permit for Thailand, but the authorities normally turn a blind eye to trespassers. You will have to leave the country every three months to renew your visa; most choose Penang Malaysia for this purpose and many have done it four or five times. There is a fine of 200 baht for every day you overstay your tourist visa. With a letter from your school, you can apply for a non-immigrant visa, which is better for teaching than a tourist visa. Teachers who have saved some of their earnings report that there is no difficulty changing baht into dollars at banks.

There are of course far fewer opportunities outside Bangkok, though language schools and institutes of higher education around the country do hire *farangs*. For a job in a university you will probably have to show a degree or teaching certificate. The best places are Chiang Mai, the popular tourist destination in the north (where there will be a certain amount of competition from other travellers) and in the booming industrial city of Hadyai in the south (where there will be none).

Murray Turner describes his job hunt in Chiang Mai:

Eagle Guest House is your best bet for info. There are seven language schools in Chiang Mai and I am now working for the English Conversation Club on Wieng Kaeo Road after only one week of looking. I hired a bicycle (100 baht for five days) and dutifully did the rounds. On your rounds take plenty of passport size photos, copies of your certificates and be ready to answer bizarre questions on application forms (name, age and profession of every member of your family). Apart from language schools, hotels often want teachers for their staff. I am getting more confidence as a teacher and am enjoying it.

Murray went on to get more hours at the Chiang Mai Academy of Tourism and Languages but unfortunately his experiences in Thailand finished on a sour note. When he returned from a visa run to Penang, he found that his teaching hours were no longer available.

There are a number of Karen tribal refugees in the Mae Sod region of northern Thailand who have fled from Myanmar (formerly Burma) in the past few years. Apparently native English speakers are much in demand, especially those who are able to stay for more than a couple of months. Anyone interested should try contacting the Burmese Relief Committee (c/o Pippa Curwen, PO Box 48, Chiang Mai University) or visit Number 4 Guest House (711 Indharakiri Road, Mae Sod, Tak 63100) where volunteers, teachers and others meet.

Americans who would like to fix up a teaching job ahead of time should ask CIEE (212-661-1414 ext 1439) about their new teaching in Thailand programme in which teachers receive a Thai salary and free accommodation for ten months.

South-East Asia

Most language schools in Indonesia and Singapore recruit only trained EFL teachers who are willing to stay for at least a year. Voluntary teaching positions may be available in the wilder parts of South-East Asia. For example try private language schools in the capital of Laos such as Advanced Training Centre (PO Box 4144, Vientiane, Lao PDR) and also in Ho Chi Minh City, since many Vietnamese people are clamouring to learn English.

HONG KONG

As Hong Kong's colonial days draw to a close there has never been a better time for Britons to experience the buzz in this last fragment of the British Empire before it is handed back to the Chinese in 1997. Opportunities for foreign workers are likely to all but vanish after the Chinese take-over, when it is estimated that up to 100,000 Chinese job-seekers will flock into the wealthy island and will fill all unskilled (and many skilled) jobs. So it's now or never.

There is already quite a lot of competition in the job market for *gweilos* (pale ghosts) however many do still find jobs in bars, restaurants, offices, building sites, etc. A recent trend is for newly arrived Europeans to do menial jobs in construction, supermarkets, delivery, etc. European nannies are popular and of course foreigners are needed to teach English (dealt with above). Hong Kong also has intriguing possiblities for any would-be entrepreneur with an idea for making money.

After arriving on a £75 flight from Bangkok, Vaughan Temby and two friends found jobs with ease and were entirely positive about working in Hong Kong:

On our very first day here, we landed well-paid jobs with Pomeroys Bar and Restaurant. Mandy was employed as a waitress and me behind the bar. After taking catering as my career in the UK, I can definitely say that this is the best catering job I've had. Excellent laid-back management, good staff benefits and good money and tips (from HK$32 an hour). All the other staff are travellers so there is a great working atmosphere. Later Mandy got a job in her field in a prestigious beauty salon and Nigel got a job in design on a great salary. So things have gone well for us and we're earning far more money than when we were in England. In summary, work is easy to find and one thing leads to another. It's a small town.

Nine months on, Vaughan had a 'real' job with a wine merchant and had come to believe in the rumour that any Briton with a trade or profession can earn double his or her UK salary in Hong Kong. Furthermore his fellow-workers at Pomeroys all had good jobs, many of which they heard about from customers at Pomeroys, a popular expat meeting place.

The worst time to look for work is just after Christmas and New Year when there is a huge influx of travellers. Things pick up during Chinese New Year when many people quit their jobs after receiving their New Year bonuses. The job hunt usually starts with the two English daily newspapers, the *Standard* and the *South China Morning Post*. Although the majority of adverts do require fluent Cantonese, a small proportion advertising for expat bar staff, office assistants and models (no experience necessary) do not. If you do not see what you are looking for, you might want to try putting an advert in yourself, as Olivia Nourse did. Within a week she was working with an American woman who ran her own garment business. The fortnightly give-away *Hong Kong Dollar Saver* has a high expat readership and is another good source of adverts.

As always, hostel notice boards are a fount of information. The Chung King Mansions are legendary. One day's offerings included adverts for teachers, financial consultants (commission only), trainee brokers (can be dodgy) and a stand-by call for film extras. The Garden Hostel (4th Floor, Mirador Mansions, Nathan Road, Kowloon) is another good bet. Vaughan Temby recommends getting out of the Chung King Travellers Hostel and into a flat as quickly as possible: 'For anyone to live in those broom cupboard dorms and conduct a life, work, look smart, etc. is an enormous achievement and one which I couldn't possibly manage'. Rents have gone up drastically in the past year or two, as has the cost of living generally.

Red Tape

All British passport holders are given a one year visa on arrival in Hong Kong (although the immigration officials routinely ask for your intended length of stay). This is extended each time you arrive in the country, so taking a trip to Macau or China gives you an automatic extra year. Commonwealth citizens get a three-month visa, Europeans one to three months and Americans one month. These can be extended in the same way.

All residents in Hong Kong are required to register for an identity card, which is a good idea in any case to persuade prospective employers that you are not a fly-by-nighter. Application can be made to any of the six Registration of Persons offices. No charge is levied for the first ID (which normally takes about a month to process) but lost or stolen cards will be replaced at a cost of about £28. The Information Office of the Immigration Department is at 7 Gloucester Road, Wanchai Tower II (3-824 6111).

Tax bills (for 15% of earnings) are sent out a year after you start work and only if you have earned more than HK$3,000 a month.

Bars and Restaurants

There are any number of bars in Hong Kong: sing-along karaoke, raucous Australian swilleries, seedy topless joints or olde English pubs. The main pub/club areas are Wanchai, Lan Kwai Fong and Tsim Tsa Tsui. Most of them are staffed by a transient population of bar men and maids, taking advantage of the free food and drink (usually soft), earning not over-substantial wages (from HK$30 per hour) and pocketing the tips (as much as HK$100 on weekdays, up to HK$200 weekends). Those on Hong Kong side normally pay slightly better than those in Kowloon, but demand a greater degree of sophistication and smartness. You are unlikely to make a fortune in your first job, but you should get some free food and drink, a share of the tips and perhaps *lai see* ('lucky money') if you are working at Chinese New Year.

In addition to the two branches of Pomeroys mentioned above (one in Central, the other in Pacific Place), pubs worth trying around Tsim Tsa Tsui are:
Ned Kellys, 11a Ashley Road (3-366 0562).
Blacksmiths Arms, Minden Row (3-369 6695).
Mad Dogs, 32-34 Nathan Road (3-301 2222).

Ricks Café, 4 Hart Avenue (3-367 2939).
Kangaroo, Haiphong Road (3-723 8293).
In Hong Kong itself, a good place to start is Speakeasy 2001 at 38 Wyndham St (3-522 5566), with many other bars in the immediate vicinity.

The Pacific Coffee shop at Star Ferry and Uncle Russ Coffee on Peking Road are always looking for staff. The upmarket sandwich bar Birleys in the Bond Centre at Admiralty has occasional openings for expatriate staff. For many of these jobs experience is not necessary but applicants must be smart and quick on their feet.

Hostessing

Hostess bars attract mainly businessmen who, in return for an enormous outlay of money, are normally content to drink, dance and chat with a hired companion. Murray Turner found himself envying his women friends:

Hostessing is a good little earner. I know women who work in karaoke bars (and they're not pros) bringing home at least HK$16,000 per month for 144 hours. Meanwhile I was working 284 hours for the same money. Women have all the luck.

Yet it isn't as easy money as it seems. Carolyn Edwards decided to give it a try in Hong Kong and found that, instead of having pressures placed on her to deliver extra favours, her company was not wanted at all:

It all sounded very legit but turned out to be a disaster. After responding to a notice in the Travellers' Hostel, we were employed by a guy called Blue to work in a karaoke club called The Singing Moon. Our instructions were to wait for the boss to tell us which table to go to and just talk to the lonely businessmen and get them to buy you as many drinks as possible (for which you got a commission of HK$10 per drink). My first and last table was in a soundproof room in which about 15 young Hong Kong men were singing their hearts out to the video. I was introduced, but no one paid any attention. I had never felt so humiliated in all my life. Sitting in there trying to talk to these kids who didn't even want me in there. I couldn't wait to get out. I decided that I didn't want to make my million from this, so I spoke to the boss, got about HK$75 for my time and left.

The scene in Kowloon's seedier bars and elsewhere can be fairly sleazy and should not be dabbled in without consulting other employees whose accounts you can trust. Few things can be more unpleasant than to discover that your boss is a pimp.

Women who don't mind sitting around in a G-string with no chance of getting a sun tan (more like flu from the air-conditioning) might consider working in a topless bar. The hourly wage is no higher than at normal bars but tips are higher and you get a percentage of the money for any drinks which are bought for you. The old red light area, Wanchai, still has topless bars, though their popularity is waning.

Models

Modelling agencies in Hong Kong may be worth seeking out, especially ones which supply fitting models, a vital ingredient in Hong Kong's fashion industry. They get paid up to HK$150 an hour for trying on endless brands of shoes and garments. White-skinned, good looking males and females (especially ones with blue eyes) are often in demand by image-conscious advertising kings. Newspaper adverts frequently offer jobs to inexperienced models or try one of the following: Irene's (115 Wanchai Road, 22F, Flat E, Tak Lee Commercial Building), Faces (4a, Ma's Mansion, 31-37 Handow Road) or Fashion Model Movement Productions.

The trade has a dubious reputation in Hong Kong and for some advertisers it seems that modelling is synonymous with sex. The sleazy side seems to rear its head in the hostels in and around Chung King where convincing agents promise easy money to penniless new arrivals. Check it out, take a friend, and retreat if you are at all unsure. Escort agencies should be avoided.

People who are able to pose comfortably with no clothes on are needed as models for life drawing classes. The pay is HK$100-120 per hour. Contact the Assistant Education Programme Manager at the Hong Kong Art Centre (2 Harbour Road, Wanchai; 3-582 0200), the Swire School of Design at Hong Kong Polytechnic and the Art & Design Department of Hong Kong University.

Film Extras

Hong Kong continues to crank out movies at a remarkable rate, and while the stars are Chinese, there is always a need for gweilo extras to act as villains, fall guys or amazed onlookers. Some people make a regular living out of this, but for most it's a one-off lark. Garden Hostel in Mirador Mansion is a good place to make contact since the manager Mohammed works as a film agent.

Carolyn Edwards is a *Work Your Way Around the World* reader in a long line who have been invited to appear in a movie while staying at Chung King Mansions, though it sounds as though it is unlikely to get to the Cannes Film Festival:

After I'd been there about a week, I was asked if I'd like to be in a movie — wow. The scene took place in a restaurant on Hong Kong Island. Work started at midnight and we worked till 9am. Make-up and costumes came out and I was done up to look like a high class prostitute. For nine hours we had to walk around smiling, drinking imitation Champagne and saying 'cheers'. It seemed to be very amateurish and was quite tiring. We were starving but never fed as promised. When we weren't needed for a scene we slept on the settees. Towards the end, our hair was looking messy and the make-up was all over the place but they still kept shooting. Eventually we were allowed to go and were paid HK$400.

Obviously Carolyn acquitted herself well in her role since she was offered subsequent chances, one of which included a kissing scene and another participating in an aerobics class, but she decided one movie was enough. As usual take a book or airmail paper for the inevitable long hiatuses between call-ups.

Business and Industry

Secretarial and personnel agencies will be interested in you only if they are convinced you intend to stay. Pay for secretaries varies from HK$8,000 a month at worst to HK$22-25,000 at best. A good English secretary with shorthand will earn HK$16,000-20,000. Hourly rates for temps vary from HK$45 to HK$85. Agencies to try are:

Prudence Tolson Personnel, 16th Floor, Kincheng Commercial Centre, 2 Carnarvon Road, Tsim Tsa Tsui (3-722 6366/fax 852-368 0823). General recruitment and garment industry.

Lindy Williams, 7th Floor, Double Building, 22 Stanley St, Central (3-845 6777/ fax 845 0689). Large temp department.

Drake, 18th Floor, Peregrine Tower, Lippo Centre, Admiralty (3-848 9288/fax 852-810 6797. General.

Margaret Sullivan, 22 Ice House St, Central (3-526 5946). Secretarial recruitment. Now Chinese-owned.

Owens Personnel Consultants Ltd, Rm 704, New World Tower, 16-18 Queen's Road, Central (3-845 6220/fax 845 5621).

Sara Beattie, 3rd Floor, Sun Hung Kei Centre, 30 Harbour Road, Wanchai (3-507 9333).

Some of the long established agencies are very helpful to new arrivals as Prudence Humble, Managing Director of Prudence Tolson Consultants explains:

> *From my 25 years in the Colony, I advise new arrivals, give insider knowledge of cheaper acccommodation and instruct them on how to live on a shoestring to get started. Then we try them on our jobs when we can. If there is nothing suitable for them on the books, we spend time advising them on where to go and who to approach, and what attributes are saleable in this market place.*

Gweilo men can earn good money in construction especially with the start of the massive new airport building project in the latter part of 1994. Digger drivers, welders, diesel mechanics, etc. should be able to find work with one of the many sub-contractors. Murray Turner was amazed at the amount of work when he arrived from Thailand in June 1994:

> *Absolutely loads of work. I've got a construction job which involves 12 hour night shifts which pay HK$615 a night. I had four jobs in five weeks before landing this one. It's very easy to get work. But it's also very very easy to get sacked, pissed off and spend all your money.*

Two months later Murray had saved an incredible HK$34,000 (nearly £3,000), though he wrote to say the work was killing him (leaving home 5pm, getting back 7.30am). He worked for Bakers (3-983 6242) and also suggests trying Flexible Office Space (3-55 99 799) for office furniture fitting work, which pays HK$400-500 a day.

Childcare

While Chinese families normally employ Cantonese speakers as babysitters and nannies, the large expatriate community often prefers English speakers to look after their precious offspring. Hong Kong is an excellent place to work as part of a household since most have at least one live-in *amah*, usually a Filipina, to wash, iron, cook, etc. Rowena Caverly visited the Rent-a-Mum Agency (1st Floor, 88B Pokfulam Road, Hong Kong Island; 3-817 9799) and was assigned her first job within three days. She had a variety of one-off jobs and did some basic home pre-school teaching. Babysitters are especially sought after December to February, the busiest time in the Hong Kong social calendar with Christmas and two new years.

Casual Opportunities

There is a small amount of money to be made handing out 'flyers' in the tourist ghetto of Tsim Tsa Tsui. For being on your feet all day you are paid a paltry HK$30 an hour (enough to eat). These jobs are regularly advertised in the hostels or you can simply contact the company after being handed a leaflet in the street.

Many world travellers arrive with jewellery they have picked up on their travels and set up a stall at the Star Ferry or in nearby Peking Road. The most popular items seem to be Thai jewellery as well as silver from Bali and Tibetan knicknacks. The mark-up is normally about 50%. Street selling is illegal without a permit, as Jeff Keeran found to his cost:

> *Duly note that there is a risk of non-chargeable arrest for hawking and obstructing pedestrian traffic. Recently after six months of successfully selling znachki [Russian for badges — Ed], I was arrested and fined HK$480. Worse, my products, worth about US$250, were confiscated. Although this*

*was my first offence, this American is currently being deported for selling.
I know several Brits who have been arrested but continue to sell items such
as insects inside walnuts for HK$20 and Australian dried flowers for HK$100.*
Britons are less likely to be deported than other nationalities, just moved on.
Hong Kong's criminal fraternity the Triads tend to leave small fry alone.

Each spring the Sevens rugby tournament draws huge crowds and many
temporary bar staff are needed for the long weekend. You get a commission for
every jug of beer you sell and can drink as much as you like. Call the headquarters
of the major breweries (Fosters, San Miguel, etc.) before the event.

A company called Abbott Leisure regularly hires outgoing itinerants as clowns
and costume characters (like Ding Dong the Dinosaur) to provide the entertainment at parties, singing telegrams, etc. Men usually get hired for costume work
('gorilla-grams'), while women may choose to be bunnygirls or do strippergrams.
The pay is HK$250-300 for an hour's clowning, HK$250 for a costume character,
HK$500 for a singing telegram, and HK$750 for a 10-minute strippergram
(male chaperone also provided). Chammiran Daniel worked for Mike Abbott
(himself a long-time traveller):

*I really liked being a clown at a party. The kids thought it was fantastic,
though it was difficult to wean them away from their computers. Being a
bunnygirl at a hotel promotion was no problem; it was just like wearing a
swim suit, but to be honest it wasn't really my scene. The important thing
is not to take it seriously.*

Buskers should head for subways and the corridors of the Mass Transit Railway
system, while the areas around the entrances to the Star Ferry very often have
two or more groups of musicians at weekends and holidays. Official hassle is
minimal as long as you don't block thoroughfares. Kim Falkingham recommends
being able to sing some songs in Chinese. She looks back fondly on one listener
who dropped the equivalent of £80 in her cap, but also remembers long days
when nobody contributed anything.

ENTERTAINMENT

Many of the opportunities like film extras, busking and modelling described
above pertain to other countries in Asia. Here are some scattered suggestions.

Hollywood does not have the world monopoly on film-making. There is an
enormous film industry in the Hindi, Chinese and Japanese speaking worlds
and it is just possible your services will be required. Foreign travellers lurking
around the Salvation Army hostel in the Colaba district of Bombay, the Broad-
lands Guest House in Madras, the main travellers' hotels in Goa, the Banglamphu
area of Bangkok (which were especially busy when there was a craze for making
Vietnam War movies), Bencoolen St in Singapore, Malate Pension in Manila,
or the 16th floor of the Chung King Mansions in Hong Kong (mentioned above)
may be invited by a film agent to become an extra. Vaughan Temby and his
two travelling companions spent a day in Bangkok working as film extras for
which they were paid 700 baht, though they heard 900 baht is possible. They
found this through the Pikanake agency (see *Modelling* below) which is a ten-
minute walk from Khao San Road. It can happen anywhere and to anyone. Even
the author of this book, while travelling in the Swat Valley of Northern Pakistan,
had to disappoint a Pakistani film director also staying at the Heaven Breeze
Hotel who wanted her to mount a horse and impersonate a colonel's daughter.

Do not ignore other branches of the media such as television and radio. Often
there will be English programmes in which you might participate, such as
'English for Today' on NHK, Japan's public broadcasting network. English
language publications such as the *Korea Times* and *China Daily* are always

worth a try. Aspiring journalists could try writing (but not about youth hostels) for some of the English language glossy business and airline magazines. For example the *Far East Traveller* published in Tokyo (which likens itself to *National Geographic*) pays from 15 cents a word or $40 a photo.

In Bangkok, Laurence Koe did a night's stint as a DJ in one of Patpong's classier strip joints. He found it a litle tricky getting past the girls to see the manager — 'No, excuse me, I am here on business'... 'Oh, you want the bees-ness'. But he was eventually shown to the manager who told him that if he could set up the equipment he could have the job. He became an instant favourite with the girls (since his relationship with them was strictly non-commercial) and enjoyed the experience of seeing their human side.

Although not very common, busking can net some worthwhile profits. With a borrowed guitar, David Hughes busked in the subways of Taipei which earned him £10 an hour tax-free. But there was a catch:

Things were fine until strange red graffiti appeared overnight near the spot where I stood. A man who 'represented' some people (gangsters? market traders?) told me to stop, or something might 'happen' to me. By this time we had just enough teaching to keep us afloat so I gladly yielded to his request.

Mimes, guitarists, dancers and musicians should go to Ginza in Tokyo or any Japanese city, especially in the evening. Once a few people gather, the Japanese herd instinct guarantees that the street will become all but impassable. Local taste favours old Beatles and Simon & Garfunkle songs.

Hostessing and Escort Work

Throughout the Far East, but especially in Japan and Singapore (as well as Hong Kong as described above), there is an institution quite alien to the West — the hostess bar. Western hostesses in Tokyo normally work at the more respectable clubs in Ginza (there are an estimated 10,000 hostess bars in Tokyo alone) and get paid an average of 4,000 yen an hour from 7pm to midnight. Monday nights are said to be the busiest after the strains of a family weekend. The reaction of most women is that this must be a cover for prostitution, but in fact that seldom seems to be the case. Inevitably some evenings are more bearable than others. It's easy money if the clientele are nice but if their English is limited, their drink intake is excessive and their intentions not of the purest, the hostess is in for a fairly miserable evening.

Anyone who wants to research the subject should try to get hold of Mark Gauthier's book *1001 Teaching, Modelling, Editing and Hostessing Job in Japan* which says, 'if you like talking about sex, think you're pretty and are curious about the seedier side of life, you'll get paid mega yen for very easy work.' The book which lists and describes some of the clubs costs 3,000 yen and can be ordered from the author (459 Maywood Road, Kitchener, Ontario N2C 2A2, Canada).

In Singapore, hostess bars also abound. Some travel-toughened women register with one of the agencies listed in the Yellow Pages, show up on the evenings of their choice (looking smart) and then accompany a client to a restaurant or nightclub. Agencies pay about S$100 for an evening (conditions differ so it's worth shopping around), plus you get a free dinner and possibly tips and gifts. Jane Roberts enjoyed this work:

Some girls who stayed at my hostel Das Travellers Inn on Beach Road were working at a hostess bar. I went along one night and have had a great time. What more can you ask for than to sit around drinking (not advised), smoking and talking to people and being paid for it. I wore the same dress every night for the ten weeks I worked there and no one said a thing.

Most of the guys I've had to sit with have been nice and polite, but it's best to make it clear, by casually dropping it into the conversation, that you will not do anything that is not right for you. When you work in one of these clubs, you will probably find that 99% of the girls are on the game. Inevitably you will be offered immense amounts of money to 'go back to someone's hotel', but you are definitely not expected to do so. Whenever I got into a position of a drunken Japanese businessman throwing his hands down my dress I would let him know that if he wanted to do that, I could arrange for another girl to be brought in as there was no way I'd allow it. If that didn't stop him, then I'd complain to the Mama-san and she would sort it out. I'd go back to a chorus of apologies. You have to have a pretty open mind about this job, and learn not to be too shocked by what you see going on. Some nights the whole place seemed to be having an orgy. And I'd just sit quietly in a corner trying to fade into the walls.

An article in *Overseas Jobs Express* puts Jane's estimate of 99% at 100%; it quotes a German woman who had been an 'escort' for ten years as saying, 'there are no Western escorts in Singapore, only prostitutes'. Jane's hostessing days in Singapore were brought to an abrupt stop when one of the other girls (a Singaporean) phoned immigration. Though Jane was not on the premises when the club was raided, Jane knew that she would no longer be able to renew her two-week visa. In a regime which cracks down on gum chewers and maintains urine detectors in lifts, there is not much future in trying to look for work without a permit, even if there are occasional opportunities for film extras and bar staff.

Modelling

There is a demand for Caucasian faces in the advertising industries of Singapore, Thailand, etc. Interested people should get some photos taken back home rather than risk being ripped off by agencies which charge you to put together a portfolio and then don't hire you. When you arrive register with one of the numerous modelling agencies. Although the hourly rate is very high, you can't expect to average more than one or two assignments per week, earning £80-100. After studying interior design in New York, Matthew Goodman set off (with a small modelling portfolio) for Singapore and managed to become a feature model in a Pepsi-Cola commercial which was aired in Saudi Arabia (and on the proceeds he took several short trips to Indonesia and Malaysia).

Bangkok sounds a promising destination. Vaughan Temby's friend Mandy got work with Kalcarrie's Modelling Agency in Siam Square:

There is big money to be made and Mandy is doing well. Oh, for a pretty face! She was with another agency first, but they were appalling, inefficient and two-faced. A portfolio is absolutely necessary. Even more important is a card which the agency can display in their office and circulate to clients. All the other models we have met have been professional, so there is stiff competition.

Men might also want to have a go. Laurence Koe went into three advertising agencies where they took photos and in one case a video of him prancing around in jeans. He was summoned back for a four-hour session for which he was paid $100. Months later he featured on the back cover of one of Thailand's two glossy fashion magazines.

Try the following agencies:

Kalcarries Models International, 412/15 Siam Square, Soi 6, Rama 4 Road, Pathumvan (3-251 2828).

International Models, Soi 128, Sukhumvit 55 (3-392 5521).

Pikanake Group, 71/13 Phasumen Road, Banpnantom, Phanakron (3-282 6932/ 282 8247). Also recruit film extras.

TOURISM

Brett Muir taught scuba in Phuket. Richard Davies funded his stay in expensive Singapore by recruiting travellers for the hostel he was staying at. Working as a croupier in Japan is said to be phenomenally lucrative because of the tips. Thailand affords the best chances as Vaughan Temby discovered:

> *We spent a great Christmas on the islands and although we weren't looking for work, we did come across some opportunities. On Koh Samui several bars along Chaweng beach needed staff during the peak season. The huge Reggae's Bar Complex, a little further inland had at least four foreign staff. On Koh Pha'Ngan a friend of mine worked as a DJ and another as a waitress/kitchen helper in the excellent German-style bakery.*

Later on Vaughan tried the hotels in Bangkok but was told that they had plenty of local labour and besides he would need a work permit.

A few years ago, Adam Jones broke new ground by finding work in a restaurant in Malaysia, but we haven't heard from anyone who has succeeded since:

> *When I arrived in Melaka, I walked around the restaurants, looking for work. Five of them had adverts in the window advertising for waiters, kitchen helpers, etc. Four of the five I visited showed interest and each invited me back for an interview. The first interview I went for at Napoleon's Grill House was a mere formality as they were so short of staff. Two days later I started work as the barman — with a wage of 240 ringgits a month, which wasn't much, but I had as many free drinks and as much food as I wanted and I negotiated free accommodation in the workers' dorm above the restaurant. I have spent a very enjoyable (and exceptionally cheap) five weeks here now, and am sad to leave. The Malaysian people are so friendly and open — they really cannot do enough for you. The locals claim that they have never seen a young traveller working in their midst which I find very surprising.*

The Black Market

These days goods are crossing borders with much greater ease than they once did; however there is still some scope for boosting finances by market speculations. Duty free whisky and cigarettes, as well as Western items such as T-shirts with slogans can sometimes be sold at a profit. In the Indian subcontinent, you are likely to be asked at some point if you have anything to sell. Myanmar (Burma) was once the mecca for black market profiteers but opportunities are much diminished under the new regime. The islands of Thailand afford opportunities; it seemed to Vaughan Temby that half the travelling population of Koh Pha'Ngan were selling black market stuff outside the infamous Tommy's.

There are some unexpected ways to work the black market which change weekly and which you will have to learn from other travellers. Past examples include taking pan (betel) leaves and coconuts from India to Pakistan, taking cheap cottons to Kathmandu tailors, taking saris from Varanasi to Bangladesh, taking watches into Iran, buying up Indian saffron to sell in the west and, oddest of all, taking breath freshener and bananas into Korea. For a while it was possible to carry a few record stylii into Bangkok in return for some pocket money, but the advent of the compact disc seems to have killed off this trivial trade. The most bizarre case we have heard of is the German resident in Taipei who tried to import a number of baby carp which, when fully grown, are very valuable. Not surprisingly, the customs officer uncovered his booty and so he never realised the vast profits.

Do not be conned at any cost into buying jewels from agents in Bangkok or anywhere else to sell in the West since you will certainly be the loser. Those who would like prolonged exposure to Nepali culture and cuisine (rice on its own, rice with lentils and lentils on their own) can try their hand at smuggling gold into Kathmandu. One agent offered Hew Stillington US$2,000, a free return ticket and promised to bail him out if he got into trouble with the authorities. He never got to use the return ticket. The misery and humiliation of being in Badraghol Prison is not worth it at any price.

You might prefer the entirely legal money-making technique of selling your blood at the main hospital on the hill in Macau, where a generous 250 patacas are paid (nearly £20). Try to arrive in good health since unless your haemoglobin count is above a certain level you will be refused as Tim Waggett was. Unfortunately the Veterans' Hospital in Taipei which used to pay US$70 for blood no longer accepts 'foreign blood'.

The old Taiwan 'Milk Run' has been redundant for several years, so there are no more free air tickets in return for 'smuggling' heavily taxed luxury items between Hong Kong, Taiwan, Korea and Japan, since most consumer durables can now be bought perfectly openly in Taiwan and elsewhere.

VOLUNTARY WORK

Many people who have travelled in Asia are dissatisfied with the role of tourist and would like to find a way of making a contribution. In very many cases this is laudable but naïve. It may be worth quoting Dominique Lapierre, author of *The City of Joy*, the bestseller which movingly describes life in a Calcutta slum. Although he is talking specifically about India, a similar situation exists in all poor countries:

> *Many of you have offered to go to Calcutta to help. This is most generous but I am afraid not very realistic. Firstly because Indian authorities only give a three-month tourist visa to foreign visitors. This is much too short a period for anyone to achieve anything really useful. Secondly because only very specialised help could really be useful. Unless you are a doctor or an experienced paramedic in the fields of leprosy, tropical diseases, malnutrition, bone tuberculosis, polio, rehabilitation of physically handicapped, I think your generous will to help could be more of a burden for the locals in charge than anything else. Moreover, you have to realise that living and working conditions on our various projects are extremely hard for unaccustomed foreigners.*

As the director of a project working with forest tribal people in the Bangalore region of India wrote:

> *As our work is in a remote area with no creature comforts, it is not easy for foreign visitors to stay there and work, and therefore I suggest that you not mention us in your book as it unnecessarily creates false hopes in the minds of your readers.*

There are exceptions of course and anyone prepared to make a fairly long-term commitment or who can afford to pay their own way may find opportunities. It must be stressed that Westerners almost invariably have to make a financial contribution to cover food and accommodation as well as their travel and insurance. Some voluntary organisations abroad such as Global Service Corps in the US (1472 Filbert St, 405, San Francisco, CA 94109) can provide a more cossetted introduction to the business of volunteering in Asia; they arrange for small groups to travel to northern Thailand to help local villagers for 16 days at a cost of $1,500 excluding air fares.

If you have not travelled widely in the Third World you may not be prepared for the scruffiness and level of disorganisation to be found in some places.

However the main difficulty with participating in local voluntary projects (of which there are many) is in fixing anything up ahead of time. Occasionally Asian charities have a representative abroad who can send information about voluntary possibilities but this is unusual. Mainstream organisations like GAP for school leavers offer a range of opportunities from teaching English to Tibetan refugees in India to working with disabled people in Hong Kong. Teaching Abroad (46 Beech View, Angmering, Sussex BN16 4DE) sends volunteers to teach in Tamil-speaking South India for short periods; the cost is £1,145. But there are not many programmes like these.

Indian Subcontinent

It is possible to become a part-time volunteer at Mother Theresa's children's home in Calcutta (Shishu Bhavan, 78 Lower Circular Road), in the Home for Dying Destitutes at Kalighat and other Homes run by the Missionaries of Charity in other Indian cities, but no accommodation can be offered. The work may consist of feeding and caring for orphaned children or the elderly. To register, visit the administrative office at 54A A.J.C. Bose Road, Calcutta 16.

Dustie Hickey found her brief time as a volunteer in India so affecting that she has returned for an extended stay:

When I was in Calcutta I decided to take a jar of horlicks to the hospital. The nuns were grateful and asked me to come back the following day to play with the children. So I went, taking with me as much paper, crayons and sweets as I could buy from the shop. I spent the morning drawing with them and it was a moving experience. In the afternoon I helped feed the babies. The nuns had their hands full. They invited me to go down to Mother Theresa's home which I did and where I met her. After I'd returned to England, she wrote to me and I plan to return, perhaps to do an arts project with the mentally handicapped. I'd also like to take some of the children to local museums, zoos and gardens if it can be arranged.

The Calcutta Rescue Fund (PO Box 52, Brentford, Middlesex TW8 0TF) works with destitute people in Calcutta, running two street clinics and one mobile clinic, a school for street children and training projects in Calcutta. For these they recruit volunteer health professionals and other self-funding volunteers who mainly work in the pharmacy section dispensing medicines via interpreters. A 'Volunteer Information Sheet' can be requested from Tom Woodhatch. Help is most needed during the monsoon. It is possible to slot in after arrival as David Hughes wrote from Calcutta:

While in England we answered an ad for nurses but there is an ongoing need for volunteers in the street clinic where the only skill needed is the ability to communicate in English and read doctors' handwriting (and that's quite a skill). Anyone prepared to give assistance can meet both new and long-stay volunteers at the Khalsa Restaurant (opposite the Salvation Army Red Shield Guest House) between 7.30am and 8am weekday mornings. It's quite hard work (mostly due to the heat) but it can be good fun. You see another side of India.

People First International offer workcamp places with local agencies in Bihar state, involved in education. Accommodation and vegetarian food are provided. For information send s.a.e. (or three IRCs from abroad) to People First Workcamps, 4 Willow Close, Saxilby, Lincoln LN1 2QL. The Indian field office is at Pachatti, Bodhgaya, Bihar 824231.

Another organisation with representation abroad is the Joint Assistance Centre (6-17/3 DLF Qutab Enclave, Phase 1, District Gurgaon, Haryana 122002; 011-835 2141) which attaches paying volunteers to a variety of workcamps for a minimum of one or three months, for example in children's homes, village tree-planting, etc. The minimum contribution of £75/US$125 covers simple accommodation and vegetarian food for one month, though the preferred stay is three months, and pressure is often put on new arrivals to pay upfront for an extended stay, as Andy Green was in 1994. His conclusions about volunteering in India are interesting:

I did two weeks' worth of workcamps and I feel that I was of no help to Indian society whatsoever. Due to differences in climate, food and culture, it is difficult to be productive. I could have paid an Indian a few pounds to do what I did in two weeks. it was however an experience I'll never forget.

Western volunteers should book in advance through Friends of JAC, 1 Ludgate Barns, Haytor, Newton Abbot, Devon TQ13 9XR or in the US c/o K. Gopalan, PO Box 14481, Santa Rosa, CA 95402. It is usually not possible to accept walk-in volunteers directly onto the workcamps, although administrative work is available at short notice.

Another UK-based organisation Indian Volunteers for Community Service (12 Eastleigh Avenue, South Harrow, Middlesex HA2 0UF) sends willing volunteers to live and learn on rural development projects in India. Living expenses are around £20 a week.

Bharat Sevak Samaj (Nehru Seva Kendra, Gugoan Bye Pass Road, Mehrauli, New Delhi 30 (011-657609) provides workers for development programmes throughout India including community centres in slum areas, nursery schools, family planning camps, disaster relief, etc. Volunteers work for two weeks to three months and are expected to be self-financing.

Bombay Sarvodaya Friendship Centre (Friendship Building, Kajupada Pipe Line Road, Kurla, Bombay 400 072; 511 3660/516 0398) is a Gandhian organisation which suggests that those seeking placement in rural areas (preferably long-term) should try to learn Hindi, be willing to work in difficult and novel situations and have a strong interest in environmental and peace issues, non-violence and social change. Enquiries should be accompanied by IRCs.

Many travellers to India stay at monasteries, temples or ashrams, which are communities for meditation, yoga, etc. There may be no official charge or at least a very small one, but it may be assumed that you are a genuine seeker after enlightenment. Jørn Borup enjoyed his stay at a Buddhist monastery in Sri Lanka:

Attached to it, there is a school and kindergarten with about 100 children whom the monks teach and take care of. The children are mainly from poor families who cannot pay for the education and food in real schools. The work (mainly in the kindergarten) will be from 8am to 1.30pm. The monastery will give free food and accommodation and help get you the necessary visa. I was asked if I could find either sponsors or people who would be interested in doing some voluntary work here.

The contact address is Ven. B. Gunaratana, Dutugamunu Viharaya, Ganegama, Baddegama (52231).

Laurence Koe followed up a lead he'd been given and visited a Catholic monastery in a suburb of Bombay where foreigners were a real oddity. The monks generously gave him their 'deluxe suite' and full board. He tried to repay their hospitality by offering to work but all they wanted was for him to discuss the western way of life with the trainee monks whenever he felt so inclined.

Conservation issues are becoming more important in India and volunteers may find something usefully green to do. Try the Youth Charitable Organization (YCO, 20-14 Urban Bank St, PB 3, Yellamanchili, 531 055 Visakhapatnam DT, Andhra Pradesh) which in the past has taken on foreign volunteers to work on soil conservation, irrigation and general community development programmes. Volunteers stay from 15 days to six months and pay 150 rupees ($5.50) a day.

An organisation listed by WWOOF (see page 114) is a botanical sanctuary in south India run by the East-West University which accepts a few volunteers to help in the garden or office, to do maintenance or join plant-collecting expeditions. A reasonable donation must be made to cover food and lodging at the Narayana Gurukula Botanical Sanctuary (Alattil PO, North Wayanad, Kerala 670645). In the neighbouring state of Tamil Nadu, the beautiful hill station of Kodaikanal has an Appropriate Technology and Agriculture Centre which may be able to use suitable volunteers; the contact address is Brian Jenkins, PO Box 57, Kodaikanal 624101.

A community organisation in Uttar Pradesh with the charming name ROSE (Rural Organization on Social Elevation, KSS Social Awareness Centre Kanda, PO Kanda, Almora, UP 263631) can assist volunteers wishing to work with poor villagers, disabled children, etc. There is a non-refundable application fee of £6. A publisher-cum-education consultant says that he can arrange for volunteer teachers from abroad to work in schools and career institutes for short periods. He also publishes a directory of homestays and free hospitality in India (for $25). Details from Jaffe International Education Service, Kunnuparambil Buildings, Kurichy, Kottayam 686549 (4826 470).

The Bangladesh Workcamps Association (289/2 Work Camp Road, North Shahjahanpur, Dhaka 1217; fax 02-86 37 97 Attn BWCA) will try to place you on seven or ten day community development camps between October and February. The participation fee is 4,000 taka per camp (about US$100). They publish detailed camp information in English. Applications must be submitted at least by mid-Septmeber for autumn camps and by the end of November for January camps, enclosing a $25 application fee.

Volunteers, especially those who are able to spend several months, are needed by Lanka Jatika Sarvodaya Shramadana Sangamaya (98 Rawatawatta Road, Moratuwa, Colombo, Sri Lanka) to help with work in villages throughout the country, and also helping with preparation of project proposals at the head-quarters. The programme is unstructured so volunteers should be able to create tasks for themselves.

Samasaveya Ltd (Anuradhapura Road, Talawa N.C.P., Sri Lanka) can use a few volunteers on their various educational and development programmes, though Laura Bowes did not find her time there very satisfactory and describes a classic case of culture shock:

> *I was collected at the airport by a Samasaveya representative and driven to his sister-in-law's house where nobody spoke English and I was generally ignored. The director Mr. Jayasinghe collected me three days later to take me to Talawa, a tiny village in the dry zone, 15km from the border. Again I was dumped on a family who spoke no English. I had been prepared to sleep in a dormitory, but nothing could have prepared me for having my clothes tried on, my toiletries used and my possessions ransacked.*
>
> *I was expected to work from 8am-5pm six days a week, but there was very little for me to do and I spent most of my time reading my book, feeling myself to be a nuisance for continually asking for something to do. I was eventually given a stack of small paper logos which had to be pasted onto forms. At this point I began to feel a little cheated that I had paid a fortune to travel over 5,000 miles to do this kind of menial task. I did manage to organise English classes for Samasaveya staff, famous for their complete lack of attendance.*

Laura goes on to say that she was asked to cycle into the jungle to visit pre-schools, but she refused, having taken the High Commission at its word when it issued general advice never to leave the main road. It is possible that 18 is too young to undertake such an isolated placement, and that people who have travelled in developing countries and are used to the lack of water and amenities might fare better. It couldn't have been that bad, since Laura offers to advise future Samasaveya volunteers on useful equipment to take.

People who find voluntary openings in Nepal will be faced with a serious visa problem. One-month tourist visas can be renewed only after exchanging US$300 into Nepali rupees. This can only be done twice. The small company Insight Nepal (PO Box 6760, Kathmandu; 418964/fax 223515) runs a 'Placement for Volunteer Service' programme (maximum three months) for volunteers to teach English, computer science and games in primary and secondary schools throughout the country. The fee of $400 includes orientation, training and a one-week trekking excursion. Volunteers must have A levels and preferably experience with sports or crafts. We have also heard of one traveller who worked at the exclusive tiger reserve Tiger Tops in Chitwan National Park in his gap year, though this may have been arranged through contacts.

Trek Aid (2 Somerset Cottages, Stoke Village, Plymouth, Devon PL3 4AZ) is a charity which has been involved with helping Tibetan refugee communities in Nepal and India for many years. People from the UK share skills in medicine, horticulture, teaching, building, etc. with the refugees for one to three months. The costs range from £600 to £1,200.

Southeast Asia

We have not come across many conservation or scientific projects in southeast Asia in which volunteers can participate. One exception is the International Scientific Support Trust and its subsidiary Trekforce Expeditions (134 Buckingham Palace Road, London SW1W 9SA; 0181-824 8890) which organise and run a series of conservation-oriented expeditions to Indonesia each year. The expeditions last six weeks and are a combination of adventurous trekking in the rainforest and conservation work (including orangutan rehabilitation and green turtle conservation) unusally in one of the national parks. ISST assists participants to raise their own contribution of £2,650.

Two possibilities in Malaysia are the Penang Organic Farm (116 Jalan Bunga Raya, Gelugor 11700, Penang; 875591 at weekends) and the Society for Christian Service in Sarawak (23-2F Long Bridge Road, 96009 Sibu, Sarawak). At the collective Penang farm, about an hour's walk from Sungai Pinang, a job sheet is posted and volunteers choose which project to join. The Sarawak organisation coordinates workcamps to improve facilities for longhouse villages.

Jørn Borup from Denmark worked for another organisation in Sarawak. IPK (PO Box 8, 96007 Sibu; 084-322795) is involved mainly in environmental issues and is encouraging tribal communities to practise sustainable agriculture:

We stayed in Sibu for about three weeks helping at the IPK office and doing some work on their organic farm. Then we stayed in a longhouse with the most friendly people. We came away with a much more intimate knowledge of the problems of the rainforest and its people.

An ashram in Bali offers full board to volunteers who stay for two months teaching English, working on the farm or maintenance work; details from Mrs Oka, Kompleks Dosen FS2, J1 Sidiman, Denpasar 80114, Bali, Indonesia.

It may be possible to get work with the UN or Hong Kong government organisations helping Vietnamese refugees in Hong Kong. Most volunteers have professional qualifications (except for English teachers) and, according to David Hughes, 'nice southern accents', in keeping with a colonial atmosphere. Philip Herklots worked with Vietnamese refugees in Hong Kong for four months and then for three months in orphanages in Singapore and Sarawak run by the Salvation Army. The first stint was fixed up through a well established link with his school. It also helps to be a committed Christian in such cases.

According to the Committee for Coordination of Services to Displaced Persons in Thailand (37-B Soi 15, Petchburi Road, Bangkok 10400), the decrease in the number of refugee camps in Thailand means that job opportunities with refugees are very limited.

Japan

The workcamp organisation in Japan (NICE, 501 View City, 2-2-1 Shinjuku, Shinjuku-ku, Tokyo 160) receives British volunteers via UNA (Wales) to carry out conservation projects, etc.

An unusual opportunity to teach local people is available at a farm in Hokkaido, the most northerly island of the Japanese archipelago, known as Shin-Shizen-Juku (Tsurui, Akan-gun, Hokkaido 085-12; 0154 64-2821), a place well known to the travelling fraternity. The owner Hiroshi Mine welcomes international travellers who want to conduct conversation classes with local businessmen, farmers, housewives, doctors and children, in exchange for board and lodging and pocket money. Mr. Mine organises the classes, provides transport and some teaching materials. The place is fairly disorganised, and much depends on the personalities of the other volunteers (often just two or three, up to a maximum of seven); whereas some travellers perceive it to be a good opportunity and enjoy a warm atmosphere and the beautiful surroundings, others find the place bleak and exploitative.

The Middle East

The areas of employment to consider are English teaching, nannying or a position in the petro-chemical or construction industries (if you happen to have senior managerial experience). Trained and experienced nannies willing to live a relatively cloistered life should contact the major nanny agencies and check adverts in the *Lady* magazine. Nurses are regularly recruited for Saudi Arabia by agencies in London.

Teaching jobs are often advertised in the UK educational press, and mostly specify advanced qualifications, for which teachers are rewarded with full expatriate packages (though the rewards are not nearly as generous as they were ten years ago). There are several English schools in Amman, Jordan which might be worth trying, for instance the Yarmouk Cultural Center, PO Box 960312.

These countries do vary in degree of Islamic restrictiveness. Oman, for example, is favoured by many British expatriates for its relatively relaxed atmosphere. The United Arab Emirates are politically stable and can provide a pleasant way of life. Not long after arrival in the UAE in September 1994, Philip Dray was optimistic that accepting a TEFL contract in Dubai was a good move: first-class accommodation in a luxury apartment complex, cheap shopping, etc. Saudi Arabia is a very different destination. Women working in Saudi Arabia sometimes begin to feel that they are treated like prisoners. A further problem for females may be that their western style of dress and behaviour could be misinterpreted as loose by male Muslims and assaults are not unknown. Liberalisation is coming very slowly to the region and it will be a long time before women are allowed to drive cars, let alone function as normal members of Saudi society. The book *Working in the Persian Gulf — Survival Secrets for Men and Women (The Real Story)* is recommended for anyone who fixes up a job in the Middle East, since it is full of practical cultural advice, though less useful for the job hunt. It is published by Desert Diamond Books, PO Box 4065, Deerfield Beach, FL 33442, for $16.95 plus postage ($3 US/$7 overseas).

If you are offered a chance to work in the Middle East, you will have to persuade yourself that the money you will save in the end justifies the boredom and hardship of living in a strict Islamic society.

TURKEY

With its ambition to join the European Union, Turkey does not fit comfortably into a chapter on Asia. However because of its adherence to Islam, it is often included under the heading of the Middle East. The situation in Turkey is very different from that of the oil states, and very much more enjoyable.

Teaching English

Turkey's ambition to join the European Union, together with a remarkable expansion in tourism during the 1980s, means that the Turkish middle classes are more eager than ever to learn English. The boom in English is not confined to private language schools *(dershane)* which have continued to mushroom in the three main cities of Istanbul, Ankara and Izmir. There are dozens of private secondary schools *(lises)* and a few universities (both private and public) which use English as the medium of instruction. In order to prepare students for an English language engineering, commerce, tourism or arts course, many secondary schools hire native speaker teachers.

Unfortunately a high proportion of foreigners who sign teaching contracts do not enjoy their year in Turkey. Bruce Lawson was offered an attractive-sounding job in Istanbul after an interview at a pub in Worthing, but two months later was very disillusioned, and his experiences are not atypical:

The contract I signed is a work of fiction that Tolstoy would have been proud of. When we arrived, the director changed our contract, denying us the 15% inflation pay rise in January, leaving us with a fixed lire rate of 7 million for all nine months. (Inflation is running about 170% at the moment.) We were told that our accommodation would be 20 minutes from the school whereas it is an hour by public transport; we were told that the resident's permit would cost £20 but it costs £60; the accommodation is a jerry-built apartment with inadequate heating (and Istanbul in winter is very cold). There are no cooking facilities so you eat out. Most people think Turkey is cheap, but a beer in the good areas is significantly more expensive than in London and you simply can't save on the salary. Private work (which pays up to £10 an hour) is prohibited in your contract, though many people risk it.

Anne Demagny echoed this warning in September 1994:

EFL teachers should be aware of what they are letting themselves in for when they sign a contract with the Turkish Ministry of Education. I found that it was no guarantee against bad treatment. On the contrary it can turn you into a prisoner since that contract cannot be broken whatever grievances you may have with the employer.

Among the main indigenous language teaching organisations in Turkey are:

English Fast, Altiyol, Yogurtcu Sukru Sokak 29, Kadikoy, Istanbul (1-338 9100). Employ about 100 native speakers in their five branches in Istanbul and one each in Ankara and Izmir. Offer an in-house training course from £500.

Kent English, Mithatpasa Caddesi No. 46, Kat. 3, Kizilay, Ankara (4-434 3833).

English Centre, Rumeli Caddesi 92/4, Zeki Bey Apt., Osmanbey, Istanbul (1-247 0983). Has branches in Ankara and Izmir.

Although Istanbul is not the capital, it is the commercial, financial and cultural centre of Turkey, so this is where most of the EFL teaching goes on. On the negative side, there may be more competition from other travelling teachers here and also in Izmir than in Ankara or less obvious cities like Mersin and Diyarbakir. Although the services of the Teachers' Centre at the British Council

(Ors Turistik Is Merkezi, Istiklal Cad. 251/253, Kat. 2-6, Beyoglu, 80060 Istanbul) are intended primarily for local Turkish teachers, they can give you a computerised list of private language schools and *lises* in Istanbul.

Without a TEFL certificate it will not be possible to get the work permit and virtually impossible to get a residence permit unless you can prove that you have sufficient funding from outside Turkey. Those who enter the country on tourist visas (which cost £5 in cash but not in coins at the border) and then find work, must leave the country every three months (normally across the border to Greece, though a trip to one of the Greek islands like Rhodes or to Northern Cyprus is more pleasant). If you do this too many times the border officials may well become suspicious.

For short-term opportunities, the youth exchange organisation Genctur (Yerebatan Cad. 15/3, Sultanahmet, 34410 Istanbul; 2-520 5274) organises summer camps for children where English is taught by native speakers who work for four hours a day in exchange for free board and lodging. Applicants must have some experience of working with children.

The Schools Unit of the Central Bureau for Educational Visits & Exchanges places teachers and sixth formers on three-week summer language camps in Turkey. Participants help with English teaching and social activities, drama, music, sports and crafts. All expenses are paid except air fares.

Childcare

The Solihull Au Pair Agency (1565 Stratford Road, Hall Green, Birmingham B28 9JA; 0121-733 6444/fax 733 6555) offers live-in jobs for one full year or for the summer. Jobs in Istanbul normally involve teaching English. On the year-long programme au pairs receive £30 a week pocket money plus a bonus of £1,000 paid in two instalments. On the summer programme (which is open to people as young as 16), au pairs receive £15 a week plus a bonus of £200 if the contract (June to September) is honoured. Summer au pairs normally spend most of the summer on holiday with the family (even outside Turkey).

The Dogan International Organization (Au Pair & Employment Agency, Sehitmuhtar Caddesi 37/7, Taksim, 80090 Istanbul; 2-235 1599) places English-speaking au pairs, preferably ones who are already in Istanbul. The pocket money is $50 a week for au pairs and $100 for au pairs plus (the latter work 10-15 hours more a week). Two UK agencies to try for au pair positions in Turkey are Tarooki Au Pairs, 1 Turnpike Close, Darlington, Co. Durham DL1 3SH and Anglo Pair Agency, 40 Wavertree Road, Streatham Hill, London SW2 3SP.

But it is possible to earn far more than pocket money. English-speaking nannies are all the rage among the wealthy of Istanbul and to a lesser extent Ankara. For example the Anglo Pair Agency promises qualified nannies a weekly wage of £150-250.

All of this sounds very rosy, though the reality can be different. Having tired of low paid washing up jobs in London, Sonia Douglas from Australia answered an advert in *TNT* placed by an agency run by a Turkish woman which specialises in handling families in Turkey: Anglo Nannies London, 20 Beverley Avenue, London SW20 0RL; 0181-944 6677. She was on a plane to Istanbul the following Wednesday to take up a live-in nanny job paying £250 a week:

> *Firstly I must say that I will never marry for money. I seem to be regarded as an English-speaking toy for the wealthy offspring and have had to get used to a complete lack of freedom and independence. Basically you are paid to talk English and play with the children. I've had to overcome my initial shock at the degree to which the children are spoilt and babied, but I've learned to bite my tongue. It is exhausting, trying and a phenomenal test of your durability.*

*But of course there is a brighter side. Since I've been in Istanbul I've had
a soft comfortable bed, an abundance of Turkish food, summer days spent
splashing in the pool, various outings and even a sailing holiday in Bodrum
without spending a single Turkish lira. The potential to save is astounding.
There's a magic about Istanbul. I've fallen for this city, but I value my
freedom also. What a dilemma.*

Sonia's high salary (equivalent to a general manager's salary in Turkey) is due
to her qualification as a primary school teacher, but apparently there were
nannies earning £200 a week whose only qualification was that they were native
English speakers.

One persistent problem is that it is generally not acceptable for young women
to go out alone in the evenings. But Turkish families are normally very generous
and allow the au pairs to share in family life on equal terms, even in their free time.

Tourism

The main Aegean resorts of Marmaris, Kusadasi and Bodrum absorb a large
number of foreign travellers as workers. Other places firmly on the travellers'
trail like Goreme in Cappadocia are also promising; Heather McCulloch received
three separate job offers in Goreme for the season after her visit, two in hostels
and one in a copper shop. 'Help Wanted' signs can sometimes be seen in the
windows of bars, carpet shops, etc. As elsewhere proprietors aim to use native
English speakers to attract more customers to buy their souvenirs or stay at their
hotels. In the majority of cases, this sort of work finds you once you make
known your willingness to undertake such jobs.

Major Turkish yachting resorts are excellent places to look for work, not just
related to boats but in hotels, bars, shops and excursions. (See section on Cyprus
for information about Northern Cyprus.) A good time to check harbourside
notice boards and to ask captains if they need anyone to clean or repair their
boats is in the lead-up to the summer season and the Marmaris Boat Show in
May. Laura O'Connor describes what she found in Marmaris:

*There's a large British community living there, retired and fed-up Brits who
have sold their houses, bought a boat and are whooping it up. There's plenty
of work opportunities in the Marina, especially for boat painting and
varnishing in April. Also girls can do hostessing on the boats. I was cleaning
boats with a friend for enough money to cover my accommodation and
evenings in the pub. Just walk around the Marina and ask.*

Laura recommends asking for advice at two English-style establishments: the
Scorpion Bar and The English Pub. She eventually found a waitressing job at
the Planet Disco in the Marmaris Palace Hotel in the neighbouring beach of
Ichmeler, popular with German tourists.

Xuela Edwards is another recent traveller who found many opportunities in
Marmaris but points out the down side:

*Affordable accommodation is hard to find and wages are appalling. The
Turkish work ethic can be difficult to handle too. Most Turkish businesses
stay open from 10am to midnight, and much later for bars and clubs. You
might not actually be doing anything but those are the hours. Turks have
said to us that the English are strange because they always want to leave
as soon as their hours are up and they want a day off. This is alien to the
Turkish mentality which regards the office or shop as an extension of the
home. Many other travellers we met also found the hanging around element
frustrating.*

*Paying and accepting commissions is the traditional way of doing business
and not regarded as ripping off the punter because these commissions are*

built into the basic price of everything. Therefore it is possible for talented salesmen/women (preferably multilingual) to make good money in Turkey.

Ian McArthur decided it would be an advantage while travelling in Turkey to be musical:

There is a great demand for musicians, particularly guitarists, in places where the 'Marlboro, Levis and Coca Cola generation' predominates. I have travelled around with my friend Vanessa and she has found work playing in bars in Istanbul, Marmaris, Olu Deniz and Patara (near Kas). Marmaris was the goldmine — £30 a night. The problem was that we both hated Marmaris — too many bloody tourists! In Patara she got a job in a bar called the Lazy Frog and played for a place to stay, food and of course beer.

Some UK tour operators hire people for Turkey. Sunsail Ltd (The Port House, Port Solent, Portsmouth, Hants. PO6 4TH; 01705 219847) has many openings for skippers, hostesses, mechanics/bosuns, dinghy sailors, cooks, bar staff and nannies to work in the watersports centres at Yedi Buku near Bodrum, Perili near Datca and an addition club at Marmaris. Try also Mark Warner (see introductory chapter *Tourism*).

Voluntary Work

The youth travel bureau of Turkey is called Genctur (Yerebatan Caddesi 15/3, Sultanahmet, 34410 Istanbul; 2-520 5274). Workcamps are among its range of activities, and recruitment takes place through all the major workcamp organisations in the UK and worldwide. The Genctur fee payable on arrival at the compulsory orientation in Istanbul is 100 Deutsch Marks.

On most camps you will have to work reasonably hard in the hot sun (and wear long sleeves and jeans in deference to Muslim customs). Mary Jelliffe recounts her experiences in Turkey:

I applied to UNA (Wales) quite late (in May/June) and heard from Turkey just one week before my camp commenced in August. My workcamp, which consisted of digging an irrigation canal from the nearby hills to the village, took place in Central Anatolia. I was told that our camp was the most easterly, since the majority are in Western Turkey.

Conditions in this remote village were fairly primitive. We lived in a half-built school-room sleeping on the floor and sharing the daily duties of collecting water and sweeping out the scorpions from under the sleeping bags. The Turkish volunteers were a great asset to the camp: through them we could have far more contact with the villagers and learn more about Turkish culture in general. In fact I later stayed in Istanbul and Izmir with two of the women volunteers I'd met on the camp.

Another workcamp organisation operates on a smaller scale: GSM Youth Activities Services (Yüksel Caddesi 44/6, 06420 Kizilay, Ankara; 312-433 22 00) places volunteers on two-week workcamps throughout the country June to October. Camps are run in cooperation with local councils. Volunteers are involved in conservation, archaeology, festival organisation, etc. The registration fee is £70. For details send an IRC to GSM.

In Extremis

The best protection against getting into serious difficulties is to have a good insurance policy (see *Introduction*). Some student cards include access to an emergency helpline. For example the Under 26 card (part of a Europe-wide network of youth cards known as Euro 26) includes among its benefits a 'Travel Helpline' telephone number that can answer specific queries and offer advice (legal, financial, etc.) in a crisis abroad. This costs £6 and does not in any way replace the need for insurance. Details from Under 26, 52 Grosvenor Gardens, London SW1W 0AG (0171-823 5363). The counterpart for Americans under 26 is the CIEE Youth Card (ring 800-GET-AN-ID) which costs $16 a year and provides minimal insurance cover (including medical evacuation). US citizens might investigate the Traveler's Emergency Network (800-275-4836) which provides 24-hour emergency medical help, prescription delivery, legal assistance, air evacuation and other services for $30 a year.

If you do end up in dire financial straits and for some reason do not have or cannot use a credit card, you should contact someone at home who is in a position to send money.

Transferring Money

If you run out of money abroad, whether through mismanagement, loss or theft, you may contact your bank back home (by telephone, fax or telegram), and ask them to telegraph some money to you. This can only be done through a bank in the town you're in — something you have to arrange with your own bank, so you know where to pick the money up. Western Union, a long-established American company, offers an international money transfer service whereby cash deposited at one branch (by, say, your mum) can be withdrawn by you from any other branch or agency, which your benefactor need not specify. Western Union agents come in all shapes and sizes, e.g. travel agencies, stationers, chemists, etc.). Unfortunately it is not well represented outside the developed world. The person sending money to you simply turns up at a Western Union counter, pays in the desired sum plus the fee, which is £8 for up to £25 transferred, £12 for £25-50, £21 for £100-200 and so on. Ring 0800-833833 for further details, a list of outlets and a complete rate schedule.

Thomas Cook offers a similar service. Cash deposited at one of their foreign exchange counters can be telexed to a named branch of Thomas Cook where it can be collected. The claim is that the money will arrive between 24 and 48 hours later, though this is optimistic in many cases. The minimum fee is £25 for sums of up to £1,000.

Barclaycard holders are entitled to make use of their 24-hour International Rescue service which covers a myriad of disasters including theft of money, tickets and cards, legal problems and medical emergencies. US citizens can ring the Overseas Citizen Service (202-647-5225), part of the State Department, which can wire cash from someone at home to any US embassy for a modest fee of $15.

One way of getting money which will not inconvenience the folks back home works best for those who know in advance where they will be when they run out of money. Before setting off, you open an account at a large bank in your destination city, which may have a branch in London. Most won't allow you to open a chequing account so instant overdrafts are not a possibility. But knowing you have £100 or £200 waiting for you in Sydney, San Francisco or Singapore is a great morale booster.

Embassies & Consulates

Your consulate can help you get in touch with friends and relations if necessary, normally by arranging a reverse charge call. According to the Foreign Office leaflet *Get it Right Before You Go,* Consulates have the authority to cash a personal cheque to the value of £100 supported by a valid banker's card, even if your cheque book has been stolen. But do not pin too much faith in your consulate. When Jane Roberts turned to the British Consulate in Toronto after having all her money stolen, they just preached at her about how she should have thought about all this before she left home.

If you are really desperate and can find no one at home or among your fellow travellers willing to lend you some money, you may ask your consulate to repatriate you by putting you on the first train or airplane heading for your home destination. If they do this your passport will be invalidated until the money is repaid. In fact permission is very rarely granted these days because of the thousands of unpaid debts incurred by indigent travellers; for example there were 83 repatriations to the UK in total last year. A British consular official advised us that in the 18 months she worked in India, only two repatriations were approved, despite the queues of desperate people. Deportation is another way of getting home which is best avoided. Although you will be transported at the expense of the government which has decided that you are an undesirable alien, there will be a black mark in your passport for several years.

Legal Problems

Everyone has heard hair-raising stories about conditions in foreign prisons, so think very carefully before engaging in illegal activities. If you do have trouble with the law in foreign countries, remain calm and polite, and demand an immediate visit from your Consul. He can at least recommend a local lawyer and interpreter if necessary. Britons should contact Prisoners Abroad (72-82 Rosebery Avenue, London EC1R 4RR; 0171-833 3467) and Americans should try the International Legal Defence Counsel (111 South 15th St, 24th Floor, Philadelphia, Pennsylvania 19102; 215-564-2859). Any travellers who would like to visit prisoners should contact these organisations for details, since many prisoners go years without a single visit.

Dire Straits

To avoid global danger spots in advance of travelling, contact the Foreign Office Advice Line on 0171-270 4129 or in the US the State Department's Hotline on 202-647-5225. To avoid being cheated, conned or robbed, you will have to proceed cautiously and even suspiciously, especially in places like Bangkok (which Vaughan Temby has dubbed Scam City).

Try not to be too downcast if destitution strikes. Elma Grey had been looking forward to leaving Greece and rejoining her old kibbutz, but she was unexpectedly turned away from the ferry because of her dire shortage of funds. She describes the 'worst down' of her travels:

Back to the Athens hotel where I'd spent the previous evening, feeling utter despair. But I found that other people's problems have an incredible way of bringing out the best in total strangers. Everyone I came into contact with was full of sympathy, advice and practical suggestions regarding possible sources of work. And quite apart from this, the feeling of much needed moral support was probably what got me through the whole thing without my degenerating into a miserable heap. Although I'd never want to feel so stranded and desperate again, in a way it was all worth it just to experience the unique feeling of just how good fellow travellers can be in a crisis.

Several travellers have insisted that when you get down to your last few dollars/pesos/marks, it is much wiser to spend them in a pub buying drinks for the locals who might then offer useful assistance than it is to spend the money on accommodation or food. David Irvine found himself in Tasmania with just $10 in his pocket. He walked into a pub and bet two men $20 each that he could drink a yard of ale, a feat he was fairly confident that he could accomplish.

Less than 24 hours after Ilka Cave from South Africa arrived in Tel Aviv, all her luggage, money and documents were stolen. One of the girls in the hostel suggested that she contact an au pair agency and soon she was living with a nice family and earning a salary. Michel Falardeau wanted to live rent-free in Sydney, so he offered his assistance to a number of charities, one of which gave him a place to live. Mark Horobin was down to his bottom dollar in San Diego and queued up outside the Rescue Mission. Several days later he had signed on as a kitchen helper and stayed for some time.

It is to be hoped that you will avoid the kind of disaster which will require the services of a lawyer, doctor or consul abroad. If you find yourself merely running short of funds, you might be interested in some of the following titbits of information, intended for entertainment as much as for practical advice.

HELP. Look out for churches that conduct services in English: the priest or vicar should be able to give you useful advice and often practical help. But be cautious about accepting help from fringe religious groups — it can be easier to accept shelter from the Moonies or the Children of God than to leave.

SOB STORIES. If you have incurred some small debt, you may be able to talk your way out of it. On several occasions David Bamford's account of being mugged was received very sympathetically, once at a police station in Holland where he was fed and a night's free bed and breakfast was arranged. Another penniless student (in Sweden) obtained a police statement that he had been robbed, which he used to wheedle money out of people. Abusing people's kindness is, however, not generally recommended.

NIGHT SHELTERS. Most large towns and some railway stations in Western Europe and North America have a night shelter run by the Salvation Army or Jesuits which provide basic but free food and accommodation. They want to help genuine vagrants, not freeloading tourists, so you must appear genuinely impoverished or a potential convert. You can find out where to find these hostels by asking around — any policeman on the night beat should be able to help you. Be warned that many of these organisations are run by religious movements, and you may be expected to show your gratitude by joining in worship.

MONASTERIES & NUNNERIES. Monastic communities often extend hospitality to indigent wayfarers. Sometimes it is freely given but try to be sensitive as to whether or not a small donation is expected.

JAIL. Travellers in Britain and America have on occasion found a free bed for the night by asking at police stations if there are any spare cells. You are most likely to be successful in peaceful country towns: the police may have other uses for their cells on a Saturday night in Glasgow.

SLEEPING OUT. It is illegal to sleep out on private property without the landowner's permission (except in Sweden); most farmers will grant their permission if you ask politely and look trustworthy. In cities try public parks and also railway or coach stations, though you may be asked for an onward ticket. Nicola Hall tries to camp discreetly near a proper campsite so that she can make use of the toilet and shower block. Ian Moody tried to avoid sleeping out on private property in Spain and one night chose a seemingly ideal shelter, a concrete covered ditch. At about 5am he was rudely awakened by a torrent of water which swept away his gear and nearly drowned him. Many people sleep on beaches; beware of early morning visits from the local constabulary and also large vacuum machines. Jonathan Galpin finds a mosquito net invaluable, not only as protection against biting insects but (when doubled over) from falling dew.

SQUATTING. Half-finished buildings usually provide enough shelter for a comfortable, uninterrupted kip. Your luggage can be safely stowed in a locker at the station during the day.

FREE MEALS. Hare Krishna have free or heavily subsidised vegetarian restaurants and take-away temples in every major city from Mexico City to Manchester. You may have to endure some minor attempts to convert you. Their food is excellent. Sometimes charities such as the Red Cross give out free food, as David Bamford discovered when he was stranded in Villefranche unable to find a grape-picking job, along with scores of North Africans.

Restaurants may be willing to give you a free meal if you promise to recommend them to a guide book. It may also be possible to do an hour's work in exchange for a meal by going to the back door, possibly at fast food outlets. Some will even give a hand-out if you are brazen enough to request one. When Safra Wightman had no money and no food in Tel Aviv, she offered to give the man at a sandwich stand a ring as security against future payment of two rolls. When she returned with the money to reclaim her ring she could see that the stone had been removed to find out if it was valuable (which it wasn't), so only trade something valueless.

BUFFET RESTAURANTS. In some countries like Sweden, the USA and Australia, reasonable restaurants offer all-you-can-eat buffets. Diners have been known to share their second and third helpings with friends who have merely bought a soft drink.

FREE WINE. You may come across free tastings at the roadside in wine producing areas from California to France (where these tastings are called *dégustations).* There will sometimes be something to eat — perhaps bread and cheese, or a local speciality such as nougat in Montelimar.

FACTORY TOURS. Ask tourist offices if there are any food or drink factories nearby that offer free guided tours; these tours normally end with the gift of free samples of whatever is being produced. For example, distilleries in Scotland hand out miniature bottles of whisky, and Kelloggs in North America provide a selection of miniature packets of cereal. Breweries are famous for their hospitality — try Heineken in Amsterdam, Guinness in Dublin, or Castlemaine XXXX in Brisbane.

FREE SAMPLES. Look out for demonstrations promoting new foods or gadgets in supermarkets and department stores. This was another of Safra Wightman's survival tips in Israel:

In supermarkets it's acceptable to taste the pick'n'mix ranges from dried fruit and nuts to chocolate, sweets, olives, pretzels, etc. On several occasions my boyfriend and I stood for ten minutes 'tasting' then bought two apples on our way out. Everybody including Israelis does the same.

HAPPY HOURS. To attract customers at off-peak times, bars and pubs sometimes offer free snacks as well as cut-price drinks.

SCAVENGING FOOD. If you are not too fussy about what you eat you can look for stale or sub-standard food that has been discarded by shops, market stalls or even restaurants. This is especially worth doing around supermarkets in America, where a large quantity of perfectly acceptable food is rejected simply because it has reached the 'sell by' date stamped on it. Fancy resort hotels are also prone to throw out good food on a regular basis. Julian Peachey and many others camping at Eilat dined like kings out of the Club Med skips. While no one he knew suffered any ill effects, the residents of a local 4-star hotel all came down with salmonella.

SELF SERVICE RESTAURANTS. The publisher of this book had an odd experience in a huge New York self-service restaurant. Having eaten his Waldorf salad he went to the water fountain for a drink. On returning to his table to conclude his repast he found a tramp-like character busily wolfing down the much anticipated apple pie: the unwanted guest promptly fled. On leaving the self-service emporium the victim spotted the culprit peering through the plate glass window with several pals, in search of customers who left their tables leaving uneaten remains still on the table.

BEGGING. Straightforward begging is normally humiliating, boring, unprofitable and illegal. The best way of achieving results is to make yourself so unbearable that people will pay you to go away — for example, two people impersonating a lunatic and his keeper around the cafés of Paris, would be soon bribed to go away by pleasure-seeking Parisians and tourists.

BEACHCOMBING. Beaches are a good place to look for lost property. After a storm in Greece, Sarah Clifford went beachcombing and found a gold necklace worth £150. A metal detector can be a valuable ally.

CLAIMING DEPOSITS. In France, Spain, Italy, Sweden, Australia, the US and many other countries you can earn some small change by taking wine, beer and coke bottles or aluminium cans for recycling back to shops for a refund of the deposit. It is best to look for bottles or cans after a beach party, a special event such as a festival or in the dustbins outside holiday villas, etc.

PUBLIC TELEPHONES. In Austria, Spain and many other countries you have to insert money in a telephone before you dial a number, you then have to press a button to get a refund if you are not connected. It is always worth pressing this button when you pass a call box in case someone has forgotten to do this — the banks of telephones in railways stations are particularly recommended.

RECLAIMING PURCHASE TAX. Some large shops in Britain, Denmark, Switzerland, Finland and Italy have special arrangements which allow foreigners to reclaim local purchase tax on goods which they plan to take out of the country. You can profit from this by looking for a local who is considering an expensive and portable purchase such as a video recorder: arrange to buy it for him and reclaim the tax, then split the difference in price. When you buy the recorder you will be given a form to be stamped by the customs when you take it out of the country. Get this stamp, wait for the shift to change, and then re-import the recorder.

BOOKS OF TICKETS. You can buy a *carnet* of ten Metro tickets in Paris at two-thirds the price of buying the tickets singly, then sell the individual tickets to travellers, splitting the difference in cost. You may even get the full face value from busy commuters who don't want to queue for tickets at rush hour. Another trick is to buy group tickets for cable car rides in Switzerland at a substantial discount on the price of buying the tickets individually. For example the journey up Mount Titlis in Engelberg, Switzerland costs about SFr340 for a single traveller compared to half the price at the group rate. You can then sell these tickets separately to individual travellers at less than the full rate. This has a better chance of success than selling single Metro tickets, since people will want to travel only once.

POSTCARDS. Tourists on beaches and in bars are often happy to pay over the odds for properly pre-stamped postcards and a pen with which to write them.

TRICKS AND SKILLS. If you know that you can drink a yard of ale, juggle four plates or smoke 27 cigars simultaneously, you might find people willing to have a sporting bet with you. For more ideas on this subject see the section on Gambling in *Enterprise*. We have heard of a traveller who erected a sign on the pavements 'Jokes — 25 Cents Each'.

MEDICAL RESEARCH. Teaching hospitals may have research clinics where new drugs and techniques are tested. Many research projects pay their volunteers very well, since in many cases they are funded by large pharmaceutical companies. Recruitment tends to take place by word of mouth in universities, especially among medical students and their friends, but there is no harm in enquiring at hospitals and drug companies. You might also enquire at university psychology departments, where there may be a need for participants for perception tests, etc. No work permits necessary; only proof of human life.

SELLING RETURN TICKETS. Ask a travel agent if it is possible to get a refund on the return part of your air or train ticket, then travel home by a cheaper method — perhaps by coach, or hitch-hiking.

SELLING BELONGINGS. By the end of your trip many of your belongings may have become expendable. You can try selling them to fellow travellers in hostels, to second-hand shops, or even to passing shoppers if you set yourself up on the edge of a market. Be ruthless about what you do and do not need: you have taken your photos, so you don't need your camera, and you can transfer your belongings from your expensive backpack to a cheaper bag. Be prepared to spend some time haggling.

If you are willing to consider selling some of your more intimate belongings, i.e. parts of your body, you may wish to acquire a copy of an American book published in 1992: *Sell Yourself to Science — The Complete Guide to Selling Your Organs, Body Fluids, Bodily Functions and Being a Human Guinea Pig* by Jim Hogshire (published by Loompanics at $16.95).

THE LAST RESORT. Sell this book — but memorise the contents first! Better still, take a couple of spare copies as recommended by Kevin Boyd:
I have met so many other travellers who would have sold their mother into slavery for my copy of your book! You should recommend that people take as many copies as they can.

Travellers' Itineraries

Heather McCulloch's Adventures

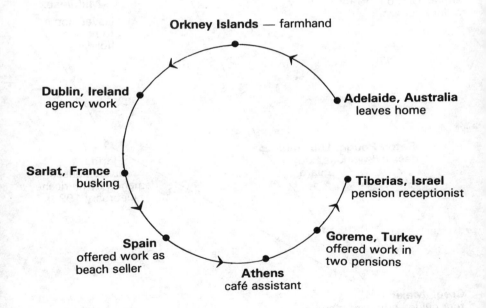

Orkney Islands — farmhand

Dublin, Ireland
agency work

Adelaide, Australia
leaves home

Sarlat, France
busking

Tiberias, Israel
pension receptionist

Spain
offered work as
beach seller

Goreme, Turkey
offered work in
two pensions

Athens
café assistant

502

Paul Donut's Trip around the Americas

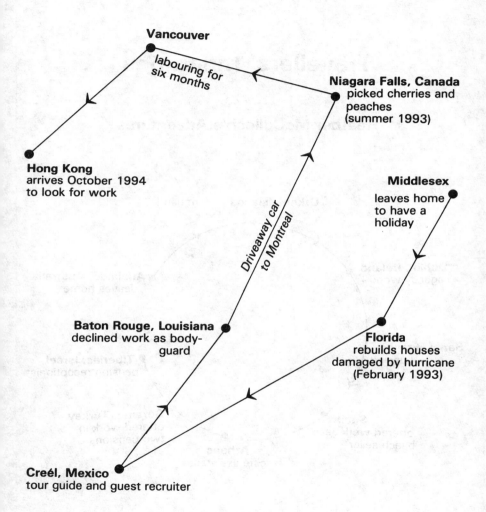

Vancouver
labouring for six months

Niagara Falls, Canada
picked cherries and peaches (summer 1993)

Hong Kong
arrives October 1994 to look for work

Middlesex
leaves home to have a holiday

Driveaway car to Montreal

Baton Rouge, Louisiana
declined work as bodyguard

Florida
rebuilds houses damaged by hurricane (February 1993)

Creél, Mexico
tour guide and guest recruiter

Nicola Sarjeant's Route around Europe

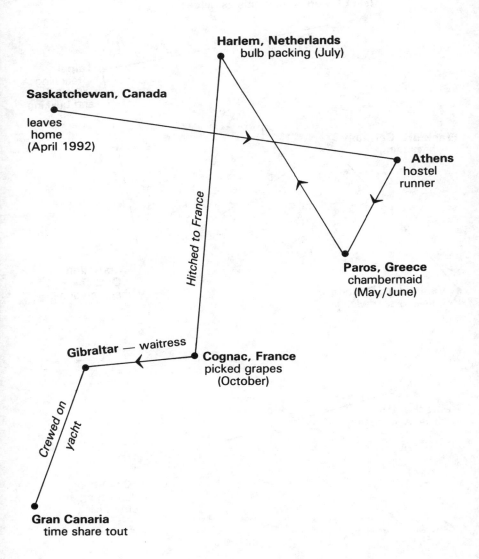

Harlem, Netherlands
bulb packing (July)

Saskatchewan, Canada

leaves
home
(April 1992)

Athens
hostel
runner

Hitched to France

Paros, Greece
chambermaid
(May/June)

Gibraltar — waitress

Cognac, France
picked grapes
(October)

*Crewed on
yacht*

Gran Canaria
time share tout

David & Greeba Hughes' Tireless Travels

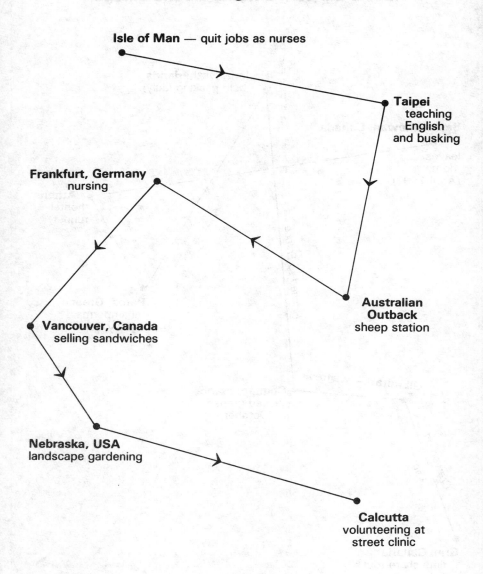

Isle of Man — quit jobs as nurses

Taipei
teaching
English
and busking

Frankfurt, Germany
nursing

**Australian
Outback**
sheep station

Vancouver, Canada
selling sandwiches

Nebraska, USA
landscape gardening

Calcutta
volunteering at
street clinic

Some Useful Phrases

English: Do you need a helper/temporary assistant?
French: Avez-vous besoin d'un aide/assistant intérimaire?
German: Brauchen Sie eine Hilfe/einen Assistenten für eine begenzte Zeit?
Dutch: Kunt U een helper/tijdelijke assistent gebruiken?
Spanish: Necesita usted un ayudante/asistente interino?
Italian: Ha bisogno d'un aiutante/d'un assistente provvisorio?
Greek: Khryázeste kanénan ypálliyo/prosorynó voythó?

GB: Do you know if there is any work in the neighbourhood?
F: Savez-vous s'il y a du travail dans les environs?
D: Wissen Sie, ob es in der Nachbarschaft irgendwelche Arbeit gibt?
NL: Weet U er werk is in de buurt?
S: Sabe usted si hay trabajo por aqui?
I: Lo sa si c'e lavoro nel vicinato?
GR: Xérete an ypárkhy dhoulyá styn peryokhý?

GB: Where is the employment office?
F: Ôu se trouve le bureau de placement?
D: Wo ist das Arbeitsamt?
NL: Waar is het kantoor voor arbeidsvoorziening?
S: Donde esta la Oficina de Empleos?
I: Dove sta l'agenzia di collocamento?
GR: Poú ýno to grafyó (evreśeos) ergasyás?

GB: What is the wage? Will it be taxed?
F: Quel est le salaire? Sera-t-il imposable?
D: Wie hoch ist der Lohn? Ist er steuerpflichtig?
NL: Hoe hoog is het loon? Is het belastbaar?
S: Cuanto es el salario? Esta sujeto al pago de impuestos?
I: Che e la paga? Sara tassata?
GR: Poso ýne to ymeromyśthyo? Tha forologhiyhý?

GB: Where can I stay? Will there be a charge for accommodation/food?
F: Ôu pourrais-je me loger? L'hébergement/les repas seront-ils payants?
D: Wo kann ich wohnen? Muss für Unterkunft und Verpflegung selb gezahlt werden?
NL: Waar kan ik onderdak vinden? Moet ik betalen voor huisvesting en maaltijden?
S: Donde puedo alojar? Hay que pagar por el alojamiento/la comida?
I: Dove posso stare? Avra una spesa per l'alloggio/il cibo?
GR: Pou boró na mýno? Tha khreothó ya ty dhyamoný/to fagytó

GB: Are there any cooking/washing facilities?
F: Est-ce qu'il y a des aménagements pour faire la cuisine/la lessive?
D: Gibt es Koch/Waschgelegenheiten?
NL: Is er kook/wasgelegenheid?
S: Se puede cocinar/lavar la ropa?
I: Ci stanno dei mezzi per cucinare/lavorare?

GR: Ypárkhoun efkolyés ya magýrema/plyśymo?

GB: When will the harvest/job begin? How long will it last?
F: Quand commencera la moisson/le travail? Combien de temps dure-t-il?
D: Wann beginnt die Ernte/Arbeit? Wie lange wird sie dauren?
NL: Wanneer begint de oogst/job? Hoe lang zal het werk duren?
S: Cuando comenzara la cosecha/el trabajo? Cuanto durara?
I: Quando incomincia la messe/il lavoro? Per quanto tempo durera?
GR: Poté tharkhyśy o theryzmos/y dhoulyá? Pośo tha dhyarkeśy?

GB: What will be the hours of work?
F: Quelles seront les heures de travail?
D: Wie lange ist die Arbeitszeit?
NL: Wat zijn de werkuren?
S: Cual sera el horario de trabajo?
I: Che saranno le ore del lavoro?
GR: Pyéz tha ýne y órez ergasyás?

GB: Thank you for your help.
F: Merci de votre aide.
D: Danke für Ihre Hilfe.
NL: Dank U voor Uw hulp.
S: Gracias por su ayuda.
GR: Sas efkharystó ya tyn voýthyá sas.

Currency Conversion Chart

COUNTRY	£1	US$1
Australia	A$2.08	A$1.34
Austria	16.8 schillings	10.8 schillings
Belgium/Luxembourg	49 francs	32 francs
Brazil	1.35 real cruzeiro	0.87 real cruzeiro
Canada	C$2.12	C$1.37
Chile	646 peso	416 peso
China	13.25 renminbi yuan	8.5 renminbi yuan
Cyprus	0.73 Cypriot pound	0.47 Cypriot pound
Czech Republic	43.2 koruna	27.9 koruna
Denmark	9.5 krone	6.1 krone
Egypt	5.25 Egyptian pound	3.4 Egyptian pound
Finland	7.76 markka	5 markka
France	8.2 franc	5.3 franc
Germany	2.4 Deutsch mark	1.54 Deutsch mark
Greece	364 drachma	235 drachma
Hong Kong	12 HK dollar	7.7 HK dollar
Hungary	165 forint	106 forint
Iceland	105 krona	68 krona
India	48.6 rupee	31.4 rupee
Indonesia	3,380 rupiah	2,180 rupiah
Ireland	1.01 punt	0.65 punt
Israel	4.68 shekel	3.02 shekel
Italy	2,437 lira	1,572 lira
Japan	154 yen	99 yen
Kenya	80 shilling	51.5 shilling
Korea	1,241 won	800 won
Malta	0.57 Maltese lira	0.37 Maltese lira
Mexico	5.28 peso	3.4 peso
Morocco	13.7 dirham	8.85 dirham
Nepal	76 rupee	49 rupee
Netherlands	2.68 guilder	1.73 guilder
New Zealand	NZ$2.57	NZ$1.65
Norway	10.5 krone	6.8 krone
Peru	3.5 new sol	2.3 new sol
Poland	35,700 złoty	23,020 złoty
Portugal	244 escudo	157 escudo
Russia (market rate)	3,500 rouble	2,250 rouble
Singapore	2.32 Singapore dollar	1.49 Singapore dollar
Slovak Republic	48.3 koruna	31.1 koruna
South Africa	5.5 rand	3.56 rand
Spain	199 peseta	128 peseta
Sweden	11.7 krona	7.56 krona
Switzerland	2 franc	1.29 franc
Taiwan	40.6 Taiwan dollar	26 Taiwan dollar
Thailand	38.7 baht	25 baht
Turkey	52,660 lira	34,000 lira
USA	1.55 dollar	—
Venezuela	263 bolivar	170 bolivar
Zimbabwe	12.6 Zimbabwe dollar	8.2 Zimbabwe dollar

Embassies/Consulates

AUSTRALIA: Australia House, The Strand, London WC2B 4LA (0171-379 4334). 1601 Massachusetts Ave NW, Washington DC 20036-2273 (202-797-3000).

AUSTRIA: 18 Belgrave Mews West, London SW1X 8HU (0171-235 3731). 3524 International Court NW, Washington DC 20008 (202-895-6700).

BELGIUM: 103-105 Eaton Square, London SW1W 9AB (0171-235 5422). 3330 Garfield St NW, Washington DC 20008 (202-333-6900).

BRAZIL: Consular Section, 6 St. Alban's St, London SW1Y 4SG (0171-930 9055). 3006 Massachusetts Ave NW, Washington DC 20008 (202-745-2700).

CANADA: 38 Grosvenor St, London W1X 0AA, (0171-258 6601). 501 Pennsylvania Ave, Washington DC 20001 (202-682-1740).

CHILE: 12 Devonshire St, London W1N 2DS (0171-580 1023). 1732 Massachusetts Ave NW, Washington DC 20036 (202-785-1746).

CHINA: 31 Portland Place, London W1N 3AG (0171-636 1835). 2300 Connecticut Ave NW, Washington DC 20008 (202-328-2500).

CZECH REPUBLIC: 26-30 Kensington Palace Gardens, London W8 4QY (0171-727 4918). 3900 Linnean Ave NW, Washington DC 20008 (202-363-6315/6).

DENMARK: 55 Sloane St, London SW1X 9SR (0171-235 1255). 3200 White Haven St NW, Washington DC 20008 (202-234-4300).

EGYPT: 2 Lowndes St, London SW1X 9ET (0171-235 9719). 2310 Decatur Place NW, Washington DC 20008 (202-232-5400).

ESTONIA: 18 Chepstow Villas, London W11 2RB (0171-229 6700).

FINLAND: 38 Chesham Place, London SW1X 8HW (0171-235 9531). 3216 New Mexico Ave NW, Washington DC 20016 (202-363-2430).

FRANCE: 21 Cromwell Road, London SW7 2DQ (0171-838 2000). 4101 Reservoir Road NW, Washington DC 20007 (202-944-6000).

GERMANY: 23 Belgrave Square, London SW1X 8PZ (0171-235 5033). 4645 Reservoir Road NW, Washington DC 20007 (202-298-4000).

GREECE: 1A Holland Park, London W11 3TP (0171-221 6467; Labour Counsellor's Office 0171-221 6774). 2221 Massachusetts Ave NW, Washington DC 20008 (202-939-5800).

HONG KONG: 6 Grafton St, London W1X 3LB (0171-499 9821).

HUNGARY: 35b Eaton Place, London SW1X 8BY (0171-235 2664). 3910 Shoemaker St NW, Washington DC 20008 (202-362-6730).

ICELAND: 1 Eaton Terrace, London SW1W 8EY (0171-730 5131/2). 2022 Connecticut Ave NW, Washington DC 20008-6194 (202-265 6653).

INDIA: India House, Aldwych, London WC2B 4NA (0171-836 8484). 2107 Massachusetts Ave NW, Washington DC 20008-2811 (202-939-7000).

INDONESIA: 38 Grosvenor Square, London W1X 9AD (0171-499 7661). 2020 Massachusetts Ave NW, Washington DC 20036 (202-775-5200).

IRELAND: 17 Grosvenor Place, London SW1X 7HR (0171-235 2171). 2234 Massachusetts Ave NW, Washington DC 20008 (202-462-3939).

ISRAEL: 2 Palace Green, London W8 4QB (0171-957 9500). 3514 International Dr NW, Washington DC 20008-3099 (202-364-5500).

ITALY: 14 Three Kings Yard, Davies St, London W1Y 2EH (0171-629 8200). 1601 Fuller St NW, Washington DC 20009 (202-328-5500).

JAPAN: 101-104 Piccadilly, London W1V 9FN (0171-465 6500). 2520 Massachusetts Ave NW, Washington DC 20008 (202-939-6700).

KENYA: 45 Portland Place, London W1N 4AS (0171-636 2371). 2249 R St NW, Washington DC 20008 (202-387-6101).

KOREA: 4 Palace Gate, London W8 5NF (0171-581 0247). 2370 Massachusetts Ave NW, Washington DC 20008 (202-939-560).

LATVIA 72 Queensborough Terrace, London W2 3SP (0171-727 1698).

LUXEMBOURG: 27 Wilton Crescent, London SW1X 8SD (0171-235 6961). 2200 Massachusetts Ave NW, Washington DC 20008 (202-265-4171).

MALAYSIA: 45 Belgrave Square, London SW1X 8QT (0171-235 8033). 2401 Massachusetts Ave NW, Washington DC 20008 (202-328-2700).

MEXICO: 42 Hertford St, London W1Y 7TF (0171-499 8586). 1911 Pennsylvania Ave NW, Washington DC 20006 (202-728-1600).

MOROCCO: Diamond House, 97-99 Praed St, London W2 (0171-724 01719). 1601 21st St NW, Washington DC 20009 (202-462-7979).

NETHERLANDS: 38 Hyde Park Gate, London SW7 5DP (0171-584 5040). 4200 Linnean Ave NW, Washington DC 20008 (202-244-5300).

NEW ZEALAND: New Zealand House, Haymarket, London SW1Y 4TE (0171-930 8422). 37 Observatory Circle NW, Washington DC 20008 (202-328-4848).

NORWAY: 25 Belgrave Square, London SW1X 8QD (0171-235 7151). 2820 34th St NW, Washington DC 20008-2799 (202-333-6000).

PERU: 52 Sloane St, London SW1X 9SP (0171-235 1917). 1700 Massachusetts Ave NW, Washington DC 20036 (202-833-9860).

POLAND: 47 Portland Place, London W1N 3AG (0171-580 4324). 2640 16th St NW, Washington DC 20009 (202-234-3800/1/2).

PORTUGAL: Silver City House, 62 Brompton Road, London SW3 1BJ (0171-581 8722/4). 2125 Kalorama Road NW, Washington DC 20008 (202-328-8610).

RUSSIA: 5 Kensington Palace Gardens, London W8 4QS (0171-229 8027). 1125 16th St NW, Washington DC 20036 (202-628-7551).

SAUDI ARABIA: 30 Belgrave Square, London SW1X 8QB (0171-235 0303). 601 New Hampshire Ave NW, Washington DC 20037 (202-342-3800).

SINGAPORE: 9 Wilton Crescent, London SW1X 8SA (0171-235 8315). 1824 R St NW, Washington DC 20009 (202-667-7555).

SLOVAK REPUBLIC: 25 Kensington Palace Gardens, London W8 4QY (0171-243 0803). 3900 Linnean Ave NW, Washington DC 20008 (202-363-6315/6).

SOUTH AFRICA: Trafalgar Square, London WC2N 5DP (0171-930 4488). 3051 Massachusetts Ave NW, Washington DC 20008-3693 (202-232-4400).

SPAIN: 20 Draycott Place, London SW3 2SB (0171-581 5921). 2700 15th St NW, Washington DC 20009 (202-265-0190).

SWEDEN: 11 Montagu Place, London W1H 2AL (0171-724 6781). 600 New Hampshire Ave NW, 1200, Washington DC 20037-2462 (202-944-5600).

SWITZERLAND: 16/18 Montagu Place, London W1H 2BQ (0171-723 0701). 2900 Cathedral Ave NW, Washington DC 20008 (202-745-7900).

TAIWAN: 50 Grosvenor Gardens, London SW1 (0171-396 9152).

THAILAND: 29/30 Queen's Gate, London SW7 5JB (0171-589 0173). 2300 Kalorama Road NW, Washington DC 20008 (202-483-7200).

TURKEY: 43 Belgrave Square, London SW1X 8PA (0171-235 5252/3/4). 1714 Massachusetts Ave NW, Washington DC 20036 (202-659-8200).

UK: 3100 Massachusetts Ave NW, Washington DC 20008 (202-462-1340).

USA: 5 Upper Grosvenor St, London W1A 2JB (0171-499 7010).

ZIMBABWE: 429 Strand, London WC2R 0SA (0171-836 7755). 1608 New Hampshire Ave NW, Washington DC 20009 (202-332-7100).

See *The London Diplomatic List* published frequently by the Foreign & Commonwealth Office and held in most public libraries in Britain.

Key Organisations

British Council, English Language Information Service, Medlock St, Manchester M15 4PR (0161-957 7000); Central Management of Direct Teaching (CMDT), 10 Spring Gardens, London SW1A 2BN (0171-389 4931/fax 389 4140).

British Trust for Conservation Volunteers, 36 St. Mary's St, Wallingford, Oxfordshire OX10 0EU (01491 839766/fax 839646).

British Universities North America Club (BUNAC), 16 Bowling Green Lane, London EC1R 0BD (0171-251 3472/fax 251 0215).

Camp America, 37a Queen's Gate, London SW7 5HR (0171-581 7373/fax 581 7377).

Campus Travel, 52 Grosvenor Gardens, London SW1W 0AG (0171-730 3402).

Central Bureau for Educational Visits & Exchanges, Seymour Mews House, Seymour Mews, London W1H 9PE (0171-486 5101/fax 935 5741).

Christian Movement for Peace (CMP), 186 St. Paul's Road, Balsall Heath, Birmingham B12 8LZ (0121-446 5704/fax 446 4060).

Concordia Youth Service Volunteers, 8 Brunswick Place, Hove, East Sussex BN3 1ET (01273 772086).

Council on International Educational Exchange (CIEE), 205 East 42nd St, New York, NY 10017, USA (212-661-1414/fax 972-3231). London office: 33 Seymour Place, London W1H 6HT (0171-706 3008/fax 724 8468).

GAP Activity Projects, 44 Queen's Road, Reading, Berkshire RG1 4BB (01734 594914/fax 576634).

International Agricultural Exchange Association (IAEA), Young Farmers' Club Centre, National Agricultural Centre, Stoneleigh Park, Kenilworth, Warwickshire CV8 2LG (01203 696578/fax 696684).

International Association for the Exchange of Students for Technical Experience (IAESTE-UK), Seymour Mews House, Seymour Mews, London W1H 9PE (0171-725 9462/fax 935 1017).

International House, 106 Piccadilly, London W1 9FL (0171-491 2598/fax 495 0284).

International Voluntary Service (IVS), Old Hall, East Bergholt, Colchester, Essex CO7 6TQ (01206 298215/fax 299043) with branch offices in Northern England (Castlehill House, 21 Otley Road, Headingley, Leeds LS6 3AA (0113 230 4600) and Scotland (7 Upper Bow, Edinburgh EH1 2JN).

Jobs in the Alps, PO Box 388, London SW1X 8LX.

Kibbutz Representatives, 1A Accommodation Road, London NW11 8ED (0181-458 9235/fax 455 7930).

Peterson's Guides, 202 Carnegie Center, PO Box 2123, Princeton, NJ, 08543-2123, USA (1-800-225-0261).

Project 67, 10 Hatton Garden, London EC1N 8AH (0171-831 7626).

Royal Geographical Society, 1 Kensington Gore, London SW7 (0171-589 5466).

STA Travel, Telephone Sales, 74 Old Brompton Road, London SW7 3LH (0171-937 9962).

Student Services Australia, SWAP Department, PO Box 399, Carlton South, Vic 3053, Australia (03-348 1777/fax 347 8070).

Trailfinders, 42-50 Earls Court Road, London W8 6EJ (0171-938 3366 (longhaul) and 0171-937 5400 (Europe and transatlantic).

Vacation Work Publications, 9 Park End St, Oxford OX1 1HJ (01865 241978/fax 790885).

WWOOF (Working for Organic Growers), 19 Bradford Road, Lewes, Sussex BN7 1RB.

Youth Hostels Association, Trevelyan House, 8 St Stephen's Hill, St. Albans, Hertford-shire AL1 2DY (01727 840211). Also: 14 Southampton St, London WC2E 7HY (0171-836 1036 membership).

Key to Symbols

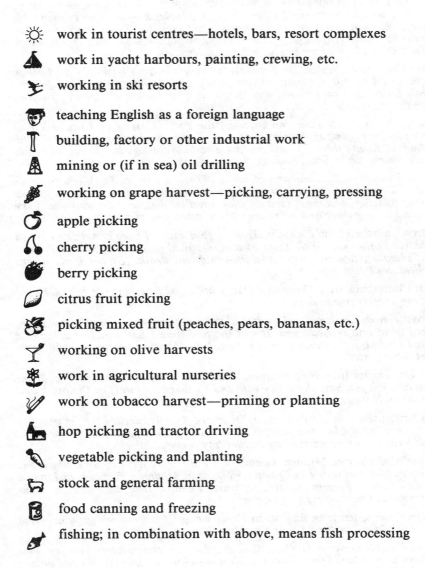

work in tourist centres—hotels, bars, resort complexes

work in yacht harbours, painting, crewing, etc.

working in ski resorts

teaching English as a foreign language

building, factory or other industrial work

mining or (if in sea) oil drilling

working on grape harvest—picking, carrying, pressing

apple picking

cherry picking

berry picking

citrus fruit picking

picking mixed fruit (peaches, pears, bananas, etc.)

working on olive harvests

work in agricultural nurseries

work on tobacco harvest—priming or planting

hop picking and tractor driving

vegetable picking and planting

stock and general farming

food canning and freezing

fishing; in combination with above, means fish processing

Readers' Comments on Past Editions

Safra Wightman from Stamford: *My first encounter with* Work Your Way Around the World *changed the direction of my life, although the inclination to just go away had always been there. Flicking through your book on a friend's coffee table I finally made my decision. Three weeks later I had sold the contents of my flat at a car boot sale, given up my job in a hairdressing salon, invested in a rucksack and a tent and booked my one-way ticket to Greece.*

Adam Cook from Wales: *Well, thanks to your amazing book, I'm in Greece, happy, and I've still got some money in my pocket. Whenever I have felt my morale lowering, I simply read any chapter of your book and all that optimism blows the blues away.*

Kathryn Kleypas, an American writing from Paris: *First of all I would like to thank you for organising a great book like* Work Your Way Around the World. *Without it, I don't think I would ever have had the courage to give up my secure (albeit boring) job in San Francisco for an au pair job in Paris.*

Arthur Solovev, a Russian writing from Paris: *I'd like to thank you for your wonderful book. I consider it to be the best and most important book for the working traveller. And maybe not only for travellers, but for those who want to be independent anywhere and who have even a little sense of adventure.*

Andrew Campbell from Australia: *How ya goin' mate? I hope everything's bonza in the land of no sun. Well, inspired and informed by your 'ripper Boris' book, I am planning my own trip-round-the-world-unto-death. (Ripper Boris means excellent, tops, like-wow, etc.).*

Heidi Clutterbuck from Germany: *Ohh, I am so addicted to your books. Please send me another one to devour.*

Zoe Willis from Scotland: *So I worked at the goat farm for two months, fed them, milked them and chased them. It was the first time I had travelled alone and worked abroad, but definitely not the last. I met loads of people and will never forget the experience.*

John Linnemeier from Bloomington, USA: *Your book really floored me. What a fantastic job you have done. My wife and I worked on farms in Denmark and in hotels in Norway.*

Jan Christensen from Fredrikshavn, Denmark: *I have travelled for the past five years, including the last two years in the US, and I am a great fan of your book. I look forward to reading the new edition (my personal bible).*

Brigitte Albrech from Munich, Germany: *Until I leave for Australia, I have my memories of tree-planting in Canada, working at Madame Tussauds in London and your book to keep my longing for travelling alive. It began with nine weeks in Mexico and now I am spoilt forever!*

Martyn Owens, teaching English in Hong Kong: *If it were not for your great book, I would not be here; it's as simple as that.*

Michel Falardeau from Quebec, Canada: *Let me congratulate you for your excellent book, which I found very useful on my 11 month journey. When I landed in Australia I used your book to find work grape-picking in Mildura.*

Glen Williams, working in the Netherlands: *Keep up the good work, 'cos it keeps inspiring just plain ordinary people like me to do something they only dreamed about doing previously.*